ARBITRATION

FOURTH EDITION

STEPHEN J. WARE
Frank Edwards Tyler Distinguished Professor of Law
University of Kansas

ALAN SCOTT RAU
Mark G. and Judy G. Yudof Chair Emeritus in Law
University of Texas

FOUNDATION
PRESS

444 Cedar Street, Suite 700
St. Paul, MN 55101
1-877-888-1330

Printed in the United States of America

ISBN: 978-1-68328-350-8

PREFACE

This arbitration book began several editions ago as a chapter of a broader book, *Processes of Dispute Resolution: The Role of Lawyers*, designed for a law school course on a wide range of alternatives to litigation, including negotiation, mediation, and other dispute resolution processes. The Alternative Dispute Resolution field has certainly come of age since. Many law schools now have standalone courses and seminars focusing specifically on arbitration. This book is written primarily for such courses.

Law students may get a glimpse of arbitration in their first-year courses, such as Contracts and Civil Procedure, but no prior knowledge of arbitration is presumed by this book. Chapters 1 and 2 aim to give readers a solid introduction to arbitration, with both a theoretical framework and plenty of real-world context. Chapter 3 is the heart of the book; it is the law, mostly the Federal Arbitration Act and Supreme Court cases interpreting it—often controversially. These cases are worthy of careful, critical attention in the classic law school manner. After doing that, students will know enough arbitration law to turn their focus to thinking like practicing lawyers representing clients in arbitration proceedings. Chapter 4 enables this, and some instructors will want their students to do various lawyering skills exercises at this point of the course. If they do, and if they were careful and thorough with Chapter 3, then they may be nearing the end of the semester without much time for Chapters 5 and 6. That approach works fine with this book's organization. Alternatively, an instructor with particular interest in transnational arbitration (Chapter 5) or processes similar to arbitration (Chapter 6) can devote significant attention to those topics.

A note on form: We have substantially edited most cases and selections to delete unnecessary material. We use spaced asterisks to indicate deletions of text, but usually do not indicate when we have deleted footnotes or citations. Where we have kept footnotes, we have kept the footnote number of the original material.

We have benefited from the helpful comments and critiques of many colleagues and students who have used the prior editions of this book, and each of the institutions at which we teach has provided substantial financial support for the completion of this project. We are also very grateful to Shelby Sternberg, Howard Mahan, Caleb Kampsen, Nick Slovikoski, Ellen Rudolph, Elliott Brewer, Bridget Brazil, Zachary Strella, Brandi Spates, Matthew Frederick, Ariel Rhines, Amanda Vescovi, Emily Thompson, Alisha Peters, Munzer Islam, and Justin Worthington for their able research assistance.

As we expect to write future editions of this book, we welcome comments and suggestions.

STEPHEN J. WARE
Frank Edwards Tyler
Distinguished Professor of Law
University of Kansas
ware@ku.edu
(785) 864-9209

ALAN SCOTT RAU
Mark G. and Judy G. Yudof
Chair Emeritus in Law
University of Texas
arau@law.utexas.edu
(512) 232-1266

July 2019

ACKNOWLEDGMENTS

The following authors and publishers gave us permission to reprint excerpts from copyrighted material; we gratefully acknowledge their assistance.

Drawing by Lorenz; copyright © 1991 The New Yorker Magazine, Inc.

Drahozal & Ware, Why Do Businesses Use (or Not Use) Arbitration Clauses, 25 Ohio St. J. on Disp. Resol. 433, 451–52 (2010).

Fuller, Collective Bargaining and the Arbitrator, 1963 Wis. L. Rev. 3, 11–12 (1963). Copyright 2018 by The Board of Regents of the University of Wisconsin System; Reprinted by permission of the Wisconsin Law Review.

Bernstein, Merchant Law in a Merchant Court: Rethinking the Code's Search for Immanent Business Norms, 144 U. Pa. L. Rev. 1765, 1771–74, 1805–07, 1819–20 (1996).

Landes & Posner, Adjudication as a Private Good, 8 J. Legal Stud. 235, 235–40, 245–47 (1979). Copyright © 1979 by The University of Chicago. All rights reserved.

Bernstein, Opting Out of the Legal System: Extralegal Contractual Relations in the Diamond Industry, 21 J. Legal Stud. 115, 117, 124, 126–28, 134, 139, 148–50, 156 (1992). Copyright © 1992 by The University of Chicago. All rights reserved.

Jones, Three Centuries of Commercial Arbitration in New York: A Brief Survey, 1956 Wash. U.L.Q. 193, 209–10, 218–19 (1956).

Mentschikoff, Commercial Arbitration, 61 Colum. L. Rev. 846, 848–54 (1961). Copyright © 1961 by the Directors of the Columbia Law Review Association Inc. All rights reserved.

Bernstein, Private Commercial Law in the Cotton Industry: Creating Cooperation through Rules, Norms, and Institutions, 99 Mich. L. Rev. 1724, 1725–28, 1731–32, 1737–39, 1740–41 (2001).

Birdthistle & Henderson, Becoming a Fifth Branch, 99 Cornell L. Rev. 1, 13–15 (2013).

Ware, What Makes Securities Arbitration Different from Other Consumer and Employment Arbitration? 76 U. Cin. L. Rev. 447, 448–52 (2008).

Black & Gross, Investor Protection Meets the Federal Arbitration Act, 1 Stan. J. Complex Litig. 1, 1–14, 26–27 (2012).

Verges, Opening the Floodgates of Small Customer Claims in FINRA Arbitration: FINRA v. Charles Schwab & Co., Inc., 15 Cardozo J. Conflict Resol. 623, 639–40 (2014).

Gross, The Customer's Nonwaivable Right to Choose Arbitration in the Securities Industry, 10 Brook J. Corp. Fin. & Com. L. 384, 384–87 (2016).

© 2016 Wasserman. All rights reserved. Distributed by Tribune Content Agency.

Gough, The High Costs of an Inexpensive Forum: An Empirical Analysis of Employment Discrimination Claims Heard in Arbitration and Civil Litigation, 35 Berkeley J. Emp. & Lab. L. 91, 94–103, 112 (2014). © 2014 by the Regents of the University of California. Reprinted from the Berkeley Journal of Employment & Labor Law by permission of the Regents of the University of California.

Ware, The Centrist Case for Enforcing Adhesive Arbitration Agreements, 23 Harv. Negot. L. Rev. 29, 69–72, 89–90, 94, 96–98, 109, 110–14 (2017).

Estlund, The Black Hole of Mandatory Arbitration, 96 N.C. L. Rev. 679, 679–92, 699–700 (2018). Reprinted with permission from the North Carolina Law Review, Vol. 96 (2018).

Horton & Chandrasekher, After the Revolution: An Empirical Study of Consumer Arbitration, 104 Geo. L.J. 57, 67–70 (2015).

Sovern, Greenberg, Kirgis & Liu, "Whimsy Little Contracts" With Unexpected Consequences: An Empirical Analysis of Consumer Understanding of Arbitration Agreements, 75 Md. L. Rev. 1, 11–14 (2015).

Larson & Dahl, Medical Malpractice Arbitration: Not Business as Usual, 8 Y.B. Arb. & Mediation 69, 69–71, 79–83, 85–87, 93 (2016).

Morrison, Can Mandatory Medical Malpractice Claims be Fair? The Kaiser Permanente System, 70 Disp. Resol. J. 35, 35–41, 43, 45–54, 59 (2015).

Movsesian, Fiqh and Cannons: Reflections on Islamic and Christian Jurisprudence, 40 Seton Hall L. Rev. 861, 879–84 (2010).

Helfand, Religious Arbitration and the New Multiculturalism: Negotiating Conflicting Legal Orders, 86 N.Y.U. L. Rev. 1231, 1237–47, 1253–55, 1265–66 (2011).

Chua-Rubenfeld & Costa, The Reverse-Entanglement Principle: Why Religious Arbitration of Federal Rights is Unconstitutional, 128 Yale L.J. 2087, 2094–99 (2014).

Pre-Dispute Arbitration Agreements Are Enforceable. © 2019 Stu's Views. All rights reserved.

Ware, A Short Defense of Southland, Casarotto, and Other Long-Controversial Arbitration Decisions, 30 Loy. Consumer L. Rev. 303, 310–15, 317–18, 327–36 (2018).

Ware, Punitive Damages in Arbitration: Contracting Out of Government's Role in Punishment and Federal Preemption of State Law, 63 Fordham L. Rev. 529, 554–55 (1994).

Horton, Arbitration About Arbitration, 70 Stan. L. Rev. 363, 394–99, 440–41 (2018).

Ricker, Jay-Z's ADR Problems: Mogul's Case Spotlights Lack of Diverse Arbitrators, ABA J. May 2019, at 9.

Fanto, Gross & Poser, Broker-Dealer Law and Regulation, § 23.0.4[B] [5th ed. 2018]. Reproduced with the permission of CCH Incorporated from Broker Dealer Law & Regulation, 5th Edition (ISBN 9781543804966), by James A. Fanto, Jill I. Gross and Norman S. Poser, © 2019 James A. Fanto and Jill I. Gross, 2017-2013 James A. Fanto, 2012-2007 Norman S. Poser and James A. Fanto.

Rossein & Hope, Disclosure and Disqualification Standards for Neutral Arbitrators: How Far to Cast the Net and What is Sufficient to Vacate Award, 81 St. John's L. Rev. 203, 235–40 (2007).

Stipanowich, Arbitration: The "New Litigation", 2010 U. Ill. L. Rev. 1, 8–9, 12–15, 19–20, 22–23 (2010).

Kaufmann-Kohler, Identifying and Applying the Law Governing the Arbitration Procedure: The Role of the Law of the Place of Arbitration, Int'l Council for Commercial Arb., Congress series no. 9 (Kluwer Law International, Paris/ 1999) 336, 342–65.

Craig, Uses and Abuses of Appeal from Awards, 4 Arb. Int'l. 174, 174–79, 182–85, 190–92 (1988).

Moses, The Principles and Practice of International Commercial Arbitration, 46–47, 50–52 (3d ed. 2017).

Sherby, A Checklist for Drafting an International Arbitration Clause, 2010 Bus. L. Today, 1, 2 (2010.

Salomon & Duffy, Enforcement Begins When the Arbitration Clause is Drafted, 22 Am. Rev. Int'l Arb. 271, 274–75 (2011).

SUMMARY OF CONTENTS

TABLE OF CONTENTS

TABLE OF CASES

The principal cases are in bold type.

ARBITRATION

FOURTH EDITION

CHAPTER 1

OVERVIEW OF ARBITRATION

Snow White and the Wicked Queen submit the fairness question to binding arbitration.

• •

Drawing by Lorenz; © 1991 The New Yorker Magazine, Inc.

A. PRIVATE ADJUDICATION

Adjudication is the process by which disputing parties present evidence and arguments to another person expected to decide the outcome of the dispute. Arbitration is private (non-government) adjudication. Arbitrators, selected by the disputing parties (directly or indirectly), are the adjudicators in arbitration. In contrast, judges and jurors are the adjudicators in litigation, which is adjudication in a government forum, a court.

Litigation is the default process of dispute resolution in the United States. Parties can, by contract, obligate themselves to use alternative processes of dispute resolution (ADR)—such as arbitration—but if they do not, then each party retains the right to have the dispute resolved in litigation. In other words, parties start with the right to litigate but can trade away this right by agreeing to arbitrate. Sometimes parties with an existing dispute contract to submit that dispute to arbitration, but such post-dispute arbitration agreements are relatively rare. More common are pre-dispute arbitration agreements. These are contracts containing a clause providing that, if a dispute arises, the parties will resolve that dispute in arbitration rather than in court. Pre-dispute arbitration clauses typically are written broadly to cover any dispute the parties' relationship might produce, but can be written more narrowly to cover just some potential disputes. Arbitration clauses appear in a wide variety of contracts formed by a wide variety of parties.

Government subsidizes litigation but not arbitration. The fees litigants pay to courts do not cover the full cost of the judge, jury, court clerk, other administrative personnel, and the courthouse itself. By contrast, parties to arbitration must pay the arbitrator's fee, as well as the fees of any organization administering the arbitration, plus any cost of the hearing room. Given this government subsidy for litigation over arbitration, why would parties choose arbitration over litigation?

Christopher R. Drahozal & Stephen J. Ware, *Why Do Businesses Use (or Not Use) Arbitration Clauses?*

25 Ohio St. J. on Disp. Resol. 433, 451–52 (2010).

We start with the expectation that well-informed people do not ordinarily pay thousands of dollars to get what they can get elsewhere for free. So, we ask, why any sophisticated parties choose to do that with respect to binding adjudication. Why do they choose arbitration over litigation? We believe that all the possible reasons fall into two categories: process and outcomes. * * * [S]ophisticated parties drafting their contract may choose arbitration because they expect that it will provide them with a better process than litigation, because they expect that it will provide them with better outcomes than litigation, or both.

Those two broad categories of reasons, of course, comprise a number of more particular reasons why parties might agree to arbitrate. For domestic [within the United States] arbitration, those reasons include:

- arbitration may be faster and cheaper than litigation, at least for some types of disputes;
- arbitration may lessen the risk of punitive damages awards or aberrational jury verdicts;
- arbitration may decrease exposure to class actions or other forms of aggregate litigation;
- arbitration may result in more accurate outcomes because of arbitrator expertise and incentives;
- arbitration may better protect confidential information from disclosure;

- arbitration may enhance the ability of parties to have their disputes resolved using trade rules; and
- arbitration may enable the parties to better preserve their relationship.

Many of the same reasons apply to transnational contracts. In that context, however, commentators emphasize two additional benefits: arbitration may provide a neutral forum and may be more likely to result in an award enforceable in another jurisdiction.

The most commonly cited reason parties choose arbitration over litigation is speed. Arbitration tends to be faster because it allows the parties to bypass long queues in court and to schedule hearings at their own convenience. In addition, as Chapter 4 explains, parties can largely choose their arbitration's procedures. Parties usually do this by agreeing to arbitrate under the rules of a particular arbitration organization. While these rules vary, procedure in arbitration tends to be less elaborate than in litigation; arbitration often streamlines pleading, motion practice, and discovery. Arbitration's speed also often comes from the fact that the arbitrator's decision is likely to be final: arbitration rarely has any appeal process, and judicial review of arbitrators' decisions is tightly restricted. So as one would expect, surveys indicate that most practicing lawyers believe arbitration is faster than either jury trial or bench trial.[1] Empirical studies comparing arbitrated cases with litigated cases seem to support the generalization that arbitration is faster,[2] although, such comparisons cannot eliminate the possibility that differences in the two sets of cases explain differing results. Arbitration's savings in time can also yield savings in expense—for example, in lawyers' fees.

Choosing arbitration over litigation may benefit the parties in other ways as well. The parties may prefer the greater privacy of arbitration. In contrast to trials, which are usually in government buildings open to the public, including journalists, arbitration hearings are generally on private property and closed to non-participants. For instance, the American Arbitration Association (AAA) Commercial Arbitration Rules, which many arbitration agreements choose, provide:

> The arbitrator and the AAA shall maintain the privacy of the hearings unless the law provides to the contrary. Any person having a direct interest in the arbitration is entitled to attend hearings. The arbitrator shall otherwise have the power to require the exclusion of any witness, other than a party or other essential person, during the testimony of any other

---

[1] See Douglas Shontz, Fred Kipperman & Vanessa Soma, *Business-to-Business Arbitration in the United States: Perceptions of Corporate Counsel* The RAND Institute for Civil Justice (2011), https://www.rand.org/content/dam/rand/pubs/technical_reports/2011/RAND_TR781.pdf (survey of business or corporate lawyers with 121 responses. . .60% of respondents agreed that arbitration saves time relative to litigation * * *").

[2] Roy Weinstein, *Efficiency and Economic Benefits of Dispute Resolution through Arbitration Compared with U.S. District Court Proceedings,* Micronomis Economic Research and Consulting (Mar. 2017), http://go.adr.org/rs/294-SFS-516/images/Economic%20Impact%20of%20Delay%20Micronomics%20Final%20Report%20%282017-03-07%29.pdf (in 2015 11.6 months was the median time from filing to award in cases administered by the American Arbitration Association and 24.2 months was the median time from filing to trial in federal district court).

witness. It shall be discretionary with the arbitrator to determine the propriety of the attendance of any other person.[3]

A few state statutes even protect arbitration materials from discovery or admissibility in litigation.[4] Absent such a statute, however, the evidence and arguments produced in arbitration may be discoverable and admissible in litigation,[5] even if there is an explicit confidentiality provision in the arbitration agreement.[6] One study found confidentiality provisions in only 13.5% of arbitration agreements studied.[7] And such provisions do not guarantee confidentiality, as demonstrated by the arbitration involving Donald Trump and Stephanie Clifford.[8] That said, most arbitrations never become the subject of litigation and thus never become the subject of public record unless the one or more of the parties wants publicity.

Another attraction of arbitration is that the parties can choose their "judges," so parties may choose arbitrators with expert knowledge of the subject matter in dispute. This attraction is illuminated in the following excerpt from Lon Fuller. A Harvard Law professor, Fuller was a giant of jurisprudence,[9] and well-described as "the 'founding' jurisprude of ADR."[10]

Lon Fuller, *Collective Bargaining and the Arbitrator*

1963 Wis. L. Rev. 3, 11–12.

Labor relations have today become a highly complicated and technical field. This field involves complex procedures that vary from industry to industry, from plant to plant, from department to department. It has developed its own vocabulary. Though the terms of this vocabulary often seem simple and familiar, their true meaning can be understood only when they are seen as parts of a larger system of practice, just as the umpire's "You're out!" can only be fully understood

---

[3] Am.Arbitration Ass'n, Commercial Arbitration Rules, R-25 (2013). However, "[t]he presumption of privacy and confidentiality in arbitration proceedings shall not apply in class arbitrations. All class arbitration hearings and filings may be made public, subject to the authority of the arbitrator to provide otherwise in special circumstances." Am.Arbitration Ass'n, Supplementary Rules for Class Arbitrations, 9(a) (2003).

[4] See, e.g., Ark.Code Ann. § 16–7–206 (1999); Cal.Evid.Code § 703.5 (West 1995); Mo.Ann.Stat. § 435.014 (West 2010); Tex.Civ.Prac. & Rem. Code Ann. § 154.073(b) (Vernon 2005). See also Group Health Plan, Inc. v. BJC Health Sys., Inc., 30 S.W.3d 198 (Mo.Ct.App.2000).

[5] United States v. Panhandle Eastern Corp., 118 F.R.D. 346 (D.Del.1988); Contship Containerlines, Ltd. v. PPG Industries, Inc., 2003 WL 1948807 (S.D.N.Y. Apr.23, 2003).

[6] Lawrence E. Jaffee Pension Plan v. Household Int'l, Inc., 2004 WL 1821968 (D.Colo.Aug.13, 2004); Urban Box Office Network v. Interfase Managers, 2004 WL 2375819 (S.D.N.Y.Oct.21, 2004).

[7] Linda J. Demaine & Deborah R. Hensler, *"Volunteering" to Arbitrate Through Predispute Arbitration Clauses: The Average Consumer's Experience*, 67 Law & Contemp. Probs. 55, 69 (2004).

[8] *See* Jim Rutenberg and Peter Baker, *Trump Lawyer Obtained Restraining Order to Silence Stormy Daniels,* N.Y. Times, Mar. 7, 2018, at A1, https://www.nytimes.com/2018/03/07/us/politics/stormy-daniels-trump.html ("Ms. Clifford's agreement, though it was made public through her lawsuit, calls for disagreements to be settled through confidential, binding arbitration. It gives Mr. Trump the right to seek financial penalties of more than $1 million in arbitration should Ms. Clifford break or threaten to break her agreement to stay silent. It also gives him the right to obtain an injunction barring her from speaking while disputes are considered in arbitration or open court.").

[9] See, e.g., Frederick Schauer, *Official Obedience and the Politics of Defining "Law"*, 86 S. Cal. L. Rev. 1165, 1194 (2013) (describing Fuller's 1964 book, The Morality of Law, as one "of the influential accounts of the rule of law").

[10] Carrie Menkel-Meadow, *Correspondences and Contradictions in International and Domestic Conflict Resolution: Lessons from General Theory and Varied Contexts*, 2003 J. Disp. Resol. 319, 341 (2003).

by one who knows the objectives, the rules and the practices of baseball. I might add that many questions of industrial relations are on a level at least equal to that of the infield fly rule. They are not suitable material for light dinner conversation.

In the nature of things few judges can have had any very extensive experience in the field of industrial relations. Arbitrators, on the other hand, are compelled to acquire a knowledge of industrial processes, modes of compensation, complex incentive plans, job classification, shift arrangements, and procedures for layoff and recall.

Naturally not all arbitrators stand on a parity with respect to this knowledge. But there are open to the arbitrator, even the novice, quick methods of education not available to courts. An arbitrator will frequently interrupt the examination of witnesses with a request that the parties educate him to the point where he can understand the testimony being received. This education can proceed informally, with frequent interruptions by the arbitrator, and by informed persons on either side, when a point needs clarification. Sometimes there will be arguments across the table, occasionally even within each of the separate camps. The end result will usually be a clarification that will enable everyone to proceed more intelligently with the case. There is in this informal procedure no infringement whatever of arbitrational due process. On the contrary, the party's chance to have his case understood by the arbitrator is seriously impaired if his representative has to talk into a vacuum, if he addresses his words to uncomprehending ears.

The education that an arbitrator can thus get, say, in a half an hour, might take days if it had to proceed by qualifying experts and subjecting them to direct and cross examination. The courts have themselves recognized the serious obstacle presented by traditional methods of proof in dealing with cases involving a complex technical background. * * *

While Fuller focuses on the value of *labor* arbitrators with expert knowledge of the subject matter in dispute, he recognizes the same value in *commercial* arbitration:

> Courts have in fact had difficulty with complicated commercial litigation. The problems here are not unlike those encountered in dealing with labor agreements. There are really few outstanding commercial judges in the history of the common law. The greatest of these, Lord Mansfield, used to sit with special juries selected from among experienced merchants and traders. To further his education in commercial practice he used to arrange dinners with his jurors. In Greek mythology it is reported that Minos prepared himself for a posthumous career as judge of shades by first exposing himself to every possible experience of life. It is not only in labor relations that the impracticability of such a program manifests itself.

Id. at 17. A commercial arbitrator may have a similar background to the parties, or be engaged in the same business, and thus likely familiar with the standard agreements, terminology, and practices of the trade. The usefulness of such expertise is particularly apparent when a dispute hinges on contract interpretation or whether the goods sold meet the necessary technical standards. In such cases arbitrators may apply substantive rules found not in statutes (like the Uniform Commercial Code) enacted by legislatures, but rather in industry rules, which may be written by trade associations. An example of such trade association arbitration is the National Grain & Feed Association (NGFA). Its website states:

> Formally established in 1901, the NGFA's Arbitration System has operated in some form since the formation of the Association on November 9, 1896. It is believed to be North America's oldest industry-based arbitration system.
>
> The Arbitration System provides a fair, cost-effective and timely way to resolve disputes involving grain, feed, barge and barge freight transactions. Its use is compulsory for resolution of disputes between Active members under the NGFA's Bylaws. The Arbitration System is also available for resolving disputes with and between Allied and Transportation members if the Arbitration Rules are referenced in the underlying contractual agreement or the parties otherwise consent The Arbitration System is kept current through the amendment process at the NGFA's annual business meeting.
>
> * * *
>
> Cases are considered by an Arbitration Committee comprised of three persons selected by the NGFA Secretary. Arbitrators are employees, active partners, principals, officers, or directors of Active, Allied and Transportation members. Arbitrators are generally selected based upon their personal experience in the type of trade practices or questions involved in the case. Arbitrators must have no commercial interest in the case.[11]

Lisa Bernstein, *Merchant Law in a Merchant Court: Rethinking the Code's Search for Immanent Business Norms*

144 U. Pa. L. Rev. 1765, 1771–74, 1805–07, 1819–20 (1996).

The NGFA is a trade association of firms and individuals who are active in the cash-markets for grain and feed. It began arbitrating disputes in 1896 and has been publishing written arbitration opinions since 1902. As a condition of membership in the Association, members must agree to submit all disputes with other members to the Association's arbitration system. A member who refuses to submit to arbitration or fails to comply with an arbitration award rendered against him may, in addition to having his actions reported in the NGFA newsletter, be suspended or expelled from the Association.[18]

---

[11] NGFA Arbitration Rules, Nat'l Grain & Feed Ass'n (Oct, 2017), https://cb4q22fdswq370gsj3m681um-wpengine.netdna-ssl.com/wp-content/uploads/Oct.-2017-Arbitration-Rules.pdf.

[18] See NGFA Bylaws, art. IX, 2(a)–(c) (explaining some of the grounds for expulsion or suspension); *id.* art. X, 1 (describing the procedure for expelling a member). Between 1975 and 1995, three members were expelled for refusing to arbitrate. *See* American Commercial Barge Line Co., NGFA Misc. Case No. 2 (1995) (expelling ACBL and noting that "it is the NGFA's long-standing interpretation of the NGFA Bylaws, Trade Rules and Arbitration Rules that compulsory arbitration of disputes is not a matter that can be altered by a member's contractual documents and is a fundamental obligation of membership"); Houston Pub. Elevator,

The NGFA has adopted four sets of substantive trade rules that are designed to "reflect trade practice and facilitate trade between NGFA members."[19] The Grain Rules and the Feed Rules each cover the basics of contract formation, performance, repudiation, breach, damages, and excuse. The Barge Rules supplement these rules whenever "shipments are designated by contract to be transported by barge," and the Barge Freight Trading Rules "govern all disputes [involving] . . . the purchase and/or sale of barge transportation." Unless they have been explicitly altered or excluded by a specific contractual provision, these rules govern all contracts between NGFA members. Together, they provide a comprehensive set of default rules governing the most important aspects of cash-market transactions in grain or feed.

The trade rules are supplemented by a highly detailed set of arbitration rules, whose applicability to disputes between NGFA members cannot be altered by contract. These rules set out the required filing fee, the guidelines for the selection of arbitrators,[23] the types of information each party must provide to the tribunal, the procedures for requesting an oral hearing, the type of information the arbitrators should include in their written opinions, and the procedures for filing and conducting an intra-association appeal.

* * *

[A]lthough the [Uniform Commercial] Code's adjudicative philosophy presupposes the existence of an embedded set of unwritten customs that are truly known and agreed to by transactors, there is some evidence that the existence of such customs might be less pervasive than the Code assumes. The codification of customary norms in written trade rules by numerous trade associations that provide commercial arbitration conducted by industry-expert adjudicators[134]

NGFA Misc. Case No. 1 (1988) (expelling Houston Public Elevator, explaining that "without compulsory arbitration, the process would be used only when convenient in defending a given position" and noting that the "equality that *all* members, large and small, now enjoy in seeking fair play would quickly evaporate"); S.M. Whitney Co. v. Mundy, Inc., NGFA Case No. 1626 (1985) (expelling Mundy, Inc.). During this period, one member was expelled for failure to comply with an arbitration award.

[19] NGFA Grain Trade R. pmbl. When the trade rules were originally adopted, custom was the starting point for the codifiers. However, changes in unwritten customary practices have not been the primary motivation for trade rule amendments. Rather, amendments have been primarily: (1) technical wording changes designed to correct typographical errors or enhance clarity; (2) changes motivated by arbitration opinions suggesting that a rule was unclear, unworkable, or undesirable; (3) changes introduced in response to technological innovations; (4) changes introduced in response to changes in state or federal regulations; and, finally, (5) changes introduced in response to important changes in the market. In addition, at least one change was explicitly designed to change an existing custom. *See* NGFA, Who's Who in the Grain Trade 37 (Nov. 1920) (reporting that the newly adopted Rule 29 provides that "the specifications of a contract cannot be altered or amended without express consent of both the buyer and the seller (this abolishes the custom of silence confirms)").

[23] The primary arbitration committee is composed of three members chosen by the National Secretary "with a view to forming each committee of prominent people experienced in the type of trade involved in the cases to be brought before it." NGFA Arb. R. 4(a). Arbitrators are required to disclose any circumstance that could affect their impartiality, *see* NGFA Arb. R. 8(a), and may recuse themselves from particular cases. Parties may also challenge the selection of an arbitrator "for prejudicial or other causes." NGFA Arb. R. 8. The National Secretary then determines whether the arbitrator should be replaced. *See id.*

[134] For example, the following associations have codified their customs into trade rules: American Cotton Shippers Association, American Fats and Oils Association, American Peanut Shellers Association, American Seed Trade Association, American Spice Trade Association, American Tin Trade Association, Association of Food Industries, Binding Industries of America, Burlap and Jute Association, Cocoa Merchants' Association of America, Colorado Grain and Feed Association, Diamond Dealers Club, General Arbitration Council of the Textile and Apparel Industries (Worth Street Rules), Green Coffee Association of New Orleans,

suggests that merchants may believe that without codification custom would be too vague and uncertain to be either a satisfactory guide to proper commercial behavior or a sufficiently certain basis for arbitrator decisionmaking.[135] One of the primary reasons NGFA decided to codify its customs was that customs differed so much from one locale to another that codification was necessary to reduce the incidence of misunderstandings and to facilitate the growth of a national market.

* * * [I]n transactions where transactors cannot reduce the "true meaning" of their agreement to a writing with sufficient specificity at a reasonable cost, but want their relationship to be governed by customary norms, they could designate an industry-expert wiseman to resolve disputes in accordance with industry norms. Given the cost and delay involved in litigation, and the need for courts to determine the content of such norms from the often conflicting testimony of expert witnesses, such approaches may be cost-effective.

In short, recognizing the undesirable effects of the Code's trade usage provision on commercial relationships suggests that while looking to usages may improve the accuracy of judicial decisions, and may be desirable in certain contexts, some merchant-transactors may nonetheless prefer either to forgo the benefits of this type of trade-specific interpretive accuracy or to obtain it in other, less costly, ways.

* * *

It is also important to note that NGFA's use of bright-line trade rules and a formalistic adjudicative philosophy severely restrict arbitrator discretion and minimize the need for arbitrators both to rely on and assess the credibility of testimony. This is particularly important in the trade-association context, where the adjudicators are themselves market transactors and the risk of adjudicative bias is perceived to be substantial. Combined with the requirement that NGFA opinions state the factual basis for their holdings, this approach makes it easier for market participants to assess whether a given case was correctly decided. This, in turn, makes it easier for a tribunal to establish and maintain a reputation for impartiality and enables more nuanced information about transactors' reputation to be disseminated to the market.

Green Coffee Association of New York, Kansas City Board of Trade, Memphis Cotton Exchange, Merchants Exchange of Portland, Mid-America Commodity Exchange, National Cottonseed Products Association, National Hay Association, National Institute of Oilseed Products, North American Wholesale Lumber Association, Pacific Coast Coffee Association, Pacific Northwest Grain and Feed Association, Pennsylvania Rice Millers' Association, Rubber Trade Association, Specialty Coffee Association of America, Tea Association of the USA, Texas Cotton Association, and the Texas Grain and Feed Association. See Lisa Bernstein, The Newest Law Merchant: Private Commercial Law in the United States, at tbl. 1 (Nov. 26, 1995) (unpublished manuscript, on file with author). Many other associations publish codes of industry standards or promulgate standard-form contracts that memorialize industry custom in contractual boilerplate. *See id.*

[135] There are, however, other explanations for these industries' decisions to codify their customs. First, codifying custom reduces arbitrators' discretion (because they do not have to determine the content of the rule), which may make arbitrator bias easier to detect and hence less likely to occur. Second, codifying custom reduces the cost of dealing with someone in a location with different unwritten customs. Finally, the codification of customs is particularly beneficial to large companies that operate in many areas, because they would otherwise have to appoint a large number of local agents familiar with local norms or would have to educate their employees about different local customs.

As we will see, arbitration occurs in a diverse variety of contexts, to resolve many different types of disputes. However, arbitration developed first and continues to flourish most thoroughly in situations where parties to a contract have or seek an ongoing relationship in which they will regularly benefit from cooperating with each other, but also anticipate that disputes will occur from time to time. The paradigm is the collective bargaining agreement between an employer and the union representing its employees, or the recurring sale of goods between merchants in the same trade association. Hence the preceding passages from Lon Fuller on labor arbitration and Lisa Bernstein on trade association arbitration.

In both the labor-management and trade-association contexts, disputes often arise within long-term relationships with a history of mutual dependence or cooperation through which each party benefits. Both sorts of relationships likely present the disputing parties with the prospect of continued benefits from future interaction. All this tends to induce the parties to agree to arbitration, participate in arbitration, and then to comply with arbitrators' decisions. Such private (non-government) incentives to arbitrate are emphasized in the following passage by early leaders of Law & Economics.

William M. Landes & Richard A. Posner, *Adjudication As a Private Good*

8 J.Legal Stud. 235, 245–47 (1979).

Imagine a purely private market in judicial services. People would offer their services as judges, and disputants would select the judge whom they mutually found most acceptable. The most popular judges would charge the highest fees, and competition among judges would yield the optimum amount and quality of judicial services at minimum social cost. This competitive process would produce judges who were not only competent but also impartial—and would thus fulfill the ideals of procedural justice—because a judge who was not regarded as impartial could not get disputes submitted to him for resolution: one party would always refuse.

A voluntary system of dispute resolution does not presuppose that the dispute has arisen from a consensual relationship (landlord-tenant, employer-employee, seller-buyer, etc.) in which the method of dispute resolution is agreed on before the dispute arose. All that is necessary is that when a dispute does arise the parties to it choose a judge to resolve it. Even if they are complete strangers, as in the typical accident case, the parties can still choose a judge to determine liability.

Although dispute resolution could thus be provided (for criminal as well as civil cases) in a market that would operate free from any obvious elements of monopoly, externality, or other sources of "market failure," it may not be efficient to banish public intervention entirely. Public intervention may be required (1) to ensure compliance with the (private) judge's decision and (2) to compel submission of the dispute to adjudication in the first place. The first of these public functions is straightforward, and no more compromises the private nature of the adjudication system described above than the law of trespass compromises the private property rights system. The second function, compelling submission of the dispute to judge, is more complex. If A accuses B of breach of contract, the next step in a system of private adjudication is for the parties to select a judge. But suppose B, knowing that any impartial judge would convict him, drags his feet in agreeing to select a judge who will hear the case, rejecting name after name submitted by A for his consideration. * * *

Two ways of overcoming the submission problem come immediately to mind. The first is for the parties to agree on the judge (or on the method of selecting him) before the dispute arises, as is done in contracts with arbitration clauses. This solution is available, however, only where the dispute arises from a preexisting voluntary relationship between the parties; the typical tort or crime does not. * * *

Another type of private solution to the problem of enforcement and the selection of a private judge is available when both parties to the dispute are members of the same (private) group or association. The group can expel any member who unreasonably refuses to submit to an impartial adjudication (perhaps by a judge selected by the group) or to abide by the judge's decision. To the extent that membership in the group confers a value over and above alternative opportunities, members will have incentives to bargain in good faith over the selection of the judge and to abide by his decision. In these circumstances dispute resolution can operate effectively without public intervention.

* * *

[I]f one party to a dispute expects that an impartial arbitrator would rule against him, he has an incentive to drag his feet in agreeing to the appointment of an arbitrator. Consistently with this point, writers on arbitration agree that the problem of selection makes arbitration a virtually unusable method of dispute resolution where there is no preexisting contractual or other relationship between the disputants. This suggests a clue to the superior ability of primitive compared to advanced societies to function without public institutions of adjudication. Primitive communities tend to be quite small and their members bound together by a variety of mutually advantageous relationships and interactions. Expulsion, outlawry, ostracism, and other forms of boycott or collective refusal to deal are highly effective sanctions in these circumstances. Another way of putting this point is that reputation, a factor recognized in the literature as deterring people from breaking contracts even in the absence of effective legal sanctions, is a more effective deterrent in a small community, where news travels rapidly throughout the entire circle of an individual's business and social acquaintances, than in large, modern, impersonal societies.

Yet even in modern society, certain trade, religious, and other associations correspond, to a degree, to the close-knit, primitive community. For example, securities or commodities exchanges whose members derive substantial benefits from membership can use the threat of expulsion as an effective sanction to induce members to submit to arbitration. So can a religious association in which excommunication is regarded by members as a substantial cost;[30] so can a

[30] The threat of excommunication was, for example, the ultimate sanction for refusal to submit to, or obey the decision of, the medieval English ecclesiastical courts, which had an immense jurisdiction covering matrimonial disputes, perjury, and a variety of other matters as well as strictly religious disputes.

university. Exchanges, religious associations, and (private) universities are in fact important examples of modern "communities" in which private adjudication (whether called arbitration or something else) is extensively utilized in preference to public adjudication.

While Chapter 3 will explain how courts enforce agreements to arbitrate and arbitrators' decisions (usually called "awards"), the preceding excerpt emphasizes private enforcement of arbitration agreements and awards. Such private enforcement may remain especially significant in close-knit religious communities.

In the Matter of the Arbitration Between Mikel and Scharf

Supreme Court, Special Term, Kings County New York, 1980.
105 Misc.2d 548, 432 N.Y.S.2d 602, aff'd, 85 A.D.2d 604, 444 N.Y.S.2d 690 (1981).

■ ARTHUR S. HIRSCH, J.

This is a motion to confirm an arbitration award rendered by a rabbinical court.

* * *

In November, 1977, respondents received notice from the Union of Orthodox Rabbis to appear before a rabbinical court for a "*Din Torah*" or arbitration of a claim brought against them by petitioner. Respondents testified they refused to appear at first on grounds that they had no knowledge of petitioner, but did appear after receiving written notice that refusal would result in the (rabbinical) court's invoking a "sirov."

* * *

Rabbinical Court—Din Torah

* * *

The beginnings of Jewish arbitral institutions are traceable to the middle of the second century. Throughout the centuries, thereafter, in every country in which Jews have been domiciled, Jewish judicial authority has existed, via the institute of arbitration conducted by special rabbinical courts. Orthodox Jews, prompted by their religious, national feelings, accepted Jewish judicial authority, by resorting to the arbitration procedure of their own free will. This method of arbitration has the imprimatur of our own judicial system, as a useful means of relieving the burdens of the inundated courts dealing with civil matters. Through Talmudic sages, it is learned that special rules or procedures have been provided under which the rabbinical courts function as a *Din Torah* (literally translated as torah judgment), with Judaic or torah law as its basis. * * *

In addition to the procedural rules established by Judaic Law, there are state, civil, procedural rules for arbitration (CPLR [Civil Practice Law and Rules] Article 75) to which the rabbinical court, as an arbitration forum, must also adhere.

* * *

Respondents [challenge] the rabbinical court's award, claiming first, the arbitration agreement was entered involuntarily, under duress and is consequently void, [and] second, charging the arbitrators with misconduct * * *.

Involuntary Agreement—Duress

Both parties are members of the orthodox Jewish community. Respondent's denial of the existence of any disputable issue between themselves and petitioner convinced them to refuse to appear for a *Din Torah* and they would not have done so had they not received the threat of a "sirov." Rabbis testifying for respondents stated that a sirov, literally translated as contempt of court, is a prohibitionary decree that subjects the recipient to shame, scorn, ridicule and ostracism by his coreligionists, fellow members of his community. Ostensibly, he is ostracized and scorned. Other Jews refuse to eat or speak with him. He is discredited and dishonored. The respondents maintain that the draconian measures of a sirov are sufficiently threatening so as to compel their compliance with the demand to appear. They claim they would have become outcasts among their friends and coreligionists. However, from other testimony, it appears that the sirov, while most assuredly ominous in its potential power, is honored in its breach. The court cannot, of course, know the actual state of mind of respondents and it may be that their fear of a sirov decree was real. However, it seems more plausible that if respondents believed the consequences so fearful, they would not, at this point, be willing to defy the rabbinical court by refusing to accept the arbitrator's determination. Undoubtedly, pressure was brought to bear to have them participate in the *Din Torah,* but pressure is not duress. Their decision to acquiesce to the rabbinical court's urgings was made without the coercion that would be necessary for the agreement to be void.

Lisa Bernstein, *Opting out of the Legal System: Extralegal Contractual Relations in the Diamond Industry*

21 J. Legal Stud. 115, 117, 124, 126–28, 134, 139, 148–50, 156 (1992).

BUSINESS disputes arise in all industries, and the diamond industry is no exception. Unlike the situation in many other industries, however, diamond industry disputes are resolved not through the courts and not by the application of legal rules announced and enforced by the state.

The diamond industry has systematically rejected state-created law. In its place, the sophisticated traders who dominate the industry have developed an elaborate, internal set of rules, complete with distinctive institutions and sanctions, to handle disputes among industry members.

* * *

The New York DDC [Diamond Dealers Club] currently has 2,000 members; in most years there is a waiting list for admission. * * * As a condition of membership, a dealer must sign an agreement to submit all disputes arising from the diamond business between himself and another member to the club's arbitration system. The agreement to arbitrate is binding. Unless the club opts not to hear the case, the member may not seek redress of his grievances in court. If he does so, he will be fined or expelled from the club. Furthermore, since the agreement to arbitrate is binding, the court will not hear the case.

* * *

Around 150 disputes per year are submitted to the DDC's arbitration system.

* * *

There are two dispute resolution bodies in the DDC, the Floor Committee and the Board of Arbitrators; both are composed of club members elected for two-year-terms.

* * *

The DDC Board of Arbitrators does not apply the New York law of contract and damages, rather it resolves disputes on the basis of trade customs and usages. Many of these are set forth with particularity in the club's bylaws, and others simply are generally known and accepted. Although at first glance diamond transactions appear to be simple buy-sell agreements, complicated controversies often arise, particularly in the sale of polished stones. In general, disputes fall into three main classes: those that have explicit remedies prescribed in the trade rules; those that have no explicit remedies prescribed but are common enough that they are dealt with consistently according to widely known customs; and those complex disputes that the arbitrators either decline to hear or decide in accordance with rules of decision and damage measures that neither party can predict ex ante.

* * *

In complex cases that are neither explicitly covered by the trade rules nor dealt with according to established custom, it is difficult to determine what substantive rules of decision are applied. Arbitrators explain that they decide complex cases on the basis of trade custom and usage, a little common sense, some Jewish law, and, last, common-law legal principles. There are no general rules of damages. When calculating damages, the arbitrators look at the stone, consider the circumstances, and apply their business experience. Many dealers feel that the arbitrators have redistributive instincts; they cite the unpredictability of the decisions as well as the arbitrators' tendency to "split the difference" as an important motivation to settle their disputes on their own. This may be a reason why, while 150 arbitration complaints are filed each year, only thirty to forty go to judgment. The arbitrators announce their judgment, but they neither make findings of fact nor explain their reasoning. The absence of explicit findings of fact and written opinions is a precaution to prevent people from complaining, rightly or wrongly, that the arbitrators were biased, unfair, or relied on evidence that lacked probative value. The arbitration board is like a jury black box. Diamond dealers eschew arbitration for many of the same reasons that businessmen in general are wary of jury trials, primarily the uncertainty of the outcome.

* * *

The DDC Bylaws provide that "[a]ll decisions of arbitration panels including floor committee arbitrations which are not complied with within 10 working days, together with the picture of the non-complying member, shall be posted in a conspicuous place in the Club rooms." This information is communicated to all bourses in the world federation. As a condition of membership in the federation, each bourse agrees to enforce the judgments of all member bourses. Since most diamond dealers frequently transact in foreign bourses, this reciprocity of enforcement greatly increases the penalty for failing to voluntarily comply with an arbitration judgment.

* * *

Secrecy is highly valued [in the diamond industry], and whoever makes public the workings of the business will suffer a loss in the value of his reputation, even if he is merely defending himself against a meritless lawsuit. Consequently, individual traders, fearful of litigation that might reveal trade practices, prefer to conclude transactions using agreements that are enforceable only in the bourse's arbitration tribunals, where the existence and outcome of a dispute are kept secret as long as the judgment is paid promptly. Given the well-established institutional premium on secrecy, parties are rarely willing to pay the reputational price of violating that norm simply to gain access to the courts. Historically, preserving the secrecy norm is one of the primary reasons that the industry uses extralegal agreements rather than legally enforceable contracts.

* * *

The Diamond Dealers Club still functions like an old-fashioned mutual-aid society. It provides kosher restaurants for its members. A Jewish health organization provides emergency medical services, and social committees are organized by neighborhood to visit sick members and their families. There is a synagogue on the premises, and contributions to a benevolent fund are required.

* * *

Although DDC arbitrators have industry expertise and sophisticated business judgment, they are not much better than courts at valuing lost profit or business opportunities forgone. Because arbitration hearings are held soon after the filing of the complaint, however, and because decisions are rendered and enforced shortly thereafter, the harm suffered by the promisee, while still difficult to quantify, is minimized.

* * *

In disputes other than breach of a promise to pay money or deliver a stone, which are dealt with in the bylaws or according to well-established custom, arbitrators' verdicts may be more accurate and predictable than those of a court since arbitrators possess industry expertise and are permitted to consider information that would be excluded in court under the rules of evidence. If a diamond dispute were decided by a court, the application of industry custom would be highly unpredictable: unlike a DDC arbitrator, who can apply his own knowledge of industry custom, a judge would have to determine the content of customary norms from the conflicting testimony of expert witnesses. The uncertainty introduced by a judge's need to resolve conflicting testimony would greatly reduce the expected benefit to the promisee of having a legally enforceable contract.

* * *

The rapid enforcement of judgments is another advantage of DDC arbitration. Unlike a court, the DDC has the ability to bring unique pressures on the losing party to pay: it can put him out of business almost instantaneously by hanging his picture in the clubroom of every bourse in the world with a notice that he failed to pay his debt. Thus, the threat of publicity and the practice of keeping disputes secret as long as judgments are paid gives the defendant an incentive to promptly comply with the arbitrators' judgment. In addition, trade rules try to minimize the likelihood of a judgment-proof debtor in two ways: by making individual members as well as the corporations they trade for liable for arbitration judgments; and by providing for the expulsion of any member who files, voluntarily or involuntarily, for personal or corporate bankruptcy in court instead of going through the club's own bankruptcy procedure, which requires the debtor to make 100 percent restitution to his diamond industry creditors.

* * *

In complex cases not covered by the trade rules or industry custom, diamond industry arbitration suffers from the same weakness as most commercial arbitration: unpredictability. The lack of written decisions and a tradition of stare decisis makes it difficult for market participants to make rational breach decisions and to determine in advance the type of sanctioned behavior. In order to increase predictability, many bourses in the world federation have relaxed the norm of complete secrecy. Arbitrators publish written announcements of the principles used to decide novel cases while keeping the parties and other identifying facts secret.

* * *

Throughout its history, the diamond business has been largely self regulating, operating outside the law of the state. Over the past thirty-five years, the private dispute-resolution mechanisms in the world's diamond bourses, combined with widespread adherence to the secrecy norm, have succeeded in maintaining a largely extralegal contractual regime where transactions are concluded on the basis of the dealers' reputations and the incidence of breach is low.

* * *

Although the DDC bylaws have always given the litigants the right to be represented by a lawyer, prior to the Rapaport case it was uncommon. Today, legal representation is the norm. The arbitrators feel that the presence of lawyers has, in some measure, altered the rules of decision they apply. The lawyers alert them to relevant parts of New York law, and, while this law still does not supply the rule of decision, the arbitrators are more conscious of the law and are increasingly reluctant to drastically depart from it, except in instances where the decisions are deeply rooted in custom or do not involve creating a new rule. Although the Board of Arbitrators has traditionally declined jurisdiction in cases involving complex statutory rights or claims that are intertwined with pending litigation, in recent years, this has become a more common practice. The older arbitrators fear that legal interference in the diamond trade will one day destroy the traditional way of doing business.

While private enforcement of arbitration agreements and awards may be especially powerful in close-knit religious communities, private enforcement can be significant in other contexts as well. For example, the above excerpt from Bernstein's *Merchant Law in a Merchant Court* notes that a member of the National Grain and Feed Association "who refuses to submit to arbitration or fails to comply with an arbitration award rendered against him may, in addition to having his actions reported in the NGFA newsletter, be suspended or expelled from the Association". It also says "Between 1975 and 1995, three members were expelled for refusing to arbitrate" and "one member was expelled for failure to comply with an arbitration award."

QUESTIONS TO REVIEW AND SYNTHESIZE

1. What is the most commonly cited reason parties choose arbitration over litigation?
2. What are some other common reasons parties choose arbitration over litigation?
3. What reason parties choose arbitration over litigation is emphasized by the above excerpts from Lon Fuller's discussions of both labor and commercial arbitration?
4. How does National Grain and Feed Association arbitration exemplify the reason emphasized by Fuller?
5. Leaving aside government enforcement of arbitration awards, what are some examples of private (non-government) enforcement of arbitration awards?
6. In disputes among what sorts of parties is private enforcement of arbitration awards particularly powerful in incentivizing parties who lose in arbitration to comply with arbitrators' orders, for example, to pay money?

B. DOES ARBITRATION ONLY RESOLVE DISPUTES, OR CAN IT FORMULATE LEGAL RULES?

William M. Landes & Richard A. Posner, *Adjudication As a Private Good*

8 J. Legal Stud. 235, 235–40 (1979).

* * *

A court system (public or private) produces two types of service. One is dispute resolution—determining whether a rule has been violated. The other is rule formulation—creating rules of law as a byproduct of the dispute-settlement process.

* * *

The two judicial services are in principle severable and in practice often are severed. Jury verdicts resolve disputes but do not create precedents. Legislatures create rules of law but do not resolve disputes. In the Anglo-American legal system rule formation is a function shared by legislatures and (especially appellate) courts; elsewhere judicial law making tends to be less important.

* * *

Rule Production. Private production of rules or precedents involves two problems. First, because of the difficulty of establishing property rights in a precedent, private judges may have little incentive to produce precedents. They will strive for a fair result between the parties in order to preserve a reputation for impartiality, but why should they make any effort to explain the result in a way that would provide guidance for future parties? To do so would be to confer an external, an uncompensated, benefit not only on future parties but also on competing judges. If anything, judges might deliberately avoid explaining their results because the demand for their services would be reduced by rules that, by clarifying the meaning of the law, reduced the incidence of disputes. Yet, despite all this, private judges just might produce precedents. We said earlier that competitive private judges would strive for a reputation for competence and impartiality. One method of obtaining such a reputation is to give reasons for a decision that convince the disputants and the public that the judge is competent and impartial. Competition could lead private judges to issue formal or informal "opinions" declaring their interpretation of the law, and these opinions—though intended simply as advertising—would function as precedents, as under a public judicial system. * * *

The second problem with a free market in precedent production is that of inconsistent precedents which could destroy the value of a precedent system in guiding behavior. If there are many judges, there is likely to be a bewildering profusion of precedents and no obvious method of harmonizing them. An individual contemplating some activity will have difficulty discovering its legal consequences because they will depend on who decides any dispute arising out of the activity.

* * *

[A] system of voluntary adjudication is strongly biased against the creation of precise rules of any sort. Any rule that clearly indicates how a judge is likely to decide a case will assure that no disputes subject to the rule are submitted to that judge since one party will know that it will lose. Judges will tend to promulgate vague standards which give each party to a dispute a fighting chance.

Landes and Posner say "a system of voluntary adjudication is strongly biased against the creation of precise rules" and toward "vague standards." They point out that "Jury verdicts resolve disputes but do not create precedents." Similarly, arbitration awards can be very brief, consisting of just two sentences finding for the claimant and ordering the respondent to pay a particular dollar amount. Such an award, which resembles the typical general verdict rendered by a jury rather than the opinion of a trial judge, is unlikely to cite much precedent or to serve as precedent for future decisions by arbitrators or courts. Such brief, conclusory awards were traditionally, and may still be, the norm in commercial arbitration in the United States. This brevity may be due in part to the reasons given by Landes and Posner—

"private judges may have little incentive to produce precedents. They will strive for a fair result between the parties in order to preserve a reputation for impartiality, but why should they make any effort to explain the result in a way that would provide guidance for future parties?" In the typical arbitration between "one-shot" disputants (as opposed to "repeat players" who expect to have similar disputes in which they might benefit from a precedent) neither the parties nor arbitrators may think the costs of a reasoned opinion are worth incurring.

In addition, the traditional norm of short, unreasoned awards may be due to the belief that such awards are less likely to be vacated by a court than are longer awards containing more reasoning with which a court might find fault. The American Arbitration Association (AAA), which has long administered much of the commercial arbitration in the U.S., traditionally discouraged arbitrators from writing reasoned awards. Soia Mentschikoff's important 1961 article, *Commercial Arbitration*, observes that the AAA:

- "from its beginning held itself out as an expert in matters that went to the enforceability of an award and set up its rules and regulations with the primary aim of rendering awards that would not be set aside by the courts"; and
- "puts enormous pressure on its arbitrators not to write opinions but to merely state the award in dollar amounts."[12]

The AAA's Commercial Arbitration Rules continue to state that "The arbitrator need not render a reasoned award unless the parties request such an award in writing prior to appointment of the arbitrator or unless the arbitrator determines that a reasoned award is appropriate."[13] While "it is increasingly common for AAA arbitrators to produce reasoned opinions rather than mere awards, these opinions are typically kept private and are of no precedential value."[14]

In contrast, labor arbitrators regularly use arbitration awards as precedents. Unlike its Commercial Arbitration Rules, the AAA's Labor Rules presume the arbitrator will accompany the award with an opinion unless the parties agree otherwise: "The parties shall advise the AAA whenever they do not require the arbitrator to accompany the award with an opinion."[15] Not only do labor arbitration awards commonly include reasoned opinions, the opinions are often published in the Bureau of National Affairs' *Labor Arbitration Reports*, and "even when awards are not published, [labor] arbitrators are often repeat players and may be well aware of how they and other arbitrators have resolved similar disputes."[16] "An extensive survey of labor arbitrators disclosed that 77 percent of the 238 responding arbitrators believed that precedents, even under *other* contracts, should be given 'some

[12] Soia Mentschikoff, *Commercial Arbitration*, 61 Colum. L. Rev. 846, 857 (1961).

[13] Rule 46(b).

[14] Lisa Bernstein, *Black Hole Apparitions*, 67 Duke L.J. Online 102, 105 (2017).

[15] Am. Arbitration Ass'n., Labor Arbitration Rule 37 (July 1, 2013), https://www.adr.org/sites/default/files/document_repository/Labor_Arbitration_Rules_1.pdf.

[16] W. Mark C. Weidemaier, *Toward a Theory of Precedent in Arbitration*, 51 WM & MARY L. REV. 1895, 1919–20 (2010).

weight.'"[17] Consequently, "labor arbitrators often justify their decisions by citing only other arbitration awards," and "arbitral precedent plays a major role [in] labor arbitration, where arbitrators are engaged primarily in building a 'common law of the workplace.'"[18]

In addition, "international commercial arbitration routinely requires arbitrators to produce fully reasoned awards."[19] In some international fields, arbitrators often cite earlier arbitration awards as precedent.[20] An example is investor-state arbitration administered by the International Centre for Settlement of Investment Disputes (ICSID): "Over time, these tribunals have come to act more like formal international courts than like traditional commercial arbitrators: they write reasoned opinions that can run hundreds of pages long; they engage in sophisticated analysis of difficult questions of international law; and they cite, interpret, and critique one another's decisions, building a sort of common law of investment on which states and investors can more or less rely."[21]

For an example of a reasoned award with calculations resulting in the award of $25,463.65, see *In re* Arb. Between Sinotrans (Bermuda) LTD. and Crossbridge Shipping Singapore LTD., SMA No. 4149, 2011 WL 6762991 (S.M.A.A.S) (N.Y. Dec. 7, 2011). In contrast, for a summary award of a much higher sum, $139,050,406.77, see *In re* Arb. Between: Eddystone Rail Company, LLC, and Jamex Transfer Services, LLC, SMA No. 4300, 2017 WL 466154 (N.Y. Jan. 24, 2017).

QUESTIONS TO REVIEW AND SYNTHESIZE

1. What are two services provided by both judges and arbitrators?
2. Why might judicial opinions be (on average) longer than arbitration awards?
3. Under what circumstances is arbitration most likely to develop a system of precedent in which later arbitrators follow or distinguish earlier arbitration awards, much like later courts follow or distinguish earlier judicial decisions?
4. How does a concise arbitration award resemble the output of a jury?

---

[17] Frank Elkouri & Edna A. Elkouri, How Arbitration Works 572 (Alan Miles Ruben et al. eds., 6th ed. 2003); see also Theodore J. St. Antoine, *The Use and Abuse of Precedent in Labor and Employment Arbitration*, 52 U. LOUISVILLE L. REV. 431 (2014) ("Yet even when not bound in any technical sense, an arbitrator may be strongly influenced by a well-reasoned decision in a prior case whose facts are closely similar to the present one").

[18] Mark C. Weidemaier, *Judging-Lite: How Arbitrators Use and Create Precedent*, 90 N.C. L. Rev. 1092, 1116 (2012).

[19] S.I. Strong, *Reasoned Awards in International Commercial Arbitration: Embracing And Exceeding The Common Law-Civil Law Dichotomy*, 37 Mich. J. Int'l L. 1, 2 (2015).

[20] Christopher S. Gibson & Christopher R. Drahozal, *Iran-United States Claims Tribunal Precedent in Investor-State Arbitration*, 23 J. Int'l Arb. 521, 537–44 (2006) ("extensive reliance on [Iran-United States Claims] Tribunal precedents" in investor-state arbitration); Gabrielle Kaufmann-Kohler, *Arbitral Precedent: Dream, Necessity, or Excuse?*, 23 Arb. Int'l 357 (2007).

[21] Julian D. Mortenson, *The Meaning of "Investment": ICSID's Travaux and the Domain of International Investment Law*, 51 Harv. Int'l L.J. 257, 264 (2010).

C. "RIGHTS" (OR "GRIEVANCE") ARBITRATION AND "INTEREST" ARBITRATION

The distinction between "rights" and "interest" arbitration is most common in labor arbitration. The paradigm of a "rights" arbitration is a hearing on the grievance (labor arbitration's word for "claim") of an employee alleging the employer's breach of a collective bargaining agreement (CBA) between the employer and a labor union. For instance, many CBAs prohibit the employer from discharging (firing) an employee without "just cause"; so many "rights" arbitrations are grievances alleging the employer lacked "just cause" for discharging the employee. In contrast, the paradigm of an "interest" arbitration is a hearing held at the expiration of a CBA to decide the terms of the next CBA. So in interest arbitration, the arbitrator determines the contract terms that will bind the parties during the life of their *new* agreement, while in rights (or grievance) arbitration, the arbitrator is merely applying an *existing* contract.[22] Interest arbitration is particularly common in the context of local government employees, such as police officers or teachers. Such public employees are usually legally-forbidden from engaging in the coordinated refusal to work (strike) that is central to how private-sector labor unions exert pressure on employers. So public sector labor law often substitutes legally-required interest arbitration for the (threatened or actual) strike of the private-sector union. Such legislation in effect gives public employee unions the right to resort to arbitration to determine the future terms of employment.

A number of statutes require the arbitration of "interest" disputes concerning the terms of a new CBA between a state or local government, and a union representing its employees. Fairly typical are Rhode Island's Fire Fighter's Arbitration Act and Policemen's Arbitration Act.[23] In recognition of "the necessity to provide some alternative method of settling disputes where employees must, as a matter of public policy, be denied the usual right to strike," the legislation requires that where a city and a union cannot reach agreement, "any and all unresolved issues" shall be submitted to arbitration. One arbitrator is to be named by each of the parties and the third, in the absence of agreement, is selected under the rules of the AAA. The legislation attempts to enumerate the "factors" which the panel must take into account—including the "interest and welfare of the public," the "community's ability to pay," and a comparison of wage rates and employment conditions with prevailing local conditions "of skilled employees of the building trades and industry" and with police or fire departments in cities of comparable size.[24]

"Interest" disputes in public sector employment are intimately connected to the political process. Many public services, such as police protection and education, raise questions that are "politically, socially, or ideologically sensitive."[25] A number of such sensitive issues have in fact been held to be "non-bargainable"—despite their obvious impact on the working conditions of public employees—and thus outside the permissible scope of "interest" arbitration. Such "non-negotiable matters of

---

[22] Charles B. Craver, *The Judicial Enforcement of Public Sector Interest Arbitration*, 21 B.C.L.Rev. 557, 558 n. 8 (1980).

[23] 28 R.I. Gen. Laws Ann. § 28–9.1–2 (West); 28 R.I. Gen. Laws Ann. § 28–9.2–2.

[24] 28 R.I. Gen. Laws Ann. § 28–9.1–10; 28 R.I. Gen. Laws Ann. § 28–9.2–10.

[25] Harry Wellington & Ralph K. Winter, Jr., The Unions and the Cities 23 (1971).

governmental policy" might in public education include questions of curriculum or of class size; in police services, questions of the personnel level of the force or a civilian review board for police discipline. See, e.g., San Jose Peace Officer's Ass'n v. City of San Jose, 78 Cal.App.3d 935, 144 Cal.Rptr. 638 (1978) (police policy governing when officer is allowed to fire weapon; "The forum of the bargaining table with its postures, strategies, trade-offs, modifications, and compromises is no place for the 'delicate balancing of different interests: the protection of society from criminals, the protection of police officers' safety, and the preservation of all human life, if possible.'"); Rutgers, State Univ. of New Jersey v. Union of Rutgers Administrators-Am. Fed'n of Teachers, Local 1766, AFL-CIO, No. A-2478-13T3, 2015 WL 2416962, at *5 (N.J. Super. Ct. App. Div. May 22, 2015) (holding that a public university's staffing decisions are "non-negotiable matters of governmental policy" because of a need for the efficient use of public resources and a sensible allocation of public funds).

In a more general sense, the resolution of *all* disputes over the terms of public employment—even disputes over nuts and bolts issues like wages—is inescapably "political." To resolve a wage dispute by applying the "factors" set out in the Rhode Island legislation requires accommodating the competing interests of employees, taxpayers, and the users of public services. The arbitrators will likely consider priorities among various government programs, the level of government services, or the desirability and feasibility of increased government revenue. Such exercises of judgment are necessarily political compromises. Should such issues be resolved "in an arbitrator's conference room as an alternative to facing up to vexing problems in the halls of state and local legislatures"?[26]

> The size of the budget, the taxes to be levied, the purposes for which tax money is to be used, the kinds and levels of governmental services to be enjoyed, and the level of indebtedness are issues that should be decided by officials who are politically responsible to those who pay the taxes and seek the services. The notion that we can or should insulate public employee bargaining from the political process either by arbitration or with some magic formula is a delusion of reality and a denigration of democratic government.[27]

Along these lines, courts have occasionally held particular authorizations of public-sector interest arbitration unconstitutional. See, e.g., Salt Lake City v. International Ass'n of Firefighters, 563 P.2d 786 (Utah 1977) (In finding a statute requiring arbitration for public employees unconstitutional, the court noted that the "legislature may not surrender its legislative authority to a body wherein the public interest is subjected to the interest of a group which may be antagonistic to the public interest"), Cty. of Riverside v. Superior Court, 66 P.3d 718, 728 (Cal. 2003) ("[E]stablishing compensation for its employees is for the county to do, and [the California constitution] prohibits the Legislature from delegating that function to a

[26] Dearborn Fire Fighters Union v. City of Dearborn, 394 Mich. 229, 231 N.W.2d 226 (1975).

[27] R. Summers, Public Sector Bargaining: *Problems of Governmental Decision-Making*, 44 U.Cinn.L.Rev. 669, 672 (1975). See also Joseph R. Grodin, *Political Aspects of Public Sector Interest Arbitration*, 64 Cal.L.Rev. 678 (1976) (examining "impact of binding interest arbitration on the political process by showing the situations in which arbitrators are, in effect, making social policy decisions that are otherwise usually reserved for elected or appointed officials.").

private body," so a statute delegating municipal functions to a private party violated the California constitution.)

On the other hand, most state supreme courts uphold the constitutionality of most interest arbitration statutes.[28] For instance, the Rhode Island Supreme Court rebuffed a constitutional attack on that state's compulsory interest arbitration statutes by characterizing the arbitrators as "public officers" rather than as mere "private persons". The arbitration panel should be considered "an administrative or governmental agency," asserted the court, because the arbitrators had been granted "a portion of the sovereign and legislative power of the government."[29] Voters in a Colorado city approved an amendment to the city charter to mandate interest arbitration to resolve collective bargaining impasses between police officers and the city. Rejecting the city's argument that this mandate unconstitutionally delegated legislative power, the Colorado Supreme Court upheld the mandate on the ground that the charter amendment provided constitutionally-sufficient political accountability and safeguards.[30]

Is the same judicial deference traditionally accorded arbitral awards appropriate in the case of compulsory "interest" arbitration in the public sector? Courts tend toward tighter review of public sector interest arbitration because of the greater public interest in the outcomes. Joseph Slater, *Interest Arbitration As Alternative Dispute Resolution: The History from 1919 to 2011*, 28 Ohio St. J. on Disp. Resol. 387, 413 (2013). In fact, many states' statutes treat such arbitration panels like an administrative agency by requiring the arbitrators to produce a record of the arbitration proceedings and a written decision, so courts may see whether it is "supported by substantial credible evidence present in the record." See Hillsdale PBA Local 207 v. Borough of Hillsdale, 137 N.J. 71, 644 A.2d 564 (1994) (award must "identify and weigh" all the factors enumerated in the statute, "analyze the evidence pertaining to those factors, and explain why other factors are irrelevant"). See Charles Craver, *The Judicial Enforcement of Public Sector Interest Arbitration*, 21 B.C.L.Rev. 557, 572 (1980) (deference to arbitral determinations would give rise to the "possibility of catastrophic consequences resulting from an entirely intemperate award").

Can an existing "interest" arbitration clause be invoked in order to obtain inclusion of a similar clause in a *new* contract? Courts that have answered "no" have reasoned in this way:

> [T]he NLRA [National Labor Relations Act] allows parties to accept or reject an arbitration provision as they see fit. However, if arbitrators were free to do as Scheinman [the arbitrator] did here, parties would have no control over the continued inclusion of an arbitration provision. This would allow for an end-run around the NLRA's public policy considerations.

---

[28] Ronald Hoh, *Interest Arbitration Its Effects on Collective Bargaining in Montana's Protective Services*, Mont. Law., March 2007, at 8, 10.

[29] City of Warwick v. Warwick Regular Firemen's Ass'n, 106 R.I. 109, 256 A.2d 206 (1969).

[30] Fraternal Order of Police, Colorado Lodge No. 19 v. City of Commerce City, 996 P.2d 133, 135, 137 (Colo. 2000), as modified on denial of reh'g (Apr. 10, 2000).

To see how this problem plays out in practice, we start with the undisputed premise that, because an arbitration provision is not a mandatory subject of bargaining, Hamilton Park was under no obligation to agree to arbitration in the 2008–2013 CBA. It is only because Hamilton Park reached a limited agreement—the inclusion of an arbitration provision in a single CBA—that Scheinman was involved in the case in the first instance. He then used this agreement to expand Hamilton Park's arbitration requirements. If an arbitrator, once empowered to decide a particular dispute, could then require all future disputes to be arbitrated, a party that has once agreed to a limited arbitration provision could forever be held hostage to it. As the Fifth Circuit explained,

> a party * * * may find itself locked into that procedure for as long as the bargaining relationship endures. Exertion of economic force to rid oneself of the clause is foreclosed, for the continued inclusion of the term is for resolution by [the arbitrator, who is] an outsider. Parties may justly fear that the tendency of arbitrators would be to continue including the clause, for that is exactly what happened in this case.

Because second generation interest arbitration provisions imposed without consent violate the contract law principles of the FAA [Federal Arbitration Act] and the public policy goals of the NLRA, we hold that they are unenforceable. As discussed, there is no evidence that Hamilton Park agreed to have such a provision. Hence it must be removed from Scheinman's award.

Hamilton Park Health Care Ctr. Ltd. v. 1199 SEIU United Healthcare Workers E., 817 F.3d 857, 865–66 (3d Cir. 2016) (quoting NLRB v. Columbus Printing Pressmen & Assistants' Union No. 252, 543 F.2d 1161, 1169–70 (5th Cir.1976)).

An example of interest arbitration in the private sector is in Major League Baseball. Under the collective bargaining agreement between the teams and the players' union, players who have been in the major leagues for at least six years can choose to become "free agents" and thus have their salaries determined through negotiation in the market with teams that might be interested in them. In contrast, players with fewer than six years service in the majors are tied to their original team unless they are traded or released. However, those with at least *three* years service do have the right to submit the question of their salary to binding arbitration. Baseball arbitration is, thus, a somewhat unique form of interest arbitration because it sets a term of an individual's contract (salary) that supplements the terms of the CBA, rather than setting terms of the CBA itself. See Benjamin A. Tulis, *Final-Offer "Baseball" Arbitration: Contexts, Mechanics & Applications*, 20 Seton Hall J.Sports & Ent.L. 85, 87 (2010).

The most distinctive feature of baseball arbitration is that arbitrators are not free to choose whatever salary figure they think is appropriate. Instead, the player and the club each submit a "final offer" on salary for the coming season. The arbitrators may then award only one or the other of the two figures submitted. This "final-offer arbitration" incentivizes each party to make concessions so its proposed salary appears more "reasonable"—and thus more likely to be chosen—than the opposing party's. Final-offer arbitration thus tends to move each party in the direction of the other, narrowing the differences between them—and at best, making any arbitration award at all completely unnecessary if the parties propose the same salary.

Final-offer arbitration is also frequently used to resolve "interest" disputes in public-sector employment. In contrast to arbitration in Major League Baseball, however, public-sector "interest" arbitrators frequently determine a wide range of issues in addition to salary—all going to make up the terms of employment in the new agreement. Some states' statutes call for each party to present to the arbitrators a "package" that includes a position on *all* issues not yet agreed. The arbitrators must then choose what they consider to be the more reasonable of the two "packages." In other states, by contrast, the arbitrators are allowed to consider each issue separately—and to choose between the positions of the parties on an issue-by-issue basis. This variation enables the arbitrators to develop their own compromise "package" by balancing the parties' positions on the various issues.

Final-offer arbitration is occasionally used outside the labor context. For example, the IRS and Apple chose final-offer arbitration to settle a "transfer pricing" dispute. The IRS had asserted a $114 million deficiency against Apple, claiming that the company had unlawfully reduced its U.S. income by overpaying for parts manufactured by its Singapore subsidiary—that is, by setting the prices higher than if the work had been done "at arm's length" for an unrelated company. Apple and the IRS spent nine months negotiating a 40-page agreement setting out the procedure for the arbitration. There would be a panel of three arbitrators—a retired federal judge, an economist, and an industry expert. For each taxable year in dispute, the parties would each present the panel with one amount, and the arbitrators must "select one of the amounts * * * and no other"; the arbitrators would not be bound by legal precedents if those cases "conflicted with industry practices." "IRS and Apple Submit Transfer Pricing Case to 'Baseball' Arbitration by Industry Experts," 10 Alternatives to High Cost Litig. 47 (1992). In another dispute, arising out of a real estate transaction in the Czech Republic, the arbitrator was instructed to choose the offer of one of the parties, but was permitted to "depart from that figure by up to $500,000 in either direction." See Al-Harbi v. Citibank, N.A., 85 F.3d 680 (D.C. Cir.1996).

The phrase "interest arbitration" is rarely used outside the labor context. But commercial and business contracts sometimes use arbitration similarly to adapt the terms of an ongoing relationship to changing conditions—for example, in long-term supply contracts or in the internal affairs of close corporations. See, e.g., Rain CII Carbon, LLC v. ConocoPhillips Co., 674 F.3d 469, 471 (5th Cir. 2012)("Conoco and Rain are parties to a long-term supply agreement, whereby Conoco agreed to sell all green anode coke produced at its Alliance refinery from August 2005 to December 2015 to Rain. The 2005 agreement includes a complex formula for capturing the market price of green coke. The agreement further provides that if a party reasonably concludes that the contract formula no longer yields market price, the party may reopen price negotiations. If such negotiations prove unfruitful, the matter would be submitted to a 'baseball' arbitration, whereby each party submits a proposal and the arbitrator selects one of the two."); Vogel v. Lewis, 268 N.Y.S.2d

237 (App. Div. 1966), aff'd, 19 N.Y.2d 589, 278 N.Y.S.2d 236, 224 N.E.2d 738 (1967) (agreement between the two owners of a close corporation; held, a dispute over whether the company should exercise an option to purchase the warehouse where the business was carried on was arbitrable; "there seems to be no reason why arbitrators may not be useful in resolving issues which involve some business judgment so long as they are not required to assume a continuing burden of management"); cf. Ringling v. Ringling Bros.-Barnum & Bailey Combined Shows, Inc., 49 A.2d 603 (Del. Ch. 1946), modified, 53 A.2d 441 (Del. 1947) (shareholders agreed to "consult and confer" with each other and to "act jointly" in exercising their voting rights, and that if they failed to agree, the disagreement would be submitted to arbitration "to the end of assuring . . . good management").

Are the following three cases examples of "rights" arbitration or "interest" arbitration?

(1) A law firm leased space in an office building. The term of the lease was ten years. At the firm's request, a clause was added to the lease by which it would have the option to renew the lease for an additional ten years; it provided that "rental for the renewal term shall be in such amount as shall be agreed upon by the parties based on the comparative rental values of similar properties as of the date of the renewal and on comparative business conditions of the two periods." The lease contained a general arbitration clause providing that "all disputes relating to" the lease shall be settled by arbitration. The parties fail to agree on a rental for the renewal term.

(2) A coal supply agreement provided that for a period of ten years a coal company would tender and a power company would buy specified quantities of coal. There was a base price per ton, and a provision for the calculation of adjustments in base price upon changes in certain labor costs and in "governmental impositions." The agreement also provided:

> Any gross proven inequity that may result in unusual economic conditions not contemplated by the parties at the time of the execution of this Agreement may be corrected by mutual consent. Each party shall in the case of a claim of gross inequity furnish the other with whatever documentary evidence may be necessary to assist in effecting a settlement.

Another clause required arbitration of "any unresolved controversy between the parties arising under this Agreement." Four years later, after a rapid escalation in the price of coal, the open market price of coal of the same quality was more than three times the current adjusted base price under the agreement. The coal company requested an adjustment in the contract price, which the power company adamantly rejected.[31]

(3) An agreement between an employer and the labor union representing its employees was to last for three years, with a provision that "this contract shall remain in effect until all terms and conditions of employment for a succeeding contract term are resolved either through

[31] See Georgia Power Co. v. Cimarron Coal Corp., 526 F.2d 101 (6th Cir.1975).

negotiation or through arbitration." After a bargaining deadlock, the union moved for arbitration. The employer presented to the arbitrator a number of items the employer wanted included in the agreement for the new term, including the right to make layoffs on account of automation or the introduction of new processes. The Union also presented a number of issues to the arbitrator, including "wages; mailers brought up to mechanical department [wage] scale; proof room brought up to composing room scale; pension; sick leave; vacations; increased mileage; grievance procedure; jurisdiction of jobs—need for job descriptions; holidays; jury and witness duty; overtime after thirty hours during holiday weeks; night differential; life insurance; option under Blue Cross for eyeglasses; option under Dental Plan for payment for dentures; paid uniforms for pressmen; addition of grandparent and guardian to funeral leave."

As these examples show, distinguishing "interest" arbitration from "rights" arbitration may be difficult. This suggests that both forms of arbitration can give parties flexibility in committing to complex, long-term contracts. When forming such a contract, parties cannot anticipate all possible disputes and then draft express terms to resolve them. Rather than try, which would consume lots of time negotiating over resolution of disputes that never arise, the parties may use broad contract language combined with an arbitration clause, thus delegating to the arbitrator their power to resolve disputes as they arise. The arbitrators' contract interpretation, ostensibly "rights" arbitration, may involve considerable flexibility to craft resolutions of disputes unaddressed or even unanticipated when the contract was formed, or where past solutions are no longer neatly adapted to changed needs. "Rights" arbitration among such parties often "involves not only the settlement of the particular dispute but also interstitial rule-making"[32]—a process aimed at creating, refining, and elaborating for the future the rules to govern their relationship. As those are the aims of interest arbitration, the supposed distinction between "rights" and "interest" arbitration may be a mere question of degree or emphasis.

QUESTIONS TO REVIEW AND SYNTHESIZE

1. Compare and contrast "rights" and "interest" arbitration.
2. Why do courts reason that an existing "interest" arbitration clause cannot be invoked in order to obtain inclusion of a similar clause in a new contract?
3. Why is interest arbitration to set the terms of public-sector employment sometimes held unconstitutional?
4. What is "final-offer arbitration?" Contrast its uses in Major League Baseball with public-sector employment.

---

[32] See David E. Feller, *A General Theory of the Collective Bargaining Agreement*, 61 Calif. L. Rev. 663, 744–45 (1973).

CHAPTER 2

SOME FREQUENT USES OF ARBITRATION

Arbitration agreements appear in a wide variety of transactions, including plans for Justin Bieber to appear at a celebration of Kylie Jenner's 18th birthday.[1] The relevant contracts, including with the event promoter, Team Productions, provided that "all disputes arising under, concerning, relating to or touching on this agreement will be submitted to binding arbitration in Los Angeles, California before a single arbitrator for prompt resolution." Apparently displeased with Team Promotions' performance, Bieber did not attend the event and tweeted to his 80 million Twitter followers: "Montreal due to the promoter of today's event breaking his contract and lying I will not be able to attend today's event. I'm sorry." Team Productions brought a defamation suit in a Canadian court against Bieber, who successfully invoked the arbitration clause, and thus persuaded the court to refer the dispute to arbitration in California.

Arbitration was also central to "Deflategate." After finding that many footballs used in a 2015 playoff game were underinflated, the National Football League (NFL) suspended star quarterback Tom Brady for four games.[2] Brady's union, the NFL

---

[1] Craig Chiasson, *Justin Bieber Tweets and an International Arbitrator Listens: Court Refers Defamation Claim to Arbitration*, LEXOLOGY (June 22, 2017), https://www.lexology.com/library/detail.aspx?g=1d55d59f-b032-499e-83b2-68a348628d8c.

[2] Martin J. Greenberg & Lori Shaw, *Deflategate*, Blog (Oct. 1, 2016), http://www.greenberglawoffice.com/deflategate/.

Players Association appealed the punishment through the arbitration process outlined in its collective bargaining agreement with the NFL. The arbitrator affirmed the suspension,[3] but the Players Association persuaded a federal court to vacate the arbitration award.[4] Ultimately, however, the Second Circuit reversed the district court, and Brady served his four game suspension.[5]

Celebs like Brady and the Biebs are not the norm in arbitration. More typical are the parties discussed in the rest of this chapter.

A. COMMERCIAL ARBITRATION

1. HISTORY

William C. Jones, *Three Centuries of Commercial Arbitration in New York: A Brief Survey*

1956 Wash.U.L.Q. 193, 209–10, 218–19.

[I]t is commonplace among those who write about arbitration that it has been in use for centuries.

* * *

[E]nough material on arbitration has been uncovered to show fairly conclusively that arbitration was in constant and widespread use throughout the colonial period in New York. * * * Seemingly, arbitration was used primarily in situations where the decision would not be entirely for one side or the other, but where there was, rather, considerable area for negotiation. The settlement of an account resulting from a long course of dealing between two merchants is an example. Land boundaries and the distribution of the proceeds from a privateering expedition are others. Evidently, from the way in which individuals felt it worthwhile to advertise in the newspapers their willingness to arbitrate, there was some social pressure to arbitrate a dispute before taking it to court, and even to submit it to arbitration after the suit was begun. This tends to substantiate a feeling that one function of arbitration was to supply a final stage in the negotiation process between two disputants and that a willingness to negotiate was highly esteemed in the community.

* * *

[T]he existence of the practice of extensive arbitration over so long a period of time in the mercantile community tends to show that, as used by merchants, arbitration is not really a substitute for court adjudication as something that is cheaper or faster or whatever,[112] but is rather a means of dispute settling quite as

---

[3] *The case for Tom Brady: An arbitrator's take*, Wash. Post (June 10, 2016), https://www.washingtonpost.com/news/early-lead/wp/2016/06/10/the-case-for-tom-brady-an-arbitrators-take/.

[4] NFL Mgmt. Council v. NFL Players Ass'n, 820 F.3d 527, 531 (2d Cir. 2016).

[5] Martin J. Greenberg & Lori Shaw, *Deflategate*, Blog (Oct. 1, 2016), http://www.greenberglawoffice.com/deflategate/.

[112] Though, interestingly enough, arbitration was presented as such an alternative in the eighteenth century in almost the same language as is used today.

ancient—for all practical purposes anyway—as court adjudication, and that it has, traditionally, fulfilled quite a different function. The primary function of arbitration is to provide the merchants fora where mercantile disputes will be settled by merchants. This, in turn, suggests that merchants wish to form, and have for a long time succeeded in forming, a separate, and, to some extent, self-governing community, independent of the larger unit. For law this means that courts may perform, in the commercial field at least, a different function from that which we usually assign to them. In many cases, they may not be the primary fora for adjudication. If this is true, when they are called upon to decide a commercial case in one of these areas, it will be either after another adjudicatory agency has acted or because the other system cannot, or will not, cope with the case. In some areas, courts may almost never get a case. * * * Insofar as this area, in which arbitration is and—most importantly—has always been the primary dispute-settling agency, is an important one (and an area which includes stockbrokers, produce brokers, coffee merchants, etc., seems to be such an area), it cannot really be said that one has studied commercial law, in the sense of the rules that actually guide the settlement of disputes involving commercial matters, if he has studied only the reports of appellate courts and legislation. We cannot even understand the significance of the "law" contained in the reports and statutes until we have studied arbitration decisions. * * *

Having gone so far with hypothesis, one may be forgiven for going a little farther and suggesting that the existence of a sufficient sense of community identity or separateness on the part of merchants to cause them to have a separate adjudicatory system tends to show that there is a mercantile community which is, to a considerable degree, self-governing. This community has existed in this form for centuries. Its existence suggests that there may be others—religious and educational communities come to mind.

The following excerpt is from a classic article by Soia Mentschikoff, the only woman actively involved in drafting the Uniform Commercial Code.[6] Mentschikoff has also been described as "the 'mother' of empirical evaluation of dispute resolution."[7]

Soia Mentschikoff, *Commercial Arbitration*

61 Col.L.Rev. 846, 848–54 (1961).

The first thing to be noted is that although commonly thought of as a single type phenomenon, both the structure and the process of commercial arbitration are determined by the different institutional contexts in which it arises. There are three major institutional settings in which commercial arbitration appears as a mechanism for the settlement of disputes.

---

6 Jennifer Trost, *The Impostor Rule and Identity Theft in America*, 35 Law & Hist. Rev. 433, 452 (2017).

7 Carrie Menkel-Meadow, *Mothers and Fathers of Invention: The Intellectual Founders of ADR*, 16 Ohio St. J. on Disp. Resol. 1, 22 (2000).

The simplest is when two persons in a contract delineating a business relationship agree to settle any disputes that may arise under the contract by resort to arbitration before named arbitrators or persons to be named at the time of the dispute. In this, which can be called individuated arbitration, the making of all arrangements, including the procedures for arbitration, rests entirely with the parties concerned. Although we do not know, we believe that the chief moving factors here are: (1) a desire for privacy as, for example, in certain crude oil situations where such arrangements exist; (2) the availability of expert deciders; (3) the avoidance of possible legal difficulties with the nature of the transaction itself; and (4) the random acceptance by many businessmen of the idea that arbitration is faster and less expensive than court action.

A second type of arbitration arises within the context of a particular trade association or exchange. The group establishes its own arbitration machinery for the settlement of disputes among its members, either on a voluntary or compulsory basis, and sometimes makes it available to nonmembers doing business in the particular trade. A particular association may also have specialist committees, which are investigatory in character, with the arbitration machinery handling only the private disputes involving nonspecialist categories of cases. * * *

The third setting for commercial arbitration is found in administrative groups, such as the American Arbitration Association, the International Chamber of Commerce, and various local chambers of commerce, which provide rules, facilities, and arbitrators for any persons desiring to settle disputes by arbitration. Many trade associations with insufficient business to warrant separate organizations make special arrangements with one of these groups to process disputes that arise among their members.

* * *

Factors Determining the Need for Arbitration

At this point it is useful to distinguish between those factors that can be said to produce a need for arbitration machinery in commercial groups and those factors that merely make it desirable. The reasons commonly given for arbitration—speed, lower expense, more expert decision, greater privacy—are appealing to all businessmen, and yet not all utilize arbitration. It seems reasonably clear, therefore, that for some trades these factors are of greater importance than for others, and that for some trades there must be countervailing values in not resorting to arbitration. We postulated three factors as being theoretically important in determining whether or not a particular trade needed institutionalized use of arbitration, and incorporated questions relating to these factors in our trade association questionnaire.

The first factor was the nature of the economic function being performed in relation to the movement of the goods by the members of the association. We postulated that persons primarily buying for resale, that is merchants in the original sense of the term, were much more likely to be interested in speed of adjudication, and that since price allowance would be a central remedy for defects in quality or, indeed, for nondelivery, the speed and low cost characteristics of arbitration would be particularly attractive to them, thus leading to the creation of institutionalized machinery. The trade associations in which such merchants constitute all or part of the membership reported as follows: 48 percent use institutionalized machinery, 34 percent make individual arrangements for arbitration, and only 18 percent never arbitrate. These figures are to be contrasted with the reports from those trade associations that stated that their memberships did not include any merchants. In those groups 23 percent reported the existence of institutionalized arbitration, 44 percent reported individual arrangements, and 33 percent reported no arbitration whatever.

The second major factor that we thought would be important in determining the need for arbitration was the participation of the members of the association in foreign trade. Apart from the enhanced possibility of delay inherent in transnational law suits, when the parties to a transaction are governed by different substantive rules of law, resort to the formal legal system poses uncertainty and relative unpredictability of result for at least one of the parties. This uncertainty and unpredictability is increased by the fact that the very rules governing the choice of the applicable law are themselves relatively uncertain and are not uniform among the nations of the world. Faced with such an uncertain formal legal situation, any affected trade group is apt to develop its own set of substantive rules or standards of behavior as the controlling rules for its members. Obviously, when a trade group develops its own rules of law, it requires as deciders of its disputes persons who are acquainted with the standards it has developed. Since this knowledgeability does not reside in the judges of any formal legal system, the drive toward institutionalized private machinery is reinforced.

* * *

The third factor that we thought would bear on the need for arbitration machinery relates to the kind of goods dealt with by the members of the association. One of the major areas of dispute among businessmen centers on the quality of the goods involved. If, therefore, the goods are such as not to be readily susceptible of quality determination by third persons, arbitration or, indeed, inspection, is an unlikely method of settling disputes. If goods are divided into raws, softs, and hards, the differences in their suitability for third party adjudication becomes relatively clear. On the whole, raws are a fungible commodity, one bushel of #1 wheat being very much like another bushel of #1 wheat. On the other hand, hards, which consist of items like refrigerators and automobiles, are not viewed by their producers as essentially fungible, however they may appear to the layman. We did not believe that Ford would like to have General Motors sitting on disputes involving the quality of Ford cars, or vice versa. Moreover, quality differentials in raws can normally be reflected by price differentials, but defects in hard goods frequently affect their usefulness and therefore price differential compensation is not feasible. Thus, the normal sales remedy for raws has come to be price allowance, whereas the normal sales remedy for hard goods has come to be repair or replacement. Raws, involving fungibility and ease of finding an appropriate remedy, are therefore highly susceptible to third party adjudication, whereas hard goods tend to move away from such adjudication. Soft goods, which are an intermediate category and range from textiles to small hardware, we thought would constitute a neutral category.

In our survey of exchanges dealing in grain and livestock, 100 percent of those responding reported the use of institutionalized arbitration. There are, of course, other reasons for such a unanimous response by the exchanges, but the nature of the goods involved is a very important one. The trade association survey showed that of all the reporting associations, dealings in raws, 46 percent had machinery, 29 percent made individual arrangements, and only 25 percent never arbitrated. On the other hand, only 4 percent of those reporting hards as their basic goods had machinery, 46 percent made individual arrangements, and 50 per cent never arbitrated. * * *

To the extent that the factors leading to institutionalized machinery reinforce each other, as, for example, in the case of an association reporting that its members have an import relationship to foreign trade, deal in raws, and consist of merchants, the existence of arbitration machinery rises to approximately 100 percent. When the contrary report is made, that is, that the membership consists of manufacturers of hard goods engaged only in domestic business, the percentage drops off to about 8 percent.

We can thus say that the presence of institutionalized arbitration is a strong index of the existence of a generally self-contained trade association having its own self-regulation machinery and that the forces leading to institutionalized arbitration also, therefore, tend to lead to the creation of self-contained, self-governing trade groups.

---

2. TRADE ASSOCIATION ARBITRATION VS. GENERAL COMMERCIAL ARBITRATION

The Mentschikoff article just excerpted distinguishes between arbitration administered by a trade association and arbitration administered by the American Arbitration Association (AAA). Mentschikoff explains elsewhere in *Commercial Arbitration* that "In almost all self-contained trade associations and exchanges, lawyer participation in the arbitration proceedings is either forbidden or discouraged, and very few of the arbitrators are lawyers or law-trained." This paucity of lawyers—because merchants play all the necessary roles—remains true in the arbitration systems of several trade associations. For example, Chapter 1 quoted the National Grain & Feed Association (NGFA) explaining that its "Arbitrators are employees, active partners, principals, officers, or directors of Active, Allied and Transportation members. Arbitrators are generally selected based upon their personal experience in the type of trade practices or questions involved in the case." More broadly, "Limiting the role of lawyers is an important common feature in [soft commodities arbitration]; lawyers are not usually included in the mandatory arbitral panel and cannot as a rule represent parties in oral hearings without both parties' express agreement, which in practice is seldom given."[8]

---

[8] See also Yuliya Chernykh, *The Last Citadel: The Restricted Role of Lawyers in Soft Commodity Arbitration*, 14 (2) Transnational Dispute Management (2017) https://www.transnational-dispute-management.com/article.asp?key=2453.

Moreover, the parties to trade association arbitration agreements rarely need litigation to enforce such agreements or to confirm or vacate trade association arbitration awards because, as we also saw in Chapter 1, self-interest and private pressures usually induce such parties to arbitrate and to comply with arbitrators' decisions. In close-knit trade associations, from Mentschikoff's time to ours, merchant parties to trade association arbitration agreements are often "repeat players" in the same industry and thus eager to remain members in good standing of their trade association. So they are vulnerable to private sanctions—culminating in expulsion from the association—if they challenge the arbitration agreement or award.[9]

Lisa Bernstein, *Private Commercial Law in the Cotton Industry: Creating Cooperation through Rules, Norms, and Institutions*

99 Mich. L. Rev. 1724, 1725–28, 1731–32, 1737–39, 1740–41 (2001).

The cotton industry has almost entirely opted out of the public legal system, replacing it with one of the oldest and most complex systems of private commercial law. Most contracts for the purchase and sale of domestic cotton, between merchants or between merchants and mills, are neither consummated under the Uniform Commercial Code ("Code") nor interpreted and enforced in court when disputes arise. Rather, most such contracts are concluded under one of several privately drafted sets of contract default rules and are subject to arbitration in one of several merchant tribunals. Similarly, most international sales of cotton are governed neither by state-supplied legal rules nor by the Convention on the International Sale of Goods, but rather by the rules of the Liverpool Cotton Association.

The institutions that create and administer the industry's private legal system work extraordinarily well. The trade rules are periodically revised to respond to technological advancements, market changes, and ambiguities revealed during disputes. Their content is known and understood by most market participants. The arbitration tribunals that resolve disputes do so expeditiously and inexpensively. Their decisions, which are recorded in written opinions, reveal a distinctive and coherent jurisprudential approach. Within the industry, arbitration awards are widely respected and complied with promptly. In short, the industry has succeeded in creating and maintaining a private legal system ("PLS") in which transactions costs, error costs, legal system costs, and collection costs are low. This system has endured since the mid-1800s, surviving widespread social change, years of extreme price volatility, and substantial changes in the background public legal regime.

This Article draws on a detailed case study of contractual relations in the cotton industry to examine the ways that the rules, norms, and institutions that constitute the industry's PLS create value for transactors. Part I describes the formal operation of the PLS and discusses the ways that its substantive rules,

---

[9] Mentschikoff, *Commercial Arbitration*, at 854 ("In exchange groups, not only is resort to arbitration on the whole compulsory for members, but failure to abide by an award is frequently considered grounds for disciplinary proceedings against the recalcitrant party."). Id. at 858 ("The ultimate sanction in many of the self-contained associations and in almost all of the exchanges is a disciplinary proceeding and thus, potential legal problems with respect to procedure are not seriously considered in these groups.").

adjudicative approaches, and arbitral procedures improve on those provided by the Code and the public legal system. Part II describes the many steps taken by cotton industry institutions to strengthen the social and informational infrastructures of trade. It discusses how these efforts combine to make reputation-based nonlegal sanctions a powerful force in the industry and explores how the availability of these sanctions makes important features of the PLS work better than they would in their absence. It also suggests that the availability of such sanctions may enable transactors to create value-enhancing contract governance structures that might be either unavailable or prohibitively expensive if their transactions were governed by the public legal system. Part III takes a step back and explores how the industry's efforts to support the legal and extralegal aspects of contracting relationships, together with certain other features of cotton institutions, have succeeded in creating conditions that are conducive to the creation, maintenance, and restoration of cooperative contracting relationships. Part IV concludes by suggesting that understanding how the cotton industry's institutions create value for transactors may help identify other industries and other contexts in which private institutions can play a positive role in supporting trade.

I. The Private Legal System

A. The Formal Operation of the Private Legal System

There are numerous sources of private commercial law in the domestic cash markets for the purchase and sale of cotton. Most merchant-to-mill transactions are governed by the Southern Mill Rules ("SMRs"), a set of trade rules that is jointly adopted by the American Cotton Shippers Association ("ACSA"), a trade association representing merchants, and the American Textile Manufacturers Institute ("ATMI"), a trade association representing mills. Most merchant-to-merchant transactions are governed by the trade rules of one of four regional cotton shippers' associations, all of which are members of ACSA, or by the rules of the Memphis Cotton Exchange ("MCE"), whose ninety member firms typically "handle about 75 percent of the U.S. cotton trade and about 35 percent of the world's cotton trade."

Both shippers' associations and regional exchanges provide arbitration services. Most require members to arbitrate disputes with other members as a condition of membership.[11] In addition, the ACSA and the ATMI have created a joint arbitration tribunal, the Board of Appeals ("BoA"), to arbitrate contract disputes that arise under the SMRs. They have also created a separate tribunal, the Cotton States Arbitration Board ("CSAB"), to make binding quality determinations. Although merchants and mills are not required to contract under the SMRs, or to arbitrate disputes with one another as a condition of membership in their respective trade associations, most merchant-to-mill contracts nevertheless provide for BoA arbitration.

* * *

[11] *See, e.g.,* [Memphis Cotton Exchange By-Laws, Art. IV, 9 (1993)] at Art. IV, 8 ("Any member refusing to submit to an arbitration when asked for by another member or a nonmember, providing the Arbitration Committee consider [sic] there exist good grounds for an arbitration, or to abide by any award or decision of said Committee when rendered," may be expelled from the Exchange).

The BoA is composed of one arbitrator appointed by the president of the ATMI and one appointed by the president of the ACSA. Arbitrators are selected for their "experience in their respective industry and their reputation for integrity and fairness." The BoA does not hold hearings. It decides cases solely on the basis of briefs and documentary evidence, most commonly: verified copies of confirmations, correspondence, mail receipts, telephone logs, weight slips, quality determination reports, and affidavits from lawyers and employees who played roles in the questioned transaction. All evidence has the names of the parties redacted.

The MCE arbitration tribunal is composed of seven arbitrators, appointed annually by the Exchange's board of directors. It holds oral hearings, complete with the calling of witnesses and cross-examination.

* * *

The BoA decides contract disputes by applying the SMRs, a comprehensive set of bright-line contract default rules that cover contract formation, performance, quality, delay, payment, repudiation, excuse, and damages, and include numerous industry-specific definitions of terms like "prompt," "raingrown," and "long staple." The MCE decides cases on the basis of the Exchange's own Trading Rules, which also define numerous industry-specific terms and contain primarily bright-line provisions. Although most SMRs and MCE Trading Rules would be enforceable under the [Uniform Commercial] Code if included in a contract, they nonetheless differ from the Code in fundamental ways.

* * *

The awards of both the BoA and the MCE's arbitration tribunals can be enforced by seeking an entry of judgment in court. However, this is rarely necessary. Failure to comply with a BoA award is grounds for expulsion from most shippers' associations, and failure to abide by an MCE award is grounds for expulsion from the Exchange. Expulsions are widely publicized. Because membership in a shippers' association strongly affects the profitability of a merchant's domestic business and is essential to participation in the international cotton trade, these association and exchange imposed penalties, together with their attendant social and reputational sanctions, are usually sufficient to induce merchants to promptly comply with arbitration decisions unless they are bankrupt or in severe financial distress.

The ATMI does not expel mills that fail to comply with arbitration decisions, perhaps because ATMI membership is not a prerequisite for maintaining a profitable mill and such a sanction would have little force. However, in part because there are far fewer mills than merchants, when mills do not comply with arbitration awards, their noncompliance quickly becomes known throughout the merchant and banking communities, and the mill typically finds itself either unable to purchase cotton, or able to purchase it only at a relatively high price or for cash prior to delivery. As a result, noncompliance with arbitral decisions is uncommon unless the mill is in severe financial distress.

* * *

The [cotton industry's "private legal system"] procedural rules reduce the cost and delay of obtaining and enforcing a judgment. They provide a streamlined process that, compared to the public system, makes it more likely that transactors will enter into new contracting relationships, makes it easier for large and small firms to transact with each other, makes smaller-sized transactions viable, limits the ability of transactors to use the arbitral process to engage in strategic behavior, and reduces the actual harm suffered by transactors who do not have access to capital on reasonable terms during the pendancy of a dispute. In addition, by providing for the appointment of industry-expert arbitrators, who can make many factual determinations more accurately and less expensively than a judge can, the rules greatly expand the "contractible" aspects of an exchange.

* * *

Lisa Bernstein's just-excerpted article on the cotton industry combines with her articles on the grain and diamond industries (both excerpted in Chapter 1) to show three industries that have developed, as Bernstein says, "Private Legal Systems." These thoroughgoing forms of private ordering use trade association arbitration to privatize all three of:

(1) adjudication (through arbitration procedures quite different from courts' rules of procedure and evidence);

(2) lawmaking (through arbitrators applying industry trade rules rather than governmental law, and through the precedential effect of arbitrators' reasoned awards); and

(3) enforcement of the adjudicator's decision (through private sanctions culminating in expulsion from the association).

By contrast, the general commercial arbitration discussed next typically privatizes only adjudication, while relying (much as courts do) on government for lawmaking and enforcement of the adjudicator's decision.

3. THE AAA AND OTHER GENERAL COMMERCIAL ARBITRATION

In contrast to the trade association arbitration just discussed, Section 2.A.1's excerpt from Soia Mentschikoff's *Commercial Arbitration* shows that the American Arbitration Association's general commercial arbitration—usually involving disputes between parties not in the same trade association—is much more like litigation. Mentschikoff's study of the AAA revealed "Lawyers represent one or more of the parties in 80 per cent of the cases, and serve as arbitrators in about 30 per cent," and those numbers are likely higher today. Moreover, in contrast to the private enforcement of trade association arbitrators' decisions, Mentschikoff says the AAA emphasizes the value of arbitration awards that courts will confirm and enforce, rather than vacate. Similarly, today's AAA staff and arbitrator trainings are attentive to how an arbitration's process will appear to a reviewing court, thus increasing lawyerly fastidiousness about arbitration procedure in the AAA, compared to trade association arbitration.

Idea Nuova, Inc. v. GM Licensing Group, Inc.

United States Court of Appeals for the Second Circuit, 2010.
617 F.3d 177.

■ REENA RAGGI, CIRCUIT JUDGE.

* * *

Idea Nuova is a New York-based company that markets novelty products. On December 16, 2002, it entered into a consulting agreement (the "Agreement") with defendant GM Licensing Group, Inc. ("GM"). In return for a commission, GM agreed to negotiate licensing agreements on behalf of Idea Nuova with the owners of various intellectual property. By its terms, the Agreement was to run for one year, from January 1, 2003, through December 31, 2003, but it could be "extended by a written agreement signed by both parties." The parties executed the requisite written renewals for both 2004 and 2005, but not for 2006. Idea Nuova maintains that negotiations as to a 2006 renewal broke down without the parties reaching agreement. GM asserts that the parties orally agreed to a three-year extension of their Agreement from 2006 through 2008.

On November 27, 2006, GM invoked the Agreement's dispute resolution provision to initiate arbitration of the parties' renewal dispute. That provision states:

> In the event of a dispute arising hereunder, the parties must attempt to resolve same for a period of forty-five (45) days after which time the dispute shall be submitted to AAA arbitration for resolution. In such arbitration, the discovery rules of the California Code of Civil Procedure shall apply.

* * *

After hearings and briefings spanning three years, the arbitrator issued four awards. In the first interim award, the arbitrator found that the parties intended "that renewals of the Agreement would be reflected in a signed, written agreement." Nevertheless, the arbitrator concluded that, under California law, an oral agreement to renew was enforceable, even without subsequent reduction of that agreement to writing, where both parties intended their oral agreement to be binding. Applying these principles to the evidence, the arbitrator found that the parties had in fact reached a binding oral agreement to renew the Agreement for the three-year period * * *.

Thereafter, the arbitrator identified the particular licensing agreements for which GM was entitled to commissions; awarded GM compensatory damages and injunctive relief; and assessed Idea Nuova fees, costs, and interest.

* * *

In the midst of these proceedings, on October 8, 2008, Idea Nuova filed a complaint in the Southern District of New York seeking to vacate the initial two arbitration awards in favor of GM * * *. The complaint was thereafter twice amended * * * to add requests to vacate the final two arbitration awards.

* * * [T]he district court granted GM's motion for confirmation of the arbitration awards, denied Idea Nuova's motion for summary judgment, and dismissed its second amended complaint.

* * *

[T]he FAA provides for judicial confirmation of arbitral awards on consent of the parties. See 9 U.S.C. § 9 (authorizing confirmation where "parties in their agreement have agreed that a judgment of the court shall be entered upon the award made pursuant to the arbitration"). Where the parties have so agreed, an arbitral award is entitled to "strong deference," and confirmation ordinarily is "a summary proceeding that merely makes what is already a final arbitration award a judgment of the court".

The thrust of Idea Nuova's appeal is the alleged lack of consent to confirmation as specified in § 9. Idea Nuova submits that its Agreement with GM does not state the parties' intent for arbitration to be "final" or "binding"; nor does the Agreement consent to judicial confirmation of any arbitral award. To be sure, in Aeronautical Industrial District Lodge 91 v. United Technologies Corp., 230 F.3d 569 (2d Cir. 2000), relied on by Idea Nuova, this court recognized a district court's jurisdiction to review an arbitration award where the parties' agreement did not state that the arbitration was "final and binding." But in the same sentence of that opinion, the court signaled that such language was not essential; there were "equivalent" ways of expressing agreement to binding arbitration and judicial confirmation of arbitral awards. Id. (stating that "district court has jurisdiction to review an arbitration award where the [underlying agreement] does not expressly provide that the arbitration is 'final and binding' or the equivalent" (emphasis added)).

Among the equivalent ways recognized by this court is a contract provision providing for arbitration to be conducted pursuant to AAA rules. See Varley v. Tarrytown Assocs., Inc., 477 F.2d 208, 210 (2d Cir. 1973) (holding that clause providing for settlement of controversies "by arbitration pursuant to the rules of the American Arbitration Association . . . is sufficient to incorporate the rules into the agreement"); accord I/S Stavborg v. Nat'l Metal Converters, Inc., 500 F.2d 424, 426 (2d Cir. 1974). Idea Nuova acknowledges this precedent, but submits that it does not apply to this case because the Agreement at issue consents to AAA arbitration without referencing AAA rules.

The argument is disingenuous. AAA arbitration is arbitration conducted according to AAA rules. See Important Notice, AAA Commercial Arbitration Rules and Mediation Procedures (indicating that "[t]hese rules and any amendment of them shall apply in the form in effect at the time the administrative filing requirements are met for a demand for arbitration or submission agreement received by the AAA"). The point is reiterated in the first subsection of the first Commercial Arbitration Rule, which further states that AAA rules will be deemed incorporated into any arbitration agreement providing for AAA arbitration of commercial disputes:

> The parties shall be deemed to have made these rules a part of their arbitration agreement whenever they have provided for arbitration by

> the American Arbitration Association (hereinafter AAA) under its Commercial Arbitration Rules or for arbitration by the AAA of a domestic commercial dispute without specifying particular rules. These rules and any amendment of them shall apply in the form in effect at the time the administrative filing requirements are met for a demand for arbitration or submission agreement received by the AAA. The parties, by written agreement, may vary the procedures set forth in these rules. After appointment of the arbitrator, such modifications may be made only with the consent of the arbitrator.

AAA Rule 1(a) (emphasis added). We thus conclude that when, as here, parties expressly agree to submit their commercial disputes "to AAA arbitration for resolution," such language is reasonably understood, without more, to agree to arbitration pursuant to AAA rules and to the incorporation of those rules into the parties' agreement.

This conclusion permits us easily to resolve this appeal. AAA Rules 7 and 48 repeatedly reference arbitral awards as "final." See AAA Rule 7(c) (indicating that arbitrator may rule on objections to arbitrability "as a preliminary matter or as part of the final award"); AAA Rule 43(b) (referencing arbitrator's ability to make decisions "in addition to a final award"); AAA Rule 43(c) (providing for arbitrator to assess fees and expenses "in the final award"). Further, Rule 48(c) states that "[p]arties to an arbitration under these rules shall be deemed to have consented that judgment upon the arbitration award may be entered in any federal or state court having jurisdiction thereof." With these rules incorporated into the parties' Agreement, see AAA Rule 1(a), we reject Idea Nuova's argument that it never agreed to binding arbitration or to the court's jurisdiction to confirm arbitral awards. This conclusion finds support not only in our previously cited precedent, but in decisions by our sister circuits. See Rainwater v. Nat'l Home Ins. Co., 944 F.2d 190, 194 (4th Cir. 1991) (holding "that resort to AAA arbitration will be deemed both binding and subject to entry of judgment unless the parties expressly stipulate to the contrary"); see also Dow Corning Corp. v. Safety Nat'l Cas. Corp., 335 F.3d 742, 745 (8th Cir. 2003) (recognizing reference to AAA rules as adequate substitute for explicit statement that parties intend binding arbitration); McKee v. Home Buyers Warranty Corp. II, 45 F.3d 981, 983 (5th Cir. 1995) (holding that reference to AAA rules indicates "that resort to AAA arbitration will be deemed both binding and subject to entry of judgment unless the parties expressly agree otherwise").

Accordingly, we conclude that the Agreement between Idea Nuova and GM satisfies the FAA's "consent to confirmation" requirement, see 9 U.S.C. § 9, and we affirm the district court judgment confirming the final arbitral award in favor of GM.

* * *

The AAA is a private non-profit organization founded in 1926 "to foster the study of arbitration, to perfect its techniques and procedures under arbitration law, and to advance generally the science of arbitration." It works actively to publicize and promote arbitration. Of far greater importance, however, is its central role in administering much of the arbitration that takes place in the United States. Many contracts include a clause requiring that any disputes go to arbitration under AAA rules. For instance, if the parties have agreed to arbitrate under the AAA's "Commercial Arbitration Rules and Mediation Procedures", these rules will resolve questions concerning the method of choosing arbitrators, their powers, time limits for various steps in the proceedings, and the conduct of the hearing. The AAA also offers alternative sets of rules available for adoption in particular industries, for example, the AAA's Construction Industry Arbitration Rules and Mediation Procedures. In addition, the AAA administers a large number of labor arbitrations under its Voluntary Labor Arbitration Rules, and uninsured motorist accident arbitrations under its Accident Claims Arbitration Rules and Mediation Procedures. In all these cases, using contracts that incorporate pre-existing bodies of rules saves the parties the burden, costs, and delay of having to negotiate and spell out an entire code for the conduct of the arbitration.

AAA in 2017 had 725 arbitrators and mediators who handled 8,560 commercial cases, 290,486 NY State No-Fault insurance cases, over 4,000 consumer cases, 1,026 international cases, and an unspecified number of labor and employment cases.[10] In most arbitration administered by the AAA, the parties select their arbitrators from a number of names suggested by AAA administrators, who furnish information concerning the background and experience of the candidates; if the parties cannot agree on a name, the AAA itself will appoint the arbitrator to hear the case. In addition, during the course of the proceeding the AAA staff furnish a variety of administrative services, concerning, for example, notice to the parties, pre-hearing conferences, and the scheduling, location, and conduct of the hearing—all intended to ensure that the process runs smoothly and that the chances of a successful later challenge to the award are minimized. Selection of arbitrators and arbitration procedure are discussed further in Chapter 4.

The AAA has in recent years been subject to increasing competition from a number of rivals. One is Judicial Arbitration & Mediation Services, Inc. (JAMS), whose neutrals are mostly retired judges,[11] which administers around 13,000 cases per year.[12] Another is ADR Services, Inc., which administers around 9,300 cases annually.[13]

4. SECURITIES ARBITRATION

The securities industry—colloquially known as "Wall Street"—has long been a heavy user of arbitration, and generated some important cases in the Supreme Court's expansion of arbitration during the 1980s and 1990s. See, e.g., Shearson/

---

[10] 2017 Annual Report, American Arbitration Association (2017), https://www.adr.org/sites/default/files/document_repository/AAA_AnnualReport_Financials_2018.pdf; Arbitration Caseload Data Press Release, American Arbitration Association (2018), https://www.adr.org/sites/default/files/document_repository/180223_AAA_ICDR_Arbitration_Caseload_Data_Press_Release.pdf.

[11] See https://www.jamsadr.com/neutrals/; see also Pollock, *"Arbitrator Finds Role Dwindling as Rivals Grow,"* Wall St. J., April 28, 1993 at B1.

[12] About JAMS, JAMS, https://www.jamsadr.com/about-jams/ (last visited Mar. 26, 2018).

[13] About ADR Services, Inc., ADS SERVICES, INC., http://www.adrservices.com/about/ (last visited Mar. 26, 2018).

Am. Exp., Inc. v. McMahon, 482 U.S. 220, 107 S. Ct. 2332, 96 L. Ed. 2d 185 (1987), Gilmer v. Interstate/Johnson Lane Corp., 500 U.S. 20 (1991).

Compared to nearly all other domestic commercial and consumer arbitration, securities arbitration is less private (more governmental). While other domestic commercial and consumer arbitration arises out of private contract and is administered by private-sector entities like the American Arbitration Association and trade associations, the duty to participate in securities arbitration is imposed by a quasi-governmental entity, the Financial Industry Regulatory Association (FINRA), which also administers and regulates such arbitration in conjunction with a federal agency—the Securities and Exchange Commission (SEC).

William A. Birdthistle & M. Todd Henderson, *Becoming A Fifth Branch*

99 Cornell L. Rev. 1, 13–15 (2013).

C. Evolving from SRO to QGO: The Case of FINRA

* * *

[A] brief sketch of the major inflection points of regulation demonstrates how the self-regulatory nature of financial SROs [Self-regulatory organizations] has grown increasingly governmental. These particular SROs are becoming or, as some have argued, have become quasi-governmental organizations (QGO).

Professor Roberta Karmel described the evolution of the SRO for Wall Street professionals this way: "From the enactment of [the Securities Exchange Act of 1934] until the present, Congress and the SEC have struggled to convert SROs from 'private clubs' to public bodies, frequently exploiting scandals to impose governance reforms on exchanges and the NASD." In a recent speech, SEC Commissioner Daniel M. Gallagher asked, "Is FINRA becoming a 'deputy SEC'?"

* * *

Regulation of stockbrokers in the United States arose originally not from the government but from the brokers themselves. The first rules emerged through a private "club" of "stockjobbers" attempting primarily to increase their value via membership and private rules and discipline. * * * From the late 1780s until 1938, these private membership rules were the primary means by which brokers were regulated.

The self-regulation of stockbrokers began not so much to fill a regulatory void but rather to forestall regulation. In 1792, the New York state legislature made contracts for the sale of stock owned by others unenforceable in New York courts. Accordingly, the only way that the growing stock brokerage industry in New York could continue to grow and flourish was by creating its own parallel legal system that could, through private rules, enforce such bargains. This early form of private enforcement built primarily on efforts at cartelization by brokers.

Just prior to the enactment of the New York stockjobbing act, the industry engaged in nascent efforts at forming a self-regulatory framework. Finally, in 1817, a group of nearly thirty brokers formed the New York Stock and Exchange Board.

* * * By 1860, the Board "dominated securities trading in New York," in part because its reputation allowed it to determine the prices at which other trades would happen most effectively.

The Board acquired this reputation in part through its creation of a "miniature legal system" that included rules governing trading and disputes among brokers. As noted above, for the entire first half of the nineteenth century, so-called time contracts, which included most broker transactions, were unenforceable in New York. Accordingly, purely private law was the only mechanism for guaranteeing the performance of such contracts. A majority vote of the Board's members originally determined the outcome of disputes: "All questions of dispute in the purchase or sale of [s]tocks" were "decided by a majority of the [B]oard." As the membership grew and the number of disputes accumulated, subsets of the Board took on this quasi-judicial role, and the decisions in individual cases took on the nature of precedent. This extragovernmental regulation increased public confidence in brokers associated with the Board and thereby attracted business.

New York's highest court explicitly blessed the nongovernmental character of the early SROs in *Belton v. Hatch*, decided in 1888. In *Belton*, a broker who was suspended from the Exchange for unsound practices sued to recover the value of its seat, which the Exchange had sold to another broker. Denying the claim for recovery of the sum, the court enforced the contract between the plaintiff and the Exchange, holding that the Exchange could use the privilege of membership as a regulatory tool. The court concluded that

> there is nothing against public policy [in this conclusion], for the reason that whatever a member acquires is subject to the self-imposed condition that his title and the rights which accrue from his membership are regulated by and dependent upon the laws adopted by [the Exchange], and expressly consented to by him when he joined.

* * *

This self-regulatory scheme survived as the primary, if not sole, source of oversight of stock transactions following the stock market crash of 1929 and the subsequent economic depression. Although contentious in light of more recent research, at the time the conventional wisdom of the cause of the crash and the depression was "unregulated speculation in securities." Accordingly, the Roosevelt Administration drew up legislation that would largely displace the private regulators by, among other things, requiring that government employees (specifically the Federal Trade Commission, in its guise as precursor to the SEC) approve all exchange rules and regulations. * * * The "happy compromise" reached in the Securities Exchange Act of 1934 was the creation of an SEC with the power to write and enforce new rules but with the preexisting regulatory apparatus largely in place.

* * *

The Securities Acts Amendments of 1975 were another watershed change in the nature of broker SROs. The statute gave the SEC its long-sought-after power to initiate as well as to approve SRO rules and rulemaking procedures.

Stephen J. Ware, *What Makes Securities Arbitration Different from Other Consumer and Employment Arbitration?*

76 U. Cin. L. Rev. 447, 448–52 (2008).

Arbitration of disputes between a member of the securities industry and its customers (investors) is, in one important respect, different from other consumer arbitration. Appreciating this difference requires a basic understanding of the securities industry's regulatory environment. Most securities trades are conducted by securities "brokers" or "dealers." The Securities Exchange Act of 1934 (Exchange Act) requires broker-dealers to register with the Securities and Exchange Commission (SEC) as a condition of doing business. The Exchange Act also requires broker-dealers to register with, and submit to the rules of, a Self Regulatory Organization (SRO) as a condition of doing business. The SEC has authority to regulate broker-dealers, but the bulk of the day-to-day regulation of broker-dealers is generally delegated to SROs by the SEC.

The SRO that a broker-dealer must join may be either "a securities association registered pursuant to [the Exchange Act]" or "a national securities exchange," which means an exchange registered pursuant to the Exchange Act. Only one securities association is registered under the Exchange Act: the Financial Industry Regulatory Authority (FINRA). There are ten national securities exchanges.

While FINRA—the result of a July 2007 merger between the National Association of Securities Dealers (NASD) and the New York Stock Exchange (NYSE)—in some ways resembles a private trade association and the securities exchanges originated as private institutions, both FINRA and the exchanges have lost much of their private character. The SROs now have many of the characteristics of government agencies. An SRO may not come into existence without SEC approval, and the SEC has oversight responsibility over the SROs. The SROs must file their proposed rule changes with the SEC, and no SRO rule change can take effect unless the SEC finds that the proposed rule is consistent with the requirements of the Exchange Act. The SEC even has the power to "abrogate, add to, and delete from . . . the rules of a[n] [SRO]." In fact, many changes in the SRO rules governing arbitration have been made "largely in response to" SEC initiatives.

In short, federal law restricts entry into the securities business to those who comply with SRO rules. To be a broker-dealer without complying with SRO rules is illegal. Therefore, SRO rules are governmental barriers to entry into the securities business. This is significant with respect to arbitration because all SRO rules require broker-dealers to arbitrate customer disputes upon customer request. In other words, to engage in the securities business, a firm must submit to arbitration. Securities firms are legally required to arbitrate.

This is a major difference between securities arbitration and other arbitration. While the law imposes on securities broker-dealers a duty to arbitrate customer disputes, the law does not do this to businesses in other industries that use consumer arbitration. If a bank that has issued a credit card, for example, is arbitrating consumer disputes, that is because the bank contracted to do so. If a computer business or a pest-control business is arbitrating consumer disputes, that is because that business contracted to do so. By contrast, securities broker-dealers are obligated to arbitrate consumer disputes whether they contract to do so or not. While consumer arbitration in other industries is contractual, consumer arbitration in the securities industry is non-contractual for the business. The broker-dealer's duty to arbitrate is imposed by law—SRO rule—rather than assumed by contract.

On the other hand, for the consumer, consumer arbitration in the securities industry is every bit as contractual as consumer arbitration in other industries. An investor is obligated to arbitrate securities disputes only if the investor has contracted to do so. The SRO rules do not require the investor to arbitrate. They only require broker-dealers to arbitrate if the investor chooses arbitration over litigation. In short, the SRO rules give the investor the choice of forum. The rules impose a one-sided duty to arbitrate.

It is against the backdrop of these SRO rules that most broker-dealers present their customers with adhesive arbitration agreements. By making the investor's agreement to arbitrate a condition of contracting, a broker-dealer negates the investor's choice of forum [arbitration or litigation] because, after the contract is formed, both parties have a duty to arbitrate.

* * *

In addition to imposing a duty to arbitrate on broker-dealers, securities law also imposes a duty to arbitrate on certain employees of broker-dealers. Pursuant to SEC mandate, the rules of each SRO require that certain employees of each of its members register with the SRO. I use the term "securities employees" to refer to such employees. The SRO rules require securities employees to sign an arbitration agreement to register with the SRO. In other words, to be a securities employee, an individual must submit to arbitration even if neither the employee nor the employer wants to condition employment on the employee assuming a duty to arbitrate.

This is a major difference between arbitration in the securities industry and arbitration in other industries.

Barbara Black & Jill I. Gross, *Investor Protection Meets the Federal Arbitration Act*

1 Stan. J. Complex Litig. 1–14, 26–27 (2012).

* * *

Virtually all brokerage firms include provisions in their standard-form customer agreements requiring arbitration of customers' disputes in the FINRA forum. * * *

The typical consumer contract containing a predispute arbitration agreement (PDAA) differs in a number of important ways from a brokerage agreement containing a PDAA. Since [the landmark case enforcing a securities PDAA,

Shearson/Am. Exp., Inc. v. McMahon, 482 U.S. 220, 107 S. Ct. 2332, 96 L. Ed. 2d 185 (1987)], FINRA, with prodding from the Securities and Exchange Commission (SEC), has engaged in ongoing review and reform of its arbitration rules in order to make the arbitration process fairer for investors. Under the Exchange Act, FINRA's rules are subject to SEC review and approval: the SEC must approve FINRA's rules, after a public comment period, if it finds they are consistent with the requirements of the Exchange Act and are designed to protect investors and the public interest. FINRA rules require broker-dealers to alert customers to the inclusion of a PDAA in the customer agreement and to provide information about the arbitration process and, in particular, how it differs from court.

Besides disclosure, FINRA also regulates the arbitration process to a degree that commercial arbitration forums may not and prohibits firms from placing any condition in a PDAA that limits or contradicts any FINRA rule. Notably, FINRA does not permit class arbitrations in its forum because it views courts as better equipped to handle complex procedures. FINRA, however, does permit, under certain circumstances, multiple claimants to combine claims containing common questions of law and fact in the same arbitration. In contrast to typical consumer agreements like the one at issue in *AT&T Mobility* [*LLC v. Concepcion*, 563 U.S. 333, 339 (2011)], FINRA does not permit brokerage agreements to contain prohibitions on judicial class actions. Accordingly, customers that have claims against a brokerage firm suitable for class action treatment are permitted to institute a class action in court, and the firm cannot enforce the PDAA against a member of the class so long as the class action appears viable.

* * *

Teresa J. Verges, *Opening the Floodgates of Small Customer Claims in FINRA Arbitration: FINRA v. Charles Schwab & Co., Inc.*

15 Cardozo J. Conflict Resol. 623, 639–40 (2014).

In October 2011, on the heels of the *Concepcion* decision, Schwab amended its Customer Account Agreement to include a provision titled, "Waiver of Class Action or Representative Action" ("Waiver"). The new provision was contained in a forty-page document Schwab mailed to its 6.8 million customers titled "Important account information you need to know," containing a series of amendments to the customers' account agreements with Schwab. The Waiver stated in relevant part:

> Neither you nor Schwab shall be entitled to arbitrate any claims as a class action or representative action, and the arbitrator(s) shall have no authority to consolidate one or more than one parties' [sic] claims or to proceed on a representative or class action basis. You and Schwab agree that any actions between us and/or Related Third Parties shall be brought solely in our individual capacities. You and Schwab hereby waive any right to bring a class action, or any type of representative action against each other or any Related Third Parties in court. You and Schwab

> waive any right to participate as a class member, or in any other capacity, in any class action or representative action brought by any other person, entity or agency against Schwab or you.

The Waiver foreclosed both judicial class actions and the consolidation of claims in FINRA arbitration, requiring that any customer claim be arbitrated solely on an individual basis.

On February 1, 2012, FINRA Enforcement brought an action for sanctions against Schwab, alleging that the Waiver provision violated FINRA Rule 2268(d)(1) and NASD Rule 3110(f)(4)(A), which prohibit member firms from including 'any condition' in PDAAs that 'limits or contradicts the rules of any self-regulatory organization,' and FINRA Rule 2268(d)(3) and NASD Rule 3110(f)(4)(C), which expressly prohibit member firms from including 'any condition' in PDAAs that 'limits the ability of a party to file any claim in court permitted to be filed in court under the rules of the forums in which a claim may be filed under the agreement. Enforcement argued that the prohibition against judicial class actions expressly "limits" and "contradicts" a customer's rights under FINRA Rule 12204(d) of the Customer Code. Enforcement further alleged that the Waiver's non-consolidation language that "the arbitrator(s) shall have no authority to consolidate one or more than one parties' [sic] claims" violated FINRA Rule 12312 of the Customer Code. Finally, by virtue of these rule violations, Enforcement alleged that Schwab violated FINRA Rule 2010, Standards of Commercial Honor and Principles of Trade.

* * *

FINRA's ban on arbitral class waivers was upheld by FINRA's Board of Governors in a 2014 ruling that the Securities Exchange Act overcomes the requirement in the FAA (as interpreted by *AT&T Mobility LLC v. Concepcion*, 563 U.S. 333, 339 (2011)), to enforce such waivers.[14] While a decision by FINRA's board can be appealed to the SEC and then finally a federal court,[15] FINRA's ban on arbitral class waivers has not been so appealed.[16] Instead, a securities firm persuaded the Second Circuit to enforce a class waiver by changing its form contract to provide for arbitration before a non-FINRA forum, the Judicial Arbitration and Mediation Service (JAMS).[17] The Second Circuit held that "a pre-dispute private

---

[14] Dep't of Enforcement v. Schwab, Disciplinary Proceeding No. 2011029760201 (FINRA Board of Governors Apr. 24, 2014), available at https://www.finra.org/sites/default/files/NACDecision/p496824.pdf. See also Jill Gross, *FINRA Reverses Hearing Panel in Schwab Enforcement Case: Class Action Waiver Violates FINRA Rules*, Indisputably (Apr. 24, 2014), http://www.indisputably.org/?p=5593.

[15] FINRA, Rule 9370 (2008) ("A Respondent aggrieved by final disciplinary action pursuant to the Rule 9200 Series or the Rule 9300 Series may apply for review by the SEC pursuant to Section 19(d)(2) of the Exchange Act."); 15 U.S.C § 78s(d) ("Any action with respect to which a self-regulatory organization is required by paragraph (1) of this subsection to file notice shall be subject to review by the appropriate regulatory agency for such member, participant, applicant, or other person, on its own motion, or upon application by any person aggrieved thereby . . . ."); FINRA, *Adjudication and Decisions*, http://www.finra.org/industry/decisions. (last visited July 11, 2018).

[16] See Teresa J. Verges, *Evolution of the Arbitration Forum as a Response to Mandatory Arbitration*, 18 Nev. L.J. 437, 451 (2018) ("FINRA has effectively used Rule 2268(d) to prohibit member firms from inserting class-action waivers in customer agreements.").

[17] Credit Suisse Sec. (USA) LLC v. Tracy, 812 F.3d 249, 252–54 (2d Cir. 2016).

agreement to arbitrate before a non-FINRA arbitral forum is enforceable."[18] FINRA responded to the Second Circuit's decision by issuing Regulatory Notice 16-25,[19] which "reminds member firms that customers have a right to request arbitration at FINRA's arbitration forum at any time and do not forfeit that right under FINRA rules by signing any agreement with a forum selection provision specifying another dispute resolution process or an arbitration venue other than the FINRA arbitration forum." It also says "A member firm's failure to comply with FINRA's rules relating to predispute arbitration agreements with customers or predispute agreements with associated persons, or failure to submit a dispute to FINRA arbitration as required by FINRA's rules, would violate FINRA rules, and member firms may be subject to disciplinary action."[20]

Jill Gross, *The Customer's Nonwaivable Right to Choose Arbitration in the Securities Industry*

10 Brook J. Corp. Fin. & Com. L. 384, 384–87 (2016).

The Securities and Exchange Commission (SEC) has long supported a brokerage customer's right to choose arbitration as a means to resolve customer disputes fairly and efficiently, and as a critical component of investor protection. Under an SEC-approved rule, broker-dealers, all of which must be members of the Financial Industry Regulatory Authority (FINRA), a securities self-regulatory organization (SRO), have an obligation to submit to arbitration at the demand of a customer. FINRA Rule 12200 provides that member firms must arbitrate a claim if "requested by a customer," "[t]he dispute is between a customer and a member or associated person of a member; and . . . [t]he dispute arises in connection with the business activities of the member or the associated person."

To prevent investors from having a unilateral right to demand arbitration, virtually all brokerage firms include provisions in their form contracts with retail customers requiring arbitration of customers' disputes in an SRO forum, primarily FINRA's Office of Dispute Resolution. Because the Federal Arbitration Act (FAA) declares the validity, irrevocability, and enforceability of arbitration agreements, which reflects "an emphatic federal policy in favor of arbitral dispute resolution," courts enforce these predispute arbitration agreements (PDAAs) strictly according to their terms. In 2010, although Congress, as part of the Dodd-Frank Wall Street Reform and Consumer Protection Act (Dodd-Frank), expressly authorized the SEC to prohibit PDAAs, the provision designates no deadline for action, and, as of 2016, the SEC has taken no action pursuant to this express power.

While some scholars criticize the fairness of mandatory or "forced" arbitration, particularly in the consumer context, I have argued that FINRA arbitration is a fair and efficient forum for the resolution of investor disputes. In particular, arbitrators can decide investors' disputes on grounds of law, equity, and

---

[18] Id. at 254. See also *You've Been Warned: Ignoring FINRA Rules in Favor of Recent Second Circuit Precedent May Invite Disciplinary Action*, Herrick Securities Alert (Aug. 2016), http://www.mondaq.com/unitedstates/x/516496/Arbitration+Dispute+Resolution/Youve+Been+Warned+Ignoring+FINRA+Rules+In+Favor+Of+Recent+Second+Circuit+Precedent+May+Invite+Disciplinary+Action.

[19] FINRA Rules, Regulatory Notice, 16–25 (2016), https://www.finra.org/rules-guidance/notices/16-25.

[20] Id.

industry custom. Equitable bases of awards may often favor investors, as current securities laws in many jurisdictions disfavor investors.

Broker-dealers, virtually all of whom are regulated by FINRA, also argue that arbitration is fair to investors and have lobbied long and hard to prevent federal regulators from prohibiting mandatory arbitration clauses in customer agreements. It is therefore surprising that, for large-dollar-value disputes primarily involving institutional (as opposed to individual) investors, broker-dealers frequently resist arbitration. Respondent firms sometimes thwart arbitration by contending that the claimant is not a "customer" of the FINRA member firm within the meaning of FINRA Customer Code Rule 12200. This contention has fallen flat in many cases, as courts have expanded the definition of "customer" to include not only traditional brokerage customers, but also issuers that purchase other services offered by broker-dealers, such as investment banking and underwriting services.

As a result, to avoid arbitration in multimillion-dollar disputes with entities that qualify as "customers" under Rule 12200, some firms have invoked forum selection clauses that had been inserted in the underlying transaction agreements with sophisticated customers. Firms argue that the clauses operate as a "waiver" of the customer's right to demand arbitration under Rule 12200. Those clauses—which drafting parties likely included at a time when courts had not yet applied Rule 12200 to broker-dealers acting in an underwriting capacity—typically provide that "all actions and proceedings" related to disputes arising out of the agreements "shall be brought in [a designated court]." The clauses examined by courts thus far contain no reference to arbitration, whether with language of waiver or otherwise. Rather, the agreements underlying those transactions more likely included these types of clauses because the drafting parties assumed disputes would be pursued in court and the clause functioned as a choice of venue provision.

The federal appellate courts, applying contract law, currently are split on the question of whether a forum selection clause supersedes the firms' obligation to arbitrate. Some courts reason that parties can contract out of the firms' "default" obligation to arbitrate, and enforce the forum selection clause as a superseding agreement. Other courts rule that the forum selection clause is not specific enough to supersede the obligation to arbitrate since the clause does not mention arbitration. The different outcomes reflect the courts' application of similar principles of contract interpretation and arbitrability, which are difficult to reconcile.

QUESTIONS TO REVIEW AND SYNTHESIZE

1. What makes arbitration "commercial" as distinguished from some other kind of arbitration?
2. How would you categorize the major types of (domestic U.S.) commercial arbitration?
3. How do these types differ in their histories and current practices?

4. How are the roles of law and government different for each type of (domestic U.S.) commercial arbitration?

5. Should government's role with respect to any type of (domestic U.S.) commercial arbitration change?

B. INTERNATIONAL COMMERCIAL ARBITRATION

1. OVERVIEW

Many of the same factors inducing parties to choose arbitration to resolve disputes in domestic commercial transactions likely apply at least as strongly when the transaction crosses national boundaries. Indeed, as Soia Mentschikoff's *Commercial Arbitration* (see Section 2.A.1) says about international commerce, the involvement of more than one body of law and more than one court system likely provides even further impetus to choose arbitration over litigation. The time, expense, and procedural complexities of litigating in another country's courts can be daunting. Litigating parties may find themselves with parallel litigation proceeding simultaneously in the courts of the United States and of a foreign country. There is likely to be far greater uncertainty with respect to the rules of decision that will govern the dispute in a foreign court, and thus as to the outcome; the rules of "conflict of laws" will not always give a reliable answer even to the question of *which* nation's law will apply to the transaction. In addition, the "foreign" party to the litigation will not only feel disadvantaged by its relative unfamiliarity with the "rules of the game," but may also doubt how fairly a foreign party will be treated in comparison to the "local" opponent. The United States Supreme Court's support for international commercial arbitration includes recognition that uncertainty concerning the law applicable to the resolution of disputes

> will almost inevitably exist with respect to any contract touching two or more countries, each with its own substantive laws and conflict-of-laws rules. A contractual provision specifying in advance the forum in which disputes shall be litigated and the law to be applied is, therefore, an almost indispensable precondition to achievement of the orderliness and predictability essential to any international business transaction. Furthermore, such a provision obviates the danger that a dispute under the agreement might be submitted to a forum hostile to the interests of one of the parties or unfamiliar with the problem area involved.
>
> A parochial refusal by the courts of one country to enforce an international arbitration agreement would not only frustrate these purposes, but would invite unseemly and mutually destructive jockeying by the parties to secure tactical litigation advantages. * * * [It would] damage the fabric of international commerce and trade, and imperil the willingness and ability of businessmen to enter into international commercial agreements.

Scherk v. Alberto-Culver Co., 417 U.S. 506, 516 (1974). See also Mitsubishi Motors Corp. v. Soler Chrysler-Plymouth, 473 U.S. 614 (1985) ("the emphatic federal policy in favor of arbitral dispute resolution * * * applies with special force in the field of international commerce.")

Another troubling cause of unpredictability in international litigation stems from uncertainty as to when and to what extent a judgment obtained in one country will be enforceable in another. A favorable decision against a French supplier in a New York court, for example, may be of little value if the courts of France will not recognize the New York judgment. Enforcement of foreign courts' judgments may become more reliable if many nations adopt the 2019 Convention on the Recognition and Enforcement of Foreign Judgments in Civil or Commercial Matters, which obliges contracting states to recognize and enforce civil and commercial judgments rendered in another contracting state.[21] But arbitration is currently well ahead of litigation in cross border enforcement because of widespread adopted and enforcement of the United Nations Convention on the Recognition and Enforcement of Foreign Arbitral Awards (reproduced in Appendix B). For decades, enforcement of a foreign arbitral award has in many countries been simpler and more assured than enforcement of a foreign judgment.[22] Some knowledgeable lawyers believe international commercial arbitration has "become the preferred means of resolving international disputes" and has "continued to grow in recent years."[23]

In addition to the American Arbitration Association's International Centre for Dispute Resolution, several organizations compete in the administration of international commercial arbitrations; by far the most important of these is the International Chamber of Commerce (ICC), based in Paris. Other prominent organizations include The London Court of International Arbitration, Swiss Chambers Arbitration Institute, Stockholm Chamber of Commerce Arbitration Institute, and the Chinese International Economic and Trade Arbitration Centre. See S.I. Strong, *Navigating the Borders Between International Commercial Arbitration and U.S. Federal Courts: A Jurisprudential GPS*, J. Disp. Resol. 119, 129–30 (2012); Gary Born, International Commercial Arbitration, 174–199 (2d. ed. 2014).

Parties to international transactions sometimes arbitrate outside of any institutional framework—administering the arbitration themselves on an "ad hoc" basis—but "although ad hoc arbitration has the advantages of greater flexibility and less expense, most experienced international practitioners prefer the more structured

---

[21] https://www.hcch.net/en/instruments/conventions/full-text/?cid=137.

[22] Yuliya Zeynalova, *The Law on Recognition and Enforcement of Foreign Judgments: Is It Broken and How Do We Fix It?*, 31 Berkeley J. Int'l L. 150, 151 (2013)("Unlike foreign arbitral awards, which are governed by the New York Convention, no treaty outlines the circumstances under which U.S. courts may recognize foreign awards and vice versa. Transnational litigants are therefore more likely to encounter difficulties enforcing their foreign court awards than parties seeking to enforce their foreign arbitral awards."); Theodore J. Folkman, Recognition and Enforcement of Foreign Arbitral Awards, Massachusetts Continuing Legal Education, Inc. (2d ed. 2016) ("[T]he absence of an international convention on the recognition and enforcement of foreign judgments makes recognition and enforcement somewhat complex. [In contrast, t]he New York Convention, the convention governing recognition and enforcement of foreign arbitral awards, greatly simplifies matters when the foreign decision is an award rather than a judgment.").

[23] Gary Born & Rachael Kent, Legal Business Arbitration Report, *Rules of the Game* (2006); Christopher R. Drahozal, *Private Ordering and International Commercial Arbitration*, 113 Penn St. L. Rev. 1031, 1048–49 (2009) ("20.6% of the material international contracts filed with the SEC contained arbitration clauses, more than doubling the percentage of U.S. contracts with arbitration clauses"); Ya-Wei Li, *Dispute Resolution Clauses in International Contracts: An Empirical Study*, 39 Cornell Int'l L.J. 789, 799 (2006) (study of significant international contracts found "only 15% contain an arbitration clause, while 67% contain a litigation clause").

character of institutional arbitration." Kevin C. Kennedy, *Invalidity of Foreign Arbitration Agreement of Arbitral Award*, 31 Am. Jur. Proof of Facts 3d 495 (1995). Dispensing with the administrative support of an established institution is particularly risky where the level of cooperation and trust between the parties is low, and where one of them may be delaying resolution. As the former president of the AAA put it, "In non-administered arbitration, burdens such as objections to the continued service of the arbitrators, scheduling of hearings, and collection and disbursement of arbitration compensation will fall upon the parties [themselves] and can produce awkward results"; many of the administrative support functions performed by institutions will, in "ad hoc" arbitrations, have to be performed by the arbitrators themselves, which may become "excessively cost prohibitive."[24] In addition, where a recognized institution has supervised the arbitration, the institution's reputation may lend credibility to the award should a court be needed to confirm and enforce it.

As discussed above, domestic commercial arbitration administered by the AAA traditionally often lacked reasoned opinions and sometimes still does. In contrast, parties in international commercial cases usually expect arbitrators to provide a written opinion that sets out the reasons for their award. The ICC requires its arbitrators to give reasoned awards.[25] This expectation of a reasoned opinion in international arbitration reflects in part the pervasive influence of Continental European legal systems, where unreasoned awards are often considered contrary to public policy and thus unenforceable. See W. Laurence Craig, William Park & Jan Paulsson, International Chamber of Commerce Arbitration § 19.04 (3rd ed. 2000); Domotique Secant Inc. v. Smart Systems Technologies Inc., 2005 CanLII 36874 (Quebec Sup. Ct.) (Quebec court refuses to recognize New Mexico award rendered "without giving reasons"; breach of the mandatory requirement "that reasons be provided" "violates * * * our notion of public order and natural justice as it applies to procedural fairness").

International commercial arbitration predictably tends to be slower and more expensive than its domestic counterpart. The fees parties in ICC arbitrations pay the ICC—as well as the fees parties pay to the arbitrators themselves—are calculated on the basis of the amount in dispute between the parties. In a $10 million case these may range from a bare—and unlikely—minimum of $102,376 to a maximum, if three arbitrators are used, of $619,715.[26] Articulate advocates of ICC arbitration respond to criticisms of excessive expense with a reminder that:

> the cost must be evaluated in relation to the alternatives. Certainly, ICC arbitration seems cheaper than abandoning one's rights altogether. Litigation, even in one's own home courts, is not necessarily a less expensive alternative, given the possibility of one or more appeals. More importantly, it simply is not always reasonable to expect that one's home forum will be acceptable to a foreign contracting party. ICC arbitration is

[24] William K. Slate II, *International Arbitration: Do Institutions Make a Difference?*, 31 Wake Forest L.Rev. 41, 53–55 (1996).

[25] Arbitration Rules, International Chamber of Commerce, Art. 32(2) (2017) ("The award shall state the reasons upon which it is based.").

[26] Cost Calculator, International Chamber of Commerce (2017), https://iccwbo.org/dispute-resolution-services/arbitration/costs-and-payments/cost-calculator/.

> too often compared—unrealistically and unfairly—with a perfect world in which there are no administrative difficulties, no judicial prejudice against foreign parties, no language problems, no uncooperative parties, and where the just always prevail at no cost to themselves.

W. Laurence Craig, William Park, & Jan Paulsson, International Chamber of Commerce Arbitration 29–30 (3d ed.2000).

Moreover, a survey of "practitioners with extensive experience in international business disputes" suggests that the usual impetus behind the search for more "informal," "alternative" methods of dispute resolution—"the desire to achieve a process that is *faster, less expensive,* and *more amicable*"—seems to have "only marginal relevance for the choice of arbitration in international commerce":

> This may be due either to the perception that, in international arbitration, these advantages do not materialize, or that these qualities are not among the real priorities of the participants. Both reasons seem to be—at least in part—true: more than half of the respondents denied that arbitration is less expensive and more than one third disputed the notion that it was faster or more amicable. And only about one tenth of the respondents affirmed that speed, cost savings and amicability were "highly relevant" factors for the choice of arbitration as a method of dispute resolution. As one practitioner explained: "parties are often not that concerned with costs because their main preoccupation is with the outcome of the procedure; the advantage of arbitration is not to cut costs, it is a tailor-made procedure that emphasizes quality."[27]

For such practitioners the most significant advantages of arbitration seem to be "the *neutrality* of the forum and the *international enforceability* of the results." Id. (in the words of one participant, "if for judgments there existed a convention similar to the New York convention, 50% of the big international commercial arbitrations would be court litigation"). See also George A. Bermann, Jack J. Coe, Jr., Christopher R. Drahozal, Catherine A. Rogers, *Restating the U.S. Law of International Commercial Arbitration*, 113 Penn St. L. Rev. 1333, 1342 (2009) ("parties choose international arbitration primarily because they fear being subject to potentially biased decisions of the national courts of the business partner turned adversary").

2. MARITIME ARBITRATION

International maritime arbitration is an important and well-established branch of international commercial arbitration, governed by the New York Convention much as it governs most other international commercial arbitration. Maritime arbitration's customs, institutions, and terminology reflect the influence of admiralty law and the unique history of the international maritime industry. While maritime disputes often involve familiar claims—like breach of contract or damage to a ship or its cargo—such claims can arise out of dramatic circumstances, like an act of war or closure of a canal constituting a crucial shipping lane. With large ships and cargo

[27] Christian Bühring-Uhle, Arbitration and Mediation in International Business 141–43 (1996).

that can be valuable, perishable, and politically sensitive, parties in the maritime industry tend to value arbitration's speed, confidentiality, and specialized expertise.

> When a vessel leaves the pier and enters international waters, it is subject to a mixture of laws, treaties, U.N. codes, and international law principles, but most significantly, it is subject to forces of nature and the unquestioned authority of the Master or Captain. The industry is also isolated by gender. Until recently, women were not allowed to serve in the U.S. Navy aboard combatant vessels, and today they are still prohibited from submarine service. These natural, cultural and industrial factors discourage gender integration at higher levels of the industry and limit the influence of outside interests.[28]

Participants in maritime arbitration often seek arbitrators expert "not only in the law of admiralty but especially in the practice of maritime operations," partly because "[t]he maritime industry uses a language that is not only unique to maritime operations, but is also unique from any other trade."[29] "The common request for 'commercial men' in model contracts as the arbitrator demonstrates the industry desire for a person with a business background, and with the skill and knowledge of the shipping industry being more highly prized than legal skills."[30]

The maritime industry also distinguishes itself with model contracts. For example, a popular model contract, code-named NORGRAIN 89 (North American Grain Charterparty), is "13 pages long with terms covering subjects such as cargo, ports, responsibility for loading fees, tolls, and collision."[31] "The arbitration clause specifies that the arbitrators shall be 'commercial men', engaged in 'Shipping and/or Grain Trades', or members of the 'Baltic Mercantile & Shipping Exchange.'" It "also gives the parties the limited choice of arbitration forums in New York under the SMA [Society of Maritime Arbitrators] or London under the LMAA."[32]

While maritime arbitration often involves large businesses with transnational disputes involving giant ships crossing the globe with exotic cargo, maritime arbitration can also involve smaller vessels closer to shore.

Farnsworth v. Towboat Nantucket Sound, Inc.

United States Court of Appeals for the First Circuit, 2015.
790 F.3d 90.

Plaintiff Rodney Farnsworth, III, entered into a salvage contract with defendant Towboat Nantucket Sound, Inc. ("TNS"), to obtain help when Farnsworth's boat went aground on rocks one night near the Weepecket Islands in Buzzards Bay. Farnsworth later tried to rescind the whole contract, claiming that he had signed it under duress, and disputed the sum owed to TNS.

---

[28] Russell J. Cortazzo, *Development and Trends of the Lex Maritime from International Arbitration Jurisprudence*, 43 J. Mar. L. & Com. 255, 264 (2012).

[29] Id. at 264-66.

[30] Id. at 266.

[31] Id. at 271.

[32] Id. at 271.

The chronology of events is important. The parties by agreement submitted the dispute to a panel of three arbitrators pursuant to a binding arbitration clause in the salvage contract. After the arbitration proceeding had started, Farnsworth chose to file this lawsuit, seeking a preliminary injunction against the arbitration and a declaration that the salvage contract was unenforceable because Farnsworth had entered into it under duress. * * * The arbitration panel found in favor of TNS and ordered Farnsworth to pay a salvage award of $60,306.85. The district court confirmed that award over Farnsworth's objection.

* * *

The contract executed by the parties is a standard form "no cure, no pay" marine salvage agreement. Farnsworth wrote by hand the following addendum to the form contract: "Aurora was hard aground, Tow Boat prevented the Boat from going further aground, and towed the boat when the Tide floated it off."

The contract contains an arbitration clause:

> Read Carefully—Arbitration Provision—In the event of any dispute arising out of this Contract including any dispute regarding this salvage or concerning the reasonableness of any fees or charges due hereunder, all parties agree to binding arbitration in the United States in accordance with the Rules for Recreational and Small Commercial Vessel Salvage Arbitration of the Society of Maritime Arbitrators, Inc. Arbitrators shall be familiar with maritime salvage. Any award hereunder shall include interest, attorneys' fees and costs, and arbitration administration expenses and shall be final and binding. For the purpose of enforcement, the Award may be entered for judgment in any court of competent jurisdiction.

Farnsworth's buyers' remorse set in quickly. Approximately five days later, on August 3, 2012, Farnsworth sent a letter to TNS purporting to rescind the salvage contract, demanding that TNS preserve evidence relating to "the prospective litigation," and intimating that TNS had engaged in illegal business practices. Farnsworth sent another letter to TNS on August 11 advising TNS of his belief that TNS had no salvage claim and threatening to "fight to preserve [his] family tradition of venerable maritime activities."

* * *

On November 15, 2013, the arbitration panel issued a decision rejecting Farnsworth's duress defense and finding that the salvage contract was valid. The panel ordered Farnsworth to pay $60,306.85 (a $50,000 salvage award plus interest) to TNS and dismissed Farnsworth's counterclaims. This was a unanimous decision, with Farnsworth's arbitrator joining.

* * *

The district court granted TNS's motion to confirm the arbitration award.

* * *

We affirm the judgment of the district court. Costs are awarded against Farnsworth.

---

3. INVESTMENT ARBITRATION

In many countries, the government assumes a far more active role in business transactions than it does in the United States. A major governmental role is particularly likely in transactions involving capital investment and the exploitation and development of national resources. The foreign state or one of its instrumentalities will often be a party to such contracts, which are likely to have political and economic implications and symbolic importance far greater than in the case of domestic transactions. This can be a factor complicating dispute resolution. A foreign state will understandably be reluctant to submit to the jurisdiction of the courts of another sovereign, and a foreign investor will be reluctant to submit to the courts of the host country, so arbitration seems a natural compromise to avoid either party's home courts.

However, capital-importing countries in particular have long been sensitive to the implications of submitting to *any* forum where the location or the decision-maker is foreign, and such reluctance has extended to foreign arbitrations as well. This unwillingness to submit to foreign arbitration may be most marked in Latin American countries, where historical memory of one-sided international "arbitrations" dominated by European or North American partners is still vivid. A Brazilian writer has argued that:

> Functioning as an active element to denationalize (or internationalize) the contract, arbitration by removing a dispute from resolution by local courts applying local law, takes it to a plane where the rules are made by the great international commercial interests, a process from which Third World countries normally are excluded.[33]

More pithily said, developing countries during the late nineteenth and early twentieth centuries "often perceived investment arbitration as little more than an extension of gunboat diplomacy."[34] For many years the "Calvo doctrine," incorporated in several Latin American constitutions or statutes, made impossible the litigation or arbitration abroad of state contracts and required foreign investors to consent to the dispute resolution processes of local courts.

This traditional opposition to arbitration has gradually been softening, due largely to a desire to attract foreign investment. One important development was creation of the International Center for Settlement of Investment Disputes (ICSID). ICSID was established by treaty in 1966 to reduce the fear of political risks that discourage the flow of private foreign capital to developing countries, by providing foreign investors with a neutral forum for the resolution of disputes. ICSID functions under the auspices of the World Bank and is a "public" body, administered by

---

[33] Quoted in Frank Nattier, *International Commercial Arbitration in Latin America: Enforcement of Arbitral Agreements and Awards*, 21 Tex.Int'l L.J. 397, 407 (1986). See also Horacio A. Grigera Náon, *Arbitration and Latin America: Progress and Setbacks*, 21 Arb. Int'l 127 (2005) ("even today, in many Latin American countries two different schools of thought uneasily coexist: one adverse to commercial arbitration and the other favouring it").

[34] Guillermo Aguilar Alvarez & William W. Park, *The New Face of Investment Arbitration: NAFTA Chapter 11*, 28 Yale J. Int'l L. 365, 367 (2003).

representatives of the various participating governments. 153 nations have ratified the treaty, including 15 Latin American states.[35] Ratification involves an unconditional commitment to enforce all ICSID awards—that is, there is no possibility of challenging an ICSID award in any national court.[36] Nevertheless, ratification is not in itself equivalent to a consent to arbitrate—such consent must be given for each case, in the particular investment contract between the state agency and the private investor.

More recently, investment arbitration has grown due to the proliferation of Bilateral Investment Treaties (BITs). Historically, the recourse available to an investor faced with adverse treatment by the host state—say, in the form of discrimination or even expropriation—was quite limited: In the absence of some supranational tribunal, neither litigation in the local courts, nor attempts to invoke the diplomatic protection of the investor's home country, were likely to be entirely satisfactory. In a BIT, by contrast, each contracting state accords important substantive and remedial rights to investors who are nationals of the other state. Typical is the 2012 U.S. Model BIT, in which each state agrees that it will:

- "observe any obligation it may have entered into" with respect to the foreign investment;
- give "fair and equitable treatment" to the other state's investors;
- treat their investment no less favorably than it treats its own nationals or the nationals of any other country; and
- take no measures "tantamount to expropriation or nationalization except for a public purpose, in a non-discriminatory manner and upon payment of prompt, adequate, and effective compensation."[37]

And at the same time—and at the insistence of capital-exporting countries like the United States—BITs give investors direct standing to enforce these provisions, by initiating arbitration proceedings against the host state; arbitration may be either through ICSID or in an "ad hoc" arbitration.[38] The largest number of ICSID cases now come to the organization through the arbitration provisions of BITs.[39]

---

[35] *Database of ICSID Member States*, International Centre for Settlement of Investment Disputes (2018), https://icsid.worldbank.org/en/Pages/about/Database-of-Member-States.aspx.

[36] Under arts. 53 and 54 of the ICSID Convention, awards "shall not be subject to any appeal or to any other remedy," and "each Contracting State shall recognize an award rendered pursuant to this Convention as binding." The treaty does, however, provide for the possibility of an internal appeal to an "*ad hoc* Committee" of ICSID, with the power to annul awards in limited circumstances—where:

(a) the Tribunal was not properly constituted;

(b) the Tribunal has manifestly exceeded its powers;

(c) there was corruption on the part of a member of the Tribunal;

(d) there has been a serious departure from a fundamental rule of procedure; or

(e) the award has failed to state the reasons on which it is based.

See art. 52.

[37] *2012 U.S. Model Bilateral Investment Treaty*, U.S. Department of State (2012) https://www.state.gov/documents/organization/188371.pdf.

[38] *Id.* Art. 24(3).

[39] See ICSID 2017 Annual Report, 31, https://icsid.worldbank.org/en/Documents/icsiddocs/ICSID%20AR%20EN.pdf.

The number of such treaties in force worldwide exceeds 2200, and the United States is a party to 58 BITs.[40] The BIT model has been generalized in Chapter 11 of the North American Free Trade Agreement (NAFTA), among Canada, Mexico, and the United States.[41]

4. OLYMPIC AND OTHER INTERNATIONAL SPORTS ARBITRATION

Athletes participating in the Olympic Games are required to sign entry forms in which they agree to settle all Games-related disputes through arbitration before the Court of Arbitration for Sport (CAS).[42] The CAS was created in 1984 by the International Olympic Committee, but is now more or less independent, and operates under the general supervision of the International Council of Arbitration for Sport (ICAS), which is composed of twenty lawyers, some of whom are Olympians. The ICAS oversees the CAS, manages its budget, and promulgates the Code of Sports Related Arbitration. The ICAS also selects the CAS panel of about 300 arbitrators. See Josephine R. Potuto & Matthew J. Mitten, *Comparing NCAA and Olympic Athlete Eligibility Dispute Resolution Systems in Light of Procedural Fairness and Substantive Justice*, 7 Harv. J. Sports & Ent. L. 1, 28 (2016).

The CAS operates an ad hoc division, consisting of 9 to 15 arbitrators selected by the ICAS, available at each site of the Olympic games "which provides expedited resolution of disputes arising during the games or within a ten day period prior to the opening ceremony." Id. However, CAS jurisdiction is not limited to the Olympics: It is a permanent body that may decide any "matters of principle relating to sport or matters of pecuniary or other interests brought into play in the practice or the development of sport." Agreements to arbitrate before CAS may be done "on a one-off basis or appear in a contract or the statutes or regulations of a sports organization."[43] A party can submit a dispute to the CAS by submitting a request for arbitration (ordinary procedure) or, if that party has exhausted all the internal remedies of the sports organization concerned, a statement of appeal (appeals procedure), the contents of which are specified by the Code of Sports-related Arbitration. The ordinary procedure applies to contractual or tort disputes, and the appeals procedure applies to actions taken by "internal bodies of sports organisations."[44] Under ordinary procedure, each party chooses one arbitrator from *the* CAS list, then the two designated arbitrators agree on who will be the required president of the panel to round out panels of three. If the arbitrators do not agree, the CAS chooses.[45] Under the appeals procedure, each party chooses an arbitrator, and the president of the panel is selected by the CAS Appeals Arbitration Division. A sole arbitrator may be selected, if necessary, and arbitrators may not have

---

[40] *Database of Bilateral Investment Treaties*, International Centre for Settlements of Investment Disputes (2018), https://icsid.worldbank.org/en/Pages/resources/Bilateral-Investment-Treaties-Database.aspx.

[41] See the U.S. Department of State website at https://www.state.gov/nafta-investor-state-arbitrations/.

[42] Maureen A. Weston, *Simply a Dress Rehearsal? U.S. Olympic Sports Arbitration and De Novo Review at the Court of Arbitration for Sport*, 38 Ga. Int'l & Comp. L. 97, 103 (2009).

[43] *Frequently Asked Questions*, COURT OF ARB. FOR SPORT, http://www.tas-cas.org/en/general-information/frequently-asked-questions.html (last visited June 21, 2018).

[44] *Id.*

[45] *Id.*

connections to parties or case in question.[46] CAS awards may be enforced under the New York Convention,[47] which applies as it does to other international commercial arbitration.

While most CAS cases involve disciplinary matters like substance abuse, or contractual disputes—involving player transfers, endorsement contracts, or contracts between athletes and agents or managers[48]—some CAS cases involve broader social issues. For instance, the following CAS decision addresses "heated debate over whether competitors who track and field's world governing body has determined are intersex athletes should be allowed in women's races. The debate has centered on a conflict between gender identity and athletic fairness, in part because it comes at a time when biology is no longer seen as the sole determinant of gender."[49]

Caster Semenya, Athletics South Africa (ASA) v. International Association of Athletics Federations (IAAF)

Court of Arbitration for Sport.
30 April 2019.

EXECUTIVE SUMMARY

Introduction

1. On 30 April 2019, the Court of Arbitration for Sport ("CAS") delivered an Award with respect to the challenges brought by Caster Semenya and Athletics South Africa ("ASA") to the validity of the IAAF's Eligibility Regulations for the Female Classification (Athletes with Differences of Sex Development) (the "g Regulations"). By a majority, the CAS Panel dismissed the requests for arbitration considering that the Claimants could not establish that the DSD Regulation were "invalid". The Panel found that the DSD Regulations are discriminatory but that, on the basis of the evidence submitted by the parties, such discrimination is a necessary, reasonable and proportionate means of achieving the legitimate objective of ensuring fair competition in female athletics in certain events and protecting the "protected class" of female athletes in those events. The Panel also expressed serious concerns about the future practical application of the DSD Regulations. While the evidence has not established that those concerns are justified, or that they negate the conclusion of prima facie proportionality, this may change in the future unless constant attention is paid to the fairness of how the Regulations are implemented.

---

[46] *Id.*

[47] *Id.*

[48] Through 2016 the CAS had received 5,057 requests for arbitration and CAS arbitrators had issued 3,123 awards. See Statistics, Court of Arbitration for Sport (2016), http://www.tas-cas.org/fileadmin/user_upload/CAS_statistics_2016_.pdf.

[49] Gina Kolata, *Track and Field Tries to Understand New Rules for Intersex Athletes*, THE NEW YORK TIMES (May 8, 2019), https://www.nytimes.com/2019/05/08/sports/semenya-xy-chromosomes.html?emc=edit_th_190508&nl=todaysheadlines&nlid=391908420508.

The DSD Regulations

2. In 2014 the Indian athlete Dutee Chand brought proceedings before the CAS challenging the IAAF Regulations Governing Eligibility of Females with Hyperandrogenism to Compete in Women's Competition (the "Hyperandrogenism Regulations"). In July 2015, the CAS delivered an Interim Award partially upholding Ms. Chand's challenge and suspending the Hyperandrogenism Regulations (CAS 2014/A/3759 *Dutee Chand v. AFI & IAAF*).

3. In *Chand*, the CAS had determined that the hormone testosterone was the primary cause for the increase in lean body mass in males at puberty and that this provided athletic advantage to male athletes over female athletes. The Panel in that case was not satisfied as to the degree of that advantage and declined to validate the Hyperandrogenism Regulations. The IAAF was given the opportunity to provide further evidence to validate those regulations, which had set the maximum level of testosterone for an athlete in female competition to 10 nmol/L, this being well above the maximum level in the female population and slightly above the minimum level in the male population.

4. In March 2018, the IAAF informed the CAS that it intended to withdraw the Hyperandrogenism Regulations and to replace them with new Regulations.

5. In April 2018, the IAAF enacted the DSD Regulations. In summary, the DSD Regulations establish new requirements governing the eligibility of women with certain differences of sex development ("DSD") to participate in the female classification in eight events (the "Restricted Events") at international athletics competitions ("International Competitions"). The Restricted Events include the 400m, 800m and 1500m races—events in which Ms. Semenya regularly participates at International Competitions.

6. During the course of the proceedings before the CAS, the IAAF explained that, following an amendment to the DSD Regulations, the DSD covered by the Regulations are limited to"46 XY DSD"—i.e. conditions where the affected individual has XY chromosomes. Accordingly, no individuals with XX chromosomes are subjected to any restrictions or eligibility conditions under the DSD Regulations.

7. Athletes with 46 XY DSD have testosterone levels well into the male range. The DSD Regulations require athletes with 46 XY DSD who have a natural testosterone level of above 5 nmol/L, and who experience a "*material androgenizing effect*" from that enhanced testosterone level, to reduce their natural testosterone level to within the normal female range (i.e. to a level below 5 nmol/L) and to maintain that reduced level for a continuous period of at least six months in order to be eligible to compete in a Restricted Event at an International Competition. There is no requirement for, or suggestion of, any surgical intervention to achieve this level.

The Claimants' challenges to the validity of the DSD Regulations

8. The DSD Regulations came into force on 1 November 2018. Prior to that date, however, Ms. Semenya and ASA (collectively, the "Claimants") commenced

arbitration proceedings before the CAS challenging the validity of the DSD Regulations.

The Claimants contended *inter alia* that the DSD Regulations unfairly discriminate against athletes on the basis of sex and/or gender because they only apply (i) to female athletes; and (ii) to female athletes having certain physiological traits. They submitted that the DSD Regulations lack a sound scientific basis; are unnecessary to ensure fair competition within the female classification; and are likely to cause grave, unjustified and irreparable harm to affected female athletes. Accordingly, the Claimants sought an award from the CAS declaring the DSD Regulations unlawful and preventing them from being brought into force on the basis that the Regulations are unfairly discriminatory, arbitrary and disproportionate and therefore violate the IAAF Constitution, the Olympic Charter, the laws of Monaco, the laws of jurisdictions in which international athletics competitions are held, as well as universally recognised fundamental human rights.

9. In response, the IAAF submitted that the DSD Regulations are based on the best available science; do not discriminate on the basis of any protected characteristic; and are a necessary, reasonable and proportionate means of pursuing the legitimate aim of safeguarding fair competition and protecting the ability of female athletes to compete on a level playing field.

10. Between 18–22 February 2019, a hearing of the Claimants' challenges was held before the CAS in Lausanne, Switzerland. The CAS Panel comprised the Hon. Dr. Annabelle Bennett AO SC (President); The Hon. Hugh L. Fraser (Arbitrator) and Dr. Hans Nater (Arbitrator). The Panel received detailed written and oral testimony from a large number of factual and expert witnesses. This included experts specialising in gynaecology, andrology and the causes, diagnosis, effects and treatment of DSD; genetics, endocrinology and pharmacology; exercise physiology and sports performance; medical and research ethics; sports regulation and governance; and statistics.

<u>The Award of the CAS Panel</u>

11. After setting out the parties' evidence and submissions, the Panel begins its analysis of the merits by noting that this case involves a complex collision of scientific, ethical and legal conundrums. It also involves incompatible, competing rights. It is not possible to give effect to one set of rights without restricting the other set of rights. Put simply, on one hand is the right of every athlete to compete in sport, to have their legal sex and gender identity respected, and to be free from any form of discrimination. On the other hand, is the right of female athletes, who are relevantly biologically disadvantaged vis-à-vis male athletes, to be able to compete against other female athletes and to achieve the benefits of athletic success. The decision is also constrained by the accepted, necessary, binary division of athletics into male events and female events, when there is no such binary division of athletes. That binary division has not been challenged.

12. The Panel has not found the issues in this case easy to decide. It is clear from the range of expert evidence presented on behalf of the parties that there are

many scientific, ethical and regulatory issues on which reasonable and informed minds may legitimately differ. The Panel is mindful that, in considering these issues, it is not acting as a policy maker or regulator. It is neither necessary nor appropriate for the Panel to step into the shoes of the IAAF by deciding how it would have approached issues had it been charged with making policies or enacting rules itself. Instead, its function is a purely judicial one. The Panel must adjudicate the disputed legal issues on the basis of the applicable legal tests and by reference to the arguments and admissible evidence on the record in these proceedings. While this inevitably requires consideration of arguments and evidence based on an array of policy and scientific matters, the Panel must be mindful of its judicial role and the limits of that role. It is also bound to make its decision based upon the evidence presented to it, taking account of the submissions made by the parties.

Discrimination

13. The Panel unanimously concludes that the DSD Regulations are prima facie discriminatory since they impose differential treatment based on protected characteristics. In particular, since the DSD Regulations establish restrictions that are targeted at a subset of the female/intersex athlete population, and do not impose any equivalent restrictions on male athletes, it follows that the Regulations are prima facie discriminatory on grounds of legal sex. Similarly, the DSD Regulations create restrictions that are targeted at a group of individuals who have certain immutable biological characteristics (namely a 46 XY DSD coupled with a material androgenising effect arising from that condition), and which do not apply to individuals who do not have those characteristics. It follows that the Regulations are also prima facie discriminatory on grounds of innate biological characteristics.

14. The conclusion that the DSD Regulations are prima facie discriminatory is merely the starting point of the Panel's legal analysis. In particular, it is common ground that a rule that imposes differential treatment on the basis of a particular protected characteristic is valid if it is a necessary, reasonable and proportionate means of attaining a legitimate objective.

Necessity

15. The majority of the Panel concludes that the IAAF has succeeded in establishing the necessity requirement.

16. The Panel begins its consideration of this question by observing that once it is recognized that it is legitimate to have separate categories of male and female competition, it inevitably follows that it is necessary to devise an objective, fair and effective means of determining which individuals may, and which may not, participate in those categories.

17. The Panel accepts the IAAF's submission that reference to a person's legal sex alone may not always constitute a fair and effective means of making that determination. This is because the reason for the separation between male and female categories in competitive athletics is ultimately founded on biology rather than legal status. The purpose of having separate categories is to protect a class of individuals who lack certain insuperable performance

advantages from having to compete against individuals who possess those insuperable advantages. In this regard, the fact that a person is recognised in law as a woman and identifies as a woman does not necessarily mean that they lack those insuperable performance advantages associated with certain biological traits that predominate in individuals who are generally (but not always) recognised in law as males and self-identify as males. It is human biology, not legal status or gender identity, that ultimately determines which individuals possess the physical traits which give rise to that insuperable advantage and which do not.

18. Accordingly, the purpose of the male-female divide in competitive athletics is not to protect athletes with a female legal sex from having to compete against athletes with a male legal sex. Nor is it to protect athletes with a female gender identity from having to compete against athletes with a male gender identity. Rather, it is to protect individuals whose bodies have developed in a certain way following puberty from having to compete against individuals who, by virtue of their bodies having developed in a different way following puberty, possess certain physical traits that create such a significant performance advantage that fair competition between the two groups is not possible. In most cases, the former group comprises individuals with a female legal sex and a female gender identity, while the latter group comprises individuals with a male legal sex and male gender identity. However, this is not true of all cases. Natural human biology does not map perfectly onto legal status and gender identity. The imperfect alignment between nature, law and identity is what gives rise to the conundrum at the heart of this case.

19. The Panel considers that, once it is recognised that the reason for organising competitive athletics into separate male and female categories rests on the need to protect one group of individuals against having to compete against individuals who possess certain insuperable performance advantages derived from biology rather than legal status, it follows that it may be legitimate to regulate the right to participate in the female category by reference to those biological factors rather than legal status alone.

20. It was common ground between the parties that there is a substantial difference in elite sports performance between males and females. It was also common ground that (a) the normal female range of serum testosterone, produced mainly in the ovaries and adrenal glands, is 0.06 to 1.68 nmol/L; and (b)the normal male range of serum testosterone concentration, produced mainly in the testes, is 7.7 to 29.4 nmol/L. On the basis of the scientific evidence presented by the parties, the Panel unanimously finds that endogenous testosterone is the primary driver of the sex difference in sports performance between males and females.

21. The IAAF submitted that all but one of the many different factors that contribute to sport performance—including training, coaching, nutrition and medical support, as well as many genetic variations—are equally available to men and women. The only factor that is available only to men is exposure to adult male testosterone levels. The IAAF submitted that if the purpose of the female category is to prevent athletes who lack that testosterone-derived

advantage from having to compete against athletes who possess that testosterone-derived advantage, then it is necessarily "category defeating" to permit any individuals who possess that testosterone-derived advantage to compete in that category. The majority of the Panel accepts the logic of the IAAF's submission.

22. Having carefully considered the expert evidence, the majority of the Panel concludes that androgen sensitive female athletes with 46 XY DSD enjoy a significant performance advantage over other female athletes without such DSD, and that this advantage is attributable to their exposure to levels of circulating testosterone in the normal adult male range, rather than the normal adult female range. The majority of the Panel observes that the evidence concerning the performances and statistical over-representation of female athletes with 46 XY DSD in certain Relevant Events demonstrates that the elevated testosterone levels that such athletes possess creates a significant and often determinative performance advantage over other female athletes who do not have a 46 XY DSD condition.

23. On this basis, the majority of the Panel accepts that the IAAF has discharged its burden of establishing that regulations governing the ability of female athletes with 46 XY DSD to participate in certain events are necessary to maintain fair competition in female athletics by ensuring that female athletes who do not enjoy the significant performance advantage caused by exposure to levels of circulating testosterone in the adult male range do not have to compete against female athletes who do enjoy that performance advantage.

Proportionality

24. The majority of the Panel concludes that, on the evidence adduced, the DSD Regulations are on their face reasonable and proportionate. In reaching this conclusion, the majority notes, amongst other things, that the DSD Regulations do not require any athlete to undergo any surgical intervention, and envisage that affected athletes can control their testosterone levels by using conventional oral contraceptives. The majority has also had regard to the possible side effects of such oral contraceptives, to the nature of the examinations that will be undertaken for the purpose of determining whether an athlete has experienced a "material androgenising effect" from their high testosterone levels, and the risk of individuals' medical confidentiality being compromised.

25. While the majority concludes that the DSD Regulations are not disproportionate on their face, the Panel highlights its serious concerns about aspects of the practical application of the DSD Regulations when they are implemented. In particular, the Panel expresses its concerns about the potential difficulty for an athlete in complying with the requirements under the Regulations(including the possibility that affected athletes may inadvertently, and through no fault of their own, be unable consistently to maintain a natural testosterone level below 5 nmol/L).The Panel also notes the paucity of evidence to justify the inclusion of two events (the 1500m and one mile events) within the category of Restricted Events. The Panel strongly encourages the IAAF to address the Panel's concerns in its implementation of

the DSD Regulations. At the same time, the majority of the Panel observes that it may be that, on implementation and with experience, certain factors, supported by evidence, may be shown to affect the overall proportionality of the DSD Regulations, either by indicating that amendments are required in order to ensure that the Regulations are capable of being applied proportionately, or by providing further support for or against the inclusion of particular events within the category of Restricted Events.

The Panel's expression of gratitude to Ms. Semenya

26. In its Award the Panel expressly pays tribute to Ms. Semenya's grace and fortitude throughout this process. The Panel expresses its profound gratitude for her dignified personal participation and the exemplary manner in which she has conducted herself throughout the proceedings.

27. The Panel also stresses that while much of the argument in this proceeding has centred around the "fairness" of permitting Ms. Semenya to compete against other female athletes, there can be no suggestion that Ms. Semenya (or any other female athletes in the same position as Ms. Semenya) has done anything wrong. This is not a case about cheating or wrongdoing of any sort. Ms. Semenya is not accused of breaching any rule. Her participation and success in elite female athletics is entirely beyond reproach and she has done nothing whatsoever to warrant any personal criticism.

QUESTIONS TO REVIEW AND SYNTHESIZE

1. How would you categorize the major types of international commercial arbitration?
2. How does each type compare to the others and to domestic U.S. commercial arbitration?
3. What factors lead parties to choose each type of international commercial arbitration?

C. LABOR ARBITRATION

Labor arbitration arises out of a collective bargaining agreement (CBA) between an employer and a labor union that represents some of the firm's employees. A CBA is likely to be a complex document. It may deal with a large number of subjects, including wages and benefits, limits on the employer's right to discharge or discipline employees, and seniority for purposes of layoffs, promotion, and job assignments. It will constitute, in short, an overall framework for employer-employee relations.

Most CBAs also spell out a process to resolve claims (grievances) alleging breach of the CBA. This process typically includes several steps: At the beginning, for example, may be informal attempts to resolve a grievance on the shop floor by consultations between the aggrieved employee's immediate supervisor and the union shop steward; if the dispute is not settled at this stage it will move to successively higher levels. The CBA is likely to say that at all stages, work is not to be interrupted because of the dispute but is to continue pending a final settlement, and is likely also to impose strict time limits to ensure that a grievance is heard and processed speedily. The final stage in the grievance process, to handle those cases that are not winnowed out by the process of day-to-day negotiation, is likely to be binding arbitration. "Virtually all of the thousands of collective bargaining agreements—negotiations between an employer and labor unions, usually on wages, hours, and working conditions—entered into annually provide for the arbitration of unresolved grievances."[50]

CBAs generally involve the union trading away the right to strike in exchange for employer promises not typically made to non-unionized employees, such as the promise not to discharge employees without "just cause." Whether the employer had "just cause" to discharge a particular employee is the sort of dispute a typical CBA would send to arbitration.

Section 301 of the Labor Management Relations Act of 1947 (the Taft-Hartley Act) granted jurisdiction to federal district courts to hear suits for violation of collective bargaining agreements "in an industry affecting commerce." In *Textile Workers Union v. Lincoln Mills*, 353 U.S. 448 (1957), the Supreme Court held that § 301 was "more than jurisdictional," and that it "authorizes federal courts to fashion a body of federal law for the enforcement of these collective bargaining agreements." "Plainly the agreement to arbitrate grievance disputes is the *quid pro quo* for an agreement not to strike." Federal policy therefore was that promises to arbitrate grievances under collective bargaining agreements should be specifically enforced, and that "industrial peace can be best obtained only in that way."

Federal courts have since engaged in "fashioning" a federal common law dealing with the enforcement of collective bargaining arbitration agreements—to such an extent that the field of "labor law" is now largely the law of labor arbitration. In 1960, in what is still the Supreme Court's most significant pronouncement on the subject, Justice Douglas described the purpose labor arbitration and its centrality to governance of a unionized workplace.

United Steelworkers of America v. Warrior & Gulf Navigation Co.

Supreme Court of the United States, 1960.
363 U.S. 574, 80 S.Ct. 1347, 4 L.Ed.2d 1409.

■ Opinion of the Court by MR. JUSTICE DOUGLAS.

* * *

The present federal policy is to promote industrial stabilization through the collective bargaining agreement. A major factor in achieving industrial peace is the

[50] American Arbitration Association, *Practice Areas*, Labor, https://www.adr.org/labor (last visited May 16, 2019). See also Gerald M. Moody, Jr., *Writing Is Reading Is Writing: Two Applications of the Parol Evidence Rule to Collective Bargaining Agreements*, 2009 Colum. Bus. L. Rev. 326, 338 (2009) (referring to "[t]he quietus presence of arbitration clauses in collective bargaining agreements"); Kenneth G. Dau-Schmidt & Timothy A. Haley, *Governance of the Workplace: The Contemporary Regime of Individual Contract*, 28 Comp. Lab. L. & Pol'y J. 313, 319 (2007) ("The Percentage of American Collective Bargaining Agreements with Contract Terms containing Grievance and Arbitration Clauses for various years: 1971: 94%; 1986: 99%; 1995: 99%.").

inclusion of a provision for arbitration of grievances in the collective bargaining agreement.

Thus the run of [commercial] arbitration cases * * * becomes irrelevant to our problem. There the choice is between the adjudication of cases or controversies in courts with established procedures or even special statutory safeguards on the one hand and the settlement of them in the more informal arbitration tribunal on the other. In the commercial case, arbitration is the substitute for litigation. Here arbitration is the substitute for industrial strife. Since arbitration of labor disputes has quite different functions from arbitration under an ordinary commercial agreement, the hostility evinced by courts toward arbitration of commercial agreements has no place here. For arbitration of labor disputes under collective bargaining agreements is part and parcel of the collective bargaining process itself.

* * *

A collective bargaining agreement is an effort to erect a system of industrial self-government. When most parties enter into [a] contractual relationship they do so voluntarily, in the sense that there is no real compulsion to deal with one another, as opposed to dealing with other parties. This is not true of the labor agreement. The choice is generally not between entering or refusing to enter into a relationship, for that in all probability preexists the negotiations. Rather it is between having that relationship governed by an agreed-upon rule of law or leaving each and every matter subject to a temporary resolution dependent solely upon the relative strength, at any given moment, of the contending forces. The mature labor agreement may attempt to regulate all aspects of the complicated relationship, from the most crucial to the most minute over an extended period of time. Because of the compulsion to reach agreement and the breadth of the matters covered, as well as the need for a fairly concise and readable instrument, the product of negotiations (the written document) is, in the words of the late Dean Shulman, "a compilation of diverse provisions: some provide objective criteria almost automatically applicable; some provide more or less specific standards which require reason and judgment in their application; and some do little more than leave problems to future consideration with an expression of hope and good faith." Gaps may be left to be filled in by reference to the practices of the particular industry and of the various shops covered by the agreement. Many of the specific practices which underlie the agreement may be unknown, except in hazy form, even to the negotiators. Courts and arbitration in the context of most commercial contracts are resorted to because there has been a breakdown in the working relationship of the parties; such resort is the unwanted exception. But the grievance machinery under a collective bargaining agreement is at the very heart of the system of industrial self-government. Arbitration is the means of solving the unforeseeable by molding a system of private law for all the problems which may arise and to provide for their solution in a way which will generally accord with the variant needs and desires of the parties. The processing of disputes through the grievance machinery is actually a vehicle by which meaning and content are given to the collective bargaining agreement.

Apart from matters that the parties specifically exclude, all of the questions on which the parties disagree must therefore come within the scope of the grievance and arbitration provisions of the collective agreement. The grievance procedure is, in other words, a part of the continuous collective bargaining process. It, rather than a strike, is the terminal point of a disagreement.

* * *

The labor arbitrator's source of law is not confined to the express provisions of the contract, as the industrial common law—the practices of the industry and the shop—is equally a part of the collective bargaining agreement although not expressed in it. The labor arbitrator is usually chosen because of the parties' confidence in his knowledge of the common law of the shop and their trust in his personal judgment to bring to bear considerations which are not expressed in the contract as criteria for judgment. The parties expect that his judgment of a particular grievance will reflect not only what the contract says but, insofar as the collective bargaining agreement permits, such factors as the effect upon productivity of a particular result, its consequence to the morale of the shop, his judgment whether tensions will be heightened or diminished. For the parties' objective in using the arbitration process is primarily to further their common goal of uninterrupted production under the agreement, to make the agreement serve their specialized needs. The ablest judge cannot be expected to bring the same experience and competence to bear upon the determination of a grievance, because he cannot be similarly informed.

Arbitration of labor disputes serves, then, to give "meaning and content" over time to the vague or ambiguous terms of the collective bargaining agreement (CBA). In addition, arbitration of grievances may affect the dynamic of the parties' relationship by communicating about potential trouble spots. Another function of labor arbitration was highlighted by Justice Douglas in a formulation which has now attained something of the status of a cliché: In a companion case to *Warrior & Gulf,* Justice Douglas noted that "[t]he processing of even frivolous claims may have therapeutic values of which those who are not a part of the plant environment may be quite unaware."[51]

Labor arbitration can have a "therapeutic" function because the ability to participate in the selection of a neutral decision-maker, and to present one's story in an informal, "non-threatening" atmosphere, may be "empowering" for each of the parties to the dispute.[52] However, while any particular grievance under a CBA is likely to be that of the individual *employee,* who may have been dismissed or whose job classification may have been changed, the parties to the CBA are the employer and the *union*. The union, as the exclusive representative of all the employees in the bargaining unit, is in exclusive control of the administration of the CBA and controls the employee's access to the grievance procedure at every stage. In these circumstances, pursuing even hopeless claims to arbitration has at least the virtue of giving employees the assurance that their cases have been heard and that they have been taken seriously. Grievance arbitration may thus serve as a "safety valve for

---

[51] United Steelworkers of America v. American Mfg. Co., 363 U.S. 564, 568 (1960).

[52] Roger Abrams, et al., *Arbitral Therapy*, 46 Rutgers L.Rev. 1751, 1765, 1767, 1769 (1994).

troublesome complaints"; the employee's presence at the hearing watching management witnesses subjected to "searching and often embarrassing cross-examination" may result in "a kind of catharsis that helps to make even eventual defeat acceptable" to the grievant.[53]

Carrying a case through the arbitration process may have other advantages for the union. It is often more politic for union representatives to "pass the buck" to the arbitrator, who they know will reject the grievance, than to be obliged *themselves* to convince their constituent, the employee, to drop the claim. In addition, a union that "arbitrarily" refuses to pursue an employee's grievance to arbitration, or that "process[s] it in a perfunctory fashion," may well be open to a suit by the employee for "unfair representation."[54] Nevertheless, the overwhelming proportion of employee grievances are resolved without resort to arbitration, much as the overwhelming proportion of lawsuits are settled before trial. If a grievance rate of 10 to 20 per 100 employees per year is still "typical,"[55] then actually taking most of those grievances to arbitration would require the labor arbitration system to expand greatly.

Awards handed down by labor arbitrators generally reveal considerable sensitivity to the considerations mentioned by Justice Douglas in his paean to labor arbitration in *Warrior & Gulf*—the need to reduce tensions and to foster a good working relationship within the plant setting, the need to pay attention to the "common law of the shop" and to the "customs and practices which the parties have come to consider as settled patterns of conduct."[56]

Labor arbitration's focus on the "law of the shop" as opposed to the "law of the land" fits with its significant number of cases in which neither party is represented by a lawyer. An analysis of a sample of unpublished grievance arbitration awards for discharge cases in Minnesota from 1982 to 2005 found the union representative was not a lawyer in approximately 45% of the cases and the employer's representative was not a lawyer in 29% of the cases. See Laura J. Cooper, Mario F. Bognanno, Stephen F. Befort, *What's the Relationship Between Labor Arbitrators' Backgrounds and Outcomes of Discipline and Discharge Awards? An Empirical Analysis*, 31 ABA J. Lab. & Emp. L. 433, 436 (2016).

> For many labor arbitrators, arbitration practice is a part-time occupation. While some part-time arbitrators are retired from other occupations or just beginning to establish an arbitration practice, some part-time arbitrators are professors—commonly in law, industrial relations, business, or economics—and some are practicing attorneys. Unlike employment arbitrators, who simultaneously may serve as attorneys representing employees in litigation, or, more frequently, representing employers in employment disputes, nearly all labor

[53] Archibald Cox, *Current Problems in the Law of Grievance Arbitration*, 30 Rocky Mt.L.Rev. 247, 261 (1958); Benjamin Aaron, *The Role of the Arbitrator in Ensuring a Fair Hearing*, 35 Proc.Nat'l Acad.Arb. 30, 32 (1983).

[54] Vaca v. Sipes, 386 U.S. 171 (1967); see also Bowen v. U.S. Postal Service, 459 U.S. 212 (1983).

[55] See David E. Feller, *A General Theory of the Collective Bargaining Agreement*, 61 Cal.L.Rev. 663, 755 (1973).

[56] *In re Standard Bag Corp. and Paper Bag, Novelty, Mounting, Finishing and Display Workers Union*, 45 Lab.Arb. 1149 (1965).

> arbitrators who simultaneously practice law must do so in an area other than labor and employment law to comply with the rules of listing agencies such as the Federal Mediation and Conciliation Service or with NAA membership rules.

Id. The NAA (National Academy of Arbitrators) is an honorary and professional organization of the most experienced labor and employment arbitrators.

QUESTIONS TO REVIEW AND SYNTHESIZE

1. What is a collective bargaining agreement and what is its role in labor arbitration?
2. Labor arbitration is most similar to which type of commercial arbitration? Why?
3. Labor arbitration differs from all commercial arbitration in what respects?

D. EMPLOYMENT ARBITRATION

https://tribunecontentagency.com/wp-content/uploads/2016/01/20160106edwas-a.jpg

While labor arbitration arises out of a collective bargaining agreement between an employer and a labor union, employment arbitration arises out of an employer's agreement with an individual employee.

Mark D. Gough, *The High Costs of an Inexpensive Forum: An Empirical Analysis of Employment Discrimination Claims Heard in Arbitration and Civil Litigation*

35 Berkeley J. Emp. & Lab. L. 91, 94, 95–96, 96–103, 112 (2014).

Beginning in the mid-1980s and continuing into the 1990s, a noticeable paradigm shift occurred in the Supreme Court's interpretation of the Federal Arbitration Act of 1926 ("FAA"), laying the legal groundwork for the ascension of employment arbitration. * * *

Multiple surveys from the early 1990s through the mid 2000s show the prolific growth of arbitration in the employment context. [A]t the same time as the Gilmer [v. Interstate/Johnson Lane Corp., 500 U.S. 20 (1991)] ruling, a Feuille and Chachere study found only four out of 107 firms, or 3.7%, used outside arbitration in 1991. In 1995, only four years later, the General Accounting Office ("GAO") found that 7.6% of employers with 100 or more employees practiced mandatory arbitration with the non-union workforce and half of these employers imposed mandatory arbitration as a condition of employment. A 1997 GAO publication reported that nineteen percent of private company respondents used arbitration. In a 2003 survey specific to the telecommunications industry, 14.1% of respondents indicated that they had adopted mandatory arbitration procedures. Adjusting for employer size, 22.7% of nonunion employees in that survey were covered by employment arbitration procedures. In a 2007 survey of 757 U.S-based nonunion companies spanning multiple industries, 46.8% of firms reported using employment arbitration. In fact, arbitration was reported to be the most common single ADR practice among the respondent firms. Finally, a survey of the US Fortune 1000 revealed that more than eighty percent of the responding companies used arbitration at least once within the past three years.

* * *

Early American Arbitration Association ("AAA") case analyses from the 1990s show surprisingly consistent, though slowly diminishing, employee win rates in arbitration. Analyzing AAA employment arbitration awards from 1992, Lisa Bingham found that employees won in seventy-eight percent of cases. In a later paper, Lisa Bingham analyzed the employee win rates in employment dispute cases heard by the AAA from 1993 to 1994, in which she found that employees won sixty-four percent of the time in cases involving "one-time player employers." Consistent with Bingham's figures, Maltby found that employees won sixty-three percent of employment disputes filed and disposed of by the AAA between 1993 and 1995.

Though these studies produced similar results, it would be wise to question their relevance to the arbitration environment today, nearly two decades later. First, these initial studies predate the adoption of the Due Process Protocol for Mediation and Arbitration of Statutory Disputes Arising Out of the Employment Relationship ("Due Process Protocol"). The Due Process Protocol was established in 1995 "in order to assure some measure of fairness and due process to employer-promulgated schemes for private resolution of statutory disputes." The Due Process Protocol recommends specific features and processes that should be present in mandatory arbitration agreements and hearings including: (1) freedom of representative choice; (2) adequate pre-hearing discovery; and (3) joint selection and compensation of arbitrators, among others. Multiple organizations endorsed the Due Process Protocol, including the National Academy of Arbitrators, the American Arbitration Association, the Society of Professionals in Dispute Resolution, the National Employment Lawyers Association, the Federal Mediation and Conciliation Service, and the American Civil Liberties Union. Theoretically, the adoption of the Due Process Protocol should make the arbitration process more friendly and fair to employees. Consequently, employee win rates, all else held constant, should be higher today than in the 1990s.

The Due Process Protocol, however, is just one reason that the cases of the early 1990s are not representative of the current employment arbitration forum. Many studies examining cases from this period include a large number of claims by highly educated employees with the power to negotiate individual contracts, typically managers and executives. In contrast, claims brought today are often forced upon employees as a condition of employment. Professor Lisa Bingham, in an analysis of 203 AAA awards from 1993 to 1995, found that employee claimants won 68.8% of the time if the cases involved employees who had negotiated their contracts individually. If, however, the arbitration agreement was written into personnel manuals or handbooks, employee claimants won only 21.3% of the time. The drastic disparity in the win rates between these two types of contracts should be considered. Individual win rates should be much lower in today's arbitration environment because the majority of claims being brought today originate from employer-promulgated mandatory arbitration agreements.

To address the changing arbitration environment, with an emphasis on the Due Process Protocol and the changing nature of arbitral cases themselves, researchers have continued mining available data on contemporary arbitrator decisions. A 2003 study found that employees won in employment arbitration 43% of the time. This overall win rate can be broken down to a 34% win rate for employees proceeding under a mandatory contract included in their hiring papers, likely to be lower-income employees, compared to a 57% rate for employees proceeding under individually-negotiated contracts, likely to be higher-income employees. A separate study examined the outcomes of fifty-nine AAA decisions between 1996 and 1997. There was an overall employee win rate of 39.7%. If the employee claimant went to arbitration as a result of an individually-negotiated contract, the employee win rate was 61.3%; if, however, a personnel handbook engendered the arbitration proceeding, the employee win rate was 27.6%. Analyzing the AAA's filings data for January 2003 through December 2007, Colvin found that the win rate for the 3,945 employment cases was only 21.4%, well below the findings from the early 1990s. Lastly, looking at a subset of AAA cases from 2008, Colvin and Pike found that plaintiff employees succeed at arbitration 24.7% of the time in cases based on employer-promulgated procedures; in cases based on individually-negotiated contracts, plaintiff employees won in 64.6% of cases.

In contrast to the research on employment arbitration, Eisenberg and Hill collected larger-scale datasets for state and federal litigation outcomes by using data gathered by government agencies. Their analysis of 1,430 employment discrimination cases heard in federal courts yielded an employee win rate of 36.4%.

They report a slightly higher employee win rate of 43.8% in 160 state court employment discrimination cases. Cases involving non-civil rights disputes tried in state court produced an employee win rate of 56.6%. Oppenheimer reports a 59% employee win rate in a sample of 117 common law discharge cases heard in California state court. Clermont and Schwab accessed the entire universe of employment discrimination cases, 265,356 in total, heard in federal court between 1979 and 2000. They found that discrimination plaintiffs won 37.8% of the time in jury trials but only 19.3% of the time in judge-only trials. A later study using data through 2006 produced similar results.

The employee win rates in litigation provided by the Eisenberg and Hill and the Clermont and Schwab studies are higher than employee win rates based on employer-promulgated agreements, which are characteristic of the post-Gilmer environment, reported in the studies conducted by Colvin, Bingham and Sarraf, Hill, and Bingham. However, the win rates in arbitration are similar to the win rates discrimination plaintiffs experience in federal judge-only trials.

B. Award Amounts

Like win rates, available empirical evidence suggests that employee plaintiffs receive lower award amounts in arbitration relative to litigation. Colvin reports the median award amount was $36,500 and the mean was $109,858 for 1,213 AAA employment arbitrations decided between 2003 and 2007. Adjusted for inflation, the median award is $43,879 and the mean award is $132,066 in 2014 dollars. Comparatively, Clermont & Schwab report federal employment discrimination cases reaching verdicts between 1991 and 2000 receive a mean award size of $890,182, which is at least $1,106,394 in 2014 dollars when adjusting for inflation. At the state level, Eisenberg & Hill find the median and mean award amount in state civil rights employment disputes going to trial were $206,976 and $478,488, respectively. Using inflation-adjusted 2014 dollars, the median and mean amounts are $282,195 and $652,380, respectively. Lastly, Oppenheimer reports the median of damages awarded in 117 California state court common law discharge cases decided between 1998 and 1999 was $296,991, or approximately $418,534 in inflation-adjusted 2014 dollars.

C. Interpretive Difficulties

An inherent limitation on using the above studies to make evaluative statements about outcomes in arbitration is the unknown comparability of cases in the arbitrated and litigated samples. Variation exists in award amounts and employee win rates between the different forums, but there is no natural way to make cases heard in arbitration identical in all respects to cases heard in civil litigation. Can the observed variance be attributed to inequities inherent in the arbitral forum or are there material differences in cases being adjudicated between the forums? First, scholars advance an "appellate effect" to explain inferior outcomes observed in arbitration summary statistics. Because arbitration is presumably adopted by large employers with developed human resource practices, often as the last step in sophisticated conflict management systems, employee grievances are exposed to several opportunities for settlement. It is plausible that formal human resource practices act to filter cases, leaving only the unmeritorious to be resolved through arbitration. Differences in formal human resource practices, some scholars argue, likely bias simple comparisons of employee win rates and monetary awards.

The same informality, lack of appeal, and due process concessions at the heart of critics' opposition to mandatory arbitration are virtues to arbitration's proponents, who argue these characteristics create a cheaper, faster, and more accessible forum over civil litigation. Indeed, because of the lower barriers to entry compared to civil litigation, employees may be more likely to bring low value and marginally weaker claims to arbitration. Notably, Samuel Estreicher argued that the speed and lower costs of the arbitration forum provides a "Saturn" in a system otherwise characterized by "Cadillacs" for the few and "rickshaws" for the many. Where only individuals with high incomes or high-value claims have meaningful access to the civil litigation system, he argues, arbitration is more accessible for claimants with average or marginally weaker (i.e., low value) claims. If low value and meritless cases that would never have been brought to court, because of cost barriers or internal filtering, are presented in the arbitration forum, it should be expected that employee win rates and award amounts are lower in arbitration, as the average arbitration case would have less merit or lower damages than the average litigated case.

However, if plaintiff attorneys accept that employees succeed less frequently and receive lower awards in arbitration, they may be reluctant to represent potential clients pursuing arbitration claims, especially because they typically work on contingency fee arrangements. Responding to the lower expected value of an arbitration case, attorneys may only agree to represent exceptional arbitration claims: those that are clearly meritorious and involve high provable damages. Opposite the appellate effect described above, attorney case selection may result in cases of higher merit and value being presented in arbitration. The tension between these effects leaves the relative merits of initial cases presented in the forums theoretically unresolved.

Lastly, arbitration proponents contend that the availability of summary judgment in civil litigation excludes cases lacking merit from court summary statistics and results in deceptively inflated employee win rates. This argument is significant but simple: a large proportion of litigated cases are dismissed prior to verdict through summary judgment, and assuming motions for summary judgment are rare in arbitration, win rates at judge or jury trials are not comparable to win rates at arbitration.

In recent years, studies using randomized vignettes have appeared in the literature to address the redoubtable task of controlling for merits of cases presented to decision-makers in various forums. One such study from 2006 looked at survey responses from 140 AAA employment arbitrators, eighty-two labor arbitrators from the National Academy of Arbitrators ("NAA"), and eighty-three jurors who had served in employment discrimination cases over the last five years. The study analyzed participant responses on thirty-two hypothetical termination cases to see if there were systematic differences in the decision-making processes between the three groups. The authors conclude employee rights are likely to be affected by increased use of employment arbitration, finding that labor arbitrators are most likely to rule in favor of the employee, followed by jurors, and employment arbitrators are the least likely to rule in favor of the employee.

III. Methods

Given the persistence of comparability concerns, how similar are cases taken to verdict in arbitration and the civil litigation system? This Article addresses this lingering issue by presenting results from a survey of approximately 1,890 attorney members of the National Employment Lawyers Association ("NELA") about their most recent employment discrimination cases taken to verdict in arbitration and litigation. Founded in 1985, NELA is the largest organization of practicing plaintiff-side employment attorneys in the country. Full membership requires attorneys to certify that a majority of their legal practice involving employment discrimination, illegal workplace harassment, wrongful termination, denial of employee benefits, and other employment-related matters is on behalf of employees. Data was initially collected through a web-administered survey, to which 521 practicing attorneys responded throughout October 2013. To increase the response rate, the survey was distributed by U.S. mail in December 2013 and January 2014, from which 175 additional responses were collected. This increased the overall survey response rate to thirty-seven percent.

Respondents were asked to record the following information relating to their most recent employment discrimination cases taken to verdict/award in arbitration and litigation: claim amount, award amount, winning party, employee salary, alleged discriminatory action, whether a motion for summary judgment was filed, defendant size, and the attorney's fee arrangement, among other variables. Responses were restricted to employment discrimination claims because they are the most common type of employment case filed in state court, federal court, and in arbitration. In total, we received information on 478 employment discrimination cases reaching verdict through litigation and 208 employment discrimination case adjudicated in arbitration.

While previous studies have reviewed large databases of employment case dispositions, this is the first study to look at a representative sample of claims across multiple states, forums, and arbitration providers. * * *

* * *

[After presenting data, the author's conclusions follow:]

[This] analysis of approximately 700 contemporary employment discrimination cases shows outcomes in arbitration are starkly inferior to outcomes reported in litigation: employees are nearly forty percent more likely to win and receive average awards nearly twice as large in cases adjudicated in the civil litigation system compared to those that are arbitrated. And where previous scholars have suggested differing case characteristics could be the culprit behind such disparities, with the exception of summary judgment and plaintiff salary, the present data provides no support for the contention that case characteristics vary to any significant degree. Though plaintiffs' salaries vary, theory suggests such variation would lead to superior outcomes being realized in arbitration. Indeed, employee arbitration-claimants on average have higher salaries than claimants found in the civil litigation system, but worked for employers of similar size and had claims evaluated as equally meritorious by their representing attorney. Further, the distribution of the alleged discriminatory acts for claims does not suggest systematic differences between cases in the two forums. And while summary judgment is more likely in litigation, the chasm between win rates and award amounts remains when controlling for this variable. Considering these findings, courts should reevaluate their permissive attitude toward mandatory arbitration procedures and acknowledge the high costs of this "inexpensive" forum.

The article just excerpted reports results of a survey. The lawyers surveyed were members of the National Employment Lawyers Association (NELA), the largest organization of practicing plaintiff-side employment attorneys in the country. In the interest group battle over employment arbitration law, NELA often opposes the US Chamber of Commerce. While the Chamber praises Supreme Court decisions increasing enforcement of employment arbitration agreements—such as *Circuit City, Inc. v. Adams*,[57] *American Express Co. v. Italian Colors Restaurant*,[58] and *Epic Systems Corp. v. Lewis*[59]—NELA condemns these decisions,[60] and in doing so sometimes describes employment arbitration as "forced arbitration."[61]

---

[57] *Circuit City Stores v. Adams*, 532 U.S. 105, 121 S. Ct. 1302 (2001); *Mandatory Arbitration Good for Workers, Businesses*, U.S. Chamber of Com. (March 20, 2001), https://www.uschamber.com/press-release/mandatory-arbitration-good-workers-businesses (last visited June 25, 2018) ("The United States Chamber of Commerce called today's 5–4 Supreme Court decision, that federal arbitration laws apply to most employment disputes, *Circuit City Stores, Inc. v. Saint Clair Adams*, good for business and good for workers.").

[58] *Am. Express Co. v. Italian Colors Rest.*, 559 U.S. 1103, 130 S. Ct. 2401 (2010); *U.S. Chamber of Commerce Commends Supreme Court for Preserving Availability of Arbitration to Consumers and Businesses*, U.S. Chamber of Com. (June 19, 2003), https://www.uschamber.com/press-release/us-chamber-commends-supreme-court-preserving-availability-arbitration-consumers-and (last visited July 7, 2018) ("The U.S. Chamber of Commerce today praised a decision by the U.S. Supreme Court that preserves the availability of arbitration—a fair, efficient, and economical method of alternative dispute resolution. In its ruling in the case American Express v. Italian Colors Restaurant . . . the Court again upheld the right of contracting parties to agree to resolve their disputes through a system that is more accessible to consumers and businesses than the judicial system.").

[59] *Epic Sys. Corp. v. Lewis*, 138 S. Ct. 1612 (2018); *Ernst & Young LLP v. Morris*, 137 S. Ct. 809 (2017); *NLRB v. Murphy Oil USA, Inc.*, 137 S. Ct. 809 (2017); *Supreme Court Affirms Validity of Employment Arbitration Agreements That Include Class Waivers*, U.S. Chamber of Comm. (May 21, 2018), https://www.uschamber.com/litigation-update/supreme-court-affirms-validity-of-employment-arbitration-agreements-include-class (last visited July 7, 2018) ("The Supreme Court issued its long awaited decision in a trilogy of cases—*Epic Systems v. Lewis, Ernst & Young v. Morris*, and *NLRB v. Murphy Oil*—addressing whether the National Labor Relations Act (NLRA) bars arbitration provisions in employment contracts that include class action waivers. By a 5–4 vote, the Court ruled in favor of employers, affirming the validity of employment agreements that require individual arbitration. The Chamber has been a staunch advocate for this result, filing over a dozen briefs on the issue in the federal courts of appeals and filing briefs at both the certiorari and merits stages of all three cases decided today.").

[60] See U.S. Supreme Court Decision Will Embolden Companies to Flout Workplace Laws—Congress Must Act, the Nat'l Emp't Lawyers Ass'n, https://www.nela.org/index.cfm?pg=20130620AMEX (last visited June 25, 2018) ("This decision [*American Express Co. v. Italian Colors Restaurant*] by a divided Court will give companies license to try to deny their workers access to our country's civil justice system when they violate our nation's employment and civil rights laws. Congress never intended the Federal Arbitration Act (FAA) to be used against America's workers or to invalidate their substantive legal rights."); Brief Amicus Curiae of the National Employment Lawyers Association in Support of Respondent Saint Clair Adams, Circuit City Stores, Inc. v. Adams, 2000 WL 1376974 ("Congress was aware of the disparity in bargaining power between employers and workers in 1925 and exempted all employment contracts from the FAA for that very reason.").

[61] U.S. Supreme Court Deals Major Blow To Employees' Basic Rights, Nat'l Emp't Lawyers Ass'n, https://www.nela.org/index.cfm?pg=MurphyOil2018 (last visited June 25, 2018).

Stephen J. Ware, *The Centrist Case for Enforcing Adhesive Arbitration Agreements*

23 Harv. Negot. L. Rev. 29, 69–72 (2017).

The facts of each case are unique, so no study can control for every variable that might distinguish the studied cases in arbitration from the studied cases in litigation. As Carrie Menkel-Meadow writes, "[r]esearch concerning the effects of ADR programs is especially difficult due to the problems of developing control groups; indeed, how can one case be subjected to both ADR and litigation?" In other words, because the same cases cannot be sent to both arbitration and, in an otherwise parallel universe, litigation, we cannot know whether the forum variable ("arbitration or litigation") or something else, like cases' merits, caused any difference in outcomes between arbitrated cases and litigated cases.

ii. Experiments and Surveys

As a way around this problem, a researcher trying to determine the effects of forum (arbitration or litigation) could conduct experiments that mimic arbitration and litigation of the same mock case. However, we could never know how different the results of such mock arbitrations and litigations would be from the results of real arbitrations and litigations because the mock arbitrators, mock judges, and mock jurors might not behave like real arbitrators, real judges, and real jurors—even if they are same people who really serve in those roles—because participants would know the case was mock, not real.

Also problematic in learning the effects of forum are surveys asking lawyers and parties to report data about their cases in arbitration and litigation. Surveys are notoriously vulnerable to inaccuracies due to respondents' ignorance, dishonesty, and self-deception. As Robert Glicksman and Dietrich Earnhart write,

> There is a risk when conducting any survey that the respondents will not provide accurate information, either because they do not have it or because they intentionally supply inaccurate or misleading information. Survey respondents may provide dishonest responses, for example, because they want to make a good impression on those asking the questions (and believe that accurate answers will not do so) or because they are convinced that inaccurate responses are in their self-interest. These kinds of responses may bias the results of any survey.

These inaccuracy problems with surveys are widely recognized across a range of research areas. Moreover, these inaccuracy problems are especially troubling when the survey's response rate is low and those who do respond have a stake in the survey's results, like businesses and lawyers surveyed about arbitration versus litigation.

2. Empirical Studies Should Try to Compare Similar Cases (Apples to Apples)

With experiments and surveys so problematic in learning the effects of forum (arbitration or litigation), the best empirical researchers can do is try to find similar cases in arbitration and litigation and then compare the results, while acknowledging that similarity is a matter of degree and will never be perfect, so no study can entirely eliminate the possibility that differences between the arbitration cases studied and the litigation cases studied might explain any differences in outcomes between the two sets of cases.

Cynthia Estlund, *The Black Hole of Mandatory Arbitration*

96 N.C. L. Rev. 679, 679, 680–82, 682–83, 684–86, 687, 688, 688–89, 689–91, 691–92, 692, 699–700 (2018).

From the early days of mandatory arbitration of statutory claims—especially employment-discrimination claims—one major critique has been the loss of transparency and publicity that attends a shift from litigation in public courts to arbitration in private tribunals. * * *

While it is important not to overstate the contrast between arbitration and litigation, there is no doubt that much more of the arbitral process is shielded from public view. In particular, the plaintiff's allegations are set out in a complaint that appears on a public docket in litigation but not in arbitration, and the hearing, if any, occurs in open court in the case of litigation but usually in a private conference room in the case of arbitration. In cases that proceed through a hearing and decision, the typically terse nature of arbitral rulings means that much of the actual rationale for the decision is hidden inside the arbitrator's head—and even these terse rulings are rarely published. The relative secrecy of arbitration is a product partly of the confidentiality norms that prevail within this private contractual forum and the community of arbitrators, and partly of confidentiality agreements that often accompany pre-dispute arbitration agreements and that bind the parties. The private and contractual nature of arbitration makes it relatively easy for firms to prevent disclosure of just about anything concerning allegations, evidence, disposition, or settlement of the disputes, not just by parties but by the tribunals themselves.

To the extent that firms do impose obligations on their employees (and customers) to arbitrate rather than litigate future legal disputes, they can often draw a heavy veil of secrecy around allegations of misconduct and their resolution. That means that firms have less to worry about if they violate the law. They face more limited "reputational sanctions," which are among the most powerful deterrents to illegal or legally questionable conduct, at least among reputable firms. The relative invisibility of particular disputes and their outcomes in arbitration thus undermines the regulatory function of private-enforcement actions, which serve not only as a dispute resolution mechanism but also as an ex post alternative or supplement to ex ante prescriptive rules of conduct.

The relative secrecy and obscurity of arbitral proceedings extends to the nature of arbitral procedures themselves. Courts follow published rules of procedure that are promulgated by publicly accountable bodies. Arbitrators are primarily bound by the agreements under which they are appointed—agreements that are written by the parties, or rather by one party in the case of most employment and consumer arbitration agreements. Some arbitration instruments adopt the procedures of reputable arbitration providers like the American Arbitration Association ("AAA"); others use more obscure providers or invent their own procedures. Either way, firms have no legal obligation to make their chosen procedures publicly available. That has made it impossible to develop an accurate empirical assessment of the shape of mandatory arbitration as a mechanism of dispute resolution and has greatly handicapped efforts to hold firms publicly accountable for the fairness of their dispute resolution procedures.

In this Article, I focus on another dimension of the obscurity surrounding mandatory arbitration: the outright disappearance of claims that are subject to this process. The secrecy and non-transparency of arbitration providers and procedures greatly impeded empirical research on arbitration, its incidence, and its outcomes for decades after the Supreme Court launched the mandatory-arbitration juggernaut. But the picture is gradually coming into focus. It now appears that the great bulk of disputes that are subject to mandatory arbitration agreements ("MAAs")—that is, a large share of all legal disputes between individuals (consumers and employees) and corporations—simply evaporate before they are even filed. It is one thing to know that mandatory arbitration draws a thick veil of secrecy over cases that are subject to that process. It is quite another to find that almost nothing lies behind that veil. Mandatory arbitration is less of an "alternative dispute resolution" mechanism than it is a magician's disappearing trick or a mirage. Metaphors beckon, but I have opted for that of the black hole into which matter collapses and no light escapes.

* * *

A word on the scope of this Article: first, the focus here is on employment disputes. Although mandatory arbitration has probably had a greater proportional impact on consumer claims (largely by way of anti-class action provisions), employment claims are distinctive in ways that matter here. Employment cases, with the exception of wage-and-hour claims, are much more likely than consumer claims to involve individual disputes with significant financial stakes for individual claimants (relative to their total resources). * * *

Within the field of employment arbitration, this Article focuses on employer-promulgated pre-dispute arbitration agreements in the non-union workplace; that is what is meant here by "mandatory arbitration." Arbitration under individually negotiated agreements (mainly for high-salaried employees) or under either post-dispute agreements to arbitrate or collective bargaining agreements is different, and more likely to be a mutually beneficial alternative to either litigation or labor-management strife. But arbitration that is imposed on employees as a condition of employment before any dispute has arisen, which is the focus of this Article, has been deservedly controversial since its inception.

* * *

The largest arbitration providers are well-established, reputable organizations like the American Arbitration Association and the Judicial Arbitration and Mediation Service ("JAMS"). Survey data indicate that the AAA is designated in about half of employment arbitration agreements, and JAMS in another twenty percent. Both organizations provide lists of qualified arbitrators and are relatively transparent in how arbitrators are chosen, who they are, and how they deal with disputes (though both organizations also promote confidentiality in the proceedings themselves). Both the AAA and JAMS also adhere to the much-touted "Due Process Protocol" ("DPP"), a set of standards for fair employment arbitration procedures that was approved by a diverse group representing employers, unions, employees, and dispute resolution professionals. But nothing in the law of arbitration requires arbitration providers to adhere to the DPP, and nothing requires employers to designate the AAA or JAMS as the arbitration provider.

An estimated thirty percent of arbitration provisions call for adjudication of disputes through other providers or ad hoc processes. In this grey zone, arbitration procedures, the pool of arbitrators, the selection process, and case outcomes may all be impossible for outside observers to ascertain. It appears that some of those providers succumb to the temptation to supply what some firms demand, and cater quite openly to the employers who unilaterally draft and impose arbitration agreements and who choose the providers. For example, consider the egregiously one-sided agreement struck down by the Fourth Circuit in Hooters of America, Inc. v. Phillips, which, among its many defects, essentially guaranteed that the employer would choose the arbitrator. But it can hardly be surprising that the overwhelmingly asymmetric process of "choosing" arbitration and arbitration providers would put pressure on the neutrality of the process.

* * *

Based on the partial early data, some commentators reached a conclusion that was quite consistent with the Gilmer Court's sanguine account of the quid pro quo of mandatory arbitration: By agreeing to arbitrate, parties trade "the procedures and opportunity for review of the courtroom for the simplicity, informality, and expedition of arbitration." Plaintiffs, for their part, lost access to juries, judges, and appellate review, but gained access to a faster and often cheaper adjudication process. Based on that early data, Professor Samuel Estreicher and others concluded that arbitration had some advantages for both sides over the expensive and "lottery-like" litigation process; recoveries were more limited, but employees—especially low-income employees—were more likely to get some kind of hearing and more likely to get some kind of remedy. On that then-plausible account, the advent of mandatory arbitration appeared likely to enhance ordinary employees' access to justice.

The picture has become a bit clearer in recent years, due in part to a handful of state laws, including California's, requiring arbitration providers to publicly disclose a modicum of information about the disputes they handle. * * *

With that in mind, it is striking how discouraging the more recent data are. It now appears not only that average recoveries are significantly lower in arbitration than in court (as previously believed), but also that employee-complainants may be significantly less likely to prevail and to recover anything. * * * Still, data on case outcomes are hotly contested, and their meaning is clouded by high rates of dismissal and summary judgment in court and by the paucity of data on settlements.

My focus here, however, is not on outcomes in arbitration versus litigation, but on the sheer number of cases in each. The single most striking fact uncovered by the recent studies is the very small number of arbitration cases that enter the process. During the eleven-year period from 2003 through 2013, an average of about 940 cases per year were filed and terminated with the AAA under employer-promulgated procedures. If the AAA is the designated provider in about half of arbitration agreements (as surveys suggest), that yields an estimate of fewer than 2000 employment arbitration cases terminated per year under MAAs. At first glance, that appears to be a very low number.

* * *

To assess the meaning of the small number of arbitrations, we might start by comparing that number with the number of employees covered by MAAs. Until recently, the prevailing scholarly estimate was that those agreements covered roughly twenty percent of nonunion private sector employees. (That compared to just over two percent coverage in 1992.) By contrast, Colvin's more comprehensive 2017 study estimated that 56 percent of non-union private sector employees, or approximately 60 million employees, are now covered by MAAs. That is a steep increase in coverage, and it sharply raises the stakes in debates over mandatory arbitration. But of course those numbers beg the question: How many such individuals each year have potential employment law claims—claims that proceed past "naming" and "blaming" to "claiming" in some forum or another?

I will focus here solely on the number of claims filed (whether or not they are terminated), as that will allow for a relatively clean comparison with federal court filing statistics, and will avoid many controversies surrounding the analysis of case outcomes. I will focus on filings in 2016, the most recent year for which solid data are available for both the AAA and federal courts. The AAA reports that 2879 individuals filed employment cases with the AAA under employer-promulgated procedures in 2016. Following the provisional assumption above that this represents half of all arbitrations under MAAs, that suggests that about 5126 cases were filed in arbitration by the approximately 60 million employees who are covered by MAAs. That appears to represent an increase above what Colvin found, on average, from 2003 to 2013, and that is what one would expect given his recent findings on growing use of MAAs. Still, it seems like a very low number. But to make sense of it, one needs to know how many claims were filed in court by those free to do so. That might make it possible to roughly estimate the number of claims one would expect to see among those covered by MAAs.

Let us begin with federal court litigation, as to which data are readily available. In 2016, approximately 31,000 federal lawsuits were filed in five categories of employment cases: "Civil rights: employment," "ADA [Americans with Disabilities Act]/employment," "FLSA" (Fair Labor Standards Act), "ERISA" (Employee Retirement Income Security Act), and "FMLA" (Family and Medical Leave Act). If those 31,000 federal court cases were all filed by the 44 percent of employees who are not covered by MAAs, then we would expect over 39,000 claims to be filed in arbitration by the other 56 percent of employees who are subject to mandatory arbitration. Given the preliminary estimate of 5,126 arbitration filings, this comparison would suggest about 34,000 "missing" arbitrations per year—that is, 34,000 cases that we would expect to enter the arbitration process, based on the general rate of employment litigation and the number of employees covered by MAAs, but that are never filed.

That is a striking number of "missing" arbitrations. But these numbers are open to several objections, two of which may call for downward adjustments * * *. First, some federal court lawsuits are filed by public employees, who are not generally subject to MAAs and should be excluded from the comparison. If government employees (who make up 15.2% of non-farm employees) are as likely as private sector employees to file an employment lawsuit in federal court, the relevant number of federal court filings would fall to 26,300. Second, some of the federal court lawsuits were presumably filed by individuals who were covered by MAAs (and thus faced a motion to compel arbitration). * * * These two adjustments lead to an estimate of "expected" arbitrations between 14,700 and 33,500, as compared to the 5,126 arbitrations that appear to have been filed, and to an estimate of between 9600 and 28,400 "missing" arbitrations.

* * *

Much is still unknown about the fate of cases in arbitration (and litigation). From whatever angle one looks at the numbers, however, it appears that a very large majority of aggrieved individuals who face the prospect of mandatory arbitration give up their claims before filing. For all the sound and fury about skewed outcomes, repeat player effects, biased arbitrators, limited discovery, and lack of adherence to or production of precedent in arbitration, it turns out that, except for a relative handful of cases, arbitration does not take place at all. That is the black hole of mandatory arbitration.

QUESTIONS TO REVIEW AND SYNTHESIZE

1. Employment arbitration differs from labor arbitration in what ways?
2. Employment arbitration differs from commercial arbitration in what ways?
3. Many employment arbitration agreements are adhesion contracts, that is, drafted by employers and presented to employees take-it-or-leave-it, so the job is available only to employees who agree to arbitrate. Similarly, many business-to-business transactions involve commercial arbitration agreements that are similarly adhesive insofar as one party refuses to do business with the other except on a form contract that includes an arbitration clause. Despite this similarity, do adhesive arbitration agreements nevertheless concern you more in the employment context?
4. What are the empirical challenges to concluding that employees' claims tend to win less often and less money in arbitration than litigation?
5. If employees win less often or less money in arbitration than litigation, does this suggest a problem with arbitration or with litigation?
6. In 2018, a Harvard Law School lecturer leaked the Munger, Tolles & Olson law firm's proposed employment arbitration agreement for summer associates, which also said that "the fact and content" of any arbitration proceeding must be held "in the strictest confidence," though the information could be disclosed to legal counsel and insurers. After the leak, Munger, Tolles & Olson tweeted that it will no longer require any of its employees to sign arbitration agreements. See Debra Cassens Weiss, After social media outcry, Munger Tolles will no longer require mandatory arbitration, ABA J. Mar. 26, 2018. http://www.abajournal.com/news/article/after_

social_media_outcry_muner_tolles_will_no_longer_require_mandatory_arb/?utm_source=maestro&utm_medium=email&utm_campaign=daily_email. How would you factor in an employment arbitration agreement to your decision whether to accept a job offer?

7. What is Due Process Protocol for Mediation and Arbitration of Statutory Disputes Arising Out of the Employment Relationship, and what effects has it had?

E. CONSUMER ARBITRATION

Bank of America announced in 1992 that all its contracts with depositors and credit-card holders would henceforth contain clauses requiring arbitration of any individual disputes under the commercial rules of the American Arbitration Association; any complaints brought as class actions would be "referred" to a neutral under California's "rent-a-judge" statute (See Chapter 6.) Notice of the arbitration clause was sent to the bank's customers as "stuffers" in their (mailed) monthly statements; cardholders, for example, were told that if they continued to use their cards after receiving the notice, the arbitration provision would apply to all past and future transactions.

During the 1980s, a number of California banks, including the Bank of America, had already begun to experiment with using arbitration in other product lines, particularly mid-range commercial loans. This was in reaction to a series of pro-borrower "lender liability" cases that seemed to broaden the scope of the duties owed to a borrower by a bank:

> [The banks] concluded that both their exposure and their transaction costs could be reduced by the adoption of arbitration provisions. First, they believed that their exposure would be both more predictable and better contained with arbitration. In their view, arbitrators generally had a better grasp of underlying contractual issues than juries and were less likely to consider factors outside those presented in the case at issue; for example, the fact that the bank is a large institution able to spread out any losses relative to the individual, who may be forced into extreme hardship. Firms also believed that arbitrators were less likely to award punitive damages. Furthermore, firms anticipated that the fact that disputes would be heard before an arbitrator would, in turn, affect plaintiffs' and plaintiffs' attorneys' calculus in deciding whether to bring suit in the first place; as possible verdicts declined, plaintiffs would be less likely to bring suit.[62]

David Horton & Andrea Cann Chandrasekher, *After the Revolution: An Empirical Study of Consumer Arbitration*

104 Geo. L.J. 57, 67–70 (2015).

[I]n the 1980s, the Court kicked its expansion of the FAA into high gear. In *Southland Corp. v. Keating*, Chief Justice Burger held that the statute—long regarded as a procedural rule for federal courts—binds state tribunals too and preempted California legislation that excluded franchise cases from arbitration.

[62] Erik Moller, et al., Private Dispute Resolution in the Banking Industry 12–13 (RAND 1993).

Chief Justice Burger reasoned that the text of section 2 only permits states to invalidate agreements to arbitrate under "grounds . . . for the revocation of any contract," and the California statute was not a generally applicable contract rule. The Court soon clarified that the FAA serves as an equal protection clause for arbitration: it forbids states from * * * "singling out arbitration provisions for suspect status" or "rely[ing] on the uniqueness of an agreement to arbitrate" to hold "that enforcement would be unconscionable."

Similarly, in *Mitsubishi Motors Corp. v. Soler Chrysler-Plymouth, Inc.*, the Court overruled the line of cases that had excluded federal statutory claims from arbitration. The Court explained that because arbitration had matured, it would not "presum[e] that the parties and arbitral body conducting a proceeding will be unable or unwilling to retain competent, conscientious, and impartial arbitrators." In a passage that the Court would repeat a half-dozen times over the course of the next three decades, it explained that the switch from litigation to arbitration did not affect the outcome of a dispute:

> By agreeing to arbitrate a statutory claim, a party does not forgo the substantive rights afforded by the statute; it only submits to their resolution in an arbitral, rather than a judicial, forum. It trades the procedures and opportunity for review of the courtroom for the simplicity, informality, and expedition of arbitration.

Thus, the Court swung from one extreme to the other. Private tribunals were no longer a cartoonish approximation of the judicial system; rather, they were equal to—in fact, arguably better than—the public model.

As firms rushed to place mandatory arbitration clauses in their standard form contracts, fine print became a divisive issue. Some Justices, the defense bar, and right-leaning commentators took the position that arbitration was good for consumers because it was faster, cheaper, and less intimidating than the court system. Yet other judges, consumer advocates, plaintiffs' lawyers, and liberal scholars posited that the opposite is true—that arbitration's limited discovery, loose evidentiary rules, narrow appellate review, and lack of reasoned awards tilted the scales of justice toward businesses.

Several of these critics also drew on Marc Galanter's canonical article, *Why the "Haves" Come Out Ahead: Speculations on the Limits of Legal Change*. [9 Law and Society Rev. 1 (1974)] Galanter famously divided participants in the legal system into repeat players, who are regularly embroiled in litigation, and one-shotters, who are not. Galanter outlined a variety of ways in which repeat players could capitalize on their experience to gain the upper hand over one-shotters, such as stockpiling information, making short-term sacrifices for long-term gains, and cultivating relationships within institutions. In the late 1990s, several influential law review articles asserted that Galanter's theory fit mandatory arbitration like a glove. After all, private judges, unlike their public counterparts, are paid by the hour. In addition, litigants cannot handpick a specific decision maker to resolve their case, but parties in arbitration can. Accordingly, as David Schwartz observed, "arbitrators have an economic stake in being selected again, and their judgment may well be shaded by a desire to build a 'track record' of decisions that corporate repeat-users will view approvingly." Likewise, Jean Sternlight noted that "[a]n arbitrator who issues a large punitive damages award against a company may not get chosen again by that company or others who hear of the award." Moreover, these scholars argued that repeat players could come out ahead even if arbitrators took pains to remain even-handed. If nothing else, firms that arbitrated regularly could compile data on particular decision makers' predilections, while one-shot plaintiffs and their lawyers could not.

But for several reasons, the repeat-player critique failed to sway courts. For one, concerns about systemic prejudice do not fit gracefully within the doctrinal framework of federal arbitration law. As noted, section 10 of the FAA allows courts to vacate awards "where there was evident partiality or corruption in the arbitrators." Yet because of the overwhelming interest in the finality of dispute resolution, judges reserve this rule for unusual situations. Indeed, "bias that might disqualify a judge will not disqualify an arbitrator." Thus, courts have overturned awards when an arbitrator failed to disclose that he was the son of the vice president of the union involved in the dispute, or that he had received a handsome consulting fee from one of the parties. Compared to these concrete and fact-specific showings, bald speculation about an arbitrator's motives rang hollow.

In addition, other forms of regulation seemed to minimize the repeat-player problem. Even under [Supreme Court cases applying the FAA], judges can exercise their prerogative under section 2 of the FAA to nullify the arbitration clause itself under the contract defense of unconscionability. Thus, courts struck down terms that gave the firm "the unilateral right to choose an arbitrator." This check against egregious system rigging made arbitral neutrality seem like a less pressing problem. Similarly, providers such as the AAA and JAMS adopted Due Process Protocols: internal standards that require arbitrators to divulge "any past or present relationship or experience with the parties or their representatives," and to give consumers an equal voice in the selection of the decision maker. These protections spurred the D.C. Circuit to declare in 1997 that "[c]orrupt arbitrators will not survive long in the business," and other jurisdictions to reject assertions that "the 'repeat player effect' is enough to render an arbitration agreement unconscionable."

Thus, by the dawn of the new millennium, arbitration had moved out of the peripheries and into the center of the civil justice landscape. Judges, scholars, and interest groups were deeply divided about whether this was a positive development.

Jeff Sovern, Elayne E. Greenberg, Paul F. Kirgis & Yuxiang Liu, *"Whimsy Little Contracts" With Unexpected Consequences: An Empirical Analysis of Consumer Understanding of Arbitration Agreements*

75 Md. L. Rev. 1, 11–14 (2015).

In a 2004 study, Linda Demaine and Deborah Hensler researched the arbitration policies of the major businesses in thirty-seven industries. They found that more than 35% of the 161 businesses they surveyed included arbitration clauses in their consumer contracts. Unsurprisingly, the numbers were highest in industries, such as financial services, in which businesses and consumers interact in ongoing relationships governed by written contracts. Demaine and Hensler found that almost 70% of the businesses in the financial sector required consumers to arbitrate. In contrast, none of the businesses in the food and entertainment industry provided for arbitration with consumers.

A 2008 study by Theodore Eisenberg, Geoffrey Miller and Emily Sherwin confirmed the prevalence of arbitration in industries where written contracts with large numbers of consumers are the norm. Eisenberg and his colleagues analyzed twenty-six consumer contracts drafted by twenty-one major companies in the telecommunications and finance industries. They found that over 75% of those contracts included an arbitration clause. Amy Schmitz reached similar results in her analysis of credit card and mobile phone contracts, finding that ten of thirteen credit card contracts and all nine mobile phone contracts she analyzed included arbitration clauses.

In a more comprehensive study of the extent of arbitration in the credit card industry, Peter Rutledge and Chris Drahozal found that, by 2009, over 95% of outstanding credit card loans were covered by an arbitration agreement. In 2009, however, two events caused a dramatic reduction in the use of arbitration agreements in credit card contracts. First, the National Arbitration Forum ("NAF"), which at the time was the largest provider of consumer credit arbitrations nationwide, ceased administering new consumer credit arbitrations as part of its settlement of a consumer fraud lawsuit filed by the Minnesota Attorney General. Second, four of the largest issuers of credit cards agreed to remove the arbitration provisions from their credit card agreements for three and a half years as part of the settlement of an antitrust lawsuit alleging that the banks conspired to force consumers to accept arbitration agreements containing class waivers. As a consequence, by the end of 2010, the percentage of outstanding credit card loans subject to an arbitration agreement had dropped to 48%.

That figure had increased only slightly as of 2012, when the Consumer Financial Protection Bureau ("CFPB"), the agency created by the Dodd-Frank Wall Street Reform and Consumer Protection Act to oversee the financial services industry, undertook a large-scale study of arbitration agreements in credit card contracts, checking account contracts, and general purpose reloadable ("GPR") prepaid cards. The CFPB found that just over half of outstanding credit card loans were covered by an arbitration agreement, while just under half of insured deposits at banks were similarly covered. In contrast, more than 68% of the dollar amount loaded on prepaid cards was covered by an arbitration agreement. The wide disparity between credit cards and prepaid cards seems to be explained by the antitrust settlement. The four issuers that agreed to remove their arbitration clauses account for almost 87% of the outstanding credit card debt not covered by an arbitration clause. The CFPB estimates that if those issuers had not removed their arbitration clauses, more than 94% of outstanding credit card debt would be covered by an arbitration agreement.

The "*Whimsy Little Contracts*" article just excerpted mentions the Minnesota Attorney General's suit against National Arbitration Forum (NAF), which at the time was the largest provider of consumer credit arbitrations nationwide.[63] This case alleged that NAF committed "consumer fraud, deceptive trade practices, and false advertising," and was hiding extensive ties to a debt collection firm that brought many of NAF's cases. NAF settled the Minnesota AG's case with an agreement to stop arbitrating consumer disputes, although it could continue arbitrating internet domain disputes and other disputes.

"*Whimsy Little Contracts*" also mentions allegations that, in violation of antitrust laws, credit card issuers "conspired" "to include compulsory arbitration clauses in their respective cardholder agreements."[64] Plaintiffs alleged that the defendants, had formed a group known as "the Arbitration Coalition" intended to "draw upon their collective market power * * * to develop, hone and implement their compulsory arbitration clauses."[65] As the court described it, "the paradigm arbitration clause in cardholder agreements" imposed by all the defendants provided that

> Any claim, dispute or controversy * * * arising from or relating in any way to this Agreement or your Account, including Claims regarding the applicability of this arbitration clause or the validity of the entire Agreement, shall be resolved by the National Arbitration Forum. * * * This arbitration agreement applies to all Claims now in existence or that may arise in the future * * *.[66]

Ultimately, the Second Circuit in 2015 affirmed a lengthy district court opinion finding that although there was "conscious parallel action in the adoption and maintenance of arbitration clauses," the "final decision to adopt class-action-barring clauses was something the Issuing Banks hashed out individually and internally," and thus not in violation of the antitrust laws. Ross v. Citigroup, Inc., 630 F. App'x 79, 82 (2d Cir. 2015), as corrected (Nov. 24, 2015).

A series of 2015 articles in the New York Times epitomized growing opposition to enforcement of consumers' adhesive arbitration agreements.[67] These articles charged that consumers party to such agreements generally do not know they are giving up their right to go to court, and particularly to take part in class actions. The New York Times articles further charge that in consumers' disputes with businesses, arbitrators "commonly consider the companies their clients" and "have twisted or outright disregarded the law" to rule favorably towards the companies,[68]

---

[63] Nancy A. Welsh, *What Is "(Im)partial Enough" in A World of Embedded Neutrals?*, 52 Ariz. L. Rev. 395, 428 (2010) ("by 2006, NAF had become this country's largest provider of consumer debt arbitration services, handling 214,000 claims in that year alone.").

[64] In re Currency Conversion Fee Antitrust Litigation, 2005 WL 2364969, 1 (S.D.N.Y. 2005).

[65] *Id.* at 9.

[66] In re Currency Conversion Fee Antitrust Litigation, 361 F.Supp.2d 237, 244 (S.D.N.Y. 2005).

[67] Jessica Silver-Greenberg & Michael Corkery, *A Privatization of the Justice System,* N.Y. TIMES, Nov. 2, 2015, at A1; Jessica Silver-Greenberg & Robert Gebeloff, *Arbitration Everywhere, Stacking Deck of Justice*, N. Y. TIMES, Nov. 1, 2015, at A1; Michael Corkery & Jessica Silver-Greenberg, *When Scripture is the Rule of Law*, N.Y. TIMES, Nov. 3, 2015, at A1.

[68] Silver-Greenberg & Corkery, N.Y. TIMES, NOV. 2, 2015, at A1.

and "the rules of arbitration largely favor companies, which can even steer cases to friendly arbitrators."[69]

Stephen J. Ware, *The Centrist Case for Enforcing Adhesive Arbitration Agreements*

23 Harv. Negot. L. Rev. 29, 89–90, 94, 96, 97, 98, 109, 110–11, 111–14 (2017).

While nearly everyone presumes that enforcement of adhesive arbitration agreements tends to lower the costs of the businesses that use them, debate centers on whether this cost-reduction for businesses tends to lower prices for consumers. More broadly, this debate about whether businesses pass on their cost savings to consumers goes beyond adhesive arbitration agreements to adhesive contract terms generally.

The standard economic analysis, as * * * [University of Chicago Law Professor Omri] Ben-Shahar puts it, is that businesses' costs are "rolled into the price" consumers pay, so higher costs to businesses (sellers) tend to raise prices to consumers (buyers), while lower costs to sellers tend to lower prices to buyers. Although Ben-Shahar directs the University of Chicago's Institute for Law and Economics, the belief that sellers' costs affect the prices they charge their customers is not unique to "Chicago School" or other conservative economists, but rather is the standard analysis across the field of economics. For example, famously liberal Nobel prize-winning economist Paul Krugman and his co-authors explain that "a fall in the price of an input makes the production of the final good less costly for seller. They are more willing to supply the good at any given price, and the supply curve shifts to the right." This "increase in supply leads to a fall in the equilibrium price and a rise in the equilibrium quantity."

This standard economic analysis—lower costs to businesses (sellers) yield lower prices to their customers (buyers)—is supported by voluminous evidence from a wide variety of sources.

* * *

The distinction between a perfectly competitive market and a monopoly (along with intermediate conditions, such as "monopolistic competition") is part of the standard economic analysis (summarized above by Omri Ben-Shahar) of the extent to which changes in businesses' costs are passed through to consumers. While the entire cost-change is passed through to consumers only under conditions of perfect competition, some of the cost-change is passed through to consumers under non-competitive conditions, even monopoly.

* * *

In short, businesses' cost savings tend, to some extent, to be passed through to consumers even in non-competitive markets. More precisely, the extent to which changes in businesses' costs are passed through to consumers is determined by the elasticity of supply and demand in the relevant markets. Therefore, considering non-competitive markets indicates that the size of the price reduction

[69] Silver-Greenberg & Gebeloff, N. Y. TIMES, Nov. 1, 2015, at A1.

caused by a cost-savings to business (such as enforcement of its adhesive arbitration agreements) will vary, while strengthening the underlying generalization that business cost-savings tend, to some extent, to lower consumer prices (or improve consumers' non-price terms) regardless of whether the business operates under perfect competition, monopoly, or anything in between.

* * *

However (un)competitive a market, if enforceable adhesive arbitration agreements reduce costs to businesses (an uncontroversial premise), then standard economic analysis suggests they also tend to reduce prices to consumers.

* * *

Even the CFPB—author of the one study finding no statistically significant evidence to support this conclusion in the arbitration context—nevertheless endorses this conclusion in that context. After anticipating that business' costs were likely to rise due to the CFPB's proposed restriction on adhesive arbitration agreements, the CFPB said it "believes that most providers would pass through at least portions of some of the costs described above to consumers." In other words, the CFPB believes the standard economic analysis's conclusion survives the CFPB's inability to find statistically significant evidence to support it.

* * *

Rather than deny that non-price contract terms (such as arbitration clauses) affect prices, sophisticated economic scholarship on adhesion contracts generally begins with that tradeoff among price and other contract terms and asks which legal rules tend to produce the best mix of price and non-price—or, more precisely, salient and nonsalient—contract terms.

* * *

[A]s Douglas Baird concludes:

> There is nothing particularly special about what the law is doing with respect to fine print as opposed to other hidden product attributes. Of course, there may not be enough sophisticated buyers to give a seller the right incentives. There are computers with microprocessors that are too slow and warranties that are too stingy that are sold to people like me every day. But the question is not whether the market is perfect, but how we should shape legal rules to make markets work more effectively with respect to all product attributes.

In other words, lawmakers' considerations in shaping legal rules to police adhesion contract terms, like warranties and arbitration, resemble lawmakers' considerations in shaping legal rules to police product attributes like the speed of a computer. The possibility that a computer's slow processor hurts some consumers more than the price increase that would result from legally-prohibiting such processors is consistent with the possibility that many other consumers would be hurt more by the price increase. Similarly, the possibility that an adhesive arbitration clause hurts some consumers more than the price increase that would result from prohibiting such clauses is consistent with the possibility that many other consumers would be hurt more by the price increase.

* * *

Much as early-1900's progressives created the FDA to mandate minimum standards of drug safety, and mid-1900's progressives created strict products liability and the Consumer Product Safety Commission to mandate minimum standards of auto safety, early 2000's progressives created the CFPB to mandate minimum standards of consumer credit safety. In these and similar regulatory incursions on consumers' freedom of contract, the strong progressive argument is not that the relevant markets lack "perfect competition, [so] such regulation may well cause prices to drop or stay the same rather than rise," but rather that the regulatory protection of consumers' safety is worth consumers paying the higher prices likely caused by the regulation.

And that is the argument I believe should incline progressives toward the Centrist Position of continuing to enforce adhesive arbitration clauses that are safe for consumers, while prohibiting those that are unsafe. "Unsafe" adhesive arbitration clauses are, this article has argued, arbitration clauses:

1) in contracts induced by duress, misrepresentation, or other contract defense;

2) that deprive consumers of class actions; or

3) that preclude correction of legally-erroneous decisions of mandatory law.

* * *

As Chris Drahozal explains, first among the "unintended consequences [that] might result from restrictions on the use of pre-dispute arbitration clauses in consumer and employment contracts" is:

> [C]onsumers and employees without disputes—who have no complaint with their treatment by a business—likely will be made worse off by legal restrictions on the use of arbitration. The cost savings that businesses achieve through arbitration benefit consumers by enabling the businesses to reduce prices and employers to increase wages. Removing those cost savings by restricting the use of arbitration will have the opposite effect.

To this sensible point, progressives sensibly reply that even consumers who have no complaint with their treatment by a business may have been harmed by the business's violations of law, but not realize it. So discovering and deterring such violations is an important role for the plaintiffs' lawyers who bring class actions, and enforcing class waivers hurts consumers who do not realize they would benefit from a class action.

QUESTIONS TO REVIEW AND SYNTHESIZE

1. In what consumer transactions' adhesion contracts have you noticed arbitration clauses? Feel free to send them to your casebook author: Professor Stephen Ware, ware@ku.edu.
2. Would you switch from Verizon or AT&T to a pre-paid cellphone to avoid a contract with an arbitration clause?
3. Why do you think businesses using consumer arbitration agreements do so? Does your answer distinguish businesses that face consumer class actions from business that face only individual claims against them?
4. Do businesses' costs to defend and pay claims tend to affect the prices they charge consumers? Does this depend on how businesses compete with each other for customers or for investors or both?

F. MEDICAL ARBITRATION

1. PHYSICIANS

David Allen Larson & Dr. David Dahl, *Medical Malpractice Arbitration: Not Business As Usual*

8 Y.B. On Arb. & Mediation 69, 69–71, 79–83, 85–87, 93 (2016).

The authors hope that no one still seriously contends that politics do not affect arbitration. In fact, it frankly is difficult to understand the most recent United States Supreme Court decisions addressing arbitration unless one appreciates how those decisions further the interests of the business community. One cannot make bold assertions of this nature without at least some explanation, of course, and more discussion will follow. But the primary focus of this article is on an interesting exception to businesses', employers', and service providers' seemingly universal embrace of arbitration processes, particularly mandatory pre-dispute arbitration. Although it may be difficult to believe given arbitration's current popularity, not everyone requires his or her clients to sign mandatory pre-dispute arbitration agreements. In fact, some service providers prefer to avoid arbitration regardless of whether it is arranged pre- or post-dispute. So which merchants or service providers are choosing to forgo arbitration and, more importantly, why do they dislike arbitration? And do politics have anything to with their choices?

* * * Physicians are not, shall we say, the world's greatest fans of arbitration. It turns out that regulatory policies and practices, in other words politics, provide one important reason why physicians prefer to avoid arbitration. And there are additional reasons that explain why this particular group of service providers has not followed the "mad rush" to arbitration. This article will explain why at least one group of service providers, physicians, do not regard arbitration as the answer to all of their prayers.

Arbitration clauses frequently appear in consumer and employment contracts, and they are not unknown in the healthcare field. Nursing homes and similar facilities use binding pre-dispute arbitration clauses to reduce litigation expenses. Contracts between patients and individual medical providers, however, are a conspicuous exception to the otherwise ever-increasing practice of inserting pre-dispute, binding arbitration agreements into contracts.

Some commentators believe that eventually medical malpractice will be resolved in arbitration. Professor Myriam Gilles has suggested, for instance, that "all manner of tort claims (including negligence, loss of chance, and other allegations of medical malpractice . . .) could soon be hashed out in the sequestered universe of arbitration." But the authors do not anticipate that physicians will embrace arbitration anytime soon.

On the one hand, is this situation merely the result of old habits dying hard? If so, then we can expect that eventually mandatory arbitration clauses will appear in physician-patient contracts much more frequently than they do today. Yet on the other hand, is there something about arbitration that is so unattractive for physicians that they will make every effort to avoid it? Keeping in mind that the medical providers are the ones drafting, and thus controlling, the arbitration clauses, is it not possible to craft arbitration clauses that provide the same benefits enjoyed by numerous businesses and employers? Perhaps surprisingly, at least at the present time the answer appears to be "no."

Many of the assumed advantages of arbitration such as faster resolutions, lower costs, and greater confidentiality may not be as compelling when it comes to medical malpractice claims. First, litigation outcomes are generally quite positive for physicians. Physicians understandably are reluctant to accept different resolution processes when they are not convinced that the outcomes will be equally favorable, much less even better. Second, physicians generally are shielded from litigation expenses by malpractice insurance. Thus, arguments about the reduced costs of arbitration are not persuasive to physicians. Third, while disputes may be resolved more quickly with arbitration than they would be through litigation, other commonly reported advantages of arbitration—such as the ability to select your decision-maker, the availability of neutrals with specific expertise, and privacy—may seem illusory to the physician. Finally, because of the regulatory environment, in other words "politics," physicians are very wary of, and opposed to, compromise judgments and awards in malpractice cases. The perception that arbitration often results in a compromise decision, a proverbial "splitting of the baby," makes arbitration uniquely unattractive to physicians seeking complete vindication for both professional and personal reasons.

II. MEDICAL MALPRACTICE CLAIMS ARE ARBITRABLE

A. In General

Courts enforce binding, pre-dispute arbitration agreements routinely and medical malpractice arbitration agreements are not treated differently.

* * *

Courts enforce binding, pre-dispute arbitration agreements routinely and, as one should expect, medical malpractice arbitration agreements are not an exception.[32] *Marmet Healthcare v. Brown*, for example, was a medical malpractice action against a nursing home in which the United States Supreme Court pre-empted a state legislature's attempt to limit pre-dispute mandatory arbitration.[33] The Court declared that West Virginia's state law "prohibition against pre-dispute agreements to arbitrate personal-injury or wrongful-death claims against nursing homes is a categorical rule prohibiting arbitration of a particular type of claim, and that rule is contrary to the terms and coverage of the FAA [Federal Arbitration Act]."[34]

* * *

III. PURPORTED ADVANTAGES OF MEDICAL MALPRACTICE ARBITRATION

Academic observers have noted the potential benefits of arbitrating medical malpractice disputes for both claimants and physicians. Chief among the advantages cited have been quality of the decision-maker, speed of resolution, and reduced litigation expenses.

A. Qualified Decision Makers

Some writers do not believe lay juries possess the competence to decide medical malpractice cases. By allowing specialist neutrals to decide medical tort cases, some scholars believe results will be more accurate. In addition, qualified decision makers enhance efficiency of dispute resolution by obviating the need to educate a jury about medical practice and science.

* * *

Physicians actually have good reason to prefer a trial by jury rather than either a trial by a judge or an arbitration before an attorney or a retired judge. Juries find for physicians in nearly eighty percent of cases. There is evidence doctors win malpractice actions only about half as often when judges decide cases compared to when juries decide. A discrepancy this large is actually quite unusual and does not exist for other personal injury litigation. This discrepancy provides confirmation for survey data that juries may be predisposed toward physician defendants in malpractice disputes.

B. Rapid Resolution

Arbitration generally is regarded as more efficient in terms of time than litigation. There is no need to select and educate a jury, for instance. There typically is less conflict over evidence because evidentiary rules usually are much more relaxed. Discovery also is much more limited. As a result of these time-savings, arbitration claimants do not have to wait as long for compensation as they do in litigation, and defendant practitioners do not have to suffer through a lengthy period of uncertainty, self-doubt, and clouded reputation.

---

[32] Marmet Health Care v. Brown, 132 S. Ct. 1201, 1203 (2012) ("The [FAA] statute's text contains no exception for personal-injury or wrongful-death claims").

[33] *Id.*

[34] *Id.* at 1204. The case ultimately was remanded, however, to determine whether the arbitration clauses were unenforceable under state common law principles that were not specific to arbitration and pre-empted by the Federal Arbitration Act. *Id.*

An analysis of 1,452 litigated malpractice claims from throughout the United States reveals that the average time from opening the claim to closing it was three years. In sharp contrast, the 604 disputes between Kaiser Permanente and its members that were arbitrated in 2014 were closed on average in less than one year. Thus, rapid resolution of claims is a real advantage of arbitration over litigation for both claimants and defendants.

C. Reduced Litigation Expenses

As one would expect, medical malpractice litigation is expensive. In addition to filing fees and attorney's fees common to any litigation, almost all medical malpractice claims require at least one, and often multiple, expert witnesses. Due to the great expense of litigating medical malpractice claims, an aggrieved patient usually needs to retain an attorney willing to pay litigation expenses until settlement. This has three consequences for the patient: (1) the patient is unlikely to find an attorney willing to take even a clear case of malpractice if the damages are small; (2) even if damages are high, and it seems malpractice occurred, an attorney still will not take the case unless the chance of winning justifies the expense of suing; and (3) even if the patient triumphs in court, her award will be substantially reduced after litigation expenses are paid. The fact that plaintiffs must overcome these consequences lends support to the perception that litigation is a more favorable dispute resolution process for medical practitioners than less costly arbitration. The first two points are particularly important and will be further discussed below.

While it is true that arbitrating medical malpractice claims probably is less expensive than litigating those same claims in court, the fact that a case will be heard by an arbitrator does not necessarily solve a claimant's financial problems. Unless the claimant can work out a contingency fee arrangement with an attorney, upfront fees and out of pocket expenses (to pay neutrals, discovery costs, and expert witnesses) may still be quite high for the plaintiff. This can discourage the plaintiff from even initiating a claim in either forum.

As compared to claimants, litigation expenses may be much less of a deterrence for physicians because many, if not almost all, of these expenses likely are covered by malpractice insurance. Although incurred litigation costs may affect future malpractice insurance premiums, the cost saving advantages of arbitration to the physician him or herself, and the benefit that defending an arbitration in lieu of a trial may have for insurance premiums, may be too small to influence a physician's preference for arbitration or litigation.

* * *

V. PHYSICIANS ARE NOT WELL SERVED BY MEDICAL MALPRACTICE ARBITRATION

In almost every medical malpractice claim, there are at least two parties with an interest in a finding of non-negligence: the insurer and the physician. The motivations of these parties are not the same, however. On the one hand, the insurer wants to keep the total cost (cost of litigation plus awarded damages) of the suit as low as possible. On the other hand, the physician is less concerned with the cost of the suit, which in most cases is entirely covered by the insurer. Instead, the physician is apprehensive about maintaining both a self-image and a reputation of competence.

Physicians are aware they likely will be sued at some point in their careers. * * *

Physicians worry that arbitration will not adequately protect their intangible interests. Physicians seek to be held blameless, and arbitration is perceived as too prone to compromise. Some writers acknowledge this point of view, but do not consider it reasonable in the context of modern arbitration which protects against trivial claims. But even if it is true that arbitration reduces unworthy claims, a physician's intangible interests are no less threatened by nontrivial claims.

A. Arbitration Perceived as Prone to Compromise

Empirical evidence that arbitration is a forum prone to compromise is scant. In this regard, however, perception can be more important than reality. Large numbers of corporate counsel believe arbitration leads to compromise awards.

* * *

A doctor sued for malpractice suffers emotionally and can interpret the lawsuit as a personal attack. Some scholars have hypothesized that the defendant physician's self-esteem is the dominant nonmonetary concern in a malpractice action. To defend herself from what she perceives as an unwarranted attack on her competence, and to protect her self-image, a physician seeks complete vindication. Complete vindication cannot be found in a forum prone to compromise.

2. Reputational Concerns

a. Name Clearing

It certainly is true that some physicians value the "name clearing" function of the judicial process. When physicians are accused of negligence, they want their day in court and the court's public declaration that the care they provided met or exceeded professional standards.

* * *

Physicians have a powerful interest in not being listed in the National Practitioner Data Bank (NPDB). [Federal legislation] requires that all payments in satisfaction of a medical malpractice claim be reported to the NPDB. This requirement includes arbitration awards. Furthermore, it requires that all hospitals access this information when first credentialing a physician, and at least every two years afterwards, so long as the physician remains on the hospital staff. A hospital that does not request this information as required is presumed to have knowledge of the information in any medical malpractice action. The NPDB can also be accessed by insurers and used to inform decision-making about whether to include a physician in a provider network. Professor Van Tassel has likened listing in the NPDB to being "blacklisted."

To avoid the potentially devastating consequences of mandatory reporting, it is believed that many physicians are willing to settle only the strongest cases against them. In all other cases, the physician has a strong incentive to litigate.

* * *

VII. CONCLUSION

Benefiting from the Federal Arbitration Act and favorable Supreme Court jurisprudence, pre-dispute arbitration agreements have become the norm in American life. Even businesses in the medical field such as nursing homes, for example, have accepted pre-dispute arbitration agreements as a strategy to control the costs of negligence actions. Physicians, however, have not embraced arbitration as a means of resolving malpractice disputes.

There are several reasons for this anomaly. First, two of the advertised advantages of arbitration over litigation—qualified decision makers and lower expenses than litigation—may not resonate with physicians. Doctors would rather entrust their fate to a jury of laypersons than a panel of attorneys and retired judges, and doctors are shielded from the cost of litigation by insurance.

When a physician is accused of malpractice, her overarching concerns are likely to be internal self-image and external reputation, not economic considerations. The doctor wants to vindicate her own competence, clear her name, avoid having to declare a malpractice settlement when credentialing, steer clear of any licensing complications a malpractice settlement might create and, above all, keep her name out of the National Practitioner Data Base. The reporting requirements, and the way that these requirements discourage physicians from choosing arbitration, is an example of how politics have affected medical malpractice arbitration. These very real concerns often are threatened as much by a small monetary settlement as by a large settlement. The danger is in the settlement, not the amount.

Doctors will choose the forum that provides the best opportunity for total vindication. Under current conditions, that forum is the courtroom. In the courtroom the physician is protected by the full array of procedural safeguards, can fully utilize depositions and discovery, and, importantly, can explain her action to a sympathetic jury. In contrast, arbitration is viewed as a process prone to undesired compromise. One development could make pre-dispute binding medical malpractice arbitration agreements more common. Judicial or legislative initiatives might make litigation less favorable for physicians. This could tip the balance toward arbitration. At present, however, the unique concerns of physicians make even pre-dispute binding arbitration unattractive compared to litigation.

Cases on medical malpractice arbitration are summarized in Marc D. Ginsberg, *The Execution of an Arbitration Provision as a Condition Precedent to a Medical Treatment: Legally Enforceable? Medically Ethical?*, 42 Mitchell Hamline L. Rev. 273, 286–306 (2016).

QUESTIONS TO REVIEW AND SYNTHESIZE

1. If the *Medical Malpractice Arbitration* article just excerpted is correct that "litigation outcomes are generally quite positive for physicians" and "arbitrating medical malpractice claims probably is less expensive than litigating those same claims in court", how far do these observations go in explaining the infrequency of

arbitration agreements in the physician-patient context compared to the employment and consumer contexts?

2. Can you think of another context in which adhesive arbitration agreements are infrequent because the parties drafting the adhesion contracts are pleased with litigation outcomes and fear arbitration would increase claims against them?

2. HMOs

In sharp contrast to the limited use by individual physicians and hospitals, a 1990s California survey revealed that 71% of the state's Health Maintenance Organizations used binding arbitration agreements with their subscribers.[70] Such arbitration agreements are usually designed by HMO's to apply to contract disputes only—and not to claims alleging medical malpractice. However, an important exception to this finding is the nation's largest HMO, Kaiser Permanente—which *does* require all of its subscribers in California to agree to arbitrate any medical malpractice claims, as well as any other disputes arising out of their health care plans.

Kaiser's arbitration program was originally designed to be self-administered—with "administrative functions performed by outside counsel retained to defend Kaiser in an adversarial capacity."[71] However, in 1997, the California Supreme Court refused to compel arbitration against the estate of a deceased plan participant—finding that Kaiser had engaged in fraud both "in the inducement" and "in the application" of the arbitration agreement: An independent statistical analysis of Kaiser arbitrations found that in only 1% of all Kaiser cases was a neutral arbitrator appointed within the 60-day period mandated by the plan; on average it took 863 days to reach a hearing in a Kaiser arbitration. For the court, a fraud claim could be premised on Kaiser's conduct in setting up a self-administered arbitration system "in which delay for its own benefit and convenience was an inherent part"—and yet nevertheless "persist[ing] in its contractual promises of expeditiousness."[72] In response to such criticisms, Kaiser promptly re-designed its arbitration mechanism to provide for independent administration.

Alan B. Morrison, *Can Mandatory Medical Malpractice Claims be Fair? The Kaiser Permanente System*

70 Disp. Resol. J. 35, 35–39, 40–41, 43, 45–54, 59 (2015).

In recent years, there has been a dramatic increase in the inclusion by businesses of mandatory arbitration clauses in contracts with consumers. Rarely are such clauses the subject of bargaining between the parties, mainly because the business simply inserts the provision in a take-it-or-leave-it form contract. Indeed,

---

[70] Elizabeth Rolph et al., *Arbitration Agreements in Health Care: Myths and Reality*, 60 Law & Contemp. Probs. 153, 171–72, 180 (1997).

[71] Engalla v. Permanente Medical Group, Inc., 15 Cal.4th 951, 64 Cal.Rptr.2d 843, 849, 938 P.2d 903 (1997).

[72] Id. at 853, 858 (held, "there is evidence to support the [plaintiff's] claims that Kaiser fraudulently induced [plaintiff] to enter the arbitration agreement in that it misrepresented the speed of its arbitration program, a misrepresentation on which [plaintiff's] employer relied by selecting Kaiser's health plan for its employees").

many consumers don't even know that the clause is there when they make their purchase, in some cases because the contract arrives in the mail with the product being acquired.

Many consumers, their lawyers, and consumer advocacy organizations oppose mandatory arbitrations because they deny consumers their right to go to court. There are many reasons for that opposition, including limitations on tools that are available in court, such as discovery, and additional costs that are not incurred in court—mainly fees for the arbitrators. Many arbitrations do not require a statement of reasons for the decision, and there are limited rights to appeal an unfavorable arbitration ruling. Finally, many people oppose giving up their right to a trial by jury, at which a state official serves as the judge, and the public can watch the proceedings.

The question that this paper seeks to answer is whether, leaving aside the absence of a public trial before a jury, can one category of mandatory arbitrations—claims of medical malpractice—be operated in a manner in which those who must use it to resolve their claims receive a fair hearing and a reasonable opportunity to recover their damages? To seek to answer that question, this paper examines the mandatory arbitration system used by the Kaiser Foundation Health Plan, Inc., which operates the Kaiser Permanente medical delivery system for its approximately 7.4 million members that it had in California as of December 31, 2014. The current arbitration program, which has been in operation since 1999, received 657 demands for arbitration in 2013. It follows one that was heavily criticized by the California Supreme Court in Engalla v. Permanente Medical Group, 64 Cal. Rpt 843, 938 P.2d 903, 15 Cal 4th 951 (1997), for the lack of an independent manager outside of Kaiser and for excessive delays in the appointment of neutral arbitrators and the holding of arbitration hearings.

After Engalla was decided, Kaiser could have litigated it further or attempted to make only the changes identified by the Court in its arbitration system. Instead, Kaiser chose to appoint a Blue Ribbon Panel that recommended sweeping changes in the system, which Kaiser accepted. The most significant change was to shift responsibility for managing the arbitration system from Kaiser to the Office of Independent Administrator (OIA), and the creation of an Arbitration Advisory Council, which later became the Arbitration Oversight Board (the Board). Working with Kaiser Permanente, the Administrator and the Council prepared and then approved the Rules that are now the basis of the current arbitration system.

* * *

Although the Kaiser Permanente arbitration system applies to all disputes that members have with Kaiser Permanente, including matters such as billing and coverage, almost all the claims are for moderate to serious injuries arising from alleged medical malpractice. These cases are generally quite complicated, almost always require expert testimony, raise factual issues that differ from case to case, and the amounts awarded, especially where there is pain and suffering, are significant. As explained below, the Kaiser Permanente arbitration system contains significant due process-like protections that would not be cost-justified for claims with much smaller amounts at stake. This paper does not take a position on whether mandatory arbitration systems that govern other cases brought by individuals, such as consumers or employees, provide basic fairness to those required to use them.

Before turning to the specifics of the Kaiser Permanente system, there is one argument made by opponents of mandatory arbitration that merits a mention. Opponents contend that if an arbitration system is fair for both sides, then it need not be mandatory, because both sides will agree to it. That contention is not an argument about whether a particular arbitration system is fair, but about whether mandatory arbitration should be permitted. Given the FAA and the manner in which the Supreme Court has construed it, that argument is one that must be addressed to Congress. Moreover, on its own terms, the fact that some claimants may choose to arbitrate and others may prefer going to court says little about the fairness of an arbitration system, but only whether a particular party believes that one system or the other is more advantageous for that party. Thus, in small dollar cases, in which an individual claimant cannot easily obtain a lawyer, arbitration might be the claimant's preferred forum, whereas the defendant might prefer a court where an unrepresented party would have serious difficulties meeting the formal requirements of litigation. Conversely, in larger value cases, the courtroom, with a jury, might well favor the interests of the claimant, but the defendant would prefer arbitration. Thus, the fact that the Kaiser-Permanente system is mandatory says nothing conclusive about its objective fairness, but it does underscore that Kaiser believes that, on an overall basis, using the system is advantageous to Kaiser.

* * *

II. DEFINING A SUCCESSFUL CLAIMS RESOLUTION SYSTEM

Before describing the Kaiser Permanente arbitration system in detail, and as part of the process of attempting to evaluate its success, it is essential to identify which criteria are relevant. No one disputes that there are some claims that should be paid and that there are others that should not. Thus, payment of a claim (or not) is not, alone, a proper measure of success; some more neutral criteria must be used. In fact, there is a neutral statement that provides a good start for assessing any claims system. Rule 1 of the Federal Rules of Civil Procedure states the goal of those Rules to be the "just, speedy, and inexpensive determination" of cases decided under them. The Kaiser Permanente system has similar goals: "to provide a fair, timely, and low cost arbitration system that respects the privacy of the parties." Of the three features in Federal Rule 1, cost and speed of individual cases in arbitration can easily be measured, although the OIA has been unable to find comparable data for the duration of cases currently litigated in the California court system. Determining whether an outcome is "just" is much more subjective, but, as discussed below, the OIA has attempted to gather reactions from the various participants that at least say something about whether the arbitration process produces results viewed as just by them.

Moreover, and perhaps more important, in the real world, there is an almost inevitable tradeoff among the three goals. Thus, an arbitration system can be made speedy and quite inexpensive, by setting abbreviated deadlines, denying all discovery, and conducting a hearing in one day, with no written explanation of the decision. But in those circumstances, the likelihood of a just result is substantially diminished. By contrast, where there is a genuine dispute about whether a doctor's negligence caused the patient permanent and serious injuries, extensive discovery and a two week trial with a dozen experts and perhaps a jury is more likely to produce a just or fair result, but at a greater cost and with additional delay.

On the other hand, if the patient suffered losses of at most $50,000, no sensible person would think that the monetary tradeoff in terms of cost and time consumed in a two-week trial is worth the price of accuracy for a claim of that magnitude. The Kaiser Permanente system includes both claims for quite modest amounts and also regularly produces substantial arbitration awards. For example, in 2013, there were twenty-six awards in favor of claimants, representing 37% of the cases that went to an arbitration hearing and decision. Recoveries ranged from $10,510 to $4,950,527, with an average of $499,027 and a median of $210,000. Thus, its overall evaluation must be done with the full range of claims covered by it in mind.

* * *

III. THE KAISER PERMANENTE CALIFORNIA ARBITRATION SYSTEM

A. The Board and the Independent Administrator

The central feature of the Kaiser Permanente arbitration system, which was created in the wake of the California Supreme Court's stinging criticism of Kaiser's prior arbitration system in Engalla, is that there is a separate independent entity—the Office of the Independent Administrator—that manages all the arbitrations, but does not conduct them. It, in turn, is under the overall supervision of the Arbitration Oversight Board. That Board, which is self-perpetuating, has thirteen members, no more than four of whom may have any current or prior association with Kaiser.

B. The Arbitrators

* * *

After an arbitration claim has been filed with the Administrator, and the filing fee is either paid or waived, her office sends to each side a list of twelve potential arbitrators randomly selected from the panel for that area. The parties are provided with three types of documents regarding each potential arbitrator: the potential arbitrator's application, which reveals significant information about the nature of the lawyer's practice (especially on which side the lawyer usually appeared); copies of any prior awards rendered by the potential arbitrator, with the claimant's name redacted; and copies of any post-arbitration evaluations of the performance of the arbitrator. The parties may agree on an arbitrator from that list or from the full panel or from outside the panel, as they did in 26% of the cases in 2013. If the parties cannot agree on an arbitrator, each side may strike four names from the list and rank the remaining names on the list in order of preference. The OIA then selects the highest ranked arbitrator and provides additional disclosures to the parties who have the right to disqualify that person without cause. Those supplemental disclosures may include information about the activities of the person's spouse or the work of that person's law firm. Persons selected as the preferred arbitrator may be disqualified by either party until the parties accept one, or under section 1281.6 of the California Code of Civil Procedure, a party asks a state court judge to appoint an arbitrator.

No process can ever eliminate all biases of arbitrators, but this system seems to address the most significant objection to many consumer arbitration programs: the fear that the sponsoring company (defendant) controls the selection of arbitrators, and thus their decisions tend to favor the company because the arbitrators wish to be re-appointed (for compensation) in the future. In this system, Kaiser Permanente has no say over who is on the arbitration panels in the first instance, the panels are not exclusive, and Kaiser Permanente has no more say over who will be an arbitrator in a given case than does the claimant. Thus, on the front end, the neutrality of the arbitrators is reasonably assured.

C. Expenses of Arbitration

One of the objections to consumer arbitration is the cost, mainly for the fees of the arbitrator, who are generally high priced lawyers or retired judges. In theory, arbitrators have every incentive to spend more time on the case because they get paid more that way. Where arbitration fees are shared, the defendant company is generally much better able to absorb the cost, and indeed cost may be a reason why an individual would simply take a pass if arbitration is the only option.

That objection could apply to the Kaiser Permanente arbitration system, but Kaiser has taken several steps that significantly reduce the likelihood that cost will discourage those who believe that they have a valid claim. First, the filing fee is only $150, which compares favorably with other filing fees: the filing fee in federal court is $400 and in California Superior Court it is $435 for claims over $25,000 and $370 for those between $10–25,000. In addition, the filing fee can also be waived by the OIA, and that seems to help those most in need. Second, in Superior Court there are substantial additional charges for filing motions and other papers, as well as the considerable daily fees for juries and the per page charges for court reporters, none of which apply to Kaiser Permanente arbitrations.

Third, and this is the most significant, although claimants are obligated under California law to pay one half of the single arbitrator's fees, Kaiser Permanente paid the full cost of the arbitrator's fee in 90% of the cases in 2013. Kaiser does that if the claimant agrees not to object that the arbitration was unfair because Kaiser paid all of the arbitrator's fees, and if a claimant agrees to waive the right to a three person arbitration, which is required under California Health & Safety Code, Section 1373.19 if a claimant seeks more than $200,000. Very few claimants turn down this offer. The idea to encourage single person arbitrations came from the Blue Ribbon Panel that recommended creation of this system because it concluded that three arbitrators were not only more expensive, but slowed down the process considerably.

Arbitrators set their own fees, which are given to the parties when selecting an arbitrator. Most bill by the hour, although some charge on a per day basis. They may change their rates once a year for new cases. In 2013, the hourly rates averaged $430, with the range from $150 to $800 per hour; daily rates ranged from $1200 to $8000 a day, with an average of $3688. Even the total fees charged by arbitrators are modest. In 2013, excluding the 30 closed cases in which no fee was charged, the average fee was $6,683.18; in cases that included a written award, the average was $26,938.24, with a median of $20,800, and that average was significantly raised by one complex case in which the fees were $160,455.62. Two other fee-related matters are worth noting: if an arbitrator charges excessive fees (either because of high rates or spending more time than is reasonable), Kaiser Permanente, which generally pays all of their fees, can strike or disqualify that person from the list without explanation in future cases. Finally, unlike other arbitration provider services, all of the fees go to the arbitrator and no portion is paid to the OIA.

* * *

D. Speedy Resolution

In general, delay is more of a problem for claimants than for defendants, including Kaiser Permanente, and it was the major problem that the Court found in Engalla. To be sure, delay creates business uncertainty, and in some situations that can be harmful for a defendant. In the Kaiser Permanente system, a doctor accused of malpractice may be anxious over whether she will be vindicated, but that concern is probably reduced because his or her employer will pay any award or settlement. For claimants, delay in getting paid means that the value of the money that is eventually received is less than had it been paid sooner, especially if the delay is significant. Delay in payment for claimants who have immediate needs can also cause them to settle sooner and for lesser amounts than they would receive if a speedy resolution were likely.

The Board's Rules on timely resolution of all cases, and the active way in which the OIA assures compliance with them, results in quite speedy determinations of all malpractice claims against Kaiser Permanente, a marked improvement over what the Court found in Engalla. * * * [A]ll cases must be completed and awards rendered within 18 months of filing, unless an exception is sought by one or both parties and granted by the arbitrator, which happened in only 16% of the cases closed in 2013. * * *

According to the public data maintained by the Administrator, virtually all cases not designated for special treatment are resolved within the 18 month window. Indeed, the average in 2013 was 11 months for all cases, with 60% resolved in less than a year. Monitoring the conduct of parties and the arbitrators is essential to keeping to this schedule, and arbitrators who fall behind may lose their place on the panel. In 2013, even the 70 cases that went to hearing were concluded in an average of 538 days, which is still within the 18 month target. The Board's Rules require that the arbitrator give reasons for every award, including findings of fact and conclusions of law, a requirement consistent with Section 632 of the California Code of Civil Procedure in cases tried without a jury. Moreover, once an arbitration is concluded by a final award, it is really final and not subject to appeal (and further delay including possibly a re-trial), except in the most extraordinary of circumstances.

* * *

Another positive for arbitrations on the issue of speedy resolution is the amount of time it takes to try an arbitration case in contrast to the time taken to try the same case before a jury. Because no two cases are identical, and judges and arbitrators are not fungible in terms of speedy completions of hearings and jury trials, any comparisons are necessarily rough. The OIA is not provided information on the number of days that hearings require, or even an average number of hearing days. In addition, the number of hearing days for arbitrations is an imprecise measure of time spent by an arbitrator, in part because the hearings need not take place on consecutive days and may occupy only a portion of the day. Among the reasons for longer court trials are the time spent on jury selection, the need for the lawyers to explain their case to the jury, and the judge's time instructing the jury on the law. Longer jury trials are also caused by time spent on objections made to prevent a jury from hearing certain evidence that would not be made if a judge were sitting alone, to side bar conferences, to waiting for jurors to arrive or return from breaks, and the actual jury deliberation itself. Although there is little doubt that the total time required for an arbitration hearing is less than for a jury trial, the amount of the difference is uncertain.

* * *

Although not all costs can be quantified, it appears likely that Kaiser's arbitration significantly reduces costs to both parties and in the process makes it more likely that a claimant with a modest value claim will be able to find an attorney to take the case.

E. Just Results

Perhaps the strongest evidence to support the Kaiser-Permanente arbitration system comes from the participants. At the conclusion of each case, the lawyers for the parties, and the claimants who do not have counsel, are asked to fill out evaluations of the system and of the arbitrator's performance. These evaluations, which are anonymous, are reviewed by the Administrator's office and, with the claimant's name redacted, forwarded to future claimants and their lawyers, and to Kaiser, to help them evaluate the attorneys on the list of 12 panel members they are provided at the outset of the arbitration selection process. In addition, the arbitrators are also asked to complete evaluation forms regarding the process and in particular how it compared to court proceedings. * * *

A large majority of the 207 lawyers from both sides in 2013 who responded supported the process and found the arbitrator to be fair on aspects such as treating parties with respect, explaining procedures clearly, and understanding the case. Unlike some arbitration systems that are criticized because they have no or only limited discovery, the Kaiser Permanente system has no such restrictions, with discovery available as if the case were in state court. On perhaps the most significant question—recommending the arbitrator to another lawyer or claimant—the average score for claimant's counsel was 4.0 (out of 5) and 4.6 for respondent's (Kaiser's) counsel. * * *

There can be no doubt that Kaiser's actions make clear that it believes that it is obtaining just results for Kaiser under its arbitration system. If it were not, it could end it tomorrow (after a transition period) and do what everyone else does: let the courts resolve these disputes. But it has not abandoned arbitration, and its willingness to pay for the substantial cost for the Independent Administrator, as well as the lesser costs for the Board, plus the claimant's half of the arbitrator's fees in most cases, removes any doubt that, given the existing state of the law on medical malpractice, it believes that its overall interests are best served by staying the course.

Part of the explanation for Kaiser's support of arbitration is related to a broader attitude that it has toward resolving claims of its members. Kaiser's stated policy is to investigate all claims of adverse medical outcomes immediately and fully and to take appropriate corrective measures, which includes an offer to compensate negligently injured parties for their losses without waiting for a demand for arbitration to be made. * * *

"Doing the right thing" is made easier because the injured person is a participant in the Kaiser Permanente system and is entitled to the additional medical services at no extra charge as long as she or he continues to be a Kaiser member. Moreover, while the literature is inconclusive on the effects on admitting fault and/or expressing regret following adverse medical outcomes, it surely make sense that a person whose medical problems have been addressed at no additional cost is less likely to file a demand for arbitration, or to file a lawsuit if that were permitted, than one whose complaints have been ignored or brushed aside as frivolous. Put another way, assuring that members are treated fairly, from the time of initial complaint of harm through the arbitration process, is seen by Kaiser as helping achieve its overall goal of providing quality health care at a reasonable cost.

* * *

IV. CONCLUSION

Although I am an arbitration skeptic, the Kaiser Permanente arbitration system is almost certainly less expensive for claimants and faster than court litigation, and neither its speed nor its low cost seems to interfere with a claimant's ability to present his or her case fully. On the output side, the results seem reasonably just, and there is no evidence that claimants would be happier (and win more often and/or obtain larger verdicts) in the civil justice system, in the same time frames and at the same costs. It also appears that, for small and medium size claims, Kaiser Permanente's arbitration program makes it more possible for them to be brought there than in court. The loss of a public trial before a jury is a negative, but whether it outweighs the positives is a question that will not be answered in the same way by everyone. What can be said is that Kaiser Permanente's arbitration system has a number of very positive aspects to it, and almost no obvious negatives beyond constraining the choice of forum, which suggests that it deserves further study.

QUESTIONS TO REVIEW AND SYNTHESIZE

1. Kaiser's arbitration differs from most consumer and employment arbitration processes in what respects?

2. The article just excerpted praises Kaiser arbitration as good for claimants. Taking this praise at face value, how much of Kaiser's system could be replicated in employment and consumer arbitration, given that for Kaiser "'Doing the right thing' is made easier because the injured person is a participant in the Kaiser Permanente system and is entitled to the additional medical services at no extra charge as long as she or he continues to be a Kaiser member."?

G. FAMILY AND RELIGIOUS ARBITRATION

Mark L. Movsesian, *Fiqh and Canons: Reflections on Islamic and Christian Jurisprudence*

40 Seton Hall L. Rev. 861, 879–84 (2010).

The different emphasis on religious law is reflected in contemporary Muslim and Christian attitudes toward religious tribunals. In countries where they constitute minority communities, some influential Muslim organizations have sought to establish Islamic law tribunals to resolve family and commercial disputes among consenting Muslims. These organizations contend that Muslims require such tribunals, whose rulings would bind parties in civil courts, in order to practice their faith. Two recent controversies, one in Canada and the other in Great Britain, illustrate the phenomenon.

In 2003, the Canadian Society of Muslims announced its intention to establish a Muslim Court of Arbitration in Ontario to resolve family disputes. The Society planned to operate the tribunal under Ontario's Arbitration Act, which allows binding family-law arbitration. The tribunal was to resolve only those disputes that Muslims voluntarily referred to it and decide cases according to "Muslim Personal/ Family Law." Such a tribunal was necessary, the Society explained, because Canadian Muslims "live in a non-Muslim country which subjects us to laws which, for the most part, do not allow us to live our faith to the best of our ability.

News of the tribunal sparked immediate resistance, with most opponents expressing concern about the potential oppression of women. The outcry did not diminish when a government report recommended allowing Islamic family law arbitration, with some safeguards. The report explained that religious organizations, including at least one Muslim group, had been conducting dispute settlement in Canada for years, thereby helping "people of faith . . . to live . . . according to their beliefs." In response to the outcry, Ontario's Premier announced a ban on all religious arbitration, but the province eventually took a more nuanced position. As of 2007, Ontario had decided to allow religious organizations to arbitrate family disputes, but only under secular law.

The British controversy began in 2008, when the Archbishop of Canterbury, Rowan Williams, gave an address in which he advocated a formal role for Islamic tribunals. In a pluralistic society, Williams argued, a supplementary role for voluntary Islamic arbitration, particularly in family and commercial disputes, seemed unavoidable. Otherwise, a "secular legal monopoly" would overwhelm citizens' religious commitments. Williams emphasized that Islamic tribunals could not be allowed to deny Muslim citizens their civil rights and pointed out that

Christian and Jewish tribunals traditionally had shared jurisdiction with civil courts in Britain without creating dire consequences. Critics excoriated Williams, but the Lord Chief Justice endorsed his position. By autumn 2008, reports surfaced that the government was advising Muslim groups that civil courts could enforce Islamic arbitration awards under the English Arbitration Act.

One such organization, the Muslim Arbitration Tribunal (MAT), would like to test the government's theory. MAT runs Islamic tribunals in London, Birmingham, and Manchester. Although informal Islamic arbitration has existed in Britain for decades, the organization's Web site proclaims that it "will . . . for the first time, offer the Muslim community a real and true opportunity to settle disputes in accordance with Islamic Sacred Law with the knowledge that the outcome as determined by MAT will be binding and enforceable." MAT advertises its services primarily in family disputes, but it also handles commercial, debt, inheritance, and mosque disputes. MAT acknowledges that civil law binds citizens but states that Islamic law also "[has] its place in this society" as "our personal and religious law." "What a great achievement it will be," its Web site proclaims, "if we can produce a result to the satisfaction of both English and Islamic law!"

Some Canadian and British Muslims have vociferously opposed the creation of these Islamic arbitration regimes. And it is true that the tribunals would cover only certain aspects of fiqh—primarily family and commercial law—not its entirety. Still, the apparent level of support for Islamic arbitration contrasts dramatically with the lack of interest contemporary Christianity shows in religious law and tribunals. Recall that ecclesiastical courts tend to be reserved nowadays for internal church matters and, in some cases, marriage annulments. The vast majority of Christians would never think to use them for lay legal disputes. Moreover, although some Christian organizations do offer arbitration services, "Christian arbitration" entails a search for ethical resolutions to legal disputes, not an application of Christian law.

Peacemaker Ministries, a prominent Christian dispute-settlement organization, offers a good illustration. The group was established "in 1982 by a group of pastors, lawyers, and business people who wanted to encourage and assist Christians to respond to conflict biblically." In addition to informal dispute-settlement mechanisms like mediation, the group offers arbitration through its "Institute for Christian Conciliation." The Institute's rules make clear that arbitrators do not resolve disputes according to some sort of Christian law. Rather, arbitrators apply secular law, subject to broad biblical principles like keeping one's word and acting justly and mercifully. The rules also state that "arbitrators may grant any remedy or relief that they deem scriptural, just and equitable, and within the scope of the agreement of the parties." In essence, the service that Peacemaker Ministries provides resembles what commercial arbitrators know as "ex aequo et bono" decision making—the resolution of legal disputes according to the broad equitable discretion of the arbitrator rather than formal legal analysis.

Michael A. Helfand, *Religious Arbitration and the New Multiculturalism: Negotiating Conflicting Legal Orders*

86 N.Y.U. L. Rev. 1231, 1237–42, 1243–47, 1253–55, 1265–66 (2011).

The mechanism to have a claim arbitrated by a religious arbitration court is the same as it is for standard arbitration courts: The parties must either sign an arbitration agreement to have a religious arbitral panel resolve the relevant dispute or include such an arbitration clause in a signed contract. In so doing, parties demonstrate their consent to exit the realm of standard legal adjudication and opt into binding arbitration. Awards issued by religious arbitration courts, like those of standard arbitration tribunals, are subject to the statutory grounds for vacatur. Thus, consent to their proceedings cannot be coerced; arbitrators must remain objective and disclose any relationship with the parties standing before them, and they cannot modify the terms of the underlying contract. As long as no such grounds exist, U.S. courts will consistently enforce religious arbitration awards.

While some have argued that enforcing religious arbitration awards violates the Establishment Clause, courts have ruled otherwise by finding that enforcing a religious arbitration award does not require them to address the merits of the underlying dispute. Accordingly, courts can avoid impermissibly insinuating themselves into religious disputes. In this way, U.S. courts treat religious arbitration courts as they treat any other arbitration panel. The existence of a religious arbitration agreement deprives a court of subject matter jurisdiction, just as any other arbitration agreement does. And the policy favoring arbitration applies to religious and secular arbitration alike. Indeed, parties voluntarily comply with most religious arbitration agreements and awards without court intervention, just as they do with secular arbitration agreements and awards.

This, however, is not to say that religious arbitration courts function like all other arbitration courts—far from it. Religious arbitration courts are unique because, rather than merely adjudicating claims based on an arbitrator's understanding of U.S. law and principles of equity, they render decisions based upon a selected body of religious law. Thus, religious arbitration agreements contain choice of law provisions that require an arbitration panel to adopt and apply selected religious rules. Accordingly, religious arbitration courts employ both the substantive and procedural machinery of an entirely different legal system. * * *

Religious arbitration takes advantage of [the contract-based understanding of the Federal Arbitration Act]. Religionists are able to structure the terms that will adjudicate their claims, choosing to resolve a dispute in accordance with religious law. Courts, in an effort to put arbitration agreements on equal footing with other contracts, enforce religious arbitration agreements and awards to advance the interests of the parties in having binding religious arbitration. * * *

[P]rioritizing first-party interests and enabling religionists to submit disputes for religious adjudication poses a number of challenges to standard arbitration doctrine. Much of the complex dynamic between religious arbitration and general arbitration doctrine stems from the underlying premise that religious arbitration entails the application of religious law.

On one hand, applying religious substantive law can undermine the enforceability of religious arbitration awards in circumstances where religious law and U.S. law conflict—most notably when a religious arbitration award is subject to the public policy ground for vacatur. Indeed, courts typically employ public policy to protect third-party interests by requiring courts to void any agreement, including an arbitration agreement, in which a private party waives rights that are intended to protect the public generally. * * *

On the other hand, the application of mandatory religious procedural law by religious arbitration courts allows religious arbitration to avoid, to a degree, some of the standard critiques leveled against secular arbitration for being procedurally lawless. Indeed, because religious arbitration courts—in contrast to their secular counterparts—employ mandatory procedural law, they may be better able to protect first-party interests by providing important procedural protections. Notwithstanding this potential advantage, the existence of mandatory procedural law does not, on its own, guarantee protection of first-party interests; the mere fact that such procedural rules are mandatory does not ensure that they will accord with standard conceptions of fairness. In this way, the existence of mandatory religious procedural law requires us to take a different approach in addressing the procedural pitfalls in the religious arbitral context. We must consider both the potential advantage of mandatory procedure and the potential disadvantage of procedural rules that do not accord with standard conceptions of fairness. * * *

[R]eligious arbitration courts employ a set of mandatory religious procedural rules that parties have limited ability to modify. In the discovery context, Jewish procedural law inverts * * * procedure in an important way. For example, where a former employee sues his former employer for back wages, Talmudic law and subsequent legal analyses have crafted shifting evidentiary burdens. To take advantage of such burden-shifting, a former employee must demonstrate the existence of the underlying employment relationship, at which point the burden of proof shifts to the former employer. Where a former employee successfully demonstrates that he did, in fact, work for the former employer, the former employer can only avoid liability by producing evidence that he had indeed paid the former employee in full. Thus, once a former employee demonstrates the existence of an employment relationship, the former employer can only avoid liability by producing evidence to substantiate his claim, such as logs with the number of hours the employee worked and receipts proving that the employee was paid for all of his work.

Islamic law has similarly developed its own burden-shifting process. At the heart of this approach stands the "most basic function of adjudication": to distinguish the claimant from the defendant. In Islamic jurisprudence, the claimant is not necessarily the party who initiated the proceedings. Instead, the claimant is the party whose claim is deemed weaker and who needs to present additional evidence to support his case. The party who is deemed the defendant—that is, the party with the stronger claim—often has secured this status by either presenting evidence to support his claim or by arguing that his claim should be granted a default presumption of correctness. Parties can jockey for position at the initial stages of litigation, each hoping to secure defendant status. Importantly, the actual plaintiffs in a case do not need to produce all relevant evidence in order to satisfy a prima facie standard. In contrast to the default in standard arbitration, the Islamic evidentiary system allows the plaintiff to shift the burden onto the defendant, forcing the hand of what might otherwise be a complacent corporation.

Importantly, such discovery rules are emblematic of a larger dynamic at work in religious arbitration. In religious arbitration, a self-standing body of rules governs procedural issues such as discovery. The drafting party does not craft these rules; instead, religious procedural law is mandatory in that it must be applied by the religious arbitration court. This ensures that repeat players have limited ability, through creative drafting, to secure favorable procedural rules. Indeed, many of these mandatory procedural rules are detailed in the collections of religious decisions and rulings compiled within the various religious communities, instead of simply leaving arbitrators with wide discretion over important procedural events. Members of religious communities can access these types of rules by reviewing the relevant law in order to better understand their rights and liabilities. Thus, the fact that religious arbitrators work within systems of procedural law limits repeat players' informational advantage. * * *

[F]or the better part of a century, courts have allowed minority groups—most notably religious groups—to piggyback on the arbitration system in order to legally enforce religious arbitration awards in U.S. courts. As a result, as long as an arbitration is conducted pursuant to a valid agreement, parties of the same religion can have religious authorities resolve their disputes in accordance with religious law, and that resolution can have the binding force of U.S. law. In this way, religious arbitration courts serve as the quintessential institution of the new multiculturalism, providing religious groups with the law-like autonomy that has been withheld under public law. * * *

Until recently, * * * backlash against religious arbitration was largely absent in the United States, and courts routinely enforced religious arbitration awards without much media fanfare. However, the attack on religious arbitration has now reached the shores of the United States. This attack, which began with questions about the procedural safeguards in religious arbitration, has slowly morphed into a national movement unwilling to cede any jurisdictional authority to religious tribunals. * * * [T]he legislatures in [Oklahoma,] Alabama, Arizona, South Carolina, South Dakota, Texas, and Wyoming have all proposed * * * bills that aim to prohibit courts from relying on, considering, or even referring to any form of religious law. * * *

It is unsurprising that attempts to formally introduce religious arbitration into state legal systems have met such ferocious resistance. Religious arbitration courts are perceived as challenging the nation-state's status as the exclusive source of legitimate law. Indeed, political philosophers since Thomas Hobbes have argued that the state is defined by its ability to monopolize the exercise of coercive legal power, and religious arbitration courts continue to be characterized as challenging this primary function of the nation-state. This is because such arbitration courts, at the request of the parties, explicitly adjudicate conflicts by applying a particular brand of religious law instead of state law. * * *

At their core, religious arbitration courts are unique because, by definition, they apply religious substantive and procedural law in adjudicating submitted disputes. This dynamic has two divergent implications. On one hand, religious arbitration courts serve particular religious communities by enabling them to resolve disputes in accordance with their own shared religious values and obligations. Thus, enforcing religious arbitration awards does more than simply enhance individual freedom of contract by allowing parties to resolve disputes within the parameters of their own agreements; it enables individuals to use arbitration agreements as a mechanism to ensure access to adjudication in accordance with shared religious beliefs and practices.

On the other hand, if the advantages of religious arbitration courts lie, in part, in their application of complete systems of procedural and substantive law, then so do their potential drawbacks. While some critics of arbitration might welcome the existence of an arbitral forum that applies mandatory procedural law, religious law lends itself to the application of procedures that are potentially discriminatory. Indeed, many of the latent concerns regarding the enforceability of religious arbitral awards stem from the possibility that religious arbitration courts will apply rules that make the resulting judgments deeply unfair. Moreover, critics wonder whether participation in religious arbitration proceedings can be viewed as truly volitional, given the specter of communal pressure to submit disputes for resolution in accordance with communal norms and values. * * *

[Religious arbitration courts serve] a unique institutional role * * * by providing an institutional solution to the new multiculturalism: They enable citizens with secondary commitments to adhere to the strictures of U.S. law without sacrificing their commitment to their religious practices. Religious arbitration courts, when properly absorbed into the United States' arbitration regime, hold out the possibility of accomplishing these goals. As a result, they serve as important religious and cultural institutions, which can potentially expand the scope of religious freedom and successfully advance the freedom-enhancing aims of the new multiculturalism.

In the article just excerpted, Professor Helfand notes that religious arbitration can "serve as the quintessential institution of the new multiculturalism, providing religious groups with the law-like autonomy." However, religious arbitration does this by "challenging the nation-state's status as the exclusive source of legitimate law," and "critics wonder whether participation in religious arbitration proceedings can be viewed as truly volitional, given the specter of communal pressure to submit disputes for resolution in accordance with communal norms and values." These grand points may apply in the following divorce case.

Judith Lieberman v. Issac Lieberman

Supreme Court, Kings County, New York, Trial Term, 1991.
149 Misc.2d 983, 566 N.Y.S.2d 490.

■ MARTIN SCHNEIER, J.

In this divorce action the plaintiff wife moves to confirm the report of the Judicial Hearing Officer dated November 3, 1989 which vacated an arbitration award dated April 7, 1987.

The plaintiff wife and defendant husband were married on March 18, 1974, in Brooklyn, New York. There are three issue of the marriage, namely: Rivka, born February 11, 1975; Moshe, born September 28, 1976, and Nosson, born January 4, 1980. The plaintiff is a high school graduate who works as a Yiddish-speaking teacher in a religious school and earns approximately $15,000 annually. The defendant is also a high school graduate who works as an office clerk and also earns approximately $15,000 per year. The sole marital asset is a one-family house located at 1439 East 7th Street, Brooklyn, New York. For the past three years, it has been occupied by the plaintiff and the three infant issue. The fair market value of the house is $175,000 to $200,000. There is no mortgage, but the parties owe $16,000 to relatives for personal loans used to purchase the house.

On February 9, 1986, the plaintiff commenced this action for divorce.

On September 29, 1986, the parties signed a binding arbitration agreement to, "settle the arguments, claims and all disputes that are between us before the Rabbinical Court" and agreed that "any decision" of the Rabbinical Court "will be obeyed by us." Each party selected one Rabbinical arbitrator and these two arbitrators selected a third. Shortly after selection of the panel was completed, the parties began attending sessions of the Beth Din or Rabbinical Court. Each party was represented by a Yiddish-speaking religious representative. A religious oath was taken by the parties prior to commencing the first session. Each session lasted several hours and cost each party $1,000 per session. The sessions were conducted in the Yiddish language.

On February 19, 1987, after six sessions with the Beth Din had been completed, the plaintiff moved [in court] for *pendente lite* relief, and did not disclose that there was a pending arbitration proceeding.

On March 12, 1987, in open court, the plaintiff was granted the *pendente lite* relief of exclusive occupancy of the marital residence, custody, unapportioned child support and maintenance in the sum of $100 per week and liberal visitation was granted to the defendant.

The *pendente lite* order was entered on April 7, 1987, which was, ironically, the same day that the Beth Din issued its award. The Beth Din, in its decision, awarded the parties joint custody with physical custody to the plaintiff and granted the defendant extensive visitation. The defendant was ordered to pay $100 a week child support and to pay for medical coverage and tuition for the children. The Rabbinical Court also ordered the parties to vacate the marital residence and that it be sold with the proceeds "deposited with the Beth Din." A religious divorce (Get) was then to "be delivered" and the proceeds thereafter were to be divided, $50,000 to the plaintiff and the balance to the defendant.

On April 30, 1987, plaintiff and defendant both appeared in Family Court, Kings County, on plaintiff's petition, and a stipulation was entered into between the parties modifying the existing *pendente lite* visitation schedule.

On May 11, 1987, the defendant moved to confirm the award of the Beth Din and to vacate the *pendente lite* award, and the plaintiff then cross-moved to vacate the award of the Beth Din. * * *

CONCLUSIONS OF LAW

It is a legal axiom that the determination by an arbitrator should not be lightly set aside. When a dispute has been moved to arbitration, the party seeking to vacate the ultimate award must meet a heavy burden to vacate that award.

The statutory grounds for vacating or modifying an arbitration award enumerated in CPLR Section 7511(b)(1)(i–iv) are: that the rights of the party were prejudiced by corruption, fraud, or misconduct in procuring the award; partiality of an arbitrator; that the arbitrator exceeded his power or failed to make a final and definite award; or a procedural failure that was not waived.

With respect to CPLR § 7511(b)(1)(i), the plaintiff claims to have been coerced by the threat of a "Sirov." A Sirov is a prohibitionary decree that subjects the recipient to shame, scorn, ridicule and public ostracism by other members of the Jewish religious community. While the threat of a Sirov may constitute pressure, it cannot be said to constitute duress.

Generally, misconduct, corruption, or fraud in procuring the award involves ex parte communications by the arbitrators with litigants; unauthorized independent investigation by an arbitrator; failure to allow a party legal representation or failure to permit a party to introduce evidence. None of these occurred in the instant proceeding.

* * *

With respect to 7511(b)(1)(iii), the plaintiff contends that the Beth Din exceeded its authority in making the award in that she expected the panel only to grant a religious divorce and not to decide matters of custody, visitation and economics.

* * *

A panel of arbitrators will only be restricted by specific limitations explicitly set forth in the arbitration agreement itself. If no such limitation exists, a broadly and generally phrased arbitration clause will be afforded the full import of its wording. Furthermore, any contention that a claim proposed to be submitted to arbitration is in excess of the arbitrator's power is waived unless raised by an application for a stay in the proceedings.

In the case at bar, the underlying subject matter of the dispute was the dissolution of the marriage between the parties. The issues of custody, visitation and economics certainly have a "reasonable relationship" to the dissolution proceedings. Additionally, the plaintiff participated in, and paid for, six full sessions of arbitration. When she did appear in this court for relief, it was not for a stay of the arbitration proceedings, but was for a determination of the identical issues which were before the Beth Din.

Additionally, an arbitrator's award will be set aside as being in excess of authority only if it is, "totally irrational" It can hardly be argued by the plaintiff that the Beth Din award was "totally irrational" when it addressed all the relief she requested in her *pendente lite* application and many of the awards were strikingly similar.

With respect to the plaintiff's objection to the proceedings, pursuant to CPLR 7511(b)(1)(iv), in that they were conducted in Yiddish, the plaintiff waived all her technical objections by her continual participation for six full sessions. It is undisputed that the plaintiff has knowledge of Yiddish and teaches elementary school in that language. Additionally, she had the opportunity to consult with her representative before and after each session of the Beth Din. The plaintiff made no effort to correct this technical flaw, or any other defects, by seeking a stay of the proceedings. It appears that her main objection was that, "nothing was being done and it was dragging on and I did not have the money anymore to go back."

In a custody dispute, an agreement between a husband and a wife will be upheld so long as the agreement is in the best interest of the children, however, the court retains supervisory power in its capacity as "*parens patriae*." To the extent that such award conflicts with the best interest of the children the agreement is a nullity insofar as it concerns the children. Hence, upon showing that a provision of an award might be *adverse* to the best interest of a child (but not simply because it "affects" the child) the court may intervene.

In the case at bar, the Beth Din award of joint custody adversely affects the best interest of the children. These parties have been embroiled in long and embittered litigation involving the children and there exists severe antagonism towards each other. In view of this, joint custody is inappropriate. Therefore, the Beth Din award regarding custody is vacated and the plaintiff is granted custody.

With respect to child support and maintenance, it is undisputed that the plaintiff and the defendant both earn approximately $300 per week. While the best interest of the children assures the court a perpetual role in an infant's welfare, a dispute over child support is one between the custodial and non-custodial parent and can be agreed upon contractually or by arbitration. Ironically, this court and the Beth Din awarded the plaintiff the identical amount for weekly support. Therefore, the award of child support by the Beth Din is confirmed. The court also confirms the portion of the Beth Din award making the defendant financially responsible for the children's medical care and school tuition.

With respect to the Beth Din's disposition of the marital residence, it is the plaintiff's contention that these provisions are not in the best interest of the children because she would have to vacate an affordable house, which the children are comfortable in, to relocate to much more expensive housing.

The defendant argues that the Beth Din award is not subject to judicial review and that he requires the larger share of the proceeds to meet his support obligation. He adds that the plaintiff can use her share of the proceeds to supplement her increased housing costs. Notwithstanding this argument, the defendant suggests that if it is not in the best interest of the children to vacate immediately, the sale of the marital residence can be deferred until such time as each child has reached maturity and that at that time the proceeds can be divided pursuant to the Beth Din award.

The court agrees with the plaintiff that the immediate needs of the custodial parent to occupy the marital residence outweigh the immediate needs of the defendant for his equitable share of the proceeds from the sale of the marital residence. Therefore, adopting the suggestion of the defendant, the court awards the plaintiff exclusive occupancy of the marital residence until the youngest child reaches the age of eighteen. At that time, the provisions of the Beth Din award with respect to the sale of the marital residence and distribution of the proceeds shall take effect.

Accordingly, the provisions of the Beth Din award consistent with this decision are confirmed and the provisions of the *pendente lite* order inconsistent with this decision are vacated.

Other divorce cases heard by Jewish courts include, e.g., Masri v. Masri, 55 Misc. 3d 487 (N.Y. Sup. Ct. 2017); Berg v. Berg, 926 N.Y.S.2d 568, 569 (App. Div. 2011); Lang v. Levi, 198 Md. App. 154 (Ct. Spec. App. 2009); Sieger v. Sieger, 747 N.Y.S.2d 102 (App. Div. 2002); Arabian v. Arabian, 915 N.Y.S.2d 513 (App. Div. 2010); Ort v. Ort, 2009 WL 1118755 (N.J. Super. Ct. App. Div. 2009). Non-divorce cases include, in addition to Chapter 1's material on diamond dealers' arbitration, e.g., Schwimmer v. Malinas, 967 N.Y.S.2d 870 (Sup. Ct. 2013) (dispute over management fees; both parties agreed to arbitration before a Beth Din and signed two arbitration agreements, one in English and one in Hebrew); Ghertner v. Solaimani, 563 S.E.2d 878 (Ga. Ct. App. 2002) (financial dispute arising out of partnership agreement); Ainsworth v. Schoen, 606 So.2d 1275 (Fla. App. 1992) (dispute over whether payment was due for a shipment of goods).

While reported cases and law review articles seem to discuss Jewish arbitration more often than other religious arbitration, Islamic and Christian arbitration have gained more notice in recent years. See, e.g., Michael Broyde: Sharia Tribunals, Rabbinical Courts, and Christian Panels (2017). Professor Helfand suggests Islamic arbitration courts are less prevalent in the United States than Jewish arbitration courts, due in part to the disagreement among Islamic jurists on whether Islamic law should apply to Muslims living in non-Muslim states. Michael A. Helfand, *Religious Arbitration and the New Multiculturalism*, 86 N.Y.U.L. REV. 1231, 1249 (2011). Nevertheless, the Fiqh Council of North America "advis[es] in the appointment of arbiters, and review[s] arbitration proceedings and decisions for their consistency with Islamic legal principles." Id. at 1250–51 (2011). See also Michael J. Broyde et al., *The Pillars of Successful Religious Arbitration: Models for American Islamic Arbitration Based on the Beth Din of America and Muslim Arbitration Tribunal Experience*, 30 Harv. J. Racial & Ethnic Just. 33, 35 (2014) ("[T]o the extent that Islamic tribunals do operate within the formal arbitration guidelines established under American law, secular judges often remain wary of enforcing their decisions because they perceive Islamic arbitration as foreign, discriminatory, arbitrary, 'informal, closed, and secret.'").

Sophia Chua-Rubenfeld & Frank J. Costa, Jr., *The Reverse-Entanglement Principle: Why Religious Arbitration of Federal Rights Is Unconstitutional*

128 Yale L.J. 2087, 2094–99 (2019).

Thousands of Americans submit to religious arbitration every year. In 2012, the Institute of Christian Conciliation (ICC) claimed to conduct around one hundred conciliations annually, with up to fifteen hundred additional religious arbitrations per year carried out by ICC-certified "conciliators" around the country. * * * Jewish arbitration is also deeply entrenched. Most major American cities have a standing beth din, or Jewish tribunal. New York City alone has four rabbinic courts. One of these four, the Beth Din of America, hears approximately three hundred divorce cases and one hundred commercial cases per year, in addition to landlord-tenant, wrongful-termination, and other disputes. The number of commercial cases has almost doubled over the past decade, suggesting that Jewish arbitration is "on the rise." The West Coast Rabbinical Court, one of multiple Jewish tribunals in Los Angeles, arbitrated around sixty-five commercial disputes last year, as well as disputes over divorces and kosher laws. These and many other tribunals advertise that they follow secular law and commercial practices only to the "extent permitted by Jewish Law." Islamic arbitration arrived in America more recently but is also starting to gain traction. There are already several reported cases of secular courts upholding the arbitral decisions of Sharia tribunals.

B. When Religious Precepts Conflict with Secular Law

The idea that religious tribunals prioritize holy law over federal statutory law is not mere speculation. It is explicitly one of the terms for which parties contract when they agree to arbitrate disputes before a religious tribunal. For example, parties who contract for the services of the ICC are bound by the Rules of Procedure for Christian Conciliation (RPCC), which provide:

> Rule 4. Conciliators shall take into consideration any state, federal, or local laws that the parties bring to their attention, but the Holy Scriptures (the Bible) shall be the supreme authority governing every aspect of the conciliation process.

Rule 4 explicitly subordinates American law to religious precepts and openly defies the Supreme Court's instruction that arbitrators should apply substantive law in the same manner that a court would. Under the rationale of cases like *Circuit City*, [excerpted in Ch. 3,] no arbitrator following this rule should be allowed to adjudicate statutory rights. And yet this clause has been upheld and enforced by at least two state courts and two federal courts.

Courts' attempts to rationalize away the problems with this rule have been unsatisfactory. In Easterly v. Heritage Christian Schools, Inc., the district court compelled a fired schoolteacher to adjudicate her age- and disability-discrimination claims before a Christian tribunal. The plaintiff argued that RPCC

Rule 4 made her arbitration contract unenforceable because she would have to "forego vindication of her substantive rights guaranteed by the ADEA and ADA . . . and instead rely on biblical scripture to define her rights." The court was unmoved.
* * *

Rule 4 also made an appearance in Spivey v. Teen Challenge of Florida, Inc., in which a mother was forced to arbitrate her son's wrongful-death claim before a Christian tribunal. Nicklaus Spivey died of a drug overdose after a religious rehabilitation center, following an attempt to "de-gay" him, threw Spivey out "[on]to the streets of Jacksonville" for violating program rules. When his mother objected to Rule 4, the court dismissed her concerns by interpreting the Rule to mean holy scripture would trump secular law only in matters of "process" rather than substance.

However, an examination of the other RPCC rules makes this reading implausible; the rules are procedural in name only. Other rules clarify that scripture can and should guide the arbitrator's substantive decisions. On the merits, the ICC's Standard of Conduct for Christian Conciliators instructs that a "Christian conciliator shall encourage and support only scripturally sound decisions and actions (Micah 6:8)." This involves encouraging "repentance, confession, forgiveness, and reconciliation whenever sin has occurred or a relationship has been broken (Luke 17:3; Gal. 6:1; 2 Tim. 4:2)." The arbitrator "shall . . . help the parties to make decisions, to take actions, and to change their lifestyles, habits, and conduct as God has instructed in the Scriptures." In crafting an arbitral award, arbitrators "may grant any remedy or relief that they deem scriptural, just and equitable, and within the scope of the agreement of the parties." And perhaps most strikingly, "the Christian conciliator shall respect the legitimate jurisdiction of civil authorities and shall cooperate with them as required by law, unless there is a clear scriptural reason to do otherwise (Acts 4:19; Rom. 13:1–7)."

These rules strongly suggest that Christian Conciliation is not just a matter of process. They seem to instruct arbitrators to steer parties toward a scripturally sanctioned outcome. They appear to give arbitrators permission to craft biblically based remedies. And they make clear that scripture, not the "jurisdiction of civil authorities," is sacrosanct.

While these examples concern the rules for Christian Conciliation, the religious principles of other faith-based tribunals also come into tension with secular law. For example, under Sharia law, a woman's testimony may be given half as much evidentiary weight as a man's. In Britain, where Islamic arbitration is widespread, the Parliament has considered legislation to prevent Sharia panels from treating "the evidence of a man [as] worth more than the evidence of a woman." Numerous civil rights groups, including the Iranian and Kurdish Women's Rights Organization, have backed the bill. Some scholars have further argued that Sharia family law may substantively disadvantage women * * *. Similarly, under traditional Jewish law, "women, non-Jews, and the handicapped cannot act as witnesses."

To put a point on it: despite protestations of district courts to the contrary, religious tribunals explicitly admit to prioritizing scriptural edicts over substantive secular law. These religious tribunals rule on thousands of disputes every year, and according to the Supreme Court's scope-of-arbitration jurisprudence, such tribunals can adjudicate issues involving federal statutory rights—including civil rights. Moreover, under the Supreme Court's narrow reading of the grounds on which an arbitration award can be vacated under the FAA, the fact that a religious tribunal failed to enforce federal rights because of a contrary scriptural commandment might not be enough to overturn an arbitral judgment. The result is that religious arbitrators can explicitly disregard the secular law, and that disregard may be insufficient to warrant review.

Cases discussing Christian arbitration are few. One mentioned by *The Reverse-Entanglement Principle* is *Spivey v. Teen Challenge of Fla., Inc.*, 122 So. 3d 986 (Fla. Dist. Ct. App. 2013).

> Nicklaus—then nineteen years old—enrolled in a year-long program at Teen Challenge's substance abuse facility in Pensacola, Florida, signing several documents, including the arbitration agreement at issue, which provides in pertinent part: "The undersigned parties accept the Bible as the inspired Word of God. They believe that God desires that they resolve their disputes with one another within the Church and that they be reconciled in their relationships in accordance with the principles stated in First Corinthians 6:1–8, Matthew 5:23–24, and Matthew 18:15–20. Accordingly, the undersigned parties hereby agree that, if any dispute or controversy that arise [sic] out of, or is related to this agreement is not resolved in private meetings between the parties pursuant to Matthew 5:23–24 and 18:15, then the dispute or controversy will be settled by biblically based mediation and, if necessary, legally binding arbitration, in accordance with the Rule[s] of Procedure for Christian Conciliation (rules) of the Association of Christian Conciliation Services (current rules available and incorporated by this reference)."

Id. at 988. The other, *Easterly v. Heritage Christian Schools, Inc.*, 2009 WL 2750099 (S.D. Indiana Aug. 26, 2009), enforced Christian school teacher's agreement to arbitrate employment discrimination claims; "Conciliators shall take into consideration any state, federal, or local laws that the parties bring to their attention, but the Holy Scriptures (the Bible) shall be the supreme authority governing every aspect of the conciliation process.") See also Maynard v. Valley Christian Acad., Inc., No. 5:16-CV-01889, 2017 WL 3594670, at *1 (N.D. Ohio Aug. 21, 2017) (enforcing Christian school's custodian's agreement to that disputes "shall be solved and settled by Christian mediation and, if necessary, legal binding arbitration in accordance with the rules of procedure for Christian Conciliation, a division of Peacemakers® Ministries, P.O. Box 81130, Billings, MT 59108 (406-256-1583). The complete text of the rules is available at www.Peacemaker.net."); Prescott v. Northlake Christian School, 244 F.Supp.2d 659 (E.D. La. 2002) (contract between school and principal required that all employment-related disputes be submitted to "biblically-based mediation and arbitration" under the Rules of Procedure for Christian Conciliation; the arbitrator concluded that the school had breached its contract "legally as well as Biblically" by wrongfully terminating the principal without following Matthew 18; held, "given the unique nature of this employment agreement," the award "was rationally related to the parties' agreement").

Not all Christian arbitration involves schools. For instance, the General Conference of the Evangelical Methodist Church won court enforcement of its arbitration agreement against individual churches in a property dispute, Gen. Conference of Evangelical Methodist Church v. Evangelical Methodist Church of Dalton, Georgia, Inc., 807 F. Supp. 2d 1291, 1300–01 (N.D. Ga. 2011), and a dispute arising out of an individual church's attempt to sever its affiliation with the conference. Gen. Conference of Evangelical Methodist Church v. Faith Evangelical Methodist Church, 809 N.W.2d 117, 121 (Iowa Ct. App. 2011).

QUESTIONS TO REVIEW AND SYNTHESIZE

1. Compare and contrast religious arbitration processes in the Jewish, Islamic, and Christian faiths.
2. The *Religious Arbitration and the New Multiculturalism* article excerpted above says "Religious arbitration courts are unique because, rather than merely adjudicating claims based on an arbitrator's understanding of U.S. law and principles of equity, they render decisions based upon a selected body of religious law." What examples have you read of trade association arbitration also not "adjudicating claims based on an arbitrator's understanding of U.S. law and principles of equity"? What different source of "law" do trade association arbitrators often use?
3. *The Reverse-Entanglement Principle* article excerpted above says "that religious tribunals prioritize holy law over federal statutory law." Does the *Religious Arbitration and the New Multiculturalism* excerpt suggest any arguments that might persuade even the secular among us to celebrate, rather than criticize, religious arbitration "prioritiz[ing] holy law over federal statutory law"?

CHAPTER 3

ARBITRATION AND THE COURTS

http://www.disputeresolutiongermany.com/wp-content/uploads/2012/10/litigate-arbitration-clause.gif

A. INTRODUCTION

Before the 1920s, if disputing parties in the United States took a case to arbitration *and* the arbitrator proceeded to render an award, the award would generally be enforceable in court. However, a party could revoke a purely *executory* agreement to arbitrate at any time. An executory agreement to arbitrate is an agreement the parties have not yet performed by participating in arbitration. A court would not specifically enforce such an agreement by ordering a party to arbitrate any disputes. Instead, a court might award money damages for breach of the promise to resolve disputes in arbitration, but how would a court calculate the dollar amount of such damages? This difficulty led courts to award zero or nominal damages,[1] rather than provide meaningful enforcement to executory arbitration agreements. So, a potential defendant could deprive the arbitration agreement of significance by ignoring the plaintiff's (claimant's) demand for arbitration and refusing to participate in arbitration. A potential plaintiff could similarly deprive its arbitration agreement of any effect by simply bringing suit, and the court would hear the case without regard to the agreement to arbitrate.

A history of this situation is in Judge Frank's opinion in *Kulukundis Shipping Co. S/A v. Amtorg Trading Corp.*, 126 F.2d 978 (2d Cir.1942):

> The English courts, while giving full effect to agreements to submit controversies to arbitration after they had ripened into arbitrators' awards, would—over a long period beginning at the end of the 17th century—do little or nothing to prevent or make irksome the breach of such agreements when they were still executory. Prior to 1687, such a breach could be made costly: a penal bond given to abide the result of an arbitration had a real bite, since a breach of the bond's condition led to a judgment for the amount of the penalty. It was so held in 1609 in Vynoir's Case, 8 CokeRep. 81b. To be sure, Coke there, in a dictum, citing precedents, dilated on the inherent revocability of the authority given to an arbitrator; such a revocation was not too important, however, if it resulted in a stiff judgment on a penal bond. But the Statute of Fines and Penalties (8 & 9 Wm.III c. 11, s. 8), enacted in 1687, provided that, in an action on any bond given for performance of agreements, while judgment would be entered for the penalty, execution should issue only for the damages actually sustained. Coke's dictum as to revocability, uttered seventy-eight years earlier, now took on a new significance, as it was now held that for breach of an undertaking to arbitrate the damages were only nominal. Recognizing the effect of the impact of this statute on executory arbitration agreements, Parliament, eleven years later, enacted a statute, 9 Wm.III c. 15 (1698), designed to remedy the situation by providing that, if an agreement to arbitrate so provided, it could be made a 'rule of court' (i.e., a court order), in which event it became irrevocable, and one who revoked it would be subject to punishment for contempt of court; but the

[1] See Munson v. Straits of Dover S.S. Co., 102 Fed. 926 (2d Cir.1900) (plaintiff sought damages, in the form of lawyer's fees and costs incurred in defending a lawsuit, for breach of agreement to arbitrate; held, plaintiff entitled to nominal damages only; judicial process is "theoretically at least, the safest and best devised by the wisdom and experience of mankind.").

submission was revocable until such a rule of court had been obtained. This statute, limited in scope, was narrowly construed and was of little help. The ordinary executory arbitration agreement thus lost all real efficacy since it was not specifically enforceable in equity, and was held not to constitute the basis of a plea in bar in, or a stay of, a suit on the original cause of action. In admiralty, the rulings were much the same

It has been well said that 'the legal mind must assign some reason in order to decide anything with spiritual quiet.' And so, by way of rationalization, it became fashionable in the middle of the 18th century to say that such agreements were against public policy because they 'oust the jurisdiction' of the courts. But that was a quaint explanation, inasmuch as an award, under an arbitration agreement, enforced both at law and in equity, was no less an ouster; and the same was true of releases and covenants not to sue, which were given full effect. Moreover, the agreement to arbitrate was not illegal, since suit could be maintained for its breach. Here was a clear instance of what Holmes called a 'right' to break a contract and to substitute payment of damages for non-performance; as, in this type of case, the damages were only nominal, that 'right' was indeed meaningful.

An effort has been made to justify this judicial hostility to the executory arbitration agreement on the ground that arbitrations, if unsupervised by the courts, are undesirable, and that legislation was needed to make possible such supervision. But if that was the reason for unfriendliness to such executory agreements, then the courts should also have refused to aid arbitrations when they ripened into awards. And what the English courts, especially the equity courts, did in other contexts, shows that, if they had had the will, they could have devised means of protecting parties to arbitrations. Instead, they restrictively interpreted successive statutes intended to give effect to executory arbitrations. No similar hostility was displayed by the Scotch courts. Lord Campbell explained the English attitude as due to the desire of the judges, at a time when their salaries came largely from fees, to avoid loss of income. Indignation has been voiced at this suggestion; perhaps it is unjustified. Perhaps the true explanation is the hypnotic power of the phrase, 'oust the jurisdiction.' Give a bad dogma a good name and its bite may become as bad as its bark.

In 1855, in Scott v. Avery, 5 H.C.L. 811, the tide seemed to have turned. There it was held that if a policy made an award of damages by arbitrators a condition precedent to a suit on the policy, a failure to submit to arbitration would preclude such a suit, even if the policy left to the arbitrators the consideration of all the elements of liability. But, despite later legislation, the hostility of the English courts to executory arbitrations resumed somewhat after Scott v. Avery, and seems never to have been entirely dissipated.

That English attitude was largely taken over in the 19th century by most courts in this country. Indeed, in general, they would not go as far as

> Scott v. Avery, supra, and continued to use the 'ouster of jurisdiction' concept: An executory agreement to arbitrate would not be given specific performance or furnish the basis of a stay of proceedings on the original cause of action. Nor would it be given effect as a plea in bar, except in limited instances, i.e., in the case of an agreement expressly or impliedly making it a condition precedent to litigation that there be an award determining some preliminary question of subsidiary fact upon which any liability was to be contingent. Hamilton v. Liverpool, 1890, etc., Ins. Co., 136 U.S. 242, 255, 10 S.Ct. 945, 34 L.Ed. 419. In the case of broader executory agreements, no more than nominal dangers would be given for a breach.
>
> Generally speaking, then, the courts of this country were unfriendly to executory arbitration agreements. The lower federal courts, feeling bound to comply with the precedents, nevertheless became critical of this judicial hostility. There were intimations in the Supreme Court that perhaps the old view might be abandoned, but in the cases hinting at that newer attitude the issue was not raised. Effective state arbitration statutes were enacted beginning with the New York Statute of 1920.
>
> The United States Arbitration Act of 1925 was sustained as constitutional, in its application to cases arising in admiralty. Marine Transit Corp. v. Dreyfus, 1932, 284 U.S. 263, 52 S.Ct. 166, 76 L.Ed. 516. The purpose of that Act was deliberately to alter the judicial atmosphere previously existing.

Kulukundis Shipping Co., 126 F.2d at 982–85.

The United States Arbitration Act was re-enacted in 1947 as the Federal Arbitration Act,[2] which is reproduced in Appendix A. Read the text of the Federal Arbitration Act ("FAA") carefully, as it is deceptively simple for such an important statute.

QUESTIONS TO REVIEW AND SYNTHESIZE

1. What does the FAA change from pre-1920s arbitration law? Which sections of the FAA effect this change?
2. The FAA enforces pre- and post-dispute agreements to arbitrate with what remedy for breach? Which sections of the FAA provide this remedy?

---

[2] See Federal Arbitration Act, Pub. L. No. 80-282, 61 Stat. 669 (1947); Judith Resnik, *Diffusing Disputes: The Public in the Private of Arbitration, the Private in Courts, and the Erasure of Rights*, 124 Yale L.J. 2804, 2939 (2015).

B. THE GROWTH OF "ARBITRABLE" CLAIMS

1. PRE-1980S

Wilko v. Swan

Supreme Court of the United States, 1953.
346 U.S. 427, 74 S.Ct. 182, 98 L.Ed.168.

■ MR. JUSTICE REED delivered the opinion of the Court.

This action by petitioner, a customer, against respondents, partners in a securities brokerage firm, was brought in the United States District Court for the Southern District of New York, to recover damages under § 12(2) of the Securities Act of 1933. The complaint alleged that on or about January 17, 1951, through the instrumentalities of interstate commerce, petitioner was induced by Hayden, Stone and Company to purchase 1,600 shares of the common stock of Air Associates, Incorporated, by false representations * * *.

Without answering the complaint, the respondent moved to stay the trial of the action pursuant to § 3 of the United States Arbitration Act [FAA] until an arbitration in accordance with the terms of identical margin agreements was had. An affidavit accompanied the motion stating that the parties' relationship was controlled by the terms of the agreements and that while the firm was willing to arbitrate petitioner had failed to seek or proceed with any arbitration of the controversy.

Finding that the margin agreements provide that arbitration should be the method of settling all future controversies, the District Court held that the agreement to arbitrate deprived petitioner of the advantageous court remedy afforded by the Securities Act, and denied the stay. A divided Court of Appeals concluded that the Act did not prohibit the agreement to refer future controversies to arbitration, and reversed.

The question is whether an agreement to arbitrate a future controversy is a 'condition, stipulation, or provision binding any person acquiring any security to waive compliance with any provision' of the Securities Act which § 14[6] declares 'void.' We granted certiorari to review this important and novel federal question affecting both the Securities Act and the United States Arbitration Act.

As the margin agreement in the light of the complaint evidenced a transaction in interstate commerce, no issue arises as to the applicability of the provisions of the United States Arbitration Act to this suit, based upon the Securities Act.

In response to a Presidential message urging that there be added to the ancient rule of caveat emptor the further doctrine of 'let the seller also beware,' Congress passed the Securities Act of 1933. Designed to protect investors, the Act requires issuers, underwriters, and dealers to make full and fair disclosure of the

---

[6] 48 Stat. 84, 15 U.S.C. s 77n, 15 U.S.C.A. s 77n. Section 14 provides:

'Any condition, stipulation, or provision binding any person acquiring any security to waive compliance with any provision of this subchapter or of the rules and regulations of the Commission shall be void.'

character of securities sold in interstate and foreign commerce and to prevent fraud in their sale. To effectuate this policy, § 12(2) created a special right to recover for misrepresentation which differs substantially from the common-law action in that the seller is made to assume the burden of proving lack of scienter. The Act's special right is enforceable in any court of competent jurisdiction—federal or state—and removal from a state court is prohibited. If suit be brought in a federal court, the purchaser has a wide choice of venue, the privilege of nation-wide service of process and the jurisdictional $3,000 requirement of diversity cases is inapplicable.

The United States Arbitration Act establishes by statute the desirability of arbitration as an alternative to the complications of litigation. The reports of both Houses on that Act stress the need for avoiding the delay and expense of litigation, and practice under its terms raises hope for its usefulness both in controversies based on statutes or on standards otherwise created. This hospitable attitude of legislatures and courts toward arbitration, however, does not solve our question as to the validity of petitioner's stipulation by the margin agreements, set out below, to submit to arbitration controversies that might arise from the transactions.

Petitioner argues that § 14 shows that the purpose of Congress was to assure that sellers could not maneuver buyers into a position that might weaken their ability to recover under the Securities Act. He contends that arbitration lacks the certainty of a suit at law under the Act to enforce his rights. He reasons that the arbitration paragraph of the margin agreement is a stipulation that waives 'compliance with' the provision of the Securities Act, set out in the margin, conferring jurisdiction of suits and special powers.

Respondent asserts that arbitration is merely a form of trial to be used in lieu of a trial at law, and therefore no conflict exists between the Securities Act and the United States Arbitration Act either in their language or in the congressional purposes in their enactment. Each may function within its own scope, the former to protect investors and the latter to simplify recovery for actionable violations of law by issuers or dealers in securities.

Respondent is in agreement with the Court of Appeals that the margin agreement arbitration paragraph does not relieve the seller from either liability or burden of proof imposed by the Securities Act. We agree that in so far as the award in arbitration may be affected by legal requirements, statutes or common law, rather than by considerations of fairness, the provisions of the Securities Act control. This is true even though this proposed agreement has no requirement that the arbitrators follow the law. This agreement of the parties as to the effect of the Securities Act includes also acceptance of the invalidity of the paragraph of the margin agreement that relieves the respondent sellers of liability for all 'representation or advice by you or your employees or agents regarding the purchase or sale by me of any property.'

The words of § 14 void any 'stipulation' waiving compliance with any 'provision' of the Securities Act. This arrangement to arbitrate is a 'stipulation,' and we think the right to select the judicial forum is the kind of 'provision' that cannot be waived under § 14 of the Securities Act. That conclusion is reached for the reasons set out above in the statement of petitioner's contention on this review. While a buyer and seller of securities, under some circumstances, may deal at arm's length on equal terms, it is clear that the Securities Act was drafted with an eye to the disadvantages under which buyers labor. Issuers of and dealers in securities have better opportunities to investigate and appraise the prospective earnings and business plans affecting securities than buyers. It is therefore reasonable for Congress to put buyers of securities covered by that Act on a different basis from other purchasers.

When the security buyer, prior to any violation of the Securities Act, waives his right to sue in courts, he gives up more than would a participant in other business transactions. The security buyer has a wider choice of courts and venue. He thus surrenders one of the advantages the Act gives him and surrenders it at a time when he is less able to judge the weight of the handicap the Securities Act places upon his adversary.

Even though the provisions of the Securities Act, advantageous to the buyer, apply, their effectiveness in application is lessened in arbitration as compared to judicial proceedings. Determination of the quality of a commodity or the amount of money due under a contract is not the type of issue here involved. This case requires subjective findings on the purpose and knowledge of an alleged violator of the Act. They must be not only determined but applied by the arbitrators without judicial instruction on the law. As their award may be made without explanation of their reasons and without a complete record of their proceedings, the arbitrators' conception of the legal meaning of such statutory requirements as 'burden of proof,' 'reasonable care' or 'material fact,' cannot be examined. Power to vacate an award is limited. While it may be true, as the Court of Appeals thought, that a failure of the arbitrators to decide in accordance with the provisions of the Securities Act would 'constitute grounds for vacating the award pursuant to section 10 of the Federal Arbitration Act,' that failure would need to be made clearly to appear. In unrestricted submission, such as the present margin agreements envisage, the interpretations of the law by the arbitrators in contrast to manifest disregard are not subject, in the federal courts, to judicial review for error in interpretation. The United States Arbitration Act contains no provision for judicial determination of legal issues such as is found in the English law. As the protective provisions of the Securities Act require the exercise of judicial direction to fairly assure their effectiveness, it seems to us that Congress must have intended § 14 to apply to waiver of judicial trial and review.

* * *

Two policies, not easily reconcilable, are involved in this case. Congress has afforded participants in transactions subject to its legislative power an opportunity generally to secure prompt, economical and adequate solution of controversies through arbitration if the parties are willing to accept less certainty of legally correct adjustment. On the other hand, it has enacted the Securities Act to protect the rights of investors and has forbidden a waiver of any of those rights. Recognizing the advantages that prior agreements for arbitration may provide for the solution of commercial controversies, we decide that the intention of Congress concerning the sale of securities is better carried out by holding invalid such an agreement for arbitration of issues arising under the Act.

Reversed.

■ MR. JUSTICE JACKSON, concurring.

I agree with the Court's opinion insofar as it construes the Securities Act to prohibit waiver of a judicial remedy in favor of arbitration by agreement made before any controversy arose. I think thereafter the parties could agree upon arbitration. However, I find it unnecessary in this case, where there has not been and could not be any arbitration, to decide that the Arbitration Act precludes any judicial remedy for the arbitrators' error of interpretation of a relevant statute.

■ MR. JUSTICE FRANKFURTER, whom MR. JUSTICE MINTON joins, dissenting.

If arbitration inherently precluded full protection of the rights § 12(2) of the Securities Act affords to a purchaser of securities, or if there were no effective means of ensuring judicial review of the legal basis of the arbitration, then, of course, an agreement to settle the controversy by arbitration would be barred by § 14, the anti-waiver provision, of that Act.

There is nothing in the record before us, nor in the facts of which we can take judicial notice, to indicate that the arbitral system as practiced in the City of New York, and as enforceable under the supervisory authority of the District Court for the Southern District of New York, would not afford the plaintiff the rights to which he is entitled.

The impelling considerations that led to the enactment of the Federal Arbitration Act are the advantages of providing a speedier, more economical and more effective enforcement of rights by way of arbitration than can be had by the tortuous course of litigation, especially in the City of New York. These advantages should not be assumed to be denied in controversies like that before us arising under the Securities Act, in the absence of any showing that settlement by arbitration would jeopardize the rights of the plaintiff.

Arbitrators may not disregard the law. Specifically they are, as Chief Judge Swan pointed out, 'bound to decide in accordance with the provisions of section 12(2).' On this we are all agreed. It is suggested, however, that there is no effective way of assuring obedience by the arbitrators to the governing law. But since their failure to observe this law 'would constitute grounds for vacating the award pursuant to section 10 of the Federal Arbitration Act,' appropriate means for judicial scrutiny must be implied, in the form of some record or opinion, however informal, whereby such compliance will appear, or want of it will upset the award.

We have not before us a case in which the record shows that the plaintiff in opening an account had no choice but to accept the arbitration stipulation, thereby making the stipulation an unconscionable and unenforceable provision in a business transaction. The Securities and Exchange Commission, as amicus curiae, does not contend that the stipulation which the Court of Appeals respected, under the appropriate safeguards defined by it, was a coercive practice by financial houses against customers incapable of self-protection. It is one thing to make out a case of overreaching as between parties bargaining not at arm's length. It is quite a different thing to find in the anti-waiver provision of the Securities Act a general limitation on the Federal Arbitration Act.

On the state of the record before us, I would affirm the decision of the Court of Appeals.

QUESTIONS TO REVIEW AND SYNTHESIZE

1. Under *Wilko*'s reasoning, should courts enforce a post-dispute agreement to arbitrate claims under the Securities Act?
2. Under *Wilko*'s reasoning, should courts enforce a post-dispute agreement to settle (for some payment by the defendant to the plaintiff) claims under the Securities Act?
3. Justice Frankfurter's dissent says "Arbitrators may not disregard the law" and are "bound to decide in accordance with § 12(2)of the Securities Act. * * * On this we are all agreed. It is suggested, however, that there is no effective way of assuring obedience by the arbitrators to the governing law. But since their failure to observe this law 'would constitute grounds for vacating the award pursuant to section 10 of the Federal Arbitration Act,' appropriate means for judicial scrutiny must be implied, in the form of some record or opinion, however informal, whereby such compliance will appear, or want of it will upset the award." Does FAA § 10 say arbitrators disregarding the law that would have applied in litigation is a ground for vacating the arbitration award?

2. 1980S

Mitsubishi Motors Corp. v. Soler Chrysler-Plymouth, Inc.

Supreme Court of the United States, 1985.
473 U.S. 614, 105 S.Ct. 3346, 87 L.Ed.2d 444.

■ JUSTICE BLACKMUN delivered the opinion of the Court.

The principal question presented by these cases is the arbitrability, pursuant to the federal Arbitration Act and the Convention on the Recognition and Enforcement of Foreign Arbitral Awards (Convention), of claims arising under the Sherman Act, 15 U.S.C. § 1 et seq., and encompassed within a valid arbitration clause in an agreement embodying an international commercial transaction.

I

Petitioner-cross-respondent Mitsubishi Motors Corporation (Mitsubishi) is a Japanese corporation which manufactures automobiles and has its principal place of business in Tokyo, Japan. Mitsubishi is the product of a joint venture between, on the one hand, Chrysler International, S.A. ("CISA"), a Swiss corporation registered in Geneva and wholly owned by Chrysler Corporation, and, on the other, Mitsubishi Heavy Industries, Inc., a Japanese corporation. The aim of the joint venture was the distribution through Chrysler dealers outside the continental United States of vehicles manufactured by Mitsubishi and bearing Chrysler and Mitsubishi trademarks. Respondent-cross-respondent Soler Chrysler-Plymouth,

Inc. (Soler), is a Puerto Rico corporation with its principal place of business in Pueblo Viejo, Guaynabo, Puerto Rico.

On October 31, 1979, Soler entered into a Distributor Agreement with CISA which provided for the sale by Soler of Mitsubishi-manufactured vehicles within a designated area, including metropolitan San Juan. On the same date, CISA, Soler, and Mitsubishi entered into a Sales Procedure Agreement (Sales Agreement) which, referring to the Distributor Agreement, provided for the direct sale of Mitsubishi products to Soler and governed the terms and conditions of such sales. Paragraph VI of the Sales Agreement, labeled "Arbitration of Certain Matters," provides:

> "All disputes, controversies or differences which may arise between [Mitsubishi] and [Soler] out of or in relation to Articles I-B through V of this Agreement or for the breach thereof, shall be finally settled by arbitration in Japan in accordance with the rules and regulations of the Japan Commercial Arbitration Association."

Initially, Soler did a brisk business in Mitsubishi-manufactured vehicles. As a result of its strong performance, its minimum sales volume, specified by Mitsubishi and CISA, and agreed to by Soler, for the 1981 model year was substantially increased. In early 1981, however, the new-car market slackened. Soler ran into serious difficulties in meeting the expected sales volume, and by the spring of 1981 it felt itself compelled to request that Mitsubishi delay or cancel shipment of several orders. About the same time, Soler attempted to arrange for the transshipment of a quantity of its vehicles for sale in the continental United States and Latin America. Mitsubishi and CISA, however, refused permission for any such diversion, citing a variety of reasons, and no vehicles were transshipped. Attempts to work out these difficulties failed. Mitsubishi eventually withheld shipment of 966 vehicles, apparently representing orders placed for May, June, and July 1981 production, responsibility for which Soler disclaimed in February 1982.

The following month, Mitsubishi brought an action against Soler in the United States District Court for the District of Puerto Rico under the federal Arbitration Act and the Convention. Mitsubishi sought an order to compel arbitration in accord with ¶ VI of the Sales Agreement. Shortly after filing the complaint, Mitsubishi filed a request for arbitration before the Japan Commercial Arbitration Association.

Soler denied the allegations and counterclaimed against both Mitsubishi and CISA. It alleged numerous breaches by Mitsubishi of the Sales Agreement, raised a pair of defamation claims, and asserted causes of action under the Sherman Act; the federal Automobile Dealers' Day in Court Act; the Puerto Rico competition statute; and the Puerto Rico Dealers' Contracts Act. In the counterclaim premised on the Sherman Act, Soler alleged that Mitsubishi and CISA had conspired to divide markets in restraint of trade. To effectuate the plan, according to Soler, Mitsubishi had refused to permit Soler to resell to buyers in North, Central, or South America vehicles it had obligated itself to purchase from Mitsubishi; had refused to ship ordered vehicles or the parts, such as heaters and defoggers, that would be necessary to permit Soler to make its vehicles suitable for resale outside Puerto Rico; and had coercively attempted to replace Soler and its other Puerto Rico distributors with a wholly owned subsidiary which would serve as the exclusive Mitsubishi distributor in Puerto Rico.

After a hearing, the District Court ordered Mitsubishi and Soler to arbitrate each of the issues raised in the complaint and in all the counterclaims save two and a portion of a third. [The Court of Appeals agreed that the arbitration clause "encompass[ed] virtually all the claims arising under the various statutes, including all those arising under the Sherman Act."[9] It held, however, against compelling arbitration of Soler's antitrust claims.]

* * *

II

At the outset, we address the contention raised in Soler's cross-petition that the arbitration clause at issue may not be read to encompass the statutory counterclaims stated in its answer to the complaint. In making this argument, Soler does not question the Court of Appeals' application of ¶ VI of the Sales Agreement to the disputes involved here as a matter of standard contract interpretation. Instead, it argues that as a matter of law a court may not construe an arbitration agreement to encompass claims arising out of statutes designed to protect a class to which the party resisting arbitration belongs "unless [that party] has expressly agreed" to arbitrate those claims, by which Soler presumably means that the arbitration clause must specifically mention the statute giving rise to the claims that a party to the clause seeks to arbitrate. Soler reasons that, because it falls within the class for whose benefit the federal and local antitrust laws and dealers' acts were passed, but the arbitration clause at issue does not mention these statutes or statutes in general, the clause cannot be read to contemplate arbitration of these statutory claims.

We do not agree, for we find no warrant in the Arbitration Act for implying in every contract within its ken a presumption against arbitration of statutory claims. * * *

[T]he first task of a court asked to compel arbitration of a dispute is to determine whether the parties agreed to arbitrate that dispute. The court is to make this determination by applying the "federal substantive law of arbitrability, applicable to any arbitration agreement within the coverage of the Act." And that body of law counsels "that * * * any doubts concerning the scope of arbitrable issues should be resolved in favor of arbitration * * *." Thus, as with any other

---

9 As the Court of Appeals saw it, "[t]he question . . . is not whether the arbitration clause mentions antitrust or any other particular cause of action, but whether the factual allegations underlying Soler's counterclaims—and Mitsubishi's bona fide defenses to those counterclaims—are within the scope of the arbitration clause, whatever the legal labels attached to those allegations." * * *

The court read the Sherman Act counterclaim to raise issues of wrongful termination of Soler's distributorship, wrongful failure to ship ordered parts and vehicles, and wrongful refusal to permit transshipment of stock to the United States and Latin America. Because the existence of just cause for termination turned on Mitsubishi's allegations that Soler had breached the Sales Agreement by, for example, failing to pay for ordered vehicles, the wrongful termination claim implicated [several] provisions within the arbitration clause [including]: Article I-D(1), which rendered a dealer's orders "firm" * * * and Article I-F, specifying payment obligations and procedures. The court therefore held the arbitration clause to cover this dispute. * * *

contract, the parties' intentions control, but those intentions are generously construed as to issues of arbitrability.

There is no reason to depart from these guidelines where a party bound by an arbitration agreement raises claims founded on statutory rights. * * * Of course, courts should remain attuned to well-supported claims that the agreement to arbitrate resulted from the sort of fraud or overwhelming economic power that would provide grounds "for the revocation of any contract." [FAA, § 2]. But, absent such compelling considerations, the Act itself provides no basis for disfavoring agreements to arbitrate statutory claims by skewing the otherwise hospitable inquiry into arbitrability.

That is not to say that all controversies implicating statutory rights are suitable for arbitration. There is no reason to distort the process of contract interpretation, however, in order to ferret out the inappropriate. Just as it is the congressional policy manifested in the federal Arbitration Act that requires courts liberally to construe the scope of arbitration agreements covered by that Act, it is the congressional intention expressed in some other statute on which the courts must rely to identify any category of claims as to which agreements to arbitrate will be held unenforceable. For that reason, Soler's concern for statutorily protected classes provides no reason to color the lens through which the arbitration clause is read. By agreeing to arbitrate a statutory claim, a party does not forego the substantive rights afforded by the statute; it only submits to their resolution in an arbitral, rather than a judicial, forum. It trades the procedures and opportunity for review of the courtroom for the simplicity, informality, and expedition of arbitration. We must assume that if Congress intended the substantive protection afforded by a given statute to include protection against waiver of the right to a judicial forum, that intention will be deducible from text or legislative history. Having made the bargain to arbitrate, the party should be held to it unless Congress itself has evinced an intention to preclude a waiver of judicial remedies for the statutory rights at issue. Nothing, in the meantime, prevents a party from excluding statutory claims from the scope of an agreement to arbitrate.

In sum, the Court of Appeals correctly conducted a two-step inquiry, first determining whether the parties' agreement to arbitrate reached the statutory issues, and then, upon finding it did, considering whether legal constraints external to the parties' agreement foreclosed the arbitration of those claims. We endorse its rejection of Soler's proposed rule of arbitration-clause construction.

III

We now turn to consider whether Soler's antitrust claims are nonarbitrable even though it has agreed to arbitrate them. In holding that they are not, the Court of Appeals followed the decision of the Second Circuit in *American Safety Equipment Corp. v. J.P. Maguire & Co.,* 391 F.2d 821 (1968). Notwithstanding the absence of any explicit support for such an exception in either the Sherman Act or the federal Arbitration Act, the Second Circuit there reasoned that "the pervasive public interest in enforcement of the antitrust laws, and the nature of the claims that arise in such cases, combine to make . . . antitrust claims . . . inappropriate for arbitration." We find it unnecessary to assess the legitimacy of the *American Safety* doctrine as applied to agreements to arbitrate arising from domestic transactions.

As in *Scherk v. Alberto-Culver Co.,* 417 U.S. 506 (1974), we conclude that concerns of international comity, respect for the capacities of foreign and transnational tribunals, and sensitivity to the need of the international commercial system for predictability in the resolution of disputes require that we enforce the parties' agreement, even assuming that a contrary result would be forthcoming in a domestic context.

* * *

> [The Court in *Scherk*] Court emphasized:
>
> "A contractual provision specifying in advance the forum in which disputes shall be litigated and the law to be applied is . . . an almost indispensable precondition to achievement of the orderliness and predictability essential to any international business transaction. . . .
>
> "A parochial refusal by the courts of one country to enforce an international arbitration agreement would not only frustrate these purposes, but would invite unseemly and mutually destructive jockeying by the parties to secure tactical litigation advantages. . . . [It would] damage the fabric of international commerce and trade, and imperil the willingness and ability of businessmen to enter into international commercial agreements."

* * *

Thus, we must weigh the concerns of *American Safety* against a strong belief in the efficacy of arbitral procedures for the resolution of international commercial disputes and an equal commitment to the enforcement of freely negotiated choice-of-forum clauses.

At the outset, we confess to some skepticism of certain aspects of the *American Safety* doctrine. As distilled by the First Circuit, the doctrine comprises four ingredients. First, private parties play a pivotal role in aiding governmental enforcement of the antitrust laws by means of the private action for treble damages. Second, "the strong possibility that contracts which generate antitrust disputes may be contracts of adhesion militates against automatic forum determination by contract." Third, antitrust issues, prone to complication, require sophisticated legal and economic analysis, and thus are "ill-adapted to strengths of the arbitral process, i.e., expedition, minimal requirements of written rationale, simplicity, resort to basic concepts of common sense and simple equity." Finally, just as "issues of war and peace are too important to be vested in the generals, . . . decisions as to antitrust regulation of business are too important to be lodged in arbitrators chosen from the business community—particularly those from a foreign community that has had no experience with or exposure to our law and values."

Initially, we find the second concern unjustified. The mere appearance of an antitrust dispute does not alone warrant invalidation of the selected forum on the undemonstrated assumption that the arbitration clause is tainted. A party resisting arbitration of course may attack directly the validity of the agreement to arbitrate. See *Prima Paint Corp*. [excerpted in Section 3.D.2.a] Moreover, the party may attempt to make a showing that would warrant setting aside the forum-selection clause—that the agreement was "[a]ffected by fraud, undue influence, or overweening bargaining power"; that "enforcement would be unreasonable and unjust"; or that proceedings "in the contractual forum will be so gravely difficult and inconvenient that [the resisting party] will for all practical purposes be deprived of his day in court." But absent such a showing—and none was attempted here—there is no basis for assuming the forum inadequate or its selection unfair.

Next, potential complexity should not suffice to ward off arbitration. We might well have some doubt that even the courts following *American Safety* subscribe fully to the view that antitrust matters are inherently insusceptible to resolution by arbitration, as these same courts have agreed that an undertaking to arbitrate antitrust claims entered into after the dispute arises is acceptable. And the vertical restraints which most frequently give birth to antitrust claims covered by an arbitration agreement will not often occasion the monstrous proceedings that have given antitrust litigation an image of intractability. In any event, adaptability and access to expertise are hallmarks of arbitration. The anticipated subject matter of the dispute may be taken into account when the arbitrators are appointed, and arbitral rules typically provide for the participation of experts either employed by the parties or appointed by the tribunal. Moreover, it is often a judgment that streamlined proceedings and expeditious results will best serve their needs that cause parties to agree to arbitrate their disputes; it is typically a desire to keep the effort and expense required to resolve a dispute within manageable bounds that prompts them mutually to forgo access to judicial remedies. In sum, the factor of potential complexity alone does not persuade us that an arbitral tribunal could not properly handle an antitrust matter.

For similar reasons, we also reject the proposition that an arbitration panel will pose too great a danger of innate hostility to the constraints on business conduct that antitrust law imposes. International arbitrators frequently are drawn from the legal as well as the business community; where the dispute has an important legal component, the parties and the arbitral body with whose assistance they have agreed to settle their dispute can be expected to select arbitrators accordingly.[18] We decline to indulge the presumption that the parties and arbitral body conducting a proceeding will be unable or unwilling to retain competent, conscientious, and impartial arbitrators.

We are left, then, with the core of the *American Safety* doctrine—the fundamental importance to American democratic capitalism of the regime of the antitrust laws. Without doubt, the private cause of action plays a central role in enforcing this regime. As the Court of Appeals pointed out:

> "A claim under the antitrust laws is not merely a private matter. The Sherman Act is designed to promote the national interest in a

[18] * * * [T]he arbitration panel selected to hear the parties' claims here is composed of three Japanese lawyers, one a former law school dean, another a former judge, and the third a practicing attorney with American legal training who has written on Japanese antitrust law.

The Court of Appeals was concerned that international arbitrators would lack "experience with or exposure to our law and values." The obstacles confronted by the arbitration panel in this case, however, should be no greater than those confronted by any judicial or arbitral tribunal required to determine foreign law. See, e.g., Fed.Rule Civ.Proc. 44.1. Moreover, while our attachment to the antitrust laws may be stronger than most, many other countries, including Japan, have similar bodies of competition law.

> competitive economy; thus, the plaintiff asserting his rights under the Act has been likened to a private attorney-general who protects the public's interest."

The treble-damages provision wielded by the private litigant is a chief tool in the antitrust enforcement scheme, posing a crucial deterrent to potential violators.

The importance of the private damages remedy, however, does not compel the conclusion that it may not be sought outside an American court. Notwithstanding its important incidental policing function, the treble-damages cause of action conferred on private parties by § 4 of the Clayton Act, and pursued by Soler here by way of its third counterclaim, seeks primarily to enable an injured competitor to gain compensation for that injury.

> "Section 4 . . . is in essence a remedial provision. It provides treble damages to '[a]ny person who shall be injured in his business or property by reason of anything forbidden in the antitrust laws. . . .' Of course, treble damages also play an important role in penalizing wrongdoers and deterring wrongdoing, as we also have frequently observed. . . . It nevertheless is true that the treble-damages provision, which makes awards available only to injured parties, and measures the awards by a multiple of the injury actually proved, is designed primarily as a remedy." *Brunswick Corp. v. Pueblo Bowl-O-Mat, Inc.*, 429 U.S. 477, 485–486 (1977).

* * *

There is no reason to assume at the outset of the dispute that international arbitration will not provide an adequate mechanism. To be sure, the international arbitral tribunal owes no prior allegiance to the legal norms of particular states; hence, it has no direct obligation to vindicate their statutory dictates. The tribunal, however, is bound to effectuate the intentions of the parties. Where the parties have agreed that the arbitral body is to decide a defined set of claims which includes, as in these cases, those arising from the application of American antitrust law, the tribunal therefore should be bound to decide that dispute in accord with the national law giving rise to the claim.[19] And so long as the prospective litigant

---

[19] In addition to the clause providing for arbitration before the Japan Commercial Arbitration Association, the Sales Agreement includes a choice-of-law clause which reads: "This Agreement is made in, and will be governed by and construed in all respects according to the laws of the Swiss Confederation as if entirely performed therein." The United States raises the possibility that the arbitral panel will read this provision not simply to govern interpretation of the contract terms, but wholly to displace American law even where it otherwise would apply. Brief for United States as Amicus Curiae 20. The International Chamber of Commerce opines that it is "[c]onceivabl[e], although we believe it unlikely, [that] the arbitrators could consider Soler's affirmative claim of anti-competitive conduct by CISA and Mitsubishi to fall within the purview of this choice-of-law provision, with the result that it would be decided under Swiss law rather than U.S. Sherman Act." Brief for International Chamber of Commerce as Amicus Curiae 25. At oral argument, however, counsel for Mitsubishi conceded that American law applied to the antitrust claims and represented that the claims had been submitted to the arbitration panel in Japan on that basis. The record confirms that before the decision of the Court of Appeals the arbitral panel had taken these claims under submission.

We therefore have no occasion to speculate on this matter at this stage in the proceedings, when Mitsubishi seeks to enforce the agreement to arbitrate, not to enforce an award. Nor need we consider now the effect of an arbitral tribunal's failure to take cognizance of the statutory cause of action on the claimant's capacity to reinitiate suit in federal court. We merely note that in the event the choice-of-forum and choice-of-law clauses operated in tandem as a prospective waiver of a party's right to pursue statutory remedies for antitrust violations, we would have little hesitation in condemning the agreement as against public policy.

effectively may vindicate its statutory cause of action in the arbitral forum, the statute will continue to serve both its remedial and deterrent function.

Having permitted the arbitration to go forward, the national courts of the United States will have the opportunity at the award enforcement stage to ensure that the legitimate interest in the enforcement of the antitrust laws has been addressed. The Convention reserves to each signatory country the right to refuse enforcement of an award where the "recognition or enforcement of the award would be contrary to the public policy of that country." Art. V(2)(b). While the efficacy of the arbitral process requires that substantive review at the award-enforcement stage remains minimal, it would not require intrusive inquiry to ascertain that the tribunal took cognizance of the antitrust claims and actually decided them.[20]

As international trade has expanded in recent decades, so too has the use of international arbitration to resolve disputes arising in the course of that trade. The controversies that international arbitral institutions are called upon to resolve have increased in diversity as well as in complexity. Yet the potential of these tribunals for efficient disposition of legal disagreements arising from commercial relations has not yet been tested. If they are to take a central place in the international legal order, national courts will need to "shake off the old judicial hostility to arbitration," and also their customary and understandable unwillingness to cede jurisdiction of a claim arising under domestic law to a foreign or transnational tribunal. To this extent, at least, it will be necessary for national courts to subordinate domestic notions of arbitrability to the international policy favoring commercial arbitration.

Accordingly, we "require this representative of the American business community to honor its bargain," by holding this agreement to arbitrate "enforce[able] . . . in accord with the explicit provisions of the Arbitration Act."

The judgment of the Court of Appeals is affirmed in part and reversed in part, and the cases are remanded for further proceedings consistent with this opinion.

■ JUSTICE STEVENS, with whom JUSTICE BRENNAN joins, and with whom JUSTICE MARSHALL joins except as to Part II, dissenting.

One element of this rather complex litigation is a claim asserted by an American dealer in Plymouth automobiles that two major automobile companies are parties to an international cartel that has restrained competition in the American market. Pursuant to an agreement that is alleged to have violated § 1 of the Sherman Act, those companies allegedly prevented the dealer from transshipping some 966 surplus vehicles from Puerto Rico to other dealers in the American market.

The petitioner denies the truth of the dealer's allegations and takes the position that the validity of the antitrust claim must be resolved by an arbitration tribunal in Tokyo, Japan. Largely because the auto manufacturers' defense to the

---

[20] See n. 19, supra. We note, for example, that the rules of the Japan Commercial Arbitration Association provide for the taking of a "summary record" of each hearing, for the stenographic recording of the proceedings where the tribunal so orders or a party requests one, and for a statement of reasons for the award unless the parties agree otherwise.* * *

antitrust allegation is based on provisions in the dealer's franchise agreement, the Court of Appeals concluded that the arbitration clause in that agreement encompassed the antitrust claim. * * *

* * * Because I am convinced that the Court of Appeals' construction of the arbitration clause is erroneous, and because I strongly disagree with this Court's interpretation of the relevant federal statutes, I respectfully dissent. In my opinion, (1) a fair construction of the language in the arbitration clause in the parties' contract does not encompass a claim that auto manufacturers entered into a conspiracy in violation of the antitrust laws; (2) an arbitration clause should not normally be construed to cover a statutory remedy that it does not expressly identify; (3) Congress did not intend § 2 of the Federal Arbitration Act to apply to antitrust claims; and (4) Congress did not intend the Convention on the Recognition and Enforcement of Foreign Arbitral Awards to apply to disputes that are not covered by the Federal Arbitration Act.

* * *

Until today all of our cases enforcing agreements to arbitrate under the Arbitration Act have involved contract claims. * * * [T]his is the first time the Court has considered the question whether a standard arbitration clause referring to claims arising out of or relating to a contract should be construed to cover statutory claims that have only an indirect relationship to the contract. In my opinion, neither the Congress that enacted the Arbitration Act in 1925, nor the many parties who have agreed to such standard clauses, could have anticipated the Court's answer to that question.

* * *

In view of the Court's repeated recognition of the distinction between federal statutory rights and contractual rights, together with the undisputed historical fact that arbitration has functioned almost entirely in either the area of labor disputes or in "ordinary disputes between merchants as to questions of fact," it is reasonable to assume that most lawyers and executives would not expect the language in the standard arbitration clause to cover federal statutory claims. Thus, in my opinion, both a fair respect for the importance of the interests that Congress has identified as worthy of federal statutory protection, and a fair appraisal of the most likely understanding of the parties who sign agreements containing standard arbitration clauses, support a presumption that such clauses do not apply to federal statutory claims.

* * *

It was Chief Justice Hughes who characterized the Sherman Anti-Trust Act as "a charter of freedom" that may fairly be compared to a constitutional provision. * * * More recently, the Court described the weighty public interests underlying the basic philosophy of the statute:

> "Antitrust laws in general, and the Sherman Act in particular, are the Magna Carta of free enterprise. They are important to the preservation of economic freedom and our free-enterprise system as the Bill of Rights is to the protection of our fundamental personal freedoms. And the

> freedoms guaranteed each and every business, no matter how small, is the freedom to compete—to assert with vigor, imagination, devotion, and ingenuity whatever economic muscle it can muster." * * * *United States v. Topco Associates, Inc.*, 405 U.S. 596, 610 (1972).

The Sherman and Clayton Acts reflect Congress' appraisal of the value of economic freedom; they guarantee the vitality of the entrepreneurial spirit. Questions arising under these Acts are among the most important in public law.

The unique public interest in the enforcement of the antitrust laws is repeatedly reflected in the special remedial scheme enacted by Congress. Since its enactment in 1890, the Sherman Act has provided for public enforcement through criminal as well as civil sanctions.

* * *

The provision for mandatory treble damages—unique in federal law when the statute was enacted—provides a special incentive to the private enforcement of the statute, as well as an especially powerful deterrent to violators. What we have described as "the public interest in vigilant enforcement of antitrust laws through the instrumentality of the private treble damage action" is buttressed by the statutory mandate that the injured party also recover costs, "including a reasonable attorney's fee." The interest in wide and effective enforcement has thus, for almost a century, been vindicated by enlisting the assistance of "private Attorneys General"; we have always attached special importance to their role because "[e]very violation of the antitrust laws is a blow to the free-enterprise system envisaged by Congress."

There are, in addition, several unusual features of the antitrust enforcement scheme that unequivocally require rejection of any thought that Congress would tolerate private arbitration of antitrust claims in lieu of the statutory remedies that it fashioned. * * * [A]n antitrust treble damage case "can only be brought in a District Court of the United States." The determination that these cases are "too important to be decided otherwise than by competent tribunals" surely cannot allow private arbitrators to assume a jurisdiction that is denied to courts of the sovereign States.

* * *

Arbitration awards are only reviewable for manifest disregard of the law, and the rudimentary procedures which make arbitration so desirable in the context of a private dispute often mean that the record is so inadequate that the arbitrator's decision is virtually unreviewable.[31] Despotic decision making of this kind is fine for parties who are willing to agree in advance to settle for a best approximation of the correct result in order to resolve quickly and inexpensively any contractual dispute that may arise in an ongoing commercial relationship. Such informality, however, is simply unacceptable when every error may have devastating consequences for

[31] The arbitration procedure in this case does not provide any right to evidentiary discovery or a written decision, and requires that all proceedings be closed to the public. Moreover, Japanese arbitrators do not have the power of compulsory process to secure witnesses and documents, nor do witnesses who are available testify under oath. Cf. [FAA] § 7 (arbitrators may summon witnesses to attend proceedings and seek enforcement in a district court).

important businesses in our national economy and may undermine their ability to compete in world markets.[32] Instead of "muffling a grievance in the cloakroom of arbitration," the public interest in free competitive markets would be better served by having the issues resolved "in the light of impartial public court adjudication."

* * *

In my opinion, the elected representatives of the American people would not have us dispatch an American citizen to a foreign land in search of an uncertain remedy for the violation of a public right that is protected by the Sherman Act. This is especially so when there has been no genuine bargaining over the terms of the submission, and the arbitration remedy provided has not even the most elementary guarantees of fair process. Consideration of a fully developed record by a jury, instructed in the law by a federal judge, and subject to appellate review, is a surer guide to the competitive character of a commercial practice than the practically unreviewable judgment of a private arbitrator.

Unlike the Congress that enacted the Sherman Act in 1890, the Court today does not seem to appreciate the value of economic freedom. I respectfully dissent.

QUESTIONS TO REVIEW AND SYNTHESIZE

1. *Mitsubishi*'s first sentence uses the word "arbitrable" and *Mitsubishi* later says: "We now turn to consider whether Soler's antitrust claims are nonarbitrable even though it has agreed to arbitrate them." What do the words "arbitrable" and "nonarbitrable" mean here? Hint: *Mitsubishi* said "We might well have some doubt that even the courts following *American Safety* subscribe fully to the view that antitrust matters are inherently insusceptible to resolution by arbitration, as these same courts have agreed that an undertaking to arbitrate antitrust claims entered into after the dispute arises is acceptable."
2. Footnote 19 of *Mitsubishi* says "that in the event the choice-of-forum and choice-of-law clauses operated in tandem as a prospective waiver of a party's right to pursue statutory remedies for antitrust violations, we would have little hesitation in condemning the agreement as against public policy." What does this mean?
3. Footnote 19 also says the International Chamber of Commerce thought it "unlikely" the arbitrators would apply Swiss law in deciding Soler's antitrust claims. In contrast, a commentator said: "what is indeed very unlikely, to say the least, is that arbitrators would accept to apply U.S. antitrust law to claims to be ruled, according to [the] parties' clear will, by Swiss law!" Jacques Werner, A Swiss Comment on *Mitsubishi,* 3 J. of Int'l Arb. 81, 83 (1986). Should a court deciding whether to enforce a pre-dispute agreement to arbitrate antitrust claims be influenced by its prediction of whether the arbitrators will apply U.S. or Swiss law to such claims?

---

[32] The greatest risk, of course, is that the arbitrator will condemn business practices under the antitrust laws that are efficient in a free competitive market. In the absence of a reviewable record, a reviewing district court would not be able to undo the damage wrought. Even a Government suit or an action by a private party might not be available to set aside the award.

4. Justice Stevens' *Mitsubishi* dissent says:

(1) "Until today all of our cases enforcing agreements to arbitrate under the Arbitration Act have involved contract claims" and

(2):

> "Arbitration awards are only reviewable for manifest disregard of the law, and the rudimentary procedures which make arbitration so desirable in the context of a private dispute often mean that the record is so inadequate that the arbitrator's decision is virtually unreviewable. Despotic decision making of this kind is fine for parties who are willing to agree in advance to settle for a best approximation of the correct result in order to resolve quickly and inexpensively any contractual dispute that may arise in an ongoing commercial relationship. Such informality, however, is simply unacceptable when every error may have devastating consequences for important businesses in our national economy and may undermine their ability to compete in world markets. Instead of muffling a grievance in the cloakroom of arbitration, the public interest in free competitive markets would be better served by having the issues resolved in the light of impartial public court adjudication."

What ties these two points together?

Two years after *Mitsubishi*, the Supreme Court's decision in *Shearson/American Express, Inc. v. McMahon*, 482 U.S. 220 (1987), enforced a pre-dispute agreement to arbitrate a customer's claims against a securities broker under the Securities Exchange Act and the Securities and Exchange Commission's Rule 10b-5. Justice O'Connor's opinion of the Court—joined by Chief Justice Rehnquist and Justices White, Powell, and Scalia—reached this conclusion by relying heavily on *Mitsubishi,* noting that "the mistrust of arbitration that formed the basis for the *Wilko* opinion in 1953 is difficult to square with the assessment of arbitration that has prevailed since that time." McMahon, 482 U.S. at 233. The *McMahon* Court pointed to the fact that the SEC had specifically approved the arbitration procedures of the various stock exchanges and has exercised its "oversight authority" to ensure that the procedures of the exchanges "adequately protect statutory rights." Id. at 233–234. Nor were arbitration agreements made unenforceable by § 29(a) of the Securities Exchange Act, which prohibits any agreement by which a party undertakes "to waive compliance with any provision of [the Act]." The *McMahon* Court said that by "agreeing to arbitrate a statutory claim, a party does not forego the substantive rights afforded by the statute; it only submits to their resolution in an arbitral, rather than a judicial, forum." Id. at 229–230.

In addition, *McMahon* held that claims under the Racketeer Influenced and Corrupt Organizations Act ("RICO") were also subject to arbitration under a pre-dispute arbitration clause. "RICO" makes it unlawful to use any money derived "from a pattern of racketeering activity" in the operation of an interstate enterprise.[3] As Justice O'Connor noted in *McMahon,* the scope of RICO has been dramatically extended far beyond the activities of "the archetypal, intimidating mobster," to reach ordinary business disputes involving "respected and legitimate" enterprises.[4] The RICO statute

---

[3] 18 U.S.C.A. § 1961.

[4] Racketeering activity" under the statute is defined as the violation of certain predicate statutes—for example, those dealing with bribery and narcotics sales, but also including "mail fraud" and "fraud in the sale

follows the model of the antitrust laws in giving a private cause of action, including the right to attorney's fees and treble damages, to persons injured by such conduct. "Although the holding in *Mitsubishi* was limited to the international context, much of its reasoning is equally applicable here." 482 U.S. at 239. Dissenting from portions of *McMahon* were Justices Blackmun, Brennan, Marshall, and Stevens.

While *McMahon* did not expressly overrule *Wilko v. Swan,* it did not take long for the Supreme Court to give *Wilko* a formal burial: In *Rodriguez de Quijas v. Shearson/American Express, Inc.*, 490 U.S. 477 (1989), the Court held that claims under the Securities Act of 1933 were also arbitrable where the parties had entered into a pre-dispute arbitration agreement. Dissenting were Justices Blackmun, Brennan, Marshall, and Stevens.

QUESTIONS TO REVIEW AND SYNTHESIZE

1. Does FAA § 10 support the *McMahon* Court's statement that by "agreeing to arbitrate a statutory claim, a party does not forego the substantive rights afforded by the statute; it only submits to their resolution in an arbitral, rather than a judicial, forum"?
2. The Supreme Court's 1980s overruling of *Wilko* occurred gradually in cases of international (*Mitsubishi*) and overseen-by-the-SEC-securities (*McMahon* and *Rodriguez de Quijas*) arbitration. What about the international and securities contexts eased the Court's path to overruling *Wilko*? See sections 2.A.4 and 2.B.
3. *Wilko* was decided by a Supreme Court entirely comprised of justices appointed by Presidents Franklin Roosevelt and Harry Truman—Democrats who led the New Deal response to the Great Depression, including the Securities Act at issue in *Wilko*, and the U.S. Government's enormous role in winning World War II. In what respects do *Wilko*'s holding and reasoning fit prevailing ideological and political views of its mid-20th-century era?
4. The Supreme Court's 1980s overruling of *Wilko* occurred—not long after the Vietnam War, Watergate, 1970s "stagflation,"[5] and the Iran Hostage Crisis—in the Reagan-Bush era of economic deregulation. In what respects do the holdings and reasoning of *Mitsubishi*, *McMahon*, and *Rodriguez de Quijas* fit prevailing ideological and political views of their era?

3. LABOR AND EMPLOYMENT

a. OVERVIEW

Chapter 2 contrasted *labor* arbitration (arising out of a labor union's collective bargaining agreement) with *employment* arbitration (arising out of an individual's employment agreement), as well as with *commercial* arbitration. Before employment arbitration grew in the 1980s and 1990s, one could comfortably speak

---

of securities"; a "pattern" of such activity is found when at least two such violations occur within a period of ten years.

[5] The 1970s combination of slow economic growth and high inflation ("stagflation") reduced confidence in government's ability to manage the economy. See, e.g., Paul Krugman, *The stagflation myth*, N.Y. Times blog, June 3, 2009, https://krugman.blogs.nytimes.com/2009/06/03/the-stagflation-myth/ ("The era of stagflation in America [which] began in 1974 and ended in the early 80s * * * was a win for conservative economics.")

of labor and commercial arbitration as the two main types of arbitration in the U.S., and the Supreme Court viewed them as quite distinct from each other. In 1960, for instance, the Court said in a landmark labor arbitration case that "[i]n the commercial case, arbitration is the substitute for litigation. Here arbitration is the substitute for industrial strife" so "the run of [commercial] arbitration cases becomes irrelevant to our problem." United Steelworkers of America v. Warrior & Gulf Navigation Co., 363 U.S. 574, 578 (1960).

The following pages begin with labor arbitration cases from this older era in which *Wilko* (1953) had not yet been superseded by *Mitsubishi* (1985), *McMahon* (1987), and *Rodriguez de Quijas* (1989). Then we discuss a 1991 Supreme Court case that put employment arbitration in the newer era of enforcing pre-dispute agreements to arbitrate statutory claims, and the 2009 Supreme Court case that brought labor arbitration into the post-*Mitsubishi* mainstream by enforcing a collective bargaining agreement's provision for the arbitration of statutory claims.

b. PRE-*MITSUBISHI* CASES

The collective bargaining agreement in *Alexander v. Gardner-Denver Co.*, 415 U.S. 36 (1974), protected employees from discharge without "just cause," and also prohibited "discrimination against any employee on account of race." After being fired, an employee claimed at an arbitration hearing that his discharge was the result of racial discrimination. The arbitrator made no explicit reference to the racial discrimination claim but found that the employee had been fired for "just cause," and denied the grievance (labor arbitration's word for "claim"). The employee then sued the employer, alleging that his discharge was in violation of Title VII of the Civil Rights Act of 1964, which makes it an "unlawful employment practice" to "fail or refuse to hire or to discharge any individual, or otherwise to discriminate against any individual with respect to his compensation, terms, conditions, or privileges of employment, because of such individual's race, color, religion, sex, or national origin."[6] The district court granted the employer's motion for summary judgment, finding "that the claim of racial discrimination had been submitted to the arbitrator and resolved adversely" to the employee: having "voluntarily elected to pursue his grievance to final arbitration under the nondiscrimination clause of the collective bargaining agreement," the employee "was bound by the arbitral decision and thereby precluded from suing his employer under Title VII." Before the Supreme Court, the employer argued that federal courts should defer to arbitral decisions on discrimination claims, at least "where (i) the claim was before the arbitrator; (ii) the collective-bargaining agreement prohibited the form of discrimination charged in the suit under Title VII; and (iii) the arbitrator has authority to rule on the claim and to fashion a remedy."

The Supreme Court, however, rejected this argument and reversed. Justice Powell's opinion for a unanimous Court said:

> The purpose and procedures of Title VII indicate that Congress intended federal courts to exercise final responsibility for enforcement of Title VII; deferral to arbitral decisions would be inconsistent with that goal. * * *

[6] 42 U.S.C. § 2000e–2(a)(1).

> [The employer's] deferral rule is necessarily premised on the assumption that arbitral processes are commensurate with judicial processes and that Congress impliedly intended federal courts to defer to arbitral decisions on Title VII issues. We deem this supposition unlikely.

Gardner-Denver was followed by two other important cases, also dealing with the effects of an arbitral award on the statutory rights of employees under a collective bargaining agreement. In *Barrentine v. Arkansas-Best Freight System, Inc.*, 450 U.S. 728 (1981), an employee had unsuccessfully submitted wage claims to arbitration. Justice Brennan's opinion for the Court held that this did not preclude a later suit, based on the same underlying facts, alleging a violation of the minimum wage provisions of the Fair Labor Standards Act (FLSA). However, foreshadowing the Court's later more conservative direction, a dissent by Chief Justice Burger (with Justice Rehnquist joining) said that while FLSA rights may not be waived, it is a:

> a totally different-proposition to say that employees and employers may not agree to a means of enforcing the employees' routine wage claims outside the costly, cumbersome judicial process of the federal courts and, specifically, that employees, acting through their union in an arm's-length negotiation with the employer, may not bind themselves—as the petitioners did here—to submit to final and binding arbitration "any controversy that might arise." rather than resolve it through litigation in the federal courts. The existence of a right and the provision of a judicial forum do not necessarily make either nonwaivable; if that were so, all the holdings of this Court and countless decisions of federal and state courts that parties are bound by contracts to arbitrate are placed in doubt.

Barrentine v. Arkansas-Best Freight Sys., Inc., 450 U.S. 728, 746–47 (1981) (Burger, C.J., dissenting).

In *McDonald v. City of West Branch*, 466 U.S. 284 (1984), a police officer was discharged by a city and filed a grievance pursuant to the city's collective bargaining agreement. Here too the arbitrator ruled against him, finding that there was "just cause" for the discharge. McDonald did not challenge the award, but later filed an action against the city under 42 U.S.C. § 1983 (imposing liability on any person who "under color of" state law deprives another "of any rights, privileges, or immunities secured by the Constitution and laws" of the United States; McDonald alleged that he had been discharged for exercising his First Amendment rights.) The court of appeals concluded that McDonald's First Amendment claims were barred by claim preclusion (res judicata) and issue preclusion (collateral estoppel) due to the arbitrator's ruling for the employer. But the Supreme Court, relying heavily on *Gardner-Denver,* reversed: While "arbitration is well suited to resolving contractual disputes," *McDonald* said, arbitration cannot in a § 1983 action "provide an adequate substitute for a judicial trial. Consequently, according preclusive effect to arbitration awards in § 1983 actions would severely undermine the protection of federal rights that the statute is designed to provide."

Justice Brennan's opinion for a unanimous *McDonald* Court buttressed this conclusion by pointing to a number of characteristics of arbitration. Noting first that "many arbitrators are not lawyers," the Court suggested that:

> [A]n arbitrator's expertise "pertains primarily to the law of the shop, not the law of the land." An arbitrator may not, therefore, have the expertise required to resolve the complex legal questions that arise in § 1983 actions.
>
> Second, because an arbitrator's authority derives solely from the contract, an arbitrator may not have the authority to enforce § 1983. As we explained in *Gardner-Denver:* "The arbitrator . . . has no general authority to invoke public laws that conflict with the bargain between the parties. . . . If an arbitral decision is based 'solely upon the arbitrator's view of the requirements of enacted legislation,' rather than on an interpretation of the collective-bargaining agreement, the arbitrator has 'exceeded the scope of the submission,' and the award will not be enforced." * * *
>
> Third, when, as is usually the case, the union has exclusive control over the "manner and extent to which an individual grievance is presented," there is an additional reason why arbitration is an inadequate substitute for judicial proceedings. The union's interests and those of the individual employee are not always identical or even compatible. As a result, the union may present the employee's grievance less vigorously, or make different strategic choices, than would the employee. Thus, were an arbitration award accorded preclusive effect, an employee's opportunity to be compensated for a constitutional deprivation might be lost merely because it was not in the union's interest to press his claim vigorously.
>
> Finally, arbitral factfinding is generally not equivalent to judicial factfinding. * * * The record of the arbitration proceedings is not as complete; the usual rules of evidence do not apply; and rights and procedures common to civil trials, such as discovery, compulsory process, cross-examination, and testimony under oath, are often severely limited or unavailable.

Even though an arbitral award would not preclude a later action by the employee, the Court nevertheless suggested that the award might still be admitted as evidence in the lawsuit. The weight to be given the award "must be determined in the court's discretion with regard to the facts and circumstances of each case":

> Relevant factors include the existence of provisions in the collective-bargaining agreement that conform substantially with [the statute or Constitution], the degree of procedural fairness in the arbitral forum, adequacy of the record with respect to the issue [in the judicial proceeding], and the special competence of particular arbitrators. Where an arbitral determination gives full consideration to an employee's [statutory or constitutional] rights, a court may properly accord it great weight. This is especially true where the issue is solely one of fact, specifically addressed by the parties and decided by the arbitrator on the basis of an adequate record.

The three cases just mentioned—*Gardner-Denver* (1974), *Barrentine* (1981), and *McDonald* (1984)—preceded *Mitsubishi* (1985) and arose out of unions' collective bargaining agreements rather than employers' contracts with individual employees not represented by a union. These two facts help contextualize the law's change of direction in *Gilmer v. Interstate/Johnson Lane Corporation*, 500 U.S. 20 (1991).

c. POST-*MITSUBISHI* CASES

Gilmer involved an individual employee who was hired as a "Manager of Financial Services" by a securities broker, and was required to register as a securities representative with the New York Stock Exchange; NYSE rules at the time required the arbitration of any dispute "arising out of the employment or termination of employment" of registered representatives. Gilmer later brought suit against his employer alleging that he had been discharged in violation of the Age Discrimination in Employment Act of 1967 (ADEA), 290 U.S.C. § 621. The Supreme Court relied on *Mitsubishi, McMahon,* and *Rodriguez de Quijas* to compel arbitration of the employee's claim. The *Gilmer* Court repeated *McMahon*'s statement that "[b]y agreeing to arbitrate a statutory claim, a party does not forgo the substantive rights afforded by the statute; it only submits to their resolution in an arbitral, rather than a judicial, forum." Again, the Court stressed that "generalized attacks" on arbitration— arguments that the arbitration process may not adequately permit vindication of the claimant's statutory rights—rested on an unwarranted "suspicion of arbitration," and were "far out of step with our current strong endorsement of the federal statutes favoring this method of resolving disputes."

For example, while it is true that discovery permitted in arbitration is more limited than in the federal courts, the Court found it "unlikely"

> that age discrimination claims require more extensive discovery than other claims that we have found to be arbitrable, such as RICO and antitrust claims. Moreover, there has been no showing in this case that the NYSE discovery provisions, which allow for document production, information requests, depositions, and subpoenas, will prove insufficient to allow ADEA claimants such as Gilmer a fair opportunity to present their claims. Although those procedures might not be as extensive as in the federal courts, by agreeing to arbitrate, a party "trades the procedures and opportunity for review of the courtroom for the simplicity, informality, and expedition of arbitration." Indeed, an important counterweight to the reduced discovery in NYSE arbitration is that arbitrators are not bound by the rules of evidence.

Gilmer, 500 U.S. at 31. Nor was the Court persuaded by the contention that "there often will be unequal bargaining power between employers and employees.":

> Mere inequality in bargaining power * * * is not a sufficient reason to hold that arbitration agreements are never enforceable in the employment context. Relationships between securities dealers and investors, for example, may involve unequal bargaining power, but we nevertheless held in *Rodriguez de Quijas* and *McMahon* that agreements to arbitrate in that context are enforceable. * * * There is no indication in this case * * * that Gilmer, an experienced businessman, was coerced or defrauded into agreeing to the arbitration clause in his registration application. As with

> the claimed procedural inadequacies discussed above, this claim of unequal bargaining power is best left for resolution in specific cases.

Gilmer, 500 U.S. at 33. A dissenting opinion from *Gilmer* was filed by Justice Stevens and joined by Justice Marshall. It objected that the majority had disregarded "any concern about the inequality of bargaining power between an entire industry, on the one hand, and an individual customer or employee, on the other," and said:

> When the FAA was passed in 1925, I doubt that any legislator who voted for it expected it to apply to statutory claims, to form contracts between parties of unequal bargaining power, or to the arbitration of disputes arising out of the employment relationship. In recent years, however, the Court "has effectively rewritten the statute", and abandoned its earlier view that statutory claims were not appropriate subjects for arbitration.

Gilmer v. Interstate/Johnson Lane Corp., 500 U.S. 20, 42–43, 111 S. Ct. 1647, 1661, 114 L. Ed. 2d 26 (1991) (Stevens, J., dissenting).

Since *Gilmer*, courts have routinely enforced employment arbitration agreements with respect to a wide variety of statutory discrimination claims. See, e.g., EEOC v. Luce, Forward, Hamilton & Scripps, 345 F.3d 742 (9th Cir. 2003) (district court enjoined law firm from requiring job applicants to agree to arbitrate Title VII claims and from enforcing existing agreements to arbitrate those claims; held, reversed; "the view that compulsory arbitration weakens Title VII conflicts with the Supreme Court's stated position that arbitration affects only the choice of forum, not substantive rights").

How could *Gilmer* be distinguished from earlier cases like *Alexander v. Gardner-Denver* and its progeny? Most notably, the *Gilmer* Court pointed out that the arbitration in the earlier employment discrimination cases occurred in the context of a collective-bargaining agreement—where the claimants were represented by their unions in the arbitration proceedings. So "an important concern [was] the tension between collective representation and individual statutory rights, a concern not applicable to the present case." Gilmer, 500 U.S. at 35.

The relationship between *Gilmer* and *Gardner-Denver* was revisited—although inconclusively—by the Supreme Court in *Wright v. Universal Maritime Service Corp.*, 525 U.S. 70 (1998). Here, an employee subject to a collective bargaining agreement filed suit alleging an employer's violation of the Americans with Disability Act of 1990. The Supreme Court acknowledged that there was "obviously some tension between these two lines of cases." The employee's contention—that "federal forum rights" could not be traded away in union-negotiated collective bargaining agreements, even if they could in individually executed contracts—"assuredly finds support in the text of *Gilmer*." The employer, on the other hand, argued that *Gilmer* "has sufficiently undermined *Gardner-Denver*" that henceforth a union too should be able to trade away an employee's right to litigate a statutory claim. The Court found it "unnecessary to resolve" this question: for "*Gardner-Denver* at least stands for the proposition that the right to a federal judicial forum is of sufficient importance to be protected against less-than-explicit union waiver in a [collective bargaining agreement]." Matters which "go beyond the interpretation and application of contract terms"—like the meaning of a federal statute—will not be *presumed* to be arbitrable, but any such requirement in a collective bargaining agreement must instead be "*particularly clear.*" And because the agreement in *Wright* could not meet such a standard, the employer's attempt to compel arbitration was denied by the Court. In *Gilmer*, by contrast—since it involved "an individual's waiver of his own rights, rather than a union's waiver of the rights of represented employees"—such a "clear and unmistakable" standard did not apply.

14 Penn Plaza LLC v. Pyett

Supreme Court of the United States, 2009.
556 U.S. 247, 129 S.Ct. 1456, 173 L.Ed.2d 398.

■ JUSTICE THOMAS delivered the opinion of the Court.

The question presented by this case is whether a provision in a collective-bargaining agreement that clearly and unmistakably requires union members to arbitrate claims arising under the Age Discrimination in Employment Act of 1967 (ADEA), 81 Stat. 602, as amended, 29 U.S.C. § 621 *et seq.*, is enforceable. The United States Court of Appeals for the Second Circuit held that this Court's decision in *Alexander* v. *Gardner-Denver Co.*, 415 U.S. 36, 94 S. Ct. 1011, 39 L. Ed. 2d 147 (1974), forbids enforcement of such arbitration provisions. We disagree and reverse the judgment of the Court of Appeals.

Respondents are members of the Service Employees International Union, Local 32BJ (Union). Under the National Labor Relations Act (NLRA), as amended, the Union is the exclusive bargaining representative of employees within the building-services industry in New York City * * *. Since the 1930's, the Union has engaged in industry wide collective bargaining with the Realty Advisory Board on Labor Relations, Inc. (RAB), a multiemployer bargaining association for the New York City real-estate industry. The agreement between the Union and the RAB is embodied in their Collective Bargaining Agreement for Contractors and Building Owners (CBA). The CBA requires union members to submit all claims of employment discrimination to binding arbitration under the CBA's grievance and dispute resolution procedures:

> "30. NO DISCRIMINATION "There shall be no discrimination against any present or future employee by reason of race, creed, color, age, disability, national origin, sex, union membership, or any characteristic protected by law, including, but not limited to, claims made pursuant to Title VII of the Civil Rights Act, the Americans with Disabilities Act, the Age Discrimination in Employment Act, the New York State Human Rights Law, the New York City Human Rights Code, . . . or any other similar laws, rules, or regulations. All such claims shall be subject to the grievance and arbitration procedure (Articles V and VI) as the sole and exclusive remedy for violations. Arbitrators shall apply appropriate law in rendering decisions based upon claims of discrimination."

Petitioner 14 Penn Plaza LLC is a member of the RAB. It owns and operates the New York City office building where, prior to August 2003, respondents worked as night lobby watchmen and in other similar capacities. Respondents were directly employed by petitioner Temco Service Industries, Inc. (Temco), a maintenance service and cleaning contractor. In August 2003, with the Union's consent, 14 Penn Plaza engaged Spartan Security, a unionized security services contractor and affiliate of Temco, to provide licensed security guards to staff the lobby and entrances of its building. Because this rendered respondents' lobby services unnecessary, Temco reassigned them to jobs as night porters and light-duty cleaners in other locations in the building. Respondents contend that these reassignments led to a loss in income, caused them emotional distress, and were otherwise less desirable than their former positions.

At respondents' request, the Union filed grievances challenging the reassignments. The grievances alleged that petitioners: (1) violated the CBA's ban on workplace discrimination by reassigning respondents on account of their age; (2) violated seniority rules by failing to promote one of the respondents to a handyman position; and (3) failed to equitably rotate overtime. After failing to obtain relief on any of these claims through the grievance process, the Union requested arbitration under the CBA.

After the initial arbitration hearing, the Union withdrew the first set of respondents' grievances—the age-discrimination claims—from arbitration. * * * But the Union continued to arbitrate the seniority and overtime claims, and, after several hearings, the claims were denied.

In May 2004, while the arbitration was ongoing but after the Union withdrew the age-discrimination claims, respondents filed a complaint with the Equal Employment Opportunity Commission (EEOC) alleging that petitioners had violated their rights under the ADEA. Approximately one month later, the EEOC issued a Dismissal and Notice of Rights, which explained that the agency's "'review of the evidence . . . fail[ed] to indicate that a violation ha[d] occurred,'" and notified each respondent of his right to sue.

Respondents thereafter filed suit against petitioners in the United States District Court for the Southern District of New York, alleging that their reassignment violated the ADEA and state and local laws prohibiting age discrimination. Petitioners filed a motion to compel arbitration of respondents' claims pursuant to §§ 3 and 4 of the Federal Arbitration Act (FAA). The District Court denied the motion because under Second Circuit precedent, "even a clear and unmistakable union-negotiated waiver of a right to litigate certain federal and state statutory claims in a judicial forum is unenforceable." * * *

The Court of Appeals affirmed. According to the Court of Appeals, it could not compel arbitration of the dispute because *Gardner-Denver*, which "remains good law," held "that a collective bargaining agreement could not waive covered workers' rights to a judicial forum for causes of action created by Congress." The Court of Appeals observed that the *Gardner-Denver* decision was in tension with this Court's more recent decision in *Gilmer* v. *Interstate/Johnson Lane Corp.*, which "held that an individual employee who had agreed individually to waive his right to a federal forum *could* be compelled to arbitrate a federal age discrimination claim." The Court of Appeals also noted that this Court previously declined to resolve this tension in *Wright* v. *Universal Maritime Service Corp.*, where the waiver at issue was not "clear and unmistakable."

The Court of Appeals attempted to reconcile *Gardner-Denver* and *Gilmer* by holding that arbitration provisions in a collective-bargaining agreement, "which purport to waive employees' rights to a federal forum with respect to statutory claims, are unenforceable." As a result, an individual employee would be free to choose compulsory arbitration under *Gilmer*, but a labor union could not collectively bargain for arbitration on behalf of its members. We granted certiorari, to address the issue left unresolved in *Wright*, which continues to divide the Courts of Appeals, and now reverse.

The NLRA governs federal labor-relations law. As permitted by that statute, respondents designated the Union as their "exclusive representativ[e] . . . for the purposes of collective bargaining in respect to rates of pay, wages, hours of employment, or other conditions of employment." As the employees' exclusive bargaining representative, the Union "enjoys broad authority . . . in the negotiation and administration of [the] collective bargaining contract." But this broad authority "is accompanied by a responsibility of equal scope, the responsibility and duty of fair representation." The employer has a corresponding duty under the NLRA to bargain in good faith "with the representatives of his employees" on wages, hours, and conditions of employment.

In this instance, the Union and the RAB, negotiating on behalf of 14 Penn Plaza, collectively bargained in good faith and agreed that employment-related discrimination claims, including claims brought under the ADEA, would be resolved in arbitration. This freely negotiated term between the Union and the RAB easily qualifies as a "conditio[n] of employment" that is subject to mandatory bargaining under § 159(a). The decision to fashion a collective bargaining agreement to require arbitration of employment-discrimination claims is no different from the many other decisions made by parties in designing grievance machinery.[5]

Respondents, however, contend that the arbitration clause here is outside the permissible scope of the collective-bargaining process because it affects the "employees' individual, non-economic statutory rights." We disagree. * * * As in any contractual negotiation, a union may agree to the inclusion of an arbitration provision in a collective-bargaining agreement in return for other concessions from the employer. Courts generally may not interfere in this bargained-for exchange. "Judicial nullification of contractual concessions . . . is contrary to what the Court has recognized as one of the fundamental policies of the National Labor Relations Act—freedom of contract."

As a result, the CBA's arbitration provision must be honored unless the ADEA itself removes this particular class of grievances from the NLRA's broad sweep. See Mitsubishi Motors Corp. v. Soler Chrysler-Plymouth, Inc. It does not. This Court has

[5] Justice Souter claims that this understanding is "impossible to square with our conclusion in [*Alexander* v.] *Gardner-Denver* that 'Title VII . . . stands on plainly different ground' from 'statutory rights related to collective activity': 'it concerns not majoritarian processes, but an individual's right to equal employment opportunities.'" As explained below, however, Justice Souter repeats the key analytical mistake made in *Gardner-Denver*'s dicta by equating the decision to arbitrate Title VII and ADEA claims to a decision to forgo these substantive guarantees against workplace discrimination. The right to a judicial forum is not the nonwaivable "substantive" right protected by the ADEA. Thus, although Title VII and ADEA rights may well stand on "different ground" than statutory rights that protect "majoritarian processes," *Gardner-Denver*, the voluntary decision to collectively bargain for arbitration does not deny those statutory antidiscrimination rights the full protection they are due.

squarely held that the ADEA does not preclude arbitration of claims brought under the statute. See *Gilmer*.

In *Gilmer,* the Court explained that "[a]lthough all statutory claims may not be appropriate for arbitration, '[h]aving made the bargain to arbitrate, the party should be held to it unless Congress itself has evinced an intention to preclude a waiver of judicial remedies for the statutory rights at issue.'" And "[i]f Congress intended the substantive protection afforded by the ADEA to include protection against waiver of the right to a judicial forum, that intention will be deducible from text or legislative history." The Court determined that "nothing in the text of the ADEA or its legislative history explicitly precludes arbitration." The Court also concluded that arbitrating ADEA disputes would not undermine the statute's "remedial and deterrent function." In the end, the employee's "generalized attacks" on "the adequacy of arbitration procedures" were "insufficient to preclude arbitration of statutory claims," because there was no evidence that "Congress, in enacting the ADEA, intended to preclude arbitration of claims under that Act".

The *Gilmer* Court's interpretation of the ADEA fully applies in the collective-bargaining context. Nothing in the law suggests a distinction between the status of arbitration agreements signed by an individual employee and those agreed to by a union representative. This Court has required only that an agreement to arbitrate statutory antidiscrimination claims be "explicitly stated" in the collective-bargaining agreement. *Wright*. The CBA under review here meets that obligation. Respondents incorrectly counter that an individual employee must personally "waive" a "[substantive] right" to proceed in court for a waiver to be "knowing and voluntary" under the ADEA. 29 U.S.C. § 626(f)(1). As explained below, however, the agreement to arbitrate ADEA claims is not the waiver of a "substantive right" as that term is employed in the ADEA. *Wright*. Indeed, if the "right" referred to in § 626(f)(1) included the prospective waiver of the right to bring an ADEA claim in court, even a waiver signed by an individual employee would be invalid as the statute also prevents individuals from "waiv[ing] rights or claims that may arise after the date the waiver is executed." § 626(f)(1)(C).

Examination of the two federal statutes at issue in this case, therefore, yields a straightforward answer to the question presented: The NLRA provided the Union and the RAB with statutory authority to collectively bargain for arbitration of workplace discrimination claims, and Congress did not terminate that authority with respect to federal age-discrimination claims in the ADEA. Accordingly, there is no legal basis for the Court to strike down the arbitration clause in this CBA, which was freely negotiated by the Union and the RAB, and which clearly and unmistakably requires respondents to arbitrate the age-discrimination claims at issue in this appeal. Congress has chosen to allow arbitration of ADEA claims. The Judiciary must respect that choice.

The CBA's arbitration provision is also fully enforceable under the *Gardner-Denver* line of cases. Respondents interpret *Gardner-Denver* and its progeny to hold that "a union cannot waive an employee's right to a judicial forum under the federal antidiscrimination statutes" because "allowing the union to waive this right would substitute the union's interests for the employee's antidiscrimination rights." The "combination of union control over the process and inherent conflict of interest with respect to discrimination claims," they argue, "provided the foundation for the Court's holding [in *Gardner-Denver*] that arbitration under a collective bargaining agreement could not preclude an individual employee's right to bring a lawsuit in court to vindicate a statutory discrimination claim." We disagree.

The holding of *Gardner-Denver* is not as broad as respondents suggest. The employee in that case was covered by a collective-bargaining agreement that prohibited "discrimination against any employee on account of race, color, religion, sex, national origin, or ancestry" and that guaranteed that "[n]o employee will be discharged . . . except for just cause." The agreement also included a "multistep grievance procedure" that culminated in compulsory arbitration for any "differences aris[ing] between the Company and the Union as to the meaning and application of the provisions of this Agreement" and "any trouble aris[ing] in the plant."

The employee was discharged for allegedly producing too many defective parts while working for the respondent as a drill operator. He filed a grievance with his union claiming that he was "'unjustly discharged'" in violation of the "'just cause'" provision within the collective-bargaining agreement. Then at the final prearbitration step of the grievance process, the employee added a claim that he was discharged because of his race.

The arbitrator ultimately ruled that the employee had been "'discharged for just cause,'" but "made no reference to [the] claim of racial discrimination." After obtaining a right-to-sue letter from the EEOC, the employee filed a claim in Federal District Court, alleging racial discrimination in violation of Title VII of the Civil Rights Act of 1964. The District Court issued a decision, affirmed by the Court of Appeals, which granted summary judgment to the employer because it concluded that "the claim of racial discrimination had been submitted to the arbitrator and resolved adversely to [the employee]." In the District Court's view, "having voluntarily elected to pursue his grievance to final arbitration under the nondiscrimination clause of the collective-bargaining agreement," the employee was "bound by the arbitral decision" and precluded from suing his employer on any other grounds, such as a statutory claim under Title VII.

This Court reversed the judgment on the narrow ground that the arbitration was not preclusive because the collective-bargaining agreement did not cover statutory claims. As a result, the lower courts erred in relying on the "doctrine of election of remedies" to bar the employee's Title VII claim. "That doctrine, which refers to situations where an individual pursues remedies that are legally or factually inconsistent" with each other, did not apply to the employee's dual pursuit of arbitration and a Title VII discrimination claim in district court. The employee's collective-bargaining agreement did not mandate arbitration of statutory antidiscrimination claims. "As the proctor of the bargain, the arbitrator's task is to effectuate the intent of the parties." Because the collective-bargaining agreement gave the arbitrator "authority to resolve only questions of contractual rights," his decision could not prevent the employee from bringing the Title VII claim in federal court "regardless of whether certain contractual rights are similar to, or duplicative of, the substantive rights secured by Title VII."

The Court also explained that the employee had not waived his right to pursue his Title VII claim in federal court by participating in an arbitration that was premised on the same underlying facts as the Title VII claim. Thus, whether the legal theory of preclusion advanced by the employer rested on "the doctrines of election of remedies" or was recast "as resting instead on the doctrine of equitable estoppel and on themes of res judicata and collateral estoppel," it could not prevail in light of the collective-bargaining agreement's failure to address arbitration of Title VII claims. "[W]e hold that the federal policy favoring arbitration does not establish that an arbitrator's resolution of a *contractual* claim is dispositive of a statutory claim under Title VII".

The Court's decisions following *Gardner-Denver* have not broadened its holding to make it applicable to the facts of this case. In *Barrentine* v. *Arkansas-Best Freight System, Inc.,* the Court considered "whether an employee may bring an action in federal district court, alleging a violation of the minimum wage provisions of the Fair Labor Standards Act, ... after having unsuccessfully submitted a wage claim based on the same underlying facts to a joint grievance committee pursuant to the provisions of his union's collective-bargaining agreement." The Court held that the unsuccessful arbitration did not preclude the federal lawsuit. Like the collective-bargaining agreement in *Gardner-Denver*, the arbitration provision under review in *Barrentine* did not expressly reference the statutory claim at issue. The Court thus reiterated that an "arbitrator's power is both derived from, and limited by, the collective-bargaining agreement" and "[h]is task is limited to construing the meaning of the collective-bargaining agreement so as to effectuate the collective intent of the parties."

McDonald v. *West Branch* was decided along similar lines. The question presented in that case was "whether a federal court may accord preclusive effect to an unappealed arbitration award in a case brought under [42 U.S.C. § 1983]." The Court declined to fashion such a rule, again explaining that "because an arbitrator's authority derives solely from the contract, *Barrentine*, an arbitrator may not have the authority to enforce § 1983" when that provision is left unaddressed by the arbitration agreement. Accordingly, as in both *Gardner-Denver* and *Barrentine*, the Court's decision in *McDonald* hinged on the scope of the collective-bargaining agreement and the arbitrator's parallel mandate.

The facts underlying *Gardner-Denver, Barrentine*, and *McDonald* reveal the narrow scope of the legal rule arising from that trilogy of decisions. Summarizing those opinions in *Gilmer*, this Court made clear that the *Gardner-Denver* line of cases "did not involve the issue of the enforceability of an agreement to arbitrate statutory claims." Those decisions instead "involved the quite different issue whether arbitration of contract-based claims precluded subsequent judicial resolution of statutory claims. Since the employees there had not agreed to arbitrate their statutory claims, and the labor arbitrators were not authorized to resolve such claims, the arbitration in those cases understandably was held not to preclude subsequent statutory actions."[7] *Gardner-Denver* and its progeny thus do not control the outcome where, as is the case here, the collective-bargaining agreement's arbitration provision expressly covers both statutory and contractual discrimination claims.[8]

We recognize that apart from their narrow holdings, the *Gardner-Denver* line of cases included broad dicta that were highly critical of the use of arbitration for the vindication of statutory antidiscrimination rights. That skepticism, however, rested on a misconceived view of arbitration that this Court has since abandoned.

First, the Court in *Gardner-Denver* erroneously assumed that an agreement to submit statutory discrimination claims to arbitration was tantamount to a waiver of those rights. See 415 U.S., at 51, 94 S. Ct. 1011, 39 L. Ed. 2d 147 ("[T]here can be no prospective *waiver* of an employee's rights under Title VII" (emphasis added)). For this reason, the Court stated, "the rights conferred [by Title VII] can form no part of the collective-bargaining process since waiver of these rights would defeat the paramount congressional purpose behind Title VII."

The Court was correct in concluding that federal antidiscrimination rights may not be prospectively waived, see 29 U.S.C. § 626(f)(1)(C); but it confused an agreement to arbitrate those statutory claims with a prospective waiver of the substantive right. The decision to resolve ADEA claims by way of arbitration instead of litigation does not waive the statutory right to be free from workplace age discrimination; it waives only the right to seek relief from a court in the first instance. See *Gilmer,* ("'[B]y agreeing to arbitrate a statutory claim, a party does not forgo the substantive rights afforded by the statute; it only submits to their resolution in an arbitral, rather than a judicial, forum'"). This "Court has been quite specific in holding that arbitration agreements can be enforced under the FAA without contravening the policies of congressional enactments giving employees specific protection against discrimination prohibited by federal law." *Circuit City Stores, Inc.* [excerpted in Section 3.C.3.b] The suggestion in *Gardner-Denver* that the decision to arbitrate statutory discrimination claims was tantamount to a substantive waiver of those rights, therefore, reveals a distorted understanding of the compromise made when an employee agrees to compulsory arbitration.

In this respect, *Gardner-Denver* is a direct descendant of the Court's decision in *Wilko* v. *Swan*, 346 U.S. 427, 74 S. Ct. 182, 98 L. Ed. 168 (1953), which held that

---

[7] Justice Souter's reliance on *Wright* v. *Universal Maritime Service Corp.*, to support its view of *Gardner-Denver* is misplaced. *Wright* identified the "tension" between the two lines of cases represented by *Gardner-Denver* and *Gilmer*, but found "it unnecessary to resolve the question of the validity of a union-negotiated waiver, since it [was] apparent . . . on the facts and arguments presented . . . that no such waiver [had] occurred." And although his dissent describes *Wright*'s characterization of *Gardner-Denver* as "raising a 'seemingly absolute prohibition of union waiver of employees' federal forum rights,'" it wrenches the statement out of context: "Although [the right to a judicial forum] is not a substantive right, see *Gilmer*], and *whether or not Gardner-Denver*'s seemingly absolute prohibition of union waiver of employees' federal forum rights *survives Gilmer, Gardner-Denver* at least stands for the proposition that the right to a federal judicial forum is of sufficient importance to be protected against less-than-explicit union waiver in a CBA". *Wright* therefore neither endorsed *Gardner-Denver*'s broad language nor suggested a particular result in this case.

[8] Because today's decision does not contradict the holding of *Gardner-Denver*, we need not resolve the *stare decisis* concerns raised by the dissenting opinions. But given the development of this Court's arbitration jurisprudence in the intervening years, *Gardner-Denver* would appear to be a strong candidate for overruling if the dissents' broad view of its holding were correct.

an agreement to arbitrate claims under the Securities Act of 1933 was unenforceable. The Court subsequently overruled *Wilko* and, in so doing, characterized the decision as "pervaded by . . . 'the old judicial hostility to arbitration.'" Rodriguez de Quijas v. Shearson/American Express, Inc., 490 U.S. 477, 480, 109 S. Ct. 1917, 104 L. Ed. 2d 526 (1989). The Court added: "To the extent that *Wilko* rested on suspicion of arbitration as a method of weakening the protections afforded in the substantive law to would-be complainants, it has fallen far out of step with our current strong endorsement of the federal statutes favoring this method of resolving disputes." Id.; see also Mitsubishi Motors Corp., supra, at 626–627, 105 S. Ct. 3346, 87 L. Ed. 2d 444 ("[W]e are well past the time when judicial suspicion of the desirability of arbitration and of the competence of arbitral tribunals inhibited the development of arbitration as an alternative means of dispute resolution"). The timeworn "mistrust of the arbitral process" harbored by the Court in *Gardner-Denver* thus weighs against reliance on anything more than its core holding. Indeed, in light of the "radical change, over two decades, in the Court's receptivity to arbitration," *Wright*, reliance on any judicial decision similarly littered with *Wilko*'s overt hostility to the enforcement of arbitration agreements would be ill advised.[9]

Second, *Gardner-Denver* mistakenly suggested that certain features of arbitration made it a forum "well suited to the resolution of contractual disputes," but "a comparatively inappropriate forum for the final resolution of rights created by Title VII." According to the Court, the "factfinding process in arbitration" is "not equivalent to judicial factfinding" and the "informality of arbitral procedure . . . makes arbitration a less appropriate forum for final resolution of Title VII issues than the federal courts." The Court also questioned the competence of arbitrators to decide federal statutory claims. See id. ("[T]he specialized competence of arbitrators pertains primarily to the law of the shop, not the law of the land"); Barrentine ("Although an arbitrator may be competent to resolve many preliminary factual questions, such as whether the employee 'punched in' when he said he did, he may lack the competence to decide the ultimate legal issue whether an employee's right to a minimum wage or to overtime pay under the statute has been violated"). In the Court's view, "the resolution of statutory or constitutional issues is a primary responsibility of courts, and judicial construction has proved especially necessary with respect to Title VII, whose broad language frequently can be given

---

[9] Justice Stevens suggests that the Court is displacing its "earlier determination of the relevant provisions' meaning" based on a "preference for arbitration." But his criticism lacks any basis. We are not revisiting a settled issue or disregarding an earlier determination; the Court is simply deciding the question identified in *Wright* as unresolved. And, contrary to Justice Stevens' accusation, it is the Court's fidelity to the ADEA's text—not an alleged preference for arbitration—that dictates the answer to the question presented. As *Gilmer* explained, nothing in the text of Title VII or the ADEA precludes contractual arbitration, and Justice Stevens has never suggested otherwise. Rather, he has always contended that permitting the "compulsory arbitration" of employment-discrimination claims conflicts with his perception of "the congressional purpose animating the ADEA." *Gilmer*, 500 U.S., at 41, 111 S. Ct. 1647, 114 L. Ed. 2d 26 (Stevens, J., dissenting). The *Gilmer* Court did not adopt Justice Stevens' personal view of the purposes underlying the ADEA, for good reason: That view is not embodied within the statute's text. Accordingly, it is not the statutory text that Justice Stevens has sought to vindicate—it is instead his own "preference" for mandatory judicial review, which he disguises as a search for congressional purpose. This Court is not empowered to incorporate such a preference into the text of a federal statute. It is for this reason, and not because of a "policy favoring arbitration," that the Court overturned *Wilko* v. *Swan*. And it is why we disavow the antiarbitration dicta of *Gardner-Denver* and its progeny today.

meaning only by reference to public law concepts." Gardner-Denver; see also McDonald ("An arbitrator may not . . . have the expertise required to resolve the complex legal questions that arise in § 1983 actions").

These misconceptions have been corrected. For example, the Court has "recognized that arbitral tribunals are readily capable of handling the factual and legal complexities of antitrust claims, notwithstanding the absence of judicial instruction and supervision" and that "there is no reason to assume at the outset that arbitrators will not follow the law." McMahon; Mitsubishi ("We decline to indulge the presumption that the parties and arbitral body conducting a proceeding will be unable or unwilling to retain competent, conscientious, and impartial arbitrators"). An arbitrator's capacity to resolve complex questions of fact and law extends with equal force to discrimination claims brought under the ADEA. Moreover, the recognition that arbitration procedures are more streamlined than federal litigation is not a basis for finding the forum somehow inadequate; the relative informality of arbitration is one of the chief reasons that parties select arbitration. Parties "trad[e] the procedures and opportunity for review of the courtroom for the simplicity, informality, and expedition of arbitration." In any event, "[i]t is unlikely . . . that age discrimination claims require more extensive discovery than other claims that we have found to be arbitrable, such as [Racketeer Influenced and Corrupt Organizations Act] and antitrust claims." Gilmer. At bottom, objections centered on the nature of arbitration do not offer a credible basis for discrediting the choice of that forum to resolve statutory antidiscrimination claims.[10]

Third, the Court in *Gardner-Denver* raised in a footnote a "further concern" regarding "the union's exclusive control over the manner and extent to which an individual grievance is presented." The Court suggested that in arbitration, as in the collective-bargaining process, a union may subordinate the interests of an individual employee to the collective interests of all employees in the bargaining unit.

We cannot rely on this judicial policy concern as a source of authority for introducing a qualification into the ADEA that is not found in its text. Absent a constitutional barrier, "it is not for us to substitute our view of . . . policy for the legislation which has been passed by Congress." * * *

The conflict-of-interest argument also proves too much. Labor unions certainly balance the economic interests of some employees against the needs of the larger work force as they negotiate collective-bargaining agreements and implement them on a daily basis. But this attribute of organized labor does not justify singling out an arbitration provision for disfavored treatment. This "principle of majority rule" to which respondents object is in fact the central premise of the NLRA. Emporium Capwell Co. v. Western Addition Community Organization, 420 U.S. 50, 62, 95 S. Ct. 977, 43 L. Ed. 2d 12 (1975). "In establishing a regime of majority

---

[10] Moreover, an arbitrator's decision as to whether a unionized employee has been discriminated against on the basis of age in violation of the ADEA remains subject to judicial review under the FAA. 9 U.S.C. § 10(a). "[A]lthough judicial scrutiny of arbitration awards necessarily is limited, such review is sufficient to ensure that arbitrators comply with the requirements of the statute." *Shearson/American Express Inc.* v. *McMahon*.

rule, Congress sought to secure to all members of the unit the benefits of their collective strength and bargaining power, in full awareness that the superior strength of some individuals or groups might be subordinated to the interest of the majority." It was Congress' verdict that the benefits of organized labor outweigh the sacrifice of individual liberty that this system necessarily demands. Respondents' argument that they were deprived of the right to pursue their ADEA claims in federal court by a labor union with a conflict of interest is therefore unsustainable; it amounts to a collateral attack on the NLRA.

In any event, Congress has accounted for this conflict of interest in several ways. As indicated above, the NLRA has been interpreted to impose a "duty of fair representation" on labor unions, which a union breaches "when its conduct toward a member of the bargaining unit is arbitrary, discriminatory, or in bad faith." This duty extends to "challenges leveled not only at a union's contract administration and enforcement efforts but at its negotiation activities as well." Thus, a union is subject to liability under the NLRA if it illegally discriminates against older workers in either the formation or governance of the collective-bargaining agreement, such as by deciding not to pursue a grievance on behalf of one of its members for discriminatory reasons. Respondents in fact brought a fair representation suit against the Union based on its withdrawal of support for their age-discrimination claims. Given this avenue that Congress has made available to redress a union's violation of its duty to its members, it is particularly inappropriate to ask this Court to impose an artificial limitation on the collective-bargaining process.

* * *

We hold that a collective-bargaining agreement that clearly and unmistakably requires union members to arbitrate ADEA claims is enforceable as a matter of federal law. The judgment of the Court of Appeals is reversed, and the case is remanded for further proceedings consistent with this opinion.

It is so ordered.

■ JUSTICE STEVENS, dissenting.

Justice Souter's dissenting opinion, which I join in full, explains why our decision in *Alexander* v. *Gardner-Denver Co.*, answers the question presented in this case. My concern regarding the Court's subversion of precedent to the policy favoring arbitration prompts these additional remarks.

Notwithstanding the absence of change in any relevant statutory provision, the Court has recently retreated from, and in some cases reversed, prior decisions based on its changed view of the merits of arbitration. Previously, the Court approached with caution questions involving a union's waiver of an employee's right to raise statutory claims in a federal judicial forum. After searching the text and purposes of Title VII of the Civil Rights Act of 1964, the Court in *Gardner-Denver* held that a clause of a collective-bargaining agreement (CBA) requiring arbitration of discrimination claims could not waive an employee's right to a judicial forum for statutory claims. The Court's decision rested on several features of the statute, including the individual nature of the rights it confers, the broad remedial powers it grants federal courts, and its expressed preference for overlapping remedies. The Court also noted the problem of entrusting a union with certain arbitration decisions given the potential conflict between the collective interest and the interests of an individual employee seeking to assert his rights. That concern later provided a basis for our decisions in *Barrentine*, and *McDonald*, which similarly held that a CBA may not commit enforcement of certain rights-creating statutes exclusively to a union-controlled arbitration process. Congress has taken no action signaling disagreement with those decisions.

The statutes construed by the Court in the foregoing cases and in *Wilko*, have not since been amended in any relevant respect. But the Court has in a number of cases replaced our predecessors' statutory analysis with judicial reasoning espousing a policy favoring arbitration and thereby reached divergent results. I dissented in those cases to express concern that my colleagues were making policy choices not made by Congress.

* * *

It is for Congress, rather than this Court, to reassess the policy arguments favoring arbitration and revise the relevant provisions to reflect its views.

■ JUSTICE SOUTER, with whom JUSTICE STEVENS, JUSTICE GINSBURG, and JUSTICE BREYER join, dissenting.

The issue here is whether employees subject to a collective-bargaining agreement (CBA) providing for conclusive arbitration of all grievances, including claimed breaches of the Age Discrimination in Employment Act of 1967 (ADEA), lose their statutory right to bring an ADEA claim in court, § 626(c). Under the 35-year-old holding in *Alexander* v. *Gardner-Denver Co.*, they do not, and I would adhere to *stare decisis* and so hold today.

Like Title VII of the Civil Rights Act of 1964, 42 U.S.C. § 2000e *et seq.*, the ADEA is aimed at "'the elimination of discrimination in the workplace'". * * *

Gardner-Denver considered the effect of a CBA's arbitration clause on an employee's right to sue under Title VII. One of the employer's arguments was that the CBA entered into by the union had waived individual employees' statutory cause of action subject to a judicial remedy for discrimination in violation of Title VII. Although Title VII, like the ADEA, "does not speak expressly to the relationship between federal courts and the grievance-arbitration machinery of collective-bargaining agreements," we unanimously held that "the rights conferred" by Title VII (with no exception for the right to a judicial forum) cannot be waived as "part of the collective bargaining process". We stressed the contrast between two categories of rights in labor and employment law. There were "statutory rights related to collective activity," which "are conferred on employees collectively to foster the processes of bargaining, [which] properly may be exercised or relinquished by the union as collective-bargaining agent to obtain economic benefits for union members." But "Title VII... stands on plainly different [categorical] ground; it concerns not majoritarian processes, but an individual's right to equal employment opportunities." Thus, as the Court previously realized, *Gardner-Denver* imposed a "seemingly absolute prohibition of union waiver of employees' federal forum rights." *Wright*.

* * *

Our analysis of Title VII in *Gardner-Denver* is just as pertinent to the ADEA in this case. The "interpretation of Title VII . . . applies with equal force in the context of age discrimination, for the substantive provisions of the ADEA 'were derived *in haec verba* from Title VII,'" and indeed neither petitioners nor the Court points to any relevant distinction between the two statutes. Given the unquestionable applicability of the *Gardner-Denver* rule to this ADEA issue, the argument that its precedent be followed in this case of statutory interpretation is equally unquestionable. * * *

The majority evades the precedent of *Gardner-Denver* as long as it can simply by ignoring it. The Court never mentions the case before concluding that the ADEA and the National Labor Relations Act, 29 U.S.C. § 151 *et seq.*, "yiel[d] a straightforward answer to the question presented," that is, that unions can bargain away individual rights to a federal forum for antidiscrimination claims. If this were a case of first impression, it would at least be possible to consider that conclusion, but the issue is settled and the time is too late by 35 years to make the bald assertion that "[n]othing in the law suggests a distinction between the status of arbitration agreements signed by an individual employee and those agreed to by a union representative". In fact, we recently and unanimously said that the principle that "federal forum rights cannot be waived in union-negotiated CBAs even if they can be waived in individually executed contracts . . . assuredly finds support in" our case law, *Wright*.

Equally at odds with existing law is the majority's statement that "[t]he decision to fashion a [CBA] to require arbitration of employment-discrimination claims is no different from the many other decisions made by parties in designing grievance machinery." That is simply impossible to square with our conclusion in *Gardner-Denver* that "Title VII . . . stands on plainly different ground" from "statutory rights related to collective activity": "it concerns not majoritarian processes, but an individual's right to equal employment opportunities."

When the majority does speak to *Gardner-Denver*, it misreads the case in claiming that it turned solely "on the narrow ground that the arbitration was not preclusive because the collective-bargaining agreement did not cover statutory claims." That, however, was merely one of several reasons given in support of the decision. * * *

See also Gilmer v. Interstate/Johnson Lane Corp., 500 U.S. 20, 35, 111 S. Ct. 1647, 114 L. Ed. 2d 26 (1991) ("An important concern" in *Gardner-Denver* "was the tension between collective representation and individual statutory rights . . .").

* * *

For that matter, Congress has unsurprisingly understood *Gardner-Denver* the way we have repeatedly explained it and has operated on the assumption that a CBA cannot waive employees' rights to a judicial forum to enforce antidiscrimination statutes. * * *

On one level, the majority opinion may have little effect, for it explicitly reserves the question whether a CBA's waiver of a judicial forum is enforceable when the union controls access to and presentation of employees' claims in arbitration, which "is usually the case". But as a treatment of precedent in statutory interpretation, the majority's opinion cannot be reconciled with the *Gardner-Denver* Court's own view of its holding, repeated over the years and generally understood, and I respectfully dissent.

QUESTIONS TO REVIEW AND SYNTHESIZE

1. Litigation in which of these cases occurred after arbitration: *Gardner-Denver*, *Barrentine*, *McDonald*, *Mitsubishi*, *McMahon*, and *Rodriguez de Quijas, Gilmer*?
2. Which of these cases arose out of a collective bargaining agreement and thus is conventionally called "labor arbitration": *Gardner-Denver*, *Barrentine*, *McDonald*, *Mitsubishi*, *McMahon*, and *Rodriguez de Quijas, Gilmer*?
3. How do your answers to the previous two questions correlate with the cases' holdings on whether federal statutory claims would be resolved in arbitration or litigation? What do you make of this correlation?
4. How did *Gilmer* respond to the dissent's concerns about applying the FAA to statutory claims arising out of "form contracts between parties of unequal bargaining power"?
5. What does *Gilmer* say about discovery and evidence in arbitration?
6. How does *Pyett* distinguish *Gardner-Denver*, *Barrentine*, and *McDonald*?
7. How does *Pyett* criticize *Gardner-Denver*, *Barrentine*, and *McDonald*?
8. In what sense does *Pyett* move labor arbitration law into the post-*Mitsubishi* mainstream of arbitration law 18 years after *Gilmer* moved employment arbitration law into that mainstream?
9. *Pyett* reiterated *McMahon*'s statement that "there is no reason to assume at the outset that arbitrators will not follow the law" and *Mitsubishi*'s implication that "competent, conscientious, and impartial arbitrators" try to apply the law. On the other hand, Chapters 1 and 2 showed what examples of arbitrators applying rules other than the law a court would have applied to the same case? Do those examples have any relevance for arbitration of the sorts of employment claims at issue in *Gilmer* and *Pyett*?

As we saw in *Wilko*, *Mitsubishi*, and *Pyett*, judges and advocates opposing enforcement of pre-dispute agreements to arbitrate claims arising under federal statutes—such as the Securities Act, Sherman Antitrust Act, and Civil Rights Act—argue that enforcing such agreements would be inconsistent, or at least in tension, with those statutes. So, the Supreme Court's transition to enforcing agreements to arbitrate such federal statutory claims involves interpreting those statutes, as well as the FAA.

Epic Systems Corp. v. Lewis

Supreme Court of the United States, 2018.
138 S.Ct. 1612, 200 L.Ed.2d 889, 211 L.R.R.M. (BNA) 3061.

■ JUSTICE GORSUCH delivered the opinion of the Court.

Should employees and employers be allowed to agree that any disputes between them will be resolved through one-on-one arbitration? Or should employees always be permitted to bring their claims in class or collective actions, no matter what they agreed with their employers?

As a matter of policy these questions are surely debatable. But as a matter of law the answer is clear. In the Federal Arbitration Act, Congress has instructed federal courts to enforce arbitration agreements according to their terms—including terms providing for individualized proceedings. Nor can we agree with the employees' suggestion that the National Labor Relations Act (NLRA) offers a conflicting command. It is this Court's duty to interpret Congress's statutes as a harmonious whole rather than at war with one another. And abiding that duty here leads to an unmistakable conclusion. The NLRA secures to employees rights to organize unions and bargain collectively, but it says nothing about how judges and arbitrators must try legal disputes that leave the workplace and enter the courtroom or arbitral forum. This Court has never read a right to class actions into the NLRA—and for three quarters of a century neither did the National Labor Relations Board. Far from conflicting, the Arbitration Act and the NLRA have long enjoyed separate spheres of influence and neither permits this Court to declare the parties' agreements unlawful.

The three cases before us differ in detail but not in substance. Take *Ernst & Young LLP v. Morris*. There Ernst & Young and one of its junior accountants, Stephen Morris, entered into an agreement providing that they would arbitrate any disputes that might arise between them. The agreement stated that the employee could choose the arbitration provider and that the arbitrator could "grant any relief that could be granted by . . . a court" in the relevant jurisdiction. The agreement also specified individualized arbitration, with claims "pertaining to different [e]mployees [to] be heard in separate proceedings."

After his employment ended, and despite having agreed to arbitrate claims against the firm, Mr. Morris sued Ernst & Young in federal court. He alleged that the firm had misclassified its junior accountants as professional employees and violated the federal Fair Labor Standards Act (FLSA) and California law by paying them salaries without overtime pay. Although the arbitration agreement provided for individualized proceedings, Mr. Morris sought to litigate the federal claim on behalf of a nationwide class under the FLSA's collective action provision, 29 U.S.C. § 216(b). He sought to pursue the state law claim as a class action under Federal Rule of Civil Procedure 23.

Ernst & Young replied with a motion to compel arbitration. The district court granted the request, but the Ninth Circuit reversed this judgment [,] * * * conclud[ing] that an agreement requiring individualized arbitration proceedings violates the NLRA by barring employees from engaging in the "concerted activit[y]," 29 U.S.C. § 157, of pursuing claims as a class or collective action.

* * *

Although the Arbitration Act and the NLRA have long coexisted—they date from 1925 and 1935, respectively—the suggestion they might conflict is something quite new. Until a couple of years ago, courts more or less agreed that arbitration agreements like those before us must be enforced according to their terms.

The National Labor Relations Board's general counsel expressed much the same view in 2010. * * *

But recently things have shifted. In 2012, the Board—for the first time in the 77 years since the NLRA's adoption—asserted that the NLRA effectively nullifies the Arbitration Act in cases like ours. D.R. Horton, Inc., 357 N.L.R.B. 2277. * * *

We begin with the Arbitration Act and the question of its saving clause.

Congress adopted the Arbitration Act in 1925 in response to a perception that courts were unduly hostile to arbitration. * * * So Congress directed courts to abandon their hostility and instead treat arbitration agreements as "valid, irrevocable, and enforceable." 9 U.S.C. § 2. * * *

Not only did Congress require courts to respect and enforce agreements to arbitrate; it also specifically directed them to respect and enforce the parties' chosen arbitration procedures. See § 3 (providing for a stay of litigation pending arbitration "in accordance with the terms of the agreement"); § 4 (providing for "an order directing that . . . arbitration proceed in the manner provided for in such agreement"). Indeed, we have often observed that the Arbitration Act requires courts "rigorously" to "enforce arbitration agreements according to their terms, including terms that specify *with whom* the parties choose to arbitrate their disputes and *the rules* under which that arbitration will be conducted."

On first blush, these emphatic directions would seem to resolve any argument under the Arbitration Act. The parties before us contracted for arbitration. They proceeded to specify the rules that would govern their arbitrations, indicating their intention to use individualized rather than class or collective action procedures. And this much the Arbitration Act seems to protect pretty absolutely. * * *

* * *

* * * Even if the Arbitration Act normally requires us to enforce arbitration agreements like theirs, the employees reply that the NLRA overrides that guidance in these cases and commands us to hold their agreements unlawful yet.

This argument faces a stout uphill climb. When confronted with two Acts of Congress allegedly touching on the same topic, this Court is not at "liberty to pick and choose among congressional enactments" and must instead strive "to give effect to both." A party seeking to suggest that two statutes cannot be harmonized, and that one displaces the other, bears the heavy burden of showing "a clearly expressed congressional intention" that such a result should follow. * * *

Seeking to demonstrate an irreconcilable statutory conflict even in light of these demanding standards, the employees point to Section 7 of the NLRA. That provision guarantees workers

> "the right to self-organization, to form, join, or assist labor organizations, to bargain collectively through representatives of their own choosing, and to engage in other concerted activities for the purpose of collective bargaining or other mutual aid or protection." 29 U.S.C. § 157.

From this language, the employees ask us to infer a clear and manifest congressional command to displace the Arbitration Act and outlaw agreements like theirs.

But that much inference is more than this Court may make. Section 7 focuses on the right to organize unions and bargain collectively. It may permit unions to bargain to prohibit arbitration. But it does not express approval or disapproval of arbitration. It does not mention class or collective action procedures. It does not even hint at a wish to displace the Arbitration Act—let alone accomplish that much clearly and manifestly, as our precedents demand.

Neither should any of this come as a surprise. The notion that Section 7 confers a right to class or collective actions seems pretty unlikely when you recall that procedures like that were hardly known when the NLRA was adopted in 1935. Federal Rule of Civil Procedure 23 didn't create the modern class action until 1966; class arbitration didn't emerge until later still; and even the Fair Labor Standards Act's collective action provision postdated Section 7 by years. * * * And while some forms of group litigation existed even in 1935, Section 7's failure to mention them only reinforces that the statute doesn't speak to such procedures.

* * *

* * * In many cases over many years, this Court has heard and rejected efforts to conjure conflicts between the Arbitration Act and other federal statutes. In fact, this Court has rejected *every* such effort to date (save one temporary exception since overruled), with statutes ranging from the Sherman and Clayton Acts to the Age Discrimination in Employment Act, the Credit Repair Organizations Act, the Securities Act of 1933, the Securities Exchange Act of 1934, and the Racketeer Influenced and Corrupt Organizations Act. Throughout, we have made clear that even a statute's express provision for collective legal actions does not necessarily mean that it precludes "individual attempts at conciliation" through arbitration. And we've stressed that the absence of any specific statutory discussion of arbitration or class actions is an important and telling clue that Congress has not displaced the Arbitration Act. Given so much precedent pointing so strongly in one direction, we do not see how we might faithfully turn the other way here.

* * *

The dissent sees things a little bit differently. In its view, today's decision ushers us back to the Lochner era when this Court regularly overrode legislative policy judgments. The dissent even suggests we have resurrected the long-dead "yellow dog" contract. But like most apocalyptic warnings, this one proves a false alarm. Cf. L. Tribe, American Constitutional Law 435 (1978) ("'Lochnerizing' has become so much an epithet that the very use of the label may obscure attempts at understanding").

Our decision does nothing to override Congress's policy judgments. As the dissent recognizes, the legislative policy embodied in the NLRA is aimed at "safeguard[ing], first and foremost, workers' rights to join unions and to engage in collective bargaining." Those rights stand every bit as strong today as they did yesterday. And rather than revive "yellow dog" contracts against union organizing that the NLRA outlawed back in 1935, today's decision merely declines to read into the NLRA a novel right to class action procedures that the Board's own general counsel disclaimed as recently as 2010.

Instead of overriding Congress's policy judgments, today's decision seeks to honor them. This much the dissent surely knows. Shortly after invoking the specter of *Lochner*, it turns around and criticizes the Court for trying *too hard* to abide the Arbitration Act's "liberal federal policy favoring arbitration agreements," saying we "ski" too far down the "slippery slope" of this Court's arbitration precedent. But the dissent's real complaint lies with the mountain of precedent itself. The dissent spends page after page relitigating our Arbitration Act precedents, rehashing arguments this Court has heard and rejected many times in many cases that no party has asked us to revisit.

* * *

Ultimately, the dissent retreats to policy arguments* * * The respective merits of class actions and private arbitration as means of enforcing the law are questions constitutionally entrusted not to the courts to decide but to the policymakers in the political branches where those questions remain hotly contested. Just recently, for example, one federal agency banned individualized arbitration agreements it blamed for underenforcement of certain laws, only to see Congress respond by immediately repealing that rule. This Court is not free to substitute its preferred economic policies for those chosen by the people's representatives. *That,* we had always understood, was *Lochner*'s sin.

The policy may be debatable but the law is clear: Congress has instructed that arbitration agreements like those before us must be enforced as written. While Congress is of course always free to amend this judgment, we see nothing suggesting it did so in the NLRA* * *

■ JUSTICE THOMAS, concurring.

I join the Court's opinion in full. I write separately to add that the employees also cannot prevail under the plain meaning of the Federal Arbitration Act. The Act declares arbitration agreements "valid, irrevocable, and enforceable, save upon such grounds as exist at law or in equity for the revocation of any contract." 9 U.S.C. § 2. As I have previously explained, grounds for revocation of a contract are those that concern "the formation of the arbitration agreement." The employees argue, among other things, that the class waivers in their arbitration agreements are unenforceable because the National Labor Relations Act makes those waivers illegal. But illegality is a public-policy defense. Because "[r]efusal to enforce a contract for public-policy reasons does not concern whether the contract was properly made," the saving clause does not apply here. For this reason, and the reasons in the Court's opinion, the employees' arbitration agreements must be enforced according to their terms.

■ JUSTICE GINSBURG, with whom JUSTICE BREYER, JUSTICE SOTOMAYOR, and JUSTICE KAGAN join, dissenting.

* * * The question presented: Does the Federal Arbitration Act permit employers to insist that their employees, whenever seeking redress for commonly experienced wage loss, go it alone, never mind the right secured to employees by the National Labor Relations Act (NLRA), *29 U.S.C. § 151 et seq.,* "to engage in . . . concerted activities" for their "mutual aid or protection"? § 157. The answer should be a resounding "No."

In the NLRA and its forerunner, the Norris-LaGuardia Act (NLGA) Congress acted on an acute awareness: For workers striving to gain from their employers decent terms and conditions of employment, there is strength in numbers. A single employee, Congress understood, is disarmed in dealing with an employer. See NLRB v. Jones & Laughlin Steel Corp., 301 U.S. 1, 33–34, 57 S.Ct. 615, 81 L.Ed. 893 (1937). The Court today subordinates employee-protective labor legislation to the Arbitration Act. In so doing, the Court forgets the labor market imbalance that gave rise to the NLGA and the NLRA, and ignores the destructive consequences of diminishing the right of employees "to band together in confronting an employer."

* * *

The end of the 19th century and beginning of the 20th was a tumultuous era in the history of our Nation's labor relations. Under economic conditions then prevailing, workers often had to accept employment on whatever terms employers dictated. See 75 Cong. Rec. 4502 (1932). Aiming to secure better pay, shorter workdays, and safer workplaces, workers increasingly sought to band together to make their demands effective.

Employers, in turn, engaged in a variety of tactics to hinder workers' efforts to act in concert for their mutual benefit. Notable among such devices was the "yellow-dog contract." Such agreements, which employers required employees to sign as a condition of employment, typically commanded employees to abstain from joining labor unions. Many of the employer-designed agreements cast an even wider net, "proscrib[ing] all manner of concerted activities." As a prominent United States Senator observed, contracts of the yellow-dog genre rendered the "laboring man ... absolutely helpless" by "waiv[ing] his right ... to free association" and by requiring that he "singly present any grievance he has."

Early legislative efforts to protect workers' rights to band together were unavailing. Courts, including this one, invalidated the legislation based on then-ascendant notions about employers' and employees' constitutional right to "liberty of contract." While stating that legislatures could curtail contractual "liberty" in the interest of public health, safety, and the general welfare, courts placed outside those bounds legislative action to redress the bargaining power imbalance workers faced.

In the 1930's, legislative efforts to safeguard vulnerable workers found more receptive audiences. As the Great Depression shifted political winds further in favor of worker-protective laws, Congress passed two statutes aimed at protecting employees' associational rights. First, in 1932, Congress passed the NLGA, which regulates the employer-employee relationship indirectly. Section 2 of the Act declares:

> "Whereas . . . the individual unorganized worker is commonly helpless to exercise actual liberty of contract and to protect his freedom of labor, . . . it is necessary that he have full freedom of association, self-organization, and designation of representatives of his own choosing, . . . and that he shall be free from the interference, restraint, or coercion of employers . . . in the designation of such representatives or in self-organization or

in other concerted activities for the purpose of collective bargaining or other mutual aid or protection." 29 U.S.C. § 102.

* * * While banning court enforcement of contracts proscribing concerted action by employees, the NLGA did not directly prohibit coercive employer practices.

But Congress did so three years later, in 1935, when it enacted the NLRA. Relevant here, § 7 of the NLRA guarantees employees "the right to self-organization, to form, join, or assist labor organizations, to bargain collectively through representatives of their own choosing, *and to engage in other concerted activities for the purpose of collective bargaining or other mutual aid or protection*." 29 U.S.C. § 157 (emphasis added). Section 8(a)(1) safeguards those rights by making it an "unfair labor practice" for an employer to "interfere with, restrain, or coerce employees in the exercise of the rights guaranteed in [§ 7]." To oversee the Act's guarantees, the Act established the National Labor Relations Board (Board or NLRB), an independent regulatory agency empowered to administer "labor policy for the Nation."

Unlike earlier legislative efforts, the NLGA and the NLRA had staying power. When a case challenging the NLRA's constitutionality made its way here, the Court, in retreat from its Lochner-era contractual-"liberty" decisions, upheld the Act as a permissible exercise of legislative authority. The Court recognized that employees have a "fundamental right" to join together to advance their common interests and that Congress, in lieu of "ignor[ing]" that right, had elected to "safeguard" it.

Despite the NLRA's prohibitions, the employers in the cases now before the Court required their employees to sign contracts stipulating to submission of wage and hours claims to binding arbitration, and to do so only one-by-one.[2] When employees subsequently filed wage and hours claims in federal court and sought to invoke the collective-litigation procedures provided for in the FLSA and Federal Rules of Civil Procedure,[3] the employers moved to compel individual arbitration. The Arbitration Act, in their view, requires courts to enforce their take-it-or-leave-it arbitration agreements as written, including the collective-litigation abstinence demanded therein.

---

[2] The Court's opinion opens with the question: "Should employees and employers be allowed to agree that any disputes between them will be resolved through one-on-one arbitration?" Were the "agreements" genuinely bilateral? Petitioner Epic Systems Corporation e-mailed its employees an arbitration agreement requiring resolution of wage and hours claims by individual arbitration. The agreement provided that if the employees "continue[d] to work at Epic," they would "be deemed to have accepted th[e] Agreement." Ernst & Young similarly e-mailed its employees an arbitration agreement, which stated that the employees' continued employment would indicate their assent to the agreement's terms. Epic's and Ernst & Young's employees thus faced a Hobson's choice: accept arbitration on their employer's terms or give up their jobs.

[3] The FLSA establishes an opt-in collective-litigation procedure for employees seeking to recover unpaid wages and overtime pay. See 29 U.S.C. § 216(b). In particular, it authorizes "one or more employees" to maintain an action "in behalf of himself or themselves and other employees similarly situated." Ibid. "Similarly situated" employees may become parties to an FLSA collective action (and may share in the recovery) only if they file written notices of consent to be joined as parties. Ibid. The Federal Rules of Civil Procedure provide two collective-litigation procedures relevant here. First, Rule 20(a) permits individuals to join as plaintiffs in a single action if they assert claims arising out of the same transaction or occurrence and their claims involve common questions of law or fact. Second, Rule 23 establishes an opt-out class-action procedure, pursuant to which "[o]ne or more members of a class" may bring an action on behalf of the entire class if specified prerequisites are met.

In resisting enforcement of the group-action foreclosures, the employees involved in this litigation do not urge that they must have access to a judicial forum. They argue only that the NLRA prohibits their employers from denying them the right to pursue work-related claims in concert in any forum. If they may be stopped by employer-dictated terms from pursuing collective procedures in court, they maintain, they must at least have access to similar procedures in an arbitral forum.

Although the NLRA safeguards, first and foremost, workers' rights to join unions and to engage in collective bargaining, the statute speaks more embracively. In addition to protecting employees' rights "to form, join, or assist labor organizations" and "to bargain collectively through representatives of their own choosing," the Act protects employees' rights "to engage in *other* concerted activities for the purpose of . . . mutual aid or protection." * * *

Suits to enforce workplace rights collectively fit comfortably under the umbrella "concerted activities for the purpose of . . . mutual aid or protection." "Concerted" means "[p]lanned or accomplished together; combined." "Mutual" means "reciprocal." When employees meet the requirements for litigation of shared legal claims in joint, collective, and class proceedings, the litigation of their claims is undoubtedly "accomplished together." By joining hands in litigation, workers can spread the costs of litigation and reduce the risk of employer retaliation.

Recognizing employees' right to engage in collective employment litigation and shielding that right from employer blockage are firmly rooted in the NLRA's design. Congress expressed its intent, when it enacted the NLRA, to "protec[t] the exercise by workers of full freedom of association," thereby remedying "[t]he inequality of bargaining power" workers faced. There can be no serious doubt that collective litigation is one way workers may associate with one another to improve their lot.

Since the Act's earliest days, the Board and federal courts have understood § 7's "concerted activities" clause to protect myriad ways in which employees may join together to advance their shared interests. * * *

Crucially important here, for over 75 years, the Board has held that the NLRA safeguards employees from employer interference when they pursue joint, collective, and class suits related to the terms and conditions of their employment. For decades, federal courts have endorsed the Board's view, comprehending that "the filing of a labor related civil action by a group of employees is ordinarily a concerted activity protected by § 7." Leviton Mfg. Co. v. NLRB, 486 F.2d 686, 689 (C.A.1 1973); see, e.g., Brady v. National Football League, 644 F.3d 661, 673 (C.A.8 2011) (similar). The Court pays scant heed to this longstanding line of decisions.

* * *

* * * For going on 80 years now, the Board and federal courts—including this one—have understood § 7 to protect numerous activities for which the Act provides no "specific" regulatory guidance.

In a related argument, the Court maintains that the NLRA does not "even whispe[r]" about the "rules [that] should govern the adjudication of class or collective actions in court or arbitration." The employees here involved, of course, do not look to the NLRA for the procedures enabling them to vindicate their employment rights in arbitral or judicial forums. They assert that the Act establishes their right to act in concert using existing, generally available procedures and to do so free from employer interference. The FLSA and the Federal Rules on joinder and class actions provide the procedures pursuant to which the employees may ally to pursue shared legal claims. Their employers cannot lawfully cut off their access to those procedures, they urge, without according them access to similar procedures in arbitral forums. See, e.g., American Arbitration Assn., Supplementary Rules for Class Arbitrations (2011).

To the employees' argument, the Court replies: If the employees "really take existing class and collective action rules as they find them, they surely take them subject to the limitations inherent in those rules—including the principle that parties may (as here) contract to depart from them in favor of individualized arbitration procedures." The freedom to depart asserted by the Court, as already underscored, is entirely one sided. Once again, the Court ignores the reality that sparked the NLRA's passage: Forced to face their employers without company, employees ordinarily are no match for the enterprise that hires them. Employees gain strength, however, if they can deal with their employers in numbers. That is the very reason why the NLRA secures against employer interference employees' right to act in concert for their "mutual aid or protection."

* * *

Moreover, the Court paints an ahistorical picture. As Judge Wood, writing for the Seventh Circuit, cogently explained, the FLSA's collective-litigation procedure and the modern class action were "not written on a clean slate." 823 F.3d 1147, 1154 (2016). By 1935, permissive joinder was scarcely uncommon in courts of equity. Nor were representative and class suits novelties. Indeed, their origins trace back to medieval times. And beyond question, "[c]lass suits long have been a part of American jurisprudence." Early instances of joint proceedings include cases in which employees allied to sue an employer. E.g., Gorley v. Louisville, 23 Ky.L.Rptr. 1782, 65 S.W. 844 (1901) (suit to recover wages brought by ten members of city police force on behalf of themselves and other officers); Guiliano v. Daniel O'Connell's Sons, 105 Conn. 695, 136 A. 677 (1927) (suit by two employees to recover for injuries sustained while residing in housing provided by their employer). It takes no imagination, then, to comprehend that Congress, when it enacted the NLRA, likely meant to protect employees' joining together to engage in collective litigation.[7]

Because I would hold that employees' § 7 rights include the right to pursue collective litigation regarding their wages and hours, I would further hold that the employer-dictated collective-litigation stoppers, *i.e.*, "waivers," are unlawful. As earlier recounted, § 8(a)(1) makes it an "unfair labor practice" for an employer to "interfere with, restrain, or coerce" employees in the exercise of their § 7 rights.

---

[7] The Court additionally suggests that something must be amiss because the employees turn to the NLRA, rather than the FLSA, to resist enforcement of the collective-litigation waivers. But the employees' reliance on the NLRA is hardly a reason to "raise a judicial eyebrow." The NLRA's guiding purpose is to protect employees' rights to work together when addressing shared workplace grievances of whatever kind.

Beyond genuine dispute, an employer "interfere[s] with" and "restrain[s]" employees in the exercise of their § 7 rights by mandating that they prospectively renounce those rights in individual employment agreements. The law could hardly be otherwise: Employees' rights to band together to meet their employers' superior strength would be worth precious little if employers could condition employment on workers signing away those rights. Properly assessed, then, the "waivers" rank as unfair labor practices outlawed by the NLRA, and therefore unenforceable in court.

Today's decision rests largely on the Court's finding in the Arbitration Act "emphatic directions" to enforce arbitration agreements according to their terms, * * *

[However,] [t]he legislative hearings and debate leading up to the FAA's passage evidence Congress' aim to enable merchants of roughly equal bargaining power to enter into binding agreements to arbitrate *commercial* disputes

The FAA's legislative history also shows that Congress did not intend the statute to apply to arbitration provisions in employment contracts. In brief, when the legislation was introduced, organized labor voiced concern. Herbert Hoover, then Secretary of Commerce, suggested that if there were "objection[s]" to including "workers' contracts in the law's scheme," Congress could amend the legislation to say: "but nothing herein contained shall apply to contracts of employment of seamen, railroad employees, or any other class of workers engaged in interstate or foreign commerce." Congress adopted Secretary Hoover's suggestion virtually verbatim in § 1 of the Act, and labor expressed no further opposition.

* * *

In recent decades, this Court has veered away from Congress' intent simply to afford merchants a speedy and economical means of resolving commercial disputes. In 1983, the Court declared, for the first time in the FAA's then 58-year history, that the FAA evinces a "liberal federal policy favoring arbitration." Moses H. Cone Memorial Hospital v. Mercury Constr. Corp., 460 U.S. 1, 24, 103 S.Ct. 927, 74 L.Ed.2d 765 (1983) (involving an arbitration agreement between a hospital and a construction contractor). Soon thereafter, the Court ruled, in a series of cases, that the FAA requires enforcement of agreements to arbitrate not only contract claims, but statutory claims as well. E.g., Mitsubishi Motors Corp. v. Soler Chrysler-Plymouth, Inc. (1985); Shearson/American Express Inc. v. McMahon (1987). Further, in 1991, the Court concluded in *Gilmer v. Interstate/Johnson Lane Corp.*, that the FAA requires enforcement of agreements to arbitrate claims arising under the Age Discrimination in Employment Act of 1967, a workplace antidiscrimination statute. Then, in 2001, the Court ruled in *Circuit City Stores, Inc. v. Adams* (2001) [excerpted in Section 3.C.3.b], that the Arbitration Act's exemption for employment contracts should be construed narrowly, to exclude from the Act's scope only transportation workers' contracts.

Employers have availed themselves of the opportunity opened by court decisions expansively interpreting the Arbitration Act. Few employers imposed arbitration agreements on their employees in the early 1990's. After *Gilmer* and

Circuit City, however, employers' exaction of arbitration clauses in employment contracts grew steadily. Moreover, in response to subsequent decisions addressing class arbitration, employers have increasingly included in their arbitration agreements express group-action waivers. It is, therefore, this Court's exorbitant application of the FAA—stretching it far beyond contractual disputes between merchants—that led the NLRB to confront, for the first time in 2012, the precise question whether employers can use arbitration agreements to insulate themselves from collective employment litigation.

* * *

Even assuming that the FAA and the NLRA were inharmonious, the NLRA should control. Enacted later in time, the NLRA should qualify as "an implied repeal" of the FAA, to the extent of any genuine conflict. Moreover, the NLRA should prevail as the more pinpointed, subject-matter specific legislation, given that it speaks directly to group action by employees to improve the terms and conditions of their employment.

* * *

The inevitable result of today's decision will be the underenforcement of federal and state statutes designed to advance the well-being of vulnerable workers. See generally Sternlight, Disarming Employees: How American Employers Are Using Mandatory Arbitration To Deprive Workers of Legal Protections, 80 Brooklyn L. Rev. 1309 (2015).

The probable impact on wage and hours claims of the kind asserted in the cases now before the Court is all too evident. Violations of minimum-wage and overtime laws are widespread. One study estimated that in Chicago, Los Angeles, and New York City alone, low-wage workers lose nearly $3 billion in legally owed wages each year. The U.S. Department of Labor, state labor departments, and state attorneys general can uncover and obtain recoveries for some violations. Because of their limited resources, however, government agencies must rely on private parties to take a lead role in enforcing wage and hours laws.

If employers can stave off collective employment litigation aimed at obtaining redress for wage and hours infractions, the enforcement gap is almost certain to widen. Expenses entailed in mounting individual claims will often far outweigh potential recoveries.

Fear of retaliation may also deter potential claimants from seeking redress alone. Further inhibiting single-file claims is the slim relief obtainable, even of the injunctive kind. The upshot: Employers, aware that employees will be disinclined to pursue small-value claims when confined to proceeding one-by-one, will no doubt perceive that the cost-benefit balance of underpaying workers tips heavily in favor of skirting legal obligations.

* * *

If these untoward consequences stemmed from legislative choices, I would be obliged to accede to them. But the edict that employees with wage and hours claims may seek relief only one-by-one does not come from Congress. It is the result of take-it-or-leave-it labor contracts harking back to the type called "yellow dog," and of the readiness of this Court to enforce those unbargained-for agreements. The FAA demands no such suppression of the right of workers to take concerted action for their "mutual aid or protection." Accordingly, I would reverse the judgment of the Fifth Circuit in No. 16–307 and affirm the judgments of the Seventh and Ninth Circuits in Nos. 16–285 and 16–300.

As discussed above, the Supreme Court permitted employees to litigate statutory claims in *Gardner-Denver* (1974), *Barrentine* (1981), and *McDonald* (1984). Two of these decisions were unanimous and in one, *Barrentine*, only two conservative justices dissented. By contrast, *Pyett* and *Epic*—requiring arbitration of employees' claims—were 5–4 decisions authored by justices appointed by Republican Presidents Bush (41) and Trump. In *Epic*, all five justices appointed by Republican presidents joined the majority, while all four justices appointed by Democratic presidents dissented.

4. MOST CLAIMS ARE "ARBITRABLE"

Since *Mitsubishi Motors Corp. v. Soler Chrysler-Plymouth, Inc.*, 473 U.S. 614, 105 S.Ct. 3346, 87 L.Ed.2d 444 (1985), no Supreme Court decision has found the FAA's command to enforce pre-dispute arbitration agreements overridden by another statute's exception to that command. However, the Court recognizes the authority of Congress to do this and several bills have been introduced in Congress to except various federal claims from enforcement of pre-dispute arbitration agreements. A few such bills have become law. Perhaps the most significant is the Dodd Frank Wall Street Reform Act, which generally banned the use of pre-dispute arbitration agreements in connection with residential mortgages and home-equity loans.[7] Other statutes prohibiting enforcement of pre-dispute arbitration agreements reach motor vehicle franchise agreements between automobile manufacturers and dealers,[8] employment agreements of military contractors,[9] and agreements extending credit to military personnel.[10]

In addition, the Supreme Court has not reversed lower court decisions denying enforcement of agreements to arbitrate core bankruptcy matters.[11] Nor has the Court

---

[7] 15 U.S.C. § 1639c.

[8] 15 U.S.C. § 1226(a)(2) ("Notwithstanding any other provision of law, whenever a motor vehicle franchise contract provides for the use of arbitration to resolve a controversy arising out of or relating to such contract, arbitration may be used to settle such controversy only if after such controversy arises all parties to such controversy consent in writing to use arbitration to settle such controversy.").

[9] Defense Appropriations Act, Pub. L. No. 111–118, § 8116, 123 Stat. 3409, 3454 (2009) (uncodified); 48 C.F.R. § 222.7402.

[10] 10 U.S.C. § 987(f)(4) ("Notwithstanding section 2 of title 9, or any other Federal or State law, rule, or regulation, no agreement to arbitrate any dispute involving the extension of consumer credit shall be enforceable against any covered member or dependent of such a member, or any person who was a covered member or dependent of that member when the agreement was made.").

[11] See, e.g., In re White Mountain Mining Co., L.L.C., 403 F.3d 164, 169–70 (4th Cir. 2005)("Congress intended to centralize disputes about a debtor's assets and legal obligations in the bankruptcy courts. Arbitration is inconsistent with centralized decision-making because permitting an arbitrator to decide a core issue would make debtor-creditor rights contingent upon an arbitrator's ruling rather than the ruling of the bankruptcy judge assigned to hear the debtor's case."); In re U.S. Lines, Inc., 197 F.3d 631, 640 (2d Cir.1999) ("there will be occasions where a dispute involving both the Bankruptcy Code and the Arbitration Act presents

overruled state court decisions denying enforcement of agreements to arbitrate child custody disputes.[12]

QUESTIONS TO REVIEW AND SYNTHESIZE

1. What agreements were the employees in *Epic* seeking to invalidate? Why were they unsuccessful?
2. What is *Lochner* and how do *Epic*'s majority and dissenting opinions use *Lochner*?
3. What federal statutes specifically ban some pre-dispute arbitration agreements?

C. THE FEDERAL ARBITRATION ACT AND STATE LAW

1. HISTORICAL AND CONSTITUTIONAL CONTEXT

Beginning with New York in 1920, almost all states have now passed statutes instructing courts to specifically enforce executory arbitration agreements, including those formed pre-dispute. The Uniform Arbitration Act, on which most of these statutes have been modeled, was adopted by the National Conference of the Commissioners on Uniform State Laws in 1955, and the Revised Uniform Arbitration Act was adopted by the Uniform Law Commissioners in 2000. About twenty states have adopted RUAA, while about 14 continue to use the UAA.[13]

Although nearly every state's law enforces most pre-dispute arbitration agreements, many states carve out exceptions for certain types of transactions, such as consumer, employment, or insurance.[14] And many states decline to enforce agreements to arbitrate certain categories of claims, such as tort claims, personal injury claims, or medical malpractice claims.[15] In contrast, the Supreme Court interprets the Federal Arbitration Act to enforce arbitration agreements in nearly all transactions and with respect to nearly all claims. Moreover, the Supreme Court has

---

a conflict of near polar extremes: bankruptcy policy exerts an inexorable pull towards centralization while arbitration policy advocates a decentralized approach towards dispute resolution.").

[12] See, e.g., Kelm v. Kelm, 92 Ohio St.3d 223, 749 N.E.2d 299 (2001)(while an arbitration clause is enforceable as to matters "relating to spousal and child support," such a rule should not be extended to allow "matters of custody and visitation" to be resolved by arbitration); Cohen v. Cohen, 600 N.Y.S.2d 996, 996–97 (App.Div.1993) (refusing to compel arbitration of custody before rabbinical tribunal because "[d]isputes over custody and visitation are not subject to arbitration").

[13] See Arbitration Act (2000), Uniform Law Commission (2019) (states and D.C. adopting RUAA), https://www.uniformlaws.org/committees/community-home?CommunityKey=a0ad71d6-085f-4648-857a-e9e893ae2736; Arbitration Act (1956), Uniform Law Commission (2019 (jurisdictions that have adopted UAA), https://www.uniformlaws.org/committees/community-home?CommunityKey=f60b379c-6378-4d9d-b271-97522fad6f89.

[14] See, e.g., Ark.Code Ann. 16–108–233 (2011)(insurance contracts); Ga.Code Ann. 9–9–2(c)(3), (6) (West 2003) (insurance contracts, consumer contracts); Md. Code Ann., Cts. & Jud. Proc. 3–206.1 (consumer insurance contracts) (West 2002); Mo.Ann.Stat. 435.350 (West 1992) (adhesion contracts, insurance contracts); N.Y.Gen.Bus.Law 399–c(2)(b) (McKinney 1996) (consumer contracts); Ohio Rev.Code Ann. 2711.01(B)(1) (West 2009) (real estate contracts); R.I.Gen.Laws 10–3–2 (2006) (employment contracts, insurance contracts); S.D.Codified Laws 21–25A–3 (2004) (insurance contracts).

[15] See, e.g., Ark. Code Ann. 16–108–230(b)(1) (personal injury); Ga. Code Ann. 9–9–2(c)(10) (personal injury); Iowa Code Ann. 679A.1(2)(c) (tort); Kan. Stat. Ann. 5–401(c)(3) (tort); Mont. Code Ann. 27–5–114(2)(a) (personal injury); Neb. Rev. Stat. 25–2602.01(e), (f) (workers compensation, personal injury tort, Fair Employment Practices Act); N.C. Gen. Stat. 90–21.60(a) ("all claims for damages for personal injury or wrongful death based on alleged negligence in the provision of health care"); S. C. Code Ann. 15–48–10(b)(3) (medical malpractice).

repeatedly held that the FAA preempts many state laws relating to arbitration. On the other hand, the Supreme Court recognizes that the FAA incorporates some state law, including much contract law. So, the FAA's relationship to state law is a hugely important topic that pervades arbitration law in the United States.

The relationship between a federal statute and state law begins with the United States Constitution's Supremacy Clause. It says that if a federal law is within the Constitution's scope of federal power then that federal law is supreme over conflicting state law, so a court (federal or state) must apply the federal law rather than the conflicting state law. However, some federal laws are written to apply only in federal court. For instance, the Federal Rules of Civil Procedure only apply in federal court and thus do not preempt the "inconsistent" state law, the state rules of civil procedure, which only apply in state court. No conflict arises because each set of rules governs only in its own forum. The same was true of federal and state arbitration law prior to the FAA's 1925 enactment. Federal arbitration law governed only in federal court, while state arbitration law governed only in state court.

2. *SOUTHLAND* AND ITS PROGENY

a. BROAD FAA PREEMPTION

Southland Corporation v. Keating

Supreme Court of the United States, 1984.
465 U.S. 1, 104 S.Ct. 852, 79 L.Ed.2d 1.

■ CHIEF JUSTICE BURGER delivered the opinion of the Court.

This case presents the questions (a) whether the California Franchise Investment Law, which invalidates certain arbitration agreements covered by the Federal Arbitration Act, violates the Supremacy Clause and (b) whether arbitration under the federal Act is impaired when a class-action structure is imposed on the process by the state courts.

Appellant Southland Corp. is the owner and franchisor of 7-Eleven convenience stores. Southland's standard franchise agreement provides each franchisee with a license to use certain registered trademarks, a lease or sublease of a convenience store owned or leased by Southland, inventory financing, and assistance in advertising and merchandising. The franchisees operate the stores, supply bookkeeping data, and pay Southland a fixed percentage of gross profits. The franchise agreement also contains the following provision requiring arbitration:

> Any controversy or claim arising out of or relating to this Agreement or the breach hereof shall be settled by arbitration in accordance with the Rules of the American Arbitration Association . . . and judgment upon any award rendered by the arbitrator may be entered in any court having jurisdiction thereof.

Appellees are 7-Eleven franchisees. Between September 1975 and January 1977, several appellees filed individual actions against Southland in California Superior Court alleging, among other things, fraud, oral misrepresentation, breach of contract, breach of fiduciary duty, and violation of the disclosure requirements of the California Franchise Investment Law, Cal.Corp.Code § 31000 et seq. Southland's answer, in all but one of the individual actions, included the affirmative defense of failure to arbitrate.

In May 1977, appellee Keating filed a class action against Southland on behalf of a class that assertedly includes approximately 800 California franchisees. Keating's principal claims were substantially the same as those asserted by the other franchisees. After the various actions were consolidated, Southland petitioned to compel arbitration of the claims in all cases, and appellees moved for class certification.

The Superior Court granted Southland's motion to compel arbitration of all claims except those claims based on the Franchise Investment Law. The court did not pass on appellees' request for class certification. Southland appealed from the order insofar as it excluded from arbitration the claims based on the California statute. Appellees filed a petition for a writ of mandamus or prohibition in the California Court of Appeal arguing that the arbitration should proceed as a class action.

The California Court of Appeal reversed the trial court's refusal to compel arbitration of appellees' claims under the Franchise Investment Law. That court interpreted the arbitration clause to require arbitration of all claims asserted under the Franchise Investment Law, and construed the Franchise Investment Law not to invalidate such agreements to arbitrate. Alternatively, the court concluded that if the Franchise Investment Law rendered arbitration agreements involving commerce unenforceable, it would conflict with § 2 of the Federal Arbitration Act and therefore be invalid under the Supremacy Clause. The Court of Appeal also determined that there was no "insurmountable obstacle" to conducting an arbitration on a classwide basis, and issued a writ of mandate directing the trial court to conduct class-certification proceedings.

The California Supreme Court, by a vote of 4–2, reversed the ruling that claims asserted under the Franchise Investment Law are arbitrable. The California Supreme Court interpreted the Franchise Investment Law to require judicial consideration of claims brought under that statute and concluded that the California statute did not contravene the federal Act.

* * *

The California Franchise Investment Law provides:

> Any condition, stipulation or provision purporting to bind any person acquiring any franchise to waive compliance with any provision of this law or any rule or order hereunder is void.
>
> Cal.Corp.Code Ann. § 31512.

The California Supreme Court interpreted this statute to require judicial consideration of claims brought under the state statute and accordingly refused to enforce the parties' contract to arbitrate such claims. So interpreted the California Franchise Investment Law directly conflicts with § 2 of the Federal Arbitration Act and violates the Supremacy Clause.

In enacting § 2 of the federal Act, Congress declared a national policy favoring arbitration and withdrew the power of the states to require a judicial forum for the resolution of claims which the contracting parties agreed to resolve by arbitration. * * *

We discern only two limitations on the enforceability of arbitration provisions governed by the Federal Arbitration Act: they must be part of a written maritime contract or a contract "evidencing a transaction involving commerce" and such clauses may be revoked upon "grounds as exist at law or in equity for the revocation of any contract." We see nothing in the Act indicating that the broad principle of enforceability is subject to any additional limitations under state law.

The Federal Arbitration Act rests on the authority of Congress to enact substantive rules under the Commerce Clause. In *Prima Paint Corp. v. Flood & Conklin Mfg. Co.*, 388 U.S. 395 (1967) [excerpted in Section 3.D.2], the Court examined the legislative history of the Act and concluded that the statute "is based upon . . . the incontestable federal foundations of 'control over interstate commerce and over admiralty.'" The contract in *Prima Paint,* as here, contained an arbitration clause. One party in that case alleged that the other had committed fraud in the inducement of the contract, although not of the arbitration clause in particular, and sought to have the claim of fraud adjudicated in federal court. The Court held that, notwithstanding a contrary state rule, consideration of a claim of fraud in the inducement of a contract "is for the arbitrators and not for the courts." The Court relied for this holding on Congress' broad power to fashion substantive rules under the Commerce Clause.

At least since 1824 Congress' authority under the Commerce Clause has been held plenary. Gibbons v. Ogden, 9 Wheat 1, 196 (1824). In the words of Chief Justice Marshall, the authority of Congress is "the power to regulate; that is, to prescribe the rule by which commerce is to be governed." The statements of the Court in *Prima Paint* that the Arbitration Act was an exercise of the Commerce Clause power clearly implied that the substantive rules of the Act were to apply in state as well as federal courts.

* * *

Although the legislative history is not without ambiguities, there are strong indications that Congress had in mind something more than making arbitration agreements enforceable only in the federal courts. The House Report plainly suggests the more comprehensive objectives:

> The purpose of this bill is to make valid and enforceable agreements for arbitration contained *in contracts involving interstate commerce* or within the jurisdiction or admiralty, *or* which may be the subject of litigation in the Federal courts.

HR Rep No. 96, 68th Cong, 1st Sess, 1 (1924). (emphasis added).

This broader purpose can also be inferred from the reality that Congress would be less likely to address a problem whose impact was confined to federal courts than a problem of large significance in the field of commerce. The Arbitration Act sought to "overcome the rule of equity, that equity will not specifically enforce an[y] arbitration agreement." The House Report accompanying the bill stated:

> The need for the law arises from. . . . the jealousy of the English courts for their own jurisdiction. . . This jealousy survived for so lon[g] a period that the principle became firmly embedded in the English common law and was adopted with it by the American courts. The courts have felt that the precedent was too strongly fixed to be overturned without legislative enactment. . . .

Surely this makes clear that the House Report contemplated a broad reach of the Act, unencumbered by state-law constraints.

* * *

Justice O'Connor argues that Congress viewed the Arbitration Act "as a procedural statute, applicable only in federal courts." If it is correct that Congress sought only to create a procedural remedy in the federal courts, there can be no explanation for the express limitation in the Arbitration Act to contracts "involving commerce." For example, when Congress has authorized this Court to prescribe the rules of procedure in the federal Courts of Appeals, District Courts, and bankruptcy courts, it has not limited the power of the Court to prescribe rules applicable only to causes of action involving commerce. We would expect that if Congress, in enacting the Arbitration Act, was creating what it thought to be a procedural rule applicable only in federal courts, it would not so limit the Act to transactions involving commerce. On the other hand, Congress would need to call on the Commerce Clause if it intended the Act to apply in state courts. Yet at the same time, its reach would be limited to transactions involving interstate commerce. We therefore view the "involving commerce" requirement in § 2, not as an inexplicable limitation on the power of the federal courts, but as a necessary qualification on a statute intended to apply in state and federal courts.

Under the interpretation of the Arbitration Act urged by Justice O'Connor, claims brought under the California Franchise Investment Law are not arbitrable when they are raised in state court. Yet it is clear beyond question that if this suit had been brought as a diversity action in a federal district court, the arbitration clause would have been enforceable. The interpretation given to the Arbitration Act by the California Supreme Court would therefore encourage and reward forum shopping. We are unwilling to attribute to Congress the intent, in drawing on the comprehensive powers of the Commerce Clause, to create a right to enforce an arbitration contract and yet make the right dependent for its enforcement on the particular forum in which it is asserted. And since the overwhelming proportion of all civil litigation in this country is in the state courts, we cannot believe Congress intended to limit the Arbitration Act to disputes subject only to *federal*-court jurisdiction.[9] Such an interpretation would frustrate congressional intent to place

---

[9] While the Federal Arbitration Act creates federal substantive law requiring the parties to honor arbitration agreements, it does not create any independent federal question jurisdiction under 28 USC § 1331 or otherwise. This seems implicit in the provisions in § 3 for a stay by a "court in which such suit is pending" and in § 4 that enforcement may be ordered by "any United States district court which, save for such agreement, would have jurisdiction under title 28, in a civil action or in admiralty of the subject matter of a suit arising out of the controversy between the parties."

"[a]n arbitration agreement . . . upon the same footing as other contracts, where it belongs." HR Rep No. 96, 68th Cong, 1st Sess, 1 (1924).

In creating a substantive rule applicable in state as well as federal courts,[10] Congress intended to foreclose state legislative attempts to undercut the enforceability of arbitration agreements.[11] We hold that § 31512 of the California Franchise Investment Law violates the Supremacy Clause.

The judgment of the California Supreme Court denying enforcement of the arbitration agreement is reversed; as to the question whether the Federal Arbitration Act precludes a class-action arbitration and any other issues not raised in the California courts, no decision by this Court would be appropriate at this time. As to the latter issues, the case is remanded for further proceedings not inconsistent with this opinion.

■ JUSTICE STEVENS, concurring in part and dissenting in part.

The Court holds that an arbitration clause that is enforceable in an action in a federal court is equally enforceable if the action is brought in a state court. I agree with that conclusion. Although Justice O'Connor's review of the legislative history of the Federal Arbitration Act demonstrates that the 1925 Congress that enacted the statute viewed the statute as essentially procedural in nature, I am persuaded that the intervening developments in the law compel the conclusion that the Court has reached. I am nevertheless troubled by one aspect of the case that seems to trouble none of my colleagues.

For me it is not "clear beyond question that if this suit had been brought as a diversity action in a federal district court, the arbitration clause would have been enforceable." The general rule prescribed by § 2 of the Federal Arbitration Act is that arbitration clauses in contracts involving interstate transactions are enforceable as a matter of federal law. That general rule, however, is subject to an exception based on "such grounds as exist at law or in equity for the revocation of any contract." I believe that exception leaves room for the implementation of certain substantive state policies that would be undermined by enforcing certain categories of arbitration clauses.

---

10 The contention is made that the Court's interpretation of § 2 of the Act renders §§ 3 and 4 "largely superfluous." This misreads our holding and the Act. In holding that the Arbitration Act preempts a state law that withdraws the power to enforce arbitration agreements, we do not hold that §§ 3 and 4 of the Arbitration Act apply to proceedings in state courts. Section 4, for example, provides that the Federal Rules of Civil Procedure apply in proceedings to compel arbitration. The Federal Rules do not apply in such state-court proceedings.

11 * * * Justice Stevens dissents in part on the ground that § 2 of the Arbitration Act permits a party to nullify an agreement to arbitrate on "such grounds as exist at law or in equity for the revocation of any contract." We agree, of course, that a party may assert general contract defenses such as fraud to avoid enforcement of an arbitration agreement. We conclude, however, that the defense to arbitration found in the California Franchise Investment Law is not a ground that exists at law or in equity "for the revocation of any contract" but merely a ground that exists for the revocation of arbitration provisions in contracts subject to the California Franchise Investment Law. Moreover, under this dissenting view, "a state policy of providing special protection for franchisees . . . can be recognized without impairing the basic purposes of the federal statute." If we accepted this analysis, states could wholly eviscerate Congressional intent to place arbitration agreements "upon the same footing as other contracts" simply by passing statutes such as the Franchise Investment Law. We have rejected this analysis because it is in conflict with the Arbitration Act and would permit states to override the declared policy requiring enforcement of arbitration agreements.

The exercise of state authority in a field traditionally occupied by state law will not be deemed preempted by a federal statute unless that was the clear and manifest purpose of Congress. Moreover, even where a federal statute does displace state authority, it "rarely occupies a legal field completely, totally excluding all participation by the legal systems of the states. . . . Federal legislation, on the whole, has been conceived and drafted on an ad hoc basis to accomplish limited objectives. It builds upon legal relationships established by the states, altering or supplanting them only so far as necessary for the special purpose." P. Bator, P. Mishkin, D. Shapiro, & H. Wechsler, Hart and Wechsler's The Federal Courts and the Federal System 470–471 (2d ed. 1973).

The limited objective of the Federal Arbitration Act was to abrogate the general common-law rule against specific enforcement of arbitration agreements, and a state statute which merely codified the general common-law rule—either directly by employing the prior doctrine of revocability or indirectly by declaring all such agreements void—would be pre-empted by the Act. However, beyond this conclusion, which seems compelled by the language of § 2 and case law concerning the Act, it is by no means clear that Congress intended entirely to displace state authority in this field. Indeed, while it is an understatement to say that "the legislative history of the . . . Act . . . reveals little awareness on the part of Congress that state law might be affected," it must surely be true that given the lack of a "clear mandate from Congress as to the extent to which state statutes and decisions are to be superseded, we must be cautious in construing the act lest we excessively encroach on the powers which Congressional policy, if not the Constitution, would reserve to the states."

The textual basis in the Act for avoiding such encroachment is the clause of § 2 which provides that arbitration agreements are subject to revocation on such grounds as exist at law or in equity for the revocation of any contract. The Act, however, does not define what grounds for revocation may be permissible, and hence it would appear that the judiciary must fashion the limitations as a matter of federal common law. In doing so, we must first recognize that as the "'saving clause' in § 2 indicates, the purpose of Congress in 1925 was to make arbitration agreements as enforceable as other contracts, but not more so." The existence of a federal statute enunciating a substantive federal policy does not necessarily require the inexorable application of a uniform federal rule of decision notwithstanding the differing conditions which may exist in the several States and regardless of the decisions of the States to exert police powers as they deem best for the welfare of their citizens. Indeed the lower courts generally look to state law regarding questions of formation of the arbitration agreement under § 2, which is entirely appropriate so long as the state rule does not conflict with the policy of § 2.

A contract which is deemed void is surely revocable at law or in equity, and the California Legislature has declared all conditions purporting to waive compliance with the protections of the Franchise Investment Laws, including but not limited to arbitration provisions, void as a matter of public policy. Given the importance to the State of franchise relationships, the relative disparity in the bargaining positions between the franchisor and the franchisee, and the remedial purposes of the California Act, I believe this declaration of state policy is entitled to respect.

* * *

[A] state policy of providing special protection for franchisees, such as that expressed in California's Franchise Investment Law, can be recognized without impairing the basic purposes of the federal statute. Like the majority of the California Supreme Court, I am not persuaded that Congress intended the preemptive effect of this statute to be "so unyielding as to require enforcement of an agreement to arbitrate a dispute over the application of a regulatory statute which a state legislature, in conformity with analogous federal policy, has decided should be left to judicial enforcement."

Thus * * * I respectfully dissent from [the Court's] conclusion concerning the enforceability of the arbitration agreement. On that issue, I would affirm the judgment of the California Supreme Court.

■ JUSTICE O'CONNOR, with whom JUSTICE REHNQUIST joins, dissenting.

The majority opinion decides three issues. First, it holds that § 2 creates federal substantive rights that must be enforced by the state courts. Second, though the issue is not raised in this case, the Court states that § 2 substantive rights may not be the basis for invoking federal-court jurisdiction under 28 U.S.C. § 1331. Third, the Court reads § 2 to require state courts to enforce § 2 rights using procedures that mimic those specified for federal courts by FAA §§ 3 and 4. The first of these conclusions is unquestionably wrong as a matter of statutory construction; the second appears to be an attempt to limit the damage done by the first; the third is unnecessary and unwise.

One rarely finds a legislative history as unambiguous as the FAA's. That history establishes conclusively that the 1925 Congress viewed the FAA as a procedural statute, applicable only in federal courts, derived, Congress believed, largely from the federal power to control the jurisdiction of the federal courts.

In 1925 Congress emphatically believed arbitration to be a matter of "procedure." At hearings on the Act congressional Subcommittees were told: "The theory on which you do this is that you have the right to tell the Federal courts how to proceed."

* * *

Since *Bernhardt* [v. *Polygraphic Co. of America, Inc.*, 350 U.S. 198, 100 L. Ed. 199, 76 S. Ct. 273 (1956)], a right to arbitration has been characterized as "substantive," and that holding is not challenged here. But Congress in 1925 did not characterize the FAA as this Court did in 1956. Congress believed that the FAA established nothing more than a rule of procedure, a rule therefore applicable only in the federal courts.

* * *

Yet another indication that Congress did not intend the FAA to govern state-court proceedings is found in the powers Congress relied on in passing the Act. The FAA might have been grounded on Congress' powers to regulate interstate and maritime affairs, since the Act extends only to contracts in those areas. There are, indeed, references in the legislative history to the corresponding federal powers. More numerous, however, are the references to Congress' pre-*Erie* power to prescribe "general law" applicable in all federal courts. At the congressional hearings, for example: "Congress rests solely upon its power to prescribe the jurisdiction and duties of the Federal courts." * * * Plainly, a power derived from Congress' Art III control over federal-court jurisdiction would not by any flight of fancy permit Congress to control proceedings in state courts.

* * *

Section 2, like the rest of the FAA, should have no application whatsoever in state courts. Assuming, to the contrary, that § 2 *does* create a federal right that the state courts must enforce, state courts should nonetheless be allowed, at least in the first instance, to fashion their own procedures for enforcing the right. Unfortunately, the Court seems to direct that the arbitration clause at issue here must be *specifically* enforced; apparently no other means of enforcement is permissible.[20]

It is settled that a state court must honor federally created rights and that it may not unreasonably undermine them by invoking contrary local procedure. "'[T]he assertion of federal rights, when plainly and reasonably made, is not to be defeated under the name of local practice.'" Brown v. Western Ry. Co. of Alabama, 338 U.S. 294, 299 (1949). But absent specific direction from Congress the state courts have always been permitted to apply their own reasonable procedures when enforcing federal rights. Before we undertake to read a set of complex and mandatory procedures into § 2's brief and general language, we should at a minimum allow state courts and legislatures a chance to develop their own methods for enforcing the new federal rights. Some might choose to award compensatory or punitive damages for the violation of an arbitration agreement; some might award litigation costs to the party who remained willing to arbitrate; some might affirm the "validity and enforceability" of arbitration agreements in other ways. Any of these approaches would vindicate § 2 rights in a manner fully consonant with the language and background of that provision.

The unelaborated terms of § 2 certainly invite flexible enforcement. At common law many jurisdictions were hostile to arbitration agreements. That hostility was reflected in two different doctrines: "revocability," which allowed parties to repudiate arbitration agreements at any time before the arbitrator's award was made, and "invalidity" or "unenforceability," equivalent rules that flatly denied any remedy for the failure to honor an arbitration agreement. In contrast, common-law jurisdictions that enforced arbitration agreements did so in at least three different ways—through actions for damages, actions for specific enforcement, or by enforcing sanctions imposed by trade and commercial

[20] If my understanding of the Court's opinion is correct, the Court has made § 3 of the FAA binding on the state courts. But * * * § 3 by its own terms governs only federal-court proceedings. Moreover, if § 2, standing alone, creates a federal right to specific enforcement of arbitration agreements §§ 3 and 4 are, of course, largely superfluous. And if § 2 implicitly incorporates §§ 3 and 4 procedures for making arbitration agreements enforceable before arbitration begins, why not also § 9 procedures concerning venue, personal jurisdiction, and notice for enforcing an arbitrator's award after arbitration ends? One set of procedures is of little use without the other.

associations on members who violated arbitration agreements. In 1925 a forum allowing any one of these remedies would have been thought to recognize the "validity" and "enforceability" of arbitration clauses.

* * *

The Court rejects the idea of requiring the FAA to be applied only in federal courts partly out of concern with the problem of forum shopping. The concern is unfounded. Because the FAA makes the federal courts equally accessible to both parties to a dispute, no forum shopping would be possible even if we gave the FAA a construction faithful to the congressional intent. In controversies involving incomplete diversity of citizenship there is simply no access to federal court and therefore no possibility of forum shopping. In controversies *with* complete diversity of citizenship the FAA grants federal-court access equally to both parties; no party can gain any advantage by forum shopping. Even when the party resisting arbitration initiates an action in state court, the opposing party can invoke FAA § 4 and promptly secure a federal court order to compel arbitration. See, e.g., Moses H. Cone Memorial Hospital v. Mercury Construction Corp., 460 U.S. 1 (1983).

* * *

Apparently confident that state courts are not competent to devise their own procedures for protecting the newly discovered federal right, the Court summarily prescribes a specific procedure, found nowhere in § 2 or its common-law origins, that the state courts are to follow.

Today's decision is unfaithful to congressional intent, unnecessary, and, in light of the FAA's antecedents and the intervening contraction of federal power, inexplicable. Although arbitration is a worthy alternative to litigation, today's exercise in judicial revisionism goes too far. I respectfully dissent.

"Several justices and almost all of the commentators who have written about *Southland* agree that this case was wrongly decided and inconsistent with congressional intent" to apply only in federal courts. Margaret L. Moses, *Statutory Misconstruction: How The Supreme Court Created A Federal Arbitration Law Never Enacted By Congress*, 34 Fla. St. U.L. Rev. 99, 125–26 (2006). However, *Southland*'s holding is consistent with the language of FAA section 2, which "broadly makes 'valid, irrevocable, and enforceable' both pre-dispute and post-dispute arbitration agreements. Nothing in the language of the section limits its application to cases in the federal courts." Christopher R. Drahozal, *In Defense of Southland: Reexamining the Legislative History of the Federal Arbitration Act*, 78 Notre Dame L. Rev. 101, 123 (2002). "By contrast, the remaining sections of the FAA by their terms apply only in federal court." Id.

Stephen J. Ware, *A Short Defense of Southland, Casarotto, and Other Long-Controversial Arbitration Decisions*

30 Loyola Consumer L. Rev. 303, 310–15 (2018).

Even if the drafters and adopters of the FAA did not intend for any of it to apply in state court and preempt state law, this original understanding of the FAA would not be conclusive because it does not account for the Supreme Court's 1938 decision in *Erie v. Tompkins*. This landmark case held that "federal courts lack the authority to create 'federal general common law,' an authority that the Supreme Court had endorsed nearly a century earlier," but rather must "apply state law in the same fashion that a state court would." *Erie* is one of the most studied cases ever because of its pervasive importance, and *Erie* posed a strong challenge to interpreting the FAA to apply only in federal courts. As I wrote over twenty years ago:

> "When it was enacted in 1925, the FAA was a procedural statute applicable only in federal courts." During the following decades, there was "universal recognition that the FAA had nothing to do with proceedings in state courts." This changed when the Supreme Court considered the effects of its landmark decisions in *Erie Railroad v. Tompkins* and *Guaranty Trust Co. v. York.*[34] *Erie* held that federal courts lack power to create substantive law, so they must decide cases according to state substantive law and federal procedural law. *Erie* thus required a line between "substance" and "procedure." *Guaranty Trust* provided such a line; it put on the substantive side any law that was "outcome determinative." The Supreme Court used that line in *Bernhardt v. Polygraphic Co. of America*[35] to conclude that the FAA is substantive law. Thus *Erie, Guaranty Trust* and *Bernhardt* moved the "FAA from the procedural side of the law, where Congress had put it in 1925, to the substantive side, where Congress had most decidedly not put it."[36]
>
> Once the FAA became understood as substantive law, a troubling issue arose about the FAA's constitutionality. If the FAA applied only in the federal courts then the Supreme Court "would have had to decide if Congress could legislate where *Erie* had forbidden the federal courts to create common law."[37] In 1967 the Court in *Prima Paint v. Flood & Conklin Mfg. Co.*[38] avoided this difficult issue by concluding, against the evidence, that Congress had enacted the FAA pursuant to its power to regulate interstate commerce. "The Court did not quite say that the FAA governs in state court, but its reasoning left little room for any other

---

[34] Guar. Tr. Co. v. York, 326 U.S. 99 (1945).

[35] Bernhardt v. Polygraphic Co. of Am., 350 U.S. 198 (1956).

[36] Stephen J. Ware, *Arbitration and Unconscionability After Doctor's Associates, Inc. v. Casarotto*, 31 Wake Forest L. Rev. 1001, 1007–08 (1996) (quoting Ian R. Macneil, Richard Speidel & Thomas Stipanowich., Federal Arbitration Law § 10.4.1 (1994)).

[37] Id. (quoting Linda R. Hirshman, The Second Arbitration Trilogy: The Federalization of Arbitration Law, 71 VA. L. REV. 1305, 1320 (1985)).

[38] 388 U.S. 395 (1967).

> result." The Supreme Court eventually concluded that the FAA governs in state court in the 1980s cases of *Moses H. Cone Memorial Hospital v. Mercury Construction Corp.*, and *Southland Corp. v. Keating*.

To recap, *Erie*'s fundamental change of the relationship between federal and state law—a change that far transcends the FAA or any other statute—may well have made the FAA unconstitutional had the Supreme Court interpreted the FAA as many argue its drafters and adopters originally understood it. In contrast, the Court's different, but still plausible, interpretation of the FAA preserved its constitutionality.

When a statute admits of more than one plausible interpretation, courts routinely choose the interpretation that preserves the statute's constitutionality. The Supreme Court has long followed this "avoidance canon," so it is quite ordinary that the Court, after *Erie*, preserved the FAA's constitutionality by interpreting its main substantive provision, section 2, to apply in state courts. * * *

* * * And while the Court's interpretation of the FAA may have disregarded the FAA's legislative history, such disregard is consistent with mainstream approaches to statutory interpretation that, for good reasons, tend to give little or no weight to legislative history. So a Supreme Court that disregards legislative history in favor of a textually plausible statutory interpretation that preserves the statute's constitutionality deserves our sympathy. The post-*Erie* Court faced a difficult predicament and worked through it pretty well—certainly better than the alternative of holding that *Erie* had rendered the FAA unconstitutional.

The preceding excerpt from *A Short Defense of Southland* quotes from, and relies heavily on, a magisterial five-volume treatise, Ian MacNeil, Richard Speidel & Thomas Stipanowich, Federal Arbitration Law (1994), which won the American Association of Publishers' Best New Legal Book Award.

QUESTIONS TO REVIEW AND SYNTHESIZE

1. Had the U.S. Supreme Court declined to hear *Southland*, the California Supreme Court's decision likely would have resulted in arbitration of all, some, or none of the franchisees' claims against Southland?
2. Justice Stevens' opinion in *Southland* said "Although Justice O'Connor's review of the legislative history of the Federal Arbitration Act demonstrates that the 1925 Congress that enacted the statute viewed the statute as essentially procedural in nature, I am persuaded that the intervening developments in the law compel the conclusion that the Court has reached." What were those "intervening developments in the law" and why might they "compel the conclusion that the court has reached"?

b. ADHESIVE ARBITRATION AGREEMENTS AND JUDGES' POLITICS

The FAA applies to any "maritime transaction" or "contract evidencing a transaction involving commerce." The FAA is the only federal statute that uses the word "involving" to describe a relation to interstate commerce, and for many years courts divided on how broadly to interpret this language. The following case interpreted it broadly to preempt inconsistent state law and increase the Supreme Court's enforcement of arbitration clauses in the form ("adhesion") contracts businesses draft and present on a take-it-or-leave-it basis to consumers, employees, franchisees, and other parties.

Allied-Bruce Terminix Cos. v. Dobson

Supreme Court of the United States, 1995.
513 U.S. 265, 115 S.Ct. 834, 130 L.Ed.2d 753.

■ JUSTICE BREYER delivered the opinion of the Court.

This case concerns the reach of § 2 of the Federal Arbitration Act. That section makes enforceable a written arbitration provision in "a contract *evidencing* a transaction *involving* commerce." 9 U.S.C. § 2 (emphasis added). Should we read this phrase broadly, extending the Act's reach to the limits of Congress' Commerce Clause power? Or, do the two italicized words—"involving" and "evidencing"—significantly restrict the Act's application? We conclude that the broader reading of the Act is the correct one, and we reverse a State Supreme Court judgment to the contrary.

In August 1987, Steven Gwin, a respondent who owned a house in Birmingham, Alabama, bought a lifetime "Termite Protection Plan" (Plan) from the local office of Allied-Bruce Terminix Companies, a franchise of Terminix International Company. In the Plan, Allied-Bruce promised "to protect" Gwin's house "against the attack of subterranean termites," to reinspect periodically, to provide any "further treatment found necessary," and to repair, up to $ 100,000, damage caused by new termite infestations. Terminix International "guaranteed the fulfillment of the terms" of the Plan. The Plan's contract document provided in writing that

> "*any controversy or claim* ... arising out of or relating to the interpretation, performance or breach of any provision of this agreement *shall be settled exclusively by arbitration.*"

In the spring of 1991, Mr. and Mrs. Gwin, wishing to sell their house to Mr. and Mrs. Dobson, had Allied-Bruce reinspect the house. They obtained a clean bill of health. But no sooner had they sold the house and transferred the Plan to Mr. and Mrs. Dobson than the Dobsons found the house swarming with termites. Allied-Bruce attempted to treat and repair the house, but the Dobsons found Allied-Bruce's efforts inadequate. They therefore sued the Gwins, and (along with the Gwins, who cross-claimed) also sued Allied-Bruce and Terminix in Alabama state court. Allied-Bruce and Terminix, pointing to the Plan's arbitration clause and § 2 of the Federal Arbitration Act, immediately asked the court for a stay, to allow arbitration to proceed. The court denied the stay. Allied-Bruce and Terminix appealed.

The Supreme Court of Alabama upheld the denial of the stay on the basis of a state statute, Ala. Code § 8–1–41(3) (1993), making written, predispute arbitration agreements invalid and "unenforceable". To reach this conclusion, the court had to find that the Federal Arbitration Act, which pre-empts conflicting state law, did not apply to the termite contract. It made just that finding. The court considered the federal Act inapplicable because the connection between the termite contract and interstate commerce was too slight. In the court's view, the Act applies to a contract only if "at the time [the parties entered into the contract] and accepted the arbitration clause, they *contemplated* substantial interstate activity." Despite some interstate activities (*e. g.*, Allied-Bruce, like Terminix, is a multistate firm and shipped treatment and repair material from out of state), the court found that the parties "contemplated" a transaction that was primarily local and not "substantially" interstate.

* * *

Before we can reach the main issues in this case, we must set forth three items of legal background.

First, the basic purpose of the Federal Arbitration Act is to overcome courts' refusals to enforce agreements to arbitrate. * * * It intended courts to "enforce [arbitration] agreements into which parties had entered," and to "place such agreements 'upon the same footing as other contracts.'"

Second, some initially assumed that the Federal Arbitration Act represented an exercise of Congress' Article III power to "ordain and establish" federal courts, U.S. Const., Art. III, § 1. In 1967, however, this Court held that the Act "is based upon and confined to the incontestable federal foundations of 'control over interstate commerce and over admiralty.'" Prima Paint Corp. v. Flood & Conklin Mfg. Co., 388 U.S. 395, 405, 18 L. Ed. 2d 1270, 87 S. Ct. 1801 (1967) (quoting H. R. Rep. No. 96, 68th Cong., 1st Sess., 1 (1924)). * * *

Third, the holding in *Prima Paint* led to a further question. Did Congress intend the Act also to apply in state courts? Did the Federal Arbitration Act pre-empt conflicting state antiarbitration law, or could state courts apply their antiarbitration rules in cases before them, thereby reaching results different from those reached in otherwise similar federal diversity cases? In *Southland Corp.* v. *Keating,* this Court decided that Congress would not have wanted state and federal courts to reach different outcomes about the validity of arbitration in similar cases. The Court concluded that the Federal Arbitration Act pre-empts state law; and it held that state courts cannot apply state statutes that invalidate arbitration agreements.

We have set forth this background because respondents, supported by 20 state attorneys general, now ask us to overrule *Southland* and thereby to permit Alabama to apply its antiarbitration statute in this case irrespective of the proper interpretation of § 2. The *Southland* Court, however, recognized that the pre-emption issue was a difficult one, and it considered the basic arguments that respondents and *amici* now raise (even though those issues were not thoroughly briefed at the time). Nothing significant has changed in the 10 years subsequent to *Southland;* no later cases have eroded *Southland*'s authority; and no unforeseen practical problems have arisen. Moreover, in the interim, private parties have likely written contracts relying upon *Southland* as authority. Further, Congress, both before and after *Southland*, has enacted legislation extending, not retracting, the scope of arbitration. See, *e. g.*, 9 U.S.C. § 15 (eliminating the Act of State doctrine as a bar to arbitration); 9 U.S.C. §§ 201–208 (international arbitration). For these reasons, we find it inappropriate to reconsider what is by now well-established law.

We therefore proceed to the basic interpretive questions aware that we are interpreting an Act that seeks broadly to overcome judicial hostility to arbitration agreements and that applies in both federal and state courts. We must decide in this case whether that Act used language about interstate commerce that nonetheless limits the Act's application, thereby carving out an important statutory niche in which a State remains free to apply its antiarbitration law or policy. We conclude that it does not.

The Federal Arbitration Act, § 2, provides that a

> "written provision in any maritime transaction or *a contract evidencing a transaction involving commerce* to settle by arbitration a controversy thereafter arising out of such contract or transaction . . . shall be valid, irrevocable, and enforceable, save upon such grounds as exist at law or in equity for the revocation of any contract." 9 U.S.C. § 2 (emphasis added).

The initial interpretive question focuses upon the words "involving commerce." These words are broader than the often-found words of art "in commerce." They therefore cover more than "'only persons or activities *within the flow* of interstate commerce.'" But how far beyond the flow of commerce does the word "involving" reach? Is "involving" the functional equivalent of the word "affecting?" That phrase—"affecting commerce"—normally signals Congress' intent to exercise its Commerce Clause powers to the full. We cannot look to other statutes for guidance for the parties tell us that this is the only federal statute that uses the word "involving" to describe an interstate commerce relation.

After examining the statute's language, background, and structure, we conclude that the word "involving" is broad and is indeed the functional equivalent of "affecting." For one thing, such an interpretation, linguistically speaking, is permissible. The dictionary finds instances in which "involve" and "affect" sometimes can mean about the same thing. V Oxford English Dictionary 466 (1st ed. 1933) (providing examples dating back to the mid-19th century, where "involve" means to "include or affect in . . . operation"). For another, the Act's legislative history, to the extent that it is informative, indicates an expansive congressional intent. See, *e. g.*, H. R. Rep. No. 96, at 1 (the Act's "control over interstate commerce reaches not only the actual physical interstate shipment of goods but also contracts relating to interstate commerce") * * *.

Further, this Court has previously described the Act's reach expansively as coinciding with that of the Commerce Clause. See, e. g., Perry v. Thomas, 482 U.S. 483, 490, 96 L. Ed. 2d 426, 107 S. Ct. 2520 (1987) (the Act "embodies Congress' intent to provide for the enforcement of arbitration agreements within the full reach of the Commerce Clause"); Southland Corp. v. Keating, 465 U.S. at 14–15 (the "'involving commerce'" requirement is a constitutionally "necessary qualification" on the Act's reach, marking its permissible outer limit).

Finally, a broad interpretation of this language is consistent with the Act's basic purpose, to put arbitration provisions on "'the same footing'" as a contract's other terms. Scherk v. Alberto-Culver Co., 417 U.S. at 511. Conversely, a narrower interpretation is not consistent with the Act's purpose, for (unless unreasonably narrowed to the flow of commerce) such an interpretation would create a new, unfamiliar test lying somewhere in a no man's land between "in commerce" and "affecting commerce," thereby unnecessarily complicating the law and breeding litigation from a statute that seeks to avoid it.

We recognize arguments to the contrary: The pre-New Deal Congress that passed the Act in 1925 might well have thought the Commerce Clause did not stretch as far as has turned out to be the case. But, it is not unusual for this Court in similar circumstances to ask whether the scope of a statute should expand along with the expansion of the Commerce Clause power itself, and to answer the question affirmatively—as, for the reasons set forth above, we do here.

* * *

The Gwins and Dobsons * * * point to * * * *Bernhardt* v. *Polygraphic Co. of America, Inc.*, 350 U.S. 198, 100 L. Ed. 199, 76 S. Ct. 273 (1956). In that case, Bernhardt, a New York resident, had entered into an employment contract (containing an arbitration clause) in New York with Polygraphic, a New York corporation. But, Bernhardt "was to perform" that contract after he "later became a resident of Vermont." This Court was faced with the question whether, in light of *Erie*, a federal court should apply the Federal Arbitration Act in a diversity case when faced with state law hostile to arbitration. The Court did not reach that question, however, for it decided that the contract itself did not "involve" interstate commerce and therefore fell outside the Act. Since Congress, constitutionally speaking, *could* have applied the Act to Bernhardt's contract, say the parties, how then can we say that the Act's word "involving" reaches as far as the Commerce Clause itself?

The best response to this argument is to point to the way in which the Court reasoned in *Bernhardt*, and to what the Court said. It said that the *reason* the Act did not apply to Bernhardt's contract was that there was

> "*no showing that petitioner* while performing his duties under the employment contract was working 'in' commerce, was producing goods for commerce, or *was engaging in activity that affected commerce*, within the meaning of our decisions."

Thus, the Court interpreted the words "involving commerce" as broadly as the words "affecting commerce"; and, as we have said, these latter words normally mean a full exercise of constitutional power. At the same time, the Court's opinion does not discuss the implications of the "interstate" facts to which the respondents now point. For these reasons, *Bernhardt* does not require us to narrow the scope of the word "involving." And, we conclude that the word "involving," like "affecting," signals an intent to exercise Congress' commerce power to the full.

Section 2 applies where there is "a contract *evidencing a transaction* involving commerce." 9 U.S.C. § 2 (emphasis added). The second interpretive question focuses on the italicized words. Does "evidencing a transaction" mean only that the transaction (that the contract "evidences") must turn out, *in fact*, to have involved interstate commerce? Or, does it mean more?

* * *

We find the interpretive choice difficult, but for several reasons we conclude that the first interpretation ("commerce in fact") is more faithful to the statute than the second ("contemplation of the parties").

* * *

The parties do not contest that the transaction in this case, in fact, involved interstate commerce. In addition to the multistate nature of Terminix and Allied-Bruce, the termite-treating and house-repairing material used by Allied-Bruce in its (allegedly inadequate) efforts to carry out the terms of the Plan, came from outside Alabama.

Consequently, the judgment of the Supreme Court of Alabama is reversed, and the case is remanded for further proceedings not inconsistent with this opinion.

It is so ordered.

■ JUSTICE O'CONNOR, concurring.

* * * I have long adhered to the view, discussed below, that Congress designed the Federal Arbitration Act to apply only in federal courts. But if we are to apply the Act in state courts, it makes little sense to read § 2 differently in that context. In the end, my agreement with the Court's construction of § 2 rests largely on the wisdom of maintaining a uniform standard.

I continue to believe that Congress never intended the Federal Arbitration Act to apply in state courts, and that this Court has strayed far afield in giving the Act so broad a compass. See Southland Corp. v. Keating, 465 U.S. 1, 21–36, 79 L. Ed. 2d 1, 104 S. Ct. 852 (1984) (O'CONNOR, J., dissenting).

* * *

Were we writing on a clean slate, I would adhere to that view and affirm the Alabama court's decision. But, as the Court points out, more than 10 years have passed since *Southland*, several subsequent cases have built upon its reasoning, and parties have undoubtedly made contracts in reliance on the Court's interpretation of the Act in the interim. After reflection, I am persuaded by considerations of *stare decisis*, which we have said "have special force in the area of statutory interpretation," to acquiesce in today's judgment. Though wrong, *Southland* has not proved unworkable, and, as always, "Congress remains free to alter what we have done."

Today's decision caps this Court's effort to expand the Federal Arbitration Act. Although each decision has built logically upon the decisions preceding it, the initial building block in *Southland* laid a faulty foundation. I acquiesce in today's judgment because there is no "special justification" to overrule *Southland*. It remains now for Congress to correct this interpretation if it wishes to preserve state autonomy in state courts.

■ JUSTICE SCALIA, dissenting.

I have previously joined two judgments of this Court that rested upon the holding of *Southland Corp.* v. *Keating*, 465 U.S. 1, 79 L. Ed. 2d 1, 104 S. Ct. 852 (1984). In neither of those cases, however, did any party ask that *Southland* be overruled, and it was therefore not necessary to consider the question. In the present case, by contrast, one of respondents' central arguments is that *Southland* was wrongly decided, and their request for its overruling has been supported by an *amicus* brief signed by the attorneys general of 20 States. For the reasons set forth in JUSTICE THOMAS' opinion, which I join, I agree with the respondents (and belatedly with JUSTICE O'CONNOR) that *Southland* clearly misconstrued the Federal Arbitration Act.

I do not believe that proper application of *stare decisis* prevents correction of the mistake. Adhering to *Southland* entails a permanent, unauthorized eviction of state-court power to adjudicate a potentially large class of disputes. Abandoning it does not impair reliance interests to a degree that justifies this evil. Primary behavior is not affected: No rule of conduct is retroactively changed, but only (perhaps) the forum in which violation is to be determined and remedied. I doubt that many contracts with arbitration clauses would have been forgone, or entered into only for significantly higher remuneration, absent the *Southland* guarantee. Where, moreover, reliance on *Southland* did make a significant difference, rescission of the contract for mistake of law would often be available.

I shall not in the future dissent from judgments that rest on *Southland*. I will, however, stand ready to join four other Justices in overruling it, since *Southland* will not become more correct over time * * *.

■ JUSTICE THOMAS, with whom JUSTICE SCALIA joins, dissenting.

I disagree with the majority at the threshold of this case, and so I do not reach the question that it decides. In my view, the Federal Arbitration Act (FAA) does not apply in state courts. I respectfully dissent.

In *Southland Corp. v. Keating*, 465 U.S. 1, 79 L. Ed. 2d 1, 104 S. Ct. 852 (1984), this Court concluded that § 2 of the FAA "appl[ies] in state as well as federal courts," and "withdr[aws] the power of the states to require a judicial forum for the resolution of claims which the contracting parties agreed to resolve by arbitration." In my view, both aspects of *Southland* are wrong.

* * *

Suppose, however, that the first aspect of *Southland* was correct: § 2 requires States to enforce the covered arbitration agreements and pre-empts all contrary state law. There still would be no textual basis for *Southland*'s suggestion that § 2 requires the States to enforce those agreements through the remedy of specific performance—that is, by forcing the parties to submit to arbitration. A contract surely can be "valid, irrevocable, and enforceable" even though it can be enforced only through actions for damages. Thus, on the eve of the FAA's enactment, this Court described executory arbitration agreements as being "valid" and as creating "a perfect obligation" under federal law even though federal courts refused to order their specific performance. See Red Cross Line v. Atlantic Fruit Co., 264 U.S. 109, 120–123, 44 S.Ct. 274, 275–277, 68 L.Ed. 582 (1924).

To be sure, §§ 3 and 4 of the FAA require that federal courts specifically enforce arbitration agreements. These provisions deal, respectively, with the potential plaintiffs and the potential defendants in the underlying dispute: § 3 holds the plaintiffs to their promise not to take their claims straight to court, while § 4 holds the defendants to their promise to submit to arbitration rather than making the other party sue them. Had this case arisen in one of the "courts of the United States," it is § 3 that would have been relevant. Upon proper motion, the court would have been obliged to grant a stay pending arbitration, unless the contract between the parties did not "evidenc[e] a transaction involving [interstate] commerce." See Bernhardt, 350 U.S., at 202, 76 S.Ct., at 275–276 (holding that § 3 is limited to the arbitration agreements that § 2 declares valid). Because this case arose in the courts of Alabama, however, petitioners are forced to contend that § 2 imposes precisely the same obligation on all courts (both federal and state) that § 3 imposes solely on federal courts. Though *Southland* supports this argument, it simply cannot be correct, or § 3 would be superfluous.

Alabama law brings these issues into sharp focus. Citing "public policy" grounds that reach back to Bozeman v. Gilbert, 1 Ala. 90 (1840), Alabama courts have declared that predispute arbitration agreements are "void." See, e.g., Wells v. Mobile County Bd. of Realtors, 387 So.2d 140, 144 (Ala.1980). But a separate state statute also includes "[a]n agreement to submit a controversy to arbitration" among the obligations that "cannot be specifically enforced" in Alabama. Ala.Code § 8–1–41 (1975). * * * [FAA] § 2—even if applicable to the States—is most naturally read to pre-empt only Alabama's common-law rule and not the state statute; the statute does not itself make executory arbitration agreements invalid, revocable, or unenforceable, any more than the inclusion of "[a]n obligation to render personal service" in the same statutory provision means that employment contracts are invalid in Alabama. In the case at hand, the specific-enforcement statute appears to provide an adequate ground for the denial of petitioners' motion for a stay.

II.

Rather than attempting to defend *Southland* on its merits, petitioners rely chiefly on the doctrine of *stare decisis* in urging us to adhere to our mistaken interpretation of the FAA. * * * In my view, that doctrine is insufficient to save *Southland*.

* * *

But suppose that *stare decisis* really did require us to abide by *Southland*'s holding that § 2 applies to the States. The doctrine still would not require us to follow *Southland*'s suggestion that § 2 requires the specific enforcement of the arbitration agreements that it covers. We accord no precedential weight to mere dicta, and this latter suggestion was wholly unnecessary to the decision in *Southland*. The arbitration agreement at issue there, if valid at all with respect to the particular claims in dispute, clearly was subject to specific performance under state law; indeed, the state trial court had already compelled arbitration for all the other claims raised in the complaint. Accordingly, the only question properly before the *Southland* Court was whether § 2 pre-empted a separate state law declaring the arbitration agreement "void" as applied to the remaining claims. The same can be said for *Perry* v. *Thomas*, 482 U.S. 483, 96 L. Ed. 2d 426, 107 S. Ct. 2520 (1987), in which we again held that § 2 pre-empted a California statute that (as we had observed in a prior case) made certain arbitration clauses "unenforceable." We have subsequently reserved judgment about the extent to which state courts must enforce arbitration agreements through the mechanisms that §§ 3 and 4 of the FAA prescribe for the *federal* courts. See Volt Information Sciences, Inc. v. Board of Trustees of Leland Stanford Junior Univ., 489 U.S. 468, 477, 103 L. Ed. 2d 488, 109 S. Ct. 1248 (1989). In short, we have never actually held, as opposed to stating or implying in dicta, that the FAA requires a state court to stay lawsuits brought in violation of an arbitration agreement covered by § 2.

Because I believe that the FAA imposes no such obligation on state courts, and indeed that the statute is wholly inapplicable in those courts, I would affirm the Alabama Supreme Court's judgment.

Allied-Bruce involved a consumer transaction—a homeowner's purchase of termite protection through a pest-control business's adhesion contract, which contained an arbitration clause. Many scholars plausibly contend that those who drafted and enacted the FAA did not intend for it to apply to consumer transactions. See, e.g., Christopher R. Leslie, *The Arbitration Bootstrap*, 94 Tex. L. Rev. 265, 308 (2015) (Congress "intended the FAA to allow enforcement only of arbitration agreements between merchants. Congress did not intend the FAA to apply to consumer contracts."); Margaret L. Moses, *How the Supreme Court's Misconstruction of the FAA Has Affected Consumers*, 30 Loy. Consumer L. Rev. 1 (2017) ("Neither the drafters of the Federal Arbitration Act nor the Congress that adopted it intended it to cover consumers or workers. . . . The FAA was simply intended to provide a means for resolving disputes among commercial entities."); Jean R. Sternlight, *Mandatory Binding Arbitration and Demise of the Seventh Amendment Right to a Jury Trial*, 16 Ohio St. J. on Disp. Resol. 669, 729–30 (2001) ("the Federal Arbitration Act was never intended to permit companies to impose arbitration on unknowing consumers and employees, but rather was merely intended to allow two sophisticated businesses to enter into predispute arbitration agreements."); Imre Stephen Szalai, *Exploring the Federal Arbitration Act Through the Lens of History*, 2016 J. Disp. Resol. 115, 118 (2016) (the FAA "was enacted to cover privately-negotiated arbitration agreements between merchants. . .the Supreme Court has expanded the statute to. . .compel arbitration of. . .consumer disputes. . .")

However, the following excerpt argues that post-FAA developments—combined with the text of the FAA—justify its application to consumer transactions.

Stephen J. Ware, *A Short Defense of Southland, Casarotto, and Other Long-Controversial Arbitration Decisions*

30 Loyola Consumer L. Rev. 303, 317–18, 327–32 (2018).

[T]he text of FAA section 2 did not make enforceable only arbitration agreements between "commercial entities" or "merchants" or "businesses." It made enforceable all arbitration agreements in all sorts of contracts "involving commerce" between all sorts of parties, except for "contracts of employment of seamen, railroad employees, or any other class of workers engaged in foreign or interstate commerce."

While the FAA's legislative history reflects concerns about non-employment adhesion contracts, such as insurance policies, these concerns did not find their way into the statute's text. So, under mainstream approaches to statutory interpretation that, for good reasons, prioritize statutory text far above legislative history, it is enough to say Congress knew how to except types of parties from FAA section 2 and chose to except some employees but not any consumers. Consequently, if consumers make arbitration agreements "involving commerce," then those agreements are covered by the FAA.

* * *

When the FAA was enacted, "very few" consumer transactions "would have involved interstate commerce and thus fallen under the jurisdiction of the FAA." The vast increase in consumer transactions now held to involve commerce under the FAA reflects not only an increase in long-distance consumer transactions, but also the Supreme Court's expansion of the U.S. Constitution's Commerce Clause to cover transactions previously considered intra-state and thus beyond the reach of federal legislation. So, if applying FAA section 2 to consumer contracts is inconsistent with the intent of the Congress that enacted it, that inconsistency is more properly blamed on the Court's post-FAA broadening of the Commerce Clause than on the Court's interpretation of the FAA.

The key moment in the Court's post-FAA broadening of the Commerce Clause was 1937 when, during the Great Depression, the Court abandoned original understanding of the Constitution to permit what would otherwise have been unconstitutional—the New Deal. In 1935 and 1936, the Court struck down several key pieces of New Deal legislation. President Franklin Delano Roosevelt thought "a recalcitrant Court was preventing the country from achieving necessary recovery and reform," and he "chastise[d] the Justices for their 'horse and buggy interpretation' of the Commerce Clause." After his landslide 1936 reelection, Roosevelt announced in February 1937 his plan to enlarge the Court's membership from nine to fifteen, which would have allowed him to appoint enough Justices to reverse the Court's recent decisions, and thus uphold the New Deal. "[T]he 1936 elections had given the Democrats dominant supermajorities in both the House and the Senate," which gave Roosevelt "good reason to hope" that his "court-packing" bill would be approved. "In April, however, before the bill came to a vote in Congress, two Supreme Court justices came over to the liberal side and by a narrow majority upheld as constitutional the National Labor Relations Act and the Social Security Act."

This "switch in time that saved nine" "provided the basis for a profound shift from federalism to nationalism [that has] effectively given Congress a police power. . .to regulate any matter under the guise of the original Commerce Clause." As Professors Eskridge and Ferejohn explain:

> The Court's switch in time averted a constitutional showdown between the Court and the political system, and between 1937 and 1943 Roosevelt remade the Court with nine nominees. The immediate agenda

> of the New Deal Court was to interpret the Commerce Clause broadly enough to embrace regulatory legislation with incidental (but demonstrable) effects on interstate commerce, and with this the coalition consolidated the new Commerce Clause jurisprudence with unanimous majorities by 1942.

In sum, "The New Deal inverted the basic orientation of Commerce Clause doctrine. As of 1932, it was still possible to say that the Commerce Clause was one of several limited and enumerated federal regulatory powers. A decade later it seemed fairer to say that the Commerce Clause gave the federal government unlimited and general powers."

The previous paragraph explained that much of the New Deal—perhaps the nation's most important progressive economic legislation—would have been unconstitutional had the 1937-Era Court adhered to the narrower understanding of (interstate) commerce prevalent during the FAA's 1925 enactment. The same can likely be said of—perhaps the nation's most important progressive social legislation—the Civil Rights Act of 1964, including Title VII prohibiting employment discrimination, and of important federal consumer protection statutes. In other words, many employment and consumer claims would not exist but for the same post-FAA expansion of "commerce" that enables FAA section 2 to enforce agreements to arbitrate those claims.

In sum, the Court's broadening of "commerce" since 1937 gave un-originalist breadth to countless areas of federal law, usually toward progressive ends. The un-originalist breadth of FAA section 2 is a rare conservative (contract-enforcing) consequence of this broadening. So, asking courts to turn back the clock to a narrow, pre-1937 understanding of "commerce" for the FAA, but not for the many other areas of broadened federal law, smacks of result-oriented inconsistency discriminating in favor of progressive statutes and against conservative statutes.

After *Allied-Bruce*, the Alabama Supreme Court continued to resist federal preemption of the state's anti-arbitration law by finding insufficient connections to interstate commerce in *Sisters of the Visitation v. Cochran Plastering Co.*, 775 So.2d 759 (2000), and *Alafabco, Inc. v. Citizens Bank*, 872 So. 2d 798 (Ala. 2002). The latter case was reversed, per curiam, by the United States Supreme Court in *Citizens Bank v. Alafabco, Inc.*, 539 U.S. 52 (2003).

The statute held preempted by the FAA in *Allied-Bruce*, Ala. Code § 8–1–41(3), prohibits courts from enforcing arbitration agreements with the remedy of specific performance. While several states prohibit specific (or any) enforcement of particular sorts of arbitration agreements,[16] Alabama may be the only state to prohibit specific enforcement of all arbitration agreements. A study of 106 decisions by the Supreme Court of Alabama from 1995 through 1999 found a "strong correlation" in the state "between a justice's source of campaign funds and how that justice votes in arbitration cases": "[j]ustices whose campaigns are funded by plaintiffs' lawyers are all Democrats and oppose arbitration, while justices whose

[16] See supra Section 3.C.1, notes 12–15.

campaigns are funded by business are nearly all Republicans and favor arbitration." Stephen J. Ware, *Money, Politics and Judicial Decisions: A Case Study of Arbitration Law in Alabama*, 15 J.L. & Pol. 645, 646 (1999).

While the politics of Alabama judicial elections—business-supported judges enforcing adhesive arbitration agreements vs. dissenters receiving heavy campaign funding from plaintiffs' trial lawyers—may have made it the first state to resist federal preemption of state law on adhesive arbitration agreements, other states' high courts followed.

Doctor's Assocs. v. Casarotto

Supreme Court of the United States, 1996.
517 U.S. 681, 116 S.Ct. 1652, 134 L.Ed.2d 902.

■ JUSTICE GINSBURG delivered the opinion of the Court.

Petitioner DAI is the national franchisor of Subway sandwich shops. In April 1988, DAI entered a franchise agreement with respondent Paul Casarotto, which permitted Casarotto to open a Subway shop in Great Falls, Montana. The franchise agreement stated, on page nine and in ordinary type: "Any controversy or claim arising out of or relating to this contract or the breach thereof shall be settled by Arbitration . . . ."

In October 1992, Casarotto sued DAI and its agent, Nick Lombardi, in Montana state court, alleging state-law contract and tort claims relating to the franchise agreement. DAI demanded arbitration of those claims, and successfully moved in the Montana trial court to stay the lawsuit pending arbitration.

The Montana Supreme Court reversed. That court left undisturbed the trial court's findings that the franchise agreement fell within the scope of the FAA and covered the claims Casarotto stated against DAI and Lombardi. The Montana Supreme Court held, however, that Mont. Code Ann. § 27–5–114(4) rendered the agreement's arbitration clause unenforceable. The Montana statute provides:

> "Notice that a contract is subject to arbitration . . . shall be typed in underlined capital letters on the first page of the contract; and unless such notice is displayed thereon, the contract may not be subject to arbitration."

Notice of the arbitration clause in the franchise agreement did not appear on the first page of the contract. Nor was anything relating to the clause typed in underlined capital letters. Because the State's statutory notice requirement had not been met, the Montana Supreme Court declared the parties' dispute "not subject to arbitration."

DAI and Lombardi unsuccessfully argued before the Montana Supreme Court that § 27–5–114(4) was preempted by § 2 of the FAA. DAI and Lombardi dominantly relied on our decisions in *Southland Corp.* v. *Keating*, 465 U.S. 1, 79 L. Ed. 2d 1, 104 S. Ct. 852 (1984), and *Perry* v. *Thomas*, 482 U.S. 483, 96 L. Ed. 2d 426, 107 S. Ct. 2520 (1987). In *Southland*, we held that § 2 of the FAA applies in state as well as federal courts and "withdr[aws] the power of the states to require a judicial forum for the resolution of claims which the contracting parties agreed to resolve by arbitration". We noted in the pathmarking *Southland* decision that the FAA established a "broad principle of enforceability," and that § 2 of the federal Act provided for revocation of arbitration agreements only upon "grounds as exist at law or in equity for the revocation of any contract." In *Perry*, we reiterated: "State law, whether of legislative or judicial origin, is applicable *if* that law arose to govern issues concerning the validity, revocability, and enforceability of contracts generally. A state-law principle that takes its meaning precisely from the fact that a contract to arbitrate is at issue does not comport with [the text of § 2]."

The Montana Supreme Court, however, read our decision in *Volt Information Sciences, Inc.* v. *Board of Trustees of Leland Stanford Junior Univ.*, 489 U.S. 468, 103 L. Ed. 2d 488, 109 S. Ct. 1248 (1989), as limiting the preemptive force of § 2 and correspondingly qualifying *Southland* and *Perry*. As the Montana Supreme Court comprehended *Volt*, the proper inquiry here should focus not on the bare words of § 2, but on this question: Would the application of Montana's notice requirement, contained in § 27–5–114(4), "undermine the goals and policies of the FAA." Section 27–5–114(4), in the Montana court's judgment, did not undermine the goals and policies of the FAA, for the notice requirement did not preclude arbitration agreements altogether; it simply prescribed "that before arbitration agreements are enforceable, they be entered knowingly."

DAI and Lombardi petitioned for certiorari. Last Term, we granted their petition, vacated the judgment of the Montana Supreme Court, and remanded for further consideration in light of *Allied-Bruce*.

* * *

On remand, without inviting or permitting further briefing or oral argument, the Montana Supreme Court adhered to its original ruling. The court stated: "After careful review, we can find nothing in the [*Allied-Bruce*] decision which relates to the issues presented to this Court in this case." * * *

Section 2 of the FAA provides that written arbitration agreements "shall be valid, irrevocable, and enforceable, save upon such grounds as exist at law or in equity for the revocation of *any* contract." 9 U.S.C. § 2 (emphasis added). Repeating our observation in *Perry*, the text of § 2 declares that state law may be applied "*if* that law arose to govern issues concerning the validity, revocability, and enforceability of contracts generally." Thus, generally applicable contract defenses, such as fraud, duress, or unconscionability, may be applied to invalidate arbitration agreements without contravening § 2.

Courts may not, however, invalidate arbitration agreements under state laws applicable *only* to arbitration provisions. By enacting § 2, we have several times said, Congress precluded States from singling out arbitration provisions for suspect status, requiring instead that such provisions be placed "upon the same footing as other contracts." Montana's § 27–5–114(4) directly conflicts with § 2 of the FAA because the State's law conditions the enforceability of arbitration agreements on compliance with a special notice requirement not applicable to contracts generally. The FAA thus displaces the Montana statute with respect to arbitration agreements covered by the Act.

* * *

The "goals and policies" of the FAA, this Court's precedent indicates, are antithetical to threshold limitations placed specifically and solely on arbitration provisions. Section 2 "mandate[s] the enforcement of arbitration agreements," *Southland*, 465 U.S. at 10, "save upon such grounds as exist at law or in equity for the revocation of any contract," 9 U.S.C. § 2. Section 27–5–114(4) of Montana's law places arbitration agreements in a class apart from "any contract," and singularly limits their validity. The State's prescription is thus inconsonant with, and is therefore preempted by, the federal law.

* * *

For the reasons stated, the judgment of the Supreme Court of Montana is reversed, and the case is remanded for further proceedings not inconsistent with this opinion.

It is so ordered.

■ JUSTICE THOMAS, dissenting.

For the reasons given in my dissent last term in *Allied-Bruce Terminix Cos.* v. *Dobson*, 513 U.S. 265, 130 L. Ed. 2d 753, 115 S. Ct. 834 (1995), I remain of the view that § 2 of the Federal Arbitration Act, 9 U.S.C. § 2, does not apply to proceedings in state courts. Accordingly, I respectfully dissent.

Despite *Casarotto*, the Montana Supreme Court continues to hold arbitration agreements to a higher standard of assent than it holds contracts generally. See Kelker v. Geneva-Roth Ventures, Inc., 303 P.3d 777, 786 (Mont. 2013).

> Outside the arbitration context, our generally applicable principles of contract law presume that '[a]bsent incapacity to contract, ignorance of the contents of a written contract is not a ground for relief from liability' under its provisions. * * * Because an arbitration provision waives fundamental rights, however, we have applied a more stringent standard when faced with a consumer's claim that she has not read or understood the arbitration clause in a contract.

Id. at 786. The Montana Supreme Court's rationale is that arbitration agreements waive a constitutional right (the right to jury trial) and Montana courts require all contracts (not just arbitration agreements) that waive constitutional rights, to the higher standard of assent, "knowing and voluntary" assent. "Montana law generally applicable to the waiver of constitutional rights, requires that the waiver will not be lightly presumed; that it must be proved to have been made voluntarily, knowingly and intelligently—typically by the party seeking the waiver; and that it will be narrowly construed." Kloss v. Edward D. Jones & Co., 54 P.3d 1, 16 (Mont.2002). See also Scott J. Burnham, *The War Against Arbitration in Montana*, 66 Mont. L. Rev. 139, 200 (2005) ("the Montana Supreme Court [in Kloss] has now accomplished what the legislature was unable to do * * * It is possible that the higher court will right this wrong, or even that a reconstituted Montana Supreme Court will see things differently. Until that time, however, arbitration is dead in Montana.")

Allied-Bruce and *Casarotto* interpreted the FAA broadly, and thus enforced adhesive arbitration agreements that would not have been enforced had state law governed. Justices who wrote the Court's opinions in *Allied-Bruce* (Breyer) and *Casarotto* (Ginsburg) where appointed by a Democratic president, Bill Clinton, while the main dissenters (Scalia and Thomas) were appointed by Republican presidents. So, in these 1990s cases the justices' votes (perhaps influenced by federalism concerns) did not line up neatly as Republican appointees enforcing businesses' adhesion contracts and Democratic appointees declining to enforce them. In contrast, the following 2011 case saw only Republican appointed justices interpreting the FAA broadly to enforce adhesive arbitration agreements that would not have been enforced had state law governed. All four dissenters were appointed by Democratic presidents. The following case addresses the arbitration-law issue that has, over the last decade or two, likely received the most attention from interest groups—class actions, and in particular adhesive arbitration agreements "waiving" the parties' rights to participate in class actions.

AT&T Mobility LLC v. Concepcion

Supreme Court of the United States, 2011.
563 U.S. 333, 131 S.Ct. 1740, 179 L.Ed.2d 742.

■ JUSTICE SCALIA delivered the opinion of the Court.

Section 2 of the Federal Arbitration Act (FAA) makes agreements to arbitrate "valid, irrevocable, and enforceable, save upon such grounds as exist at law or in equity for the revocation of any contract." 9 U.S.C. § 2. We consider whether the FAA prohibits States from conditioning the enforceability of certain arbitration agreements on the availability of classwide arbitration procedures.

In February 2002, Vincent and Liza Concepcion entered into an agreement for the sale and servicing of cellular telephones with AT&T Mobility LLC (AT&T). The contract provided for arbitration of all disputes between the parties, but required that claims be brought in the parties' "individual capacity, and not as a plaintiff or class member in any purported class or representative proceeding."[2] The agreement authorized AT&T to make unilateral amendments, which it did to the arbitration provision on several occasions. The version at issue in this case reflects revisions made in December 2006, which the parties agree are controlling.

The revised agreement provides that customers may initiate dispute proceedings by completing a one-page Notice of Dispute form available on AT&T's Web site. AT&T may then offer to settle the claim; if it does not, or if the dispute is not resolved within 30 days, the customer may invoke arbitration by filing a separate Demand for Arbitration, also available on AT&T's Web site. In the event the parties proceed to arbitration, the agreement specifies that AT&T must pay all costs for nonfrivolous claims; that arbitration must take place in the county in which the customer is billed; that, for claims of $10,000 or less, the customer may choose whether the arbitration proceeds in person, by telephone, or based only on submissions; that either party may bring a claim in small claims court in lieu of arbitration; and that the arbitrator may award any form of individual relief, including injunctions and presumably punitive damages. The agreement,

[2] That provision further states that "the arbitrator may not consolidate more than one person's claims, and may not otherwise preside over any form of a representative or class proceeding."

moreover, denies AT&T any ability to seek reimbursement of its attorney's fees, and, in the event that a customer receives an arbitration award greater than AT&T's last written settlement offer, requires AT&T to pay a $7,500 minimum recovery and twice the amount of the claimant's attorney's fees.

The Concepcions purchased AT&T service, which was advertised as including the provision of free phones; they were not charged for the phones, but they were charged $30.22 in sales tax based on the phones' retail value. In March 2006, the Concepcions filed a complaint against AT&T in the United States District Court for the Southern District of California. The complaint was later consolidated with a putative class action alleging, among other things, that AT&T had engaged in false advertising and fraud by charging sales tax on phones it advertised as free.

In March 2008, AT&T moved to compel arbitration under the terms of its contract with the Concepcions. The Concepcions opposed the motion, contending that the arbitration agreement was unconscionable and unlawfully exculpatory under California law because it disallowed classwide procedures. The District Court denied AT&T's motion. It described AT&T's arbitration agreement favorably, noting, for example, that the informal dispute-resolution process was "quick, easy to use," and likely to "promp[t] full or . . . even excess payment to the customer *without* the need to arbitrate or litigate"; that the $7,500 premium functioned as "a substantial inducement for the consumer to pursue the claim in arbitration" if a dispute was not resolved informally; and that consumers who were members of a class would likely be worse off. Nevertheless, relying on the California Supreme Court's decision in *Discover Bank* v. *Superior Court*, 36 Cal. 4th 148, 30 Cal. Rptr. 3d 76, 113 P. 3d 1100 (2005), the court found that the arbitration provision was unconscionable because AT&T had not shown that bilateral arbitration adequately substituted for the deterrent effects of class actions.

The Ninth Circuit affirmed, also finding the provision unconscionable under California law as announced in *Discover Bank*. It also held that the *Discover Bank* rule was not pre-empted by the FAA because that rule was simply "a refinement of the unconscionability analysis applicable to contracts generally in California." In response to AT&T's argument that the Concepcions' interpretation of California law discriminated against arbitration, the Ninth Circuit rejected the contention that "class proceedings will reduce the efficiency and expeditiousness of arbitration" and noted that "*Discover Bank* placed arbitration agreements with class action waivers on the *exact same footing* as contracts that bar class action litigation outside the context of arbitration."

We granted certiorari.

The FAA was enacted in 1925 in response to widespread judicial hostility to arbitration agreements. Section 2, the "primary substantive provision of the Act," provides, in relevant part, as follows:

> "A written provision in any maritime transaction or a contract evidencing a transaction involving commerce to settle by arbitration a controversy thereafter arising out of such contract or transaction . . . shall be valid, irrevocable, and enforceable, save upon such grounds as exist at law or in equity for the revocation of any contract." 9 U.S.C. § 2.

We have described this provision as reflecting both a "liberal federal policy favoring arbitration," and the "fundamental principle that arbitration is a matter of contract". In line with these principles, courts must place arbitration agreements on an equal footing with other contracts, and enforce them according to their terms.

The final phrase of § 2, however, permits arbitration agreements to be declared unenforceable "upon such grounds as exist at law or in equity for the revocation of any contract." This saving clause permits agreements to arbitrate to be invalidated by "generally applicable contract defenses, such as fraud, duress, or unconscionability," but not by defenses that apply only to arbitration or that derive their meaning from the fact that an agreement to arbitrate is at issue. Doctor's Associates, Inc. v. Casarotto, 517 U.S. 681, 687, 116 S. Ct. 1652, 134 L. Ed. 2d 902 (1996). The question in this case is whether § 2 pre-empts California's rule classifying most collective-arbitration waivers in consumer contracts as unconscionable. We refer to this rule as the *Discover Bank* rule.

Under California law, courts may refuse to enforce any contract found "to have been unconscionable at the time it was made," or may "limit the application of any unconscionable clause." A finding of unconscionability requires "a 'procedural' and a 'substantive' element, the former focusing on 'oppression' or 'surprise' due to unequal bargaining power, the latter on 'overly harsh' or 'one-sided' results."

In *Discover Bank*, the California Supreme Court applied this framework to class-action waivers in arbitration agreements and held as follows:

> "[W]hen the waiver is found in a consumer contract of adhesion in a setting in which disputes between the contracting parties predictably involve small amounts of damages, and when it is alleged that the party with the superior bargaining power has carried out a scheme to deliberately cheat large numbers of consumers out of individually small sums of money, then . . . the waiver becomes in practice the exemption of the party 'from responsibility for [its] own fraud, or willful injury to the person or property of another.' Under these circumstances, such waivers are unconscionable under California law and should not be enforced."

California courts have frequently applied this rule to find arbitration agreements unconscionable.

The Concepcions argue that the *Discover Bank* rule, given its origins in California's unconscionability doctrine and California's policy against exculpation, is a ground that "exist[s] at law or in equity for the revocation of any contract" under FAA § 2. Moreover, they argue that even if we construe the *Discover Bank* rule as a prohibition on collective-action waivers rather than simply an application of unconscionability, the rule would still be applicable to all dispute-resolution contracts, since California prohibits waivers of class litigation as well.

When state law prohibits outright the arbitration of a particular type of claim, the analysis is straightforward: The conflicting rule is displaced by the FAA. But the inquiry becomes more complex when a doctrine normally thought to be generally applicable, such as duress or, as relevant here, unconscionability, is alleged to have been applied in a fashion that disfavors arbitration. In *Perry* v. *Thomas*, 482 U.S. 483, 107 S. Ct. 2520, 96 L. Ed. 2d 426 (1987), for example, we noted that the FAA's pre-emptive effect might extend even to grounds traditionally thought to exist "at law or in equity for the revocation of any contract." We said that a court may not "rely on the uniqueness of an agreement to arbitrate as a basis for a state-law holding that enforcement would be unconscionable, for this would enable the court to effect what . . . the state legislature cannot."

An obvious illustration of this point would be a case finding unconscionable or unenforceable as against public policy consumer arbitration agreements that fail to provide for judicially monitored discovery. The rationalizations for such a holding are neither difficult to imagine nor different in kind from those articulated in *Discover Bank*. A court might reason that no consumer would knowingly waive his right to full discovery, as this would enable companies to hide their wrongdoing. Or the court might simply say that such agreements are exculpatory—restricting discovery would be of greater benefit to the company than the consumer, since the former is more likely to be sued than to sue. And, the reasoning would continue, because such a rule applies the general principle of unconscionability or public-policy disapproval of exculpatory agreements, it is applicable to "any" contract and thus preserved by § 2 of the FAA. In practice, of course, the rule would have a disproportionate impact on arbitration agreements; but it would presumably apply to contracts purporting to restrict discovery in litigation as well.

Other examples are easy to imagine. The same argument might apply to a rule classifying as unconscionable arbitration agreements that fail to abide by the Federal Rules of Evidence, or that disallow an ultimate disposition by a jury (perhaps termed "a panel of twelve lay arbitrators" to help avoid pre-emption). Such examples are not fanciful, since the judicial hostility towards arbitration that prompted the FAA had manifested itself in "a great variety" of "devices and formulas" declaring arbitration against public policy. And although these statistics are not definitive, it is worth noting that California's courts have been more likely to hold contracts to arbitrate unconscionable than other contracts.

The Concepcions suggest that all this is just a parade of horribles, and no genuine worry. "Rules aimed at destroying arbitration" or "demanding procedures incompatible with arbitration," they concede, "would be preempted by the FAA because they cannot sensibly be reconciled with Section 2." The "grounds" available under § 2's saving clause, they admit, "should not be construed to include a State's mere preference for procedures that are incompatible with arbitration and would wholly eviscerate arbitration agreements."

We largely agree. Although § 2's saving clause preserves generally applicable contract defenses, nothing in it suggests an intent to preserve state-law rules that stand as an obstacle to the accomplishment of the FAA's objectives. * * *

We differ with the Concepcions only in the application of this analysis to the matter before us. We do not agree that rules requiring judicially monitored discovery or adherence to the Federal Rules of Evidence are "a far cry from this case." The overarching purpose of the FAA, evident in the text of §§ 2, 3, and 4, is to ensure the enforcement of arbitration agreements according to their terms so as to facilitate streamlined proceedings. Requiring the availability of classwide arbitration interferes with fundamental attributes of arbitration and thus creates a scheme inconsistent with the FAA.

The "principal purpose" of the FAA is to "ensur[e] that private arbitration agreements are enforced according to their terms." * * *

The point of affording parties discretion in designing arbitration processes is to allow for efficient, streamlined procedures tailored to the type of dispute. * * *

The dissent quotes *Dean Witter Reynolds Inc.* v. *Byrd*, 470 U.S. 213, 219, 105 S. Ct. 1238, 84 L. Ed. 2d 158 (1985), as "reject[ing] the suggestion that the overriding goal of the Arbitration Act was to promote the expeditious resolution of claims." That is greatly misleading. After saying (accurately enough) that "the overriding goal of the Arbitration Act was [not] to promote the expeditious resolution of claims," but to "ensure judicial enforcement of privately made agreements to arbitrate," *Dean Witter* went on to explain: "This is not to say that Congress was blind to the potential benefit of the legislation for expedited resolution of disputes. Far from it . . . ." It then quotes a House Report saying that "the costliness and delays of litigation . . . can be largely eliminated by agreements for arbitration." The concluding paragraph of this part of its discussion begins as follows:

> "We therefore are not persuaded by the argument that the conflict between two goals of the Arbitration Act—enforcement of private agreements and encouragement of efficient and speedy dispute resolution—must be resolved in favor of the latter in order to realize the intent of the drafters."

In the present case, of course, those "two goals" do not conflict—and it is the dissent's view that would frustrate *both* of them.

Contrary to the dissent's view, our cases place it beyond dispute that the FAA was designed to promote arbitration. * * * Thus, in *Preston* v. *Ferrer*, holding preempted a state-law rule requiring exhaustion of administrative remedies before arbitration, we said: "A prime objective of an agreement to arbitrate is to achieve 'streamlined proceedings and expeditious results,'" which objective would be "frustrated" by requiring a dispute to be heard by an agency first. That rule, we said, would, "at the least, hinder speedy resolution of the controversy."[5]

California's *Discover Bank* rule similarly interferes with arbitration. Although the rule does not *require* classwide arbitration, it allows any party to a consumer contract to demand it *ex post*. The rule is limited to adhesion contracts, but the

---

[5] Relying upon nothing more indicative of congressional understanding than statements of witnesses in committee hearings and a press release of Secretary of Commerce Herbert Hoover, the dissent suggests that Congress "thought that arbitration would be used primarily where merchants sought to resolve disputes of fact . . . [and] possessed roughly equivalent bargaining power." Such a limitation appears nowhere in the text of the FAA and has been explicitly rejected by our cases. "Relationships between securities dealers and investors, for example, may involve unequal bargaining power, but we [have] nevertheless held . . . that agreements to arbitrate in that context are enforceable." Gilmer v. Interstate/Johnson Lane Corp., 500 U.S. 20, 33, 111 S. Ct. 1647, 114 L. Ed. 2d 26 (1991); see also id., at 32–33, 111 S. Ct. 1647, 114 L. Ed. 2d 26 (allowing arbitration of claims arising under the Age Discrimination in Employment Act of 1967 despite allegations of unequal bargaining power between employers and employees). Of course the dissent's disquisition on legislative history fails to note that it contains nothing—not even the testimony of a stray witness in committee hearings—that contemplates the existence of class arbitration.

times in which consumer contracts were anything other than adhesive are long past.[6] The rule also requires that damages be predictably small, and that the consumer allege a scheme to cheat consumers. The former requirement, however, is toothless and malleable (the Ninth Circuit has held that damages of $4,000 are sufficiently small), and the latter has no limiting effect, as all that is required is an allegation. Consumers remain free to bring and resolve their disputes on a bilateral basis under *Discover Bank*, and some may well do so; but there is little incentive for lawyers to arbitrate on behalf of individuals when they may do so for a class and reap far higher fees in the process. And faced with inevitable class arbitration, companies would have less incentive to continue resolving potentially duplicative claims on an individual basis.

Although we have had little occasion to examine classwide arbitration, our decision in *Stolt-Nielsen* [*S.A. v. AnimalFeeds International Corp.*, 130 S. Ct. 1758 (2010)] is instructive. In that case we held that an arbitration panel exceeded its power under § 10(a)(4) of the FAA by imposing class procedures based on policy judgments rather than the arbitration agreement itself or some background principle of contract law that would affect its interpretation. We then held that the agreement at issue, which was silent on the question of class procedures, could not be interpreted to allow them because the "changes brought about by the shift from bilateral arbitration to class-action arbitration" are "fundamental." This is obvious as a structural matter: Classwide arbitration includes absent parties, necessitating additional and different procedures and involving higher stakes. Confidentiality becomes more difficult. And while it is theoretically possible to select an arbitrator with some expertise relevant to the class-certification question, arbitrators are not generally knowledgeable in the often-dominant procedural aspects of certification, such as the protection of absent parties. The conclusion follows that class arbitration, to the extent it is manufactured by *Discover Bank* rather than consensual, is inconsistent with the FAA.

First, the switch from bilateral to class arbitration sacrifices the principal advantage of arbitration—its informality—and makes the process slower, more costly, and more likely to generate procedural morass than final judgment. "In bilateral arbitration, parties forgo the procedural rigor and appellate review of the courts in order to realize the benefits of private dispute resolution: lower costs, greater efficiency and speed, and the ability to choose expert adjudicators to resolve specialized disputes." But before an arbitrator may decide the merits of a claim in classwide procedures, he must first decide, for example, whether the class itself may be certified, whether the named parties are sufficiently representative and typical, and how discovery for the class should be conducted. A cursory comparison of bilateral and class arbitration illustrates the difference. According to the American Arbitration Association (AAA), the average consumer arbitration between January and August 2007 resulted in a disposition on the merits in six months, four months if the arbitration was conducted by documents only. As of September 2009, the AAA had opened 283 class arbitrations. Of those, 121

[6] Of course States remain free to take steps addressing the concerns that attend contracts of adhesion—for example, requiring class-action-waiver provisions in adhesive agreements to be highlighted. Such steps cannot, however, conflict with the FAA or frustrate its purpose to ensure that private arbitration agreements are enforced according to their terms.

remained active, and 162 had been settled, withdrawn, or dismissed. Not a single one, however, had resulted in a final award on the merits. For those cases that were no longer active, the median time from filing to settlement, withdrawal, or dismissal—not judgment on the merits—was 583 days, and the mean was 630 days.[7]

Second, class arbitration *requires* procedural formality. The AAA's rules governing class arbitrations mimic the Federal Rules of Civil Procedure for class litigation. Compare AAA, Supplementary Rules for Class Arbitrations (effective Oct. 8, 2003), online at http://www.adr.org/sp.asp?id=21936, with Fed. Rule Civ. Proc. 23. And while parties can alter those procedures by contract, an alternative is not obvious. If procedures are too informal, absent class members would not be bound by the arbitration. For a class-action money judgment to bind absentees in litigation, class representatives must at all times adequately represent absent class members, and absent members must be afforded notice, an opportunity to be heard, and a right to opt out of the class. At least this amount of process would presumably be required for absent parties to be bound by the results of arbitration.

We find it unlikely that in passing the FAA Congress meant to leave the disposition of these procedural requirements to an arbitrator. Indeed, class arbitration was not even envisioned by Congress when it passed the FAA in 1925; as the California Supreme Court admitted in *Discover Bank*, class arbitration is a "relatively recent development." And it is at the very least odd to think that an arbitrator would be entrusted with ensuring that third parties' due process rights are satisfied.

Third, class arbitration greatly increases risks to defendants. Informal procedures do of course have a cost: The absence of multilayered review makes it more likely that errors will go uncorrected. Defendants are willing to accept the costs of these errors in arbitration, since their impact is limited to the size of individual disputes, and presumably outweighed by savings from avoiding the courts. But when damages allegedly owed to tens of thousands of potential claimants are aggregated and decided at once, the risk of an error will often become unacceptable. Faced with even a small chance of a devastating loss, defendants will be pressured into settling questionable claims. Other courts have noted the risk of "in terrorem" settlements that class actions entail and class arbitration would be no different.

Arbitration is poorly suited to the higher stakes of class litigation. In litigation, a defendant may appeal a certification decision on an interlocutory basis and, if unsuccessful, may appeal from a final judgment as well. Questions of law are reviewed *de novo* and questions of fact for clear error. In contrast, 9 U.S.C. § 10 allows a court to vacate an arbitral award *only* where the award "was procured by corruption, fraud, or undue means"; "there was evident partiality or corruption in the arbitrators"; "the arbitrators were guilty of misconduct in refusing to postpone the hearing . . . or in refusing to hear evidence pertinent and material to the controversy[,] or of any other misbehavior by which the rights of any party have

---

[7] The dissent claims that class arbitration should be compared to class litigation, not bilateral arbitration. Whether arbitrating a class is more desirable than litigating one, however, is not relevant. A State cannot defend a rule requiring arbitration-by-jury by saying that parties will still prefer it to trial-by-jury.

been prejudiced"; or if the "arbitrators exceeded their powers, or so imperfectly executed them that a mutual, final, and definite award . . . was not made." The AAA rules do authorize judicial review of certification decisions, but this review is unlikely to have much effect given these limitations; review under § 10 focuses on misconduct rather than mistake. And parties may not contractually expand the grounds or nature of judicial review. Hall Street Assocs., 552 U.S., at 578, 128 S. Ct. 1396, 170 L. Ed. 2d 254. We find it hard to believe that defendants would bet the company with no effective means of review, and even harder to believe that Congress would have intended to allow state courts to force such a decision.[8]

The Concepcions contend that because parties may and sometimes do agree to aggregation, class procedures are not necessarily incompatible with arbitration. But the same could be said about procedures that the Concepcions admit States may not superimpose on arbitration: Parties *could* agree to arbitrate pursuant to the Federal Rules of Civil Procedure, or pursuant to a discovery process rivaling that in litigation. Arbitration is a matter of contract, and the FAA requires courts to honor parties' expectations. But what the parties in the aforementioned examples would have agreed to is not arbitration as envisioned by the FAA, lacks its benefits, and therefore may not be required by state law.

The dissent claims that class proceedings are necessary to prosecute small-dollar claims that might otherwise slip through the legal system. But States cannot require a procedure that is inconsistent with the FAA, even if it is desirable for unrelated reasons. Moreover, the claim here was most unlikely to go unresolved. As noted earlier, the arbitration agreement provides that AT&T will pay claimants a minimum of $7,500 and twice their attorney's fees if they obtain an arbitration award greater than AT&T's last settlement offer. The District Court found this scheme sufficient to provide incentive for the individual prosecution of meritorious claims that are not immediately settled, and the Ninth Circuit admitted that aggrieved customers who filed claims would be "essentially guarantee[d]" to be made whole. Indeed, the District Court concluded that the Concepcions were *better off* under their arbitration agreement with AT&T than they would have been as participants in a class action, which "could take months, if not years, and which may merely yield an opportunity to submit a claim for recovery of a small percentage of a few dollars."

* * *

Because it "stands as an obstacle to the accomplishment and execution of the full purposes and objectives of Congress," California's *Discover Bank* rule is pre-empted by the FAA. The judgment of the Ninth Circuit is reversed, and the case is remanded for further proceedings consistent with this opinion.

---

[8] The dissent cites three large arbitration awards (none of which stems from classwide arbitration) as evidence that parties are willing to submit large claims before an arbitrator. *Post*, at ___–___, 179 L. Ed. 2d, at 766. Those examples might be in point if it could be established that the size of the arbitral dispute was predictable when the arbitration agreement was entered. Otherwise, all the cases prove is that arbitrators can give huge awards—which we have never doubted. The point is that in class-action arbitration huge awards (with limited judicial review) will be entirely predictable, thus rendering arbitration unattractive. It is not reasonably deniable that requiring consumer disputes to be arbitrated on a classwide basis will have a substantial deterrent effect on incentives to arbitrate.

■ JUSTICE THOMAS, concurring.

Section 2 of the Federal Arbitration Act (FAA) provides that an arbitration provision "shall be valid, irrevocable, and enforceable, save upon such grounds as exist at law or in equity for the revocation of any contract." 9 U.S.C. § 2. The question here is whether California's *Discover Bank* rule is a "groun[d] . . . for the revocation of any contract."

It would be absurd to suggest that § 2 requires only that a defense apply to "any contract." If § 2 means anything, it is that courts cannot refuse to enforce arbitration agreements because of a state public policy against arbitration, even if the policy nominally applies to "any contract." There must be some additional limit on the contract defenses permitted by § 2.

I write separately to explain how I would find that limit in the FAA's text. As I would read it, the FAA requires that an agreement to arbitrate be enforced unless a party successfully challenges the formation of the arbitration agreement, such as by proving fraud or duress. 9 U.S.C. §§ 2, 4. Under this reading, I would reverse the Court of Appeals because a district court cannot follow both the FAA and the *Discover Bank* rule, which does not relate to defects in the making of an agreement.

This reading of the text, however, has not been fully developed by any party and could benefit from briefing and argument in an appropriate case. Moreover, I think that the Court's test will often lead to the same outcome as my textual interpretation and that, when possible, it is important in interpreting statutes to give lower courts guidance from a majority of the Court. Therefore, although I adhere to my views on purposes-and-objectives pre-emption, I reluctantly join the Court's opinion.

* * *

■ JUSTICE BREYER, with whom JUSTICE GINSBURG, JUSTICE SOTOMAYOR, and JUSTICE KAGAN join, dissenting.

The California law in question consists of an authoritative state-court interpretation of two provisions of the California Civil Code. The first provision makes unlawful all contracts "which have for their object, directly or indirectly, to exempt anyone from responsibility for his own . . . violation of law." The second provision authorizes courts to "limit the application of any unconscionable clause" in a contract so "as to avoid any unconscionable result."

The specific rule of state law in question consists of the California Supreme Court's application of these principles to hold that "some" (but not "all") "class action waivers" in consumer contracts are exculpatory and unconscionable under California "law." In particular, in *Discover Bank* the California Supreme Court stated that, when a class-action waiver,

> "is found in a consumer contract of adhesion in a setting in which disputes between the contracting parties predictably involve small amounts of damages, and when it is alleged that the party with the superior bargaining power has carried out a scheme to deliberately cheat large numbers of consumers out of individually small sums of money, then . . . the waiver becomes in practice the exemption of the party 'from

> responsibility for [its] own fraud, or willful injury to the person or property of another.'"

In such a circumstance, the "waivers are unconscionable under California law and should not be enforced."

The *Discover Bank* rule does not create a "blanket policy in California against class action waivers in the consumer context. Instead it represents the "application of a more general [unconscionability] principle." Courts applying California law have enforced class-action waivers where they satisfy general unconscionability standards.

The *Discover Bank* rule is consistent with the federal Act's language. It "applies equally to class action litigation waivers in contracts without arbitration agreements as it does to class arbitration waivers in contracts with such agreements." Linguistically speaking, it falls directly within the scope of the Act's exception permitting courts to refuse to enforce arbitration agreements on grounds that exist "for the revocation of *any* contract." 9 U.S.C. § 2 (emphasis added). The majority agrees.

The *Discover Bank* rule is also consistent with the basic "purpose behind" the Act. * * *

Congress was fully aware that arbitration could provide procedural and cost advantages. * * *

But we have also cautioned against thinking that Congress' primary objective was to guarantee these particular procedural advantages. Rather, that primary objective was to secure the "enforcement" of agreements to arbitrate. The relevant Senate Report points to the Act's basic purpose when it says that "[t]he purpose of the [Act] is *clearly set forth in section 2*," namely, the section that says that an arbitration agreement "shall be valid, irrevocable, and enforceable, save upon such grounds as exist at law or in equity for the revocation of any contract," 9 U.S.C. § 2.

Thus, insofar as we seek to implement Congress' intent, we should think more than twice before invalidating a state law that does just what § 2 requires, namely, puts agreements to arbitrate and agreements to litigate "upon the same footing."

The majority's contrary view (that *Discover Bank* stands as an "obstacle" to the accomplishment of the federal law's objective) rests primarily upon its claims that the *Discover Bank* rule increases the complexity of arbitration procedures, thereby discouraging parties from entering into arbitration agreements, and to that extent discriminating in practice against arbitration. These claims are not well founded.

For one thing, a state rule of law that would sometimes set aside as unconscionable a contract term that forbids class arbitration is not (as the majority claims) like a rule that would require "ultimate disposition by a jury" or "judicially monitored discovery" or use of "the Federal Rules of Evidence." Unlike the majority's examples, class arbitration is consistent with the use of arbitration. It is a form of arbitration that is well known in California and followed elsewhere. Indeed, the AAA has told us that it has found class arbitration to be "a fair, balanced, and efficient means of resolving class disputes." And unlike the majority's examples, the *Discover Bank* rule imposes equivalent limitations on litigation; hence it cannot fairly be characterized as a targeted attack on arbitration.

Where does the majority get its contrary idea—that individual, rather than class, arbitration is a "fundamental attribut[e]" of arbitration? The majority does not explain. And it is unlikely to be able to trace its present view to the history of the arbitration statute itself.

When Congress enacted the Act, arbitration procedures had not yet been fully developed. Insofar as Congress considered detailed forms of arbitration at all, it may well have thought that arbitration would be used primarily where merchants sought to resolve disputes of fact, not law, under the customs of their industries, where the parties possessed roughly equivalent bargaining power. This last mentioned feature of the history—roughly equivalent bargaining power—suggests, if anything, that California's statute is consistent with, and indeed may help to further, the objectives that Congress had in mind.

Regardless, if neither the history nor present practice suggests that class arbitration is fundamentally incompatible with arbitration itself, then on what basis can the majority hold California's law pre-empted?

For another thing, the majority's argument that the *Discover Bank* rule will discourage arbitration rests critically upon the wrong comparison. The majority compares the complexity of class arbitration with that of bilateral arbitration. And it finds the former more complex. But, if incentives are at issue, the *relevant* comparison is not "arbitration with arbitration" but a comparison between class arbitration and judicial class actions. After all, in respect to the relevant set of contracts, the *Discover Bank* rule similarly and equally sets aside clauses that forbid class procedures—whether arbitration procedures or ordinary judicial procedures are at issue.

* * *

The majority's related claim that the *Discover Bank* rule will discourage the use of arbitration because "[a]rbitration is poorly suited to . . . higher stakes" lacks empirical support. Indeed, the majority provides no convincing reason to believe that parties are unwilling to submit high-stake disputes to arbitration. And there are numerous counterexamples.

Further, even though contract defenses, *e.g.*, duress and unconscionability, slow down the dispute resolution process, federal arbitration law normally leaves such matters to the States. A provision in a contract of adhesion (for example, requiring a consumer to decide very quickly whether to pursue a claim) might increase the speed and efficiency of arbitrating a dispute, but the State can forbid it. The *Discover Bank* rule amounts to a variation on this theme. California is free to define unconscionability as it sees fit, and its common law is of no federal concern so long as the State does not adopt a special rule that disfavors arbitration.

Because California applies the same legal principles to address the unconscionability of class arbitration waivers as it does to address the unconscionability of any other contractual provision, the merits of class proceedings should not factor into our decision. * * *

Regardless, the majority highlights the disadvantages of class arbitrations, as it sees them. But class proceedings have countervailing advantages. In general agreements that forbid the consolidation of claims can lead small-dollar claimants to abandon their claims rather than to litigate. I suspect that it is true even here, for as the Court of Appeals recognized, AT&T can avoid the $7,500 payout (the payout that supposedly makes the Concepcions' arbitration worthwhile) simply by paying the claim's face value, such that "the maximum gain to a customer for the hassle of arbitrating a $30.22 dispute is still just $30.22."

What rational lawyer would have signed on to represent the Concepcions in litigation for the possibility of fees stemming from a $30.22 claim? See, e.g., Carnegie v. Household Int'l, Inc., 376 F.3d 656, 661 (CA7 2004) ("The *realistic* alternative to a class action is not 17 million individual suits, but zero individual suits, as only a lunatic or a fanatic sues for $30"). In California's perfectly rational view, nonclass arbitration over such sums will also sometimes have the effect of depriving claimants of their claims (say, for example, where claiming the $30.22 were to involve filling out many forms that require technical legal knowledge or waiting at great length while a call is placed on hold). *Discover Bank* sets forth circumstances in which the California courts believe that the terms of consumer contracts can be manipulated to insulate an agreement's author from liability for its own frauds by "deliberately cheat[ing] large numbers of consumers out of individually small sums of money." Why is this kind of decision—weighing the pros and cons of all class proceedings alike—not California's to make?

* * *

With respect, I dissent.

Concepcion's partisan pattern of justices' votes—five justices appointed by Republican presidents ruling for a business while four justices appointed by Democratic presidents dissent—continues on FAA preemption issues related to adhesive arbitration agreements' class waivers. In *Lamps Plus Inc. v Varela*, 139 S. Ct. 1407 (2019), an employee filed a class action against his employer, which responded by seeking to compel arbitration on an individual (not classwide) basis, pursuant to an employment arbitration agreement. The district court and Ninth Circuit compelled arbitration—but on a class basis—after finding that the arbitration agreement was ambiguous about the availability of class arbitration and that California law resolves adhesion contract ambiguities against the party that drafted the contract. The Ninth Circuit thus distinguished *Stolt-Nielsen S. A. v. AnimalFeeds Int'l Corp.*, 559 U.S. 662 (2010), arguing that in *Stolt-Nielsen* the parties had stipulated to the fact that the agreement was silent about class arbitration, while the Lamps Plus parties had no such stipulation. Varela v. Lamps Plus, Inc., 701 F. App'x 670, 672 (9th Cir. 2017).

A slim majority of the Supreme Court disagreed and held that courts cannot find the necessary consent to class arbitration in an ambiguous arbitration clause.

Lamps Plus, Inc. v. Varela, 139 S. Ct. at 1411. While construing ambiguous contract terms against the drafter is a rule California applies generally to all adhesion contracts, not just to arbitration agreements, the *Lamps Plus* majority reiterated *Concepcion*'s points that class arbitration is sharply different from traditional bilateral arbitration—including class arbitration's challenge of providing due process for absent parties—and held that "[c]lass arbitration, to the extent it is manufactured by [state law] rather than consen[t], is inconsistent with the FAA." Id. at 1417–1418. In contrast, Justice Ginsburg's dissent saw "irony [in the majority] invoking 'the first principle' that 'arbitration is strictly a matter of consent' . . . to justify imposing individual arbitration on employees who surely would not choose to proceed solo."

While *Concepcion* and *Lamps Plus* greatly limit states' ability to prevent enforcement of arbitral class waivers, federal law can prohibit enforcement of them. For instance, class waivers are prohibited by the Financial Industry Regulatory Authority (FINRA), overseen by the Securities Exchange Commission, so they are not enforceable in securities brokers' contracts with their customers and employees.[17] In 2017, the Consumer Financial Protection Bureau, then directed by a Democrat, issued a rule that would have prohibited arbitral class waivers in consumer financial services,[18] but the Republican President and Congress overturned it and several Obama-era regulations reducing enforcement of adhesive arbitration agreements.[19] This partisan divide recurs in Congress, where bills to reduce enforcement of adhesive arbitration agreements receive little support from Republicans—who tend to emphasize the costs of class actions—and heavy support from Democrats, who tend to emphasize the benefits of class actions.

Some states' laws permit representative actions that are not technically class actions—for instance, the California Labor Code's Private Attorneys General Act ("PAGA") allows an employee to bring, on behalf of the state, a civil action as a representative. "Because an aggrieved employee's action under the [PAGA] functions as a substitute for an action brought by the government itself, a judgment in that action binds all those, including nonparty aggrieved employees, who would be bound by a judgment in an action brought by the government." Iskanian v. CLS Transportation Los Angeles, LLC, 59 Cal. 4th 348, 381 (2014) (internal quotations omitted). In *Iskanian*, the California Supreme Court prohibited arbitration agreement waivers of an employee's right to bring a representative PAGA action. Both *Iskanian* and a later Ninth Circuit case held that this "*Iskanian* rule" is not preempted by the FAA. Sakkab v. Luxottica Retail N. Am., Inc., 803 F.3d 425, 432 (9th Cir. 2015). Similarly, both the California Supreme Court and the Ninth Circuit

[17] See Section 2.A.4.

[18] *See* CFPB Arbitration Agreements Rule, 82 Fed. Reg. 33,210, 1 (Jul. 19, 2017) (to be codified at 40 C.F.R. pt. 1040), http://files.consumerfinance.gov/f/documents/201707_cfpb_Arbitration-Agreements-Rule.pdf ("[T]he final rule prohibits covered providers of certain consumer financial products and services from using an agreement with a consumer that provides for arbitration of any future dispute between the parties to bar the consumer from filing or participating in a class action concerning the covered consumer financial product or service.").

[19] Sylvan Lane, *Trump repeals consumer arbitration rule, wins banker praise*, The Hill (Nov. 1, 2017), http://thehill.com/policy/finance/358297-trump-repeals-consumer-bureau-arbitration-rule-joined-by-heads-of-banking; Perry Cooper, *Arbitration Update: CFPB Rule Uncertain, Mixed Fates for Others*, Bloomberg News (June 1, 2017) ("A half dozen Obama-era rules to limit mandatory arbitration have met a variety of fates in the four months since Donald Trump became president.").

hold that the FAA does not preempt California law prohibiting arbitration agreement waivers of statutory consumer protection claims for a public injunction "which is defined as 'injunctive relief that has the primary purpose and effect of prohibiting unlawful acts that threaten future injury to the general public.'" Blair v. Rent-A-Ctr., Inc., No. 17-17221, 928 F.3d 819, 2019 WL 2701333, at *3 (9th Cir. June 28, 2019) (quoting McGill v. Citibank, N.A., 2 Cal.5th 945 (2017)).

The preceding materials show the highest courts of three states—Alabama, Montana, and California—resisting FAA preemption of state law in the context of adhesive arbitration agreements. Other states have also resisted the U.S. Supreme Court's expansive view of FAA preemption, so the Court has several times since *Allied-Bruce* (1995) unanimously (per curiam) reversed various state courts resisting FAA preemption:

- Citizens Bank v. Alafabco, Inc., 539 U.S. 52 (2003) (reversing Alabama supreme court's decision that the dispute did not contain a contract evidencing a transaction involving commerce and thus was not preempted by FAA);
- Marmet Health Care Ctr., Inc. v. Brown, 565 U.S. 530 (2012) (reversing West Virginia supreme court's decision that FAA did not preempt state law precluding enforcement of predispute agreements to arbitrate personal injury or wrongful death claims against nursing homes); and
- Nitro-Lift Techs., L.L.C. v. Howard, 568 U.S. 17 (2012) (reversing Oklahoma supreme court's decision that FAA's separability doctrine did not preempt Oklahoma law).

See also Kindred Nursing Ctrs. Ltd. P'ship v. Clark, 137 S. Ct. 1421 (2017) (reversing Kentucky supreme court's decision that a person holding a general power of attorney must possess some specific authority to waive rights under the Kentucky constitution to access the courts and to trial by jury was not preempted by FAA) (7 justices in majority, with one not participating, and Justice Thomas's brief dissent adhering to his view that the FAA does not apply in state court).

QUESTIONS TO REVIEW AND SYNTHESIZE

1. In each of the preceding four major cases (*Southland*, *Allied-Bruce*, *Casarotto*, and *Concepcion*) what was the content of the state law preempted by the FAA?
2. For each of these state laws, what is the best argument that the state law is consistent with FAA § 2, and thus not preempted by it, even though FAA § 2 is (as *Southland* and *Allied-Bruce* hold) federal substantive law reaching as far the Constitution's Commerce Clause allows?
3. What is the source and importance of the view that the FAA places "[a]n arbitration agreement . . . upon the same footing as other contracts"?
4. Does *Concepcion* place arbitration agreements upon an even stronger footing than other contracts?
5. What reasons does *Concepcion* give to show that the *Discover Bank* rule is inconsistent with the FAA? How does the dissent respond to each of these reasons?

6. A Utah statute says that no patient may "be denied health care on the sole basis that [the patient] refused to enter into a binding arbitration agreement with a health care provider." Utah Code § 78B–3–421(3). Is this statute preempted by the FAA if a hospital refuses to provide services (even emergency room services) to patients who have not signed the hospital's arbitration agreement?

7. What plausible state regulation of arbitration agreements between lawyers and their clients is and is not preempted by the FAA? Compare Smith v. Lindemann, 710 Fed. Appx. 101, 105 (3d Cir. 2017) ("A New Jersey rule prohibiting the inclusion of an arbitration provision in an attorney-client representation agreement (whether inferred by this Court or the New Jersey Supreme Court) would be preempted by the FAA"), with Smith v. Jem Group, Inc., 737 F.3d 636, 642 (9th Cir. 2013)(FAA did not preempt Washington Rules of Professional Conduct enforcing attorney-client arbitration agreements only if "fully disclosed" because that rule did not single out or place any additional burden on arbitration provisions compared to other material provisions of attorney-client agreements); Snow v. Bernstein, Shur, Sawyer & Nelson, P.A., 176 A.3d 729, 738 (2017) ("the requirement in question—that attorneys fully inform a client of the scope and effect of a contractual provision requiring the client to submit any malpractice claims against the firm to arbitration—does not 'singl[e] out' arbitration agreements, and is therefore not preempted by the FAA.")

c. THE FAA GRANTS NO INDEPENDENT FEDERAL JURISDICTION

Why, a future litigator reading the previous pages might ask, do businesses struggling to persuade state courts to enforce adhesive arbitration agreements not remove state cases to (generally more friendly) federal courts? After all, a party asserting its federal rights is ordinarily entitled to have a federal court hear its arguments, as federal courts generally have jurisdiction to hear questions of federal law. But that is not true of parties asserting FAA rights. The Supreme Court's 1984 decision in *Southland Corp v. Keating* held that, while FAA § 2 is substantive law, it is unusual federal substantive law because

> it does not create any independent federal-question jurisdiction under 28 U.S.C. § 1331 (1976) or otherwise. This seems implicit in the provisions in [FAA] § 3 for a stay by a "court in which such suit is pending" and in § 4 that enforcement may be ordered by "any United States district court which, save for such agreement, would have jurisdiction under Title 28, in a civil action or in admiralty of the subject matter of a suit arising out of the controversy between the parties."

Southland, 465 U.S. 1, 16 n.9 (1984). Consequently, parties asserting their FAA rights must use state court unless they can point to some other source of federal jurisdiction.

Vaden v. Discover Bank

Supreme Court of the United States, 2009.
556 U.S. 49, 129 S.Ct. 1262, 173 L.Ed.2d 206.

■ JUSTICE GINSBURG delivered the opinion of the Court.

Section 4 of the Federal Arbitration Act, 9 U.S.C. § 4, authorizes a United States district court to entertain a petition to compel arbitration if the court would have jurisdiction, "save for [the arbitration] agreement," over "a suit arising out of the controversy between the parties." We consider in this opinion two questions concerning a district court's subject-matter jurisdiction over a § 4 petition: Should a district court, if asked to compel arbitration pursuant to § 4, "look through" the petition and grant the requested relief if the court would have federal-question jurisdiction over the underlying controversy? And if the answer to that question is yes, may a district court exercise jurisdiction over a § 4 petition when the petitioner's complaint rests on state law but an actual or potential counterclaim rests on federal law?

The litigation giving rise to these questions began when Discover Bank's servicing affiliate filed a complaint in Maryland state court. Presenting a claim arising solely under state law, Discover sought to recover past-due charges from one of its credit cardholders, Betty Vaden. Vaden answered and counterclaimed, alleging that Discover's finance charges, interest, and late fees violated state law. Invoking an arbitration clause in its cardholder agreement with Vaden, Discover then filed a § 4 petition in the United States District Court for the District of Maryland to compel arbitration of Vaden's counterclaims. The District Court had subject-matter jurisdiction over its petition, Discover maintained, because Vaden's state-law counterclaims were completely preempted by federal banking law. The District Court agreed and ordered arbitration. Reasoning that a federal court has jurisdiction over a § 4 petition if the parties' underlying dispute presents a federal question, the Fourth Circuit eventually affirmed.

We agree with the Fourth Circuit in part. A federal court may "look through" a § 4 petition and order arbitration if, "save for [the arbitration] agreement," the court would have jurisdiction over "the [substantive] controversy between the parties." We hold, however, that the Court of Appeals misidentified the dimensions of "the controversy between the parties." Focusing on only a slice of the parties' entire controversy, the court seized on Vaden's counterclaims, held them completely preempted, and on that basis affirmed the District Court's order compelling arbitration. Lost from sight was the triggering plea—Discover's claim for the balance due on Vaden's account. Given that entirely state-based plea and the established rule that federal-court jurisdiction cannot be invoked on the basis of a defense or counterclaim, the whole "controversy between the parties" does not qualify for federal-court adjudication. Accordingly, we reverse the Court of Appeals' judgment.

* * *

As this case shows, if the underlying dispute is the proper focus of a § 4 petition, a further question may arise. The dispute brought to state court by Discover concerned Vaden's failure to pay over $ 10,000 in past-due credit card charges. In support of that complaint, Discover invoked no federal law. When Vaden answered and counterclaimed, however, Discover asserted that federal law, specifically § 27(a) of the FDIA [Federal Deposit Insurance Act], displaced the state laws on which Vaden relied. What counts as the underlying dispute in a case so postured? May Discover invoke § 4, not on the basis of its own complaint, which had no federal element, but on the basis of counterclaims asserted by Vaden? To answer these questions, we first review relevant provisions of the FAA, 9 U.S.C. § 1 *et seq.*, and controlling tenets of federal jurisdiction.

* * *

The "body of federal substantive law" generated by elaboration of FAA § 2 is equally binding on state and federal courts. "As for jurisdiction over controversies touching arbitration," however, the Act is "something of an anomaly" in the realm of federal legislation: It "bestow[s] no federal jurisdiction but rather requir[es] [for access to a federal forum] an independent jurisdictional basis" over the parties' dispute. Hall Street Associates, L.L.C. v. Mattel, Inc., 552 U.S. 576, 581–582, 128 S. Ct. 1396, 170 L. Ed. 2d 254 (2008) (quoting Moses H. Cone, 460 U.S., at 25, n. 32, 103 S. Ct. 927, 74 L. Ed. 2d 765). Given the substantive supremacy of the FAA, but the Act's nonjurisdictional cast, state courts have a prominent role to play as enforcers of agreements to arbitrate

The independent jurisdictional basis Discover relies upon in this case is 28 U.S.C. § 1331, which vests in federal district courts jurisdiction over "all civil actions arising under the Constitution, laws, or treaties of the United States." Under the longstanding well-pleaded complaint rule, however, a suit "arises under" federal law "only when the plaintiff's statement of his own cause of action shows that it is based upon [federal law]." Federal jurisdiction cannot be predicated on an actual or anticipated defense: "It is not enough that the plaintiff alleges some anticipated defense to his cause of action and asserts that the defense is invalidated by some provision of [federal law]."

Nor can federal jurisdiction rest upon an actual or anticipated counterclaim. * * * [A] federal counterclaim, even when compulsory, does not establish "arising under" jurisdiction. Adhering assiduously to the well-pleaded complaint rule, the Court observed, *inter alia*, that it would undermine the clarity and simplicity of that rule if federal courts were obliged to consider the contents not only of the complaint but also of responsive pleadings in determining whether a case "arises under" federal law. A *complaint* purporting to rest on state law, we have recognized, can be recharacterized as one "arising under" federal law if the law governing the complaint is exclusively federal. Under this so-called "complete preemption doctrine," a plaintiff's "state cause of action [may be recast] as a federal claim for relief, making [its] removal [by the defendant] proper on the basis of federal question jurisdiction." A state-law-based *counterclaim*, however, even if similarly susceptible to recharacterization, would remain nonremovable. Under our precedent construing § 1331, as just explained, counterclaims, even if they rely exclusively on federal substantive law, do not qualify a case for federal-court cognizance.

Attending to the language of the FAA and the above-described jurisdictional tenets, we approve the "look through" approach to this extent: A federal court may "look through" a § 4 petition to determine whether it is predicated on an action that "arises under" federal law; in keeping with the well-pleaded complaint rule * * *, however, a federal court may not entertain a § 4 petition based on the contents, actual or hypothetical, of a counterclaim.

* * *

Having determined that a district court should "look through" a § 4 petition, we now consider whether the court "would have [federal-question] jurisdiction" over "a suit arising out of the controversy" between Discover and Vaden. 9 U.S.C. § 4. As explained above, § 4 of the FAA does not enlarge federal-court jurisdiction; rather, it confines federal courts to the jurisdiction they would have "save for [the arbitration] agreement." Mindful of that limitation, we read § 4 to convey that a party seeking to compel arbitration may gain a federal court's assistance only if, "save for" the agreement, the entire, actual "controversy between the parties," as they have framed it, could be litigated in federal court. We conclude that the parties' actual controversy, here precipitated by Discover's state-court suit for the balance due on Vaden's account, is not amenable to federal-court adjudication. Consequently, the § 4 petition Discover filed in the United States District Court for the District of Maryland must be dismissed.

* * *

Discover, we note, is not left without recourse. Under the FAA, state courts as well as federal courts are obliged to honor and enforce agreements to arbitrate. Discover may therefore petition a Maryland court for aid in enforcing the arbitration clause of its contracts with Maryland cardholders.

True, Maryland's high court has held that §§ 3 and 4 of the FAA prescribe federal-court procedures and, therefore, do not bind the state courts.[20] But Discover scarcely lacks an available state remedy. Section 2 of the FAA, which does bind the state courts, renders agreements to arbitrate "valid, irrevocable, and *enforceable*." This provision "carries with it duties [to credit and enforce arbitration agreements] indistinguishable from those imposed on federal courts by FAA §§ 3 and 4." Notably, Maryland, like many other States, provides a statutory remedy nearly identical to § 4. See Md. Cts. & Jud. Proc. Code Ann. § 3–207 ("If a party to an arbitration agreement . . . refuses to arbitrate, the other party may file a petition with a court to order arbitration. . . . If the court determines that the agreement exists, it shall order arbitration. Otherwise it shall deny the petition."). Even before it filed its debt-recovery action in a Maryland state court, Discover could have sought from that court an order compelling arbitration of any agreement-related dispute between itself and cardholder Vaden. At no time was federal-court intervention needed to place the controversy between the parties before an arbitrator.

---

[20] This Court has not decided whether §§ 3 and 4 apply to proceedings in state courts, see *Volt Information Sciences, Inc.* v. *Board of Trustees of Leland Stanford Junior Univ.*, 489 U.S. 468, 477, n. 6, 109 S. Ct. 1248, 103 L. Ed. 2d 488 (1989), and we do not do so here.

* * *

■ CHIEF JUSTICE ROBERTS, with whom JUSTICE STEVENS, JUSTICE BREYER, and JUSTICE ALITO join, concurring in part and dissenting in part.

I agree with the Court that a federal court asked to compel arbitration pursuant to § 4 of the Federal Arbitration Act should "look through" the dispute over arbitrability in determining whether it has jurisdiction to grant the requested relief. But look through to what? The statute provides a clear and sensible answer: The court may consider the § 4 petition if the court "would have" jurisdiction over "the subject matter of a suit arising out of the controversy between the parties." 9 U.S.C. § 4.

The § 4 petition in this case explains that the controversy Discover seeks to arbitrate is whether "Discover Bank charged illegal finance charges, interest and late fees." Discover contends in its petition that the resolution of this dispute is controlled by federal law—specifically § 27(a) of the Federal Deposit Insurance Act (FDIA), 12 U.S.C. § 1831d(a) (setting forth the interest rates a state-chartered, federally insured bank may charge "notwithstanding any State constitution or statute which is hereby preempted"). Vaden agrees that the legality of Discover's charges and fees is governed by the FDIA. A federal court therefore "would have jurisdiction . . . of the subject matter of a suit arising out of the controversy" Discover seeks to arbitrate. That suit could be an action by Vaden asserting that the charges violate the FDIA, or one by Discover seeking a declaratory judgment that they do not.

The majority is diverted off this straightforward path by the fortuity that a complaint happens to have been filed in this case. Instead of looking to the controversy the § 4 petitioner seeks to arbitrate, the majority focuses on the controversy underlying that complaint, and asks whether "the *whole* controversy," as reflected in "the parties' state-court filings," arises under federal law. Because that litigation was commenced as a state-law debt-collection claim, the majority concludes there is no § 4 jurisdiction.

This approach is contrary to the language of § 4, and sharply restricts the ability of federal courts to enforce agreements to arbitrate. The "controversy" to which § 4 refers is the dispute alleged to be subject to arbitration. The § 4 petitioner must set forth the nature of that dispute—the one he seeks to arbitrate—in the § 4 petition seeking an order to compel arbitration. Section 4 requires that the petitioner be "aggrieved" by the other party's "failure, neglect, or refusal . . . to arbitrate under a written agreement for arbitration"; that language guides the district court to the specific controversy the other party is unwilling to arbitrate.

That is clear from the FAA's repeated and consistent use of the term "controversy" to mean the specific dispute asserted to be subject to arbitration, not to some broader, "full flavor[ed]" or "full-bodied" notion of the disagreement between the parties. In § 2, for example, the "controversy" is the one "to [be] settle[d] by arbitration" and the one "to [be] submit[ted] to arbitration." 9 U.S.C. § 2. In § 10(a)(3), it is a ground for vacating an arbitration award that the arbitrator refused to hear evidence "pertinent and material to the controversy"—obviously the "controversy" subject to arbitration, or the arbitrator's refusal to consider the evidence would hardly be objectionable. In § 11(c), an award may be modified if "imperfect in matter of form not affecting the merits of the controversy"—again, necessarily the controversy submitted to arbitration, and therefore the subject of the award.

There is no reason to suppose "controversy" meant the controversy subject to arbitration everywhere else in the FAA, but something quite different in § 4. The issue is whether there is jurisdiction to compel arbitration to resolve a controversy; why would the pertinent controversy for assessing jurisdiction be anything other than the same one asserted to be subject to arbitration?

The majority looks instead to the controversy the state-court litigation seeks to resolve. This produces the odd result of defining "controversy" more broadly than the § 4 petition itself. Discover's petition does not seek to arbitrate its state-law debt-collection claims, but rather Vaden's allegation that the fees Discover has been charging her (and other members of her proposed class) violate the FDIA. The majority does not appear to question that there would be federal jurisdiction over a suit arising out of the subject matter of that dispute. The majority finds no jurisdiction here, however, because "a federal court could not entertain Discover's state-law debt-collection claim." There is no jurisdiction to compel arbitration of a plainly federal controversy—the FDIA dispute—because there is no jurisdiction to compel arbitration of the debt-collection dispute. But why Discover should have to demonstrate federal jurisdiction over a state-court claim it does not seek to arbitrate is a mystery. Cf. Moses H. Cone Memorial Hospital v. Mercury Constr. Corp., 460 U.S. 1, 19–21, 103 S. Ct. 927, 74 L. Ed. 2d 765 (1983) (affirming federal-court jurisdiction over a § 4 petition seeking to arbitrate only one of two disputes pending in state-court litigation); Dean Witter Reynolds Inc. v. Byrd, 470 U.S. 213, 218–221, 105 S. Ct. 1238, 84 L. Ed. 2d 158 (1985) (when litigation involves multiple claims, only some of which are covered by an arbitration agreement, district court must compel arbitration of the covered claims if so requested).

The majority's approach will allow federal jurisdiction to compel arbitration of *entirely* state-law claims. Under that approach the "controversy" is not the one the § 4 petitioner seeks to arbitrate, but a broader one encompassing the "whole controversy" between the parties. If that broader dispute involves both federal and state-law claims, and the "originating" dispute is federal, a party could seek arbitration of just the state-law claims. The "controversy" under the majority's view would qualify as federal, giving rise to § 4 jurisdiction to compel arbitration of a purely state-law claim.

Take this case as an example. If Vaden had filed her FDIA claim first, and Discover had responded with a state-law debt-collection counterclaim, that suit is one that "could be litigated in federal court." As a result, the majority's approach would seem to permit Vaden to file a § 4 petition to compel arbitration of the entirely state-law-based debt-collection dispute, because that dispute would be part and parcel of the "full flavor[ed]," "originating" FDIA controversy. Defining the controversy as the dispute the § 4 petitioner seeks to arbitrate eliminates this problem by ensuring that the *actual dispute* subject to arbitration is federal.

* * * The majority's rule thus makes § 4 jurisdiction over the same controversy entirely dependent upon the happenstance of how state-court litigation has unfolded.

Nothing in § 4 suggests such a result.

The majority glosses over another problem inherent in its approach: In many if not most cases under § 4, no complaint will have been filed. See Hartford Financial Systems, Inc. v. Florida Software Servs., Inc., 712 F.2d 724, 728 (CA1 1983) (Breyer, J.) ("Normally, [§ 4] motions are brought in independent proceedings"). What to "look through" to then? The majority instructs courts to look to the "full-bodied controversy." But as this case illustrates, that would lead to a different result had the state-court complaint not been filed. Discover does not seek to arbitrate whether an outstanding debt exists; indeed, Discover's § 4 petition does not even allege any dispute on that point. A district court would therefore not understand the § 4 "controversy" to include the debt-collection claim in the absence of the state-court suit. Under the majority's rule, the FDIA dispute would be treated as a "controversy" qualifying under § 4 before the state suit and counterclaims had been filed, but not after.

The far more concrete and administrable approach would be to apply the same rule in all instances: Look to the controversy the § 4 petitioner seeks to arbitrate—as set forth in the § 4 petition—and assess whether a federal court would have jurisdiction over the subject matter of a suit arising out of that controversy. The controversy the moving party seeks to arbitrate and the other party will not would be the same controversy used to assess jurisdiction to compel arbitration.

The majority objects that this would allow a court to "hypothesiz[e] discrete controversies of its own design," in an apparent effort to find federal jurisdiction where there is none. Not so. A district court entertaining a § 4 petition is required to determine what "a suit" arising out of the allegedly arbitrable controversy would look like. There is no helping that, given the statute's subjunctive language. But that does not mean the inquiry is the free-form one the majority posits.

To the contrary, a district court must look to the specific controversy—the concrete dispute that one party has "fail[ed], neglect[ed], or refus[ed]" to arbitrate—and determine whether *that* controversy would give rise to a suit under federal law.

* * *

Discover and Vaden have agreed to arbitrate any dispute arising out of Vaden's account with Discover. Vaden's allegations against Discover have given rise to such a dispute. Discover seeks to arbitrate that controversy, but Vaden refuses to do so. Resolution of the controversy is governed by federal law, specifically the FDIA. There is no dispute about that. In the absence of the arbitration agreement, a federal court "would have jurisdiction . . . of the subject matter of a suit arising out of the controversy between the parties," 9 U.S.C. § 4, whether the suit were brought by Vaden or Discover. The District Court therefore may exercise jurisdiction over this petition under § 4 of the Federal Arbitration Act.

Footnote 20 of *Vaden* notes the Supreme Court "has not decided whether §§ 3 and 4 apply to proceedings in state courts." *Vaden* also says "Maryland's high court has held that §§ 3 and 4 of the FAA prescribe federal-court procedures and, therefore, do not bind the state courts. But Discover scarcely lacks an available state remedy. * * * Maryland, like many other States, provides a statutory remedy nearly identical to § 4."

Suppose though, instead of Maryland, the case arose in the courts of a state (like Alabama) that lacks an analog to FAA § 3 and 4?

> While the Supreme Court has been curiously and consistently coy on the question of whether state courts are bound by §§ 3 and 4, it seems obvious enough that these provisions exist to supply the remedial mechanisms necessary to make the core substantive mandate of § 2 effective. Once it is held that the states are bound by § 2 to treat arbitration agreements as enforceable, the suggestion that the remedy of specific performance is not necessary to vindicate the federal interest simply flies in the face of history, returning us to the era before modern arbitration statutes, when predispute arbitration clauses were enforceable only through the dubious means of actions for damages. In addition to the obligation to grant stays or compel arbitration, other provisions of §§ 3 and 4 may also call on states to align their procedures to some extent with the demands of federal arbitration policy. To say, for example, that courts "shall proceed summarily to the trial" of any issue concerning the making of the arbitration agreement may require applications to be heard under a state's local version of motion practice, or at least in some expeditious and summary hearing rather than in a plenary action.
>
> Other aspects of §§ 3 and 4 may not, however, "dig into" substantive rights in quite the same way. Section 4 provides for a jury determination of contested issues concerning the "making of the arbitration agreement." But a state might prefer that these issues be decided by the court. [See Rosenthal v. Great Western Fin. Securities Corp., 14 Cal.4th 394, 58 Cal.Rptr.2d 875, 926 P.2d 1061 (Cal. 1996)].
>
> To have a court rather than a jury pass on the existence of an arbitration agreement hardly appears to undermine or frustrate the arbitration process; moreover, a bench trial of the issue should not be expected to "frequently and predictably" lead to different outcomes. State rules denying a jury trial are certainly consistent both with the summary nature of the proceeding, and with the traditional treatment of these specific performance actions as equitable—and they can only result in making arbitration a speedier and more efficient process. It is not particularly clear in any event what role the choice of a jury in § 4 was intended to play in the overall statutory scheme: For some reason it is only "the party alleged to be in default"—presumably the party who has "failed, neglected, or refused" to proceed with arbitration—who under § 4 is entitled to ask for a jury trial; the party "aggrieved" by such "failure,

> neglect, or refusal" has no equivalent right. After such an analysis it might be concluded that state law ought to govern on such matters, even where the parties themselves have not expressly chosen to adopt such law.

Alan Scott Rau, Does State Arbitration Law Matter At All? Part II: A Continuing Role for State Law, in ADR & The Law 208, 211 (15th ed. 1999).

QUESTIONS TO REVIEW AND SYNTHESIZE

1. What makes FAA § 2 unusual federal substantive law? What impact does this have on parties going to court to enforce their FAA rights?
2. What is the well-pleaded-complaint rule, and what role does it play in *Vaden*?
3. *Vaden* instructs federal courts to "look through" a FAA § 4 petition how?
4. Compared to the *Vaden* majority, would the dissent shift more arbitration cases to federal or state court?

3. FEDERAL PREEMPTION OF STATE LAW IN THE LABOR AND EMPLOYMENT CONTEXTS

The previous section summarizes FAA preemption of state law, generally. Federal preemption has a somewhat different history and doctrine in the contexts of labor and employment arbitration. To reiterate, *labor* arbitration generally refers to arbitration arising out of a labor union's collective bargaining agreement ("CBA"), while *employment* arbitration arises out of an individual's employment contract.

a. LABOR

The foundational labor arbitration case, *Textile Workers* v. *Lincoln Mills of Ala.,* 353 U.S. 448, 1 L. Ed. 2d 972, 77 S. Ct. 912 (1957), held that CBAs' arbitration clauses are enforceable. However, *Lincoln Mills* did not mention the FAA, but rather rested its holding on Section 301 of the Labor Management Relations Act of 1947 ("LMRA"), which provides in pertinent part:

> (a) * * * Suits for violation of contracts between an employer and a labor organization representing employees in an industry affecting commerce as defined in this chapter, or between any such labor organizations, may be brought in any district court of the United States having jurisdiction of the parties, without respect to the amount in controversy or without regard to the citizenship of the parties.
>
> (b) * * * Any labor organization which represents employees in an industry affecting commerce as defined in this chapter and any employer whose activities affect commerce as defined in this chapter shall be bound by the acts of its agents. Any such labor organization may sue or be sued as an entity and in behalf of the employees whom it represents in the courts of the United States. Any money judgment against a labor organization in a district court of the United States shall be enforceable only against the organization as an entity and against its assets, and shall not be enforceable against any individual member or his assets.

29 U.S.C. § 185(a)–(b).

Before enactment of the LMRA, the legal status of unions was uncertain, and different state courts had ruled differently on whether unions could sue and be sued.[20] By subjecting unions to suit, the LMRA strengthened employers' ability to compel unions to comply with no-strike clauses in CBAs. *Lincoln Mills* said "the entire tenor of the [LMRA's legislative] history indicates that the agreement to arbitrate grievance disputes was considered as quid pro quo of a no-strike agreement."[21] That is, CBAs generally involve unions trading away the right to strike, in exchange for employers' promises and the union's right to arbitrate alleged breaches of those promises.

Because the LMRA says nothing about arbitration, courts must make case law (common law) to govern labor arbitration. *Lincoln Mills* held that this is *federal* common law. LMRA § 301 grants jurisdiction to federal courts and *Lincoln Mills* held that this provision does not merely give federal courts jurisdiction to apply *state* law, but rather gives them authority to create substantive *federal* law.[22] So with respect to labor arbitration, federal common law generally preempts inconsistent state law, but to what extent is that federal common law (rooted in the LMRA) supplemented by the FAA?

Because *Lincoln Mills* did not mention the FAA, the "most natural reading" of *Lincoln Mills* is that the FAA does not govern labor arbitration.[23] Justice Frankfurter's dissent in *Lincoln Mills* said:

> Naturally enough, I find rejection, though not explicit, of the availability of the Federal Arbitration Act to enforce arbitration clauses in collective-bargaining agreements in the silent treatment given that Act by the Court's opinion. If an Act that authorizes the federal courts to enforce arbitration provisions in contracts generally, but specifically denies authority to decree that remedy for 'contracts of employment,' were available, the Court would hardly spin such power out of the empty darkness of § 301. I would make this rejection explicit, recognizing that when Congress passed legislation to enable arbitration agreements to be enforced by the federal courts, it saw fit to exclude this remedy with respect to labor contracts.[24]

The Supreme Court's subsequent opinions on labor arbitration did not address the FAA until *United Paperworkers Int'l Union v. Misco, Inc.*, 484 U.S. 29, 40 n.9 (1987), when the Court said the FAA "does not apply to 'contracts of employment of . . . workers engaged in foreign or interstate commerce,' 9 U.S.C. § 1, but the federal courts have often looked to the Act for guidance in labor arbitration cases."

---

[20] Stewart J. Schwab, *Union Raids, Union Democracy, And The Market For Union Control*, 1992 U. Ill. L. Rev. 367, 407–08 ("In many states, because the union had no independent legal identity, it could not sue or be sued. . . Congress finally resolved the legal status of unions by enacting section 301 of the Labor Management Relations Act.").

[21] Lincoln Mills, 353 U.S. 448, 455. See also Local 174, Teamsters v. Lucas Flour Co., 369 U.S. 95 (1962)(courts should imply a no-strike clause with respect to any dispute which a CBA "provides shall be settled exclusively and finally by compulsory arbitration.").

[22] Lincoln Mills, 353 U.S. at 456 (the "substantive law to apply in suits under [the LMRA] is federal law, which the courts must fashion from the policy of our national labor laws.").

[23] Ian R. Macneil, Richard E. Speidel & Thomas J. Stipanowich, *Federal Arbitration Law: Agreements, Awards, and Remedies under the Federal Arbitration Act* § 11.3.1, at 11:9 (1994).

[24] Lincoln Mills, 353 U.S. at 466 (Frankfurter, J., dissenting).

The Court went further in *14 Penn Plaza LLC v. Pyett*, 556 U.S. 247, 129 S. Ct. 1456, 173 L. Ed. 2d 398 (2009), which resolved a labor arbitration case by applying the FAA without referring to the LMRA. *Pyett* (excerpted above in Section 3.B.3.c) enforced CBA arbitration clauses that "clearly and unmistakably require[ ] union members to arbitrate" statutory discrimination claims. 556 U.S. at 274.

Pyett leaves doubt about the extent to which the FAA applies to labor arbitration, but on some issues this will not matter due to the substantive similarities between the FAA and the federal common law developed under the LMRA. See, e.g., Wiregrass Metal Trades Council AFL-CIO v. Shaw Envtl. & Infrastructure, Inc., 837 F.3d 1083, 1087 n.1, 1093 (11th Cir. 2016) ("The LMRA clearly applies to labor cases. Whether the FAA also applies does not matter in this case. Shaw sought to vacate the arbitration award on the ground that the arbitrator exceeded her authority. That is a recognized ground for vacatur under both the FAA and federal common law developed under the LMRA."); Nat'l Football League Mgmt. Council v. Nat'l Football League Players Ass'n, 820 F.3d 527, 546 (2d Cir. 2016) ("Regardless of which position we adopt, our result is the same, and thus we need not decide whether the [standard] of the FAA ought to be imported to our review of arbitrations conducted pursuant to the LMRA").

b. EMPLOYMENT

Circuit City Stores v. Adams

Supreme Court of the United States, 2001.
532 U.S. 105, 121 S.Ct. 1302, 149 L.Ed.2d 234.

■ JUSTICE KENNEDY delivered the opinion of the Court.

Section 1 of the Federal Arbitration Act (FAA) excludes from the Act's coverage "contracts of employment of seamen, railroad employees, or any other class of workers engaged in foreign or interstate commerce." 9 U.S.C. § 1. All but one of the Courts of Appeals which have addressed the issue interpret this provision as exempting contracts of employment of transportation workers, but not other employment contracts, from the FAA's coverage. A different interpretation has been adopted by the Court of Appeals for the Ninth Circuit, which construes the exemption so that all contracts of employment are beyond the FAA's reach, whether or not the worker is engaged in transportation. It applied that rule to the instant case. We now decide that the better interpretation is to construe the statute, as most of the Courts of Appeals have done, to confine the exemption to transportation workers.

In October 1995, respondent Saint Clair Adams applied for a job at petitioner Circuit City Stores, Inc., a national retailer of consumer electronics. Adams signed an employment application which included the following provision:

> "I agree that I will settle any and all previously unasserted claims, disputes or controversies arising out of or relating to my application or candidacy for employment, employment and/or cessation of employment with Circuit City, *exclusively* by final and binding *arbitration* before a neutral Arbitrator. By way of example only, such claims include

> claims under federal, state, and local statutory or common law, such as the Age Discrimination in Employment Act, Title VII of the Civil Rights Act of 1964, as amended, including the amendments of the Civil Rights Act of 1991, the Americans with Disabilities Act, the law of contract and the law of tort."

Adams was hired as a sales counselor in Circuit City's store in Santa Rosa, California.

Two years later, Adams filed an employment discrimination lawsuit against Circuit City in state court, asserting claims under California's Fair Employment and Housing Act, Cal. Govt. Code Ann. § 12900 *et seq.*, and other claims based on general tort theories under California law. Circuit City filed suit in the United States District Court for the Northern District of California, seeking to enjoin the state-court action and to compel arbitration of respondent's claims pursuant to the FAA, 9 U.S.C. §§ 1–16. The District Court entered the requested order. Respondent, the court concluded, was obligated by the arbitration agreement to submit his claims against the employer to binding arbitration. An appeal followed.

While respondent's appeal was pending in the Court of Appeals for the Ninth Circuit, the court ruled on the key issue in an unrelated case. The court held the FAA does not apply to contracts of employment. In the instant case, following the rule announced in *Craft*, the Court of Appeals held the arbitration agreement between Adams and Circuit City was contained in a "contract of employment," and so was not subject to the FAA. Circuit City petitioned this Court, noting that the Ninth Circuit's conclusion that all employment contracts are excluded from the FAA conflict with every other Court of Appeals to have addressed the question. We granted certiorari to resolve the issue.

Congress enacted the FAA in 1925. As the Court has explained, the FAA was a response to hostility of American courts to the enforcement of arbitration agreements, a judicial disposition inherited from then-longstanding English practice. To give effect to this purpose, the FAA compels judicial enforcement of a wide range of written arbitration agreements. The FAA's coverage provision, § 2, provides that

> "[a] written provision in any maritime transaction or a contract evidencing a transaction involving commerce to settle by arbitration a controversy thereafter arising out of such contract or transaction, or the refusal to perform the whole or any part thereof, or an agreement in writing to submit to arbitration an existing controversy arising out of such a contract, transaction, or refusal, shall be valid, irrevocable, and enforceable, save upon such grounds as exist at law or in equity for the revocation of any contract." 9 U.S.C. § 2.

We had occasion in *Allied-Bruce* to consider the significance of Congress' use of the words "involving commerce" in § 2. The analysis began with a reaffirmation of earlier decisions concluding that the FAA was enacted pursuant to Congress' substantive power to regulate interstate commerce and admiralty and that the Act was applicable in state courts and pre-emptive of state laws hostile to arbitration. Relying upon these background principles and upon the evident reach of the words "involving commerce," the Court interpreted § 2 as implementing Congress' intent "to exercise [its] commerce power to the full."

The instant case, of course, involves not the basic coverage authorization under § 2 of the Act, but the exemption from coverage under § 1. The exemption clause provides the Act shall not apply "to contracts of employment of seamen, railroad employees, or any other class of workers engaged in foreign or interstate commerce." 9 U.S.C. § 1. Most Courts of Appeals conclude the exclusion provision is limited to transportation workers, defined, for instance, as those workers "actually engaged in the movement of goods in interstate commerce."

* * *

Respondent, endorsing the reasoning of the Court of Appeals for the Ninth Circuit that the provision excludes all employment contracts, relies on the asserted breadth of the words "contracts of employment of . . . any other class of workers engaged in . . . commerce." Referring to our construction of § 2's coverage provision in *Allied-Bruce*—concluding that the words "involving commerce" evidence the congressional intent to regulate to the full extent of its commerce power—respondent contends § 1's interpretation should have a like reach, thus exempting all employment contracts. The two provisions, it is argued, are coterminous; under this view the "involving commerce" provision brings within the FAA's scope all contracts within the Congress' commerce power, and the "engaged in . . . commerce" language in § 1 in turn exempts from the FAA all employment contracts falling within that authority.

This reading of § 1, however, runs into an immediate and, in our view, insurmountable textual obstacle. Unlike the "involving commerce" language in § 2, the words "any other class of workers engaged in . . . commerce" constitute a residual phrase, following, in the same sentence, explicit reference to "seamen" and "railroad employees." Construing the residual phrase to exclude all employment contracts fails to give independent effect to the statute's enumeration of the specific categories of workers which precedes it; there would be no need for Congress to use the phrases "seamen" and "railroad employees" if those same classes of workers were subsumed within the meaning of the "engaged in . . . commerce" residual clause. The wording of § 1 calls for the application of the maxim *ejusdem generis*, the statutory canon that "where general words follow specific words in a statutory enumeration, the general words are construed to embrace only objects similar in nature to those objects enumerated by the preceding specific words." Under this rule of construction the residual clause should be read to give effect to the terms "seamen" and "railroad employees," and should itself be controlled and defined by reference to the enumerated categories of workers which are recited just before it; the interpretation of the clause pressed by respondent fails to produce these results.

Canons of construction need not be conclusive and are often countered, of course, by some maxim pointing in a different direction. The application of the rule *ejusdem generis* in this case, however, is in full accord with other sound considerations bearing upon the proper interpretation of the clause. For even if the term "engaged in commerce" stood alone in § 1, we would not construe the provision to exclude all contracts of employment from the FAA. Congress uses different modifiers to the word "commerce" in the design and enactment of its statutes. The phrase "affecting commerce" indicates Congress' intent to regulate to the outer limits of its authority under the Commerce Clause. The "involving commerce" phrase, the operative words for the reach of the basic coverage provision in § 2, was at issue in *Allied-Bruce*. That particular phrase had not been interpreted before by this Court. Considering the usual meaning of the word "involving," and the pro-arbitration purposes of the FAA, *Allied-Bruce* held the "word 'involving,' like 'affecting,' signals an intent to exercise Congress' commerce power to the full." Unlike those phrases, however, the general words "in commerce" and the specific phrase "engaged in commerce" are understood to have a more limited reach. In *Allied-Bruce* itself the Court said the words "in commerce" are "often-found words of art" that we have not read as expressing congressional intent to regulate to the outer limits of authority under the Commerce Clause. Id. at 273; see also United States v. American Building Maintenance Industries, 422 U.S. 271, 279–280, 45 L. Ed. 2d 177, 95 S. Ct. 2150 (1975) (the phrase "engaged in commerce" is "a term of art, indicating a limited assertion of federal jurisdiction"); Jones v. United States, 529 U.S. 848, 855, 146 L. Ed. 2d 902, 120 S. Ct. 1904 (2000) (phrase "used in commerce" "is most sensibly read to mean active employment for commercial purposes, and not merely a passive, passing, or past connection to commerce").

It is argued that we should assess the meaning of the phrase "engaged in commerce" in a different manner here, because the FAA was enacted when congressional authority to regulate under the commerce power was to a large extent confined by our decisions. See United States v. Lopez, 514 U.S. 549, 556, 131 L. Ed. 2d 626, 115 S. Ct. 1624 (1995) (noting that Supreme Court decisions beginning in 1937 "ushered in an era of Commerce Clause jurisprudence that greatly expanded the previously defined authority of Congress under that Clause"). When the FAA was enacted in 1925, respondent reasons, the phrase "engaged in commerce" was not a term of art indicating a limited assertion of congressional jurisdiction; to the contrary, it is said, the formulation came close to expressing the outer limits of Congress' power as then understood. Were this mode of interpretation to prevail, we would take into account the scope of the Commerce Clause, as then elaborated by the Court, at the date of the FAA's enactment in order to interpret what the statute means now.

A variable standard for interpreting common, jurisdictional phrases would contradict our earlier cases and bring instability to statutory interpretation. The Court has declined in past cases to afford significance, in construing the meaning of the statutory jurisdictional provisions "in commerce" and "engaged in commerce," to the circumstance that the statute predated shifts in the Court's Commerce Clause cases.

* * * The Court's reluctance to accept contentions that Congress used the words "in commerce" or "engaged in commerce" to regulate to the full extent of its commerce power rests on sound foundation, as it affords objective and consistent significance to the meaning of the words Congress uses when it defines the reach of a statute. To say that the statutory words "engaged in commerce" are

subject to variable interpretations depending upon the date of adoption, even a date before the phrase became a term of art, ignores the reason why the formulation became a term of art in the first place: The plain meaning of the words "engaged in commerce" is narrower than the more open-ended formulations "affecting commerce" and "involving commerce." It would be unwieldy for Congress, for the Court, and for litigants to be required to deconstruct statutory Commerce Clause phrases depending upon the year of a particular statutory enactment.

* * *

In sum, the text of the FAA forecloses the construction of § 1 followed by the Court of Appeals in the case under review, a construction which would exclude all employment contracts from the FAA. While the historical arguments respecting Congress' understanding of its power in 1925 are not insubstantial, this fact alone does not give us basis to adopt, "by judicial decision rather than amendatory legislation," an expansive construction of the FAA's exclusion provision that goes beyond the meaning of the words Congress used. While it is of course possible to speculate that Congress might have chosen a different jurisdictional formulation had it known that the Court would soon embrace a less restrictive reading of the Commerce Clause, the text of § 1 precludes interpreting the exclusion provision to defeat the language of § 2 as to all employment contracts. Section 1 exempts from the FAA only contracts of employment of transportation workers.

As the conclusion we reach today is directed by the text of § 1, we need not assess the legislative history of the exclusion provision.

* * *

Nor can we accept respondent's argument that our holding attributes an irrational intent to Congress. "Under petitioner's reading of § 1," he contends, "those employment contracts *most* involving interstate commerce, and thus most assuredly within the Commerce Clause power in 1925 . . . are *excluded* from [the] Act's coverage; while those employment contracts having a *less* direct and less certain connection to interstate commerce . . . would come *within* the Act's affirmative coverage and would not be excluded."

We see no paradox in the congressional decision to exempt the workers over whom the commerce power was most apparent. To the contrary, it is a permissible inference that the employment contracts of the classes of workers in § 1 were excluded from the FAA precisely because of Congress' undoubted authority to govern the employment relationships at issue by the enactment of statutes specific to them. By the time the FAA was passed, Congress had already enacted federal legislation providing for the arbitration of disputes between seamen and their employers, see Shipping Commissioners Act of 1872, 17 Stat. 262. When the FAA was adopted, moreover, grievance procedures existed for railroad employees under federal law, see Transportation Act of 1920, §§ 300–316, 41 Stat. 456, and the passage of a more comprehensive statute providing for the mediation and arbitration of railroad labor disputes was imminent, see Railway Labor Act of 1926, 44 Stat. 577, 46 U.S.C. § 651 (repealed). It is reasonable to assume that Congress excluded "seamen" and "railroad employees" from the FAA for the simple reason that it did not wish to unsettle established or developing statutory dispute resolution schemes covering specific workers.

As for the residual exclusion of "any other class of workers engaged in foreign or interstate commerce," Congress' demonstrated concern with transportation workers and their necessary role in the free flow of goods explains the linkage to the two specific, enumerated types of workers identified in the preceding portion of the sentence. It would be rational for Congress to ensure that workers in general would be covered by the provisions of the FAA, while reserving for itself more specific legislation for those engaged in transportation. Indeed, such legislation was soon to follow, with the amendment of the Railway Labor Act in 1936 to include air carriers and their employees.

Various *amici,* including the attorneys general of 22 States, object that the reading of the § 1 exclusion provision adopted today intrudes upon the policies of the separate States. They point out that, by requiring arbitration agreements in most employment contracts to be covered by the FAA, the statute in effect pre-empts those state employment laws which restrict or limit the ability of employees and employers to enter into arbitration agreements. It is argued that States should be permitted, pursuant to their traditional role in regulating employment relationships, to prohibit employees like respondent from contracting away their right to pursue state-law discrimination claims in court.

It is not our holding today which is the proper target of this criticism. The line of argument is relevant instead to the Court's decision in *Southland Corp.* v. *Keating,* 465 U.S. 1, 79 L. Ed. 2d 1, 104 S. Ct. 852 (1984), holding that Congress intended the FAA to apply in state courts, and to pre-empt state antiarbitration laws to the contrary. [The Court declined to revisit *Southland.*]

* * *

■ JUSTICE STEVENS, with whom JUSTICE GINSBURG and JUSTICE BREYER join, and with whom JUSTICE SOUTER joins as to Parts II and III, dissenting.

JUSTICE SOUTER has cogently explained why the Court's parsimonious construction of § 1 of the Federal Arbitration Act (FAA or Act) is not consistent with its expansive reading of § 2. I join his opinion, but believe that the Court's heavy reliance on the views expressed by the Courts of Appeals during the past decade makes it appropriate to comment on three earlier chapters in the history of this venerable statute.

Section § 2 of the FAA makes enforceable written agreements to arbitrate "in any maritime transaction or a contract evidencing a transaction involving commerce." If we were writing on a clean slate, there would be good reason to conclude that neither the phrase "maritime transaction" nor the phrase "contract evidencing a transaction involving commerce" was intended to encompass employment contracts.

The history of the Act, which is extensive and well-documented, makes clear that the FAA was a response to the refusal of courts to enforce commercial arbitration agreements, which were commonly used in the maritime context. The original bill was drafted by the Committee on Commerce, Trade, and Commercial

Law of the American Bar Association (ABA) upon consideration of "the further extension of the principle of *commercial* arbitration." As drafted, the bill was understood by Members of Congress to "simply provide for one thing, and that is to give an opportunity to enforce an agreement in *commercial* contracts and *admiralty* contracts." It is no surprise, then, that when the legislation was first introduced in 1922, it did not mention employment contracts, but did contain a rather precise definition of the term "maritime transactions" that underscored the commercial character of the proposed bill. Indeed, neither the history of the drafting of the original bill by the ABA, nor the records of the deliberations in Congress during the years preceding the ultimate enactment of the Act in 1925, contains any evidence that the proponents of the legislation intended it to apply to agreements affecting employment.

Nevertheless, the original bill was opposed by representatives of organized labor, most notably the president of the International Seamen's Union of America,[5] because of their concern that the legislation might authorize federal judicial enforcement of arbitration clauses in employment contracts and collective-bargaining agreements. In response to those objections, the chairman of the ABA committee that drafted the legislation emphasized at a Senate Judiciary Subcommittee hearing that "it is not intended that this shall be an act referring to labor disputes at all," but he also observed that "if your honorable committee should feel that there is any danger of that, they should add to the bill the following language, 'but nothing herein contained shall apply to seamen or any class of workers in interstate and foreign commerce.'" Similarly, another supporter of the bill, then Secretary of Commerce Herbert Hoover, suggested that "if objection appears to the inclusion of workers' contracts in the law's scheme, it might be well amended by stating 'but nothing herein contained shall apply to contracts of employment of seamen, railroad employees, or any other class of workers engaged in interstate or foreign commerce.'" The legislation was reintroduced in the next session of Congress with Secretary Hoover's exclusionary language added to § 1, and the amendment eliminated organized labor's opposition to the proposed law.

That amendment is what the Court construes today. History amply supports the proposition that it was an uncontroversial provision that merely confirmed the fact that no one interested in the enactment of the FAA ever intended or expected that § 2 would apply to employment contracts. It is particularly ironic, therefore, that the amendment has provided the Court with its sole justification for refusing to give the text of § 2 a natural reading. Playing ostrich to the substantial history behind the amendment, ("We need not assess the legislative history of the exclusion provision"), the Court reasons in a vacuum that "if all contracts of employment are beyond the scope of the Act under the § 2 coverage provision, the separate exemption" in § 1 "would be pointless". But contrary to the Court's suggestion, it is not "pointless" to adopt a clarifying amendment in order to

---

[5] He stated: "This bill provides for reintroduction of forced or involuntary labor, if the freeman through his necessities shall be induced to sign. Will such contracts be signed? Esau agreed, because he was hungry. It was the desire to live that caused slavery to begin and continue. With the growing hunger in modern society, there will be but few that will be able to resist. The personal hunger of the *seaman,* and the hunger of the wife and children of the *railroad man* will surely tempt them to sign, and so with *sundry other workers in 'Interstate and Foreign Commerce.'*"

eliminate opposition to a bill. Moreover, the majority's reasoning is squarely contradicted by the Court's approach in *Bernhardt* v. *Polygraphic Co. of America,* 350 U.S. 198, 200, 201, n. 3, 100 L. Ed. 199, 76 S. Ct. 273 (1956), where the Court concluded that an employment contract did not "evidence 'a transaction involving commerce' within the meaning of § 2 of the Act," and therefore did not "reach the further question whether in any event petitioner would be included in 'any other class of workers' within the exceptions of § 1 of the Act."

The irony of the Court's reading of § 2 to include contracts of employment is compounded by its cramped interpretation of the exclusion inserted into § 1. As proposed and enacted, the exclusion fully responded to the concerns of the Seamen's Union and other labor organizations that § 2 might encompass employment contracts by expressly exempting not only the labor agreements of "seamen" and "railroad employees," but also of *"any other class of workers* engaged in foreign or interstate commerce." 9 U.S.C. § 1 (emphasis added). Today, however, the Court fulfills the original—and originally unfounded—fears of organized labor by essentially rewriting the text of § 1 to exclude the employment contracts *solely* of "seamen, railroad employees, or any other class of *transportation* workers engaged in foreign or interstate commerce." In contrast, whether one views the legislation before or after the amendment to § 1, it is clear that it was not intended to apply to employment contracts at all.

* * *

In *Textile Workers* v. *Lincoln Mills of Ala.,* 353 U.S. 448, 1 L. Ed. 2d 972, 77 S. Ct. 912 (1957), the Court granted certiorari to consider the union's claim that, in a suit brought under § 301 of the Labor Management Relations Act, 1947 (LMRA), a federal court may enforce the arbitration clause in a collective-bargaining agreement. The union argued that such authority was implicitly granted by § 301 and explicitly granted by § 2 of the FAA. In support of the latter argument, the union asked the Court to rule either that a collective-bargaining agreement is not a "contract of employment" within the meaning of the exclusion in § 1, or that the exclusion is limited to transportation workers. The Court did not accept either argument, but held that § 301 itself provided the authority to compel arbitration. The fact that the Court relied on § 301 of the LMRA, a statutory provision that does not mention arbitration, rather than the FAA, a statute that expressly authorizes the enforcement of arbitration agreements, strongly implies that the Court had concluded that the FAA simply did not apply because § 1 exempts labor contracts.

* * *

Times have changed. Judges in the 19th century disfavored private arbitration. The 1925 Act was intended to overcome that attitude, but a number of this Court's cases decided in the last several decades have pushed the pendulum far beyond a neutral attitude and endorsed a policy that strongly favors private arbitration. * * * There is little doubt that the Court's interpretation of the Act has given it a scope far beyond the expectations of the Congress that enacted it.

* * *

It is not necessarily wrong for the Court to put its own imprint on a statute. But when its refusal to look beyond the raw statutory text enables it to disregard countervailing considerations that were expressed by Members of the enacting Congress and that remain valid today, the Court misuses its authority. As the history of the legislation indicates, the potential disparity in bargaining power between individual employees and large employers was the source of organized labor's opposition to the Act, which it feared would require courts to enforce unfair employment contracts. That same concern underlay Congress' exemption of contracts of employment from mandatory arbitration. When the Court simply ignores the interest of the unrepresented employee, it skews its interpretation with its own policy preferences.

* * *

■ JUSTICE SOUTER, with whom JUSTICE STEVENS, JUSTICE GINSBURG, and JUSTICE BREYER join, dissenting.

Section 2 of the Federal Arbitration Act (FAA or Act) provides for the enforceability of a written arbitration clause in "any maritime transaction or a contract evidencing a transaction involving commerce" 9 U.S.C. § 2, while § 1 exempts from the Act's coverage "contracts of employment of seamen, railroad employees, or any other class of workers engaged in foreign or interstate commerce." Whatever the understanding of Congress's implied admiralty power may have been when the Act was passed in 1925, the commerce power was then thought to be far narrower than we have subsequently come to see it. As a consequence, there are two quite different ways of reading the scope of the Act's provisions. One way would be to say, for example, that the coverage provision extends only to those contracts "involving commerce" that were understood to be covered in 1925; the other would be to read it as exercising Congress's commerce jurisdiction in its modern conception in the same way it was thought to implement the more limited view of the Commerce Clause in 1925. The first possibility would result in a statutory ambit frozen in time, behooving Congress to amend the statute whenever it desired to expand arbitration clause enforcement beyond its scope in 1925; the second would produce an elastic reach, based on an understanding that Congress used language intended to go as far as Congress could go, whatever that might be over time.

In *Allied-Bruce Terminix Cos.* v. *Dobson*, 513 U.S. 265, 130 L. Ed. 2d 753, 115 S. Ct. 834 (1995), we decided that the elastic understanding of § 2 was the more sensible way to give effect to what Congress intended when it legislated to cover contracts "involving commerce," a phrase that we found an apt way of providing that coverage would extend to the outer constitutional limits under the Commerce Clause. The question here is whether a similarly general phrase in the § 1 exemption, referring to contracts of "any . . . class of workers engaged in foreign or interstate commerce," should receive a correspondingly evolutionary reading, so as to expand the exemption for employment contracts to keep pace with the enhanced reach of the general enforceability provision.

* * *

When the Act was passed (and the commerce power was closely confined) our case law indicated that the only employment relationships subject to the commerce power were those in which workers were actually engaged in interstate commerce. Thus, by using "engaged in" for the exclusion, Congress showed an intent to exclude to the limit of its power to cover employment contracts in the first place, and it did so just as clearly as its use of "involving commerce" showed its intent to legislate to the hilt over commercial contracts at a more general level.

* * *

The Court has no good reason, therefore, to reject a reading of "engaged in" as an expression of intent to legislate to the full extent of the commerce power over employment contracts. The statute is accordingly entitled to a coherent reading as a whole by treating the exemption for employment contracts as keeping pace with the expanded understanding of the commerce power generally.

* * *

[I]t is imputing something very odd to the working of the congressional brain to say that Congress took care to bar application of the Act to the class of employment contracts it most obviously had authority to legislate about in 1925, contracts of workers employed by carriers and handlers of commerce, while covering only employees "engaged" in less obvious ways, over whose coverage litigation might be anticipated with uncertain results. It would seem to have made more sense either to cover all coverable employment contracts or to exclude them all. In fact, exclusion might well have been in order based on concern that arbitration could prove expensive or unfavorable to employees, many of whom lack the bargaining power to resist an arbitration clause if their prospective employers insist on one.[3] And excluding all employment contracts from the Act's enforcement of mandatory arbitration clauses is consistent with Secretary Hoover's suggestion that the exemption language would respond to any "objection . . . to the inclusion of workers' contracts."

The Court tries to deflect the anomaly of excluding only carrier contracts by suggesting that Congress used the reference to seamen and rail workers to indicate the class of employees whose employment relations it had already legislated about and would be most likely to legislate about in the future. This explanation, however, does nothing to eliminate the anomaly. On the contrary, the explanation tells us why Congress might have referred specifically to the sea and rail workers; but, if so, it also indicates that Congress almost certainly intended the catchall phrase to be just as broad as its terms, without any interpretive squeeze in the name of *ejusdem generis*.

The very fact, as the Court points out, that Congress already had spoken on the subjects of sailors and rail workers and had tailored the legislation to the particular circumstances of the sea and rail carriers may well have been reason for

---

[3] Senator Walsh expressed this concern during a subcommittee hearing on the FAA: "'The trouble about the matter is that a great many of these contracts that are entered into are really not voluntary things at all . . . . It is the same with a good many contracts of employment. A man says, "There are our terms. All right, take it or leave it." Well, there is nothing for the man to do except to sign it; and then he surrenders his right to have his case tried by the court, and has to have it tried before a tribunal in which he has no confidence at all.'"

mentioning them specifically. But making the specific references was in that case an act of special care to make sure that the FAA not be construed to modify the existing legislation so exactly aimed; that was no reason at all to limit the general FAA exclusion from applying to employment contracts that had not been targeted with special legislation. Congress did not need to worry especially about the FAA's effect on legislation that did not exist and was not contemplated. As to workers uncovered by any specific legislation, Congress could write on a clean slate, and what it wrote was a general exclusion for employment contracts within Congress's power to regulate. The Court has understood this point before, holding that the existence of a special reason for emphasizing specific examples of a statutory class can negate any inference that an otherwise unqualified general phrase was meant to apply only to matters *ejusdem generis*. On the Court's own reading of the history, then, the explanation for the catchall is not *ejusdem generis*; instead, the explanation for the specifics is *ex abundanti cautela*, abundance of caution.

Nothing stands in the way of construing the coverage and exclusion clauses together, consistently and coherently. I respectfully dissent.

Stephen J. Ware, *A Short Defense of Southland, Casarotto, and Other Long-Controversial Arbitration Decisions*

30 Loyola Consumer L. Rev. 303, 333–36 (2018).

[*Circuit City*] produces what I have described as the "strange result of a *federal* statute governing employees *less* closely connected to interstate commerce, while *state* law governs employees *most* closely connected to it."

This strange result could have been avoided by emphasizing that section 1 excludes from the FAA's coverage, not only "seamen" and "railroad employees," but also "any other class of workers engaged in foreign or interstate commerce," and then interpreting "workers engaged in . . . commerce" flexibly to broaden along with the Court's broadening of "commerce" in post-FAA constitutional decisions. Under this statutory interpretation, as the types of jobs in "commerce" expanded to bring employees under FAA section 2, the types of employees excluded from the FAA by section 1 would have similarly expanded, thus leaving most employment arbitration agreements excluded from the FAA. This interpretation of section 1 was advocated, before *Circuit City*, by Matthew Finkin, who wrote: "As the commerce power has been expanded by the United States Supreme Court, the [FAA section 1 employment] exemption has expanded along with it, leaving the status of these employees' contracts in practical effect just as they were when the Act was passed."

While this interpretation has much appeal, *Circuit City*'s counter-argument is also coherent. The *Circuit City* Court distinguished FAA section 2's "involving commerce"—construed as extending to the full reach of Congress's Commerce power—from section 1's "in commerce"—a term of art the Court has, in several contexts, construed more narrowly. *Circuit City* said, "the word 'involving,' like 'affecting,' signals an intent to exercise Congress' commerce power to the full.

Unlike those phrases, however, the general words 'in commerce' and the specific phrase 'engaged in commerce' are understood to have a more limited reach." This distinction was not fabricated by the *Circuit City* majority, as the Court cited non-arbitration cases reading "in commerce" more narrowly than the full reach of Congress's Commerce power.

In addition, *Circuit City* cited non-arbitration cases declining to "afford significance, in construing the meaning of the statutory jurisdictional provisions 'in commerce' and 'engaged in commerce,' to the circumstance that the statute predated shifts in the Court's Commerce Clause cases." *Circuit City* rejected giving FAA section 1 "a broader construction than justified by its evident language simply because it was enacted in 1925 rather than 1938." The Court concluded:

> While it is of course possible to speculate that Congress might have chosen a different jurisdictional formulation [in FAA section 1] had it known that the Court would soon embrace a less restrictive reading of the Commerce Clause, the text of § 1 precludes interpreting the exclusion provision to defeat the language of § 2 as to all employment contracts.
>
> As the conclusion we reach today is directed by the text of § 1, we need not assess the legislative history of the exclusion provision.

However confident one is that Congress would have written FAA section 1 differently had it anticipated the Court's 1937 broadening of "commerce," *Circuit City* can at least be defended on the ground that it is consistent with mainstream approaches to statutory interpretation that, for good reasons, prioritize statutory text over legislative history, and with non-arbitration decisions declining to give significance, in construing statutory text, to its enactment before 1937's constitutional change.

In sum, *Circuit City*'s strange result has a defensible basis in statutory text and the Court's post-FAA broadening of "commerce." Whether defensible enough to outweigh Professor Finkin's argument seems to me a close call.

Lower courts have followed *Circuit City* in not applying the FAA to "transportation workers," while applying it to other employees. Compare, e.g., Palcko v. Airborne Express, Inc., 372 F.3d 588, 593 (3d Cir. 2004) (employee was a "transportation worker" because "she was responsible for 'monitoring and improving the performance of drivers under [her] supervision to insure [sic] timely and efficient delivery of packages.' Such direct supervision of package shipments makes Palcko's work "so closely related [to interstate and foreign commerce] as to be in practical effect part of it."), with Lenz v. Yellow Transp., Inc., 431 F.3d 348, 351–52 (8th Cir. 2005) (customer service representative for interstate trucking company, who fielded calls from customers regarding their shipment orders, was not a transportation worker and thus was governed by FAA).

Transportation workers' arbitration agreements are governed by state arbitration law. While many states enforce employment arbitration agreements as readily as other arbitration agreements, some states do not. Transportation workers excluded from the FAA, and thus governed by state arbitration law, can be independent contractors as well as employees, the Supreme Court unanimously held in *New Prime Inc. v. Oliveira*, 139 S.Ct. 532 (2019).

While a consequence of *Circuit City* is that most employment arbitration agreements are now generally enforceable against the employees who sign them, such agreements do not bind the Equal Employment Opportunity Commission (EEOC), so it can obtain victim-specific remedies in court on behalf of an employee who has agreed to arbitrate. The Supreme Court's opinion in *Equal Employment Opportunity Commission v. Waffle House*, 534 U.S. 279 (2002) said:

> It goes without saying that a contract cannot bind a nonparty. Accordingly, the proarbitration policy goals of the FAA do not require the [EEOC] to relinquish its statutory authority if it has not agreed to do so. * * * [W]e are persuaded that, pursuant to Title VII and the ADA, whenever the EEOC chooses from among the many charges filed each year to bring an enforcement action in a particular case, the agency may be seeking to vindicate a public interest, not simply provide make-whole relief for the employee, even when it pursues entirely victim-specific relief. To hold otherwise would undermine the detailed enforcement scheme created by Congress simply to give greater effect to an agreement between private parties that does not even contemplate the EEOC's statutory function.

Id. at 295–96.[25]

QUESTIONS TO REVIEW AND SYNTHESIZE

1. Did those who drafted and enacted the FAA expect it to govern many employment contracts?
2. After *Circuit City*, what employment contracts are governed by the FAA?
3. What developments between 1925 and 2001 help explain your contrasting answers to the previous two questions?

4. FEDERAL PREEMPTION OF STATE LAW IN THE INSURANCE CONTEXT

Federal preemption of state arbitration law related to the "*business of insurance*" involves not only the FAA but also the McCarran-Ferguson Act, which provides that:

> No Act of Congress shall be construed to invalidate, impair, or supersede any law enacted by any State for the purpose of regulating the business of insurance * * * unless such Act specifically relates to the business of insurance.

15 U.S.C. § 1012(b).

---

[25] See United States Equal Employment Opportunity Commission v. River Oaks Imaging and Diagnostic, 1995 WL 264003 (S.D.Tex.Apr.19, 1995).

Citizens of Humanity LLC v. Applied Underwriters, Inc.

Court of Appeal, Second District, Division 2, California, 2017.
17 Cal.App.5th 806, 226 Cal.Rptr.3d 1, 17 Cal. Daily Op. Serv. 11,240,
2017 Daily Journal D.A.R. 11,135.

■ Opinion CHAVEZ, J.

Defendants and appellants Applied Underwriters, Inc. (Applied Underwriters), California Insurance Company (CIC), Continental Indemnity Company, Applied Risk Services, Inc., Joan Sheppard, Westin Fredrick Penfield, and Michael Scott Wichman (collectively, defendants) appeal from an order denying their petition to compel arbitration of a dispute with plaintiffs and respondents Citizens of Humanity, LLC, and CM Laundry, LLC (collectively, plaintiffs). We affirm the trial court's order.

BACKGROUND

The RPA

In 2012, plaintiffs purchased from defendants a workers' compensation insurance package known as the EquityComp program. As part of that program, plaintiffs entered into a Reinsurance Participation Agreement (RPA) with Applied Underwriters Captive Risk Assurance Company, Inc. (AUCRA), a company affiliated with defendants. The RPA contains an arbitration provision that provides in relevant part:

> "13. Nothing in this section shall be deemed to amend or alter the due date of any obligation under this Agreement. Rather, this section is only intended to provide a mechanism for resolving accounting disputes in good faith.
>
> "(A) It is the express intention of the parties to resolve any disputes arising under this Agreement without resort to litigation in order to protect the confidentiality of their relationship and their respective businesses and affairs. Any dispute or controversy that is not resolved informally pursuant to sub paragraph (B) of Paragraph 13 arising out of or related to this Agreement shall be fully determined in the British Virgin Islands under the provisions of the American Arbitration Association.
>
> "(B) All disputes between the parties relating in any way to (1) the execution and delivery, construction or enforceability of this Agreement, (2) the management or operation of the Company, or (3) any other breach or claimed breach of this Agreement or the transactions contemplated herein shall be settled amicably by good faith discussion among all of the parties hereto, and, failing such amicable settlement, finally determined exclusively by binding arbitration in accordance with the procedures provided herein. The reference to this arbitration clause in any specific provision of this Agreement is for emphasis only, and is not intended to limit the scope, extent or intent of this arbitration clause or to mean that any other provision of this Agreement shall not be fully subject to the terms of this arbitration clause. All disputes arising with respect to any provision of this Agreement shall be fully subject to the terms of this arbitration clause."

None of the other agreements between the parties contains an arbitration provision.

The RPA also contains a choice of law provision that states:

> "16. This Agreement shall be exclusively governed by and construed in accordance with the laws of Nebraska and any matter concerning this Agreement that is not subject to the dispute resolution provisions of Paragraph 13 hereof shall be resolved exclusively by the courts of Nebraska without reference to its conflict of laws."

<u>The instant action</u>

In February 2015, plaintiffs filed a complaint against defendants and AUCRA alleging causes of action against AUCRA for fraudulent inducement in entering into the arbitration agreement, breach of contract, and breach of the covenant of good faith and fair dealing; and against all of the defendants for fraud, false advertising, breach of fiduciary duty, professional negligence, and declaratory relief.

The parties filed competing motions to compel and to stay arbitration of their dispute. * * *

Before the hearing on defendants' motion to compel arbitration, plaintiffs dismissed AUCRA as a defendant. Plaintiffs then argued that the motion to compel arbitration should be denied because the only defendant that had signed the RPA had been dismissed. * * * The trial court denied the motion to compel arbitration and this appeal followed.

* * *

The instant case involves the intersection of three different statutory schemes: the FAA, the McCarran-Ferguson Act, and the NUAA [Nebraska Uniform Arbitration Act].

A. The NUAA

Section 25–2602.01(b) of the NUAA provides that a written agreement to arbitrate disputes between the contracting parties "is valid, enforceable, and irrevocable, except upon such grounds as exist at law or in equity for the revocation of any contract, if the provision is entered into voluntarily and willingly." (Neb. Rev. Stats., § 25–2602.01(b).) Subsection (f)(4) of that statute, however, excepts from this provision "any agreement concerning or relating to an insurance policy," thereby prohibiting agreements to arbitrate certain insurance-related disputes.[1]

B. The FAA

The FAA reflects the fundamental principle that arbitration is "a matter of contract." Section 2 of the FAA makes arbitration agreements in contracts "involving commerce ... valid irrevocable, and enforceable" (9 U.S.C. § 2), and section 4 of the FAA provides for federal district court enforcement of such

[1] Section 25–2602.01 of the NUAA provides in relevant part: "(b) A provision in a written contract to submit to arbitration any controversy thereafter arising between the parties is valid, enforceable, and irrevocable, except upon such grounds as exist at law or in equity for the revocation of any contract, if the provision is entered into voluntarily and willingly. [¶] . . . [¶] (f) Subsection (b) of this section does not apply to: [¶] . . . [¶] . . . any agreement concerning or relating to an insurance policy other than a contract between insurance companies including a reinsurance contract." (Neb. Rev. Stats., § 25–2602.01.)

agreements. The "'body of federal substantive law'" created by the FAA is applicable, however, in both state and federal courts. (Southland Corp. v. Keating (1984) 465 U.S. 1, 12, 104 S.Ct. 852, 79 L.Ed.2d 1.) State law therefore cannot bar enforcement of the FAA, even in the context of state law claims brought in state court. The FAA thus ordinarily preempts conflicting state laws that prohibit arbitration of particular types of claims. (AT&T Mobility LLC v. Concepcion (2011) 563 U.S. 333, 341, 131 S.Ct. 1740, 179 L.Ed.2d 742.)

C. *McCarran-Ferguson Act*

The federal McCarran-Ferguson Act provides a narrow exception to federal preemption of conflicting state laws that regulate the business of insurance. Section 1012(b) of the McCarran-Ferguson Act provides: "No Act of Congress shall be construed to invalidate, impair, or supersede any law enacted by any State for the purpose of regulating the business of insurance, . . . unless such Act specifically relates to the business of insurance." (15 U.S.C. § 1012(b).) "The McCarran-Ferguson Act thus allows state law to reverse-preempt an otherwise applicable federal statute, because the McCarran-Ferguson Act does not permit an 'Act of Congress' to be 'construed to invalidate, impair, or supersede' state law unless the Act of Congress 'specifically relates to the business of insurance.'" (Safety Nat'l Cas. Corp. v. Certain Underwriters (5th Cir. 2009) 587 F.3d 714, 720.)

* * *

The validity of the parties' arbitration agreement turns on whether the McCarran-Ferguson Act applies, whether section 25-2602.01(f) of the NUAA applies, and whether those two statutes together preempt the FAA.

A. *Applicability of the McCarran-Ferguson Act*

Courts apply a three-part test for determining whether the McCarran-Ferguson Act causes a state law to reverse preempt a federal statute: (1) whether the federal statute to be preempted specifically relates to the business of insurance, (2) whether the state law was enacted for regulating the business of insurance, and (3) whether application of the federal statute operates to invalidate, impair, or supersede the state law. (Am. Bankers Ins. Co. v. Inman (5th Cir. 2006) 436 F.3d 490, 493 (Am. Bankers); Std. Sec. Life Ins. Co. v. West (8th Cir. 2001) 267 F.3d 821 (Std. Sec.); Kremer v. Rural Comty. Ins. Co. (2010) 280 Neb. 591, 788 N.W.2d 538, 551 (Kremer).)

It is undisputed that the FAA does not regulate the business of insurance, and that application of the FAA in this case would invalidate section 25–2602.01(f) of the NUAA. The determinative inquiry is whether section 25–2602.01(f) of the NUAA was enacted for the purpose of regulating the business of insurance within the meaning of the McCarran-Ferguson Act. That inquiry is guided by principles articulated by the United States Supreme Court in *United States Dep't of Treasury v. Fabe* (1993) 508 U.S. 491, 500–503, 113 S.Ct. 2202, 124 L.Ed.2d 449 (*Fabe*).

In *Fabe,* the Supreme Court held that an Ohio statute governing the priority of claims against an insolvent insurer is a "law enacted for the purpose of regulating the business of insurance" within the meaning of the McCarran-Ferguson Act and rejected the argument that the Ohio statute was a bankruptcy law rather than a law "regulating the business of insurance." The court reasoned that although "the Ohio statute does not directly regulate the 'business of insurance' by prescribing the terms of the insurance contract or by setting the rate charged by the insurance company," the business of insurance is not "confined entirely to the writing of insurance contracts, as opposed to their performance."

The court in *Fabe* emphasized that the focus of the McCarran-Ferguson Act is the relationship between insurer and insured and that "'[s]tatutes aimed at protecting or regulating this relationship [between insurer and insured], directly or indirectly, are laws regulating the "business of insurance."'" The Supreme Court concluded that "[t]he broad category of laws enacted 'for the purpose of regulating the business of insurance' consists of laws that possess the 'end, intention, or aim' of adjusting, managing, or controlling the business of insurance."

Applying the principles articulated in *Fabe,* the Nebraska Supreme Court in *Kremer, supra,* 788 N.W.2d 538, addressed the precise issue presented here—whether section 25–2602.01(f) of the NUAA is a state law enacted for the purpose of regulating the business of insurance within the meaning of the McCarran-Ferguson Act. The court in *Kremer* held that it was, and that section 25–2602.01(f) accordingly reverse preempts the FAA through application of the McCarran-Ferguson Act. * * *

Federal courts applying *Fabe* have likewise concluded that the FAA is reverse preempted under state laws similar to the Nebraska statute at issue here. (See, e.g., Am. Bankers, supra, 436 F.3d 490 [FAA reverse preempted under McCarran-Ferguson Act by Mississippi statute prohibiting arbitration of disputes regarding uninsured and underinsured motorist coverage of personal automobile insurance policies]; McKnight v. Chicago Title Ins. Co. (11th Cir. 2004) 358 F.3d 854, 858–859 [FAA reverse preempted by Georgia law prohibiting arbitration clauses in insurance contracts]; Std. Sec., supra, 267 F.3d 821 [FAA reverse preempted by Missouri Arbitration Act's prohibition on arbitration clauses in insurance contracts]; Mutual Reinsurance Bureau v. Great Plains Mut. Ins. Co. (10th Cir. 1992) 969 F.2d 931, 934–935 [FAA reverse preempted by Kansas statute barring arbitration provision in insurance contracts].)

Consistent with the principles articulated in *Fabe,* as applied by federal appellate courts and the Nebraska Supreme Court, we agree with the trial court's conclusion in the instant case that section 25–2602.01(f) of the NUAA is a state law enacted for the purpose of regulating the business of insurance. * * *

* * *

The trial court did not err by concluding that section 25–2602.01(f) of the NUAA is a statute that regulates the business of insurance within the meaning of the McCarran-Ferguson Act.

Application of the FAA would operate to invalidate or impair section 25–2602.01(f) of the NUAA. The trial court did not err by concluding that the McCarran-Ferguson Act applies and reverse preempts the FAA.

Section 25–2602.01(f) of the NUAA applies to the RPA and renders the arbitration provision contained in the RPA unenforceable. The trial court accordingly did not err by denying the petition to compel arbitration.

DISPOSITION

The order denying the petition to compel arbitration is affirmed. * * *

Citizens of Humanity mentions several cases holding "that the FAA is reverse preempted under state laws similar to the Nebraska statute at issue here." For other cases of the McCarran-Ferguson Act protecting state anti-arbitration laws from FAA preemption, see, e.g., *Munich American Reinsurance Co. v. Crawford*, 141 F.3d 585 (5th Cir. 1998) (Oklahoma has formulated a "complex and comprehensive scheme of insurance regulation" which vests state courts with "exclusive original jurisdiction" over all delinquency proceedings involving insolvent insurance companies; held, petition to compel arbitration was properly dismissed); *State, Dept. of Transp. v. James River Ins. Co.*, 292 P.3d 118, 121 (Wash.2013) (enforcing state statute that prohibits binding arbitration agreements in insurance contracts).

In contrast, the McCarran-Ferguson Act does not protect from FAA preemption state laws regulating arbitration generally, even when those laws are applied to insurance arbitration. See, e.g., Miller v. Nat'l Fidel. Life Ins. Co., 588 F.2d 185, 187 (5th Cir.1979) (where state insurance code contains no provisions relating to arbitration, applying the FAA to an insurance arbitration clause does not—to use McCarran-Ferguson's language—"invalidate, impair, or supersede any state law regulating the business of insurance."); Hamilton Life Ins. Co. v. Republic Nat'l Life Ins. Co., 408 F.2d 606, 611 (2d Cir.1969) ("arbitration statutes * * * are not statutes regulating the business of insurance, but statutes regulating the method of handling contract disputes generally.")

QUESTIONS TO REVIEW AND SYNTHESIZE

1. What is "reverse preemption" of the FAA by the McCarran-Ferguson Act?
2. What sorts of state laws are preempted by the FAA outside the insurance context but not in the insurance context?

5. CONTRACTING OUT OF FAA PREEMPTION

Stephen J. Ware, *Punitive Damages in Arbitration: Contracting Out of Government's Role in Punishment and Federal Preemption of State Law*

63 Fordham L. Rev. 529, 554–55 (1994).

[Generally,] courts do not permit parties to choose whether state or federal law governs their disputes. That choice is made by the federal government in deciding whether to enact federal law. If federal law is enacted, then it governs the parties who have no choice in the matter. Federal preemption of state law is a mandatory rule, not a default rule that the parties are free to contract around—except for the FAA.

The FAA is special because its core provision, Section 2, gives the terms of arbitration agreements the force of federal law. If an arbitration agreement evidencing a transaction involving interstate commerce states that arbitration is to be conducted under the arbitration law of California, then federal law states that arbitration of disputes covered by that agreement is to be conducted under the arbitration law of California.

Section 2 of the FAA makes federal preemption of state law a default rule rather than a mandatory rule. It allows the parties to an arbitration agreement evidencing a transaction involving interstate commerce to choose whether to be governed by state or federal arbitration law. If the parties choose state law, then it would be inconsistent with Section 2 to apply any substantive arbitration law other than that of the chosen state.

On this fundamental and somewhat startling point, the majority and dissent in *Volt [Information Sciences, Inc. v. Board of Trustees of Leland Stanford Jr. Univ.,* 489 U.S. 468, 478–79 (1989)] agree. The [*Volt*] majority opinion affirms the California Court of Appeal's holding that the parties contracted around preemption of state law by the FAA. The [*Volt*] dissent agrees that parties "are free if they wish to write an agreement to arbitrate outside the coverage of the FAA. Such an agreement would permit a state rule, otherwise preempted by the FAA, to govern their arbitration." The importance of *Volt*, then, is the unanimous view of the Justices that FAA preemption of state law is not a mandatory rule. It is a default rule that the parties are free to contract around.

In *Volt*, the Supreme Court's majority found, over a thoughtful dissent, that the parties' use of standard choice-of-law clause contracted out of FAA preemption and thus into state arbitration law. *Volt* is explained more in the following (later) case.

Mastrobuono v. Shearson Lehman Hutton

Supreme Court of the United States, 1995.
514 U.S. 52, 115 S.Ct. 1212, 131 L.Ed.2d 76.

■ JUSTICE STEVENS delivered the opinion of the Court.

New York law allows courts, but not arbitrators, to award punitive damages. In a dispute arising out of a standard-form contract that expressly provides that it "shall be governed by the laws of the State of New York," a panel of arbitrators awarded punitive damages. The District Court and Court of Appeals disallowed that award. The question presented is whether the arbitrators' award is consistent with the central purpose of the Federal Arbitration Act to ensure "that private agreements to arbitrate are enforced according to their terms." *Volt Information Sciences, Inc.* v. *Board of Trustees of Leland Stanford Junior Univ.*, 489 U.S. 468, 479, 103 L. Ed. 2d 488, 109 S. Ct. 1248 (1989).

In 1985, petitioners, Antonio Mastrobuono, then an assistant professor of medieval literature, and his wife Diana Mastrobuono, an artist, opened a securities trading account with respondent Shearson Lehman Hutton, Inc. (Shearson), by executing Shearson's standard-form Client's Agreement. Respondent Nick DiMinico, a vice president of Shearson, managed the Mastrobuonos' account until they closed it in 1987. In 1989, petitioners filed this action in the United States District Court for the Northern District of Illinois, alleging that respondents had mishandled their account and claiming damages on a variety of state and federal law theories.

Paragraph 13 of the parties' agreement contains an arbitration provision and a choice-of-law provision. Relying on the arbitration provision and on §§ 3 and 4 of the Federal Arbitration Act (FAA), respondents filed a motion to stay the court proceedings and to compel arbitration pursuant to the rules of the National Association of Securities Dealers. The District Court granted that motion, and a panel of three arbitrators was convened. After conducting hearings in Illinois, the panel ruled in favor of petitioners.

In the arbitration proceedings, respondents argued that the arbitrators had no authority to award punitive damages. Nevertheless, the panel's award included punitive damages of $400,000, in addition to compensatory damages of $159,327. Respondents paid the compensatory portion of the award but filed a motion in the District Court to vacate the award of punitive damages. The District Court granted the motion and the Court of Appeals for the Seventh Circuit affirmed. Both courts relied on the choice-of-law provision in paragraph 13 of the parties' agreement, which specifies that the contract shall be governed by New York law. Because the New York Court of Appeals has decided that in New York the power to award punitive damages is limited to judicial tribunals and may not be exercised by arbitrators, *Garrity* v. *Lyle Stuart, Inc.*, 40 N.Y.2d 354, 353 N.E.2d 793, 386 N.Y.S.2d 831 (1976), the District Court and the Seventh Circuit held that the panel of arbitrators had no power to award punitive damages in this case.

We granted certiorari because the Courts of Appeals have expressed differing views on whether a contractual choice-of-law provision may preclude an arbitral award of punitive damages that otherwise would be proper. We now reverse.

Earlier this Term, we upheld the enforceability of a predispute arbitration agreement governed by Alabama law, even though an Alabama statute provides that arbitration agreements are unenforceable. Writing for the Court, JUSTICE BREYER observed that Congress passed the FAA "to overcome courts' refusals to enforce agreements to arbitrate." After determining that the FAA applied to the parties' arbitration agreement, we readily concluded that the federal statute pre-empted Alabama's statutory prohibition.

Petitioners seek a similar disposition of the case before us today. Here, the Seventh Circuit interpreted the contract to incorporate New York law, including the *Garrity* rule that arbitrators may not award punitive damages. Petitioners ask us to hold that the FAA pre-empts New York's prohibition against arbitral awards of punitive damages because this state law is a vestige of the "ancient" judicial hostility to arbitration. * * *

* * * Regardless of whether the FAA pre-empts the *Garrity* decision in contracts not expressly incorporating New York law, respondents argue that the

parties may themselves agree to be bound by *Garrity*, just as they may agree to forgo arbitration altogether. In other words, if the contract says "no punitive damages," that is the end of the matter, for courts are bound to interpret contracts in accordance with the expressed intentions of the parties—even if the effect of those intentions is to limit arbitration.

We have previously held that the FAA's proarbitration policy does not operate without regard to the wishes of the contracting parties. In *Volt Information Sciences, Inc.* v. *Board of Trustees of Leland Stanford Junior Univ.*, 489 U.S. 468, 103 L. Ed. 2d 488, 109 S. Ct. 1248 (1989), the California Court of Appeal had construed a contractual provision to mean that the parties intended the California rules of arbitration, rather than the FAA's rules, to govern the resolution of their dispute. Noting that the California rules were "manifestly designed to encourage resort to the arbitral process," and that they "generally fostered the federal policy favoring arbitration," we concluded that such an interpretation was entirely consistent with the federal policy "to ensure the enforceability, according to their terms, of private agreements to arbitrate." After referring to the holdings in *Southland* and *Perry*, which struck down state laws limiting agreed-upon arbitrability, we added:

> "But it does not follow that the FAA prevents the enforcement of agreements to arbitrate under different rules than those set forth in the Act itself. Indeed, such a result would be quite inimical to the FAA's primary purpose of ensuring that private agreements to arbitrate are enforced according to their terms. Arbitration under the Act is a matter of consent, not coercion, and parties are generally free to structure their arbitration agreements as they see fit. Just as they may limit by contract the issues which they will arbitrate, see *Mitsubishi* [*Motors Corp.* v. *Soler Chrysler-Plymouth, Inc.*, 473 U.S. 614, 628, 87 L. Ed. 2d 444, 105 S. Ct. 3346 (1985)], so too may they specify by contract the rules under which that arbitration will be conducted." Volt, 489 U.S. at 479.

Relying on our reasoning in *Volt*, respondents thus argue that the parties to a contract may lawfully agree to limit the issues to be arbitrated by waiving any claim for punitive damages. On the other hand, we think our decisions in *Allied-Bruce*, *Southland*, and *Perry* make clear that if contracting parties agree to *include* claims for punitive damages within the issues to be arbitrated, the FAA ensures that their agreement will be enforced according to its terms even if a rule of state law would otherwise exclude such claims from arbitration. Thus, the case before us comes down to what the contract has to say about the arbitrability of petitioners' claim for punitive damages.

Shearson's standard-form "Client Agreement," which petitioners executed, contains 18 paragraphs. The two relevant provisions of the agreement are found in paragraph 13. The first sentence of that paragraph provides, in part, that the entire agreement "shall be governed by the laws of the State of New York." The second sentence provides that "any controversy" arising out of the transactions between the parties "shall be settled by arbitration" in accordance with the rules of the National Association of Securities Dealers (NASD), or the Boards of Directors of the New York Stock Exchange and/or the American Stock Exchange. The agreement contains no express reference to claims for punitive damages. To ascertain whether paragraph 13 expresses an intent to include or exclude such claims, we first address the impact of each of the two relevant provisions, considered separately. We then move on to the more important inquiry: the meaning of the two provisions taken together. See Restatement (Second) of Contracts § 202(2) (1979) ("A writing is interpreted as a whole").

The choice-of-law provision, when viewed in isolation, may reasonably be read as merely a substitute for the conflict-of-laws analysis that otherwise would determine what law to apply to disputes arising out of the contractual relationship. Thus, if a similar contract, without a choice-of-law provision, had been signed in New York and was to be performed in New York, presumably "the laws of the State of New York" would apply, even though the contract did not expressly so state. In such event, there would be nothing in the contract that could possibly constitute evidence of an intent to exclude punitive damages claims. Accordingly, punitive damages would be allowed because, in the absence of contractual intent to the contrary, the FAA would pre-empt the *Garrity* rule.

Even if the reference to "the laws of the State of New York" is more than a substitute for ordinary conflict-of-laws analysis and, as respondents urge, includes the caveat, "detached from otherwise-applicable federal law," the provision might not preclude the award of punitive damages because New York allows its courts, though not its arbitrators, to enter such awards. See Garrity, 40 N.Y.2d at 358, 353 N.E.2d, at 796. In other words, the provision might include only New York's substantive rights and obligations, and not the State's allocation of power between alternative tribunals.[3] Respondents' argument is persuasive only if "New York law" means "New York decisional law, including that State's allocation of power between courts and arbitrators, notwithstanding otherwise-applicable federal law." But, as we have demonstrated, the provision need not be read so broadly. It is not, in itself, an unequivocal exclusion of punitive damages claims.[4]

The arbitration provision (the second sentence of paragraph 13) does not improve respondents' argument. On the contrary, when read separately this clause strongly implies that an arbitral award of punitive damages is appropriate. It explicitly authorizes arbitration in accordance with NASD rules; the panel of arbitrators in fact proceeded under that set of rules. The NASD's Code of Arbitration Procedure indicates that arbitrators may award "damages and other relief." While not a clear authorization of punitive damages, this provision appears broad enough at least to contemplate such a remedy. Moreover, as the

[3] In a related point, respondents argue that there is no meaningful distinction between "substance" and "remedy," that is, between an entitlement to prevail on the law and an entitlement to a specific form of damages. We do not rely on such a distinction here, nor do we pass upon its persuasiveness.

[4] The dissent makes much of the similarity between this choice-of-law clause and the one in *Volt Information Sciences, Inc.* v. *Board of Trustees of Leland Stanford Junior Univ.*, 489 U.S. 468, 103 L. Ed. 2d 488, 109 S. Ct. 1248 (1989), which we took to incorporate a California statute allowing a court to stay arbitration pending resolution of related litigation. In *Volt*, however, we did not interpret the contract *de novo*. Instead, we deferred to the California court's construction of its own State's law. Id., at 474 ("The interpretation of private contracts is ordinarily a question of state law, which this Court does not sit to review"). In the present case, by contrast, we review a *federal* court's interpretation of this contract, and our interpretation accords with that of the only decision maker arguably entitled to deference—the arbitrator.

Seventh Circuit noted, a manual provided to NASD arbitrators contains this provision:

> "B. Punitive Damages
>
> "The issue of punitive damages may arise with great frequency in arbitrations. Parties to arbitration are informed that arbitrators can consider punitive damages as a remedy."

Thus, the text of the arbitration clause itself surely does not support—indeed, it contradicts—the conclusion that the parties agreed to foreclose claims for punitive damages.

* * *

Moreover, respondents cannot overcome the common-law rule of contract interpretation that a court should construe ambiguous language against the interest of the party that drafted it. * * * As a practical matter, it seems unlikely that petitioners were actually aware of New York's bifurcated approach to punitive damages, or that they had any idea that by signing a standard-form agreement to arbitrate disputes they might be giving up an important substantive right. In the face of such doubt, we are unwilling to impute this intent to petitioners.

Finally[,] respondents' reading of the two clauses violates another cardinal principle of contract construction: that a document should be read to give effect to all its provisions and to render them consistent with each other. We think the best way to harmonize the choice-of-law provision with the arbitration provision is to read "the laws of the State of New York" to encompass substantive principles that New York courts would apply, but not to include special rules limiting the authority of arbitrators. Thus, the choice-of-law provision covers the rights and duties of the parties, while the arbitration clause covers arbitration; neither sentence intrudes upon the other. In contrast, respondents' reading sets up the two clauses in conflict with one another: one foreclosing punitive damages, the other allowing them. This interpretation is untenable.

We hold that the Court of Appeals misinterpreted the parties' agreement. The arbitral award should have been enforced as within the scope of the contract. The judgment of the Court of Appeals is, therefore, reversed.

It is so ordered.

■ JUSTICE THOMAS, dissenting.

In *Volt Information Sciences, Inc.* v. *Board of Trustees of Leland Stanford Junior Univ.*, 489 U.S. 468, 478, 103 L. Ed. 2d 488, 109 S. Ct. 1248 (1989), we held that the Federal Arbitration Act (FAA) simply requires courts to enforce private contracts to arbitrate as they would normal contracts—according to their terms. This holding led us to enforce a choice-of-law provision that incorporated a state procedural rule concerning arbitration proceedings. Because the choice-of-law provision here cannot reasonably be distinguished from the one in *Volt*, I dissent.

* * *

In this case, as in *Volt*, the parties agreed to mandatory arbitration of all disputes. As in *Volt*, the contract at issue here includes a choice-of-law clause.

Indeed, the language of the two clauses is functionally equivalent: Whereas the choice-of-law clause in *Volt* provided that "the Contract shall be governed by the law of [the State of California]," the one before us today states, in paragraph 13 of the Client's Agreement, that "this agreement . . . shall be governed by the laws of the State of New York." New York law prohibits arbitrators from awarding punitive damages, *Garrity* v. *Lyle Stuart, Inc.*, 40 N.Y.2d 354, 353 N.E.2d 793, 386 N.Y.S.2d 831 (1976), and permits only courts to award such damages. As in *Volt*, petitioners here argue that the New York rule is "antiarbitration," and hence is pre-empted by the FAA. In concluding that the choice-of-law clause is ambiguous, the majority essentially accepts petitioners' argument. *Volt* itself found precisely the same argument irrelevant, however, and the majority identifies no reason to think that the state law governing the interpretation of the parties' choice-of-law clause supports a different result.

The majority claims that the incorporation of New York law "need not be read so broadly" as to include both substantive and procedural law, and that the choice of New York law "is not, in itself, an unequivocal exclusion of punitive damages claims." But we rejected these same arguments in *Volt*, and the *Garrity* rule is just the sort of "state rule governing the conduct of arbitration" that *Volt* requires federal courts to enforce. "Just as [the parties] may limit by contract the issues which they will arbitrate, so too may they specify by contract the rules under which that arbitration will be conducted." To be sure, the majority might be correct that *Garrity* is a rule concerning the State's allocation of power between "alternative tribunals," although *Garrity* appears to describe itself as substantive New York law. Nonetheless, *Volt* makes no distinction between rules that serve only to distribute authority between courts and arbitrators (which the majority finds unenforceable) and other types of rules (which the majority finds enforceable).

* * *

Thankfully, the import of the majority's decision is limited and narrow. This case amounts to nothing more than a federal court applying Illinois and New York contract law to an agreement between parties in Illinois. Much like a federal court applying a state rule of decision to a case when sitting in diversity, the majority's interpretation of the contract represents only the understanding of a single federal court regarding the requirements imposed by state law. As such, the majority's opinion has applicability only to this specific contract and to no other. But because the majority reaches an erroneous result on even this narrow question, I respectfully dissent.

After *Mastrobuono*, the Supreme Court's decision in *Preston v. Ferrer*, 552 U.S. 346 (2008), similarly held that the parties did not contract out of FAA preemption. *Preston* involved a contract with an arbitration clause and a clause providing that the "agreement shall be governed by the laws of the state of California."[26] Preston sought to arbitrate his claim for payment for services he rendered to Ferrer. Preston's demand for arbitration was countered by Ferrer's

[26] *Id.* at 361.

petition to the California Labor Commissioner charging that the contract was unenforceable under the California Talent Agencies Act (CTAA),[27] which vests the Labor Commissioner with exclusive original jurisdiction to determine whether a particular agreement is subject to a California statute that requires parties to exhaust administrative remedies before resorting to arbitration.[28] In other words, Preston wanted the case decided in arbitration, while Ferrer wanted at least some preliminary portion of the case decided by the Labor Commissioner.

Had the contract contained no choice-of-law clause, a court would have compelled arbitration simply because that is what the agreement provided, and the agreement is enforceable under the FAA. The CTAA purports to make portions of that arbitration agreement unenforceable, but the FAA preempts conflicting state law.

> "Procedural prescriptions of the TAA thus conflict with the FAA's dispute resolution regime in two basic respects: First, the TAA, in § 1700.44(a), grants the Labor Commissioner exclusive jurisdiction to decide an issue that the parties agreed to arbitrate, see Buckeye, * * *; second, the TAA, in § 1700.45, imposes prerequisites to enforcement of an arbitration agreement that are not applicable to contracts generally, see Doctor's Associates, Inc., * * *."

Preston, 552 U.S. at 356. One question in *Preston* was whether the parties contracted out of this preemption by including in their contract a California choice-of-law clause. In answering "no," the *Preston* Court distinguished *Volt* and was "guided by [its] more recent decision" in *Mastrobuono*. Id. at 361. The *Preston* Court concluded that the California choice-of law clause should be read to incorporate "prescriptions governing the substantive rights and obligations of the parties, but not the State's 'special rules limiting the authority of arbitrators.'" Id. at 363 (quoting Mastrobuono, 514 U.S. at 63–64).

In sum, *Mastrobuono* and *Preston* reinforce *Volt*'s main holding—that parties can contract out of at least some aspects of FAA preemption—but indicate that doing so typically requires more explicit language than a standard, general choice-of-law clause. Similarly, most lower-court cases treat a general choice-of-law clause as a choice among states, rather than a choice of the chosen state over the FAA. For parties to contract out of FAA preemption, they need more specific language stating not only which state's law they choose to govern the merits of any dispute, but also that they want this state's arbitration law. See BNSF R. Co. v. Alstom Transp., Inc., 777 F.3d 785, 790 (5th Cir. 2015) ("arbitration under non-FAA [state] rules [only] if a contract expressly references state arbitration law"); Foulger-Pratt Residential Contracting, LLC v. Madrigal Condominiums, LLC, 779 F. Supp. 2d 100, 110 (D.D.C. 2011) (while "a generic choice of law clause is insufficient to displace the FAA, * * * In this case * * * the parties included a specific clause stating that '[t]his [a]greement to arbitrate shall be specifically enforceable pursuant to and interpreted under the laws of the District of Columbia.' [This clause] specifically and

---

[27] Cal.Lab.Code Ann. § 1700 et seq. (West 2003 and Supp.2008).

[28] Preston, 552 U.S. at 356 (citing Cal.Lab.Code Ann. § 1700.44(a)).

unambiguously evidences their clear choice of D.C. law rather than the FAA to govern their agreement to arbitrate.")

A variation of this contracting-out-of-FAA-preemption question was addressed by the Supreme Court's 2015 opinion in *DirecTV v. Imburgia*, 136 S. Ct. 463, 467 (2015). The California Court of Appeal acknowledged that—pursuant to *AT & T Mobility LLC v. Concepcion*, 563 U.S. 333 (2011), excerpted above in Section 3.C.2.b—the FAA enforces arbitration agreement "class-waiver" provisions requiring individual (rather than class) arbitration, and preempts state law to the contrary. However, the California Court of Appeal found that California law does not enforce such clauses and that the particular contract at issue evidenced the parties' choice to be governed by California, rather than federal, law on this question. The Supreme Court's opinion by Justice Breyer reiterated the *Volt* principle that parties can contract out of at least some aspects of FAA preemption:

> As the Court of Appeal noted, the Federal Arbitration Act allows parties to an arbitration contract considerable latitude to choose what law governs some or all of its provisions, including the law governing enforceability of a class-arbitration waiver. In principle, they might choose to have portions of their contract governed by the law of Tibet, the law of pre-revolutionary Russia, or (as is relevant here) the law of California including the Discover Bank rule and irrespective of that rule's invalidation in Concepcion.

DIRECTV, Inc. v. Imburgia, 136 S. Ct. 463, 468 (2015). However, the Supreme Court concluded (as in *Mastrobuono* and *Preston*) that the parties' contract did not in fact contract out of FAA preemption. The California Court of Appeal interpreted the contract's phrase "law of your state" to include law (the *Discover Bank* rule) that had been invalidated by federal preemption (*Concepcion*). But the Supreme Court could find nothing in the California Court of Appeals' "opinion (nor in any other California case) suggesting that California would generally interpret words such as 'law of your state' to include state laws held invalid because they conflict with, say, federal labor statutes, federal pension statutes, federal antidiscrimination laws, the Equal Protection Clause, or the like." Id. at 469. So the Supreme Court concluded the California Court of Appeals' "interpretation of the phrase 'law of your state' does not place arbitration contracts 'on equal footing with all other contracts,'" and thus "is pre-empted by the Federal Arbitration Act." Id. at 471.

QUESTIONS TO REVIEW AND SYNTHESIZE

1. What sorts of contract language leads courts to apply state arbitration law rather than the FAA?
2. Parties using that contract language may contractually avoid FAA preemption of what sorts of state arbitration law?

D. THE AGREEMENT TO ARBITRATE

1. FORMATION OF ARBITRATION AGREEMENTS

This chapter has shown the Supreme Court interpreting the FAA broadly to enforce arbitration agreements in nearly all sorts of transactions and with respect to nearly all sorts of claims. Consequently, much can turn on whether particular parties formed an arbitration agreement. Whether they did is generally governed by plain old contract law—largely made at the state level. See First Options of Chicago, Inc. v. Kaplan, 514 U.S. 938, 944 (1995) ("When deciding whether the parties agreed to arbitrate a certain matter * * * courts generally * * * should apply ordinary state-law principles that govern the formation of contracts."); Arthur Anderson LLP v. Carlisle, 556 U.S. 624, 129 S.Ct.1896, 173 L.Ed.2d 832 (2009) (FAA section 2 "explicitly retains an external body of law governing revocation (such grounds 'as exist at law or in equity'); * * * 'state law,' therefore, is applicable to determine which contracts are binding under § 2").

Plain old contract law now addresses 21st Century methods of communication centering on cell phones, as indicated by at least one court enforcing an arbitration agreement formed by the exchange of text messages, *Storace v. Lexington*, 2019 U.S. Dist. LEXIS 108155 (E.D. Cal. June 27, 2019), and by the following two cases. These two cases include images of phone screens. Seeing these images in color helps appreciate the courts' reasoning. To view these cases with color images, go to store.westacademic.com and view the PDF on the product detail page for this book.

Cullinane v. Uber Technologies, Inc.

United States Court of Appeals, First Circuit, 2018.
893 F.3d 53.

■ TORRUELLA, CIRCUIT JUDGE:

This case concerns the enforceability of an arbitration clause contained in an online contract. Plaintiffs-Appellants Rachel Cullinane, Jacqueline Núñez, Elizabeth Schaul, and Ross McDonagh, (collectively, "Plaintiffs"), filed this putative class action in Massachusetts Superior Court on behalf of themselves and other users of a ride-sharing service in the Boston area against Defendant-Appellee Uber Technologies, Inc. ("Uber"). In their complaint, Plaintiffs alleged that Uber violated a Massachusetts consumer-protection statute by knowingly imposing certain fictitious or inflated fees. Uber removed the case to the United States District Court for the District of Massachusetts, and filed a motion to compel arbitration and stay or dismiss the case. The district court granted Uber's motion to compel arbitration and dismissed the complaint. For the reasons explained below, we reverse and remand.

* * *

Uber provides a ride-sharing service that transports customers throughout some cities, including Boston, for a fee. Uber licenses the Uber mobile application (the "Uber App") to the public so that users may request transportation services from independent third party providers in the users' local area. To be able to request and pay for third party transportation services, Uber App users must first register with Uber by creating an account. At the time Plaintiffs created their accounts, prospective users could either register through the Uber App or register directly through Uber's website.

All four named Plaintiffs downloaded the Uber App on iPhones and used the Uber App to create Uber accounts between December 31, 2012 and January 10, 2014. On September 13, 2013, Plaintiff Jacqueline Núñez ("Núñez") used the Uber App to order transportation to Boston Logan International Airport ("Logan Airport") and was charged, in addition to the cost of the transportation, $8.75 for a Massport Surcharge & Toll[1] (the "Massport Surcharge"). Plaintiff Rachel Cullinane ("Cullinane") used the Uber App to request transportation from Logan Airport on June 29, 2014, and was charged $5.25 for the East Boston toll[2] and the same $8.75 Massport Surcharge. Plaintiff Elizabeth Schaul ("Schaul") used the Uber App to obtain transportation both to and from Logan Airport on multiple occasions. Each time, Uber charged her the $8.75 Massport Surcharge. The last named Plaintiff, Ross McDonagh ("McDonagh") claims he used the Uber App for several trips—not all of them to or from Logan Airport—and was charged $5.25 for the East Boston toll and the $8.75 surcharge, even when he did not travel to or from Logan Airport. The Plaintiffs object to the Massport Surcharge and the East Boston toll because they maintain that Uber charged these fees unnecessarily (i.e. there was no requirement from the Commonwealth of Massachusetts that these fees be charged to Uber passengers). Now, the Plaintiffs seek to represent a class of Massachusetts-resident Uber passengers who have been charged the Massport Surcharge and East Boston toll, and have not received a refund for these charges.

B. Uber App Registration Process

All prospective Uber passengers must go through Uber's registration process. When Plaintiffs used the Uber App to register, the process included three different screens that asked for user information. The first screen, titled "Create an Account," asked users to enter an e-mail address, a mobile phone number, and a password for the account. Immediately above the phone's keyboard—which occupied half of the phone screen—written in dark gray against a black background, was the text: "We use your email and mobile number to send you ride confirmations and receipts."

The second screen, entitled "Create a Profile," prompted the user to enter their first and last name, and to upload a picture. This screen also included dark gray text on a black background which read: "Your name and photo helps [sic] your driver identify you at pickup."

The third screen varied slightly during the thirteen-month period during which the Plaintiffs registered. The first two plaintiffs to register, Núñez and Schaul, saw

---

[1] According to the Plaintiffs, at the time Uber explained in its Boston website that the Massport Surcharge "cover[ed] Massport fees and other costs related to airport trips."

[2] Also according to the Plaintiffs, Uber charged an East Boston toll to passengers traveling through East Boston.

a third screen titled "Link Card." The last two plaintiffs to register, Cullinane and McDonagh, saw a third screen titled "Link Payment." Irrespective of its title, the third and final screen prompted the user to enter the appropriate payment information for Uber's services. Because the design and content of both versions of the third screen are particularly relevant to this case, we discuss them in greater detail.

1. "Link Card"

When confronted with the third screen, Núñez and Schaul were presented with the "Link Card" screen. This is what it looked like:[3] [To view this image in color, go to store.westacademic.com and view the PDF on the product detail page for this book.]

[3] The parties do not dispute that the screenshots attached to Uber's motion to compel arbitration accurately depict the content of the Uber App screens presented to the Plaintiffs. The screenshots, however, are larger than the actual size of the average smartphone's display. Because the Plaintiffs contend that the iPhones they used to register with Uber had 3.5-inch displays, we reproduce the screenshots found in the record as they would appear in a smartphone's display that is approximately 3.5 inches, measured diagonally. Uber does not concede that the Plaintiffs' iPhone displays were this size.

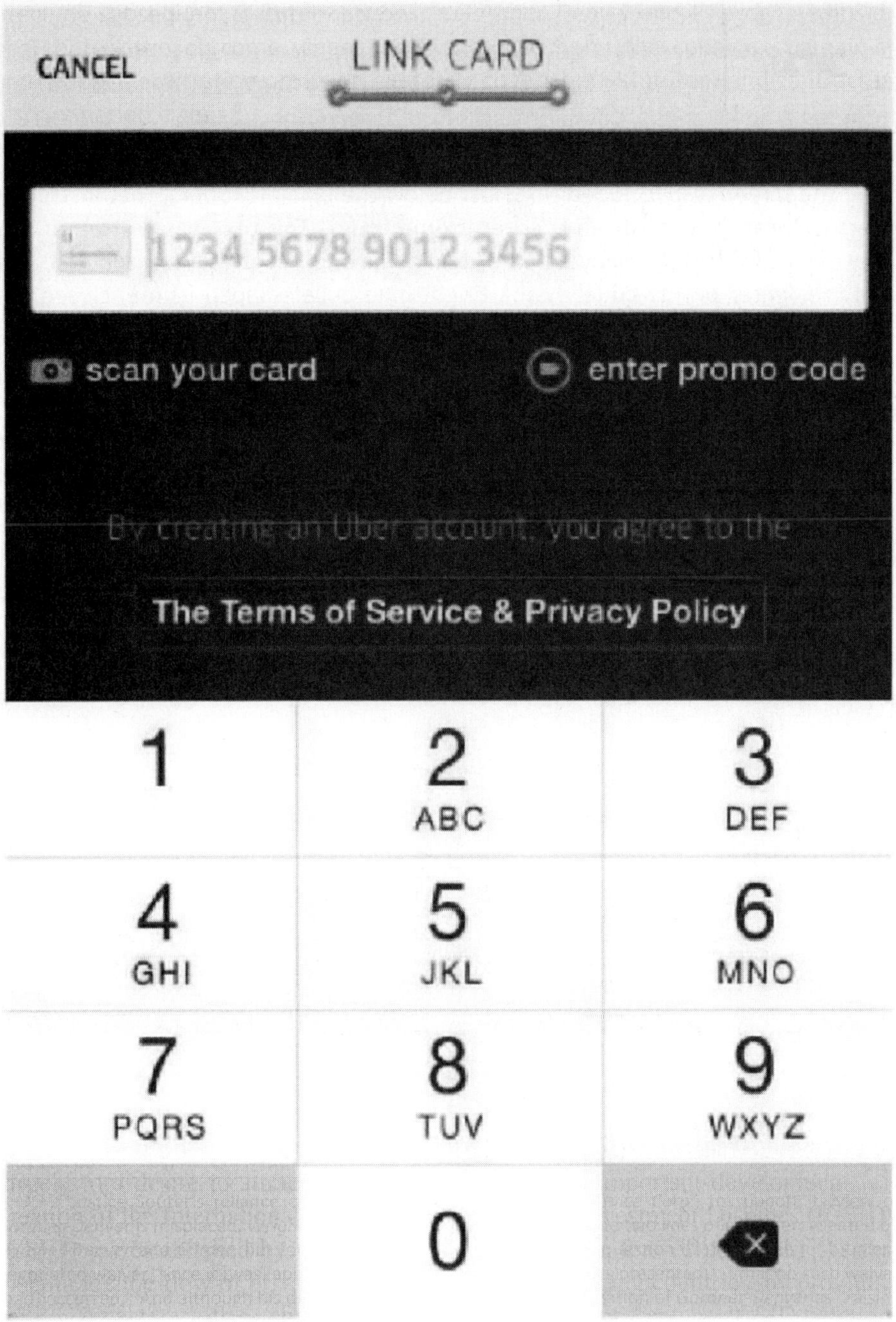

As depicted in the screenshot above, the screen contained a thick gray bar at the top of the screen with the title "Link Card." To the left of the title was a "CANCEL" button and to the right was an inoperative and barely visible "DONE" button. Below the thick gray title bar was a blank text field where users could enter their credit card information. The blank text field was white, contrasting with the black background, horizontally traversing the screen, and included some light gray numbers to exemplify the type of information required. In addition, at the beginning of the blank text field, and to the left of the light gray numbers, there was an icon representing a credit card. The "Link Card" screen automatically included a number pad, covering half of the screen, for users to type their credit card information into the blank text field.

The screen also included text, just below the blank text field, that instructed users to "scan your card" and "enter promo code." This text was written in light gray bolded font. The "scan your card" text had a bright blue camera icon to its left, and the "enter promo code" had a bright blue bullet-shaped icon enclosed in a circle. The record is unclear as to whether the "scan your card" and "enter promo code" texts were clickable buttons.[4]

Finally, the "Link Card" screen also included dark gray text which read: "By creating an Uber account, you agree to the." Below this text was the phrase "Terms of Service & Privacy Policy" in bold white text enclosed in a gray rectangle. According to Uber, this rectangular box indicated that this phrase was a "clickable button."

2. "Link Payment"

Plaintiffs Cullinane and McDonagh confronted a third screen that looked like this: [To view this image in color, go to store.westacademic.com and view the PDF on the product detail page for this book.]

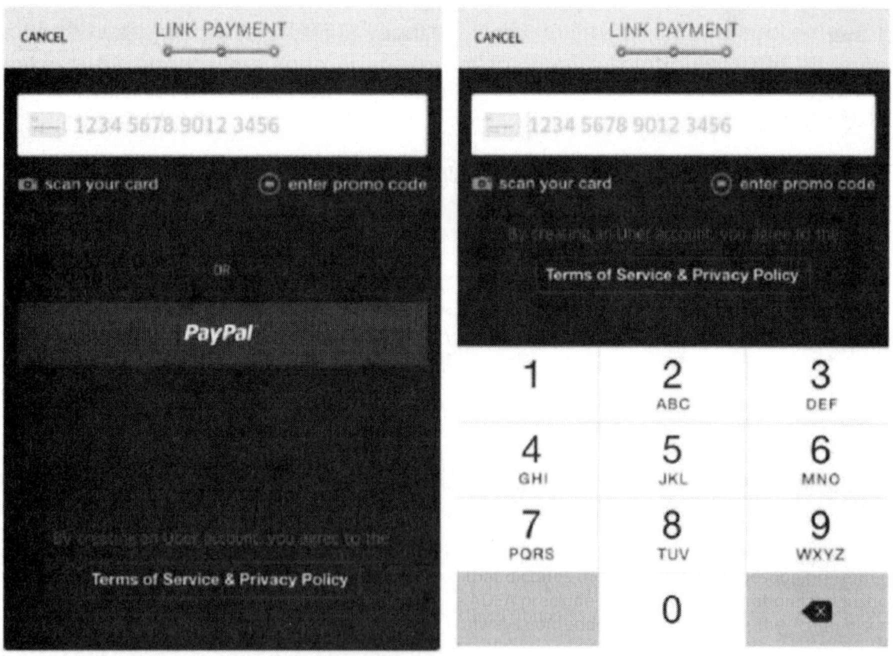

[4] A clickable button is "[a]n icon on screen that is 'pressed' by clicking it with the mouse or, if a touchscreen, tapping it with a finger." PC Mag., https://www.pcmag.com/encyclopedia/term/39092/button (last visited June 15, 2018).

The "Link Payment" screen was very similar to the "Link Card" screen, except that it provided for an additional payment option that altered the screen's initial presentation. Instead of a blank text field for credit card information and the aforementioned number pad, the "Link Payment" screen displayed the blank text field and a large blue button with the PayPal logo.[5] The blue PayPal button was located immediately below a centralized dark gray text reading "OR," indicating the existence of two payment options. Below the PayPal button, at the bottom of the screen, the texts "[b]y creating an Uber account you agree to the" and "Terms of Service & Privacy Policy" were presented in the same manner as previously described.

If the user selected the blank text field to input his or her credit card information, the user would then "engage[ ] the keyboard" and the "Link Payment" screen would resemble the "Link Card" screen.

Notwithstanding the differences in the third screen, the design and general mechanics of the Uber App interface remained fairly uniform. For example, all screens included a gray bar at the top. Within this bar the user was presented with the screen title written in capital letters in a dark colored font. Below the title, but within the gray bar, was an illustration of three circles connected by a green line. These circles indicated the user's progress through Uber's registration process.

In addition, on all screens, the gray bar incorporated two buttons: one to the left and one to the right of the screen's title. The left button was a "CANCEL" button, written in all capital letters. This button was enabled throughout the registration process, even before the user interacted with the screen. On the first two screens the right button was a "NEXT" button, also written in all capital letters. The "NEXT" button would remain barely visible and inoperative until after the user had entered the required information for each screen. In both versions of the third screen, the "NEXT" button was replaced by a "DONE" button. This "DONE" button also remained inoperative and barely visible until the user had entered the requested payment information.

C. Uber's Terms and Conditions

Uber's Terms and Conditions (the "Agreement") consisted of an approximately ten-page document that was available to Uber App users during the registration process via hyperlink. If the user "clicked" on the "Terms of Service & Privacy Policy" button[8] in either version of the third screen, he or she would be taken to another screen that contained two additional clickable buttons entitled "Terms & Conditions" and "Privacy Policy." The Agreement was displayed on the user's screen once the "Terms & Conditions" button was clicked. However, the Uber App did not require prospective users to "click" any of these buttons or access the Agreement before they could complete the registration process.

---

5 PayPal is "an internet service to pay for transactions online." *United States v. Frechette*, 583 F.3d 374, 377 n.1 (6th Cir. 2009).

8 In this sense, Uber's "Terms of Service & Privacy Policy" button was a hyperlink. "[When accessed on a computer a] hyperlink is a 'string of text or a computer graphic that a user can 'click' with the mouse pointer' to open a new browser page." *iLOR, LLC v. Google, Inc.*, 631 F.3d 1372, 1374 (Fed. Cir. 2011) (citation omitted). And hyperlinks found on phone applications (like the Uber App) can generally be accessed with the mere touch of the finger. *See* PC Mag., *supra* n.4.

The Agreement contained a "Dispute Resolution" section that provided that the user and Uber:

> [A]gree that any dispute, claim or controversy arising out of or relating to this Agreement or the breach, termination, enforcement, interpretation or validity thereof or the use of the Service or Application (collectively, **"Disputes"**) will be settled by binding arbitration. . . . **You acknowledge and agree that you and [Uber] are each waiving the right to a trial by jury or to participate as a plaintiff or class User in any purported class action or representative proceeding.**

(Emphasis in original). Furthermore, the Agreement stipulated that "[t]he arbitration [would] be administered by the American Arbitration Association ('AAA') in accordance with the Commercial Arbitration Rules and the Supplementary Procedures for Consumer Related Disputes (the 'AAA Rules')" and that the Federal Arbitration Act ("FAA") would govern the interpretation and enforcement of the Agreement's arbitration.

D. Procedural Background

In November 2014, plaintiffs filed this putative class action against Uber in Massachusetts Superior Court. * * * Uber filed a Notice of Removal to the United States District Court for the District of Massachusetts pursuant to the Class Action Fairness Act (CAFA), 28 U.S.C. § 1332(d). * * * Uber moved to compel arbitration and stay proceedings or, in the alternative, to dismiss the case, relying on the arbitration clause of the Agreement. * * *

After a hearing, the district court granted Uber's motion to compel arbitration and dismissed the case. This timely appeal followed.

* * *

Under the FAA, "[a] written provision in . . . a contract . . . to settle by arbitration a controversy thereafter arising out of such contract . . . shall be valid, irrevocable, and enforceable." 9 U.S.C. § 2 (2012). The Supreme Court has stated that the FAA reflects "a federal liberal policy favoring arbitration agreements." AT&T Mobility LLC v. Concepcion, 563 U.S. 333, 346, 131 S.Ct. 1740, 179 L.Ed.2d 742 (2011) (quoting Moses H. Cone Mem'l Hosp. v. Mercury Constr. Corp., 460 U.S. 1, 24, 103 S.Ct. 927, 74 L.Ed.2d 765 (1983)). It was Congress's intention to "place arbitration agreements 'upon the same footing as other contracts.'" Scherk v. Alberto-Culver Co., 417 U.S. 506, 511, 94 S.Ct. 2449, 41 L.Ed.2d 270 (1974) (quoting H.R. Rep. No. 68-96, at 2 (1924)). Nevertheless, the "FAA does not require parties to arbitrate when they have not agreed to do so." Volt Info. Scis., Inc. v. Bd. of Trs. of Leland Stanford Jr. Univ., 489 U.S. 468, 478, 109 S.Ct. 1248, 103 L.Ed.2d 488 (1989). Therefore, in deciding a motion to compel arbitration, a court must first determine "whether '. . . there exists a written agreement to arbitrate.'"

It is well settled that "arbitration is a matter of contract." Rent-A-Center, West, Inc. v. Jackson, 561 U.S. 63, 67, 130 S.Ct. 2772, 177 L.Ed.2d 403 (2010). "When deciding whether the parties agreed to arbitrate a certain matter (including arbitrability), courts generally . . . should apply ordinary state-law principles that govern the formation of contracts." First Options of Chi., Inc. v. Kaplan, 514 U.S.

938, 944, 115 S.Ct. 1920, 131 L.Ed.2d 985 (1995). The district court applied Massachusetts law and the parties do not challenge that decision. In any event, we agree with the district court that Massachusetts contract law applies.

The Massachusetts Supreme Judicial Court ("SJC") has not addressed the issue of contract formation for online agreements. However, in Ajemian v. Yahoo!, Inc., 83 Mass.App.Ct. 565, 987 N.E.2d 604, 611–15 (2013), the Massachusetts Appeals Court ("Appeals Court") addressed the enforceability of forum selection and limitation clauses within an online contract and that court's decision is "trustworthy data for ascertaining state law." While the clauses at issue in *Ajemian* did not include an arbitration clause, "the essential question presented was the same: what level of notice and assent is required in order for a court to enforce an online adhesion contract?" Consequently, we apply the principles stated in *Ajemian*.

In *Ajemian*, the Appeals Court determined that there was "no reason to apply different legal principles [of contract enforcement] simply because a forum selection clause . . . is contained in an online contract." Therefore, "such clauses will be enforced provided they have been reasonably communicated and accepted." The Appeals Court explained that "[r]easonably conspicuous notice of the existence of contract terms and unambiguous manifestation of assent to those terms by consumers *are essential* if electronic bargaining is to have integrity and credibility." With this in mind, the Appeals Court set forth a two-step inquiry for the enforceability of forum selection clauses in online agreements. The first inquiry is whether the contract terms were "reasonably communicated to the plaintiffs." The second is whether the record shows that those terms were "accepted and, if so, the manner of acceptance." The court further clarified that the burden to show that the terms were reasonably communicated and accepted lies on the party seeking to enforce the forum selection clause.

With the legal framework determined, we proceed to our analysis keeping in mind that our sole focus is on the enforceability of Uber's mandatory arbitration clause found in the Agreement.

A. Reasonable Notice

Uber makes no claim that any of the Plaintiffs actually saw the arbitration clause or even clicked on the "Terms of Service & Privacy Policy" button. Rather, it relies solely on a claim that its online presentation was sufficiently conspicuous as to bind the Plaintiffs whether or not they chose to click through the relevant terms. Therefore, we must determine whether the terms of the Agreement were "reasonably communicated" to the Plaintiffs. We note that "in the context of web-based contracts . . . clarity and conspicuousness are a function of the design and content of the relevant interface." Meyer v. Uber Techs., Inc., 868 F.3d 66, 75 (2d Cir. 2017).

Under Massachusetts law, "conspicuous" means that a terms is "so written, displayed or presented that a reasonable person against which it is to operate ought to have noticed it." Mass. Gen. Laws ch. 106, § 1–201(b)(10); *see also* Mass. Gen. Laws ch. 156 D, § 1.40 (defining the term "conspicuous" as "written so that a reasonable person against whom the writing is to operate should have noticed it").

Whether or not a term is conspicuous is for the court to decide. Several nonexhaustive examples of general characteristics that make a term conspicuous include using larger and contrasting font, the use of headings in capitals, or somehow setting off the term from the surrounding text by the use of symbols or other marks.

In addition, when the terms of the agreement are only available by following a link, the court must examine "the language that was used to notify users that the terms of their arrangement with [the service provider] could be found by following the link, how prominently displayed the link was, and any other information that would bear on the reasonableness of communicating [the terms]." Ajemian, 987 N.E.2d at 612.

After reviewing the Uber App registration process, we find that the Plaintiffs were not reasonably notified of the terms of the Agreement. We note at the outset that Uber chose not to use a common method of conspicuously informing users of the existence and location of terms and conditions: requiring users to click a box stating that they agree to a set of terms, often provided by hyperlink, before continuing to the next screen. Instead, Uber chose to rely on simply displaying a notice of deemed acquiescence and a link to the terms. In order to determine whether that approach reasonably notified users of the Agreement, we begin our analysis with how this link was displayed.

Uber contends that the gray rectangular box with the language "Terms of Service & Privacy Policy" was reasonably conspicuous, both visually and contextually, because it was displayed in a larger font, in bold, contrasting in color, and highlighted by the box around it. Furthermore, Uber argues that the screen contained a total of twenty-six words, making it difficult for a user to miss it.

While the language and the number of words found on the "Link Card" and "Link Payment" screens could be seen to favor Uber's position, the reading of Uber's "Terms of Service & Privacy Policy" hyperlink must be contextualized. That is, it may not be read in a vacuum. Other similarly displayed terms presented simultaneously to the user in both versions of the third screen diminished the conspicuousness of the "Terms of Service & Privacy Policy" hyperlink. We explain.

First, Uber's "Terms of Service & Privacy Policy" hyperlink did not have the common appearance of a hyperlink. While not all hyperlinks need to have the same characteristics, they are "commonly blue and underlined." CR Assocs. L.P. v. Sparefoot, Inc., No. 17-10551-LTS, 2018 WL 988056, at *4 n.4 (D. Mass. Feb. 20, 2018); see also e.g., Meyer, 868 F.3d at 78 ("[T]he hyperlinks are in blue and underlined."); Adelson v. Harris, 774 F.3d 803, 808 (2d Cir. 2014) ("[T]he hyperlinks were not hidden but visible in the customary manner, that is, by being embedded in blue, underlined text."); Fteja v. Facebook, Inc., 841 F.Supp.2d 829, 835 (S.D.N.Y. 2012) ("The phrase 'Terms of Service' is underlined, an indication that the phrase is a hyperlink, a phrase that is 'usually highlighted or underlined' and 'sends users who click on it directly to a new location—usually an internet address or a program of some sort.'"). Here, the "Terms of Service & Privacy Policy" hyperlink was presented in a gray rectangular box in white bold text. Though not dispositive, the characteristics of the hyperlink raise concerns as to whether a reasonable user would have been aware that the gray rectangular box was actually a hyperlink.

Next, the overall content of the "Link Card" and "Link Payment" screens show that the "Terms of Service & Privacy Policy" hyperlink was not a conspicuous term as defined by Massachusetts law. Again, this hyperlink was displayed in white bold font within a gray rectangular box. While these features may have been sufficient to accentuate a hyperlink found within a registration process interface with a plain design and limited content, that was not the case here.

Along with the "Terms of Service & Privacy Policy" hyperlink, the "Link Card" and "Link Payment" screens contained other terms displayed with similar features. For example, the terms "scan your card" and "enter promo code" were also written in bold and with a similarly sized font as the hyperlink. Both versions of the third screen also included the words "CANCEL" and "DONE,"—the latter being barely visible until the user had entered the required payment information—in all capital letters and dark colored font. Meanwhile, the top of the screens featured the terms "Link Card" or "Link Payment" in large capital letters and dark colored font. These had the largest-sized font in both versions of the third screen.

Uber's "Terms of Service & Privacy Policy" hyperlink was even less conspicuous on the "Link Payment" screen. The inclusion of the additional payment option and the placement of a large blue PayPal button in the middle of the screen were more attention-grabbing and displaced the hyperlink to the bottom of the screen.

It is thus the design and content of the "Link Card" and "Link Payment" screens of the Uber App interface that lead us to conclude that Uber's "Terms of Service & Privacy Policy" hyperlink was not conspicuous. Even though the hyperlink did possess some of the characteristics that make a term conspicuous, the presence of other terms on the same screen with a similar or larger size, typeface, and with more noticeable attributes diminished the hyperlink's capability to grab the user's attention. If everything on the screen is written with conspicuous features, then nothing is conspicuous.

Furthermore, when we consider the characteristics of the text used to notify potential users that the creation of an Uber account would bind them to the linked terms, we note that this phrase was even less conspicuous than the "Terms of Service & Privacy Policy" hyperlink. This notice was displayed in a dark gray small-sized non-bolded font against a black background. The notice simply did not have any distinguishable feature that would set it apart from all the other terms surrounding it.

Because both the "Link Card" and "Link Payment" screens were filled with other very noticeable terms that diminished the conspicuousness of the "Terms of Service & Privacy Policy" hyperlink and the notice, we find that the terms of the Agreement were not reasonably communicated to the Plaintiffs. As such, Uber's motion to compel arbitration fails.

IV. Conclusion

Because the Plaintiffs were not reasonably notified of the terms of the Agreement, they did not provide their unambiguous assent to those terms. We therefore find that Uber has failed to carry its burden on its motion to compel arbitration. For these reasons we reverse the district court's grant of Uber's motion to compel arbitration, and remand the case for further proceedings consistent with this opinion.

Reversed and Remanded.

One of the cases *Cullinane* cites, *Meyer v. Uber Techs., Inc.*, 868 F.3d 66 (2d Cir. 2017), enforced an Uber arbitration clause. As *Cullinane* quotes, in *Meyer* the Second Circuit observed that "the hyperlinks are in blue and underlined."

Meyer v. Uber Techs., Inc.

United States Court of Appeals, Second Circuit, 2017.
868 F.3d 66.

* * *

[B]efore an agreement to arbitrate can be enforced, the district court must first determine whether such agreement exists between the parties. This question is determined by state contract law.

* * *

We agree with the district court's determination that California state law applies, and note that New York and California apply "substantially similar rules for determining whether the parties have mutually assented to a contract term."

To form a contract, there must be "[m]utual manifestation of assent, whether by written or spoken word or by conduct." California law is clear, however, that "an offeree, regardless of apparent manifestation of his consent, is not bound by inconspicuous contractual provisions of which he is unaware, contained in a document whose contractual nature is not obvious." "Thus, California contract law measures assent by an objective standard that takes into account both what the offeree said, wrote, or did and the transactional context in which the offeree verbalized or acted."

Where there is no evidence that the offeree had actual notice of the terms of the agreement, the offeree will still be bound by the agreement if a reasonably prudent user would be on inquiry notice of the terms. Whether a reasonably prudent user would be on inquiry notice turns on the "[c]larity and conspicuousness of arbitration terms"; in the context of web-based contracts, as discussed further below, clarity and conspicuousness are a function of the design and content of the relevant interface.

Thus, only if the undisputed facts establish that there is "[r]easonably conspicuous notice of the existence of contract terms and unambiguous manifestation of assent to those terms" will we find that a contract has been formed.

* * * "Courts around the country have recognized that [an] electronic 'click' can suffice to signify the acceptance of a contract," and that "[t]here is nothing automatically offensive about such agreements, as long as the layout and language of the site give the user reasonable notice that a click will manifest assent to an agreement."

With these principles in mind, one way in which we have previously distinguished web-based contracts is the manner in which the user manifests assent—namely, "clickwrap" (or "click-through") agreements, which require users to click an "I agree" box after being presented with a list of terms and conditions of use, or "browsewrap" agreements, which generally post terms and conditions on a website via a hyperlink at the bottom of the screen. Courts routinely uphold clickwrap agreements for the principal reason that the user has affirmatively assented to the terms of agreement by clicking "I agree." Browsewrap agreements, on the other hand, do not require the user to expressly assent. "Because no affirmative action is required by the website user to agree to the terms of a contract other than his or her use of the website, the determination of the validity of the browsewrap contract depends on whether the user has actual or constructive knowledge of a website's terms and conditions."

Of course, there are infinite ways to design a website or smartphone application, and not all interfaces fit neatly into the clickwrap or browsewrap categories. Some online agreements require the user to scroll through the terms before the user can indicate his or her assent by clicking "I agree." Other agreements notify the user of the existence of the website's terms of use and, instead of providing an "I agree" button, advise the user that he or she is agreeing to the terms of service when registering or signing up.

In the interface at issue in this case, a putative user is not required to assent explicitly to the contract terms; instead, the user must click a button marked "Register," underneath which the screen states "By creating an Uber account, you agree to the TERMS OF SERVICE & PRIVACY POLICY," with hyperlinks to the Terms of Service and Privacy Policy. * * *

* * *

Meyer attests that he was not on actual notice of the hyperlink to the Terms of Service or the arbitration provision itself, and defendants do not point to evidence from which a jury could infer otherwise. Accordingly, we must consider whether Meyer was on inquiry notice of the arbitration provision by virtue of the hyperlink to the Terms of Service on the Payment Screen and, thus, manifested his assent to the agreement by clicking "Register."

* * *

In considering the question of reasonable conspicuousness, precedent and basic principles of contract law instruct that we consider the perspective of a reasonably prudent smartphone user.

* * *

[W]e conclude that the design of the screen and language used render the notice provided reasonable as a matter of California law.[9] The Payment Screen is uncluttered, with only fields for the user to enter his or her credit card details, buttons to register for a user account or to connect the user's pre-existing PayPal account or Google Wallet to the Uber account, and the warning that "By creating

[9] In evaluating the application interface, we use the actual-size screenshot of the last step in the registration process, as it would have appeared on Meyer's Samsung Galaxy S5.

an Uber account, you agree to the TERMS OF SERVICE & PRIVACY POLICY." The text, including the hyperlinks to the Terms and Conditions and Privacy Policy, appears directly below the buttons for registration. The entire screen is visible at once, and the user does not need to scroll beyond what is immediately visible to find notice of the Terms of Service. Although the sentence is in a small font, the dark print contrasts with the bright white background, and the hyperlinks are in blue and underlined. This presentation differs sharply from the screen we considered in *Nicosia* [v. Amazon.com, Inc., 834 F.3d 220 (2d Cir. 2016)], which contained, among other things, summaries of the user's purchase and delivery information, "between fifteen and twenty-five links," "text . . . in at least four font sizes and six colors," and several buttons and advertisements. Furthermore, the notice of the terms and conditions in *Nicosia* was "not directly adjacent" to the button intended to manifest assent to the terms, unlike the text and button at issue here.

In addition to being spatially coupled with the mechanism for manifesting assent—*i.e.*, the register button—the notice is temporally coupled. As we observed in *Schnabel* [v. Trilegiant Corp., 697 F.3d 110 (2d Cir. 2012)],

> inasmuch as consumers are regularly and frequently confronted with non-negotiable contract terms, particularly when entering into transactions using the Internet, the presentation of these terms at a place and time that the consumer will associate with the initial purchase or enrollment, or the use of, the goods or services from which the recipient benefits at least indicates to the consumer that he or she is taking such goods or employing such services subject to additional terms and conditions that may one day affect him or her.

Schnabel, 697 F.3d at 127. Here, notice of the Terms of Service is provided simultaneously to enrollment, thereby connecting the contractual terms to the services to which they apply. We think that a reasonably prudent smartphone user would understand that the terms were connected to the creation of a user account.

That the Terms of Service were available only by hyperlink does not preclude a determination of reasonable notice. See Fteja [v. Facebook, Inc., 841 F.Supp.2d 829, 839 (S.D.N.Y. 2012)] ("[C]licking [a] hyperlinked phrase is the twenty-first century equivalent of turning over the cruise ticket. In both cases, the consumer is prompted to examine terms of sale that are located somewhere else."). Moreover, the language "[b]y creating an Uber account, you agree" is a clear prompt directing users to read the Terms and Conditions and signaling that their acceptance of the benefit of registration would be subject to contractual terms. As long as the hyperlinked text was itself reasonably conspicuous—and we conclude that it was—a reasonably prudent smartphone user would have constructive notice of the terms. While it may be the case that many users will not bother reading the additional terms, that is the choice the user makes; the user is still on inquiry notice.

* * *

Accordingly, we conclude that the Uber App provided reasonably conspicuous notice of the Terms of Service as a matter of California law and turn to the question of whether Meyer unambiguously manifested his assent to those terms.

2. Manifestation of assent

Although Meyer's assent to arbitration was not express, we are convinced that it was unambiguous in light of the objectively reasonable notice of the terms, as discussed in detail above. * * * there is ample evidence that a reasonable user would be on inquiry notice of the terms, and the spatial and temporal coupling of the terms with the registration button "indicate[d] to the consumer that he or she is . . . employing such services subject to additional terms and conditions that may one day affect him or her." A reasonable user would know that by clicking the registration button, he was agreeing to the terms and conditions accessible via the hyperlink, whether he clicked on the hyperlink or not.

The fact that clicking the register button had two functions—creation of a user account and assent to the Terms of Service—does not render Meyer's assent ambiguous. The registration process allowed Meyer to review the Terms of Service prior to registration, unlike web platforms that provide notice of contract terms only after the user manifested his or her assent. Furthermore, the text on the Payment Screen not only included a hyperlink to the Terms of Service, but expressly warned the user that by creating an Uber account, the user was agreeing to be bound by the linked terms. Although the warning text used the term "creat[e]" instead of "register," as the button was marked, the physical proximity of the notice to the register button and the placement of the language in the registration flow make clear to the user that the linked terms pertain to the action the user is about to take.

The transactional context of the parties' dealings reinforces our conclusion. Meyer located and downloaded the Uber App, signed up for an account, and entered his credit card information with the intention of entering into a forward-looking relationship with Uber. The registration process clearly contemplated some sort of continuing relationship between the putative user and Uber, one that would require some terms and conditions, and the Payment Screen provided clear notice that there were terms that governed that relationship.

Accordingly, we conclude on the undisputed facts of this case that Meyer unambiguously manifested his assent to Uber's Terms of Service as a matter of California law.

Addendum A

[To view these images in color, go to store.westacademic.com and view the PDF on the product detail page for this book.]

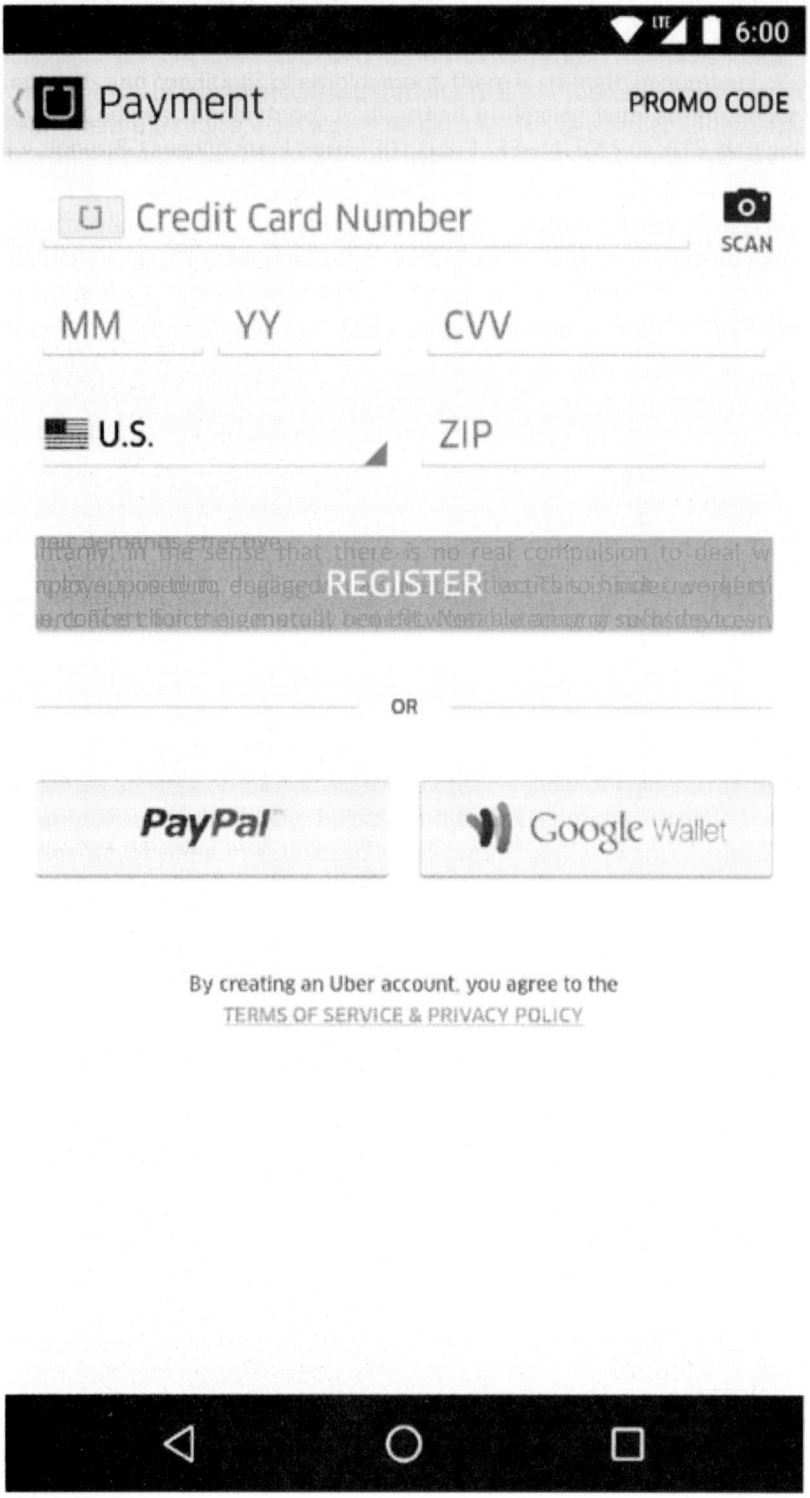
6:00
Payment
PROMO CODE
Credit Card Number
SCAN
MM
YY
CVV
U.S.
ZIP
REGISTER
OR
PayPal
Google Wallet
By creating an Uber account, you agree to the
TERMS OF SERVICE & PRIVACY POLICY

Addendum B

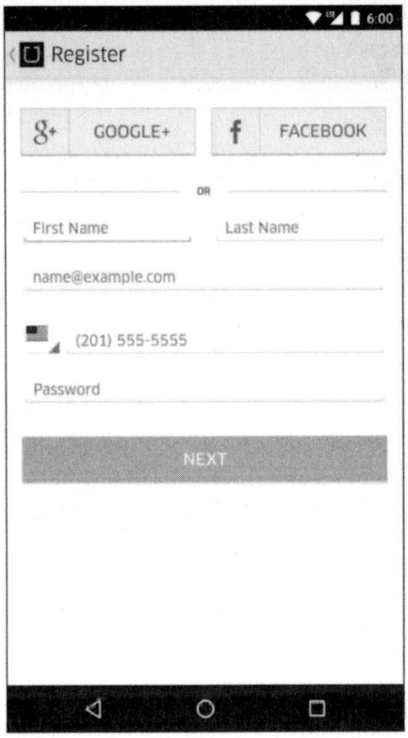

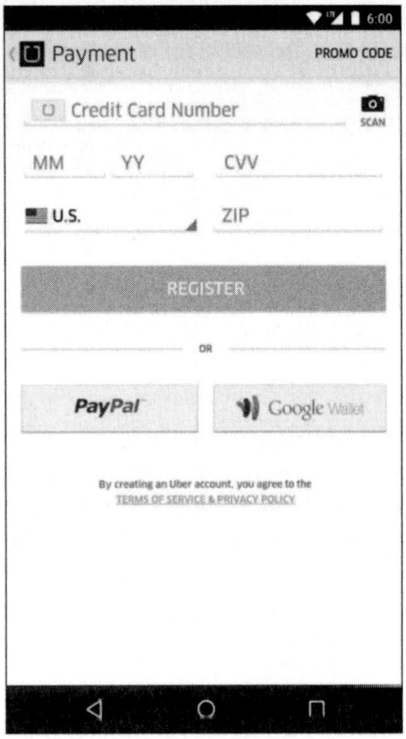

QUESTIONS TO REVIEW AND SYNTHESIZE

1. What led *Meyer* and *Cullinane* to different decisions on whether to enforce an Uber arbitration agreement?
2. What bodies of law determine whether parties have formed an arbitration agreement?

Issues surrounding the manifestation-of-assent requirement to form a contract can arise in a number of ways and most of them can apply to an arbitration agreement. In a category of such cases, the document containing the arbitration clause was never signed (or clicked on) by all of the parties and the issue is whether the non-signing parties manifested assent to the arbitration clause by performing the contract. For instance, if goods or services are delivered by the seller to the buyer with documents that purport to be a contract including an arbitration clause, does the buyer's acceptance and use of the goods or services manifest assent to the document's arbitration clause? Compare Stenzel v. Dell, Inc., 870 A.2d 133 (Me.2005) (by "accepting delivery of the computers, and then failing to exercise their right to return the computers as provided by the agreement, [the plaintiffs] expressly manifested their assent to be bound by the agreement"), with DeFontes v. Dell, Inc., 984 A.2d 1073 (R.I.2009)("We are not persuaded that a reasonably prudent offeree would understand that by keeping the Dell computer he or she was agreeing to be bound by the terms and conditions agreement and retained, for a specified time, the power to reject the terms by returning the product.")

Or suppose the document containing the arbitration clause was never signed (or clicked on) by the parties but they did sign a document that does not contain an arbitration clause. One party may argue the signed document effectively incorporates by reference the document containing an arbitration clause. Compare CompuCredit Corp. v. Greenwood, 565 U.S. 95, 96 (2012)(enforcing an arbitration agreement incorporated by reference in a consumer's application for a credit card); Ward v. Hilliard, 116 N.E.3d 1011 (Ill.App.Ct.2018) (holding retirement account terms of service were incorporated by reference into signed application to open account), with State ex rel. U-Haul Co. of W. Virginia v. Zakaib, 752 S.E.2d 586, 598 (W.V. 2013) (holding that U-Haul's rental contract did not incorporate an addendum's arbitration agreement because the rental agreement's mention of the addendum was "brief" and "general" and "U-Haul's practice was to provide customers a copy of the Addendum only after the Rental Agreement had been executed.")

In addition to incorporation-by-reference, another example of the contract's terms spread over multiple documents is when a sale of goods involves two documents (the buyer's purchase order or the seller's price quote or acknowledgment) only one of which contains an arbitration clause. The Uniform Commercial Code tries, not always successfully, to solve the "battle of the forms" problem. UCC § 2–207 provides that

> (1) A definite and seasonable expression of acceptance or a written confirmation which is sent within a reasonable time operates as an acceptance even though it states terms additional to or different from those offered or agreed upon, unless acceptance is expressly made conditional on assent to the additional or different terms.
>
> (2) The additional terms are to be construed as proposals for addition to the contract. Between merchants such terms become part of the contract unless:
>
> (a) the offer expressly limits acceptance to the terms of the offer;
>
> (b) they materially alter it; or
>
> (c) notification of objection to them has already been given or is given within a reasonable time after notice of them is received.

Assume that an exchange of forms creates a contract under UCC 2–207(1) but that only the *second* form contains a clause providing for the arbitration of future disputes. Does this clause become part of the contract? New York's highest court (the Court of Appeals) considered this question in *In the Matter of the Arbitration Between Marlene Industries Corp. v. Carnac Textiles*, Inc., 45 N.Y.2d 327, 408 N.Y.S.2d 410, 380 N.E.2d 239 (1978). This case involved conflicting forms sent in confirmation of an *oral order* placed by the buyer; the seller's "acknowledgment" form, sent last, alone provided for arbitration but was not made "expressly conditional" on the buyer's assent to that or any other term. The Court of Appeals held that:

> the inclusion of an arbitration agreement materially alters a contract for the sale of goods, and thus, pursuant to section 2–207(2)(b) it will not become a part of such a contract unless both parties explicitly agree to it.
>
> It has long been the rule in this State that the parties to a commercial transaction "will not be held to have chosen arbitration as the forum for the resolution of their disputes in the absence of an express, unequivocal agreement to that effect; absent such an explicit commitment neither party may be compelled to arbitrate." The reason for this requirement, quite simply,

> is that by agreeing to arbitrate a party waives in large part many of his normal rights under the procedural and substantive law of the State, and it would be unfair to infer such a significant waiver on the basis of anything less than a clear indication of intent.
>
> Since an arbitration agreement in the context of a commercial transaction "must be clear and direct, and must not depend upon implication, inveiglement or subtlety . . . [its] existence . . . should not depend solely upon the conflicting fine print of commercial forms which cross one another but never meet." Thus, at least under this so-called "New York Rule", it is clear that an arbitration clause is a material addition which can become part of a contract only if it is expressly assented to by both parties. Applying these principles to this case, we conclude that the contract between Marlene and Carnac does not contain an arbitration clause; hence, the motion to permanently stay arbitration should have been granted.

More recent cases have been more willing to find agreements to arbitrate. See Aceros Prefabricados, S.A. v. TradeArbed, Inc., 282 F.3d 92, 100 (2d Cir.2002) ("arbitration agreements do not, as a matter of law, constitute material alterations to a contract; rather, the question of their inclusion in a contract under section 2–207(2)(b) is answered by examining, on a case-by-case basis, their materiality under a preponderance of the evidence standard as we would examine any other agreement."); ICC Chem. Corp. v. Vitol, Inc., 425 F. App'x 57, 59 (2d Cir. 2011) (arbitration agreement became part of contract under UCC 2–207(2)(b) because it was not a "material alteration").

Assent to arbitration can also be an issue of agency: whether a party (the principal) who did not assent to an arbitration agreement is nevertheless bound by it because someone else (the agent) assented to it on behalf of the principal. One such case rose to the Supreme Court and prompted seven of the eight participating justices to hold that Kentucky's clear-statement rule—requiring an explicit statement in a power of attorney that the attorney-in-fact has authority to waive the principal's state constitutional rights to access the courts and to a jury trial—disfavors arbitration agreements and therefore is preempted by the FAA. Kindred Nursing Ctrs. Ltd. P'ship v. Clark, 137 S. Ct. 1421 (2017). Other agency cases find, for example, that a parent had authority to bind a minor to an arbitration clause. See Hojnowski v. Vans Skate Park, 901 A.2d 381 (N.J.2006).

In sum, asking whether parties have formed an arbitration agreement can raise many of the same questions that might arise in asking whether parties have formed any contract.

QUESTIONS TO REVIEW AND SYNTHESIZE

1. When a business buys goods through a voice call and then later receives with the goods a document containing an arbitration clause, what will determine whether a court finds that buyer to have manifested assent to that arbitration agreement?

2. What is another way (not addressed in the previous question) a court can find manifestation-of-assent to arbitrate without a signed contract containing the arbitration provision?

2. CONTRACT-LAW DEFENSES TO ENFORCEMENT OF ARBITRATION AGREEMENTS

a. THE "SEVERABILITY" OF THE ARBITRATION CLAUSE

Even if parties have formed an arbitration agreement, one party may argue that the agreement is unenforceable due to a contract-law defense to contract enforcement, such as misrepresentation or duress. Arguments about such defenses are typically heard by arbitrators rather than courts.

Prima Paint Corp. v. Flood & Conklin Mfg. Co.

Supreme Court of the United States, 1967.
388 U.S. 395, 87 S.Ct. 1801, 18 L.Ed.2d 1270.

■ MR. JUSTICE FORTAS delivered the opinion of the Court.

This case presents the question whether the federal court or an arbitrator is to resolve a claim of "fraud in the inducement," under a contract governed by the United States Arbitration Act of 1925, where there is no evidence that the contracting parties intended to withhold that issue from arbitration.

The question arises from the following set of facts. On October 7, 1964, respondent, Flood & Conklin Manufacturing Company, a New Jersey corporation, entered into what was styled a "Consulting Agreement," with petitioner, Prima Paint Corporation, a Maryland corporation. This agreement followed by less than three weeks the execution of a contract pursuant to which Prima Paint purchased F & C's paint business. The consulting agreement provided that for a six-year period F & C was to furnish advice and consultation "in connection with the formulae, manufacturing operations, sales and servicing of Prima Trade Sales account." These services were to be performed personally by F & C's chairman, Jerome K. Jelin, "except in the event of his death or disability." F & C bound itself for the duration of the contractual period to make no "Trade Sales" of paint or paint products in its existing sales territory or to current customers. To the consulting agreement were appended lists of F & C customers, whose patronage was to be taken over by Prima Paint. In return for these lists, the covenant not to compete, and the services of Mr. Jelin, Prima Paint agreed to pay F & C certain percentages of its receipts from the listed customers and from all others, such payments not to exceed $25,000 over the life of the agreement. The agreement took into account the possibility that Prima Paint might encounter financial difficulties, including bankruptcy, but no corresponding reference was made to possible financial problems which might be encountered by F & C. The agreement states that it "embodies the entire understanding of the parties on the subject matter." Finally, the parties agreed to a broad arbitration clause, which read in part:

> "Any controversy or claim arising out of or relating to this Agreement, or the breach thereof, shall be settled by arbitration in the City of New York, in accordance with the rules then obtaining of the American Arbitration Association. . . ."

The first payment by Prima Paint to F & C under the consulting agreement was due on September 1, 1965. None was made on that date. Seventeen days later, Prima Paint did pay the appropriate amount, but into escrow. It notified attorneys for F & C that in various enumerated respects their client had broken both the consulting agreement and the earlier purchase agreement. Prima Paint's principal contention, so far as presently relevant, was that F & C had fraudulently represented that it was solvent and able to perform its contractual obligations, whereas it was in fact insolvent and intended to file a petition under Chapter XI of the Bankruptcy Act shortly after execution of the consulting agreement. Prima Paint noted that such a petition was filed by F & C on October 14, 1964, one week after the contract had been signed. F & C's response, on October 25, was to serve a "notice of intention to arbitrate." On November 12, three days before expiration of its time to answer this "notice," Prima Paint filed suit in the United States District Court for the Southern District of New York, seeking rescission of the consulting agreement on the basis of the alleged fraudulent inducement. The complaint asserted that the federal court had diversity jurisdiction.

Contemporaneously with the filing of its complaint, Prima Paint petitioned the District Court for an order enjoining F & C from proceeding with the arbitration. F & C cross-moved to stay the court action pending arbitration. F & C contended that the issue presented—whether there was fraud in the inducement of the consulting agreement—was a question for the arbitrators and not for the District Court. * * *

The District Court granted F & C's motion to stay the action pending arbitration, holding that a charge of fraud in the inducement of a contract containing an arbitration clause as broad as this one was a question for the arbitrators and not for the court. * * * The Court of Appeals for the Second Circuit dismissed Prima Paint's appeal.

* * *

[The Court first determined that "[t]here could not be a clearer case of a contract evidencing a transaction in interstate commerce."]

Having determined that the contract in question is within the coverage of the Arbitration Act, we turn to the central issue in this case: whether a claim of fraud in the inducement of the entire contract is to be resolved by the federal court, or whether the matter is to be referred to the arbitrators. The courts of appeals have differed in their approach to this question. The view of the Court of Appeals for the Second Circuit, as expressed in this case and in others, is that—except where the parties otherwise intend—arbitration clauses as a matter of federal law are "separable" from the contract in which they are embedded, and that where no claim is made that fraud was directed to the arbitration clause itself, a broad arbitration clause will be held to encompass arbitration of the claim that the contract itself was induced by fraud.[9] The Court of Appeals for the First Circuit, on the other hand, has taken the view that the question of "severability" is one of

[9] The Court of Appeals has been careful to honor evidence that the parties intended to withhold such issues from the arbitrators and to reserve them for judicial resolution. We note that categories of contracts otherwise within the Arbitration Act but in which one of the parties characteristically has little bargaining power are expressly excluded from the reach of the Act. See § 1.

state law, and that where a State regards such a clause as inseparable a claim of fraud in inducement must be decided by the court.

With respect to cases brought in federal court involving maritime contracts or those evidencing transactions in "commerce," we think that Congress has provided an explicit answer. That answer is to be found in § 4 of the Act, which provides a remedy to a party seeking to compel compliance with an arbitration agreement. Under § 4, with respect to a matter within the jurisdiction of the federal courts save for the existence of an arbitration clause, the federal court is instructed to order arbitration to proceed once it is satisfied that "the making of the agreement for arbitration or the failure to comply [with the arbitration agreement] is not in issue." Accordingly, if the claim is fraud in the inducement of the arbitration clause itself—an issue which goes to the "making" of the agreement to arbitrate—the federal court may proceed to adjudicate it. But the statutory language does not permit the federal court to consider claims of fraud in the inducement of the contract generally. Section 4 does not expressly relate to situations like the present in which a stay is sought of a federal action in order that arbitration may proceed. But it is inconceivable that Congress intended the rule to differ depending upon which party to the arbitration agreement first invokes the assistance of a federal court. We hold, therefore, that in passing upon a § 3 application for a stay while the parties arbitrate, a federal court may consider only issues relating to the making and performance of the agreement to arbitrate. In so concluding, we not only honor the plain meaning of the statute but also the unmistakably clear congressional purpose that the arbitration procedure, when selected by the parties to a contract, be speedy and not subject to delay and obstruction in the courts.

* * *

In the present case no claim has been advanced by Prima Paint that F & C fraudulently induced it to enter into the agreement to arbitrate "[a]ny controversy or claim arising out of or relating to this Agreement, or the breach thereof." This contractual language is easily broad enough to encompass Prima Paint's claim that both execution and acceleration of the consulting agreement itself were procured by fraud. Indeed, no claim is made that Prima Paint ever intended that "legal" issues relating to the contract be excluded from arbitration, or that it was not entirely free so to contract. Federal courts are bound to apply rules enacted by Congress with respect to matters—here, a contract involving commerce—over which it has legislative power. The question which Prima Paint requested the District Court to adjudicate preliminarily to allowing arbitration to proceed is one not intended by Congress to delay the granting of a § 3 stay. Accordingly, the decision below dismissing Prima Paint's appeal is Affirmed.

■ MR. JUSTICE BLACK, with whom MR. JUSTICE DOUGLAS and MR. JUSTICE STEWART join, dissenting.

The Court here holds that the United States Arbitration Act, as a matter of federal substantive law, compels a party to a contract containing a written arbitration provision to carry out his "arbitration agreement" even though a court might, after a fair trial, hold the entire contract—including the arbitration agreement—void because of fraud in the inducement. The Court holds, what is to me fantastic, that the legal issue of a contract's voidness because of fraud is to be decided by persons designated to arbitrate factual controversies arising out of a valid contract between the parties. And the arbitrators who the Court holds are to adjudicate the legal validity of the contract need not even be lawyers, and in all probability will be nonlawyers, wholly unqualified to decide legal issues, and even if qualified to apply the law, not bound to do so. I am by no means sure that thus forcing a person to forgo his opportunity to try his legal issues in the courts where, unlike the situation in arbitration, he may have a jury trial and right to appeal, is not a denial of due process of law. I am satisfied, however, that Congress did not impose any such procedures in the Arbitration Act. And I am fully satisfied that a reasonable and fair reading of that Act's language and history shows that both Congress and the framers of the Act were at great pains to emphasize that non-lawyers designated to adjust and arbitrate factual controversies arising out of valid contracts would not trespass upon the courts' prerogative to decide the legal question of whether any legal contract exists upon which to base an arbitration.

* * *

Let us look briefly at the language of the Arbitration Act itself as Congress passed it. Section 2, the key provision of the Act, provides that "[a] written provision in . . . a contract . . . involving commerce to settle by arbitration a controversy thereafter arising out of such contract . . . shall be valid, irrevocable, and enforceable, *save upon such grounds as exist at law or in equity for the revocation of any contract*." (Emphasis added.) Section 3 provides that "[i]f any suit . . . be brought . . . *upon any issue referable to arbitration* under an agreement in writing for such arbitration, the court . . . *upon being satisfied that the issue involved in such suit . . . is referable to arbitration under such an agreement*, shall . . . stay the trial of the action until such arbitration has been had . . ." (Emphasis added.) The language of these sections could not, I think, raise doubts about their meaning except to someone anxious to find doubts. They simply mean this: an arbitration agreement is to be enforced by a federal court unless the court, not the arbitrator, finds grounds "at law or in equity for the revocation of any contract." Fraud, of course, is one of the most common grounds for revoking a contract. If the contract was procured by fraud, then, unless the defrauded party elects to affirm it, there is absolutely no contract, nothing to be arbitrated. Sections 2 and 3 of the Act assume the existence of a valid contract. They merely provide for enforcement where such a valid contract exists. These provisions were plainly designed to protect a person against whom arbitration is sought to be enforced from having to submit his legal issues as to validity of the contract to the arbitrator. * * *

Finally, it is clear to me from the bill's sponsors' understanding of the function of arbitration that they never intended that the issue of fraud in the inducement be resolved by arbitration. They recognized two special values of arbitration: (1) the expertise of an arbitrator to decide factual questions in regard to the day-to-day performance of contractual obligations,[13] and (2) the speed with which

[13] "Not all questions arising out of contracts ought to be arbitrated. It is a remedy peculiarly suited to the disposition of the ordinary disputes between merchants as to questions of fact—quantity, quality, time of delivery, compliance with terms of payment, excuses for non-performance, and the like. It has a place also in the determination of the simpler questions of law—the questions of law which arise out of these daily relations between merchants as to the passage of title, the existence of warranties, or the questions of law

arbitration, as contrasted to litigation, could resolve disputes over performance of contracts and thus mitigate the damages and allow the parties to continue performance under the contracts. Arbitration serves neither of these functions where a contract is sought to be rescinded on the ground of fraud. On the one hand, courts have far more expertise in resolving legal issues which go to the validity of a contract than do arbitrators.[14] On the other hand, where a party seeks to rescind a contract and his allegation of fraud in the inducement is true, an arbitrator's speedy remedy of this wrong should never result in resumption of performance under the contract. And if the contract were not procured by fraud, the court, under the summary trial procedures provided by the Act, may determine with little delay that arbitration must proceed. The only advantage of submitting the issue of fraud to arbitration is for the arbitrators. Their compensation corresponds to the volume of arbitration they perform. If they determine that a contract is void because of fraud, there is nothing further for them to arbitrate. I think it raises serious questions of due process to submit to an arbitrator an issue which will determine his compensation.

* * *

The avowed purpose of the Act was to place arbitration agreements "upon the same footing as other contracts." The separability rule which the Court applies to an arbitration clause does not result in equality between it and other clauses in the contract. I had always thought that a person who attacks a contract on the ground of fraud and seeks to rescind it has to seek rescission of the whole, not tidbits, and is not given the option of denying the existence of some clauses and affirming the existence of others. Here F & C agreed both to perform consulting services for Prima and not to compete with Prima. Would any court hold that those two agreements were separable, even though Prima in agreeing to pay F & C not to compete did not directly rely on F & C's representations of being solvent? The simple fact is that Prima would not have agreed to the covenant not to compete or to the arbitration clause but for F & C's fraudulent promise that it would be financially able to perform consulting services.

* * *

Prima here challenged in the courts the validity of its alleged contract with F & C as a whole, not in fragments. If there has never been any valid contract, then there is not now and never has been anything to arbitrate. If Prima's allegations are true, the sum total of what the Court does here is to force Prima to arbitrate a contract which is void and unenforceable before arbitrators who are given the power to make final legal determinations of their own jurisdiction, not even subject to effective review by the highest court in the land. That is not what Congress said Prima must do. It seems to be what the Court thinks would promote the policy of

---

which are complementary to the questions of fact which we have just mentioned." Cohen & Dayton, The New Federal Arbitration Law, 12 Va.L.Rev. 265, 281 (1926).

[14] "It [arbitration] is not a proper remedy for . . . questions with which the arbitrators have no particular experience and which are better left to the determination of skilled judges with a background of legal experience and established systems of law." Cohen & Dayton, supra, at 281.

arbitration. I am completely unable to agree to this new version of the Arbitration Act * * *.

For decades after *Prima Paint*, many courts did not apply its severability doctrine, in part because of doubt about whether *state* courts were bound by it. The belief that states were free to depart from the severability doctrine followed from the fact that *Prima Paint*'s reasoning rested on FAA §§ 3 and 4, which by their terms appear to apply only to proceedings in federal court. In the following case, however, the Supreme Court held that "*Prima Paint*'s rule of severability" applies in state court and preempts any inconsistent state law.

Buckeye Check Cashing, Inc. v. Cardegna

Supreme Court of the United States, 2006.
546 U.S. 440, 126 S.Ct. 1204, 163 L.Ed.2d 1038.

■ JUSTICE SCALIA delivered the opinion of the Court.

We decide whether a court or an arbitrator should consider the claim that a contract containing an arbitration provision is void for illegality.

Respondents John Cardegna and Donna Reuter entered into various deferred-payment transactions with petitioner Buckeye Check Cashing (Buckeye), in which they received cash in exchange for a personal check in the amount of the cash plus a finance charge. For each separate transaction they signed a "Deferred Deposit and Disclosure Agreement" (Agreement), which included the following arbitration provisions:

> "1. *Arbitration Disclosure* By signing this Agreement, you agree that if a dispute of any kind arises out of this Agreement or your application therefore or any instrument relating thereto, then either you or we or third-parties involved can choose to have that dispute resolved by binding arbitration as set forth in Paragraph 2 below . . . .
>
> "2. *Arbitration Provisions* Any claim, dispute, or controversy . . . arising from or relating to this Agreement . . . or the validity, enforceability, or scope of this Arbitration Provision or the entire Agreement (collectively 'Claim'), shall be resolved, upon the election of you or us or said third-parties, by binding arbitration . . . . This arbitration Agreement is made pursuant to a transaction involving interstate commerce, and shall be governed by the Federal Arbitration Act ('FAA'), 9 U.S.C. Sections 1–16. The arbitrator shall apply applicable substantive law constraint *[sic]* with the FAA and applicable statutes of limitations and shall honor claims of privilege recognized by law . . . ."

Respondents brought this putative class action in Florida state court, alleging that Buckeye charged usurious interest rates and that the Agreement violated various Florida lending and consumer-protection laws, rendering it criminal on its face. Buckeye moved to compel arbitration. The trial court denied the motion, holding that a court rather than an arbitrator should resolve a claim that a contract is illegal and void *ab initio*. The District Court of Appeal of Florida for the Fourth

District reversed, holding that because respondents did not challenge the arbitration provision itself, but instead claimed that the entire contract was void, the agreement to arbitrate was enforceable, and the question of the contract's legality should go to the arbitrator.

Respondents appealed, and the Florida Supreme Court reversed, reasoning that to enforce an agreement to arbitrate in a contract challenged as unlawful "'could breathe life into a contract that not only violates state law, but also is criminal in nature . . . .'" We granted certiorari.

* * *

Challenges to the validity of arbitration agreements "upon such grounds as exist at law or in equity for the revocation of any contract" can be divided into two types. One type challenges specifically the validity of the agreement to arbitrate. See, e.g., Southland Corp. v. Keating, 465 U.S. 1, 4–5, 104 S. Ct. 852, 79 L. Ed. 2d 1 (1984) (challenging the agreement to arbitrate as void under California law insofar as it purported to cover claims brought under the state Franchise Investment Law). The other challenges the contract as a whole, either on a ground that directly affects the entire agreement (*e.g.*, the agreement was fraudulently induced), or on the ground that the illegality of one of the contract's provisions renders the whole contract invalid.[1] Respondents' claim is of this second type. The crux of the complaint is that the contract as a whole (including its arbitration provision) is rendered invalid by the usurious finance charge.

In *Prima Paint Corp.* v. *Flood & Conklin Mfg. Co.,* 388 U.S. 395, 87 S. Ct. 1801, 18 L. Ed. 2d 1270 (1967), we addressed the question of who—court or arbitrator—decides these two types of challenges. The issue in the case was "whether a claim of fraud in the inducement of the entire contract is to be resolved by the federal court, or whether the matter is to be referred to the arbitrators. Guided by § 4 of the FAA,[2] we held that "if the claim is fraud in the inducement of the arbitration clause itself—an issue which goes to the making of the agreement to arbitrate—the federal court may proceed to adjudicate it. But the statutory language does not permit the federal court to consider claims of fraud in the inducement of the contract generally." We rejected the view that the question of "severability" was one of state law, so that if state law held the arbitration provision not to be severable a challenge to the contract as a whole would be decided by the court.

---

[1] The issue of the contract's validity is different from the issue whether any agreement between the alleged obligor and obligee was ever concluded. Our opinion today addresses only the former, and does not speak to the issue decided in the cases cited by respondents (and by the Florida Supreme Court), which hold that it is for courts to decide whether the alleged obligor ever signed the contract, Chastain v. Robinson-Humphrey Co., 957 F.2d 851 (CA11 1992), whether the signor lacked authority to commit the alleged principal, Sandvik AB v. Advent Int'l Corp., 220 F.3d 99 (CA3 2000); Sphere Drake Ins. Ltd. v. All American Ins. Co., 256 F.3d 587 (CA7 2001), and whether the signor lacked the mental capacity to assent, Spahr v. Secco, 330 F.3d 1266 (CA10 2003).

[2] In pertinent part, § 4 reads:

> "A party aggrieved by the alleged failure, neglect, or refusal of another to arbitrate under a written agreement for arbitration may petition any United States district court [with jurisdiction] . . . for an order directing that such arbitration proceed in a manner provided for in such agreement . . . . Upon being satisfied that the making of the agreement for arbitration or the failure to comply therewith is not in issue, the court shall make an order directing the parties to proceed to arbitration in accordance with the terms of the agreement . . . ."

Subsequently, in *Southland Corp.*, we held that the FAA "created a body of federal substantive law," which was "applicable in state and federal courts." We rejected the view that state law could bar enforcement of § 2, even in the context of state-law claims brought in state court.

Prima Paint and *Southland* answer the question presented here by establishing three propositions. First, as a matter of substantive federal arbitration law, an arbitration provision is severable from the remainder of the contract. Second, unless the challenge is to the arbitration clause itself, the issue of the contract's validity is considered by the arbitrator in the first instance. Third, this arbitration law applies in state as well as federal courts. The parties have not requested, and we do not undertake, reconsideration of those holdings. Applying them to this case, we conclude that because respondents challenge the Agreement, but not specifically its arbitration provisions, those provisions are enforceable apart from the remainder of the contract. The challenge should therefore be considered by an arbitrator, not a court.

In declining to apply *Prima Paint's* rule of severability, the Florida Supreme Court relied on the distinction between void and voidable contracts. "Florida public policy and contract law," it concluded, permit "no severable, or salvageable, parts of a contract found illegal and void under Florida law." *Prima Paint* makes this conclusion irrelevant. That case rejected application of state severability rules to the arbitration agreement *without discussing* whether the challenge at issue would have rendered the contract void or voidable. Indeed, the opinion expressly disclaimed any need to decide what state-law remedy was available (though Justice Black's dissent *asserted* that state law rendered the contract void). Likewise in *Southland*, which arose in state court, we did not ask whether the several challenges made there—fraud, misrepresentation, breach of contract, breach of fiduciary duty, and violation of the California Franchise Investment Law—would render the contract void or voidable. We simply rejected the proposition that the enforceability of the arbitration agreement turned on the state legislature's judgment concerning the forum for enforcement of the state-law cause of action. So also here, we cannot accept the Florida Supreme Court's conclusion that enforceability of the arbitration agreement should turn on "Florida public policy and contract law".

Respondents assert that *Prima Paint*'s rule of severability does not apply in state court. They argue that *Prima Paint* interpreted only §§ 3 and 4—two of the FAA's procedural provisions, which appear to apply by their terms only in federal court—but not § 2, the only provision that we have applied in state court. This does not accurately describe *Prima Paint*. Although § 4, in particular, had much to do with *Prima Paint*'s understanding of the rule of severability, this rule ultimately arises out of § 2, the FAA's substantive command that arbitration agreements be treated like all other contracts. The rule of severability establishes how this equal-footing guarantee for "a written [arbitration] provision" is to be implemented. Respondents' reading of *Prima Paint* as establishing nothing more than a federal-court rule of procedure also runs contrary to *Southland*'s understanding of that case. One of the bases for *Southland's* application of § 2 in state court was precisely *Prima Paint*'s "reliance for [its] holding on Congress' broad power to fashion substantive rules under the Commerce Clause." 465 U.S., at 11, 104 S. Ct. 852, 79 L. Ed. 2d 1; see also Prima Paint, *supra*, at 407, 87 S. Ct. 1801, 18 L. Ed. 2d 1270 (Black, J., dissenting) ("the Court here holds that the [FAA], as a matter of *federal substantive law* . . ." (emphasis added)). *Southland* itself refused to "believe Congress intended to limit the Arbitration Act to disputes subject only to *federal*-court jurisdiction."

Respondents point to the language of § 2, which renders "valid, irrevocable, and enforceable" "a written provision in" or "an agreement in writing to submit to arbitration an existing controversy arising out of" a "contract." Since, respondents argue, the only arbitration agreements to which § 2 applies are those involving a "contract," and since an agreement void *ab initio* under state law is not a "contract," there is no "written provision" in or "controversy arising out of" a "contract," to which § 2 can apply. This argument echoes Justice Black's dissent in *Prima Paint:* "Sections 2 and 3 of the Act assume the existence of a valid contract. They merely provide for enforcement where such a valid contract exists." 388 U.S., at 412–413, 87 S. Ct. 1801, 18 L. Ed. 2d 1270. We do not read "contract" so narrowly. The word appears four times in § 2. Its last appearance is in the final clause, which allows a challenge to an arbitration provision "upon such grounds as exist at law or in equity for the revocation of any *contract*." (Emphasis added.) There can be no doubt that "contract" as used this last time must include contracts that later prove to be void. Otherwise, the grounds for revocation would be limited to those that rendered a contract voidable—which would mean (implausibly) that an arbitration agreement could be challenged as voidable but not as void. Because the sentence's final use of "contract" so obviously includes putative contracts, we will not read the same word earlier in the same sentence to have a more narrow meaning.[3] We note that neither *Prima Paint* nor *Southland* lends support to respondents' reading; as we have discussed, neither case turned on whether the challenge at issue would render the contract voidable or void.

* * *

It is true, as respondents assert, that the *Prima Paint* rule permits a court to enforce an arbitration agreement in a contract that the arbitrator later finds to be void. But it is equally true that respondents' approach permits a court to deny effect to an arbitration provision in a contract that the court later finds to be perfectly enforceable. *Prima Paint* resolved this conundrum—and resolved it in favor of the separate enforceability of arbitration provisions. We reaffirm today that, regardless of whether the challenge is brought in federal or state court, a challenge to the validity of the contract as a whole, and not specifically to the arbitration clause, must go to the arbitrator.

The judgment of the Florida Supreme Court is reversed, and the case is remanded for further proceedings not inconsistent with this opinion.

---

[3] Our more natural reading is confirmed by the use of the word "contract" elsewhere in the United States Code to refer to putative agreements, regardless of whether they are legal. For instance, the Sherman Act, ch. 647, 26 Stat. 209, as amended, states that "every contract, combination . . ., or conspiracy, in restraint of trade [is] hereby declared to be illegal." 15 U.S.C. § 1. Under respondents' reading of "contract," a bewildering circularity would result: A contract illegal because it was in restraint of trade would not be a "contract" at all, and thus the statutory prohibition would not apply.

It is so ordered.

■ JUSTICE ALITO took no part in the consideration or decision of this case.

■ JUSTICE THOMAS, dissenting.

I remain of the view that the Federal Arbitration Act (FAA), 9 U.S.C. § 1 *et seq.*, does not apply to proceedings in state courts. Thus, in state-court proceedings, the FAA cannot be the basis for displacing a state law that prohibits enforcement of an arbitration clause contained in a contract that is unenforceable under state law. Accordingly, I would leave undisturbed the judgment of the Florida Supreme Court.

Buckeye said "The issue of the contract's validity is different from the issue of whether any agreement between the alleged obligor and obligee was ever concluded." Accordingly, post-*Buckeye* courts generally send to arbitrators questions about defenses to enforcement of contracts containing arbitration agreements, but (like the two *Uber* cases excerpted in Section 3.D.1), generally resolve in court questions about whether a particular party formed an arbitration agreement. *Prima Paint* and *Buckeye* also left a presumption that courts, rather than arbitrators, resolve contract defenses "directed to the arbitration clause itself,"[29] but the following case holds that presumption is rebuttable.

b. THE FURTHER SEVERABILITY OF THE DELEGATION CLAUSE

Rent-A-Center, W., Inc. v. Jackson

Supreme Court of the United States, 2010.
561 U.S. 63, 130 S.Ct. 2772, 177 L.Ed.2d 403.

■ JUSTICE SCALIA delivered the opinion of the Court.

We consider whether, under the Federal Arbitration Act (FAA or Act), 9 U.S.C. §§ 1–16, a district court may decide a claim that an arbitration agreement is unconscionable, where the agreement explicitly assigns that decision to the arbitrator.

On February 1, 2007, the respondent here, Antonio Jackson, filed an employment-discrimination suit under Rev. Stat. § 1977, 42 U.S.C. § 1981, against his former employer in the United States District Court for the District of Nevada. The defendant and petitioner here, Rent-A-Center, West, Inc., filed a motion under the FAA to dismiss or stay the proceedings, 9 U.S.C. § 3, and to compel arbitration, § 4. Rent-A-Center argued that the Mutual Agreement to Arbitrate Claims (Agreement), which Jackson signed on February 24, 2003, as a condition of his employment there, precluded Jackson from pursuing his claims in court. The Agreement provided for arbitration of all "past, present or future" disputes arising out of Jackson's employment with Rent-A-Center, including "claims for discrimination" and "claims for violation of any federal . . . law." It also provided that "[t]he Arbitrator, and not any federal, state, or local court or agency, shall have exclusive authority to resolve any dispute relating to the interpretation,

---

[29] Prima Paint, 388 U.S. at 402.

applicability, enforceability or formation of this Agreement including, but not limited to any claim that all or any part of this Agreement is void or voidable."

Jackson opposed the motion on the ground that "the arbitration agreement in question is clearly unenforceable in that it is unconscionable" under Nevada law. Rent-A-Center responded that Jackson's unconscionability claim was not properly before the court because Jackson had expressly agreed that the arbitrator would have exclusive authority to resolve any dispute about the enforceability of the Agreement. It also disputed the merits of Jackson's unconscionability claims.

The District Court granted Rent-A-Center's motion to dismiss the proceedings and to compel arbitration. The court found that the Agreement "'"clearly and unmistakenly *[sic]*"'" gives the arbitrator exclusive authority to decide whether the Agreement is enforceable, and, because Jackson challenged the validity of the Agreement *as a whole*, the issue was for the arbitrator. The court noted that even if it were to examine the merits of Jackson's unconscionability claims, it would have rejected the claim that the agreement to split arbitration fees was substantively unconscionable under Nevada law. It did not address Jackson's procedural or other substantive unconscionability arguments.

Without oral argument, a divided panel of the Court of Appeals for the Ninth Circuit reversed in part, affirmed in part, and remanded. The court reversed on the question of who (the court or arbitrator) had the authority to decide whether the Agreement is enforceable. It noted that "Jackson does not dispute that the language of the Agreement clearly assigns the arbitrability determination to the arbitrator," but held that where "a party challenges an arbitration agreement as unconscionable, and thus asserts that he could not meaningfully assent to the agreement, the threshold question of unconscionability is for the court." The Ninth Circuit affirmed the District Court's alternative conclusion that the fee-sharing provision was not substantively unconscionable and remanded for consideration of Jackson's other unconscionability arguments. Judge Hall dissented on the ground that "the question of the arbitration agreement's validity should have gone to the arbitrator, as the parties 'clearly and unmistakably provide[d]' in their agreement."

* * *

The FAA reflects the fundamental principle that arbitration is a matter of contract. Section 2, the "primary substantive provision of the Act," provides:

> "A written provision in . . . a contract evidencing a transaction involving commerce to settle by arbitration a controversy thereafter arising out of such contract . . . shall be valid, irrevocable, and enforceable, save upon such grounds as exist at law or in equity for the revocation of any contract." 9 U.S.C. § 2.

The FAA thereby places arbitration agreements on an equal footing with other contracts, *Buckeye*, and requires courts to enforce them according to their terms. Like other contracts, however, they may be invalidated by "generally applicable contract defenses, such as fraud, duress, or unconscionability." Doctor's Associates, Inc. v. Casarotto, 517 U.S. 681, 687, 116 S. Ct. 1652, 134 L. Ed. 2d 902 (1996).

The Act also establishes procedures by which federal courts implement § 2's substantive rule. Under § 3, a party may apply to a federal court for a stay of the trial of an action "upon any issue referable to arbitration under an agreement in writing for such arbitration." Under § 4, a party "aggrieved" by the failure of another party "to arbitrate under a written agreement for arbitration" may petition a federal court "for an order directing that such arbitration proceed in the manner provided for in such agreement." The court "shall" order arbitration "upon being satisfied that the making of the agreement for arbitration or the failure to comply therewith is not in issue."

The Agreement here contains multiple "written provision[s]" to "settle by arbitration a controversy," § 2. Two are relevant to our discussion. First, the section titled "Claims Covered By The Agreement" provides for arbitration of all "past, present or future" disputes arising out of Jackson's employment with Rent-A-Center. Second, the section titled "Arbitration Procedures" provides that "[t]he Arbitrator . . . shall have exclusive authority to resolve any dispute relating to the . . . enforceability . . . of this Agreement including, but not limited to any claim that all or any part of this Agreement is void or voidable." The current "controversy" between the parties is whether the Agreement is unconscionable. It is the second provision, which delegates resolution of that controversy to the arbitrator, that Rent-A-Center seeks to enforce. Adopting the terminology used by the parties, we will refer to it as the delegation provision.

The delegation provision is an agreement to arbitrate threshold issues concerning the arbitration agreement. We have recognized that parties can agree to arbitrate "gateway" questions of "arbitrability," such as whether the parties have agreed to arbitrate or whether their agreement covers a particular controversy. This line of cases merely reflects the principle that arbitration is a matter of contract.[1] An agreement to arbitrate a gateway issue is simply an additional, antecedent agreement the party seeking arbitration asks the federal court to enforce, and the FAA operates on this additional arbitration agreement

[1] There is one caveat. *First Options of Chicago, Inc.* v. *Kaplan*, 514 U.S. 938, 944, 115 S. Ct. 1920, 131 L. Ed. 2d 985 (1995), held that "[c]ourts should not assume that the parties agreed to arbitrate arbitrability unless there is 'clea[r] and unmistakabl[e]' evidence that they did so." The parties agree the heightened standard applies here. The District Court concluded the "Agreement to Arbitrate clearly and unmistakenly *[sic]* provides the arbitrator with the exclusive authority to decide whether the Agreement to Arbitrate is enforceable." The Ninth Circuit noted that Jackson did not dispute that the text of the Agreement was clear and unmistakable on this point. 581 F.3d 912, 917 (2009). He also does not dispute it here. What he argues now, however, is that it is not "clear and unmistakable" that his *agreement* to that text was valid, because of the unconscionability claims he raises. The dissent makes the same argument. See *post*, at 80–82, 177 L. Ed. 2d, at 418–419 (opinion of Stevens, J.). This mistakes the subject of the First Options "clear and unmistakable" requirement. It pertains to the parties' *manifestation of intent*, not the agreement's *validity*. As explained in *Howsam* v. *Dean Witter Reynolds, Inc.*, 537 U.S. 79, 83, 123 S. Ct. 588, 154 L. Ed. 2d 491 (2002), it is an "interpretive rule," based on an assumption about the parties' expectations. In "circumstance[s] where contracting parties would likely have expected a court to have decided the gateway matter," ibid., we assume that is what they agreed to. Thus, "[u]nless the parties clearly and unmistakably provide otherwise, the question of whether the parties agreed to arbitrate is to be decided by the court, not the arbitrator." AT&T Technologies, Inc. v. Communications Workers, 475 U.S. 643, 649, 106 S. Ct. 1415, 89 L. Ed. 2d 648 (1986). The validity of a written agreement to arbitrate (whether it is legally binding, as opposed to whether it was in fact agreed to—including, of course, whether it was void for unconscionability) is governed by § 2's provision that it shall be valid "save upon such grounds as exist at law or equity for the revocation of any contract." Those grounds do not include, of course, any requirement that its lack of unconscionability must be "clear and unmistakable." And they are not grounds that *First Options* added for agreements to arbitrate gateway issues; § 2 applies to all written agreements to arbitrate.

just as it does on any other. The additional agreement is valid under § 2 "save upon such grounds as exist at law or in equity for the revocation of any contract," and federal courts can enforce the agreement by staying federal litigation under § 3 and compelling arbitration under § 4. The question before us, then, is whether the delegation provision is valid under § 2.

There are two types of validity challenges under § 2: "One type challenges specifically the validity of the agreement to arbitrate," and "[t]he other challenges the contract as a whole, either on a ground that directly affects the entire agreement (*e.g.*, the agreement was fraudulently induced), or on the ground that the illegality of one of the contract's provisions renders the whole contract invalid." *Buckeye*. In a line of cases neither party has asked us to overrule, we held that only the first type of challenge is relevant to a court's determination whether the arbitration agreement at issue is enforceable.[2] See Prima Paint Corp.; Buckeye; Preston v. Ferrer, 552 U.S. 346, 353–354, 128 S. Ct. 978, 169 L. Ed. 2d 917 (2008). That is because § 2 states that a "written provision" "to settle by arbitration a controversy" is "valid, irrevocable, and enforceable" *without mention* of the validity of the contract in which it is contained. Thus, a party's challenge to another provision of the contract, or to the contract as a whole, does not prevent a court from enforcing a specific agreement to arbitrate. "[A]s a matter of substantive federal arbitration law, an arbitration provision is severable from the remainder of the contract." *Buckeye*.

* * *

Here, the "written provision . . . to settle by arbitration a controversy," 9 U.S.C. § 2, that Rent-A-Center asks us to enforce is the delegation provision—the provision that gave the arbitrator "exclusive authority to resolve any dispute relating to the . . . enforceability . . . of this Agreement". The "remainder of the contract," is the rest of the agreement to arbitrate claims arising out of Jackson's employment with Rent-A-Center. To be sure this case differs from *Prima Paint*, *Buckeye*, and *Preston*, in that the arbitration provisions sought to be enforced in those cases were contained in contracts unrelated to arbitration—contracts for consulting services, *Prima Paint*, check-cashing services, *Buckeye*, and "personal management" or "talent agent" services, *Preston*. In this case, the underlying contract is itself an arbitration agreement. But that makes no difference.[3] Application of the severability rule does not depend on the substance of the remainder of the contract. Section 2 operates on the specific "written provision" to "settle by arbitration a controversy" that the party seeks to enforce. Accordingly, unless Jackson challenged the delegation provision specifically, we must treat it as valid under § 2, and must enforce it under §§ 3 and 4, leaving any challenge to the validity of the Agreement as a whole for the arbitrator.

---

[2] The issue of the agreement's "validity" is different from the issue whether any agreement between the parties "was ever concluded," and, as in *Buckeye*, we address only the former.

[3] The dissent calls this a "breezy assertion," but it seems to us self-evident. When the dissent comes to discussing the point, it gives no logical reason why an agreement to arbitrate one controversy (an employment-discrimination claim) is not severable from an agreement to arbitrate a different controversy (enforceability). There is none. Since the dissent accepts that the invalidity of one provision *within an arbitration agreement* does not necessarily invalidate its other provisions, it cannot believe in some sort of magic bond between arbitration provisions that prevents them from being severed from each other. * * *

The District Court correctly concluded that Jackson challenged only the validity of the contract as a whole. * * *

As required to make out a claim of unconscionability under Nevada law [Jackson] contended that the Agreement was both procedurally and substantively unconscionable. It was procedurally unconscionable, he argued, because it "was imposed as a condition of employment and was non-negotiable." But we need not consider that claim because none of Jackson's substantive unconscionability challenges was specific to the delegation provision. First, he argued that the Agreement's coverage was one sided in that it required arbitration of claims an employee was likely to bring—contract, tort, discrimination, and statutory claims—but did not require arbitration of claims Rent-A-Center was likely to bring—intellectual property, unfair competition, and trade secrets claims. This one-sided-coverage argument clearly did not go to the validity of the delegation provision.

Jackson's other two substantive unconscionability arguments assailed arbitration procedures called for by the contract—the fee-splitting arrangement and the limitations on discovery—procedures that were to be used during arbitration under *both* the agreement to arbitrate employment-related disputes *and* the delegation provision. It may be that had Jackson challenged the delegation provision by arguing that these common procedures *as applied* to the delegation provision rendered *that provision* unconscionable, the challenge should have been considered by the court. To make such a claim based on the discovery procedures, Jackson would have had to argue that the limitation upon the number of depositions causes the arbitration of his claim that the Agreement is unenforceable to be unconscionable. That would be, of course, a much more difficult argument to sustain than the argument that the same limitation renders arbitration of his factbound employment-discrimination claim unconscionable. Likewise, the unfairness of the fee splitting arrangement may be more difficult to establish for the arbitration of enforceability than for arbitration of more complex and fact-related aspects of the alleged employment discrimination. Jackson, however, did not make any arguments specific to the delegation provision; he argued that the fee-sharing and discovery procedures rendered the *entire* Agreement invalid.

Jackson's appeal to the Ninth Circuit confirms that he did not contest the validity of the delegation provision in particular.

* * *

■ JUSTICE STEVENS, with whom JUSTICE GINSBURG, JUSTICE BREYER, and JUSTICE SOTOMAYOR join, dissenting.

Neither petitioner nor respondent has urged us to adopt the rule the Court does today: Even when a litigant has specifically challenged the validity of an agreement to arbitrate he must submit that challenge *to the arbitrator* unless he has lodged an objection to the particular line in the agreement that purports to assign such challenges to the arbitrator—the so-called "delegation clause."

The Court asserts that its holding flows logically from *Prima Paint*, in which the Court held that consideration of a contract revocation defense is generally a matter for the arbitrator, unless the defense is specifically directed at the arbitration clause. We have treated this holding as a severability rule: When a party challenges a contract, "but not specifically its arbitration provisions, those provisions are enforceable apart from the remainder of the contract." Buckeye Check Cashing, Inc. v. Cardegna. The Court's decision today goes beyond *Prima Paint*. Its breezy assertion that the subject matter of the contract at issue—in this case, an arbitration agreement and nothing more—"makes no difference," is simply wrong. This written arbitration agreement is but one part of a broader employment agreement between the parties, just as the arbitration clause in *Prima Paint* was but one part of a broader contract for services between those parties. Thus, that the subject matter of the agreement is exclusively arbitration makes *all* the difference in the *Prima Paint* analysis.

Under the Federal Arbitration Act (FAA), 9 U.S.C. §§ 1–16, parties generally have substantial leeway to define the terms and scope of their agreement to settle disputes in an arbitral forum. "[A]rbitration is," after all, "simply a matter of contract between the parties; it is a way to resolve those disputes—but only those disputes—that the parties have agreed to submit to arbitration." First Options of Chicago, Inc. v. Kaplan, 514 U.S. 938, 943, 115 S. Ct. 1920, 131 L. Ed. 2d 985 (1995). The FAA, therefore, envisions a limited role for courts asked to stay litigation and refer disputes to arbitration.

Certain issues—the kind that "contracting parties would likely have expected a court to have decided"—remain within the province of judicial review. Howsam v. Dean Witter Reynolds, Inc., 537 U.S. 79, 83, 123 S. Ct. 588, 154 L. Ed. 2d 491 (2002). These issues are "gateway matter[s]" because they are necessary antecedents to enforcement of an arbitration agreement; they raise questions the parties "are not likely to have thought that they had agreed that an arbitrator would" decide. *Howsam*. Quintessential gateway matters include "whether the parties have a valid arbitration agreement at all," "whether the parties are bound by a given arbitration clause," and "whether an arbitration clause in a concededly binding contract applies to a particular type of controversy." It would be bizarre to send these types of gateway matters to the arbitrator as a matter of course, because they raise a "'question of arbitrability.'"

* * *

Two different lines of cases bear on the issue of *who* decides a question of arbitrability respecting validity, such as whether an arbitration agreement is unconscionable. Although this issue, as a gateway matter, is typically for the court, we have explained that such an issue can be delegated to the arbitrator in some circumstances. When the parties have purportedly done so, courts must examine two distinct rules to decide whether the delegation is valid.

The first line of cases looks to the parties' intent. In *AT&T Technologies*, we stated that "question[s] of arbitrability" may be delegated to the arbitrator, so long as the delegation is clear and unmistakable. We reaffirmed this rule, and added some nuance, in *First Options*. Against the background presumption that questions of arbitrability go to the court, we stated that federal courts should "generally" apply "ordinary state-law principles that govern the formation of contracts" to assess "whether the parties agreed to arbitrate a certain matter (including arbitrability)." But, we added, a more rigorous standard applies when the inquiry is whether the parties have "agreed to arbitrate arbitrability": "Courts should not assume that the parties agreed to arbitrate arbitrability unless there is clear and unmistakable evidence that they did so." Justice Breyer's unanimous opinion for the Court described this standard as a type of "revers[e]" "presumption"[4]—one in favor of a judicial, rather than an arbitral, forum. * * *

The second line of cases bearing on who decides the validity of an arbitration agreement, as the Court explains, involves the *Prima Paint* rule. That rule recognizes two types of validity challenges. One type challenges the validity of the arbitration agreement itself, on a ground arising from an infirmity in that agreement. The other challenges the validity of the arbitration agreement tangentially—via a claim that the entire contract (of which the arbitration agreement is but a part) is invalid for some reason. Under *Prima Paint*, a challenge of the first type goes to the court; a challenge of the second type goes to the arbitrator. * * *

In sum, questions related to the validity of an arbitration agreement are usually matters for a court to resolve before it refers a dispute to arbitration. But questions of arbitrability may go to the arbitrator in two instances: (1) when the parties have demonstrated, clearly and unmistakably, that it is their intent to do so; or (2) when the validity of an arbitration agreement depends exclusively on the validity of the substantive contract of which it is a part.

We might have resolved this case by simply applying the *First Options* rule: Does the arbitration agreement at issue "clearly and unmistakably" evince petitioner's and respondent's intent to submit questions of arbitrability to the arbitrator?[6] The answer to that question is no. Respondent's claim that the arbitration agreement is unconscionable undermines any suggestion that he "clearly" and "unmistakably" assented to submit questions of arbitrability to the arbitrator. See Restatement (Second) of Contracts § 208, Comment *d* (1979) ("[G]ross inequality of bargaining power, together with terms unreasonably favorable to the stronger party, may confirm indications that the transaction involved elements of deception or compulsion, or may show that the weaker party had no meaningful choice, no real alternative, or did not in fact assent or appear to assent to the unfair terms"); American Airlines, Inc. v. Wolens, 513 U.S. 219, 249, 115 S. Ct. 817, 130 L. Ed. 2d 715 (1995) (O'Connor, J., concurring in judgment and dissenting in part) ("[A] determination that a contract is 'unconscionable' may in fact be a determination that one party did not intend to agree to the terms of the contract"). The fact that the agreement's "delegation" provision suggests assent is beside the point, because the gravamen of respondent's claim is that he never consented to the terms in his agreement.

In other words, when a party raises a good-faith validity challenge to the arbitration agreement itself, that issue must be resolved before a court can say that

---

[4] It is a "revers[e]" presumption because it is counter to the presumption we usually apply in favor of arbitration when the question concerns whether a particular dispute falls within the scope of a concededly binding arbitration agreement. First Options, 514 U.S., at 944–945, 115 S. Ct. 1920, 131 L. Ed. 2d 985.

[6] Respondent has challenged whether he "meaningfully agreed to the terms of the form Agreement to Arbitrate, which he contends is procedurally and substantively unconscionable." Even if *First Options* relates only to "manifestation of intent," as the Court states, whether there has been meaningful agreement surely bears some relation to whether one party has manifested intent to be bound to an agreement.

he clearly and unmistakably intended to *arbitrate* that very validity question. This case well illustrates the point: If respondent's unconscionability claim is correct—*i.e.*, if the terms of the agreement are so one-sided and the process of its making so unfair—it would contravene the existence of clear and unmistakable assent to arbitrate the very question petitioner now seeks to arbitrate. Accordingly, it is necessary for the court to resolve the merits of respondent's unconscionability claim in order to decide whether the parties have a valid arbitration agreement under § 2. Otherwise, that section's preservation of revocation issues for the Court would be meaningless.

* * *

Prima Paint and its progeny allow a court to pluck from a potentially invalid *contract* a potentially valid *arbitration agreement*. Today the Court adds a new layer of severability—something akin to Russian nesting dolls—into the mix: Courts may now pluck from a potentially invalid *arbitration agreement* even narrower provisions that refer particular arbitrability disputes to an arbitrator. I do not think an agreement to arbitrate can ever manifest a clear and unmistakable intent to arbitrate its own validity. But even assuming otherwise, I certainly would not hold that the *Prima Paint* rule extends this far.

* * *

The Court, however, reads the delegation clause as a distinct mini-arbitration agreement divisible from the contract in which it resides—which just so happens also to be an arbitration agreement. Although the Court simply declares that it "makes no difference" that the underlying subject matter of the agreement is itself an arbitration agreement that proposition does not follow from—rather it is at odds with—*Prima Paint*'s severability rule.

* * *

Before today, however, if respondent instead raised a challenge specific to "the validity of the agreement to arbitrate"—for example, that the agreement to arbitrate was void under state law—the challenge would have gone to the court. That is what *Buckeye* says. But the Court now declares that *Prima Paint*'s pleading rule requires more: A party must lodge a challenge with even greater specificity than what would have satisfied the *Prima Paint* Court. A claim that an *entire* arbitration agreement is invalid will not go to the court unless the party challenges the *particular sentences* that delegate such claims to the arbitrator, on some contract ground that is particular and unique to those sentences.

It would seem the Court reads *Prima Paint* to require, as a matter of course, infinite layers of severability: We must always pluck from an arbitration agreement the specific delegation mechanism that would—but for present judicial review—commend the matter to arbitration, even if this delegation clause is but one sentence within one paragraph within a standalone agreement. And, most importantly, the party must identify this one sentence and lodge a specific challenge to its validity. Otherwise, he will be bound to pursue his validity claim in arbitration.

Even if limited to separately executed arbitration agreements, however, such an infinite severability rule is divorced from the underlying rationale of *Prima Paint*. The notion that a party may be bound by an arbitration clause in a contract that is nevertheless invalid may be difficult for any lawyer—or any person—to accept, but this is the law of *Prima Paint*. It reflects a judgment that the "national policy favoring arbitration," outweighs the interest in preserving a judicial forum for questions of arbitrability—*but only when questions of arbitrability are bound up in an underlying dispute*. When the two are so bound up, there is actually no gateway matter at all: The question "Who decides" is the entire ball game. Were a court to decide the fraudulent inducement question in *Prima Paint*, in order to decide the antecedent question of the validity of the included arbitration agreement, then it would also, necessarily, decide the merits of the underlying dispute. Same, too, for the question of illegality in *Buckeye;* on its way to deciding the arbitration agreement's validity, the court would have to decide whether the contract was illegal, and in so doing, it would decide the merits of the entire dispute.

In this case, however, resolution of the unconscionability question will have no bearing on the merits of the underlying employment dispute. It will only, as a preliminary matter, resolve who should decide the merits of that dispute. Resolution of the unconscionability question will, however, decide whether the arbitration agreement *itself* is "valid" under "such grounds as exist at law or in equity for the revocation of any contract." 9 U.S.C. § 2. As *Prima Paint* recognizes, the FAA commits those gateway matters, specific to the arbitration agreement, to the court. Indeed, it is clear that the present controversy over whether the arbitration agreement is unconscionable is *itself severable* from the merits of the underlying dispute, which involves a claim of employment discrimination. This is true for all gateway matters, and for this reason *Prima Paint* has no application in this case. * * *

David Horton, *Arbitration About Arbitration*

70 Stan. L. Rev. 363, 394–99, 440–41 (2018).

In 2010, the Court decided *Rent-A-Center, West, Inc. v. Jackson*, which transformed arbitration about arbitration. Rent-A-Center, a nationwide rent-to-own company, required its at-will workers to sign a freestanding "Mutual Agreement to Arbitrate Claims." In the middle of a paragraph entitled "Arbitration Procedures" was a clause that gave the arbitrator the "exclusive authority to resolve . . . any claim that all or any part of this agreement is void or voidable." Antonio Jackson, a former employee, sued the company for racial discrimination and retaliation. When Rent-A-Center moved to compel arbitration, Jackson countered by arguing that "the arbitration agreement as a whole" was unconscionable because it forced him to pay a portion of the arbitrator's fees and restricted discovery. The Ninth Circuit held that Jackson could pursue his unconscionability theory in federal district court, rather than arbitration, because any arbitration clause that might be unconscionable cannot pass the "clear and unmistakable" test. According to the appellate panel, this was because an allegation of unconscionability translates into a claim that a party "could not meaningfully assent to the agreement."

The Supreme Court offered a fundamentally different take. Justice Scalia, writing for the Court, began by refuting the Ninth Circuit's bright-line rule that drafters cannot task the arbitrator with deciding whether the agreement to arbitrate the merits is unconscionable. According to Justice Scalia, the *First Options* "clear and unmistakable" rule "pertains to the parties' manifestation of intent"—not their actual assent—and is thus satisfied by mere written words on a page. Thus, he concluded that the Mutual Agreement to Arbitrate Claims contained a presumptively valid delegation clause.

Justice Scalia then addressed Jackson's unconscionability challenge by fusing the Court's separability and arbitrating arbitrability case law. Section 2 of the FAA states in part that "[a] written provision . . . to settle by arbitration a controversy . . . shall be valid, irrevocable, and enforceable." Justice Scalia opined that a delegation clause is its own "written [arbitration] provision" within the meaning of the statute:

> The delegation provision is an agreement to arbitrate threshold issues concerning the arbitration agreement. . . . An agreement to arbitrate a gateway issue is simply an additional, antecedent agreement the party seeking arbitration asks the federal court to enforce, and the FAA operates on this additional arbitration agreement just as it does on any other.

In turn, by deeming delegation clauses to be self-contained arbitration clauses, Justice Scalia brought the separability doctrine into play. *Prima Paint* decreed that a challenge to the container contract (but not the arbitration provision) is a matter to be resolved in arbitration. In *Rent-A-Center*, Justice Scalia extended this principle and held that if an arbitration agreement includes a delegation clause, a challenge to the validity of the arbitration agreement (but not the delegation clause specifically) is also for the arbitrator. As a result, a plaintiff cannot ask a judge to review the fairness of the agreement to arbitrate the merits of the dispute unless she first proves that the delegation clause is invalid.

To see why this is a formidable hurdle for plaintiffs, consider how Justice Scalia disposed of Jackson's efforts to avoid arbitration. At the district court, Jackson had argued that the Mutual Agreement to Arbitrate Claims was unconscionable because it limited discovery in his fact-sensitive civil rights lawsuit and called for him to pay a portion of the arbitrator's fees. But he had not offered any reason that the delegation clause itself was invalid. Thus, the Court concluded that Jackson had conceded the relevant issue and held that he must arbitrate the question whether the arbitration clause was unconscionable. Moreover, Justice Scalia took pains to point out that even if Jackson had contested the enforceability of the delegation clause, he likely would have lost. As Justice Scalia noted, the aspects of the arbitration clause that Jackson claimed made it unfair for him to arbitrate his substantive claim—the fee-sharing provision and discovery limitations—had little bearing on whether it would be unfair for him to arbitrate the discrete question whether the arbitration clause was unconscionable.

Lower courts interpreted *Rent-A-Center* broadly. For one, they understood the opinion to establish a kind of "super-separability" rubric in which every contract that contains a delegation clause breaks down into "three agreements[,] each nested inside the other": (1) a delegation clause, (2) an arbitration clause, and (3) the container contract. In addition, they took to extremes the idea that plaintiffs needed to argue that the delegation provision itself is unconscionable. If a plaintiff failed to mention the magic words "delegation clause" in her pleadings, she—like Jackson in *Rent-A-Center*—would be forced to challenging the fairness of the arbitral process in arbitration itself.

Then, on the heels of *Rent-A-Center*, the Supreme Court decided a rash of cases about the FAA and class actions that had the collateral consequence of further insulating delegation clauses. For example, in *AT&T Mobility LLC v. Concepcion*, the Court held that the statute preempts a California common law doctrine that deemed most class arbitration waivers in adhesion contracts to be unconscionable. Although *Concepcion*'s holding remains contested, some courts read the opinion as signaling that "any general state-law contract defense, based in unconscionability or otherwise, that has a disproportionate effect on arbitration is displaced by the FAA."

Delegation clauses rode the wake of these decisions. Recall that some judges refused to compel arbitration of unconscionability challenges on the ground that as "a repeat player, the arbitrator has a unique self-interest in deciding that a dispute is arbitrable." Nevertheless, after *Concepcion*, the same courts were constrained to find that this theory is preempted by the FAA because it "discriminates against arbitration, putting agreements to arbitrate on a lesser footing than agreements to select any judicial forum for dispute resolution." Thus, they uniformly "rejected the argument, however practical it may be, that an arbitrator will be unable to determine the question of arbitrability because he or she may potentially be driven by an ulterior interest in keeping the case in arbitration to generate fees."

* * * For decades, courts applied closer scrutiny to agreements to arbitrate substantive arbitrability than they did to agreements to arbitrate the merits. Yet *Rent-A-Center* seemed to obliterate that distinction by declaring that delegation clauses qualify for the same protections under federal law as arbitration provisions. As this Article: explains next, that view is flawed.

* * *

When Congress passed the FAA, it established a price of admission into the arbitral forum: convincing a court that the parties had entered into a valid agreement to arbitrate that encompassed the plaintiff's allegations. But in rising numbers, companies are attempting to privatize this gatekeeping function. The Supreme Court has encouraged this movement by insisting that delegation clauses are independent arbitration provisions.

But arbitration about arbitration has never been fungible with arbitration about the merits. As a result, delegation clauses should not be seen as fully functional arbitration clauses entitled to all the privileges of the FAA. Instead, they ought to be treated like the weaker cousins of agreements to arbitrate the merits:

terms that are presumptively valid but also laden with commonsense exceptions. In turn, this shift would allow judges to maintain the legitimacy of alternative dispute resolution.

QUESTIONS TO REVIEW AND SYNTHESIZE

1. When an arbitration agreement has a delegation clause similar to the delegation clause in *Rent-A-Center v. Jackson*, what does that Supreme Court decision require a party to allege to lead a court decide which allegations of unconscionability?
2. What are the main disagreements between the Court's *Rent-A-Center v. Jackson* opinion and the dissent?

c. DELEGATION AND UNCONSCIONABILITY AFTER *RENT-A-CENTER V. JACKSON*

Since *Rent-A-Center*, many courts have grappled with delegation clauses. A few fairly representative cases follow.

Bowles v. OneMain Financial Group, L.L.C.

United States Court of Appeals, Fifth Circuit, 2019.
927 F.3d 878.

■ E. GRADY JOLLY, CIRCUIT JUDGE:

Cathy Bowles appeals the district court's order compelling the arbitration of her federal age discrimination suit against OneMain Financial. Bowles objected to arbitration on the grounds that a valid arbitration agreement was never formed between her and OneMain for two reasons: first, there was no meeting of the minds and, second, the circumstances surrounding the arbitration agreement's formation render it procedurally unconscionable. Although the district court correctly rejected Bowles's meeting of the minds argument, it erroneously referred her procedural unconscionability[1] challenge to the arbitrator. Because procedural unconscionability goes to contract formation under Mississippi law, the district court should have ruled on this objection. Accordingly, we REVERSE and VACATE the district court's order and REMAND to the district court to decide the merits of Bowles's procedural unconscionability claim.

---

[1] We recently set out the difference between procedural and substantive unconscionability under Mississippi law:

> Under substantive unconscionability, we look within the four corners of an agreement in order to discover any abuses relating to the specific terms which violate the expectations of, or cause gross disparity between, the contracting parties. Procedural unconscionability may be proved by showing a lack of knowledge, lack of voluntariness, inconspicuous print, the use of complex legalistic language, disparity in sophistication or bargaining power of the parties and/or a lack of opportunity to study the contract and inquire about the contract terms.

Begole v. N. Miss. Med. Ctr., Inc., 761 F. App'x 248, 251 (5th Cir. 2019) (internal citations and quotation marks omitted). Neither party disputes that Bowles's objection is to procedural rather than substantive unconscionability. Furthermore, by using the term "procedural unconscionability" and grounding her objection in disparate bargaining power, her lack of a meaningful opportunity to bargain, and fraud in procuring her assent, we are convinced that Bowles's objection is indeed to procedural unconscionability.

I.

Bowles had worked for OneMain Financial Group and its predecessors since 1998. Over that period she had agreed several times through employment contracts and acknowledgments of employee handbooks to refer all employment disputes to arbitration. In 2016, Bowles was again required to review and acknowledge OneMain's Employee Dispute Resolution Program/Agreement ("Arbitration Agreement"). This Arbitration Agreement provides that any employment-related dispute will be referred to arbitration in accordance with the rules and procedures of the American Arbitration Association. In addition, the Arbitration Agreement contained a delegation clause, which delegated to the arbitrator as follows: "any legal dispute . . . arising out of, relating to, or concerning the validity, enforceability or breach of this Agreement, shall be resolved by final and binding arbitration." On November 15, 2016, Bowles viewed the Arbitration Agreement[2] and electronically signed a certificate that reads: "I hereby certify that I have carefully read the Employment Dispute Resolution Program/Agreement within and that I understand and agree to its terms."

In October 2017, OneMain terminated Bowles for allegedly inappropriate interactions with employees under her supervision. Bowles filed an unsuccessful administrative complaint with the EEOC. She next filed suit in federal court alleging that her termination violated the Age Discrimination in Employment Act and Title VII of the Civil Rights Act of 1964. In response, OneMain moved the district court, under the Federal Arbitration Act, to compel Bowles to arbitrate her claims pursuant to the 2016 Arbitration Agreement.

Bowles objected to OneMain's motion to compel by challenging the formation of the Arbitration Agreement itself on two grounds. First, she argued that there was no "meeting of the minds" because she did not understand that she was agreeing to a binding arbitration agreement and therefore there was not the mutual assent necessary for contract formation under Mississippi law. Second, she argued that the Agreement was procedurally unconscionable because her assent was obtained through misrepresentation, she never had a meaningful opportunity to bargain, and there was a gross disparity in the parties' bargaining power.

The district court granted OneMain's motion to compel and dismissed the case with prejudice. * * *

* * *

* * * To determine whether the parties entered a valid arbitration agreement, "courts generally . . . should apply ordinary state-law principles that govern the formation of contracts." First Options of Chi., Inc. v. Kaplan, 514 U.S. 938, 944, 115 S.Ct. 1920, 131 L.Ed.2d 985 (1995). * * *

Furthermore, courts must follow a two-step analysis to determine whether a claim must be arbitrated. "At step one, the court must determine whether the parties entered into *any arbitration agreement at all*." Lloyd's Syndicate 457 v. FloaTEC, L.L.C., 921 F.3d 508, 514 (5th Cir. 2019). At step two, "we engage in a 'limited' inquiry: '[W]hether the [parties'] agreement contains a valid delegation

[2] Before signing, the software required Bowles to open the Arbitration Agreement.

clause.'" If the agreement contains such a delegation clause, "a motion to compel arbitration should be granted in almost all cases."

Our concern in this appeal relates only to step one. Courts may not refer the step one inquiry—whether an arbitration agreement was formed in the first place—to the arbitrator. See Lloyd's Syndicate, 457, 921 F.3d at 514 ("The first step is a question of contract formation only—did the parties form a valid agreement to arbitrate some set of claims. This inquiry is for the court."); Will-Drill Res., Inc. v. Samson Res. Co., 352 F.3d 211, 218 (5th Cir. 2003) ("Where the very existence of any [arbitration] agreement is disputed, it is for the courts to decide at the outset whether an agreement was reached."); see also Begole, 761 F. App'x at 251 ("[W]here a party challenges the validity of the agreement to arbitrate in particular, the district court must weigh in on whether the specific decision to agree to arbitrate was unconscionable.").

* * *

Bowles first argues that there was no meeting of the minds because she did not intend to agree to arbitrate employment-related disputes. The district court correctly found that this objection is a challenge to contract formation under Mississippi law and examined the merits of Bowles's meeting of the minds argument. We can find no error in the district court's ruling on the merits of Bowles's meeting of the minds objection. The court correctly found that the electronic communications transmitting the Arbitration Agreement clearly identified an arbitration agreement as the subject of the communications. Furthermore, Bowles was given the opportunity to read the Agreement and certified that she had "carefully read the Employment Dispute Resolution Program/Agreement within and that I understand and agree to its terms." Bowles cannot deny that she thus agreed to the Arbitration Agreement. Instead, she argues that she thought she was "simply acknowledging receipt of another policy or directive" and did not understand she was agreeing to arbitrate her employment disputes. The district court correctly held that such a unilateral lack of diligence does not preclude contract formation under Mississippi law. See Hicks v. Bridges, 580 So. 2d 743, 746 (Miss. 1991) ("A person cannot avoid a signed, written contract on the grounds that he did not read it . . . . To permit a party when sued on a written contract to admit that he signed it but to deny that it expresses the agreement or to allow him to admit that he signed it but did not read it or know its stipulations would absolutely destroy the value of all contracts.") The district court thus made no error in concluding that there was the meeting of the minds between Bowles and OneMain necessary for contract formation, and this portion of the district court's ruling is affirmed.

B.

We turn now to the district court's holding that Bowles's procedural unconscionability objection must be decided by the arbitrator. Although the district court considered Bowles's meeting of the minds objection on the merits, it held that her procedural unconscionability argument was for the arbitrator to resolve. Accordingly, the dispositive question here is whether, under Mississippi law,

Bowles's procedural unconscionability objection is a challenge to contract enforcement, as the district court reasoned, or contract formation.

We think the district court plainly erred. In Mississippi, it is pellucid that "[p]rocedural unconscionability goes to the formation of the contract." West, 891 So. 2d at 213 (citing East Ford, Inc., 826 So. 2d at 714). Because Bowles's procedural unconscionability objection challenges the formation of the Arbitration Agreement itself, the district court had the duty to resolve this challenge.[5] See Lloyd's Syndicate, 457, 921 F.3d at 514; Banc One Acceptance Corp. v. Hill, 367 F.3d 426, 431 (5th Cir. 2004) (district court applying Mississippi law had the "authority and the responsibility to adjudicate whether the arbitration agreement . . . was procedurally unconscionable"). The district court thus erred in dismissing the case without adjudicating Bowles's procedural unconscionability challenge to the Arbitration Agreement's formation. We therefore remand for the district court to decide the merits of Bowles's procedural unconscionability objection. We have nothing to say about the merits of that question.

* * *

QUESTIONS TO REVIEW AND SYNTHESIZE

1. In *Bowles* (excerpted above), the arbitration agreement's delegation clause said: "any legal dispute . . . arising out of, relating to, or concerning the validity, enforceability or breach of this Agreement, shall be resolved by final and binding arbitration." So why did the Fifth Circuit rule that the district court, rather than the arbitrator, should address Bowles' argument that the arbitration agreement "was procedurally unconscionable because her assent was obtained through misrepresentation, she never had a meaningful opportunity to bargain, and there was a gross disparity in the parties' bargaining power"?
2. How does what *Bowles* describes as a "pellucid" (clear) rule of Mississippi law—"[p]rocedural unconscionability goes to the formation of the contract"—relate to footnote 6 of Justice Stevens' *Rent-A-Center* dissent?

State ex rel. Pinkerton v. Fahnestock

Supreme Court of Missouri, en banc., 2017.
531 S.W.3d 36, 349 Ed. Law Rep. 827.

■ PATRICIA BRECKENRIDGE, JUDGE

Steven Pinkerton seeks a writ * * * requiring the circuit court to overrule the motion to compel arbitration filed by Aviation Institute of Maintenance (the school). * * *

---

[5] Although "generally, allegations of unconscionability[ ] related to the formation of the contract as a whole, are for the arbitrator . . . where a party challenges the validity of the agreement to arbitrate in particular, the district court must weigh in on whether the specific decision to agree to arbitrate was unconscionable." Begole, 761 F. App'x at 251 (citing Prima Paint Corp. v. Flood & Conklin Mfg. Co., 388 U.S. 395, 403–04, 87 S.Ct. 1801, 18 L.Ed.2d 1270 (1967)). Here, Bowles's procedural unconscionability "line of attack, aim[s] at the arbitration [agreement] alone." Banc One Acceptance Corp., 367 F.3d at 431.

This Court * * * now holds the incorporation of the American Arbitration Association (AAA) rules into the arbitration agreement provided clear and unmistakable evidence the parties intended to delegate threshold issues of arbitrability to the arbitrator. Mr. Pinkerton's only specific challenge to the delegation provision—that it would be unconscionable to delegate a determination of unconscionability to a person with a direct financial interest in the outcome—was without merit, and he did not otherwise specifically challenge the validity or enforceability of the delegation provision. Accordingly, the circuit court properly sustained the school's motion to compel arbitration, stayed the case, and ordered the parties to arbitrate threshold issues of arbitrability. * * *

Factual and Procedural Background

In 2009, Mr. Pinkerton * * * received a tour of the school and * * * he returned to the school to sign the two-page enrollment agreement for the aviation maintenance technical engineer program.

The enrollment agreement listed information about the program's duration, graduation requirements, tuition and fees, scheduling, and its policies regarding cancellation, termination, withdrawal, and refunds. The enrollment agreement also included an arbitration agreement. The arbitration agreement was about three-fourths from the top of the enrollment agreement's first page. The heading "Arbitration Agreement" was in bold face type, and the terms of the arbitration agreement were in the same type size as the remainder of the enrollment agreement. The arbitration agreement provided:

> I agree that any controversy, claim or dispute of any sort arising out of or relating to matters including, but not limited to: student admission, enrollment, financial obligations and status as a student, which cannot be first resolved by way of applicable internal dispute resolution practices and procedures, shall be submitted for arbitration, to be administered by the American Arbitration Association located within Virginia Beach, Virginia, in accordance with its commercial arbitration rules. All fees and expenses of arbitration shall be shared equally and any award rendered in favor of a student will be limited to the total amount paid to the School by the student. Any award or determination rendered by the arbitrator(s) shall be final and entered as a judgment by a court of competent jurisdiction.

Mr. Pinkerton did not receive a copy of the AAA commercial rules.

Rule R-7 of the commercial rules defined the scope of the arbitrator's "jurisdiction." It read, in relevant part:

> The arbitrator shall have the power to rule on his or her own jurisdiction, including any objections with respect to the existence, scope, or validity of the arbitration agreement or to the arbitrability of any claim or counterclaim.

Mr. Pinkerton signed the enrollment agreement and received a copy. An admissions representative and another school official also signed the agreement.

* * *

In 2011, Mr. Pinkerton graduated from the school as the valedictorian of the night program. Having fulfilled the graduation requirements, he received a certificate of aviation maintenance, which entitled him to take the federal aviation administration examinations to become an airline mechanic. He took both required examinations and received his temporary airman certificate from the federal aviation administration in 2012. Despite having obtained his certification, Mr. Pinkerton alleges he cannot find employment in the aviation field.

In 2014, Mr. Pinkerton filed a lawsuit * * * alleging the school engaged in fraud, misrepresentation, and deception related to the school's graduation and job placement rates, starting salaries, and the costs and benefits of its educational programs. The lawsuit included claims for violations of the Missouri Merchandising Practices Act, fraudulent misrepresentation, negligent misrepresentation, money had and received, and unjust enrichment.

The school moved to dismiss, or in the alternative, to compel arbitration and stay the proceedings, citing the arbitration agreement in the enrollment agreement requiring Mr. Pinkerton to arbitrate "any controversy, claim or dispute." The school further contended the arbitration agreement delegated threshold arbitrability disputes, such as whether an arbitration clause is enforceable or its applicability to the dispute at issue, to the arbitrator by incorporating by reference the AAA's jurisdictional rule into the arbitration agreement. The school requested the circuit court enforce this delegation provision if Mr. Pinkerton challenged the arbitration agreement. * * *

After conducting a hearing on the matter, the circuit court sustained the school's motion to compel arbitration. * * *

* * *

The Delegation Provision

The circuit court determined the arbitration agreement contained an enforceable delegation provision delegating issues of arbitrability to the arbitrator. Mr. Pinkerton contends his signature on the enrollment agreement was not evidence he agreed to delegate threshold issues of arbitrability to the arbitrator because the delegation provision was not included as part of the arbitration agreement but was instead incorporated by reference to the AAA commercial rules. Mr. Pinkerton argues that incorporating a delegation provision by reference does not meet the "clear and unmistakable" standard required to show the parties intended an arbitrator to decide issues of arbitrability.

Generally, any silence or ambiguity "concerning the scope of arbitrable issues should be resolved in favor of arbitration." Mitsubishi Motors Corp. v. Soler Chrysler-Plymouth, Inc., 473 U.S. 614, 626, 105 S.Ct. 3346, 87 L.Ed.2d 444 (1985). * * *

This presumption of arbitrability, however, is reversed when considering whether a court or an arbitrator should decide threshold questions of arbitrability. * * * Disputes over the formation of the parties' arbitration agreement and its enforceability or applicability to the dispute at issue have been considered threshold issues of arbitrability. When considering whether parties have intended to delegate threshold questions of arbitrability to an arbitrator, "[c]ourts should not assume that the parties agreed to arbitrate arbitrability unless there is clea[r] and unmistakabl[e] evidence that they did so." Rent-A-Ctr., W., Inc. v. Jackson, 561 U.S. 63, 69 n.1, 130 S.Ct. 2772, 177 L.Ed.2d 403 (2010). * * *

* * *

Mr. Pinkerton interprets the "clear and unmistakable" standard to prohibit the delegation provision from being incorporated by reference into an arbitration agreement. He contends that no clear and unmistakable evidence exists of the parties' mutual assent to the delegation provision unless the delegation provision is expressly written into an arbitration agreement. * * *

* * *

Missouri [law] recognizes that "matters incorporated into a contract by reference are as much a part of the contract as if they had been set out in the contract in haec verba." Generally, "[t]erms not explicit in a contract may be incorporated into the contract by reference" so long as the "intent to incorporate [is] clear." "To incorporate terms from another document, the contract must make [ ] clear reference to the document and describe[ ] it in such terms that its identity may be ascertained beyond a doubt." Parties may, therefore, "incorporate contractual terms by reference to a separate, noncontemporaneous document, including a separate agreement to which they are not parties, including a separate document which is unsigned." There is no requirement that an incorporated document be attached to the contract or provided to the parties prior to the execution of the contract.

Here, the parties' arbitration agreement specifically references the AAA's commercial arbitration rules. At the time Mr. Pinkerton signed the enrollment agreement, the AAA's "Commercial Arbitration Rules with Supplementary Procedures for Consumer-Related Disputes" governed all consumer arbitration disputes. The reference to the AAA's commercial rules in the arbitration agreement was not a mere passing reference to these rules; instead, it was a clear reference to an identifiable, ascertainable set of rules. Such a reference establishes the parties' intent to incorporate the AAA commercial arbitration rules into the enrollment agreement.

This finding is consistent with most federal circuit courts, which have concluded arbitration agreements containing similar language were sufficient to incorporate by reference the delegation provision in the AAA rules. * * *

* * *

The dissenting opinion asserts whether Mr. Pinkerton intended to incorporate the AAA rules is a factual question that should be put to the parties' proof. But for purposes of contract interpretation, the intent of the parties is a question of law to be determined from the four corners of the contract. It is only when an ambiguity arises and cannot be resolved within the four corners of the contract that "the parties' intent can be determined by use of parol evidence." Only then does the parties' intent become "a factual issue to be resolved by the finder of fact."

* * *

* * * [N]one of the cases [cited by the dissent] considering the sophistication of the parties addresses arbitration agreements, and each case presents an exception to general principles of contract law. The United States Supreme Court has held arbitration can be limited only by application of principles of general contract law, AT&T Mobility LLC v. Concepcion, 563 U.S. 333, 339, 131 S.Ct. 1740, 179 L.Ed.2d 742 (2011), so this Court cannot make a rule specifically applicable to arbitration delegation clauses.

The dissenting opinion also relies on several federal district court cases—all from the Ninth Circuit—and a few state cases. This is because Missouri courts have never considered the sophistication of the contractual parties in determining the parties' intent with respect to arbitration agreements. Rather, Missouri courts apply the longstanding principle that a party's failure to read or understand the terms of a contract is not a defense to enforcement of those terms. Missouri contract law, therefore, generally does not support differential treatment for consumers for purposes of contract interpretation.

Finally, were this Court to adopt the dissenting opinion's approach, its impact would extend beyond interpretation of arbitration agreements. Arbitration agreements are placed "on an equal footing with other contracts, and courts will examine arbitration agreements in the same light as they would examine any contractual agreement." Triarch Indus., Inc. v. Crabtree, 158 S.W.3d 772, 776 (Mo. banc 2005). Therefore, this Court would have to consider the parties' sophistication in determining intent in all contracts.

Applying Missouri's general contract principles to this case, Mr. Pinkerton agreed the AAA commercial arbitration rules, which include a delegation provision, would govern arbitration disputes. By clearly referencing the AAA commercial arbitration rules, the parties expressed their intent to arbitrate any dispute under these rules, including the AAA's "jurisdiction" rule providing that the "[a]rbitrator shall have the power to rule on his or her own jurisdiction, including any objections with respect to the existence, scope or validity of the arbitration agreement." Accordingly, the delegation provision clearly and unmistakably evidences the parties' intent to delegate threshold issues of arbitrability to the arbitrator.

Enforceability of the Delegation Provision

Upon finding the parties clearly and unmistakably intended to delegate threshold issues to the arbitrator, the circuit court concluded the delegation provision was enforceable and compelled arbitration. Mr. Pinkerton asserts the circuit court erroneously compelled arbitration because state and federal arbitration law require the circuit court to adjudicate the threshold question of whether an arbitration agreement was formed. But such an argument ignores the nature of his challenges to the arbitration agreement, the severability of the delegation provision, and his failure to specifically challenge the enforceability of such provision.

First, Mr. Pinkerton contends threshold issues of the formation of an arbitration agreement cannot be delegated to an arbitrator. Under the Federal Arbitration Act (FAA), * * * a court must be satisfied that the parties have "concluded" or formed an arbitration agreement before the court may order arbitration to proceed according to the terms of the agreement. Buckeye Check Cashing, Inc. v. Cardegna, 546 U.S. 440, 444 n.1, 126 S.Ct. 1204, 163 L.Ed.2d 1038 (2006). * * *

Nevertheless, Mr. Pinkerton does not challenge whether the arbitration agreement was formed or concluded. Instead, Mr. Pinkerton challenges the conscionability of such arbitration agreement. While this Court has held unconscionability is a state law defense to contract formation, *see Brewer v. Mo. Title Loans*, 364 S.W.3d 486, 493 (Mo. banc 2012), conscionability is not an essential element of contract formation. As recognized by the Supreme Court, unconscionability is a "generally applicable contract defense[ ]" like fraud and duress. Rent-A-Ctr., 561 U.S. at 68, 130 S.Ct. 2772. As such, while unconscionability is a defense to contract formation and, therefore, a contract's validity and enforceability, Eaton v. CMH Homes, Inc., 461 S.W.3d 426, 432 (Mo. banc 2015), it is not an issue of whether a contract has ever been "concluded."[9] See Buckeye, 546 U.S. at 444 n.1, 126 S.Ct. 1204.

Mr. Pinkerton's mischaracterization of the issue of unconscionability as a formation issue rather than enforceability has no impact on the resolution of this case, however, because both issues of formation and enforceability of arbitration clauses can be delegated to an arbitrator. Mr. Pinkerton does not cite any case law prohibiting issues of formation from being delegated to the arbitrator. Mr. Pinkerton relies on *Baker v. Bristol Care, Inc.*, 450 S.W.3d 770 (Mo. banc 2014), for the proposition that formation issues can never be delegated to an arbitrator. In *Baker*, this Court held a delegation provision that provided the "arbitrator [would] resolve disputes 'relating to the applicability or enforceability' of the agreement" did not delegate issues of contract formation to the arbitrator. *Baker*, however, does not state that issues related to contract formation can never be delegated to an arbitrator but only that the delegation provision at issue in *Baker* was limited to issues of "applicability" or "enforceability." In contrast, the delegation provision at issue here is broader than in *Baker*. It delegates to the arbitrator "the power to rule on his or her own jurisdiction, including any objections with respect to the existence, scope, or validity of the arbitration agreement or to the arbitrability of any claim or counterclaim."

* * *

Mr. Pinkerton further asserts the circuit court erroneously concluded the delegation provision was enforceable. * * *

* * *

The only specific challenge Mr. Pinkerton raised before the circuit court as to the enforceability of the delegation provision was his contention the delegation provision was unconscionable on the sole ground that "[i]t would be unconscionable to delegate such a determination [of unconscionability] to a person with a direct financial interest in the outcome." Such a contention, however, is defeated by the Supreme Court's holding in *Rent-A-Center* that issues of

---

[9] Issues as to whether a contract has been "concluded" include whether: a contract was signed by the obligor, a signor lacked authority to sign a contract to commit a principal, or a signor lacked the mental capacity to sign a contract. Buckeye, 546 U.S. at 444 n.1, 126 S.Ct. 1204.

unconscionability can be delegated to an arbitrator. 561 U.S. at 73–74, 130 S.Ct. 2772. Mr. Pinkerton's challenge to the delegation provision, therefore, is without merit.

* * *

Although Mr. Pinkerton challenges the validity of the arbitration agreement as a whole, his only specific challenge to the delegation agreement—that it was unconscionable to delegate formation issues to an arbitrator—is without merit, and he did not otherwise direct any specific challenges to the delegation provision.[12] This Court must, therefore, treat the delegation provision "as valid under § 2 [of the FAA], and must enforce it under §§ 3 and 4, leaving any challenge to the validity of the [a]greement as a whole," or to other provisions within the arbitration agreement, "for the arbitrator." The circuit court, therefore, did not err in ordering the parties to arbitrate threshold issues of arbitrability. The preliminary writ of prohibition is quashed, and the case shall proceed to arbitration.

* * *

■ FISCHER, C.J., WILSON AND RUSSELL, JJ., concur;

■ LAURA DENVIR STITH, JUDGE, dissenting.

I dissent.

The United States Supreme Court has held, "When deciding whether the parties agreed to arbitrate a certain matter (including arbitrability), courts generally . . . should apply ordinary state-law principles that govern the formation of contracts." First Options of Chi., Inc. v. Kaplan, 514 U.S. 938, 944, 115 S.Ct. 1920, 131 L.Ed.2d 985 (1995). But the Supreme Court added an important qualification "applicable when courts decide whether a party has agreed that arbitrators should decide arbitrability: Courts should not assume that the parties agreed to arbitrate arbitrability *unless there is 'clea[r] and unmistakabl[e]' evidence* that they did so." *Id.* (emphasis added); accord Rent-A-Ctr., W., Inc. v. Jackson, 561 U.S. 63, 68, 130 S.Ct. 2772, 177 L.Ed.2d 403 (2010). Therefore, the record must provide "clear and unmistakable" evidence the parties intended to delegate questions of arbitrability to the arbitrator.

The majority fails to give meaning to this high standard of proof when it holds "clear and unmistakable" evidence of such intent is irrebuttably provided based solely on the fact Mr. Pinkerton signed a contract referencing the American Arbitration Association's rules of arbitration and one of the unattached commercial AAA rules at that time delegated issues of arbitrability to an arbitrator. Regardless of whether this is a valid conclusion for commercial or sophisticated parties—as numerous federal courts have held—Mr. Pinkerton undeniably is an

[12] The dissenting opinion contends the record clearly shows Mr. Pinkerton specifically challenged the delegation provision and points to a motion he filed stating in capital letters that he "disputes the existence and enforceability of any agreement to delegate issues of arbitrability to an arbitrator." What the dissenting opinion ignores is that Mr. Pinkerton then proceeded to challenge the arbitration agreement as a whole. Again, a delegation provision is a severable agreement that is enforceable unless a specific challenge is levied against the provision. Rent-A-Ctr., 561 U.S. at 71, 130 S.Ct. 2772. Therefore, despite his contentions to the contrary, Mr. Pinkerton failed to levy a direct challenge to the delegation provision.

unsophisticated consumer, and only one of the cases on which the majority relies involved an unsophisticated party.

Despite the majority's refusal to so recognize, Missouri historically has required greater specificity and protection for consumer contracts purporting to waive the consumer's litigation rights—including the right to jury trial, forum selection clauses, and waiver of negligence clauses—than it has for such provisions in a contract between sophisticated parties. Rather than presuming the consumer understands the contract, the courts look to the record to determine whether the waiver is valid on a case-by-case basis.

Applying these principles here, it is error to find the contract's mere incorporation of the unattached and undescribed AAA rules would have unambiguously signaled to an unsophisticated consumer that an arbitrator rather than a judge would determine whether the arbitration provision itself was valid. The contract's reference to the AAA rules is but one fact among many the courts must consider in determining the factual issue of whether the parties "clearly and unmistakably" intended to delegate the arbitrability issue to the arbitrator.

* * *

* * * This Court should recognize a generally applicable principle of Missouri contract law that when a consumer contract purports to incorporate by reference another writing, the court should determine whether the parties actually know and understand the provisions to be included.

Applying these principles here, Mr. Pinkerton was a young, non-college educated student who was trying to go to school to learn how to repair aircraft engines. The school he attended is a large for-profit corporation. The school did not provide Mr. Pinkerton with a copy of the AAA rules. Nothing in the contract explains the content of the AAA rules even generally, nor does the contract explain where and how to find them. The contract does not explain that, while the referenced rules were called "commercial" rules at that time, they nonetheless applied to consumers like Mr. Pinkerton and precluded him from having a court decide whether the agreement or the delegation provision was enforceable or binding. An average consumer might well presume the rules are simply that: rules governing the procedural aspects of arbitration, not "rules" that actually take away the consumer's rights. Certainly nothing in the contract mentioned delegation of arbitration decisions to an arbitrator. It is not surprising that both Mr. Pinkerton and the school's agent testified they had no idea what the AAA rules contained and no idea what they required the arbitrator or the court to decide. Neither said they understood the rules delegated to an arbitrator the arbitrability issue itself.

On these facts, a trial court certainly could find Mr. Pinkerton did not "clearly and unmistakably" intend to delegate arbitrability to an arbitrator. This Court should remand the case for a factual determination whether Mr. Pinkerton actually knew and understood what the provisions of the AAA rules were, where he could find them, and whether, as a matter of fact, he clearly and unmistakably showed an intent to delegate arbitrability issues to an arbitrator.

* * *

III. UNCONSCIONABILITY IS A CONTRACT FORMATION ISSUE

While the majority recognizes "this Court has held that unconscionability is a state law defense to contract formation," the majority nonetheless unnecessarily creates uncertainty by suggesting it is not sure why this is the case because "conscionability is not an essential element of contract formation. As such, while unconscionability is a defense to contract formation and, therefore, a contract's validity and enforceability, it is not an issue of whether a contract has ever been concluded."

This dicta interprets the term "contract formation" more narrowly than does the Supreme Court. Indeed, as this Court explained in *Brewer v. Missouri Title Loans*, 364 S.W.3d at 492 n.3:

> While Missouri courts traditionally have discussed unconscionability under the lens of *procedural* unconscionability and *substantive* unconscionability, *Concepcion* instead dictates a review that limits the discussion to whether state law defenses such as unconscionability impact the *formation* of a contract. . . . Accordingly, the analysis in this Court's ruling today—as well as this Court's ruling in *Robinson v. Title Lenders, Inc.,*—no longer focuses on a discussion of procedural unconscionability or substantive unconscionability, but instead is limited to a discussion of facts relating to unconscionability impacting the formation of the contract.

In other words, the unconscionability of the terms of a contract may be such that it negates the formation of the contract at all, or the unconscionability may instead impact enforcement of particular terms or of the contract as a whole. *Robinson* pointed out the former type of unconscionability in formation is exemplified by "procedural" unconscionability such as "high pressure sales tactics, unreadable fine print, or misrepresentation among other unfair issues in the contract formation process." Robinson v. Title Lenders, Inc., 364 S.W.3d 505, 508 n.2 (Mo. banc 2012). *Brewer* advised that in cases otherwise subject to arbitration, "Future decisions by Missouri's courts addressing unconscionability likewise shall limit review of the defense of unconscionability to the context of its relevance to contract formation."

The Supreme Court has recognized unconscionability may affect contract formation or may be an issue of contract enforcement.[5] The same reasoning applies to other defenses such as duress or fraud. *Brewer* and relevant Supreme Court cases recognize duress as a defense against formation, but lack of duress is not an essential element of contract formation. Baker v. Bristol Care, Inc., 450

---

[5] E.g., Granite Rock Co. v. Int'l Bhd. of Teamsters, 561 U.S. 287, 304 n.9, 130 S.Ct. 2847, 177 L.Ed.2d 567 (2010) ("The parties' dispute about the [contract]'s ratification date presents a formation question in the sense above, and is therefore not on all fours with, for example, the formation disputes we referenced in Buckeye Check Cashing, Inc. v. Cardegna, 546 U.S. 440, 444, n. 1, 126 S.Ct. 1204, 163 L.Ed.2d 1038 (2006), which concerned whether, not when, an agreement to arbitrate was 'concluded.'"); Buckeye, 546 U.S. at 444 n.1, 126 S.Ct. 1204 ("The issue of the contract's validity is different from the issue whether any agreement between the alleged obligor and obligee was ever concluded."). *Buckeye* went on to list several examples of formation questions, including "whether [a party] ever signed the contract, whether the signor lacked authority to commit the alleged principal, and whether the signor lacked the mental capacity to assent." 546 U.S. at 444 n.1, 126 S.Ct. 1204 (citations omitted).

S.W.3d 770, 782 (Mo. 2014) ("[A] contract is *voidable* due to . . . duress . . . but such [a] defense [has] nothing to do with contract formation. In fact, [duress] defenses assume a contract was formed."). It does not follow that a party alleging duress is not raising a contract formation challenge. The same is true of fraud.

* * * The case should be remanded for determination of the factual question whether an unsophisticated student such as Mr. Pinkerton clearly and unmistakably intended to delegate the issue of arbitrability to the arbitrator.

Rent-A-Center, Inc. v. Ellis

Supreme Court of Appeals of West Virginia, 2019.
827 S.E.2d 605.

■ WALKER, CHIEF JUSTICE:

After Respondent Anita Ellis was terminated from employment, she filed workers' compensation discrimination claims against Petitioners Rent-A-Center, Inc. and Rent-A-Center East, Inc. Relying on the arbitration agreement that Respondent signed at the time she was hired, Petitioners moved to compel arbitration. Respondent challenged the arbitration agreement's delegation clause, which required that any challenge to the interpretation, applicability, enforceability or formation of the agreement be resolved by the arbitrator and not any court, on the grounds that it was ambiguous, unconscionable and in violation of West Virginia Code § 23–2–7 (2017)["No employer or employee shall exempt himself from the burden or waive the benefits of this chapter by any contract, agreement, rule or regulation, and any such contract, agreement, rule or regulation shall be pro tanto void."]. The circuit court found the delegation clause unconscionable and refused to enforce the arbitration agreement. * * * Because the delegation clause was neither unconscionable nor unenforceable, we reverse the circuit court and remand this case for an order compelling arbitration.

I. FACTUAL AND PROCEDURAL BACKGROUND

When Respondent was hired by Petitioners in March of 2011 as an assistant manager, she signed a "Mutual Agreement to Arbitrate Claims" (arbitration agreement). The agreement states that it is governed by the Federal Arbitration Act (FAA), that it applies mutually to both parties, and that the mutual obligation to arbitrate differences "[p]rovide[s] consideration for each other." The arbitration agreement includes a "Claims Covered by the Agreement" section that states:

> The Company and I mutually consent to the resolution by arbitration of all claims or controversies ("claims"), past, present or future, including without limitation, claims arising out of my application for employment, assignment/employment, and/or the termination of my assignment/ employment
>
> * * *
>
> * * * The claims covered by this Agreement include, but are not limited to: * * * tort or statutory claims for discrimination (including, but not

> limited to, * * * workers' compensation); * * * and claims for violation of any federal, state or other governmental law, statute, regulation, or ordinance * * *

Under the "Arbitration Procedures" section, the agreement includes the following delegation clause:

> The Arbitrator, and not any federal, state, or local court or agency, shall have exclusive authority to resolve any dispute relating to the interpretation, applicability, enforceability, or formation of this Agreement, including, but not limited to, any claim that all or part of this Agreement is void or voidable.

Just above the Respondent's signature line on the agreement, the following appears in bold, capitalized letters:

> I ACKNOWLEDGE THAT I HAVE CAREFULLY READ THIS AGREEMENT; THAT I UNDERSTAND ITS TERMS; THAT ALL UNDERSTANDINGS AND AGREEMENTS BETWEEN THE COMPANY AND ME RELATING TO THE SUBJECTS COVERED IN THE AGREEMENT ARE CONTAINED IN IT; AND THAT I HAVE ENTERED INTO THE AGREEMENT NOT IN RELIANCE ON ANY PROMISES OR REPRESENTATIONS BY THE COMPANY OTHER THAN THOSE CONTAINED IN THIS AGREEMENT ITSELF. I UNDERSTAND THAT BY SIGNING THIS AGREEMENT THE COMPANY AND I ARE GIVING UP OUR RIGHTS TO A JURY TRIAL AND THAT PURSUANT TO THE TERMS OF THIS AGREEMENT, I AM AGREEING TO ARBITRATE CLAIMS COVERED BY THIS AGREEMENT.
>
> I FURTHER ACKNOWLEDGE THAT I HAVE BEEN GIVEN THE OPPORTUNITY TO DISCUSS THIS AGREEMENT WITH MY PRIVATE COUNSEL AND HAVE AVAILED MYSELF OF THAT OPPORTUNITY TO THE EXTENT THAT I WISH TO DO SO.

On April 8, 2014, Respondent injured her right shoulder while moving a refrigerator at work. She filed a workers' compensation claim and received temporary total disability (TTD) benefits for the period April 23, 2014, through May 15, 2014. By letter dated November 28, 2014, Petitioners terminated Respondent from employment effective November 11, 2014. The stated reason for termination was Respondent's absences from work.

On October 8, 2015, Respondent sought to re-open her workers' compensation claim. She was awarded TTD benefits for the period of May 19, 2014, through December 17, 2014. Respondent then filed a complaint in the Circuit Court of Mercer County in which she alleged that Petitioners unlawfully terminated her while she was off work due to a compensable injury and for which she received or was eligible to receive TTD benefits in violation of West Virginia Code §§ 23–5A–1 and –3(a) (2017).

Petitioners filed a motion to dismiss or stay the case and compel arbitration * * *.

* * *

In an order entered June 22, 2017, the circuit court denied Petitioners' motion to compel. The court determined that the arbitration agreement was both procedurally and substantively unconscionable and that there was no mutual agreement to arbitrate. In finding that the arbitration agreement was procedurally unconscionable, the circuit court placed significance on the fact that the arbitration provision was a non-negotiable term in an adhesion contract, and the Respondent was not permitted to opt out of or alter the provision. The circuit court also noted that the Respondent did not have the same level of sophistication or understanding about the arbitration clause as the Petitioners' attorneys who drafted the language, and found that she likely had no meaningful opportunity to seek counsel.

In finding substantive unconscionability, the circuit court determined that the agreement substantially impaired a plaintiff's right to pursue remedies for their losses such as a class action suit, which was expressly waived in the agreement, and that it would deprive the Respondent of a statutory remedy that exists to benefit and protect workers that have the claims set forth in West Virginia Code § 23–5A–3. The circuit court also concluded that there was a lack of a real and voluntary meeting of the minds, there was an overall imbalance and one-sidedness to the agreement, and there was no real choice or bargaining on the part of the Respondent, as her only alternative to signing the agreement was not taking the job. Further, it found that the consideration for the agreement "that both parties agree to arbitrate," was an "illusory promise" and was therefore inadequate. This appeal followed.

* * *

The parties assert various assignments and cross-assignments of error, all of which pertain to one central issue—whether the delegation clause in the arbitration agreement between the parties should have been enforced. Petitioners assert that the circuit court erred in denying their motion to compel arbitration because the delegation clause clearly assigns the arbitrator "the exclusive authority to resolve any dispute relating to the * * * applicability, enforceability, or formation of * * * the arbitration agreement." Petitioners contend that in *Rent-A-Center, West, Inc. v. Jackson*, the United States Supreme Court enforced the identical delegation clause and found that it clearly delegated the gateway issues of arbitrability to the arbitrator. Thus, Petitioners contend the FAA mandates that an arbitrator and not the circuit court should have determined whether the arbitration agreement is unenforceable.

Reiterating the arguments she made below, Respondent asserts that the delegation clause is (1) ambiguous and fails to reflect an unmistakable intent to delegate to the arbitrator the determination of gateway issues of arbitrability; (2) unconscionable under West Virginia common law contract principles; and (3) invalid because it violates West Virginia Code § 23–2–7. Before we consider the parties' arguments, we set forth the legal framework that controls the arbitration agreement and delegation clause at issue.

A. Delegation of Arbitrability

As the United States Supreme Court has explained, "[p]arties can agree to arbitrate 'gateway' questions of 'arbitrability,' such as whether the parties have agreed to arbitrate or whether their agreement covers a particular controversy." This can be accomplished by a specific term in the arbitration agreement, known as a delegation provision. As we have held, "[a] 'delegation provision' is a clause, within an agreement to arbitrate, which clearly and unmistakably provides that the parties to the agreement give to the arbitrator the power to decide the validity, revocability or enforceability of the arbitration agreement under general state contract law."

In discussing delegation provisions, we have described their purely contractual nature:

> The way that courts treat a delegation provision within an arbitration agreement should reflect the principle that arbitration is purely a matter of contract. In their contract, the parties may agree that questions about the validity, revocability or enforceability of an arbitration agreement under state contract law will be delegated from a court to an arbitrator. "Because the parties are the masters of their collective fate, they can agree to arbitrate almost any dispute—even a dispute over whether the underlying dispute is subject to arbitration."

In considering a challenge to the same arbitration agreement we examine in this case, the United States Supreme Court discussed how the severability doctrine applies to delegation provisions in *Rent-A-Center, West*. In that case, * * *

* * * the Supreme Court severed the delegation provision from the remainder of the arbitration agreement and explained that, unless Jackson challenged the delegation provision specifically, it must be treated as valid and must be enforced, leaving any challenge to the to the validity of the arbitration agreement as a whole for the arbitrator. It concluded that Jackson had only challenged the validity of the contract as a whole because he raised a challenge to the delegation provision for the first time in his appeal to the Supreme Court, which the Court determined was too late and would not be considered. However, the high court went on to illustrate how Jackson *could have* argued that the delegation provision, as opposed to the arbitration agreement as a whole, was "unconscionable"—and therefore unenforceable—because of the limitations on arbitral discovery and the fee-splitting procedures. It reasoned:

> Jackson's other two substantive unconscionability arguments assailed arbitration procedures called for by the contract—the fee-splitting arrangement and the limitations on discovery—procedures that were to be used during arbitration under *both* the agreement to arbitrate employment-related disputes *and* the delegation provision. It may be that had Jackson challenged the delegation provision by arguing that these common procedures *as applied* to the delegation provision rendered *that provision* unconscionable, the challenge should have been considered by the court. To make such a claim based on the discovery procedures, Jackson would have had to argue that the limitation upon the number of depositions causes the arbitration of his claim that the [arbitration] Agreement is unenforceable to be unconscionable. That would be, of course, a much more difficult argument to sustain than the argument that the same limitation renders arbitration of his factbound

> employment-discrimination claim unconscionable. Likewise, the unfairness of the fee-splitting arrangement may be more difficult to establish for the arbitration of enforceability than for arbitration of more complex and fact-related aspects of the alleged employment discrimination. Jackson, however, did not make any arguments specific to the delegation provision; he argued that the fee-sharing and discovery procedures rendered the *entire* Agreement invalid.

We examined the *Rent-A-Center, West* holding in *Schumacher Homes of Circleville, Inc. v. Spencer* (*Schumacher Homes II*), and held that delegation clauses will be enforced if there is a "clear and unmistakable intent" to delegate these gateway issues to the arbitrator, and if the delegation provision is valid and enforceable under general principles of state contract law. * * *

Applying *Rent-A-Center, West*, we determined in *Schumacher Homes II* that because a delegation provision is a mini-arbitration agreement divisible from both the broader arbitration clause and the even broader contract in which the delegation provision and arbitration clause are found, a party must specifically object to the delegation provision in order for a court to consider the challenge. A party resisting delegation to an arbitrator of any question about the enforceability of an arbitration agreement must specifically challenge the delegation provision first. * * *

* * *

B. Challenging the Delegation Clause

Although we acknowledged that the rule created by the Supreme Court in *Rent-A-Center, West* seemed to be "intricate and complex," we made it clear in *Schumacher Homes II* that it is possible to oppose enforcement of a delegation provision. As we cautioned, "the FAA does not require all claims to be sent to arbitration merely because there is a delegation provision." Because delegation clauses and "agreements to arbitrate are severable does not mean that they are unassailable."

(1) *Clear and Unmistakable Intent*

In determining whether the delegation clause in this case is enforceable, we must first discern whether the language of the delegation provision reflects "a clear and unmistakable intent by the parties to delegate state contract law questions about the validity, revocability and enforceability of the arbitration agreement to an arbitrator." * * *

Respondent contends the delegation clause is ambiguous—meaning that it does not clearly and unmistakably reflect the parties' intent to arbitrate the question of arbitrability—because it does not state that the arbitrator shall determine what is "arbitrable" nor is it explicitly labeled as a "delegation clause." The delegation clause in this case states:

> The Arbitrator, and not any federal, state, or local court or agency, shall have exclusive authority to resolve any dispute relating to the interpretation, applicability, enforceability or formation of this

> Agreement including, but not limited to, a claim that all or any part of this Agreement is void or voidable.

* * *

* * * [W]hen we examine the delegation clause at issue, here, we find that it clearly and unmistakably designates authority to the arbitrator to decide whether the arbitration agreement is enforceable. In footnote twenty-seven of *Schumacher Homes II*, we noted that the very delegation clause at issue in this case, which was examined by the United States Supreme Court in *Rent-A-Center, West*, provided "an example of a clear delegation provision." Also, in *House v. Rent-A-Center Franchising International, Inc.*, the United States District Court for the Southern District of West Virginia determined that this same delegation provision was "clear and concise." In examining this delegation clause, the district court stated:

> Language designating authority to an arbitrator cannot be made any clearer. If agreements incorporating by reference the rules of the American Arbitration Association (AAA), which in turn references a delegation provision, have been upheld by courts, surely a concise statement within the agreement itself satisfies the clear and unmistakable test.

* * * [W]e reject Respondent's assertion that the clause is ambiguous and find that it clearly and unmistakably demonstrates the parties' intent to delegate the issues of arbitrability to the arbitrator.

(2) *Validity*

We must next decide, under *Schumacher Homes II*, whether the delegation clause itself is valid, irrevocable and enforceable under general principles of state contract law. On this issue, we stated in *Schumacher Homes II* that:

> Questions about the validity, revocability, and enforceability of a provision delegating a problem with the enforceability or scope of an arbitration clause are resolved by looking to state contract law. "When deciding whether the parties agreed to arbitrate a certain matter (including arbitrability), courts generally * * * should apply ordinary state-law principles that govern the formation of contracts."

* * *

* * * Respondent argues that the delegation clause was invalid because it was unconscionable under state law and in violation of West Virginia Code § 23–2–7. * * *

* * *

(a) *Unconscionability*

In examining unconscionability, this Court has used a two-step approach. "Under West Virginia law, we analyze unconscionability in terms of two components parts: procedural unconscionability and substantive unconscionability. * * * To conclude that a contractual term is unenforceable on grounds of unconscionability requires a finding that the provision in issue 'is both procedurally and substantively unconscionable.'" We have explained that "[a]lthough both forms of unconscionability need to be present, the court 'should apply a sliding scale' to determine whether a contract is unconscionable, finding that "the more substantively oppressive the contract term, the less evidence of procedural unconscionability [will be] required." We are mindful that

> "[t]he doctrine of unconscionability means that, because of an overall and gross imbalance, one-sidedness or lop-sidedness in a contract, a court may be justified in refusing to enforce the contract as written. The concept of unconscionability must be applied in a flexible manner, taking into consideration all of the facts and circumstances of a particular case."

As we observed in *Brown I*, "[t]he burden of proving that a contract term is unconscionable rests with the party attacking the contract."

(i) *Procedural Unconscionability*

In *Brown I*, we explained what courts should consider in assessing procedural unconscionability:

> Procedural unconscionability is concerned with inequities, improprieties, or unfairness in the bargaining process and formation of the contract. Procedural unconscionability involves a variety of inadequacies that results in the lack of a real and voluntary meeting of the minds of the parties, considering all the circumstances surrounding the transaction. These inadequacies, include, but are not limited to, the age, literacy, or lack of sophistication of a party; hidden or unduly complex contract terms; the adhesive nature of the contract; and the manner and setting in which the contract was formed, including whether each party had a reasonable opportunity to understand the terms of the contract.

Respondent contends that the arbitration agreement and the delegation clause at issue are part of a contract of adhesion, as they are part of a preprinted, form contract drafted by the defendant with no opportunity for her to alter any terms of the agreement—a take-it-or-leave-it deal. Respondent maintains that both the arbitration agreement and the delegation clause are procedurally unconscionable because there is grossly unequal bargaining power and sophistication between her (a high school graduate with little understanding of the law) and Petitioners (large corporate entities that are highly experienced in drafting and litigating arbitration agreements and delegation clauses). Respondent asserts that while Petitioners have extensive experience regarding the litigation of this delegation clause, she had never before seen it and certainly not before entering into her agreement with the Petitioners.

Respondent also argues that the circumstances under which she reviewed and signed the document containing the delegation clause were controlled by her employer, making it difficult for her to review and understand the clause. Respondent contends that on her first day of employment, she was directed by her manager to sign numerous documents in quick succession and she did not see the arbitration agreement again until the motion to compel was filed. She argues that she was never advised that the forms she was signing "involved legal matters;" and the delegation clause consists of "one sentence of text" in four to five pages of "densely fine print." She maintains that there was simply no time for her to read the documents that were placed in front of her or to reasonably understand the terms of the delegation clause.

Petitioners contend that their motion to compel arbitration should have been enforced—despite the fact that the circuit court found that (1) the agreement to arbitrate was nonnegotiable; (2) Respondent could not opt out or alter it; (3) the parties' levels of sophistication were unequal; (4) Respondent had no chance to seek counsel; and (5) there was no true bargained-for exchange—because similar findings were recently rejected by this Court in *Nationstar Mortgage, LLC v. West*.

In *Nationstar Mortgage, LLC v. West*, a case involving a mortgagee's motion to compel arbitration, we found that, although the arbitration agreement very likely was a contract of adhesion, the fact that it was prepared by a party with more power, lacked an opt-out provision allowing for some choice in the matter, and was perceived to lack separate consideration did not make the agreement procedurally unconscionable.

In so finding, we acknowledged the realities of consummating standardized business transactions and the attendant unworkability of individualized bargaining, and stated:

> [c]ourts around the country have recognized that the need for pre-printed form contracts is a stark reality of today's mass-production/consumer culture. Despite even severe disparities in bargaining power, these agreements are most often enforced, at least as long as they comport with the reasonable expectations of the parties. A contrary rule would slow commerce to a crawl.

As we explained, contracts of adhesion are routinely executed without the signatory's full reading or comprehension of the specified terms:

> [c]ustomers do not in fact ordinarily understand or even read the standard terms. They trust to the good faith of the party using the form and to the tacit representation that like terms are being accepted regularly by others similarly situated. *But they understand that they are assenting to the terms not read or not understood, subject to such limitations as the law may impose.*

We noted that in reviewing an adhesion contract, we must examine whether "it imposes terms beyond the reasonable expectations of an ordinary person, or oppressive or unconscionable terms." Because contracts of adhesion are by definition typically prepared by a party with more power, we did not view that factor as persuasive by itself. Further, in assessing the circuit court's determination that Nationstar's failure to include an opt-out provision in its arbitration rider was significant in ruling on the issue of procedural unconscionability, we held in Syllabus Point 2 that:

> The omission of an "opt out" provision in an agreement that permits the signatories to reject arbitration is just one of multiple factors to consider in evaluating a claim of procedural unconscionability. As a result, the omission of an "opt out" provision is not in itself sufficient evidence that an arbitration agreement is grossly unfair and thus unenforceable on grounds of procedural unconscionability.

Like Respondent here, the petitioners in *Nationstar* contended that their loan closing was conducted in a hurried manner, not allowing the opportunity to appreciate their relinquishment of the right to utilize the court system. In rejecting the petitioners' argument, we noted that the petitioners were not complaining (1) that they had been denied the right to read the arbitration agreement; (2) that they lacked the capacity to understand the arbitration clause; (3) that they were coerced into signing the document; or (4) that they were denied the opportunity to take more time to read and review the loan documents, or to have a third party review them. We also reiterated that "a party to a contract has a duty to read the instrument," and the fact that the petitioners "may have signed a document without reading it first [did] not excuse them from the binding effect of the agreements contained in the executed document." For these reasons, we find Respondent's argument unavailing.

Respondent also asserts that the very arcane nature of the delegation clause, "agreeing to arbitrate issues of arbitrability," supports the fact that there was no real and voluntary meeting of the minds. Respondent notes that in *First Options Chicago v. Kaplan*, Justice Breyer noted:

> On the other hand, the former question—the "who (primarily) should decide arbitrability" question—is rather arcane. A party often might not focus upon that question or upon the significance of having arbitrators decide the scope of their own powers. And, given the principle that a party can be forced to arbitrate only those issues it specifically has agreed to submit to arbitration, one can understand why courts might hesitate to interpret silence or ambiguity on the "who should decide arbitrability" point as giving the arbitrators that power, for doing so might too often force unwilling parties to arbitrate a matter they reasonably would have thought a judge, not an arbitrator, would decide.

Conversely, Petitioners contend, and we agree, that while the issue of who decides arbitrability is arcane when an agreement is silent or ambiguous in this regard, it is for that very reason that FAA jurisprudence requires that parties must "clearly and unmistakably" agree to arbitrate questions of arbitrability in order for that agreement to be enforceable. Because we have determined that the delegation clause at issue is clear and unmistakable, this issue has no merit. For these reasons, we conclude that the grounds relied upon by the circuit court to find the delegation clause procedurally unconscionable were erroneous.

(ii) *Substantive Unconscionability*

To prevail on her unconscionability argument involving the delegation clause at issue here, Respondent must show both procedural and substantive unconscionability, at least in some measure. Because we conclude that no procedural unconscionability exists with respect to the delegation clause, we need not evaluate whether substantive unconscionability exists. But, even if Respondent had succeeded in her procedural unconscionability argument, she has failed to demonstrate substantive unconscionability.

This Court recently reiterated in *Nationstar* that "the focus of substantive unconscionability is on the nature of the contractual provisions rather than on the circumstances surrounding the contract's formation." We stated:

> Substantive unconscionability involves unfairness in the contract itself and whether a contract term is one-sided and will have an overly harsh effect on the disadvantaged party. The factors to be weighed in assessing substantive unconscionability vary with the content of the agreement. Generally, courts should consider the commercial reasonableness of the contract terms, the purpose and effect of the terms, the allocation of the risks between the parties, and public policy concerns.

Respondent challenges the delegation clause as substantively unconscionable under West Virginia Code § 23–2–7 because it results in an improper exemption from burdens and a waiver of benefits under our workers' compensation statute. West Virginia Code § 23–5A–3 provides, in part, that

> (a) It shall be a discriminatory practice within the meaning of section one of this article to terminate an injured employee while the injured employee is off work due to a compensable injury within the meaning of article four of this chapter and is receiving or is eligible to receive temporary total disability benefits, unless the injured employee has committed a separate dischargeable offense.

West Virginia Code § 23–2–7 also provides that, "No employer or employee shall exempt himself from the burden or waive the benefits of this chapter by any contract, agreement, rule or regulation, and any such contract, agreement, rule or regulation shall be pro tanto void." Respondent argues that § 23–5A–3 and § 23–5A–1 allow access to the circuit court and to a jury to enforce and address claims of unlawful discrimination when the worker is fired while in a protected status or because he or she filed a workers compensation claim.

Conversely, Petitioners maintain that because the delegation clause itself does not affect any burdens or benefits arising under the worker's compensation statute, Respondent's challenge under West Virginia Code § 23–2–7 is actually directed at the provision of the agreement requiring arbitration of her underlying worker's compensation discrimination claim. We agree. Numerous courts have similarly rejected substantive unconscionability arguments directed at the arbitration agreement, itself, rather than the terms of the delegation provision. Thus, under the FAA and U.S. Supreme Court precedent, the question of whether the parties' arbitration agreement violates West Virginia Code § 23–2–7 is for an arbitrator to decide, not this Court.

Respondent also alleges that the delegation clause is substantively unconscionable because it lacks mutuality. Specifically, she claims that the threshold question of arbitrability is decided by an arbitrator who has a financial interest in ruling in favor of the defendant and for arbitration, rather than for the plaintiff and against arbitration. In several opinions discussing the unconscionability doctrine, we have noted that "the lack of mutuality in a contractual obligation—particularly in the context of arbitration—is an element a court may consider in assessing the substantive unconscionability of a contract term." For instance, in *Brown v. Genesis Healthcare Corp.* (*Brown II*), we stated that:

> Substantive unconscionability may manifest itself in the form of "an agreement requiring arbitration only for the claims of the weaker party but a choice of forums for the claims of the stronger party." "Some courts suggest that mutuality of obligation is the locus around which substantive unconscionability analysis revolves." "Agreements to arbitrate must contain at least 'a modicum of bilaterality' to avoid unconscionability."

Petitioners contend that Respondent's argument is antiquated and based on a mistrust of arbitration, which has been repeatedly rejected by the United States Supreme Court. Further, they claim that the delegation clause here does not lack mutuality because both parties are bound by it equally. It requires arbitration for "any dispute relating to the interpretation, applicability, enforceability, or formation of this Agreement, including, but not limited to, any claim that all or part of this Agreement is void or voidable" whether by or against the employee or employer. Petitioners contend, and we agree, that the arbitration agreement also contains mutual promises by both parties to arbitrate disputes covered by the agreement, which constitutes sufficient consideration to support the agreement. This mutuality is far more than the "modicum of bilaterality" required by our Court in employment arbitration agreements. Thus, we find nothing in the delegation clause upon which to conclude that it lacks mutuality.

IV. CONCLUSION

Because we have determined that the delegation clause clearly and unmistakably evinces the parties' intent to send gateway questions of arbitration to an arbitrator and that is also valid, the circuit court should have referred the parties' arguments about the enforceability of the arbitration agreement to the arbitrator. For these reasons, we reverse the circuit court's June 23, 2017 order, and remand the case to the circuit court with directions to refer the Respondent's challenge to the enforceability of the arbitration agreement to an arbitrator, in accordance with the parties' contract.

Reversed and remanded.

Justice Workman concurs and reserves the right to file a concurring opinion.

■ WORKMAN, JUSTICE, concurring:

I concur with the majority's decision as it correctly follows the pro-arbitration law established by Congress, repeatedly upheld by the United States Supreme Court, and adopted by this Court. But as I have previously explained in concurring opinions * * *, arbitration agreements are "trump[ing] an individual's right to a jury trial," which is a fundamental right that should be zealously guarded.

The plaintiff below, Anita Ellis, was required to sign an arbitration agreement as part of her employment with Rent-A-Center, Inc. When she was suffered an injury to her right shoulder while moving a refrigerator as part of her employment, she filed a workers' compensation claim and her injury was found compensable. She was then terminated from her employment based upon her absences from work as a result of her compensable injury. She filed a civil action against her employer alleging that her employer had unlawfully terminated her employment by discriminating against her in violation of West Virginia Code §§ 23–5A–1, –3 (2017), which prohibit discriminatory practices by an employer against an employee, including the filing of a workers' compensation claim and the termination of an injured employee who is receiving or eligible to receive workers' compensation temporary total disability benefits.

The arbitration agreement deprived Ms. Ellis of the right to have a jury determine the facts surrounding the issue of whether her statutory rights were violated. I will continue to express my judicial disdain for these mandatory arbitration agreements prepared by sophisticated businesses and forced upon people as a condition of employment.

For the foregoing reasons, I respectfully concur.

Despite *Rent-A-Center v. Jackson*, courts occasionally decline to enforce arbitration agreements with delegation clauses. See, e.g., MacDonald v. CashCall, Inc, 883 F.3d 220, 227–28 (3d Cir. 2018).

> The Loan Agreement's arbitration provision states that disputes "will be resolved by Arbitration, which shall be conducted by the Cheyenne River Sioux Tribal Nation by an authorized representative in accordance with its consumer dispute rules and the terms of this Agreement." This language requires the Tribe's involvement in the arbitration, but as our sister circuit courts have noted, such a tribal arbitral forum does not exist.

Id. at 227.

> Here, unlike in *Rent-A-Center*, MacDonald specifically challenged the delegation clause. His Complaint alleges that "[b]ecause the arbitration procedure described in the agreement is fabricated and illusory, any provision requiring that the enforceability of the arbitration procedure must be decided through arbitration is also illusory and unenforceable." Similarly, his brief opposing Defendants' motion to compel arbitration states that "the delegation clause suffers from the same defect as the arbitration provision," and includes a section discussing this challenge. These explicit references to the delegation clause are sufficient to contest it. Therefore, the District Court did not err in assessing the delegation clause's enforceability.
>
> MacDonald asserts that the Loan Agreement's delegation clause and arbitration provisions are unenforceable for the same reasons—the arbitration mechanism articulated in the Loan Agreement is illusory * * *. [W]e conclude that the arbitral forum provided for in the Loan Agreement is nonexistent. As a result, and as explained herein, there is no arbitration forum in which an arbitrator could evaluate whether the arbitration provision is enforceable.

Id. See also Citizens of Humanity, LLC v. Applied Underwriters Captive Risk Assurance Co., Inc., 299 Neb. 545, 909 N.W.2d 614 (2018) (finding that manufacturer specifically challenged validity of delegation clause, rather than entire arbitration clause, of reinsurance participation agreement as contrary to state law; and reinsurance participation agreement was subject to the McCarran-Ferguson Act's "reverse preemption" of FAA (see Section 3.C.4) so state anti-arbitration statute rendered arbitration provision invalid.)

Moreover, *Rent-A-Center* does not preclude courts from denying enforcement to arbitration agreements lacking delegation clauses. See, e.g., Cullinane v. Beverly Enterprises-Nebraska, Inc., 300 Neb. 210, 225, 912 N.W.2d 774, 789 (2018) (affirming denial of motion to compel arbitration; evidence supported trial court's determination that agreement was unenforceable for having been obtained by fraud; "plain language of the ADR Agreement does not clearly and unmistakably empower an arbitrator to determine enforceability issues such as the challenge Thomas raises here").

In *Subcontracting Concepts (CT), LLC v. De Melo*, 34 Cal. App. 5th 201, 216, 245 Cal. Rptr. 3d 838, 849 (Ct. App. 2019), the California Court of Appeal affirmed a denial of employer's motion to compel arbitration of workers' wage claims:

> We agree with the trial court and the parties that the arbitration clause was procedurally unconscionable.
>
> First, the Agreement containing that clause was adhesive in that it was imposed on respondent "as a condition of employment" and with "no opportunity to negotiate."
>
> Second, respondent, who was not fluent enough in English to fully understand legal documents written in English, did not understand what arbitration was and no one explained to him the meaning of any of the 27 clauses in the five-page Agreement, including the arbitration clause.
>
> Third, the arbitration clause referred to the American Arbitration Association, but did not clearly state what rules would govern arbitration, nor was respondent provided with a copy of the governing rules.
>
> Having determined that the arbitration clause contains at least a moderate level of procedural unconscionability, we will consider whether the clause is also substantively unconscionable.
>
> * * *
>
> Substantive unconscionability addresses the fairness of the term in dispute. [It] "traditionally involves contract terms that are so one-sided as to 'shock the conscience,' or that impose harsh or oppressive terms."
>
> * * *
>
> We agree with the trial court that the arbitration clause contains numerous substantively unconscionable provisions.
>
> * * *
>
> * * * [F]irst, the arbitration clause requires respondent to bear his own costs for arbitration. As the Labor Commissioner points out in her briefing, "it is fair to assume that the cost [to respondent] would be substantial given that the Agreement requires three arbitrators, each

having both a transportation and legal background." The trial court correctly found that this term was substantively unconscionable. (See *Armendariz*, 24 Cal.4th at pp. 110–111, 99 Cal.Rptr.2d 745, 6 P.3d 669 ["when an employer imposes mandatory arbitration as a condition of employment, the arbitration agreement or arbitration process cannot generally require the employee to bear any type of expense that the employee would not be required to bear if he or she were free to bring the action in court"].)

Second, the clause bars respondent from recovering any attorney fees or other costs. Our Supreme Court has "held that the FAA does not require enforcement of a provision in an arbitration agreement that, in violation of generally applicable California contract law, 'limit[s] statutorily imposed remedies such as punitive damages and attorney fees.'"

Third, the arbitration clause states that the arbitrators "have authority to award actual monetary damages only. No punitive or equitable relief is authorized." Under these provisions, respondent is barred from seeking statutory remedies, including punitive damages, statutory penalties, and equitable relief. This would preclude respondent from pursuing statutory penalties against SCI for (1) failing to provide accurate itemized wage statements pursuant to section 226 and (2) failing to timely pay all wages upon his separation from employment pursuant to section 203.10. These Labor Code provisions cannot "in any way be contravened or set aside by a private agreement." (§ 219, subd. (a).) Hence, like the provision precluding an award of attorney fees, this limitation improperly "undermine[s] statutory protections" to which respondent would otherwise be entitled.

Fourth, the clause improperly bars respondent from arbitrating any PAGA [Private Attorneys General Act] claims. Our Supreme Court has held that "an employee's right to bring a PAGA action is unwaivable." As the court explained, "an agreement by employees to waive their right to bring a PAGA action serves to disable one of the primary mechanisms for enforcing the Labor Code. Because such an agreement has as its 'object, . . . indirectly, to exempt [the employer] from responsibility for [its] own . . . violation of law,' it is against public policy and may not be enforced."

Fifth, as the trial court found, the arbitration clause precluded respondent "from taking advantage of the relatively inexpensive remedy before the Labor Commissioner." Appellants observe that "[i]n *Sonic II*, our Supreme Court held that an otherwise valid arbitration agreement may not be deemed substantively unconscionable merely on the basis that it requires an employee to waive his right to a Berman hearing." [A Berman hearing is a dispute resolution forum established by California's Legislature to help employees recover wages owed.] However, as appellants also acknowledge, the *Sonic II* court further held that an arbitration agreement requiring waiver of the protections provided in a Berman hearing in favor of arbitration that "does not provide an employee

> with an accessible and affordable arbitral forum for resolving wage disputes may support a finding of unconscionability."
>
> The arbitration clause in the present case would deprive respondent of the protections provided in the Berman hearing process, replacing those protections with costs and obstacles he would not otherwise face. It would also significantly limit the remedies that would otherwise be available, as discussed above. Therefore, because the arbitration clause requires respondent to waive all of the protections and many of the remedies available at a Berman hearing, without providing him "with an accessible and affordable arbitral forum for resolving wage disputes," we conclude the trial court correctly found the clause substantively unconscionable on this ground as well.

Subcontracting Concepts (CT), LLC v. De Melo, 34 Cal. App. 5th 201, 211–15, 245 Cal. Rptr. 3d 838, 844–48 (Ct. App. 2019).

Although states can differ in their unconscionability doctrines, the FAA constrains the extent to which courts may hold arbitration clauses unconscionable. The United States Supreme Court has shown that it will police state courts' expansive use of the unconscionability doctrine against arbitration agreements. In the 1980s and 1990s, the Court warned that state courts may not "rely on the uniqueness of an agreement to arbitrate as a basis for a state-law holding that enforcement would be unconscionable, for this would enable the court to effect what * * * the state legislature cannot." Doctor's Associates, 517 U.S. at 687–88 n.3; Perry v. Thomas, 482 U.S. 483, 493 n.9 (1987). Then in the 2011 case of *AT&T Mobility LLC v. Concepcion*, 563 U.S. 333 (2011) (excerpted above in Section 3.C.2.b), the Court followed through on this warning and held that a California case law rule on the unconscionability of arbitration agreements prohibiting class actions was preempted by the FAA.

As we saw above, *Concepcion* said "The overarching purpose of the FAA, evident in the text of §§ 2, 3, and 4, is to ensure the enforcement of arbitration agreements according to their terms so as to facilitate streamlined proceedings." The Court's reasoning built on this premise that an important purpose of the FAA was to enforce agreements in which parties choose the more streamlined process (arbitration) over the more elaborate process (litigation). The Court suggested that the FAA would preempt (hypothetical) state law deeming unconscionable arbitration agreements lacking "judicially monitored discovery," "adherence to the Federal Rules of Evidence," or "arbitration-by-jury" because requiring arbitration to include these aspects of litigation would effectively convert the more streamlined process into the more elaborate process, so it would no longer be "arbitration," as that process was envisioned by those who enacted the FAA. Similarly, the Court held that state law "[r]equiring the availability of classwide arbitration interferes with fundamental attributes of arbitration and thus creates a scheme inconsistent with the FAA."

QUESTIONS TO REVIEW AND SYNTHESIZE

1. How would you, as a Missouri trial court judge, rule in a case identical to *Pinkerton* (excerpted above), except that in your case the student denies signing or even seeing the enrollment agreement and the school is not able to produce any arbitration agreement with the student's signature? The school's lawyer quotes to you *Pinkerton*'s statement that "both issues of formation and enforceability of arbitration clauses can be delegated to an arbitrator. Mr. Pinkerton does not cite any case law prohibiting issues of formation from being delegated to the arbitrator."
2. To render an arbitration agreement unenforceable under West Virginia law, must a court find both procedural and substantive unconscionability, or is one type of unconscionability enough? Same question for California law?
3. Had English been the first language of the respondent in *Subcontracting Concepts* (block quoted three paragraphs before these questions), would the California Court of Appeals still have held that "the arbitration clause contains at least a moderate level of procedural unconscionability"? Same question under West Virginia law?

3. SCOPE OF ARBITRATION AGREEMENTS

a. PRESUMPTIVELY DECIDED BY COURTS

Even if disputing parties agree that they formed a valid agreement to arbitrate, they may not agree on whether their dispute falls within the scope of the agreement—that is, whether the parties have agreed to submit *this* matter in controversy to arbitration. Most nations' laws give arbitrators, not courts, the initial power to rule on the agreement's scope. In contrast, FAA § 3 presumptively[30] sends disputes about an arbitration agreement's scope to courts, rather than to arbitrators:

> If any suit or proceeding be brought in any of the courts of the United States upon any issue referable to arbitration under an agreement in writing for such arbitration, the court in which such suit is pending, *upon being satisfied that the issue involved in such suit or proceeding is referable to arbitration under such an agreement*, shall on application of one of the parties stay the trial of the action until such arbitration has been had in accordance with the terms of the agreement, providing the applicant for the stay is not in default in proceeding with such arbitration.

Similarly, labor arbitration law (primarily federal common law under the Labor Management Relations Act, rather than the FAA), also presumptively sends disputes about an arbitration agreement's scope to courts, rather than arbitrators.

[30] See infra Section 3.D.3.b.

AT & T Technologies, Inc. v. Communications Workers of America

Supreme Court of the United States, 1986.
475 U.S. 643, 106 S.Ct. 1415, 89 L.Ed.2d 648.

■ JUSTICE WHITE delivered the opinion of the Court.

The issue presented in this case is whether a court asked to order arbitration of a grievance filed under a collective-bargaining agreement must first determine that the parties intended to arbitrate the dispute, or whether that determination is properly left to the arbitrator.

I

AT & T Technologies, Inc. (AT & T or the Company) and the Communications Workers of America (the Union) are parties to a collective-bargaining agreement which covers telephone equipment installation workers. Article 8 of this agreement establishes that "differences arising with respect to the interpretation of this contract or the performance of any obligation hereunder" must be referred to a mutually agreeable arbitrator upon the written demand of either party. This Article expressly does not cover disputes "excluded from arbitration by other provisions of this contract."[1] Article 9 provides that, "subject to the limitations contained in the provisions of this contract, but otherwise not subject to the provisions of the arbitration clause," AT & T is free to exercise certain management functions, including the hiring and placement of employees and the termination of employment.[2] "When lack of work necessitates Layoff," Article 20 prescribes the order in which employees are to be laid off.[3]

On September 17, 1981, the Union filed a grievance challenging AT & T's decision to lay off 79 installers from its Chicago base location. The Union claimed that, because there was no lack of work at the Chicago location, the planned layoffs would violate Article 20 of the agreement. Eight days later, however, AT & T laid off all 79 workers, and soon thereafter, the Company transferred approximately the same number of installers from base locations in Indiana and Wisconsin to the Chicago base. AT & T refused to submit the grievance to arbitration on the ground

---

1 Article 8 provides, in pertinent part, as follows:

If the National and the Company fail to settle by negotiation any differences arising with respect to the interpretation of this contract or the performance of any obligation hereunder, such differences shall (provided that such dispute is not excluded from arbitration by other provisions of this contract, and provided that the grievance procedures as to such dispute have been exhausted) be referred upon written demand of either party to an impartial arbitrator mutually agreeable to both parties.

2 Article 9 states:

The Union recognizes the right of the Company (subject to the limitations contained in the provisions of this contract, but otherwise not subject to the provisions of the arbitration clause) to exercise the functions of managing the business which involve, among other things, the hiring and placement of Employees, the termination of employment, the assignment of work, the determination of methods and equipment to be used, and the control of the conduct of work.

3 Article 20 provides, in pertinent part, "[w]hen lack of work necessitates Layoff, Employees shall be Laid-Off in accordance with Term of Employment and by Layoff groups as set forth in the following [subparagraphs stating the order of layoff]." Article 1.11 defines the term "Layoff" to mean "a termination of employment arising out of a reduction in the force due to lack of work."

that under Article 9, the Company's decision to lay off workers when it determines that a lack of work exists in a facility is not arbitrable.

The Union then sought to compel arbitration by filing suit in federal court pursuant to § 301(a) of the Labor Management Relations Act, 29 U.S.C. § 185(a). Ruling on cross-motions for summary judgment, the District Court reviewed the provisions of Articles 8, 9, and 20 and set forth the parties' arguments as follows:

> "Plaintiffs interpret Article 20 to require that there be an actual lack of work prior to employee layoffs and argue that there was no such lack of work in this case. Under plaintiffs' interpretation, Article 20 would allow the union to take to arbitration the threshold issue of whether the layoffs were justified by a lack of work. Defendant interprets Article 20 as merely providing a sequence for any layoffs which management, in its exclusive judgment, determines are necessary. Under defendant's interpretation, Article 20 would not allow for an arbitrator to decide whether the layoffs were warranted by a lack of work but only whether the company followed the proper order in laying off the employees."

Finding that "the union's interpretation of Article 20 was at least 'arguable,'" the court held that it was "for the arbitrator, not the court to decide whether the union's interpretation has merit," and accordingly, ordered the Company to arbitrate.

The Court of Appeals for the Seventh Circuit affirmed. The Court of Appeals understood the District Court to have ordered arbitration of the threshold issue of arbitrability. The court acknowledged the "general rule" that the issue of arbitrability is for the courts to decide unless the parties stipulate otherwise, but noted that this Court's decisions in *Steelworkers v. Warrior & Gulf Navigation Co.*, 363 U.S. 574 (1960), and *Steelworkers v. American Mfg. Co.*, 363 U.S. 564 (1960), caution courts to avoid becoming entangled in the merits of a labor dispute under the guise of deciding arbitrability. From this observation, the court announced an "exception" to the general rule, under which "a court should compel arbitration of the arbitrability issue where the collective bargaining agreement contains a standard arbitration clause, the parties have not clearly excluded the arbitrability issue from arbitration, and deciding the issue would entangle the court in interpretation of substantive provisions of the collective bargaining agreement and thereby involve consideration of the merits of the dispute."

All of these factors were present in this case. Article 8 was a "standard arbitration clause," and there was "no clear, unambiguous exclusion from arbitration of terminations predicated by a lack of work determination." Moreover, although there were "colorable arguments" on both sides of the exclusion issue, if the court were to decide this question it would have to interpret not only Article 8, but Articles 9 and 20 as well, both of which are "substantive provisions of the Agreement." The court thus "decline[d] the invitation to decide arbitrability," and ordered AT & T "to arbitrate the arbitrability issue."

* * *

We granted certiorari and now vacate the Seventh Circuit's decision and remand for a determination of whether the Company is required to arbitrate the Union's grievance.

II

The principles necessary to decide this case are not new. They were set out by this Court over 25 years ago in a series of cases known as the *Steelworkers Trilogy: Steelworkers v. American Mfg. Co.; Steelworkers v. Warrior & Gulf Navigation Co.*; and *Steelworkers v. Enterprise Wheel & Car Corp.,* 363 U.S. 593 (1960). These precepts have served the industrial relations community well, and have led to continued reliance on arbitration, rather than strikes or lockouts, as the preferred method of resolving disputes arising during the term of a collective-bargaining agreement. We see no reason either to question their continuing validity, or to eviscerate their meaning by creating an exception to their general applicability.

The first principle gleaned from the *Trilogy* is that "arbitration is a matter of contract and a party cannot be required to submit to arbitration any dispute which he has not agreed so to submit." This axiom recognizes the fact that arbitrators derive their authority to resolve disputes only because the parties have agreed in advance to submit such grievances to arbitration.

The second rule, which follows inexorably from the first, is that the question of arbitrability—whether a collective-bargaining agreement creates a duty for the parties to arbitrate the particular grievance—is undeniably an issue for judicial determination. Unless the parties clearly and unmistakably provide otherwise, the question of whether the parties agreed to arbitrate is to be decided by the court, not the arbitrator.

The Court expressly reaffirmed this principle in *John Wiley & Sons, Inc. v. Livingston,* 376 U.S. 543 (1964). The "threshold question" there was whether the court or an arbitrator should decide if arbitration provisions in a collective-bargaining contract survived a corporate merger so as to bind the surviving corporation. The Court answered that there was "no doubt" that this question was for the courts. "'Under our decisions, whether or not the company was bound to arbitrate, as well as what issues it must arbitrate, is a matter to be determined by the Court on the basis of the contract entered into by the parties.' . . . The duty to arbitrate being of contractual origin, a compulsory submission to arbitration cannot precede judicial determination that the collective bargaining agreement does in fact create such a duty."

The third principle derived from our prior cases is that, in deciding whether the parties have agreed to submit a particular grievance to arbitration, a court is not to rule on the potential merits of the underlying claims. Whether "arguable" or not, indeed even if it appears to the court to be frivolous, the union's claim that the employer has violated the collective-bargaining agreement is to be decided, not by the court asked to order arbitration, but as the parties have agreed, by the arbitrator. "The courts, therefore, have no business weighing the merits of the grievance, considering whether there is equity in a particular claim, or determining whether there is particular language in the written instrument which will support the claim. The agreement is to submit all grievances to arbitration, not merely those which the court will deem meritorious."

Finally, it has been established that where the contract contains an arbitration clause, there is a presumption of arbitrability in the sense that "[a]n order to arbitrate the particular grievance should not be denied unless it may be said with positive assurance that the arbitration clause is not susceptible of an interpretation that covers the asserted dispute. Doubts should be resolved in favor of coverage." Warrior & Gulf, 363 U.S. at 582–583. Such a presumption is particularly applicable where the clause is as broad as the one employed in this case, which provides for arbitration of "any differences arising with respect to the interpretation of this contract or the performance of any obligation hereunder. . . ." In such cases, "[i]n the absence of any express provision excluding a particular grievance from arbitration, we think only the most forceful evidence of a purpose to exclude the claim from arbitration can prevail." Warrior & Gulf, 363 U.S., at 584–585.

This presumption of arbitrability for labor disputes recognizes the greater institutional competence of arbitrators in interpreting collective bargaining agreements, "furthers the national labor policy of peaceful resolution of labor disputes and thus best accords with the parties' presumed objectives in pursuing collective bargaining." The willingness of parties to enter into agreements that provide for arbitration of specified disputes would be "drastically reduced," however, if a labor arbitrator had the "power to determine his own jurisdiction. . . ." Cox, Reflections Upon Labor Arbitration, 72 Harv.L.Rev. 1482, 1509 (1959). Were this the applicable rule, an arbitrator would not be constrained to resolve only those disputes that the parties have agreed in advance to settle by arbitration, but instead, would be empowered "to impose obligations outside the contract limited only by his understanding and conscience." This result undercuts the longstanding federal policy of promoting industrial harmony through the use of collective-bargaining agreements, and is antithetical to the function of a collective-bargaining agreement as setting out the rights and duties of the parties.

With these principles in mind, it is evident that the Seventh Circuit erred in ordering the parties to arbitrate the arbitrability question. It is the court's duty to interpret the agreement and to determine whether the parties intended to arbitrate grievances concerning layoffs predicated on a "lack of work" determination by the Company. If the court determines that the agreement so provides, then it is for the arbitrator to determine the relative merits of the parties' substantive interpretations of the agreement. It was for the court, not the arbitrator, to decide in the first instance whether the dispute was to be resolved through arbitration.

The Union does not contest the application of these principles to the present case. Instead, it urges the Court to examine the specific provisions of the agreement for itself and to affirm the Court of Appeals on the ground that the parties had agreed to arbitrate the dispute over the layoffs at issue here. But it is usually not our function in the first instance to construe collective-bargaining contracts and arbitration clauses, or to consider any other evidence that might unmistakably demonstrate that a particular grievance was not to be subject to arbitration. The issue in the case is whether, because of express exclusion or other forceful evidence, the dispute over the interpretation of Article 20 of the contract, the layoff provision, is not subject to the arbitration clause. That issue should have been decided by the District Court and reviewed by the Court of Appeals; it should not have been referred to the arbitrator.

The judgment of the Court of Appeals is vacated, and the case is remanded for proceedings in conformity with this opinion.

■ JUSTICE BRENNAN, with whom THE CHIEF JUSTICE and JUSTICE MARSHALL join, concurring.

I join the Court's opinion and write separately only to supplement what has been said in order to avoid any misunderstanding on remand and in future cases.

The Seventh Circuit's erroneous conclusion that the arbitrator should decide whether this dispute is arbitrable resulted from that court's confusion respecting the "arbitrability" determination that we have held must be judicially made. Despite recognizing that Article 8 of the collective-bargaining agreement "is a standard arbitration clause, providing for arbitration of 'any differences arising with respect to the interpretation of this contract or the performance of any obligation hereunder,'" and that "there is no clear, unambiguous exclusion [of this dispute] from arbitration," the Court of Appeals thought that "there [were] colorable arguments both for and against exclusion." The "colorable arguments" referred to by the Court of Appeals were the parties' claims concerning the meaning of Articles 9 and 20 of the collective-bargaining agreement: the Court of Appeals thought that if the Union's interpretation of Article 20 was correct and management could not order lay-offs for reasons other than lack of work, the dispute was arbitrable; but if AT & T's interpretation of Article 20 was correct and management was free to order lay-offs for other reasons, the dispute was not arbitrable under Article 9. Because these were the very issues that would be presented to the arbitrator if the dispute was held to be arbitrable, the court reasoned that "determining arbitrability would enmesh a court in the merits of th[e] dispute," and concluded that the arbitrability issue should be submitted to the arbitrator.

The Court of Appeals was mistaken insofar as it thought that determining arbitrability required resolution of the parties' dispute with respect to the meaning of Articles 9 and 20 of the collective-bargaining agreement. This is clear from our opinion in *Steelworkers v. Warrior & Gulf Navigation Co.* In *Warrior & Gulf,* the Union challenged management's contracting out of labor that had previously been performed by Company employees. The parties failed to resolve the dispute through grievance procedures, and the Union requested arbitration; the Company refused, and the Union sued to compel arbitration under § 301 of the Labor Management Relations Act, 29 U.S.C. § 185. The collective-bargaining agreement contained a standard arbitration clause similar to Article 8 of the AT & T/CSA contract, i.e., providing for arbitration of all differences with respect to the meaning or application of the contract. We held that, in light of the congressional policy making arbitration the favored method of dispute resolution, such a provision requires arbitration "unless it may be said with positive assurance that the arbitration clause is not susceptible of an interpretation that covers the asserted dispute. Doubts should be resolved in favor of coverage."

The Company in *Warrior & Gulf* relied for its argument that the dispute was not arbitrable on a "Management Functions" clause which, like Article 9 of the AT & T/CWA agreement, excluded "matters which are strictly a function of management" from the arbitration provision. We recognized that such a clause "might be thought to refer to any practice of management in which, under particular circumstances prescribed by the agreement, it is permitted to indulge." However, we also recognized that to read the clause this way would make arbitrability in every case depend upon whether management could take the action challenged by the Union; the arbitrability of every dispute would turn upon a resolution of the merits, and "the arbitration clause would be swallowed up by the exception." Therefore, we held that, where a collective-bargaining agreement contains a standard arbitration clause and the "exception" found in the Management Functions clause is general, "judicial inquiry . . . should be limited to the search for an explicit provision which brings the grievance under the cover of the [Management Functions] clause. . . ." "In the absence of any express provision excluding a particular grievance from arbitration, . . . only the most forceful evidence of a purpose to exclude the claim from arbitration can prevail. . . ."

The Seventh Circuit misunderstood these rules of contract construction and did precisely what we disapproved of in *Warrior & Gulf*—it read Article 9, a general Management Functions clause, to make arbitrability depend upon the merits of the parties' dispute. As *Warrior & Gulf* makes clear, the judicial inquiry required to determine arbitrability is much simpler. The parties' dispute concerns whether Article 20 of the collective-bargaining agreement limits management's authority to order lay-offs for reasons other than lack of work. The question for the court is "strictly confined" to whether the parties agreed to submit disputes over the meaning of Article 20 to arbitration. Because the collective-bargaining agreement contains a standard arbitration clause, the answer must be affirmative unless the contract contains explicit language stating that disputes respecting Article 20 are not subject to arbitration, or unless the party opposing arbitration—here AT & T—adduces "the most forceful evidence" to this effect from the bargaining history. Under *Warrior & Gulf,* determining arbitrability does not require the court even to consider which party is correct with respect to the meaning of Article 20.

The presumption of arbitrability established by the *Steelworkers* "Trilogy" continues, but the Supreme Court has not found every labor dispute arbitrable. The collective bargaining agreement in *Litton Financial Printing Div. v. NLRB*, 501 U.S. 190, 111 S.Ct. 2215, 115 L.Ed.2d 177 (1991), provided that any layoffs would be in order of seniority, provided that "aptitude and ability [were] equal." One year after the agreement expired, the employer laid off a number of senior employees, and the Union brought a grievance. The Supreme Court (in a 5–4 decision) held that this dispute did not "arise under" the expired agreement and was therefore not arbitrable. The grievances "would be arbitrable only if they involve rights which accrued or vested under the Agreement, or rights which carried over after expiration of the Agreement * * * as continuing obligations under the contract," and this was not the case: Since aptitude and ability "do not remain constant, but change over time," they "cannot be said to vest or accrue." The Court rejected the Union's argument that this was an issue of contract interpretation that should be submitted in the first instance to the arbitrator: The presumption of arbitrability cannot be applied "wholesale in the context of an expired bargaining agreement, for to do so would make limitless the contractual obligation to arbitrate. * * * [W]e must determine whether the parties agreed to arbitrate this dispute, and we cannot avoid that duty because it requires us to interpret a provision of a bargaining agreement." A footnote in the opinion conceded that the Court's determination that the dispute was not arbitrable "does, of necessity, determine that * * * the employees lacked any vested contractual right to a particular order of layoff."

Is *Litton* consistent with *AT & T*? See also Independent Lift Truck Builders Union v. Hyster Co., 2 F.3d 233 (7th Cir.1993) (after *Litton,* "the rule that courts must decide arbitrators' jurisdiction takes precedence over the rule that courts are not to decide the merits of the underlying dispute"); Commun. Workers of Am. v. Avaya, Inc., 693 F.3d 1295, 1300 (10th Cir. 2012) ("court's duty to determine whether the party intended the dispute to be arbitrable trumps its duty to avoid reaching the merits"); Paper, Allied-Industrial Chem. & Energy Workers Int'l Union, Local 4-12 v. Exxon Mobil Corp., 657 F.3d 272, 277–78 (5th Cir. 2011) ("the question of arbitrability is a question for the court * * * even if answering the arbitrability question requires a construction of the contract.")

While the alternative to arbitration of a labor grievance is "industrial strife," (a strike or lockout,) a likely alternative to arbitration of a non-labor claim is litigation of that claim. Nevertheless, the presumption of arbitrability applies outside the labor context, as the Supreme Court has found the FAA's "policy favoring arbitration agreements" to warrant a presumption that "any doubts concerning the scope of arbitrable issues should be resolved in favor of arbitration." Moses H. Cone Memorial Hospital v. Mercury Construction Corp., 460 U.S. 1, 24–25, 103 S.Ct. 927, 941, 74 L.Ed.2d 765 (1983). See also Mastrobuono v. Shearson Lehman Hutton, Inc., 514 U.S. 52, 62, 115 S. Ct. 1212, 1218, 131 L. Ed. 2d 76 (1995) ("due regard must be given to the federal policy favoring arbitration, and ambiguities as to the scope of the arbitration clause itself resolved in favor of arbitration") (quoting Volt Information Sciences, Inc. v. Board of Trustees of Leland Stanford Junior Univ., 489 U.S. 468, 477, 103 L. Ed. 2d 488, 109 S. Ct. 1248 (1989)).

Moreover, in non-labor cases, courts continue to cite the Supreme Court's labor cases (such as *AT&T* and *Steelworkers*) in emphasizing that:

> Whether parties have agreed to arbitrate a matter is fundamentally a question of contractual interpretation. But "[t]he analysis differs from ordinary contract interpretation in that 'any doubts concerning the scope of arbitrable issues should be resolved in favor of arbitration.'" Bensadoun v. Jobe-Riat, 316 F.3d 171, 176 (2d Cir. 2003). This arbitration-friendly approach effectuates the "federal policy favoring arbitration" found in the Federal Arbitration Act. Shearson/American Express, Inc. v. McMahon, 482 U.S. 220, 226, 107 S.Ct. 2332, 96 L.Ed.2d 185 (1987). Under these principles, an order to arbitrate "should not be denied unless it may be said with positive assurance that the arbitration clause is not susceptible of an interpretation that covers the asserted

> dispute." AT&T Tech., Inc. v. Commc'ns Workers of Am., 475 U.S. 643, 650, 106 S.Ct. 1415, 89 L.Ed.2d 648 (1986).

Safra Sec., LLC v. Gonzalez, 764 F. App'x 125, 126 (2d Cir.2019). And:

> The Supreme Court has "interpreted the Federal Arbitration Act as establishing that, 'as a matter of federal law, any doubts concerning the scope of arbitrable issues should be resolved in favor of arbitration." Even more forcefully, we have stated that arbitration is required "'unless it may be said with positive assurance that the arbitration clause is not susceptible of an interpretation that covers the asserted dispute.'"; see also United Steelworkers v. Warrior & Gulf Navigation Co., 363 U.S. 574, 584–85, 80 S.Ct. 1347, 4 L.Ed.2d 1409 (1960) ("In the absence of any express provision excluding a particular grievance from arbitration, we think only the most forceful evidence of a purpose to exclude the claim from arbitration can prevail. . . .").

Panepucci v. Honigman Miller Schwartz & Cohn LLP, 281 F. App'x 482, 486 (6th Cir.2008).

After all, said one district court judge, "the more the arbitrators do, the less I have to do." Block 175 Corp. v. Fairmont Hotel Management Co., 648 F.Supp. 450, 454 (D. Colo. 1986).

b. AGREEMENTS TO ARBITRATE DISPUTES ABOUT THE SCOPE OF THE AGREEMENT TO ARBITRATE

The first paragraph of Section 3.D.3 quoted FAA § 3, which allows parties to receive a court's decision on whether a claim is arbitrable (within the scope of the arbitration agreement) before compelling arbitration. However, the rule that courts, rather than arbitrators, resolve disputes about the scope of the arbitration agreement is merely a default rule. Parties can contract around this rule by using an arbitration agreement that says such disputes shall be resolved by the arbitrator rather than the court, provided that they do so "clearly and unmistakably." Howsam v. Dean Witter Reynolds, Inc., 537 U.S. 79, 83 (2002) ("the question whether the parties have submitted a particular dispute to arbitration, i.e., the 'question of arbitrability,' is an issue for judicial determination unless the parties clearly and unmistakably provide otherwise.")

For example, an agreement can incorporate the American Arbitration Association's Commercial Arbitration Rules, which provide that "[t]he arbitrator shall have the power to rule on his or her own jurisdiction, including any objections with respect to the existence, *scope* or validity of the arbitration agreement or to the arbitrability of any claim or counterclaim."[31] Sleeper Farms v. Agway, Inc., 211 F.Supp.2d 197, 200–03 (D.Me.2002)(since the AAA rules constitute "a clear and unmistakable delegation of scope-determining authority to an arbitrator," the court "refers this dispute" to the arbitrator "to determine * * * what issues * * * are covered by the arbitration clause.")

---

[31] Am.Arbitration Ass'n, Commercial Arbitration Rules, R-7(a) (2013) (emphasis added).

The Supreme Court unanimously enforced this AAA rule in *Henry Schein, Inc. v. Archer and White Sales, Inc.*, 139 S.Ct. 524 (2019). The relevant contract said:

> "Any dispute arising under or related to this Agreement (except for actions seeking injunctive relief and disputes related to trademarks, trade secrets, or other intellectual property of [Schein]), shall be resolved by binding arbitration in accordance with the arbitration rules of the American Arbitration Association."

Id. at 528. Archer brought suit, seeking both money damages and injunctive relief, and Schein moved to compel arbitration. The Fifth Circuit affirmed a denial of that motion because—although AAA rules delegate to the arbitrator the power to rule on his or her own jurisdiction, including the scope of the arbitration agreement—Schein's argument that Archer's action seeking injunctive relief was covered by the arbitration agreement was "wholly groundless" because the agreement excepted from arbitration "actions seeking injunctive relief." The Supreme Court unanimously reversed. Quoting *AT&T Technologies, Inc. v. Communications Workers* for the principle that "a court may not 'rule on the potential merits of the underlying' claim that is assigned by contract to an arbitrator, 'even if it appears to the court to be frivolous,'" the *Henry Schein* Court said this "principle applies with equal force to the threshold issue of arbitrability." Id. at 530.

The question discussed in the previous three paragraphs (whether parties to an arbitration agreement delegated to their arbitrator issues about the *scope* of that agreement) is different from the question whether parties delegated to an arbitrator issues about whether someone is a party to an arbitration agreement at all. Whether a particular party *formed* an arbitration agreement is generally for the court (rather than arbitrator) to decide under the Supreme Court's 1995 decision in *First Options of Chicago v. Kaplan*, 514 U.S. 938, 944 (1995). In *First Options*, an options trader ("MKI") owed money to a clearinghouse firm ("First Options"), and the parties entered into a series of agreements aimed at "working out" the debt. Kaplan, the President and sole shareholder of MKI, signed several of these, containing an arbitration clause, on behalf of MKI; in addition, he signed one such agreement in his individual capacity that did *not* contain an arbitration clause. First Options initiated arbitration proceedings against both MKI and Kaplan individually; the arbitrators took jurisdiction and issued an award against both. The Supreme Court held that the award should be vacated: Where a proper objection has been raised, a court must make a *de novo* determination of consent to arbitration without any deference to the arbitrators' findings. And in 2019, the *Henry Schein* Court reiterated that "before referring a dispute to an arbitrator, the court determines whether a valid arbitration agreement exists. But if a valid agreement exists, and if the agreement delegates the arbitrability issue to an arbitrator, a court may not decide the arbitrability issue." 139 S.Ct. at 530.

The Supreme Court similarly holds in labor arbitration that "courts should order arbitration of a dispute only where the court is satisfied that neither the formation of the parties' arbitration agreement nor (absent a valid provision specifically committing such disputes to an arbitrator) its enforceability or applicability to the dispute is in issue. Where a party contests either or both matters, 'the court' must resolve the disagreement." Granite Rock Co. v. Int'l Bhd. of Teamsters, 561 U.S. 287, 299–300 (2010) (citing *First Options*).

QUESTIONS TO REVIEW AND SYNTHESIZE

1. What presumption is endorsed by both *AT&T* and *Moses H. Cone Memorial Hospital v. Mercury Construction Corp.*, 460 U.S. 1, 24–25, 103 S.Ct. 927, 941, 74 L.Ed.2d 765 (1983)?
2. *Howsam* and *Henry Schein* support enforcing arbitration agreements that do what?
3. What one broad holding can be found in *First Options*, *Henry Schein*, and *Granite Rock*? Is this holding in tension with *Rent-A-Center v. Jackson* or cases we saw in Section 3.D.2.c applying *Rent-A-Center v. Jackson*?

4. CONDITIONS TO ARBITRATION

A party opposing arbitration may assert that arbitration should not occur because a contractual time limit to start arbitration has expired or contractual preconditions to start arbitration have not been satisfied. Such "procedural questions which grow out of the dispute and bear on its final disposition are presumptively not for the judge, but for an arbitrator, to decide", the Supreme Court held in *Howsam v. Dean Witter Reynolds, Inc.,* 537 U.S. 79, 84–85 (2002). As examples, *Howsam* endorsed authorities stating that the "arbitrator should decide whether the first two steps of a grievance procedure were completed, where these steps are prerequisites to arbitration," and "whether prerequisites such as time limits, notice, laches, estoppel, and other conditions precedent to an obligation to arbitrate have been met, are for the arbitrators to decide." Other courts have added to this list the place (venue) of arbitration. LodgeWorks, L.P. v. C.F. Jordan Const., LLC, 506 F. App'x 747, 750 (10th Cir.2012); Fin. Servs. v. W. Va. Univ. Hosps., Inc., 660 F.3d 643, 655 (2d Cir.2011) ("venue is a procedural issue that [the] arbitrators should address in the first instance.")

5. REMEDIES IN ARBITRATION

Remedies, like other aspects of arbitration, are primarily determined by the arbitration agreement. For example, the Supreme Court used a contractual analysis to determine whether the arbitrator could award punitive damages in *Mastrobuono v. Shearson Lehman Hutton, Inc.*, 514 U.S. 52 (1995) (excerpted above in Section 3.C.5). As the *Mastrobuono* Court said, "the case before us comes down to what the contract has to say about the arbitrability of petitioners' claim for punitive damages." *Mastrobuono* stated that this contractual analysis is mandated by the FAA and that it preempts any state law requiring a non-contractual analysis. New York law, at the time, required a non-contractual analysis. New York law prohibited arbitrators from awarding punitive damages regardless of the arbitration agreement's terms. *Mastrobuono* found that the FAA preempted that New York law. *Mastrobuono* pointed out that the contract authorized arbitration in accordance with the rules of the National Association of Securities Dealers ("NASD") and a NASD manual provided to NASD arbitrators contained this provision: "The issue of punitive damages may arise with great frequency in arbitrations. Parties to arbitration are informed that arbitrators can consider punitive damages as a remedy." Thus, the Court found that the arbitration clause "contradicts * * * the conclusion that the parties agreed to foreclose claims for punitive damages." *Mastrobuono* then went on to cite two further reasons for interpreting the contract to permit arbitrators to award punitive damages: (1) "the federal policy favoring arbitration," which means that "ambiguities as to the scope of the arbitration clause itself are resolved in favor of arbitration," and (2) "the common-law rule of contract interpretation that a court should construe ambiguous language against the interest of the party that drafted it." These final two points suggest that the Court favors interpretations of arbitration agreements that preserve the full remedies of the parties, especially parties who sign form arbitration agreements presented to them on a take-it-or-leave-it basis.

Section 3.D.2.c, discussing unconscionability, quotes *Subcontracting Concepts (CT), LLC v. De Melo*, 34 Cal. App. 5th 201, 216, 245 Cal. Rptr. 3d 838, 849 (Ct. App. 2019), which affirmed a denial of employer's motion to compel arbitration in part because the California Supreme Court had "held that the FAA does not require enforcement of a provision in an arbitration agreement that, in violation of generally applicable California contract law, 'limit[s] statutorily imposed remedies such as punitive damages and attorney fees.'" In *Subcontracting Concepts*, the California Court of Appeals held the arbitration clause unconscionable in part because it "states that the arbitrators 'have authority to award actual monetary damages only. No punitive or equitable relief is authorized.'" Several other courts have similarly declined to enforce remedy limitations in arbitration agreements, typically in the context of adhesive arbitration agreements presented by businesses to employees and consumers.

However, the Supreme Court case of *Pacificare Health Systems, Inc. v. Book*, 538 U.S. 401 (2003), indicates that in at least some cases involving contractual remedy-limitations, courts should send to the arbitrators the question whether to enforce those limitations. In *Book*, physicians brought claims under a statute (RICO) that provides for treble damages. The defendants' motion to compel arbitration was denied by the lower courts because the agreement's ban on "punitive damages" could bar recovery of treble damages as provided for by the RICO statute, and such bar would be unenforceable as a matter of public policy because it would prevent the plaintiffs "from obtaining any meaningful relief for [their] statutory claims." The Supreme Court, however, reversed: Writing for a unanimous court, Justice Scalia thought that to address the public-policy related question was simply "premature": The terms of the agreement were "ambiguous," and the intent of the parties "uncertain"—in particular, whether the contractual limitation was even applicable to RICO claims for treble damages "is, to say the least, in doubt." So the arbitration clause was "at least initially, enforceable": Courts should not take upon themselves "the authority to decide the antecedent question of how the ambiguity is to be resolved," and the arbitrators must first be called on to tell us just what the agreement meant. "Since we do not know how the arbitrator will construe the remedial limitations," the Court concluded "the proper course is to compel arbitration." Id. at 407.

Many arbitration agreements provide that the arbitrator may order any remedy that a court could order. And this seems to be the usual default interpretation of arbitration agreements that are silent on remedies. For example, arbitrators order parties to pay punitive damages and issue injunctions even though the arbitration agreement may not expressly authorize those remedies.

In contrast, arbitration is generally less suited than litigation as a forum for an emergency remedy, such as a temporary restraining order. This is because arbitration cannot award any remedy until an arbitrator has been appointed. The party against whom a restraining order is sought likely can delay that appointment until it does whatever the other party sought to restrain. For this reason, the American Arbitration Association maintains an emergency panel of arbitrators that can quickly rule on requests for provisional remedies before the appointment of the arbitrators who will hear the rest of the case,[32] but that option appears to be used only rarely.

Suppose a party to an arbitration agreement asks a court to issue preliminary injunctive relief in disputes that are ultimately to be resolved by an arbitration panel. Most courts are willing to do this. See, e.g., Toyo Tire Holdings of Americas, Inc. v. Continental Tire North America, Inc., 609 F.3d 975, 978–81, 983 (9th Cir. 2010) ("If Toyo loses its customers before interim relief is possible, any subsequent relief could be useless"; "court may issue interim injunctive relief on arbitrable claims if interim relief is necessary to preserve the status quo and the meaningfulness of the arbitration process"); Janvey v. Alguire, 647 F.3d 585, 589–90 (5th Cir. 2011) (affirming preliminary injunction requested by the receiver appointed to "to conserve, hold, manage, and preserve the value of the receivership estate" and freezing various investment accounts containing proceeds from the Ponzi scheme until court decides whether to compel arbitration). But at least one circuit has held that "courts should not grant injunctive relief unless there is 'qualifying contractual language' which permits it." Manion v. Nagin, 255 F.3d 535, 538–39 (8th Cir.2001) (quoting Merrill Lynch, Pierce, Fenner & Smith, Inc. v. Hovey, 726 F.2d 1286, 1292 (8th Cir.1984)).

The previous paragraph's discussion of courts ordering preliminary injunctive relief in disputes likely to be resolved later in arbitration is an example of judicial supervision of arbitration, the focus of the next section.

QUESTION TO REVIEW AND SYNTHESIZE

1. When do courts enforce contractual limitations on remedies arbitrators may award?

E. JUDICIAL SUPERVISION AND REVIEW OF ARBITRATION

1. INTRODUCTION

Although arbitration's usual confidentiality leaves some doubt, the usual belief is that most arbitrations never encounter a court, and those that do often involve just a court's perfunctory confirmation of the arbitration award. In other words, significant judicial supervision or review of arbitration is the exception, rather than the rule.

---

[32] See Am.Arbitration Ass'n, Commercial Arbitration Rules, R-38 (2013).

This judicial deference to arbitration serves a practical purpose. For arbitration to resolve disputes quickly and inexpensively—let alone to realize the benefits of an expert adjudicator—litigation challenging the arbitration process, or aimed at vacating the resulting award, must be minimized. Failure to minimize litigation about arbitration poses the danger exemplified by a tongue-in-cheek comment of a lawyer from Latin America, a region where arbitration was for many decades neither familiar nor generally accepted: "We lawyers like arbitration. It assures us three litigations: one before, one during and one after the arbitration."[33] When arbitration does that for lawyers, arbitration's appeal to disputing parties shrinks.

On the other hand, some sort of public (government) supervision and control of arbitration may be necessary to protect wider social interests that may be ignored or jeopardized by private arbitrators. The inevitable tension between these two values is a theme that figures in much of these materials.

2. CONFIRMATION AND CLAIM PRECLUSION (RES JUDICATA)

As a general rule, arbitration awards are final and binding on the parties with only very limited grounds for judicial review. If all parties comply with the award, that ends the dispute. If a party refuses to comply, however, then any other party may seek court enforcement of the award beginning with a court order *confirming* the award. 9 U.S.C. § 9. An order confirming an award "shall have the same force and effect, in all respects, as, and be subject to all the provisions of law relating to, a judgment in an action; and it may be enforced as if it had been rendered in an action in the court in which it is entered." 9 U.S.C. § 13. A confirmed award in favor of the claimant is enforced in the same manner as other court judgments: through orders to turn over property, judicial liens, garnishment, etc.

In addition, arbitration awards generally have claim-preclusive effect—that is, the arbitrator's ruling precludes litigating or re-arbitrating the claims resolved in arbitration—whether or not a court has confirmed the award. Jacobson v. Fireman's Fund Ins. Co., 111 F.3d 261, 267 (2d Cir.1996) ("[the] contention that only a judicially confirmed arbitration award may form the basis for the defenses of *res judicata* and collateral estoppel is without merit * * * [These] doctrines are applicable to issues resolved by arbitration where there has been a final determination on the merits, notwithstanding a lack of confirmation of the award."); Freecharm Ltd. v. Atlas Wealth Holdings Corp., 2011 WL 4591929, 2011 U.S. Dist. LEXIS 113172, at *14 (S.D. Fla. Sep. 30, 2011) ("an unconfirmed arbitration award has a preclusive effect on subsequent litigation proceedings"); Thibodeau v. Crum, 6 Cal.Rptr.2d 27 (Cal.Ct.App.1992) (unconfirmed award in arbitration between homeowner and general contractor is *res judicata* barring homeowner's identical claim against subcontractor).

The claim-preclusive effect of arbitration awards can be less clear in labor arbitration because many collective bargaining agreements prohibit discrimination that is also prohibited by statute, so arbitration of alleged discrimination might be resolving both statutory and contractual claims or just resolving contractual claims.

---

[33] Quoted in Nattier, *International Commercial Arbitration in Latin America: Enforcement of Arbitral Agreements and Awards*, 21 Tex.Int'l L.J. 397, 408 (1986).

In such ambiguous circumstances, *Alexander v. Gardner-Denver Co.*, 415 U.S. 36 (1974), discussed in Section 3.B.3.b, allowed a Title VII suit to proceed even after the arbitrator rejected the employee's contractual claim for discrimination in violation of the collective bargaining agreement. In contrast, *14 Penn Plaza LLC v. Pyett*, 556 U.S. 247 (2009), excerpted above in Section 3.B.3.c, criticized *Gardner-Denver*,[34] and distinguished it to enforce collective bargaining arbitration clauses that "clearly and unmistakably require[ ] union members to arbitrate" statutory discrimination claims.[35] Nevertheless, since *Pyett*, lower courts have resisted finding that an arbitration *award* on an employee's statutory discrimination claim precludes suit on that claim. See, e.g., Mathews v. Denver Newspaper Agency LLP, 649 F.3d 1199, 1207–08 (10th Cir. 2011) (employee's suit on statutory claims not precluded by arbitration award denying contract claim, but not addressing statutory claim; "Because the arbitration agreement empowered the arbitrator to resolve only the dispute submitted, and because the dispute submitted made no mention of statutory claims, the arbitral decision could in no way determine the question of Mathews's statutory rights"); Siddiqua v. New York State Dep't of Health, 642 F. App'x 68, 71 (2d Cir. 2016) ("because Siddiqua did not agree to arbitrate her statutory claims, and the labor arbitrator was not authorized to resolve such claims, the Arbitrator's award in this case cannot preclude subsequent statutory actions.") (internal quotations omitted).

3. ISSUE PRECLUSION (COLLATERAL ESTOPPEL)

The doctrine of issue preclusion bars adjudication of issues that have been decided in a prior case, and it "can apply if that prior case was an arbitration. Generally, final arbitral awards are afforded the same preclusive effects as are prior court judgments." Manganella v. Evanston Ins. Co., 700 F.3d 585, 591 (1st Cir. 2012) (affirming ruling that company president could not receive indemnity from his insurer for charges of sexual harassment brought against him by former employee because, under the doctrine of issue preclusion, a prior arbitration between president and purchaser of his business conclusively established that president's conduct was excluded by relevant insurance policy.)

However, "there may be particular difficulties in applying preclusion principles to an arbitral award, especially where the reasoning behind the award is unexplained" because "[f]or issue preclusion to apply," "the arbitrators must have decided an issue the same as the one presented" in the case in which preclusion is sought. Id.

While issue preclusion can only be asserted *against* one who was a party to the prior case, it can be asserted *by* one who was a stranger to that prior case. When issue preclusion is asserted by one who was a stranger to the prior case, it is called "non-mutual" issue preclusion. See, e.g., Riverdale Dev. Co. v. Ruffin Bldg. Sys.

[34] See, e.g., id. at 265 ("We recognize that apart from their narrow holdings, the *Gardner-Denver* line of cases included broad dicta that were highly critical of the use of arbitration for the vindication of statutory antidiscrimination rights. That skepticism, however, rested on a misconceived view of arbitration that this Court has since abandoned."); see also id. ("The suggestion in *Gardner-Denver* that the decision to arbitrate statutory discrimination claims was tantamount to a substantive waiver of those rights, therefore, reveals a distorted understanding of the compromise made when an employee agrees to compulsory arbitration.").

[35] Id. at 274.

Inc., 146 S.W.3d 852, 854 (Ark.2004) ("a third party * * * is entitled to rely upon an arbitration award such as [the one] here under the doctrines of collateral estoppel or *res judicata*"). However, under the law of some states, arbitration awards have non-mutual issue-preclusive effect only if the arbitration agreement provides that they will have such effect. Buckner v. Kennard, 99 P.3d 842, 846 (Utah 2004) ("a private arbitration award does not have nonmutual collateral estoppel effect unless the parties expressly provide for such preclusive effect beforehand"). For example, in Vandenberg v. Superior Court, 21 Cal.4th 815, 88 Cal.Rptr.2d 366, 982 P.2d 229 (1999), the earlier arbitration had been between a landowner and its lessee for contamination of soil and groundwater. The California Supreme Court held that the arbitrator's findings adverse to the lessee did not prevent the lessee, in a later indemnification action against his insurers, from arguing that the discharge was "sudden and accidental" and thus not excluded from pollution coverage under the policy. The court noted that while in arbitration the parties have voluntarily traded "the safeguards and formalities of court litigation for an expeditious, sometimes roughshod means of resolving their dispute," "these same features can be serious, unexpected disadvantages if issues decided by the arbitrators are given leveraged effect in favor of strangers to the arbitration."

QUESTIONS TO REVIEW AND SYNTHESIZE

1. What are the differences between courts' judgments and arbitration awards with regard to ease of enforcement?
2. What is claim preclusion and what are the differences between courts' judgments and arbitration awards with regard to claim preclusion?
3. What is issue preclusion and what are the differences between courts' judgments and arbitration awards with regard to issue preclusion?

4. VACATUR OF ARBITRATION AWARDS

a. DEFERENTIAL REVIEW OF ARBITRATION AWARDS UNDER THE FAA

A party disappointed with an arbitrator's decision may ask a court to vacate the arbitration award. The conventional wisdom is that challenges to arbitration awards usually fail, especially in federal courts. For instance, a study of employment arbitration awards found them confirmed by federal district courts in 92.7% of cases, federal appellate courts in 87.7% of cases, state trial courts in 78.8% of cases, and state appellate courts in 71.4% of cases. Michael H. LeRoy, *Misguided Fairness? Regulating Arbitration by Statute: Empirical Evidence of Declining Award Finality*, 83 Notre Dame L. Rev. 551, 587–89 (2008).

In some ways, a court considering whether to vacate an arbitration award is like an appellate court considering whether to reverse the decision of a trial court. But "the grounds on which courts review arbitration awards are much narrower than the grounds on which appeals courts review decisions of trial courts."[36] In particular, when appellate courts reverse trial courts they generally do so on the ground that the trial court has erred in its findings of fact or conclusions of law. Appellate courts

[36] Christopher R. Drahozal, Commercial Arbitration: Cases and Problems 494 (2d ed.2006).

usually give some deference to trial courts' factual findings—reversing only those that are "clearly erroneous"—but give no deference to trial courts' legal rulings, reviewing them de novo.[37] So the typical appeal of a trial court's decision centers on the appellant's argument that the trial court made an error of law.

By contrast, arbitrators' legal rulings are rarely given de novo review by courts considering a motion to vacate an arbitration award. In fact, the FAA may not allow courts to review arbitrators' legal rulings at all—because "error of law" by the arbitrator is not even a ground for vacating an arbitration award. The FAA only permits courts to vacate:

> (1) Where the award was procured by corruption, fraud, or undue means;
>
> (2) Where there was evident partiality or corruption in the arbitrators, or either of them;
>
> (3) Where the arbitrators were guilty of misconduct in refusing to postpone the hearing, upon sufficient cause shown, or in refusing to hear evidence pertinent and material to the controversy; or of any other misbehavior by which the rights of any party have been prejudiced; or
>
> (4) Where the arbitrators exceeded their powers, or so imperfectly executed them that a mutual, final, and definite award upon the subject matter submitted was not made.

9 U.S.C. § 10(a). While many parties, at the time they agree to arbitrate, may like committing to these narrow grounds of vacatur to speed resolution of their disputes, suppose particular parties are willing to incur the time and expense of a court scrutinizing the arbitration award more closely for errors of law or clearly erroneous factual findings?

Hall St. Assocs., L.L.C. v. Mattel, Inc.

Supreme Court of the United States, 2008.
552 U.S. 576, 128 S.Ct. 1396, 170 L.Ed.2d 254.

■ JUSTICE SOUTER delivered the opinion of the Court.

The Federal Arbitration Act (FAA or Act), provides for expedited judicial review to confirm, vacate, or modify arbitration awards. The question here is whether statutory grounds for prompt vacatur and modification may be supplemented by contract. We hold that the statutory grounds are exclusive.

This case began as a lease dispute between landlord, petitioner Hall Street Associates, L. L. C., and tenant, respondent Mattel, Inc. The property was used for many years as a manufacturing site, and the leases provided that the tenant would indemnify the landlord for any costs resulting from the failure of the tenant or its predecessor lessees to follow environmental laws while using the premises.

---

[37] "For purposes of standard of review, decisions by judges are traditionally divided into three categories, denominated questions of law (reviewable de novo), questions of fact (reviewable for clear error), and matters of discretion (reviewable for 'abuse of discretion')." Pierce v. Underwood, 487 U.S. 552 (1988).

Tests of the property's well water in 1998 showed high levels of trichloroethylene (TCE), the apparent residue of manufacturing discharges by Mattel's predecessors between 1951 and 1980. * * *

After Mattel gave notice of intent to terminate the lease in 2001, Hall Street filed this suit, contesting Mattel's right to vacate on the date it gave, and claiming that the lease obliged Mattel to indemnify Hall Street for costs of cleaning up the TCE, among other things. Following a bench trial before the United States District Court for the District of Oregon, Mattel won on the termination issue, and after an unsuccessful try at mediating the indemnification claim, the parties proposed to submit to arbitration. The District Court was amenable, and the parties drew up an arbitration agreement, which the court approved and entered as an order. One paragraph of the agreement provided that

> "[t]he United States District Court for the District of Oregon may enter judgment upon any award, either by confirming the award or by vacating, modifying or correcting the award. The Court shall vacate, modify or correct any award: (i) where the arbitrator's findings of facts are not supported by substantial evidence, or (ii) where the arbitrator's conclusions of law are erroneous."

Arbitration took place, and the arbitrator decided for Mattel. * * *

Hall Street then filed a District Court Motion for Order Vacating, Modifying And/Or Correcting Arbitration Accord, on the ground that failing to treat the Oregon Act as an applicable environmental law under the terms of the lease was legal error. The District Court agreed, vacated the award, and remanded for further consideration by the arbitrator. The court expressly invoked the standard of review chosen by the parties in the arbitration agreement, which included review for legal error, and cited *LaPine Technology Corp. v. Kyocera Corp.*, 130 F.3d 884, 889 (CA9 1997), for the proposition that the FAA leaves the parties "free . . . to draft a contract that sets rules for arbitration and dictates an alternative standard of review."

On remand, the arbitrator followed the District Court's ruling that the Oregon Act was an applicable environmental law and amended the decision to favor Hall Street. This time, each party sought modification, and again the District Court applied the parties' stipulated standard of review for legal error, correcting the arbitrator's calculation of interest but otherwise upholding the award. Each party then appealed to the Court of Appeals for the Ninth Circuit, where Mattel switched horses and contended that the Ninth Circuit's recent en banc action overruling *LaPine* in *Kyocera Corp. v. Prudential-Bache Trade Servs., Inc.*, 341 F.3d 987, 1000 (2003), left the arbitration agreement's provision for judicial review of legal error unenforceable. Hall Street countered that *Kyocera* (the later one) was distinguishable, and that the agreement's judicial review provision was not severable from the submission to arbitration.

The Ninth Circuit reversed in favor of Mattel in holding that, "[u]nder *Kyocera* the terms of the arbitration agreement controlling the mode of judicial review are unenforceable and severable." The Circuit instructed the District Court on remand to "return to the application to confirm the original arbitration award (not the subsequent award revised after reversal), and . . . confirm that award, unless . . . the award should be vacated on the grounds allowable under 9 U.S.C. § 10, or modified or corrected under the grounds allowable under 9 U.S.C. § 11."

After the District Court again held for Hall Street and the Ninth Circuit again reversed,[1] we granted certiorari to decide whether the grounds for vacatur and modification provided by §§ 10 and 11 of the FAA are exclusive. We agree with the Ninth Circuit that they are, but vacate and remand for consideration of independent issues.

Congress enacted the FAA to replace judicial indisposition to arbitration with a "national policy favoring [it] and plac[ing] arbitration agreements on equal footing with all other contracts." * * * [T]he Act makes contracts to arbitrate "valid, irrevocable, and enforceable," so long as their subject involves "commerce." § 2. * * *

The Act also supplies mechanisms for enforcing arbitration awards: a judicial decree confirming an award, an order vacating it, or an order modifying or correcting it. §§ 9–11. An application for any of these orders will get streamlined treatment as a motion, obviating the separate contract action that would usually be necessary to enforce or tinker with an arbitral award in court. § 6. Under the terms of § 9, a court "must" confirm an arbitration award "unless" it is vacated, modified, or corrected "as prescribed" in §§ 10 and 11. Section 10 lists grounds for vacating an award, while § 11 names those for modifying or correcting one.

The Courts of Appeals have split over the exclusiveness of these statutory grounds when parties take the FAA shortcut to confirm, vacate, or modify an award, with some saying the recitations are exclusive, and others regarding them as mere threshold provisions open to expansion by agreement.[5] As mentioned already, when this litigation started, the Ninth Circuit was on the threshold side of the split from which it later departed en banc in favor of the exclusivity view, which it followed in this case. We now hold that §§ §§ 10 and 11 respectively provide the FAA's exclusive grounds for expedited vacatur and modification.

Hall Street makes two main efforts to show that the grounds set out for vacating or modifying an award are not exclusive, taking the position, first, that expandable judicial review authority has been accepted as the law since *Wilko v.*

---

[1] On remand, the District Court vacated the arbitration award because it supposedly rested on an implausible interpretation of the lease and thus exceeded the arbitrator's powers, in violation of 9 U.S.C. § 10. Mattel appealed, and the Ninth Circuit reversed, holding that implausibility is not a valid ground for vacating or correcting an award under § 10 or § 11. 196 Fed. Appx. 476, 477–478 (2006).

[5] The Ninth and Tenth Circuits have held that parties may not contract for expanded judicial review. See Kyocera Corp. v. Prudential-Bache Trade Servs., Inc., 341 F.3d 987, 1000 (CA9 2003) (en banc); Bowen v. Amoco Pipeline Co., 254 F.3d 925, 936 (CA10 2001). The First, Third, Fifth, and Sixth Circuits, meanwhile, have held that parties may so contract. See Puerto Rico Tel. Co. v. U.S. Phone Mfg. Corp., 427 F.3d 21, 31 (CA1 2005); Jacada (Europe), Ltd. v. International Marketing Strategies, Inc., 401 F.3d 701, 710 (CA6 2005); Roadway Package System, Inc. v. Kayser, 257 F.3d 287, 288 (CA3 2001); Gateway Technologies, Inc. v. MCI Telecommunications Corp., 64 F.3d 993, 997 (CA5 1995). The Fourth Circuit has taken the latter side of the split in an unpublished opinion, see Syncor Int'l Corp. v. McLeland, 120 F.3d 262 (1997), while the Eighth Circuit has expressed agreement with the former side in dicta, see UHC Management Co. v. Computer Sciences Corp., 148 F.3d 992, 997–998 (1998).

Swan, 346 U.S. 427, 74 S. Ct. 182, 98 L. Ed. 168 (1953). This, however, was not what *Wilko* decided, which was that § 14 of the Securities Act of 1933 voided any agreement to arbitrate claims of violations of that Act, a holding since overruled by *Rodriguez de Quijas v. Shearson/American Express, Inc.*, 490 U.S. 477, 484, 109 S. Ct. 1917, 104 L. Ed. 2d 526 (1989). Although it is true that the Court's discussion includes some language arguably favoring Hall Street's position, arguable is as far as it goes.

The *Wilko* Court was explaining that arbitration would undercut the Securities Act's buyer protections when it remarked (citing FAA § 10) that "[p]ower to vacate an [arbitration] award is limited," and went on to say that "the interpretations of the law by the arbitrators in contrast to manifest disregard [of the law] are not subject, in the federal courts, to judicial review for error in interpretation." Hall Street reads this statement as recognizing "manifest disregard of the law" as a further ground for vacatur on top of those listed in § 10, and some Circuits have read it the same way. Hall Street sees this supposed addition to § 10 as the camel's nose: if judges can add grounds to vacate (or modify), so can contracting parties.

But this is too much for *Wilko* to bear. Quite apart from its leap from a supposed judicial expansion by interpretation to a private expansion by contract, Hall Street overlooks the fact that the statement it relies on expressly rejects just what Hall Street asks for here, general review for an arbitrator's legal errors. Then there is the vagueness of *Wilko*'s phrasing. Maybe the term "manifest disregard" was meant to name a new ground for review, but maybe it merely referred to the § 10 grounds collectively, rather than adding to them. Or, as some courts have thought, "manifest disregard" may have been shorthand for § 10(a)(3) or § 10(a)(4), the paragraphs authorizing vacatur when the arbitrators were "guilty of misconduct" or "exceeded their powers." We, when speaking as a Court, have merely taken the *Wilko* language as we found it, with out embellishment, see *First Options*, and now that its meaning is implicated, we see no reason to accord it the significance that Hall Street urges.

Second, Hall Street says that the agreement to review for legal error ought to prevail simply because arbitration is a creature of contract, and the FAA is "motivated, first and foremost, by a congressional desire to enforce agreements into which parties ha[ve] entered." Dean Witter Reynolds Inc. v. Byrd, 470 U.S. 213, 220, 105 S. Ct. 1238, 84 L. Ed. 2d 158 (1985). But, again, we think the argument comes up short. Hall Street is certainly right that the FAA lets parties tailor some, even many, features of arbitration by contract, including the way arbitrators are chosen, what their qualifications should be, which issues are arbitrable, along with procedure and choice of substantive law. But to rest this case on the general policy of treating arbitration agreements as enforceable as such would be to beg the question, which is whether the FAA has textual features at odds with enforcing a contract to expand judicial review following the arbitration.

To that particular question we think the answer is yes, that the text compels a reading of the §§ 10 and 11 categories as exclusive. To begin with, even if we assumed §§ 10 and 11 could be supplemented to some extent, it would stretch basic interpretive principles to expand the stated grounds to the point of evidentiary and legal review generally. Sections 10 and 11, after all, address egregious departures from the parties' agreed-upon arbitration: "corruption," "fraud," "evident partiality," "misconduct," "misbehavior," "exceed[ing]. . . powers," "evident material miscalculation," "evident material mistake," "award[s] upon a matter not submitted;" the only ground with any softer focus is "imperfect[ions]," and a court may correct those only if they go to "[a] matter of form not affecting the merits." Given this emphasis on extreme arbitral conduct, the old rule of *ejusdem generis* has an implicit lesson to teach here. Under that rule, when a statute sets out a series of specific items ending with a general term, that general term is confined to covering subjects comparable to the specifics it follows. Since a general term included in the text is normally so limited, then surely a statute with no textual hook for expansion cannot authorize contracting parties to supplement review for specific instances of outrageous conduct with review for just any legal error. "Fraud" and a mistake of law are not cut from the same cloth.

That aside, expanding the detailed categories would rub too much against the grain of the § 9 language, where provision for judicial confirmation carries no hint of flexibility. On application for an order confirming the arbitration award, the court "must grant" the order "unless the award is vacated, modified, or corrected as prescribed in sections 10 and 11 of this title." There is nothing malleable about "must grant," which unequivocally tells courts to grant confirmation in all cases, except when one of the "prescribed" exceptions applies. This does not sound remotely like a provision meant to tell a court what to do just in case the parties say nothing else.

In fact, anyone who thinks Congress might have understood § 9 as a default provision should turn back to § 5 for an example of what Congress thought a default provision would look like:

> "[i]f in the agreement provision be made for a method of naming or appointing an arbitrator. . . such method shall be followed; but if no method be provided therein, or if a method be provided and any party thereto shall fail to avail himself of such method, . . . then upon the application of either party to the controversy the court shall designate and appoint an arbitrator. . . ."

"[I]f no method be provided" is a far cry from "must grant . . . unless" in § 9.

Instead of fighting the text, it makes more sense to see the three provisions, §§ 9–11, as substantiating a national policy favoring arbitration with just the limited review needed to maintain arbitration's essential virtue of resolving disputes straightaway. Any other reading opens the door to the full-bore legal and evidentiary appeals that can "rende[r] informal arbitration merely a prelude to a more cumbersome and time-consuming judicial review process," and bring arbitration theory to grief in postarbitration process.

Nor is *Dean Witter,* to the contrary, as Hall Street claims it to be. *Dean Witter* held that state-law claims subject to an agreement to arbitrate could not be remitted to a district court considering a related, nonarbitrable federal claim; the state-law claims were to go to arbitration immediately. Despite the opinion's language "reject[ing] the suggestion that the overriding goal of the [FAA] was to promote the expeditious resolution of claims," the holding mandated immediate enforcement of an arbitration agreement; the Court was merely trying to explain that the inefficiency and difficulty of conducting simultaneous arbitration and federal-court litigation was not a good enough reason to defer the arbitration.

When all these arguments based on prior legal authority are done with, Hall Street and Mattel remain at odds over what happens next. Hall Street and its *amici* say parties will flee from arbitration if expanded review is not open to them. One of Mattel's *amici* foresees flight from the courts if it is. We do not know who, if anyone, is right, and so cannot say whether the exclusivity reading of the statute is more of a threat to the popularity of arbitrators or to that of courts. But whatever the consequences of our holding, the statutory text gives us no business to expand the statutory grounds.

In holding that §§ 10 and 11 provide exclusive regimes for the review provided by the statute, we do not purport to say that they exclude more searching review based on authority outside the statute as well. The FAA is not the only way into court for parties wanting review of arbitration awards: they may contemplate enforcement under state statutory or common law, for example, where judicial review of different scope is arguable. But here we speak only to the scope of the expeditious judicial review under §§ 9, 10, and 11, deciding nothing about other possible avenues for judicial enforcement of arbitration awards.

* * *

Although we agree with the Ninth Circuit that the FAA confines its expedited judicial review to the grounds listed in 9 U.S.C. §§ 10 and 11, we vacate the judgment and remand the case for proceedings consistent with this opinion.

It is so ordered.

■ JUSTICE STEVENS, with whom JUSTICE KENNEDY joins, dissenting.

May parties to an ongoing lawsuit agree to submit their dispute to arbitration subject to the caveat that the trial judge should refuse to enforce an award that rests on an erroneous conclusion of law? Prior to Congress' enactment of the Federal Arbitration Act (FAA or Act) in 1925, the answer to that question would surely have been "Yes."[1] Today, however, the Court holds that the FAA does not merely authorize the vacation or enforcement of awards on specified grounds, but also forbids enforcement of perfectly reasonable judicial review provisions in arbitration agreements fairly negotiated by the parties and approved by the district court. Because this result conflicts with the primary purpose of the FAA and ignores the historical context in which the Act was passed, I respectfully dissent.

Prior to the passage of the FAA, American courts were generally hostile to arbitration. They refused, with rare exceptions, to order specific enforcement of executory agreements to arbitrate.[2] Section 2 of the FAA responded to this hostility by making written arbitration agreements "valid, irrevocable, and enforceable." 9

---

[1] See Kleine v. Catara, 14 F. Cas. 732, 735, F. Cas. No. 7869 (CC Mass. 1814) (Story, J.) ("If the parties wish to reserve the law for the decision of the court, they may stipulate to that effect in the submission; they may restrain or enlarge its operation as they please").

[2] See Red Cross Line v. Atlantic Fruit Co., 264 U.S. 109, 120–122, 44 S. Ct. 274, 68 L. Ed. 582 (1924); The Atlanten, 252 U.S. 313, 315–316, 40 S. Ct. 332, 64 L. Ed. 586 (1920). Although agreements to arbitrate were not specifically enforceable, courts did award nominal damages for the breach of such contracts.

U.S.C. § 2. This section, which is the centerpiece of the FAA, reflects Congress' main goal in passing the legislation: "to abrogate the general common-law rule against specific enforcement of arbitration agreements," and to "ensur[e] that private arbitration agreements are enforced according to their terms". Given this settled understanding of the core purpose of the FAA, the interests favoring enforceability of parties' arbitration agreements are stronger today than before the FAA was enacted. As such, there is more—and certainly not less—reason to give effect to parties' fairly negotiated decisions to provide for judicial review of arbitration awards for errors of law.

* * *

While § 9 of the FAA imposes a 1-year limit on the time in which any party to an arbitration may apply for confirmation of an award, the statute does not require that the application be given expedited treatment. Of course, the premise of the entire statute is an assumption that the arbitration process may be more expeditious and less costly than ordinary litigation, but that is a reason for interpreting the statute liberally to favor the parties' use of arbitration. An unnecessary refusal to enforce a perfectly reasonable category of arbitration agreements defeats the primary purpose of the statute.

That purpose also provides a sufficient response to the Court's reliance on statutory text. It is true that a wooden application of "the old rule of *ejusdem generis*," might support an inference that the categories listed in §§ 10 and 11 are exclusive, but the literal text does not compel that reading—a reading that is flatly inconsistent with the overriding interest in effectuating the clearly expressed intent of the contracting parties. A listing of grounds that must always be available to contracting parties simply does not speak to the question whether they may agree to additional grounds for judicial review.

Moreover, in light of the historical context and the broader purpose of the FAA, §§ 10 and 11 are best understood as a shield meant to protect parties from hostile courts, not a sword with which to cut down parties' "valid, irrevocable and enforceable" agreements to arbitrate their disputes subject to judicial review for errors of law.[3] § 2.

Even if I thought the narrow issue presented in this case were as debatable as the conflict among the courts of appeals suggests, I would rely on a presumption of overriding importance to resolve the debate and rule in favor of petitioner's position that the FAA permits the statutory grounds for vacatur and modification of an award to be supplemented by contract. A decision *"not to regulate"* the terms of an agreement that does not even arguably offend any public policy whatsoever "is adequately justified by a presumption in favor of freedom.

Accordingly, while I agree that the judgment of the Court of Appeals must be set aside, and that there may be additional avenues available for judicial enforcement of parties' fairly negotiated review provisions, I respectfully dissent

[3] In the years before the passage of the FAA, arbitration awards were subject to thorough and broad judicial review. See Cohen & Dayton, The New Federal Arbitration Law, 12 Va. L. Rev. 265, 270–271 (1926); Cullinan, Contracting for an Expanded Scope of Judicial Review in Arbitration Agreements, 51 Vand. L. Rev. 395, 409 (1998). In §§ 10 and 11 of the FAA, Congress significantly limited the grounds for judicial vacatur or modification of such awards in order to protect arbitration awards from hostile and meddlesome courts.

from the Court's interpretation of the FAA, and would direct the Court of Appeals to affirm the judgment of the District Court enforcing the arbitrator's final award.

■ JUSTICE BREYER, dissenting.

The question presented in this case is whether "the Federal Arbitration Act . . . *precludes* a federal court from enforcing" an arbitration agreement that gives the court the power to set aside an arbitration award that embodies an arbitrator's mistake about the law. Like the majority and Justice Stevens, and primarily for the reasons they set forth, I believe that the Act does not *preclude* enforcement of such an agreement. See ante, at 590, 170 L. Ed. 2d, at 266 (opinion of the Court) (The Act "is not the only way into court for parties wanting review of arbitration awards"); ante, at 595, 170 L. Ed. 2d, at 269–270 (Stevens, J., dissenting) (The Act is a "shield meant to protect parties from hostile courts, not a sword with which to cut down parties' 'valid, irrevocable and enforceable' agreements to arbitrate their disputes subject to judicial review for errors of law").

At the same time, I see no need to send the case back for further judicial decisionmaking. The agreement here was entered into with the consent of the parties and the approval of the District Court. Aside from the Federal Arbitration Act itself, 9 U.S.C. § 1 *et seq.*, respondent below pointed to no statute, rule, or other relevant public policy that the agreement might violate. The Court has now rejected its argument that the agreement violates the Act, and I would simply remand the case with instructions that the Court of Appeals affirm the District Court's judgment enforcing the arbitrator's final award.

For over a century, courts have warned that "if an arbitrator makes a mistake either as to law or fact, it is the misfortune of the party, and there is no help for it. There is no right of appeal, and the court has no power to revise the decisions of 'judges who are of the parties' own choosing.'" Patton v. Garrett, 116 N.C. 847, 21 S.E. 679, 682–83 (1895). On the other hand, recent decades' enforcement of adhesive arbitration agreements sending consumer, employment, and similar claims to arbitration has seen occasional judicial interest in more closely policing arbitrators' rulings, especially on such claims.

For example, although a discharged employee in *Halligan v. Piper Jaffray, Inc.*, 148 F.3d 197, 203 (2d Cir. 1998), had presented the arbitrators with "overwhelming evidence" of age-based discrimination, an arbitration panel denied any relief in an award that contained no explanation or rationale. The Second Circuit held that the award should be vacated: An arbitration award may be vacated if it is in "'manifest disregard' of the law," which requires findings both that the arbitrators "knew of a governing legal principle yet refused to apply it or ignored it altogether," and that the law was "well defined, explicit, and clearly applicable." "In view of the strong evidence that Halligan was fired because of his age and the agreement of the parties that the arbitrators were correctly advised of the applicable legal principles, we are inclined to hold that they ignored the law or the evidence or both." The court stressed that in making this decision, the arbitrators' failure to explain their award "can be taken into account." If the arbitrators had given as their rationale that they had simply believed the employer's witnesses rather than the employee's, "on this record it would have been extremely hard to accept—but they did not do even that." The court disclaimed any holding that arbitrators must write reasoned awards in every case or "even in most cases"—but it observed that "where a reviewing court is inclined to find that arbitrators manifestly disregarded the law or the evidence and that an explanation, if given, would have strained credulity, the absence of explanation may reinforce the reviewing court's confidence that the arbitrators engaged in manifest disregard."

While *Halligan* suggested greater judicial scrutiny of arbitrators' legal rulings, other courts moved in the opposite direction—weakening the "manifest disregard" ground for vacatur, with the Seventh Circuit even suggesting that it could be eliminated. See, e.g., Wise v. Wachovia Securities, LLC, 450 F.3d 265, 268–69 (7th Cir.2006) (Posner, J.) ("we have defined 'manifest disregard of the law' so narrowly that it fits comfortably under the first clause of the [FAA's] fourth statutory ground [for vacatur]—'where the arbitrators exceeded their powers.' For we have confined it to cases in which arbitrators 'direct the parties to violate the law.'"); Sarofim v. Trust Company Of The West, 440 F.3d 213, 217 (5th Cir.2006) (confining manifest disregard doctrine to cases in which enforcement of the award would "result in significant injustice."). This narrower view received support from the Supreme Court's 2008 *Hall Street* opinion excerpted above.

In *Hall Street*, the Supreme Court stated that the FAA's four grounds for vacatur are "exclusive." The Court viewed the FAA's provisions on confirmation and vacatur of arbitration awards

> as substantiating a national policy favoring arbitration with just the limited review needed to maintain arbitration's essential virtue of resolving disputes straightaway. Any other reading opens the door to the full-bore legal and evidentiary appeals that can render informal arbitration merely a prelude to a more cumbersome and time-consuming judicial review process and bring arbitration theory to grief in post-arbitration process.

This rationale, along with *Hall Street*'s statement that the FAA's four grounds for vacatur are "exclusive," led some courts and commentators to conclude that *Hall Street* prohibits judicially-created grounds for vacatur, including "manifest disregard." See Medicine Shoppe Int'l, Inc. v. Turner Investments, Inc., 614 F.3d 485, 489 (8th Cir.2010) (citing *Hall Street* for the proposition that a "claim that the arbitrator disregarded the law" is "not included among those specifically enumerated in § 10 and [ ] therefore not cognizable"); Frazier v. CitiFinancial Corp., LLC, 604 F.3d 1313, 1322–24 (11th Cir.2010) ("Although our prior precedents have recognized these three non-statutory grounds for vacatur [arbitrary and capricious, public policy, and manifest disregard] * * * We hold that our judicially-created bases for vacatur are no longer valid in light of Hall Street").

By contrast, other courts continue to use "manifest disregard" to vacate awards, often reasoning that so-called "non-statutory" grounds, such as "manifest disregard," are better characterized as statutory grounds because they are shorthand to define what constitutes arbitrators' "exceed[ing] their powers" under FAA § 10(a)(4). Comedy Club, Inc. v. Improv West Assocs., 553 F.3d 1277, 1283 (9th Cir. 2009) (vacating an award on manifest disregard grounds post-*Hall Street*); Wachovia Securities, LLC v. Brand, 671 F.3d 472, 483 (4th Cir.2012) ("manifest disregard continues to exist either 'as an independent ground for review or as a judicial gloss on the enumerated grounds for vacatur set forth at 9 U.S.C. § 10.' Therefore, we decline to adopt the position of the Fifth and Eleventh Circuits that manifest disregard no longer exists."); Sharp v. Downey, 13 A.3d 1, 21 (Md.Ct.App.2010) (vacating award due to manifest disregard of law, which continues to be a ground for vacatur under Maryland Arbitration Act); Daesang Corporation v. NutraSweet Company, 167 AD3d 1, 85 NYS3d 6 (NY App. Div. 2018) (award may be vacated for manifest disregard of the law only if both: (1) the arbitrators knew of a governing legal principle yet refused to apply it or ignored it altogether, and (2) the law ignored by the arbitrators was well defined, explicit, and clearly applicable to the case.)

The Supreme Court left uncertainty in the post-*Hall Street* case of *Stolt-Nielsen S.A. v. AnimalFeeds International Corp.*, 559 U.S. 662 (2010), in which it said "We do not decide whether 'manifest disregard' survives our decision in [*Hall Street*], as an independent ground for review or as a judicial gloss on the enumerated grounds for vacatur set forth at 9 U.S.C. § 10." With this uncertainty in the law, we do not know whether courts will vacate awards on the ground that arbitrators did not apply the law correctly. The Supreme Court left unresolved the very important question of whether arbitrators are bound to apply the law in all, some, or none of the cases they hear, not to mention the subsidiary question of whether they must do so correctly. Until these questions are resolved, much doubt will surround the Supreme Court's repeated statement that "judicial scrutiny of arbitration awards * * * is sufficient to ensure that arbitrators comply with the requirements of the statute" giving rise to the claim asserted in arbitration. Shearson/Am. Express, Inc. v. McMahon, 482 U.S. 220, 232 (1987); Gilmer v. Interstate/Johnson Lane Corp., 500 U.S. 20, 32 n.4 (1991); 14 Penn Plaza LLC v. Pyett, 556 U.S. 247, 269 n.10 (2009).

QUESTIONS TO REVIEW AND SYNTHESIZE

1. How did the Supreme Court reply to Hall Street's argument "that the agreement to review for legal error ought to prevail simply because arbitration is a creature of contract, and the FAA is [as earlier Court decisions said] 'motivated, first and foremost, by a congressional desire to enforce agreements into which parties have entered.'"
2. Do courts currently vacate arbitration awards that "manifestly disregard" the law?
3. What are the policy arguments for and against courts confirming arbitration awards that make errors of law?

b. STATE LAW GROUNDS FOR VACATUR

In somewhat mysterious dicta, *Hall Street* said:

> In holding that [FAA] §§ 10 and 11 provide exclusive regimes for the review provided by the statute, we do not purport to say that they exclude more searching review based on authority outside the statute as well. The FAA is not the only way into court for parties wanting review of arbitration awards: they may contemplate enforcement under state statutory or common law, for example, where judicial review of different

> scope is arguable. But here we speak only to the scope of the expeditious judicial review under §§ 9, 10, and 11, deciding nothing about other possible avenues for judicial enforcement of arbitration awards.

Assessing this passage, Professor Thomas Carbonneau writes:

> In dicta, the [*Hall Street*] Court tries to temper the effect of its exclusivity holding by contending that the supervision of arbitral awards is available outside the framework of the FAA. In other words, although the statutory grounds are "exclusive" (otherwise stated, not modifiable by contract), the parties could obtain "more searching review" of awards (i.e., review of the merits) under other frameworks for judicial supervision. The assertion is mesmerizing. By way of illustration, the Court explains that parties "may contemplate enforcement under state statutory or common law . . . where judicial review of different scope is arguable." It is difficult to divine what Justice Souter means by "arguable" in this statement; the word is another fastidious understatement that makes understanding difficult. More importantly, the contention does not seem to account for the impact of the federal preemption doctrine.[38]

If parties want "more searching [judicial] review" of arbitration awards "under state statutory or common law," what do they have to do to get it? One possibility is to use an arbitration agreement with a clause—similar to the one in *Hall Street*—requiring arbitrators to apply the law correctly, but then move to vacate an award in state rather than federal court. Several post-*Hall Street* state supreme court decisions have relied on state law to enforce agreements requiring arbitrators to apply the law correctly. See, e.g., Cable Connection, Inc. v. DirectTV, Inc., 190 P.3d 586, 589 (Cal. 2008) (discussing *Hall Street* and concluding that FAA does not preempt state law enforcing arbitration agreement providing that "The arbitrators shall not have the power to commit errors of law or legal reasoning, and the award may be vacated or corrected on appeal to a court of competent jurisdiction for any such error."); Nafta Traders, Inc. v. Quinn, 339 S.W.3d 84, 88 (Tex.2011) (enforcing an arbitration agreement that said "[t]he arbitrator does not have authority (i) to render a decision which contains a reversible error of state or federal law, or (ii) to apply a cause of action or remedy not expressly provided for under existing state or federal law.").

Suppose though, the arbitration agreement does not purport to expand grounds for vacatur beyond those in the FAA, but state law does? Some federal courts before *Hall Street* held that the FAA preempts state grounds for vacatur not found in federal law.[39] And after *Hall Street*, New York's highest court applied the FAA's grounds

---

[38] Thomas E. Carbonneau, The Rise in Judicial Hostility to Arbitration: Revisiting Hall Street Associates, 14 Cardozo J. Conflict Resol. 593, 608–09 (2013).

[39] See Alston v. UBS Fin. Servs., Inc., No. Civ.A. 04-01798(HHK), 2006 WL 20516, at *1 n.3 (D.D.C. 2006) ("The Alstons attempt to rely on Virginia law as a basis for vacatur as well [as the FAA]. The court, however, need not analyze the Alstons' motion under Virginia law because, to the extent that the FAA and Virginia law conflict, state law is preempted"); see also In re Arbitration between Lemoine Skinner III v. Donaldson, Lufkin & Jenrette Secs. Corp., No. C 03-2625 VRW, 2003 WL 23174478, at *8 (N.D. Cal. Dec. 29, 2003) ("the [FAA] sets out the exclusive grounds upon which an arbitration award may be vacated . . . . Any state law that allows for additional grounds for dismissal of an arbitration award would be preempted by the FAA."); M & L Power Servs., Inc. v. Am. Networks Int'l, 44 F. Supp. 2d 134, 141–42 (D.R.I. 1999) ("the FAA only preempts state law to the extent that said state law provides lesser protection for arbitration agreements and awards than does federal law . . . . In this case, the "'complete irrationality' ground for vacating

for vacatur to proceedings in state court. US Elecs., Inc. v. Sirius Satellite Radio, Inc., 958 N.E.2d 891, 892 (N.Y. 2011) ("As this matter affects interstate commerce, the vacatur of the arbitration award is governed by the Federal Arbitration Act."). On the other hand, the New Hampshire Supreme Court rejected an FAA-preemption argument in affirming vacatur of an award under a ground—"plain mistake of law or fact" by the arbitrator—found in state law, but not in the FAA. See Finn v. Ballentine Partners, L.L.C., 143 A.3d 859 (N.H. 2016).

> The fact that a state law affecting arbitration is less deferential to an arbitrator's decision than the FAA does not create an obstacle so insurmountable as to preempt state law. Volt demonstrates that not all obstacles to arbitration are repugnant to the FAA. The procedural rule in Volt delayed arbitration, and simplified it, by staying the proceedings until non-arbitral issues had been resolved. On the other hand, the state rule at issue in AT&T Mobility contemplated an extreme alteration of arbitration procedure, risks, and efficiency, and failure to comply with its requirement would make the agreement to arbitrate unenforceable. It thus had such a profound effect upon arbitration as to effectively deter parties from choosing arbitration.
>
> 12RSA 542:8 [which the court construed as "grant[ing] the trial court the power to vacate an arbitration award for a "plain mistake" of law or fact"] is more like the rule at issue in Volt than that at issue in AT & T Mobility. * * *
>
> In this case, the trial court did not refuse to enforce the parties' agreement to arbitrate. Instead it applied RSA 542:8 to review the second panel's award, which was produced because the trial court had complied with the FAA and enforced their agreement to arbitrate. RSA 542:8 does not interfere with the FAA's principal purpose of protecting arbitration agreements from perceived judicial hostility. Because our state standard of review does not impede the enforcement of an arbitration agreement nor mandate drastic changes to the procedures by which arbitration is to be conducted, it is not preempted by the FAA.
>
> Finn nonetheless insists that the Court's discussion in Hall Street about the dangers of "full-bore legal and evidentiary appeals that can render informal arbitration merely a prelude to a more cumbersome and time-consuming judicial review process," thus "bring[ing] arbitration theory to grief in postarbitration process," Hall Street, 552 U.S. at 588, 128 S.Ct. 1396 (quotation and brackets omitted), demands that we hold RSA 542:8 preempted by the FAA. She argues that, although the Court acknowledged that parties may seek review of arbitral decisions through other avenues of enforcement, these "are only permissible where they are more restrictive than federal standards of review." See Hall Street, 552 U.S. at 584, 590–92, 128 S.Ct. 1396. We do not believe that Hall Street stands for this proposition.

---

an arbitration award violates Congress' policy as set forth in the FAA. As such, it is preempted and may not be applied to any case to which the FAA applies").

* * *

> Here, the Agreement included a choice-of-law clause, and Finn and the other shareholders selected New Hampshire law as the governing law: "This Agreement shall be governed by and construed in accordance with the internal laws of the State of New Hampshire, without regard to conflict of laws principles." Their choice to govern their agreement by New Hampshire law includes the agreement to arbitrate; the arbitration clause does not reference the use of any other governing law. The parties opted for judicial review through a mechanism other than the FAA, an avenue left undisturbed by the Court in Hall Street. See Hall Street, 552 U.S. at 590, 128 S.Ct. 1396. By applying RSA 542:8 to the arbitral award, the trial court was faithful to the parties' intent. Not only does Hall Street contemplate the possibility of such an outcome, enforcing parties' agreements according to their terms remains at the heart of the FAA. We therefore conclude that the FAA does not preempt RSA 542:8, and that the trial court did not err by applying it to the second arbitral award.

143 A.3d at 869–72. Professor Jill Gross argues that the FAA does "not preempt state vacatur law in state court, except in the rare circumstance where state vacatur law permits broad de novo review of award." Jill I. Gross, *Over-Preemption of State Vacatur Law: State Courts and the FAA*, 3 J. Am. Arb. 1 (2004). Agreeing on that rare case, the proposed final draft of the Restatement of the U.S. Law of International Commercial and Investor-State Arbitration says:

> Although FAA § 10 does not apply in state court, the Supreme Court has repeatedly held that FAA § 2—which makes arbitration agreements valid, irrevocable, and enforceable—does apply in state court. A state law ground for post-award relief could, in an extreme case, so substantially impair the parties' arbitration agreement as to be preempted by the FAA.

Restatement of the U.S. Law of International Commercial and Investor-State Arbitration § 1.9 cmt. b. (Am. Law Inst., Proposed Final Draft (April 24, 2019). Illustration 1 to this section says a state statute "permitting a court to review an arbitration award de novo" would be "preempted because it substantially impairs the parties' agreement to arbitrate."

QUESTIONS TO REVIEW AND SYNTHESIZE

1. Why might parties have a better chance of vacating an arbitration award in state rather than federal court?

c. DEFERENTIAL REVIEW OF LABOR ARBITRATION AWARDS

While the Supreme Court has not directly held that labor arbitration is governed by the FAA, see Section 3.B.3.a above, labor arbitration awards also receive deferential review by courts, as discussed briefly at the below baseball game and more extensively in the case that follows.

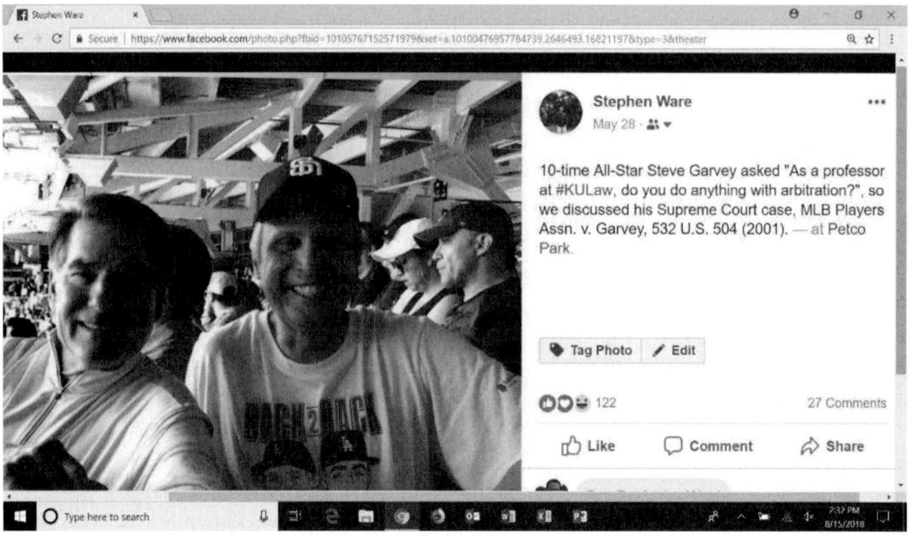

Major League Baseball Players Ass'n v. Garvey

Supreme Court of the United States, 2001.
532 U.S. 504, 121 S.Ct. 1724, 149 L.Ed.2d 740.

■ PER CURIAM.

The Court of Appeals for the Ninth Circuit here rejected an arbitrator's factual findings and then resolved the merits of the parties' dispute instead of remanding the case for further arbitration proceedings. Because the Court's determination conflicts with our cases limiting review of an arbitrator's award entered pursuant to an agreement between an employer and a labor organization and prescribing the appropriate remedy where vacation of the award is warranted, we grant the petition for a writ of certiorari and reverse. The motions for leave to file briefs amicus curiae of the National Academy of Arbitrators and the Office of the Commissioner of Baseball are granted.

In the late 1980's, petitioner Major League Baseball Players Association (Association) filed grievances against the Major League Baseball Clubs (Clubs), claiming the Clubs had colluded in the market for free-agent services after the 1985, 1986 and 1987 baseball seasons, in violation of the industry's collective-bargaining agreement. A free agent is a player who may contract with any Club, rather than one whose right to contract is restricted to a particular Club. In a series of decisions, arbitrators found collusion by the Clubs and damage to the players. The Association and Clubs subsequently entered into a Global Settlement Agreement (Agreement), pursuant to which the Clubs established a $280 million fund to be distributed to injured players. The Association also designed a "Framework" to evaluate the individual player's claims, and, applying that Framework, recommended distribution plans for claims relating to a particular season or seasons.

The Framework provided that players could seek an arbitrator's review of the distribution plan. The arbitrator would determine "only whether the approved

Framework and the criteria set forth therein have been properly applied in the proposed Distribution Plan." Garvey v. Roberts, 203 F.3d 580, 583 (CA9 2000) *(Garvey I)*. The Framework set forth factors to be considered in evaluating players' claims, as well as specific requirements for lost contract-extension claims. Such claims were cognizable "'only in those cases where evidence exists that a specific offer of an extension was made by a club prior to collusion only to thereafter be withdrawn when the collusion scheme was initiated.'"

Respondent Steve Garvey, a retired, highly regarded first baseman, submitted a claim for damages of approximately $ 3 million. He alleged that his contract with the San Diego Padres was not extended to the 1988 and 1989 seasons due to collusion. The Association rejected Garvey's claim in February 1996, because he presented no evidence that the Padres actually offered to extend his contract. Garvey objected, and an arbitration hearing was held. He testified that the Padres offered to extend his contract for the 1988 and 1989 seasons and then withdrew the offer after they began colluding with other teams. He presented a June 1996 letter from Ballard Smith, Padres' President and CEO from 1979 to 1987, stating that, before the end of the 1985 season, Smith offered to extend Garvey's contract through the 1989 season, but that the Padres refused to negotiate with Garvey thereafter due to collusion.

The arbitrator denied Garvey's claim, after seeking additional documentation from the parties. In his award, he explained that "'there exists . . . substantial doubt as to the credibility of the statements in the Smith letter.'" He noted the "stark contradictions" between the 1996 letter and Smith's testimony in the earlier arbitration proceedings regarding collusion, where Smith, like other owners, denied collusion and stated that the Padres simply were not interested in extending Garvey's contract. The arbitrator determined that, due to these contradictions, he "'must reject [Smith's] more recent assertion that Garvey did not receive [a contract] extension'" due to collusion, and found that Garvey had not shown a specific offer of extension. He concluded that:

> "'the shadow cast over the credibility of the Smith testimony coupled with the absence of any other corroboration of the claim submitted by Garvey compels a finding that the Padres declined to extend his contract not because of the constraints of the collusion effort of the clubs but rather as a baseball judgment founded upon [Garvey's] age and recent injury history.'"

Garvey moved in Federal District Court to vacate the arbitrator's award, alleging that the arbitrator violated the Framework by denying his claim. The District Court denied the motion. The Court of Appeals for the Ninth Circuit reversed by a divided vote. The court acknowledged that judicial review of an arbitrator's decision in a labor dispute is extremely limited. But it held that review of the merits of the arbitrator's award was warranted in this case, because the arbitrator "'dispensed his own brand of industrial justice.'" The court recognized that Smith's prior testimony with respect to collusion conflicted with the statements in his 1996 letter. But in the court's view, the arbitrator's refusal to credit Smith's letter was "inexplicable" and "bordered on the irrational," because a panel of arbitrators, chaired by the arbitrator involved here, had previously concluded that the owners' prior testimony was false. The court rejected the arbitrator's reliance on the absence of other corroborating evidence, attributing that fact to Smith and Garvey's direct negotiations. The court also found that the record provided "strong support" for the truthfulness of Smith's 1996 letter. The Court of Appeals reversed and remanded with directions to vacate the award.

The District Court then remanded the case to the arbitration panel for further hearings, and Garvey appealed. The Court of Appeals, again by a divided vote, explained that *Garvey I* established that "the conclusion that Smith made Garvey an offer and subsequently withdrew it because of the collusion scheme was the only conclusion that the arbitrator could draw from the record in the proceedings." *(Garvey II)*. Noting that its prior instructions might have been unclear, the Court clarified that *Garvey I* "left only one possible result—the result our holding contemplated—an award in Garvey's favor." The Court of Appeals reversed the District Court and directed that it remand the case to the arbitration panel with instructions to enter an award for Garvey in the amount he claimed.

The parties do not dispute that this case arises under § 301 of the Labor Management Relations Act, 1947, 61 Stat. 156, 29 U.S.C. § 185(a), as the controversy involves an assertion of rights under an agreement between an employer and a labor organization. Although Garvey's specific allegation is that the arbitrator violated the Framework for resolving players' claims for damages, that Framework was designed to facilitate payments to remedy the Clubs' breach of the collective-bargaining agreement. Garvey's right to be made whole is founded on that agreement.

Judicial review of a labor-arbitration decision pursuant to such an agreement is very limited. Courts are not authorized to review the arbitrator's decision on the merits despite allegations that the decision rests on factual errors or misinterprets the parties' agreement. Paperworkers v. Misco, Inc., 484 U.S. 29, 36, 98 L. Ed. 2d 286, 108 S. Ct. 364 (1987). We recently reiterated that if an "'arbitrator is even arguably construing or applying the contract and acting within the scope of his authority,' the fact that 'a court is convinced he committed serious error does not suffice to overturn his decision.'" Eastern Associated Coal Corp. v. Mine Workers, 531 U.S. 57, 62, 148 L. Ed. 2d 354, 121 S. Ct. 462 (2000). It is only when the arbitrator strays from interpretation and application of the agreement and effectively "dispenses his own brand of industrial justice" that his decision may be unenforceable. Steelworkers v. Enterprise Wheel & Car Corp., 363 U.S. 593, 597, 4 L. Ed. 2d 1424, 80 S. Ct. 1358 (1960). When an arbitrator resolves disputes regarding the application of a contract, and no dishonesty is alleged, the arbitrator's "improvident, even silly, factfinding" does not provide a basis for a reviewing court to refuse to enforce the award. *Misco*.

In discussing the courts' limited role in reviewing the merits of arbitration awards, we have stated that "'courts . . . have no business weighing the merits of the grievance [or] considering whether there is equity in a particular claim.'" When the judiciary does so, "it usurps a function which . . . is entrusted to the arbitration tribunal." ("It is the arbitrator's construction [of the agreement] which was bargained for . . ."). Consistent with this limited role, we said in *Misco* that "even in the very rare instances when an arbitrator's procedural aberrations rise to the level of affirmative misconduct, as a rule the court must not foreclose further proceedings by settling the merits according to its own judgment of the appropriate result." That step, we explained, "would improperly substitute a judicial determination for the arbitrator's decision that the parties bargained for" in their agreement. Instead, the court should "simply vacate the award, thus leaving open the possibility of further proceedings if they are permitted under the terms of the agreement."

To be sure, the Court of Appeals here recited these principles, but its application of them is nothing short of baffling. The substance of the Court's discussion reveals that it overturned the arbitrator's decision because it disagreed with the arbitrator's factual findings, particularly those with respect to credibility. The Court of Appeals, it appears, would have credited Smith's 1996 letter, and found the arbitrator's refusal to do so at worst "irrational" and at best "bizarre." But even "serious error" on the arbitrator's part does not justify overturning his decision, where, as here, he is construing a contract and acting within the scope of his authority.

In *Garvey II*, the court clarified that *Garvey I* both rejected the arbitrator's findings and went further, resolving the merits of the parties' dispute based on the court's assessment of the record before the arbitrator. For that reason, the court found further arbitration proceedings inappropriate. But again, established law ordinarily precludes a court from resolving the merits of the parties' dispute on the basis of its own factual determinations, no matter how erroneous the arbitrator's decision. Even when the arbitrator's award may properly be vacated, the appropriate remedy is to remand the case for further arbitration proceedings. The dissent suggests that the remedy described in *Misco* is limited to cases where the arbitrator's errors are procedural. *Misco* did involve procedural issues, but our discussion regarding the appropriate remedy was not so limited. If a remand is appropriate *even* when the arbitrator's award has been set aside for "procedural aberrations" that constitute "affirmative misconduct," it follows that a remand ordinarily will be appropriate when the arbitrator simply made factual findings that the reviewing court perceives as "irrational." The Court of Appeals usurped the arbitrator's role by resolving the dispute and barring further proceedings, a result at odds with this governing law.[2]

For the foregoing reasons, the Court of Appeals erred in reversing the order of the District Court denying the motion to vacate the arbitrator's award, and it erred further in directing that judgment be entered in Garvey's favor. The judgment of the Court of Appeals is reversed, and the case is remanded for further proceedings consistent with this opinion.

---

[2] In any event, no serious error on the arbitrator's part is apparent in this case. The fact that an earlier panel of arbitrators rejected the owners' testimony as a whole does not compel the conclusion that the panel found Smith's specific statements with respect to Garvey to be false. The arbitrator's explanation for his decision indicates that he simply found Smith an unreliable witness and that, in the absence of corroborating evidence, he could only conclude that Garvey failed to show that the Padres had offered to extend his contract. The arbitrator's analysis may have been unpersuasive to the Court of Appeals, but his decision hardly qualifies as serious error, let alone irrational or inexplicable error. And, as we have said, any such error would not justify the actions taken by the court.

■ JUSTICE GINSBURG, concurring in part and concurring in the judgment.

I agree with the Court that in *Garvey* v. *Roberts*, 203 F.3d 580 (CA9 2000) (*Garvey I*), the Ninth Circuit should not have disturbed the arbitrator's award. Correction of that error sets this case straight. I see no need to say more.

■ JUSTICE STEVENS, dissenting.

It is well settled that an arbitrator "does not sit to dispense his own brand of industrial justice." Steelworkers v. Enterprise Wheel & Car Corp., 363 U.S. 593, 597, 4 L. Ed. 2d 1424, 80 S. Ct. 1358 (1960). We have also said fairly definitively, albeit in dicta, that a court should remedy an arbitrator's "procedural aberrations" by vacating the award and remanding for further proceedings. Paperworkers v. Misco, Inc., 484 U.S. 29, 40–41, n. 10, 98 L. Ed. 2d 286, 108 S. Ct. 364 (1987). Our cases, however, do not provide significant guidance as to what standards a federal court should use in assessing whether an arbitrator's behavior is so untethered to either the agreement of the parties or the factual record so as to constitute an attempt to "dispense his own brand of industrial justice." Nor, more importantly, do they tell us how, having made such a finding, courts should deal with "the extraordinary circumstance in which the arbitrator's own rulings make clear that, more than being simply erroneous, his finding is completely inexplicable and borders on the irrational." Garvey v. Roberts, 203 F.3d 580, 590 (CA9 2000) (case below). Because our caselaw is not sufficiently clear to allow me to conclude that the case below was wrongly decided—let alone to conclude that the decision was so wrong as to require the extraordinary remedy of a summary reversal—I dissent from the Court's disposition of this petition.

Without the benefit of briefing or argument, today the Court resolves two difficult questions. First, it decides that even if the Court of Appeals' appraisal of the merits is correct—that is to say, even if the arbitrator did dispense his own brand of justice untethered to the agreement of the parties, and even if the correct disposition of the matter is perfectly clear—the only course open to a reviewing court is to remand the matter for another arbitration. That conclusion is not compelled by any of our cases, nor by any analysis offered by the Court. As the issue is subject to serious arguments on both sides, the Court should have set this case for argument if it wanted to answer this remedial question.

Second, without reviewing the record or soliciting briefing, the Court concludes that, in any event, "no serious error on the arbitrator's part is apparent in this case." At this stage in the proceedings, I simply cannot endorse that conclusion. After examining the record, obtaining briefing, and hearing oral argument, the Court of Appeals offered a reasoned explanation of its conclusion. Whether or not I would ultimately agree with the Ninth Circuit's analysis, I find the Court's willingness to reverse a factbound determination of the Court of Appeals without engaging that court's reasoning a troubling departure from our normal practice.*

* The Court's opinion is somewhat ambiguous as to its reasons for overturning the portion of the Court of Appeals' decision setting aside the arbitration. It is unclear whether the majority is saying that a court may never set aside an arbitration because of a factual error, no matter how perverse, or whether the Court merely holds that the error in this case was not sufficiently severe to allow a court to take that step. If

Accordingly, I respectfully dissent.

While *Garvey* reiterates longstanding labor law about judicial deference to arbitrators, *Garvey* "only address[es] the relationship between arbitrators and the courts, not arbitrators and the NLRB." Part-Time Faculty Ass'n at Columbia Coll. Chicago v. Columbia Coll. Chicago, 892 F.3d 860, 867 (7th Cir. 2018) (affirming vacatur of arbitration award that conflicted with ruling by Regional Director of the National Labor Relations Board that employees were included in bargaining unit for relevant purposes).

QUESTIONS TO REVIEW AND SYNTHESIZE

1. See Section 3.B.3.a. To what extent is labor arbitration governed by the FAA?
2. What are the similarities between judicial review of labor arbitration awards and awards in cases governed by the FAA, what more specific similarities characterize judicial review in both the labor and FAA contexts?
3. What differences separate judicial review of labor arbitration awards and awards in cases governed by the FAA?
4. What does *Garvey* say a court should do if "set[s] aside" an arbitration award for "procedural aberrations" that constitute "affirmative misconduct" or factual findings that the court perceives as "irrational"?
5. The U.S. Court of Appeals for which circuit was reversed or vacated by the Supreme Court in the last two decisions excerpted in this chapter and several others earlier in this chapter. Is this just a coincidence? Do you see any pattern in how the Supreme Court differs from this circuit?

---

it is the latter, the Court offers no explanation of what standards it is using or of its reasons for reaching that conclusion.

CHAPTER 4

THE ARBITRATION PROCEEDING

A. ARBITRATION AS "THE PARTIES' DREAM"

While arbitration is a form of binding adjudication, and thus importantly distinct from mediation and "the gentler arts of reconciliation and accommodation,"[1] arbitration can nevertheless involve abundant cooperation between the parties. Possible areas of cooperation include choosing:

- the number of arbitrators and the process for selecting them;
- the time and place for arbitration; and
- the procedural and substantive rules governing the arbitration.

To a large extent, all these issues are directly or indirectly resolved by "agreement—and giving thought to such matters may thus make the same calls on the parties' creativity and imagination as do more openly 'empowering' ADR processes,"[2] such as mediation.

> Within broad limits * * * private parties who submit an existing dispute to arbitration may write their own ticket about the terms of submission, if they can agree to a ticket. [The authors refer to an old story about a person who, in a dream, was threatened by an ominous character and who asked,

---

[1] Derek Bok, *A Flawed System of Law Practice and Training*, 33 J. Legal Educ. 570, 582–83 (1983).

[2] See Alan Rau, *Integrity in Private Judging*, 38 So. Tex. L. Rev. 485, 486 (1997).

> tremulously, "Wh-what are you going to do now?"—only to receive the answer, "How do I know? This is *your* dream."] The arbitration of an existing dispute is the parties' dream, and they can make it what they want it to be.
>
> The trouble is that it takes time and money to draft elaborate private laws * * *. Only in the most exceptional circumstances can a private disputant stop to negotiate and draft a complete constitution, together with a substantive and procedural code, for the governance of his private court.[3]

Rather than draft their own "substantive and procedural code," parties to arbitration agreements usually incorporate by reference the standard arbitration rules prepared by their trade association, religious organization, or (probably most commonly) by institutions like the American Arbitration Association (AAA) that specialize in administering arbitration for a wide variety of parties. Using standard arbitration rules allows parties to avoid having to reinvent the wheel through lengthy negotiation and drafting, and instead to build upon the experience of others. The following materials frequently reference the widely-used Commercial Arbitration Rules of the AAA, but arbitration remains largely "the parties' dream," so parties and their lawyers can consider the special circumstances of each individual transaction, with a view to adding to the pre-existing structure or adapting it in light of the parties' particular situation.

B. THE ARBITRATORS

1. SELECTION OF ARBITRATORS

As Chapter 1 explained more thoroughly, one of arbitration's attractions is the ability to have a dispute decided by "judges" the parties choose. Arbitrator selection is thus an important aspect of the arbitration process.

One simple way to select an arbitrator is for the parties to name the individual who will arbitrate their dispute. The parties may name the arbitrator in a pre-dispute agreement. Or the parties may wait to name the arbitrator if and when a dispute arises, because the appropriate arbitrator may depend on the nature of the dispute. For instance, in labor arbitration, the parties may prefer lawyers as arbitrators when the issue is one of arbitrability (whether a dispute should be sent to arbitration at all) but prefer economists for wage disputes in "interest" arbitration, and industrial engineers for disputes over job evaluation.[4]

However, reliance on this by-name method of arbitrator selection has downsides. When the parties name an arbitrator in advance, that individual may be unwilling or unable to serve by the time a dispute later arises. This requires some means to select a replacement, and may even open up a challenge to the whole arbitration process, as one party may argue that its agreement to arbitrate was conditioned on the choice of the earlier-named "known and trusted expert," so arbitration should not proceed in that arbitrator's absence. Such arguments rarely

---

[3] Henry Melvin Hart, et al., The Legal Process 310 (1994).

[4] See Retzer and Petersen, *Strategies of Arbitrator Selection*, 70 Lab.Arb. 1307, 1319 (1978).

persuade courts,[5] because the FAA and many state statutes provide that if the parties cannot agree on an arbitrator, the court will appoint one. FAA § 5 provides:

> If in the agreement provision be made for a method of naming or appointing an arbitrator or arbitrators or an umpire, such method shall be followed; but if no method be provided therein, or if a method be provided and any party thereto shall fail to avail himself of such method, or if for any other reason there shall be a lapse in the naming of an arbitrator or arbitrators or umpire, or in filling a vacancy, then upon the application of either party to the controversy the court shall designate and appoint an arbitrator or arbitrators or umpire, as the case may require, who shall act under the said agreement with the same force and effect as if he or they had been specifically named therein; and unless otherwise provided in the agreement the arbitration shall be by a single arbitrator.

Nevertheless, delays and acrimony are generally reduced by a previously-agreed means of selecting an arbitrator that does not depend on any particular individual who may be unwilling or unable to serve.

Where an arbitration agreement contemplates only that the parties will select their arbitrator *after* a dispute arises, a recalcitrant party can easily slow progress, especially in a large case. Consider for example the agonizingly prolonged contract dispute between the Hunt brothers of Texas and the major oil-producing companies, a complex case arising out of various interests in Libyan oil concessions and involving sixteen parties and a welter of legal issues. The arbitration extended over a period of seven years; more than *two years* were consumed by the process of screening arbitrators, "as arbitrators proposed by one party were rejected by one or more of the other parties." The complexity of the issues in the case made the search for the requisite "arbitrators of unusual legal qualifications and broad experience in complicated transactions" particularly difficult. The court, however, made it clear that much of the delay was due to the tactics of the Hunts and their "campaign of obstruction to impede and defeat the arbitration."[6]

2. TRIPARTITE ARBITRATION

A common pattern in arbitration is the "tripartite" arbitral panel, in which each party is allowed to select one arbitrator and a third, "neutral" chairman is chosen by the other two. What effects might this kind of panel have on the adjudication process? The AAA's Commercial Arbitration Rules provide that where there is a panel of more than one arbitrator, decision is to be by *majority vote* unless the agreement provides otherwise.[7] To the same effect is § 4 of the Uniform Arbitration

---

[5] See, e.g., Singleton v. Grade A Market, Inc., 607 F. Supp. 2d 333, 341 (D. Conn. 2009) ("as a general rule, where the arbitrator named in the arbitration agreement cannot or will not arbitrate the dispute, a court does not void the agreement but instead appoints a different arbitrator.") (quoting Astra Footwear Indus. v. Harwyn Int'l, Inc., 442 F. Supp. 907, 910 (S.D.N.Y. 1978), *aff'd. mem.*, 578 F.2d 1366 (2d Cir. 1978)).

[6] See Hunt v. Mobil Oil Corp., 654 F.Supp. 1487 (S.D.N.Y. 1987).

[7] Rule 44, Commercial Arbitration Rules and Mediation Procedures, Am. Arbitration Ass'n (Oct. 1 2013).

Act,[8] and § 13 of the Revised Uniform Arbitration Act which states "If there is more than one arbitrator, the powers of an arbitrator must be exercised by a majority of the arbitrators, but all of them shall conduct the hearing under Section 15(c)."[9]

If the party-appointed arbitrators agree on a particular result and persuade the neutral arbitrator to acquiesce in this result, is it in reality a negotiated settlement masquerading as an arbitral award? And if the two party-appointed arbitrators *disagree,* may the neutral arbitrator be forced to trim or compromise the neutral's own views in order to obtain a majority? Consider *In re Publishers' Ass'n of N.Y. and N.Y. Typographical Union*, 36 Lab.Arb. 706 (1961), in which the neutral arbitrator voted with the employer to discharge a worker but wrote, in an unusually candid opinion, that this penalty had been "forced upon" him. While he would have preferred a lesser penalty, such as a disciplinary suspension, his most "patient and painstaking efforts" had convinced him that "there was no possibility whatever of an award issuing which would reflect a view intermediate to the polar position of my colleagues." He therefore saw no choice other than to join in the position which was *closest* to the one he preferred.

Having three arbitrators, rather than one, tends to raise parties' costs of both time and money, but the tripartite panel remains common for several reasons long identified by commentators. See Arnold M. Zack, *Tripartite Panels: Asset or Hindrance in Dispute Settlement?*, Proceedings, 34th Annual Meeting, Nat'l Academy of Arbitrators 273, 279 (1982) (deliberations between neutral and party-appointed arbitrators can help clarify technical issues, provide assurance that the neutral fully understands the issues and background of the case, and allow discussion and review of the possible implications of the neutral's written opinion); Andreas F. Lowenfeld, *The Party-Appointed Arbitrator in International Controversies: Some Reflections*, 30 Tex.Int'l L.J. 59, 65–67 (1995) (in international disputes a party-appointed arbitrator can help in the "translation of legal culture * * * when matters that are self-evident to lawyers from one country are puzzling to lawyers from another"; such an arbitrator also gives some "confidence that at least one member of the tribunal is listening, and listening sympathetically, to the submission of counsel").

3. ARBITRATOR SELECTION UNDER INSTITUTIONAL RULES—AND THE IMPACT OF JAY-Z

Arbitrator selection often occurs in two steps. First, parties agree (before or after a dispute arises) to arbitrate under the rules of a particular arbitration organization, such as the Commercial Arbitration Rules of the American Arbitration Association. Then, when a dispute arises, the arbitration organization follows those rules for selecting arbitrators. For example, when the AAA receives a demand for arbitration under its Commercial Rules, the AAA distributes to the parties a short list of potential arbitrators. The AAA chooses these from its extensive panel of

[8] Unif. Arbitration Act, § 4 (Rules effective 1955), https://www.uniformlaws.org/committees/community-home/librarydocuments?communitykey=f60b379c-6378-4d9d-b271-97522fad6f89&tab=library documents.

[9] Revised Unif. Arbitration Act § 13 (Rules effective 2000), https://www.uniformlaws.org/view document/final-act-1?CommunityKey=a0ad71d6-085f-4648-857a-e9e893ae2736&tab=librarydocuments.

arbitrators, trying to match the names to the nature of the dispute and the industry involved.[10] It may, for example, suggest arbitrators who have had experience in solar heating or landscape architecture if the dispute centers on practice in those trades. The parties' agreement may specify that their arbitrator shall have some particular qualifications (e.g., a Certified Practical Accountant for at least 10 years), which would further guide the AAA.

When the AAA sends parties a list of potential arbitrators, it also sends information about the arbitrators on the list: the arbitrator's profession, present and past employment, education, areas of expertise, and rate of compensation. The AAA uses no mechanism analogous to voir dire in which the parties can question potential arbitrators prior to selection—although they may do extensive research on their own. Under AAA procedure, each party may cross off the list any names it finds unacceptable. Each then ranks the remaining names in order of preference, and from these the AAA is supposed to appoint an arbitrator "in accordance with the designated order of mutual preference."[11] In the unlikely event that every name turns out to be objectionable to one or both of the parties, the AAA may at that point simply choose another name from its panel without submitting any further lists; barring disqualification for cause, this selection is final.[12]

Arbitration can proceed before any number of arbitrators—it is, again, "the parties' dream." But parties most often use one arbitrator or a tribunal of three arbitrators. The AAA rules call for a single arbitrator unless the parties specify otherwise or unless the AAA "in its discretion" selects a larger number.[13] The AAA administers claims of $75,000 or less under its "Expedited Procedures" which always use a single arbitrator.[14] However, in complex or high-stakes cases, parties commonly use three arbitrators.

What does Jay-Z have to do with all this?

> In a dispute stemming from the $200 million sale of his clothing line, rapper and entrepreneur Jay-Z (whose real name is Shawn Carter) in November [2018] challenged an arbitration clause as discriminatory, stating it would force him to select an arbitrator from a list nearly devoid of his ethnic group. Only three of 200 arbitrators on the large and complex case roster provided by the American Arbitration Association identified

---

[10] Rule 12, Commercial Arbitration Rules and Mediation Procedures, American Arbitration Association (Oct. 1 2013).

[11] Rule 12, Commercial Arbitration Rules and Mediation Procedures, American Arbitration Association (Oct. 1 2013); Bernstein, *Nudging and Shoving All Parties to a Jurisdictional Dispute Into Arbitration: The Dubious Procedure of National Steel,* 78 Harv.L.Rev. 784, 790–91 (1965).

[12] Rule 12(b), Commercial Arbitration Rules and Mediation Procedures, Am. Arbitration Ass'n (Oct. 1 2013).

[13] Rule 16(a), Commercial Arbitration Rules and Mediation Procedures, Am. Arbitration Ass'n (Oct. 1 2013).

[14] Rule 1(b), Commercial Arbitration Rules and Mediation Procedures, Am. Arbitration Ass'n (Oct. 1, 2013) ("[T[he Expedited Procedures shall apply in any case in which no disclosed claim or counterclaim exceeds $75,000, exclusive of interest, attorneys' fees, and arbitration fees and costs"); Rule 16(a), Commercial Arbitration Rules and Mediation Procedures, Am. Arbitration Ass'n (Oct. 1, 2013) ("If the arbitration agreement does not specify the number of arbitrators, the dispute shall be heard and determined by one arbitrator").

> themselves as African-American, and one of them had a conflict, he argued.
>
> Jay-Z recently reached a compromise with the AAA, which offered him additional African-American arbitrators to choose from and expressed a willingness to implement other means of improving diverse representation in future arbitrations. * * *
>
> ADR providers are offering possible solutions. JAMS, for example, drafted a diversity inclusion rider that may be incorporated into a dispute resolution clause. Through it, the parties agree to appoint a "fair representation" of diverse arbitrators—taking into account ethnicity, gender and sexual orientation—and to request providers to include a significant number of diverse neutrals on their rosters.
>
> * * *
>
> While acknowledging there should be diversity in arbitration, Justice Saliann Scarpulla stated at a hearing on the Jay-Z matter in November: "This is a private agreement between two individuals. You could have said in your contract, 'I want the Dalai Lama to decide my case,' and that's your private right." She added, "If people are dissatisfied with the diversity of the AAA, don't put the AAA panel in your agreement. Go somewhere else."

Darlene Ricker, *Jay-Z's ADR Problems: Mogul's Case Spotlights Lack of Diverse Arbitrators*, ABA J. May 2019, at 9.

For comparison to arbitrator selection by the AAA, consider the following discussion of arbitrator selection by FINRA (the Financial Industry Regulation Authority) which, as we saw in Section 2.A.4, administers nearly all securities arbitration in the U.S.

James A. Fanto, Jill I. Gross & Norman S. Poser, Broker-Dealer Law and Regulation

§ 23.0.4[B] (5th ed. 2018).

* * *

For all disputes at FINRA (except for those subject to special proceedings for promissory notes), "[i]f the amount of a claim is $50,000 or less, exclusive of interest and expenses, the panel will consist of one arbitrator." If the amount of the claim is more than $50,000 but not more than $100,000, the panel will be composed of one arbitrator, unless the parties agree in writing to a panel of three arbitrators; if the amount of the claim is more than $100,000 or if the claim is for unspecified or non-monetary relief, the panel will consist of three arbitrators, unless the parties agree in writing to one arbitrator.

[2] Arbitrator classification

FINRA maintains rosters of arbitrators classified as public or nonpublic, and chair-qualified. * * *

Over the years, in response to steady complaints about the myriad of conflicts of interest faced by industry-affiliated arbitrators and the various sources of possible bias for even public arbitrators, FINRA has adopted rule amendments tightening the definition of the term *public arbitrator* in order to exclude individuals with significant ties to the securities industry. Under today's very complex definition in Rule 12100(y), a person is classified as a public arbitrator if he or she is otherwise qualified to serve as an arbitrator and is not subject to either a listed permanent or temporary disqualification. Permanent disqualifications include:

> (1) association with a broker-dealer, investment adviser, hedge fund, or mutual fund;
>
> (2) registration through, under or with the Commodity Exchange Act or the Commodities Future Trading Commission, or a member of the National Futures Association, or the Municipal Securities Rulemaking Board;
>
> (3) association with an entity that is organized under or registered pursuant to the Securities Exchange Act of 1934, Investment Company Act of 1940, or the Investment Advisers Act of 1940;
>
> (4) "for a total of 15 years or more, an attorney, accountant, or other professional who has devoted 20 percent or more of his or her professional time annually" to the entities mentioned above;
>
> (5) "for a total of 15 years or more, an attorney, accountant, expert witness or other professional who has devoted 20 percent or more of his or her professional time annually to representing or providing services to parties in disputes concerning investment accounts or transactions, or employment relationships within the financial industry"; and
>
> (6) "for a total of 15 years or more, an employee of a bank or other financial institution who effects transactions in securities, including government or municipal securities, commodities, futures, or options or supervises or monitors the compliance with the securities and commodities laws of employees who engage in such activities."

Temporary disqualifications are too numerous to list here, but include disqualifications based on a person's own activities within the last five years, activities by others at one's employer or the financial industry affiliation of an immediate family member.

Conversely, as the definition of a public arbitrator became more complex, FINRA simplified the definition of a "nonpublic arbitrator," which now "means a person who is otherwise qualified to serve as an arbitrator, and is disqualified from service as a public arbitrator * * *."

Arbitrators are eligible to be chairpersons if they have completed FINRA chairperson training, are attorneys, and have served on a panel in at least one prior arbitration in which hearings have been held. If they are not attorneys, they must have served on a panel in at least three prior arbitrations through award in which hearings have been held.

[3] Composition of Panels

In a customer-broker arbitration, if the panel consists of one arbitrator, the arbitrator must be from the public chairperson roster, unless the parties agree otherwise. For a three-arbitrator customer dispute panel, customers have a choice of an all-public panel, or a panel with two public and one nonpublic arbitrators, with a public chairperson. Arbitration panels in disputes between member firms consist of nonpublic arbitrators only. In a dispute between associated persons, or between or among members and associated persons, a one-member panel is public; a three-member panel consists of one nonpublic and two public arbitrators, with a public chairperson. In an arbitration involving a claim of statutory employment discrimination, a one-member panel is public; a three-member panel is all public, unless the parties agree otherwise in writing.

Under FINRA's "neutral list selection system," [FINRA] sends all parties at the same time lists of arbitrators within a designated geographic hearing site, generated in a random fashion by a computer program. In the case of single-arbitrator arbitration, FINRA sends one list of 10 public arbitrators, unless the parties agree otherwise. In three-arbitrator customer arbitrations, FINRA sends three lists to the parties: 10 names of Chair-qualified public arbitrators, 15 names of public arbitrators, and 10 names of nonpublic (i.e., industry) arbitrators. In addition to the lists, FINRA sends each potential panelist's current Arbitrator Disclosure Report, which contains the employment history of each listed arbitrator for the past 10 years and other background information. Every arbitrator is required to disclose to the Director [of FINRA's Office of Dispute Resolution] any personal interest he or she may have in the outcome of the arbitration; and any existing or past associations that they or their family members or business associates may have that might create partiality or an appearance of partiality. The Director is required to pass this information on to the parties.

The parties may strike up to four arbitrators from the Chair-qualified list; up to six arbitrators from the public list, and any and all names from the nonpublic list, thus guaranteeing a customer an all-public panel if the customer wants one. Any arbitrators remaining on any list must be ranked in order of preference. If a party does not return the lists to the Director within 20 days after the Director sends the lists, the Director shall treat the party as having retained all the arbitrators on the list or lists and as having no preferences.

When the parties return the lists, the Director consolidates the parties' rankings of the listed arbitrators, subject to availability and disqualification, and excludes any arbitrators whose names were stricken. If there are not enough names left to make up an arbitration panel, the Director shall appoint one or more additional arbitrators and provide the parties with information about them, subject to the parties' right to request that the additional arbitrator(s) be disqualified for conflict of interest or bias. The Rules also specify procedures for appointing replacement arbitrators if FINRA removes an arbitrator or one withdraws from the panel.

"Either upon request of a party or on the Director's own initiative," the Director has the authority to remove an arbitrator for "conflict of interest or bias," but only before the first hearing session begins. After the first hearing session, "the

Director may remove an arbitrator based only on information required to be disclosed under Rule 12405 that was not previously known by the parties." Parties can also ask that an arbitrator recuse himself for good cause, but the targeted arbitrator decides this request. As long as the forum follows its own prescribed rules, courts will uphold the arbitrator selection process.

On the Harvard Law School Forum on Corporate Governance and Financial Regulation, three professors summarize their research "examin[ing] consumer arbitration in the securities industry using a new detailed data covering 9,000 arbitration disputes between consumers and their financial advisers" as follows:

> The arbitrator selection process is based on the premise that arbitrators differ, and do so in terms of how favorable they will be to either party. Consistent with this intuition, we find empirical evidence suggesting that there are large persistent differences across arbitrators. Some arbitrators are systematically industry friendly while others are consumer friendly, and the differences are substantial. * * *
>
> Given that both firms and consumers can eliminate arbitrators on the randomly generated list who are biased against them, one might expect that the selected arbitrators would not be biased. Instead, we find that industry friendly arbitrators, those that grant lower awards, are more likely to be selected again relative to arbitrators who are consumer friendly. * * *
>
> Firms' informational advantage in selecting arbitrators likely comes from their additional experience in arbitration. While most consumers will participate in arbitration typically at most once in their lifetime, the average firm in our sample participates in roughly 100 different arbitration cases. We find that some consumers are able to compensate for their lack of personal experience by hiring attorneys who specialize in arbitration (PIABA members), faring better in arbitration. Of course, the knowledge that specialized attorneys exist, and how to find them already requires a certain level of familiarity and sophistication with arbitration. Overall, these findings suggest that the parties' level of sophistication and experience plays a potentially critical role in the arbitrator selection process.
>
> Unlike judges, arbitrators are only compensated if they are selected to arbitrate a case. Because industry friendly arbitrators are more likely to be selected, arbitrators are potentially incentivized to develop a reputation for being industry friendly. Arbitrators therefore compete to be selected on the arbitration panel by choosing their slant: how industry or consumer friendly they will act. * * *
>
> A key result of the model is that even though the underlying population of arbitrators may be unbiased, competition among arbitrators can drive all arbitrators to intentionally slant their case decisions. In fact, under a benchmark in which arbitrators only want to maximize their monetary payoffs, no arbitrator wants to be the least industry friendly arbitrator.

> This induces extreme competition between arbitrators, resulting in all arbitrators being maximally industry friendly. Intuitively, competition between arbitrators exacerbates the informational advantage of firms in equilibrium when consumers are uninformed. Our model estimates suggest that randomly selecting arbitrators—as opposed to selecting them using the current mechanism where firms have informational advantage over consumers—would increase investor awards by 5pp, or $40,000 on average. * * *
>
> While our analysis focuses on arbitration in the securities industry, the insights from our setting likely extend to consumer arbitration more broadly. In our setting, the arbitrator selection process results in biased outcomes because (i) both firms and consumers have control over the arbitrator selection process, and (ii) firms have an informational advantage in selecting arbitrators over consumers. Both of these features are common across other consumer arbitration forums such as the American Arbitration Association (AAA) and the Judicial Arbitration and Mediation Services, Inc. (JAMS). Using data on JAMS and AAA arbitration proceedings available online, we replicate our main findings in these settings, with the caveat that data are relatively sparse and span a wide range of industries and cases, leading to noisier estimates of arbitrator bias and selection. Nevertheless, our analysis suggests that our results may apply to consumer arbitration beyond just financial services.

Arbitration with Uninformed Consumers, posted by Mark Egan (Harvard Business School), Gregor Matvos (University of Texas at Austin), Amit Seru (Stanford University), on Monday, January 28, 2019, https://corpgov.law.harvard.edu/2019/01/28/arbitration-with-uninformed-consumers/.

4. PAYING THE ARBITRATORS AND THE ARBITRATION ORGANIZATION

Arbitrators are generally free to state their own rate of compensation and see who hires them. Regular fees of $1000 per day or more allow some people to make a full-time job of serving as an arbitrator of labor disputes. The supply of commercial arbitrators is more elastic, and the "full-time" commercial arbitrator is less common, but growing. Commercial rates tend to be higher than in labor cases—with $2000 per day long ago termed not "excessively high" or "far beyond the applicable standard for such services."[15] Section 2.F.2's excerpt on HMO arbitration noted an average daily rate of $3688 in 2013. International commercial arbitrators tend to earn even more, and a 2009 commentator said "[i]t is generally known that the going rate for ICC [International Chamber of Commerce] and other international arbitrators is $600/hour or $5,000/day."[16]

---

[15] Polin v. Kellwood Co., 103 F.Supp.2d 238, 257 n. 27 (S.D.N.Y.2000), aff'd, 34 Fed. Appx. 406 (2d Cir. 2002).

[16] Ronald J. Offenkrantz, *Arbitrating Commercial Issues: Do You Really Know the Out-of-Pocket Costs?*, 81 N.Y. ST. B.J. 30,31–32 (2009).

In addition to arbitrator fees, parties pay fees, often based on the amount of the claim, to arbitration organizations like the AAA and the ICC for their services in supervising the arbitration. Much like court filing fees, arbitration organization fees must usually be paid at the time a case is filed. These arbitration filing fees can vary widely, and they usually depend on the remedy sought by the claimant, which acts as a measure of the size of the case. In other words, the more money the claimant demands, the higher the fee charged by the arbitration organization.[17] For consumers in small arbitrations, the required filing fees are usually comparable to a court fee,[18] while for larger commercial cases, filing fees can exceed court fees by thousands of dollars.[19] Additional administrative fees and arbitrator's fees may add up as required to hold hearings and complete the arbitration.[20] This usually has the result that arbitrators or arbitration organizations have higher fees for parties who require more work because of the size of the case; in contrast, courts usually have the same fees for parties regardless of the case size.

Arbitration fees, especially in the context of consumers' and employees' adhesive arbitration agreements, have contributed to courts' refusals to enforce such agreements. See, e.g., Ting v. AT&T, 319 F.3d 1126, 1151 (9th Cir.2003) (fees excessive and unconscionable). Relatedly, the Supreme Court said in *Green Tree Financial Corp.-Alabama v. Randolph*, 531 U.S. 79, 90 (2000), that courts should not enforce agreements to arbitrate when enforcement would prevent the prospective litigant from "*effectively vindicating* his or her [federal] statutory cause of action." Cases applying the "effectively vindicate" doctrine typically involve federal employment discrimination claims or claims arising under federal legislation regulating consumer finance. These cases have refused to enforce arbitration agreements due to the amount of arbitration fees the claimant is required to pay, although courts differ on how to determine when the fees are too high.[21] Although this sort of argument did not persuade the Supreme Court to invalidate an arbitral class waiver in *American Express Co. v. Italian Colors Restaurant*, 570 U.S. 228 (2013), that decision left open the possibility that the "effectively vindicate" doctrine still applies to cases in which the "filing and administrative fees attached to arbitration [ ] are so high as to make access to the forum impracticable." Id. at 2310–11.

---

[17] See, e.g., *Administrative Fee Schedule, Commercial Arbitration Rules and Mediation Procedures*, Am. Arbitration Ass'n (May. 1, 2018) ("[A]dministrative fees are based on the amount of the claim or counterclaim and are to be paid by the party bringing the claim or counterclaim at the time the demand or claim is filed with the AAA."), https://www.adr.org/sites/default/files/Commercial_Arbitration_Fee_Schedule_0.pdf.

[18] *Cost of Arbitration, Consumer Arbitration Rules*, Am. Arbitration Ass'n (Feb. 21, 2018) ("Filing Fee: $200 (nonrefundable)"), https://www.adr.org/sites/default/files/Consumer_Fee_Schedule.pdf.

[19] *Administrative Fee Schedule, Commercial Arbitration Rules and Mediation Procedures*, Am. Arbitration Ass'n (May 1, 2018) (initial filing fee for amount of claim "$500,000 to less than $1,000,000" is $5,500 on the standard fee schedule), https://www.adr.org/sites/default/files/Commercial_Arbitration_Fee_Schedule_0.pdf.

[20] Consumer Arbitration Rules, Cost of Arbitration § (i), Am. Arbitration Ass'n (Feb. 21, 2018) ("The AAA reserves the right to assess additional administrative fees for services performed by the AAA beyond those provided for in these Rules and which may be required by the parties' agreement or stipulation").

[21] Compare Morrison v. Circuit City Stores, Inc., 317 F.3d 646 (6th Cir.2003), with Bradford v. Rockwell Semiconductor Sys., Inc., 238 F.3d 549 (4th Cir.2001); Muriithi v. Shuttle Exp., Inc. 712 F.3d 173, 181–83 (4th Cir.2013).

To avoid the fees of an arbitration organization, parties can choose to arbitrate without such an organization. However, this requires the parties to agree to an arbitrator and only use the arbitrator's help in conducting the arbitration. Consequently, the arbitrator may be required to perform administrative tasks that an arbitration organization would normally perform. Depending on the arbitrator's hourly rate, it may in fact be cheaper for the parties to use an arbitration organization.

QUESTIONS TO REVIEW AND SYNTHESIZE

1. In what scenario does the AAA always use only one arbitrator?
2. How are arbitrators selected under the AAA Commercial Rules?
3. Section 2.E excerpts David Horton & Andrea Cann Chandrasekher, *After the Revolution: An Empirical Study of Consumer Arbitration*, which says:

   Marc Galanter's canonical article, Why the "Haves" Come Out Ahead: Speculations on the Limits of Legal Change. [9 Law and Society Rev. 1 (1974)] Galanter famously divided participants in the legal system into repeat players, who are regularly embroiled in litigation, and one-shotters, who are not. Galanter outlined a variety of ways in which repeat players could capitalize on their experience to gain the upper hand over one-shotters, such as stockpiling information, making short-term sacrifices for long-term gains, and cultivating relationships within institutions. In the late 1990s, several influential law review articles asserted that Galanter's theory fit mandatory arbitration like a glove. After all, private judges, unlike their public counterparts, are paid by the hour. In addition, litigants cannot handpick a specific decision maker to resolve their case, but parties in arbitration can. Accordingly, as David Schwartz observed, "arbitrators have an economic stake in being selected again, and their judgment may well be shaded by a desire to build a 'track record' of decisions that corporate repeat-users will view approvingly." Likewise, Jean Sternlight noted that "[a]n arbitrator who issues a large punitive damages award against a company may not get chosen again by that company or others who hear of the award." Moreover, these scholars argued that repeat players could come out ahead even if arbitrators took pains to remain even-handed. If nothing else, firms that arbitrated regularly could compile data on particular decision makers' predilections, while one-shot plaintiffs and their lawyers could not.

To what extent do these concerns apply to arbitrator selection under the AAA Commercial and FINRA rules?

4. Section 2.A.4 showed that securities arbitration differs from other commercial arbitration in what ways? How do these differences relate to FINRA arbitration selection?
5. What is the "effectively vindicate" doctrine and how does it relate to arbitration fees?
6. Which arbitrators tend to be the most expensive? Why?

5. ARBITRATOR IMPARTIALITY AND DISCLOSURE

a. LEGAL REGULATION VS. CONSENSUAL AND REPUTATIONAL FACTORS

Commonwealth Coatings Corp. v. Continental Casualty Co.

Supreme Court of the United States, 1968.
393 U.S. 145, 89 S.Ct. 337, 21 L.Ed.2d 301.

■ MR. JUSTICE BLACK delivered the opinion of the Court.

At issue in this case is the question whether elementary requirements of impartiality taken for granted in every judicial proceeding are suspended when the parties agree to resolve a dispute through arbitration. [Having read this far, what do you think the answer is going to be?—Eds.]

The petitioner, Commonwealth Coatings Corp., a subcontractor, sued the sureties on the prime contractor's bond to recover money alleged to be due for a painting job. The contract for painting contained an agreement to arbitrate such controversies. Pursuant to this agreement petitioner appointed one arbitrator, the prime contractor appointed a second, and these two together selected the third arbitrator. This third arbitrator, the supposedly neutral member of the panel, conducted a large business in Puerto Rico, in which he served as an engineering consultant for various people in connection with building construction projects. One of his regular customers in this business was the prime contractor that petitioner sued in this case. This relationship with the prime contractor was in a sense sporadic in that the arbitrator's services were used only from time to time at irregular intervals, and there had been no dealings between them for about a year immediately preceding the arbitration. Nevertheless, the prime contractor's patronage was repeated and significant, involving fees of about $12,000 over a period of four or five years, and the relationship even went so far as to include the rendering of services on the very projects involved in this lawsuit. An arbitration was held, but the facts concerning the close business connections between the third arbitrator and the prime contractor were unknown to petitioner and were never revealed to it by this arbitrator, by the prime contractor, or by anyone else until after an award had been made. Petitioner challenged the award on this ground, among others, but the District Court refused to set aside the award. The Court of Appeals affirmed.

* * * [B]oth sides here assume that [the FAA] governs this case. Section 10 sets out the conditions upon which awards can be vacated. The two courts below held, however, that § 10 could not be construed in such a way as to justify vacating the award in this case. We disagree and reverse. Section 10 does authorize vacation of an award where it was "procured by corruption, fraud, or undue means" or "[w]here there was evident partiality * * * in the arbitrators." These provisions show a desire of Congress to provide not merely for *any* arbitration but for an impartial one. It is true that petitioner does not charge before us that the third arbitrator was actually guilty of fraud or bias in deciding this case, and we have no reason, apart from the undisclosed business relationship, to suspect him of any improper motives. But neither this arbitrator nor the prime contractor gave to

petitioner even an intimation of the close financial relations that had existed between them for a period of years. We have no doubt that if a litigant could show that a foreman of a jury or a judge in a court of justice had, unknown to the litigant, any such relationship, the judgment would be subject to challenge. This is shown beyond doubt by *Tumey v. State of Ohio*, 273 U.S. 510 (1927), where this Court held that a conviction could not stand because a small part of the judge's income consisted of court fees collected from convicted defendants. Although in *Tumey* it appeared the amount of the judge's compensation actually depended on whether he decided for one side or the other, that is too small a distinction to allow this manifest violation of the strict morality and fairness Congress would have expected on the part of the arbitrator and the other party in this case. Nor should it be at all relevant, as the Court of Appeals apparently thought it was here, that "[t]he payments received were a very small part of [the arbitrator's] income * * *." For in *Tumey* the Court held that a decision should be set aside where there is "the slightest pecuniary interest" on the part of the judge, and specifically rejected the State's contention that the compensation involved there was "so small that it is not to be regarded as likely to influence improperly a judicial officer in the discharge of his duty * * *." Since in the case of courts this is a *constitutional* principle, we can see no basis for refusing to find the same concept in the broad statutory language that governs arbitration proceedings and provides that an award can be set aside on the basis of "evident partiality" or the use of "undue means." It is true that arbitrators cannot sever all their ties with the business world, since they are not expected to get all their income from their work deciding cases, but we should, if anything, be even more scrupulous to safeguard the impartiality of arbitrators than judges, since the former have completely free rein to decide the law as well as the facts and are not subject to appellate review. We can perceive no way in which the effectiveness of the arbitration process will be hampered by the simple requirement that arbitrators disclose to the parties any dealings that might create an impression of possible bias.

[Justice Black then referred to the AAA rules of procedure which, "while not controlling in this case," called on an arbitrator "to disclose any circumstances likely to create a presumption of bias or which he believes might disqualify him as an impartial Arbitrator."]

[B]ased on the same principle as this Arbitration Association rule is that part of the 33d Canon of Judicial Ethics which provides:

> 33. Social Relations
>
> * * * [A judge] should, however, in pending or prospective litigation before him be particularly careful to avoid such action as may reasonably tend to awaken the suspicion that his social or business relations or friendships, constitute an element in influencing his judicial conduct.

This rule of arbitration and this canon of judicial ethics rest on the premise that any tribunal permitted by law to try cases and controversies not only must be unbiased but also must avoid even the appearance of bias. We cannot believe that it was the purpose of Congress to authorize litigants to submit their cases and controversies to arbitration boards that might reasonably be thought biased against one litigant and favorable to another.

Reversed.

■ MR. JUSTICE WHITE, with whom MR. JUSTICE MARSHALL joins, concurring.

While I am glad to join my Brother Black's opinion in this case, I desire to make these additional remarks. The Court does not decide today that arbitrators are to be held to the standards of judicial decorum of Article III judges, or indeed of any judges. It is often because they are men of affairs, not apart from but of the marketplace, that they are effective in their adjudicatory function. This does not mean the judiciary must overlook outright chicanery in giving effect to their awards; that would be an abdication of our responsibility. But it does mean that arbitrators are not automatically disqualified by a business relationship with the parties before them if both parties are informed of the relationship in advance, or if they are unaware of the facts but the relationship is trivial. I see no reason automatically to disqualify the best informed and most capable potential arbitrators.

The arbitration process functions best when an amicable and trusting atmosphere is preserved and there is voluntary compliance with the decree, without need for judicial enforcement. This end is best served by establishing an atmosphere of frankness at the outset, through disclosure by the arbitrator of any financial transactions which he has had or is negotiating with either of the parties. In many cases the arbitrator might believe the business relationship to be so insubstantial that to make a point of revealing it would suggest he is indeed easily swayed, and perhaps a partisan of that party.* But if the law requires the disclosure, no such imputation can arise. And it is far better that the relationship be disclosed at the outset, when the parties are free to reject the arbitrator or accept him with knowledge of the relationship and continuing faith in his objectivity, than to have the relationship come to light after the arbitration, when a suspicious or disgruntled party can seize on it as a pretext for invalidating the award. The judiciary should minimize its role in arbitration as judge of the arbitrator's impartiality. That role is best consigned to the parties, who are the architects of their own arbitration process, and are far better informed of the prevailing ethical standards and reputations within their business.

Of course, an arbitrator's business relationships may be diverse indeed, involving more or less remote commercial connections with great numbers of people. He cannot be expected to provide the parties with his complete and unexpurgated business biography. But it is enough for present purposes to hold, as the Court does, that where the arbitrator has a substantial interest in a firm which has done more than trivial business with a party, that fact must be disclosed. If arbitrators err on the side of disclosure, as they should, it will not be difficult for courts to identify those undisclosed relationships which are too insubstantial to warrant vacating an award.

* In fact, the District Court found—on the basis of the record and petitioner's admissions—that the arbitrator in this case was entirely fair and impartial. I do not read the majority opinion as questioning this finding in any way.

■ MR. JUSTICE FORTAS, with whom MR. JUSTICE HARLAN and MR. JUSTICE STEWART join, dissenting.

I dissent and would affirm the judgment.

* * *

Both courts below held, and petitioner concedes, that the third arbitrator was innocent of any actual partiality, or bias, or improper motive. There is no suggestion of concealment as distinguished from the innocent failure to volunteer information.

The third arbitrator is a leading and respected consulting engineer who has performed services for "most of the contractors in Puerto Rico." He was well known to petitioner's counsel and they were personal friends. Petitioner's counsel candidly admitted that if he had been told about the arbitrator's prior relationship "I don't think I would have objected because I know Mr. Capacete [the arbitrator]."

Clearly, the District Judge's conclusion, affirmed by the Court of Appeals for the First Circuit, was correct, that "the arbitrators conducted fair, impartial hearings; that they reached a proper determination of the issues before them, and that plaintiff's objections represent a 'situation where the losing party to an arbitration is now clutching at straws in an attempt to avoid the results of the arbitration to which it became a party.'"

* * *

Arbitration is essentially consensual and practical. The United States Arbitration Act is obviously designed to protect the integrity of the process with a minimum of insistence upon set formulae and rules. The Court applies to this process rules applicable to judges and not to a system characterized by dealing on faith and reputation for reliability. Such formalism is not contemplated by the Act nor is it warranted in a case where no claim is made of partiality, of unfairness, or of misconduct in any degree.

Each of the three opinions in *Commonwealth Coatings* displays a different level of judicial comfort with binding adjudication—not by judges elevated above the parties by courtroom architecture and black robes—but rather by "men of affairs" in a "consensual and practical" "system characterized by dealing on faith and reputation for reliability." While discomfort with such adjudicators leads Justice Black's plurality opinion to analogize arbitrators to judges and jurors, Justice White's concurrence (essential to a majority of the Court) begins by distinguishing arbitrators from judges and emphasizes that arbitrators are appropriately "not apart from but of the marketplace." Going further, Justice Fortas' dissent contrasts the formal legal rules governing judges with the consensual and reputational factors constraining arbitrators.

The consensual and reputational factors constraining arbitrators often appear through the work of arbitration organizations like the AAA. While the FAA allows courts to vacate an arbitration award where "there was evident partiality or corruption in the arbitrators,"[22] arbitration organizations often resolve partiality issues well before an award is rendered, during the arbitrator-selection process. For example, the AAA's Commercial Arbitration Rules requires any person named as an arbitrator to "disclose to the AAA any circumstance likely to give rise to justifiable doubt as to the arbitrator's impartiality or independence, including any bias or any financial or personal interest in the result of the arbitration or any past or present relationship with the parties or their representatives." The AAA communicates this information to the parties and if any of them objects, "the AAA shall determine whether the arbitrator should be disqualified * * * and shall inform the parties of its decision, which decision shall be conclusive." (Rules 17, 18).

In addition, the AAA and the American Bar Association adopted a "Code of Ethics for Arbitrators in Commercial Disputes." Canon II of this Code provides that "an arbitrator shall disclose any interest or relationship likely to affect impartiality or which might create an appearance of partiality":

> A. Persons who are requested to serve as arbitrators should, before accepting, disclose:
>
> (1) any known direct or indirect financial or personal interest in the outcome of the arbitration;
>
> (2) any known existing or past financial, business, professional or personal relationships which might reasonably affect impartiality or lack of independence in the eyes of any of the parties. For example, prospective arbitrators should disclose any such relationships which they personally have with any party or its lawyer, with any coarbitrator, or with any individual whom they have been told will be a witness. They should also disclose any such relationships involving their families or household members or their current employers, partners, or professional or business associates that can be ascertained by reasonable efforts;
>
> (3) the nature and extent of any prior knowledge they may have of the dispute. * * *
>
> B. Persons who are requested to accept appointment as arbitrators should make a reasonable effort to inform themselves of any interests or relationships described in paragraph A. * * *
>
> G. If an arbitrator is requested by all parties to withdraw, the arbitrator must do so. If an arbitrator is requested to withdraw by less than all of the parties because of alleged partiality, the arbitrator should withdraw unless either of the following circumstances exists:
>
> (1) An agreement of the parties, or arbitration rules agreed to by the parties, or applicable law establishes procedures for determining challenges to arbitrators, in which case those procedures should be followed; or
>
> (2) In the absence of applicable procedures, if the arbitrator, after carefully considering the matter, determines that the reason for the

[22] 9 U.S.C. § 10(a)(2).

> challenge is not substantial, and that he or she can nevertheless act and decide the case impartially and fairly.

Notes to the Code also warn that

> A prospective arbitrator is not necessarily partial or prejudiced by having acquired knowledge of the parties, the applicable law or the customs and practices of the business involved. Arbitrators may also have special experience or expertise in the areas of business, commerce, or technology which are involved in the arbitration. Arbitrators do not contravene this Canon if, by virtue of such experience or expertise, they have views on certain general issues likely to arise in the arbitration, but an arbitrator may not have prejudged any of the specific factual or legal determinations to be addressed during the arbitration.

An arbitrator's failure to make disclosures required by these ethical canons or the rules of the AAA or Rules and Canons will not necessarily lead a court to vacate the arbitrator's award. For the Seventh Circuit, Judge Posner has written that:

> [E]ven if the failure to disclose was a material violation of the ethical standards applicable to arbitration proceedings, it does not follow that the arbitration award may be nullified judicially. * * * The arbitration rules and code do not have the force of law. If [a party] is to get the arbitration award set aside it must bring itself within the statute * * *.
>
> The American Arbitration Association is in competition not only with other private arbitration services but with the courts in providing—in the case of the private services, selling—an attractive form of dispute settlement. It may set its standards as high or as low as it thinks its customers want. The [FAA] has a different purpose—to make arbitration effective by putting the coercive force of the federal courts behind arbitration decrees that affect interstate commerce or are otherwise of federal concern. * * * The standards for judicial intervention are therefore narrowly drawn to assure the basic integrity of the arbitration process without meddling in it. Section 10 is full of words like corruption and misbehavior and fraud. The standards it sets are minimum ones. * * * The fact that the AAA went beyond the statutory standards in drafting its own code of ethics does not lower the threshold for judicial intervention.

Merit Ins. Co. v. Leatherby Ins. Co., 714 F.2d 673 (7th Cir.1983). However, Judge Posner may be more sensitive than most judges about the necessary "tradeoff between impartiality and expertise." Id. at 679. See also Lefkovitz v. Wagner, 395 F.3d 773, 780 (7th Cir. 2005) (Posner, J.) ("[s]tricter rules cabin the generalist [judge] because he is more apt to be led astray by the lawyers and witnesses in a matter in which his only knowledge comes from them. When disputants repose their trust in a specific individual rather than having to take the luck of the draw, it is right that they should have to take the bad with the good unless the individual runs completely off the rails").

A good example of the "tradeoff between impartiality and expertise" is *International Produce, Inc. v. A/S Rosshavet*, 638 F.2d 548 (2d Cir.1981), a maritime arbitration in which the neutral arbitrator was Vice President of a management firm retained by owners of various commercial vessels. After the hearings began, this arbitrator's firm became involved in an unrelated arbitration involving another vessel. It happened that the law firms representing the parties in the second arbitration were the same firms that were handling the *International Produce* arbitration; in this second proceeding the arbitrator appeared as a non-party witness, prepared in his testimony by one of the law firms and cross-examined by the other. Although requested to withdraw from serving as arbitrator in the *International Produce* case, the arbitrator refused to do so, and his award was successfully challenged in district court. However, the Second Circuit held that the award should not have been vacated:

> It is not unusual that those who are selected as arbitrators in maritime arbitrations have had numerous prior dealings with one or more of the parties or their counsel. * * * Arbitrator Klosty aptly analogized New York's maritime-arbitration community to a busy harbor, where the wakes of the members often cross. The most sought-after arbitrators are those who are prominent and experienced members of the specific business community in which the dispute to be arbitrated arose. Since they are chosen precisely because of their involvement in that community, some degree of overlapping representation and interest inevitably results. Those chosen as arbitrators in important shipping arbitrations have typically participated in a great number of prior maritime disputes, not only as arbitrators but also as parties and witnesses. They have therefore almost inevitably come into contact with a significant proportion of the relatively few lawyers who make up the New York admiralty bar. Under these circumstances, a decision on our part to vacate arbitration awards whenever a mere appearance of bias can be made out would seriously disrupt the salutary process of settling maritime disputes through arbitration.

Of course, the alleged conflict of interest in *International Produce* was immediately known to both of the parties in the case as soon as it arose. In contrast, courts are more likely to vacate awards by arbitrators who failed to disclose facts unknown to one of the parties. See, e.g., Positive Software Solutions, Inc. v. New Century Mortgage Corp., 436 F.3d 495 (5th Cir. 2006) (vacating award where arbitrator failed to disclose that seven years before the arbitration, he and his former law firm were co-counsel in a lengthy litigation matter with law firm and particular lawyer representing winning party in arbitration); Gray v. Chiu, 151 Cal.Rptr.3d 791, 797 (Ct.App. 2013) (vacating award because neutral arbitrator failed to disclose, as required by California Arbitration Act and Ethics Standards [both discussed below], that a lawyer in the arbitration was a member of the neutral arbitrator's administering dispute resolution agency, ADR Services, Inc.).

On the other hand, in *Sphere Drake Ins. Ltd. v. All American Life Ins. Co.*, 307 F.3d 617, 620 (7th Cir. 2002), an arbitrator had—four years previously—worked on an unrelated matter as counsel to the Bermuda subsidiary of the party who had appointed him. Writing for the Seventh Circuit, Judge Easterbrook held that the arbitrator's failure to make a full disclosure of these facts "may sully his reputation for candor but does not demonstrate 'evident partiality' and thus does not spoil the award." On those same facts, after all, the arbitrator could even "have served as a federal judge * * * without challenge on grounds of partiality"—and if "the full truth would not have disclosed even a risk of partiality," his failure to make a complete disclosure should not be treated differently: *Commonwealth Coatings* "did not hold * * * that disclosure is compulsory for its own sake, and its absence fatal even if the arbitrator meets judicial standards of impartiality."

> Industry arbitration, the modern law merchant, often uses panels composed of industry insiders, the better to understand the trade's norms of doing business and the consequences of proposed lines of decision. The more experience the panel has, and the smaller the number of repeat players, the more likely it is that the panel will contain some actual or potential friends, counselors or business rivals of the parties. Yet all participants may think the expertise-impartiality tradeoff worthwhile; the Arbitration Act does not fasten on every industry the model of the disinterested generalist judge.

Sphere Drake Ins. Ltd. v. All American Life Ins. Co., 307 F.3d 617, 620 (7th Cir. 2002) (Easterbrook, J.)

QUESTIONS TO REVIEW AND SYNTHESIZE

1. If an arbitrator fails to disclose a potentially disqualifying conflict, but you represent the party seeking to confirm, rather than vacate, the award, what facts will help your case?
2. What is the "tradeoff between impartiality and expertise"?
3. Whose ruling is more likely to be overturned: (A) an arbitrator who received from one of the parties $12,000 for periodic work as an engineering consultant two-to-five years before ruling for that party, or (B) a trial court judge whose re-election campaign received from one the parties a total of $12,000 in campaign contributions two-to-five years before ruling for that party? Compare *Caperton v. A.T. Massey Coal Co.*, 556 U.S. 868, 888–90 (2009) (Due Process required recusal in a case involving, not contributions to the judge's campaign, but independent expenditures by corporate party's president criticizing the judge's opponent).

b. STATE LAW, PARTICULARLY CALIFORNIA

California goes beyond federal law in imposing more explicit and stringent obligations of disclosure on potential arbitrators. See Cal.Code.Civ.Pro. § 1281.85. The California Arbitration Act requires any potential arbitrator to disclose the existence of any facts that would warrant the disqualification of a *judge*. Id. § 1281.9(a)(1). It further provides that any potential arbitrator must disclose the "names of the parties to all prior or pending * * * cases in which the proposed neutral arbitrator served or is serving as * * * arbitrator for any party to the arbitration proceeding or for a lawyer for a party," as well as "the results of each case arbitrated to conclusion * * * and the amount of monetary damages awarded, if any." Id. §§ 1281.9(a)(3). The proposed arbitrator "shall be disqualified on the basis of the disclosure statement" if any party "serves a notice of disqualification;" failure to make the requisite disclosures gives rise to vacatur. Id. §§ 1281.91(b)(1); 1286.2(a)(6).

At the same time the California legislature delegated to the state Judicial Council the task of promulgating additional minimum ethical standards, which could "expand but may not limit" those in the statute. The resulting "Ethics Standards for Neutral Arbitrators in Contractual Arbitration" came into effect in 2002 and are highly complex and detailed: They would apparently require disqualification of an arbitrator whose "spouse used to serve on a bar committee with an associate of a party's lawyer, even if the associate is uninvolved in the case."[23] They also require disclosure of an arbitrator's membership in any organization that practices "invidious discrimination on the basis of race, sex, religion, national origin, or sexual orientation."[24]

Most extensive are the requirements for consumer and employment arbitrations administered by an organization like the AAA: In such cases, the arbitrator shall disclose any financial or professional relationship between the *organization* and a party or lawyer to the arbitration, as well as whether the organization had ever administered any other arbitrations in which a present party or lawyer was involved—and in such cases, the result and the amount of damages awarded.[25] "The sheer collective volume of disclosure requirements is enough to make a conscientious arbitrator nervous, and provide a disappointed lawyer potential ammunition with which to pursue another try or an improved negotiated outcome." Jay Folberg, *Arbitration Ethics: Is California the Future?*, 18 Ohio St. J. on Disp. Res. 343, 352 (2003) (the author chaired the California Judicial Council Blue Ribbon Panel of Experts on Arbitrator Ethics).

Data generated by California's disclosure requirements are generally readily available online and published quarterly. See, e.g., AAA Consumer Report, https://www.adr.org/consumer (last visited June 28, 2019) (click on "Consumer and Employment Arbitration Statistics"); JAMS Consumer Report, https://www.jamsadr.com/consumercases/ (last visited June 28, 2019) (click on "JAMS Consumer Case Information Spreadsheet"). Leading scholars rely on this data in drawing conclusions about consumer and employment arbitration. See, e.g., David Horton & Andrea Cann Chandrasekher, *After the Revolution: An Empirical Study of Consumer Arbitration*, 104 Geo. L.J. 57, 79 (2015) (using 2009–13 AAA consumer arbitration data, which was generated by compliance with California's disclosure requirements, to analyze effectiveness of arbitration, particularly for consumers); Alexander J.S. Colvin, *Empirical Research on Employment Arbitration: Clarity Amidst the Sound and Fury?*, 11 Emp. Rts. & Emp. Pol'y J. 405, 407 (2007) (using 2003–06 AAA employment arbitration data, which was published in compliance with California's disclosure requirements to analyze employment arbitration; "filings by the AAA

---

[23] Credit Suisse First Boston Corp. v. Grunwald, 400 F.3d 1119, 1134 n.23 (9th Cir. 2005) ("Standard 7(d)(8) requires the disclosure of '[a]ny other professional relationship . . . that the arbitrator or a member of the arbitrator's immediately family has or has had with a party or lawyer for a party.' Standard (2)(m) defines 'Lawyer for a party' to include the law firm and associates of the lawyer representing the party. Thus, read together, these two provisions require an arbitrator to disclose any professional relationship his spouse had with anyone associated with a party's lawyer's law firm").

[24] 2019 Cal. Rules of Court, Ethics Standards for Neutral Arbitrators in Contractual Arbitration, Standard 7(d)(14), https://www.courts.ca.gov/cms/rules/index.cfm?title=ethics&linkid=ethics7.

[25] *Id.* Standard 8.

under this California law include all arbitration cases filed nationally involving consumers, not just those from California").

Merrick T. Rossein & Jennifer Hope, *Disclosure and Disqualification Standards for Neutral Arbitrators: How Far to Cast the Net and What Is Sufficient to Vacate Award*

81 St. John's L. Rev. 203, 235–40 (2007).

In response to consumer frustration over mandatory arbitration agreements, the California legislature took action in 2001 to curb what was perceived as arbitrator and arbitration-provider abuses. It enacted section 1286.2(a)(6)(A) of the California Code of Civil Procedure as a solution to the growing "lack of public confidence" in arbitration in consumer contexts. The statute codified the new California Ethics Standards requiring additional and extremely comprehensive arbitrator "disclosures about the relationships between the provider organization and a party or lawyer involved in a consumer arbitration," including disclosures about past service as a dispute resolution neutral for any party or attorney, other interests, relationships and affiliations that may constitute conflicts of interest, as well as "establishment of future professional relationships."

If an arbitrator wishes to entertain offers from other professional relationships, such as that of a mediator or other dispute resolution neutral, the arbitrator must disclose to all parties in writing within ten days of nomination that he or she will entertain such offers of employment. A party may then disqualify the arbitrator based on this disclosure. If no disclosure is made, the arbitrator is prohibited from entering into any new dispute resolution relationships with the parties or attorneys while the arbitration is pending.

The duty of an arbitrator to make reasonable inquiry into her potential conflicts was expanded as well. Section 9 lays out an obligation for an arbitrator to "inform himself or herself of relationships or other matters involving her or her extended family and former spouse" by inquiring with immediate and extended family members and indicating in writing that he or she did such an inquiry. Further, an arbitrator must "inform himself or herself of relationships with any lawyer associated in the practice of law with the lawyer in the arbitration."

The new statutes provide for disclosure of "specific data about arbitrations they have administered within the past five years" and "post the data on an internet website in a computer-searchable format." Broader than disclosure rules promulgated by the NASD and the New York Stock Exchange, the California rules extend to all neutral arbitrators throughout the period of the arbitration.

Most dramatically, the California statute provides for vacating decision when arbitrators don't properly disclose[,] transforming once optional guidelines into a mandate "with consequences for failure to comply." If an arbitrator fails to comply with the statutory Ethics Standards, a party may serve a notice of disqualification. Some of the specific mandatory disclosure requirements include: family relationships with a party or a lawyer in the arbitration, a relationship between a family members and an arbitrator, any service within the last five years in a case involving a party or attorney in the current arbitration, financial interests of the arbitrator or a family member in a party, or anything that "otherwise leads the arbitrator to believe that his or her disqualification will further the interests of justice."

Since state legislation cannot treat arbitration agreement in contracts differently than it treats provisions in contracts as a whole, California sought to avoid preemption under the Federal Arbitration Act by shifting the focus away from arbitration contracts and onto the arbitrators themselves. But, will codes such as California's Ethic Standards pass preemption? In *Ovitz v. Schulman*, [133 Cal.App.4th 830, 35 Cal.Rptr.3d 117 (2005),] the California Court of Appeal held that the FAA does not preempt the new standards based on the court's "review of the relevant statutory language, the congressional purpose of the FAA, and the parties' arbitration agreement." After submitting to mandatory arbitration, an award was rendered in favor of Ovitz. However, during the arbitration proceeding, the arbitrator, Campbell Lucas, disclosed that he had accepted an offer a few months ago for a future matter with Ovitz's counsel's firm. When the opposing party sought disqualification of Lucas, the AAA refused. In opposition to Ovitz's motion to confirm the award, Shulman argued that Lucas' failure to disclose his business relationship at the time of appointment warranted vacatur under California Ethics Standard 12(b).

Ovitz argued that the FAA preempted the California Ethics Standards, such that an award vacatur is limited to the statutory language of the Act, specifically evident partiality. An example of how California is attempting to avoid preemption by placing emphasis on an arbitrators duties, the court distinguished between the FAA's "evident partiality" as a basis for vacatur and the California Ethics Standards requirements for arbitrator disclosure. The court found that the arbitrator did not comply with section 12(b) [of the California Ethics Standards for Neutral Arbitrators in Contractual Arbitration] by failing to note a relevant relationship in his initial disclosure and then failing to disclose after accepting a position in another case, "knowing of the involvement of the law firm representing [one of the parties] in the . . . arbitration." The issue, therefore, was explicitly about disclosure, not about vacatur. And since the FAA does not contain a provision regarding disclosure (i.e., Congress has not spoken on the issue), there is no conflict of law and, therefore, not a preemption issue.

In response to the new rules, however, provider organizations such as the NASD protested that California could not provide for more stringent standards than those of the Securities Exchange Commission ("SEC"). In response, the NASD and the New York Stock Exchange ("NYSE") "asked the federal court to exempt them from [the Standards, claiming] there was already extensive federal oversight" and that the FAA preempted the standards. The court denied the NASD and NYSE relief. Two years later, however, the district court in *Mayo v. Dean Witter Reynolds, Inc.*, [258 F. Supp. 2d 1097, 1116 (N.D. Cal. 2003)] held that:

> [A]pplication of the California standards to the NYSE and other self-regulatory organizations is preempted by the Exchange Act and the comprehensive system of federal regulations of the securities industry established pursuant to the Exchange Act. Moreover, at least as they are applied here, the California standards are preempted by § 2 of the FAA.

In 2005, the Ninth Circuit, in *Credit Suisse First Boston Corp. v. Grunwald*, [400 F.3d 1119 (9th Cir. 2005)] held that the California Ethics Standards were preempted by the NASD and NYSE disclosure rules. Also citing congressional intent and jurisdiction, the court affirmed that the NASD is not bound by California's ethics rules because they were preempted by a provision in the 1934 Securities Exchange Act. Preemption applied because Congress' goal was inhibited by California's ethics rules where it made the SEC responsible for regulating self-regulating organizations; since it would be impossible to comply with both the federal rules and the California rules, the Supremacy Clause mandates that the NASD rules govern. The NASD's Code does not mandate, but rather allows for removal of an arbitrator if she fails to make a required disclosure; even though an arbitration can be disqualified, parties may opt to prevent such disqualification by "unanimously agreeing that the arbitrator should not be disqualified." And, the battle seems hardly over as the court failed to address whether the FAA also preempted the California rules.

Those in favor of the new standards hold it as more efficient because it places the burden on those affected by the violation, as opposed to a government agency. It also provides for increased transparency with consequences to follow for failures to disclose, which give consumers some semblance of legitimacy and provide incentives for disclosure prior to arbitration. Those in opposition to the new disclosure revisions see formal ethical regulations as another way that parties will avoid liability by using the standards to overturn otherwise legitimate arbitration awards.

For now, California's Ethics Standard is the most demanding in the nation, and whether or not the FAA preempts the standards has yet to be addressed. Caution is essential, as one commentator noted:

> The California disclosure rules for neutral arbitrators are complex and unforgiving. Knowing the rules and complying with them to the letter are essential not only for arbitrators, obviously, but also for the parties and their counsel. The latter must be aware of what the arbitrator has disclosed and, based on those disclosures, whether or not they or their opponents may offer the arbitrator additional employment as a neutral while the arbitration is pending. The consequences of failing to keep track can be significant. In the Ovitz case, even if the parties were to go through a second arbitration, the $1.9 million award of attorneys' fees and costs in the first arbitration still would be lost forever.

In *Ovitz*, the California Court of Appeal said the California Ethics Standards:

> require arbitrators to make comprehensive disclosures of potential grounds for disqualification. On a showing that the arbitrator failed timely to disclose a ground for disqualification of which he or she was aware, the California Code of Civil Procedure requires the vacating of any award rendered by the arbitrator. (Code Civ. Proc., § 1286.2, subd. (a)(6)(A).

By contrast, the Federal Arbitration Act employs a different standard: it permits the vacating of an arbitration award only on a showing of "evident partiality" by the arbitrator. (9 U.S.C. § 10(a)(2).)

* * *

In the instant case, the Arbitrator failed in his initial disclosure statement to disclose timely a ground for disqualification under standard 12(b), i.e., a disclosure "if" he would entertain other offers of employment from the parties or their lawyers. He then violated standard 12(c) by accepting appointment in the California National Bank case, knowing of the involvement of the law firm representing the APG parties in the Schulman arbitration. He also violated standards 7(d)(4)(A)(i) and 7(c) by failing to disclose his service in that case within 10 calendar days of his appointment.

* * *

The APG parties contend that even if the Arbitrator failed in his disclosure obligations, the failure does not require the vacating of the arbitration award. The reason: the FAA preempts California law governing the vacating of an arbitration award. We conclude, however, that a review of the relevant statutory language, the congressional purpose of the FAA, and the parties' arbitration agreement demonstrates that the FAA does not preempt section 1286.2(a)(6)(A).

* * *

In cases to which it applies, the FAA has a "limited preemptive effect" on state law. "The FAA contains no express pre-emptive provision, nor does it reflect a congressional intent to occupy the entire field of arbitration. But even when Congress has not completely displaced state regulation in an area, state law may nonetheless be pre-empted to the extent that it actually conflicts with federal law—that is, to the extent that it "stands as an obstacle to the accomplishment and execution of the full purposes and objectives of Congress."

* * *

Thus, the FAA 'establishes that, as a matter of federal law, any doubts concerning the scope of arbitrable issues should be resolved in favor of arbitration, whether the problem at hand is the construction of the contract language itself or an allegation of waiver, delay, or a like defense to arbitrability. * * * By its terms, section 1286.2(a)(6)(A) does not undermine the enforceability of arbitration agreements. It neither limits the rights of contracting parties to submit disputes to arbitration, nor discourages persons from using arbitration. Section 1286.2(a)(6)(A) merely requires the vacating of an award if the arbitrator failed timely to disclose a ground for disqualification of which he was aware.

* * *

Further, the agreement provided that judicial review of the arbitration award would occur under section 1286.2 or other applicable law. To the

> extent there is any conflict on the subject of judicial review between this specific term and the more general provision that the arbitration would be governed by AAA rules, the specific provision controls.
>
> * * *
>
> To the extent the parties meant the FAA, we have now resolved the question: the FAA does not preempt section 1286.2(a)(6)(A). Thus, vacating the arbitration award under section 1286.2(a)(6)(A) does not violate the parties' contract. Based on this conclusion, combined with our review of the relevant federal statutory language and the purpose of the FAA, we hold that section 10(a)(2) of the FAA does not preempt section 1286.2(a)(6)(A).

Ovitz v. Schulman, 35 Cal.Rptr.3d at 833, 845, 849, 851, 852, 853, 855.

c. SUING ARBITRATORS

While vacating awards and ethical rules like California's are ways of influencing arbitrators' behavior, another way to influence arbitrators is to sue them. Parties who lose a case in arbitration sometimes sue the arbitrator or the administering organization, claiming that the arbitrator did not decide fairly or violated the organization's rules. Such claims usually lose due to "arbitral immunity." Courts often conclude that "the independence necessary for principled and fearless decision-making can best be preserved by protecting these persons from bias or intimidation caused by the fear of a lawsuit arising out of the exercise of official functions within their jurisdiction." Corey v. New York Stock Exchange, 691 F.2d 1205 (6th Cir.1982). See also Sacks v. Dietrich, 663 F.3d 1065, 1069 (9th Cir. 2011) ("The doctrine of arbitral immunity provides that arbitrators are immune from civil liability for acts within their jurisdiction arising out of their arbitral functions in contractually agreed upon arbitration hearings"; "[a]s with judicial immunity * * *, arbitral immunity is essential to protect the decision-maker from undue influence and protect the decision-making process from reprisals by dissatisfied litigants. Of course, arbitral immunity does not extend to every act of an arbitrator. Arbitral immunity extends only to those acts taken by arbitrators within the scope of their duties and within their jurisdiction") (internal quotations omitted); Serna v. Webster, 2017 WL 4386359, at *7 (D.N.M. Sept. 30, 2017) ("Every Court of Appeals to have considered the issue recognizes the doctrine of arbitral immunity. * * * Indeed, even the Supreme Court supports the doctrine of arbitral immunity. . . . These courts uniformly hold that arbitration forums and sponsors, like courts of law, are immune from liability for actions taken in connection with administering arbitration").

On the other hand, California courts have held "immunity does not apply to the arbitrator's breach of contract by failing to make any decision at all * * *, arbitral immunity does not protect an arbitrator who unjustifiably fails to complete the job". Greenspan v. LADT, LLC, 185 Cal.App.4th 1413,1458, 111 Cal.Rptr.3d 468,504 (Cal. Ct. App 2010); Morgan Phillips, Inc. v. JAMS/Endispute, L.L.C., 140 Cal. App. 4th 795, 797–98, 44 Cal. Rptr. 3d 782, 783 (2006) ("If an arbitrator withdraws from an arbitration proceeding for no stated ethical reason following evidence and argument, and offers to continue mediation efforts but refuses to render an arbitration award, does the doctrine of arbitral immunity protect the arbitrator from suit? We hold that because such conduct defeats rather than serves the adjudicatory purpose of arbitration, arbitral immunity does not apply"). See also Hopper v. Am. Arbitration Ass'n, Inc., 708 F. App'x 373 (9th Cir. 2017) (reversing trial court dismissal of false advertising claim against AAA on the basis of arbitral immunity; "advertisement, designed to sway individuals to choose AAA over its competitors—as Hopper alleges occurred here—is distinct and distant from the decisional act of an arbitrator. Therefore, adjudication of claims, like false advertising, that arise before a formal arbitration relationship between parties to arbitration, arbitrators, and arbitration companies like AAA will not lead to 'undue influence' over the arbitration process, nor will it expose arbitrators' decisions to "reprisals by dissatisfied litigants.")

Much like arbitrator immunity, a similar interest in protecting arbitrators also means that when courts hear motions to vacate arbitration awards, the court is unlikely to permit examination of the arbitrators themselves aimed at developing a factual basis for impeaching the award. See, e.g., Woods v. Saturn Distribution Corp., 78 F.3d 424 (9th Cir. 1996) (although "it may be difficult to prove actual bias without deposing the arbitrators, deposition of arbitrators are repeatedly condemned by courts" and they must be "limited to situations where clear evidence of impropriety has been presented"; in arbitration between franchisee and automobile manufacturer, the franchisee "could have compiled evidence showing, e.g., the percentage of arbitration decisions that have been in favor of Saturn * * * to provide some indicia of improper motive"); Fitta v. Burke, 2011 WL 4917051, 716 S.E.2d 876 (N.C. Ct. App 2011) (plaintiff moved to vacate arbitration award and filed a motion to compel arbitrators "to make themselves available for oral deposition"; "plaintiff seeks to inquire of the arbitrators the reason for their decision. This is contrary to our law. * * * the trial court properly denied plaintiff's motion to compel"); Perik v. JP Morgan Chase Bank, N.A., 2017 IL App (1st) 151593-U, 54, appeal denied, 89 N.E.3d 763 (Ill. 2017) (affirming denial of plaintiff's petition to vacate arbitration award and plaintiff's motion to depose arbitrator: "this court has expressed its hesitation to allow a party to conduct discovery into the arbitration process after the arbitration has concluded. * * * Other courts are similarly skeptical of allowing parties to depose arbitrators after the fact. * * * We see no basis in the record by which [Plaintiff] could have justified her request to depose the arbitrator").

The Revised Uniform Arbitration Act also provides that "an arbitrator or an arbitration organization acting in such capacity is immune from civil liability to the same extent as a judge of a court of this State acting in a judicial capacity"; where a suit against an arbitrator or an arbitral institution is dismissed on the ground of immunity, the defendants are entitled to recover "reasonable attorney's fees and other reasonable expenses of litigation." Section 14(a), (e). While arbitrators might *by contract choose to accept* potential liability for negligence, thereby giving rise to a market for insurance, RUAA prohibits this by making the rule of arbitrator immunity mandatory and unwaivable. See Section 4(c) (a party "may not waive," and the parties "may not vary the effect of," Section 14).

QUESTIONS TO REVIEW AND SYNTHESIZE

1. Do California's Ethics Standards for Neutral Arbitrators in Contractual Arbitration ("Ethics Standards") focus on arbitrators or arbitration agreements? Why?
2. What are the pros and cons of California's Ethics Standards?
3. When are arbitrators generally immune, and not immune, from suit?

C. CONDUCT OF THE ARBITRATION PROCEEDING

1. INTRODUCTION

Arbitration procedures tend to be more streamlined than litigation, as arbitration tends to have less extensive pleadings, discovery, motion practice, and evidentiary rules. To lawyers and judges accustomed to the more elaborate procedures of litigation, the procedures of arbitration may be unsettling: "Submission of disputes to arbitration always risks an accumulation of procedural and evidentiary shortcuts that would properly frustrate counsel in a formal trial."[26] However, generations of thoughtful commentators have observed that arbitration procedure can vary widely. This, from 1955, is still true of arbitration's variety:

> At one extreme, we have what is practically courtroom procedure, with carefully drawn submissions, formal procedures, emphasis upon technicalities, formal opening and closing statements, arguments as to the admissibility and relevance of evidence, qualifications of witnesses, and the burden of proof, and briefs, rebuttal briefs, and sur-rebuttal briefs. At the other extreme, we have an atmosphere which is barely distinguishable from a mediation proceeding; the issue is vague and ill-defined, everybody talks at the same time, says irrelevant things, no standards of evidence appear, and the arbitrator seems to be working chiefly at the task of securing agreement between the disputants. Between the extremes are innumerable shadings and variations.[27]

The personality and the professional background of the arbitrator, the attitudes and the relationship of the parties, the issues in contention—all will influence the way the arbitration proceeds. So will the arbitration organization and the context. For instance, is it arbitration before the AAA, which seeks awards that will be confirmed by courts, or before a trade association that relies on private, rather than judicial, enforcement of its awards? (See Section 2.A.2's comparison of these two sorts of commercial arbitration.)

We should not be surprised to find a considerable amount of procedural innovation in the practice of arbitration—stemming, first, from the large freedom of the parties to "write their own ticket," and, second, from the traditionally broad discretion of arbitrators in structuring the proceedings. "Indeed, short of authorizing trial by battle or ordeal or, more doubtfully, by a panel of three monkeys, parties can stipulate to whatever procedures they want to govern the arbitration of their

---

[26] Forsythe Int'l, S.A. v. Gibbs Oil Co. of Texas, 915 F.2d 1017, 1022 (5th Cir.1990).

[27] Stein, *The Selection of Arbitrators*, N.Y.U. Eighth Annual Conference on Labor 291, 293 (1955).

disputes."[28] In one large and complex antitrust dispute, for example, the parties selected as their arbitrator a noted antitrust scholar and law professor:

> Based on his reading of briefs and affidavits, [the arbitrator] advised counsel which witnesses he wanted to have at the hearing. Rather than putting on the plaintiff's case in full, followed by defendant's case in full, [the arbitrator] proceeded by topic or category of witness; and in several instances, he put corresponding witnesses for the two sides on the stand at the same time. In so doing, he was able to let both parties' witnesses respond in succession to the same question and then engage in dialogue to explore differences of opinion. Throughout the proceeding, [he] peppered counsel with questions to explore the bases for and merits of various legal theories.[29]

This technique avoided both the rigidity of traditional direct and cross-examination, and the usual "ships-passing-in-the-night" quality of most competing expert testimony. In fact, most of the questioning at the hearing was done by the arbitrator, and only "limited follow-up questioning" was conducted by counsel. In addition, the parties agreed that the arbitrator would write a reasoned opinion that "could be published because of its potential value to other parties who might be faced with similar issues." Id.

Another illustration of the enormous flexibility permitted by the arbitration process is provided by an international arbitration, involving the dissolution of a joint venture. After the closing of the hearings, the arbitral tribunal

> Issued an Order by which it gave its tentative "inclination" regarding the outcome of the dispute and—simultaneously—put some additional questions to the parties, * * * reserving any modifications of its final judgment depending upon the parties' answers to the questions put. This Order actually gave the parties the possibility to see—before the final award was issued—that any and all issues raised were duly taken into consideration by the tribunal and also to realize that the tribunal had actually understood the core of the dispute. Indeed, the losing party tried— through the answers required by the tribunal—to redress the situation through what it considered its strongest arguments. In that case, it was in vain. But clearly, the losing party had been given a "voice" in a very efficient process.[30]

2. THE ROLE OF LAWYERS

Lawyers used to be less common in arbitration than they are today. Back in 1947, Lon Fuller (remember him from Section 1.A?) could advise advocates that the commercial arbitrator, "who will usually be a layman, * * * will be unimpressed by

---

[28] Baravati v. Josephthal, Lyon & Ross, Inc., 28 F.3d 704, 709 (7th Cir.1994)(Posner, C.J.).

[29] Baker, Alexander, Cohan & Heike, "The First Texas-Pulse Arbitration: A Case Study," reprinted in John Murray, Alan Rau, and Edward Sherman, Dispute Resolution: Materials for Continuing Legal Education IV-136, IV-141 (NIDR 1991).

[30] Teresa Giovannini, *"The Psychological Aspects of Dispute Resolution: Commentary," in* International Council for Commercial Arbitration, Congress series no. 11, International Commercial Arbitration: Important Contemporary Questions 348, 351 (2003).

arguments resting upon the abstract 'rights' of the parties. The arbitrator will chiefly want to know whether the parties conducted themselves honorably and fairly and made a genuine effort to settle their differences by negotiation."[31] By 1962, Soia Mentschikoff (remember her from Section 2.A.1?) distinguished between arbitration administered by a trade association and arbitration administered by the AAA: "In almost all self-contained trade associations and exchanges, lawyer participation in the arbitration proceedings is either forbidden or discouraged, and very few of the arbitrators are lawyers or law-trained." This paucity of lawyers—because merchants play all the necessary roles—remains true in the arbitration systems of several trade associations. For example, Section 1.A showed us arbitration before the National Grain & Feed Association in which lawyers typically neither represent the parties nor serve as arbitrators.[32] But nowadays "[l]egal representation is taken for granted in most commercial arbitration processes,"[33] including AAA arbitration, and has for decades increased in labor arbitration as well.

The growth in lawyer-ized arbitration has largely tracked arbitration's expansion from commercial and labor disputes about contract interpretation and performance to encompass all sorts of (often statutory) claims among a wide variety of parties, including individual consumers and employees. When the paradigm arbitration case changes from a dispute about the quality of goods one merchant delivered another to alleged violations of an employment discrimination statute or a technical, financial regulation, then attention to legal rules and procedural formality grows along with the role of lawyers.

The growing role of lawyers in arbitration has even led to rulings that a non-attorney who represents a party in arbitration is engaged in the "unauthorized practice of law." See In re Advisory Opinion on Nonlawyer Representation in Securities Arbitration, 696 So.2d 1178 (Fla. 1997) ("we think that compensated nonlawyer representatives in securities arbitration are engaged in the unauthorized practice of law and the protection of the public requires us to step in where there is no [federal] legislation or regulation"). See also In re Town of Little Compton, 37 A.3d 85, 95 (R.I.2012) ("although the conduct involved in this case may be the practice of law pursuant to the language of § 11–27–2, because of the long-standing involvement of nonlawyer union employees at public grievance arbitrations, we will not limit this involvement at this time. We may in the future, however."); Disciplinary Counsel v. Alexicole, Inc., 822 N.E.2d 348 (Ohio 2004) (A non-attorney who was not licensed to practice law in Ohio cannot represent his or her client in an arbitration taking place in Ohio); In re Creasy, 12 P.3d 214, 217 (Ariz.2000) (examining witness in arbitration constitutes practice of law).

An "unauthorized practice of law" argument has been used to challenge the representation of parties in arbitration by out-of-state lawyers. Compare Birbrower, Montalbano, Condon & Frank v. Superior Court, 949 P.2d 1 (Cal.1998) (New York

---

[31] Lon Fuller, Basic Contract Law 713 (1947).

[32] See also Yuliya Chernykh, *The Last Citadel: The Restricted Role of Lawyers in Soft Commodity Arbitration*, 14 (2) Transnational Dispute Management (2017) https://www.transnational-dispute-management.com/article.asp?key=2453 ("Limiting the role of lawyers is an important common feature in [soft commodities arbitration]; lawyers are not usually included in the mandatory arbitral panel and cannot as a rule represent parties in oral hearings without both parties' express agreement, which in practice is seldom given.")

[33] Thomas J. Stipanowich, *Arbitration: The "New Litigation"*, 2010 U. Ill. L. Rev. 1, 45 (2010).

lawyers barred from recovering fees for work performed in California in connection with an impending California arbitration, because they had done so in violation of the California Business and Professions Code § 6125 which states "No person shall practice law in California unless the person is an active member of the State Bar."), with Cal.Civ.P. Code § 1282.4 (West 2007) (allows non-resident lawyers to participate in California arbitrations, creating limited exception to *Birbrower*); Fla.Bar Rule 1–3.11 (permitting out-of-state attorneys to participate in Florida arbitrations under limited circumstances); Williamson v. John D. Quinn Constr. Corp., 537 F.Supp. 613, 616 (S.D.N.Y.1982) (rejecting claim that out-of-state attorney and firm were foreclosed from recovery obtained in connection with services rendered in arbitration proceeding because not authorized to practice law in that State); Prudential Equity Group, LLC v. Ajamie, 538 F.Supp.2d 605, 607–08 (S.D.N.Y.2008) (same, following *Williamson*); Colmar, Ltd. v. Fremantlemedia North America, Inc., 801 N.E.2d 1017, 1026 (Ill.App.2003) (relying on Model Rule of Professional Responsibility 5.5(c) as persuasive authority that "an out-of-state attorney's representation of a client during arbitration does not violate the rules prohibiting the unlicensed practice of law").

ABA Model Rule of Professional Conduct 5.5(c) provides that:

> A lawyer admitted in another United States jurisdiction, and not disbarred or suspended from practice in any jurisdiction, may provide legal services on a temporary basis in this jurisdiction that:
>
> * * *
>
> (3) are in or reasonably related to a pending or potential arbitration, mediation, or other alternative dispute resolution proceeding in this or another jurisdiction, if the services arise out of or are reasonably related to the lawyer's practice in a jurisdiction in which the lawyer is admitted to practice and are not services for which the forum requires pro hac vice admission.

Thomas J. Stipanowich, *Arbitration: The "New Litigation"*

2010 U. Ill. L. Rev. 1, 8–9, 12–15, 19–20, 22–23 (2010).

* * *

Early in the twentieth century, the dawn of the modern era of American arbitration was heralded by the passage of a federal statute underpinning the enforcement of contractual agreements to arbitrate future disputes; advocates championed arbitration as a means of avoiding the "needless contention that [is] incidental to the atmosphere of trials in court." Arbitration was popularly touted as a more efficient, less costly, and more final method for resolving disputes; there was little or no discovery, motion practice, judicial review, or other trappings of litigation. By the beginning of the twenty-first century, however, it was common to speak of U.S. business arbitration in terms similar to civil litigation—"judicialized," formal, costly, time-consuming, and subject to hardball advocacy.

Contractual provisions for the resolution of disputes by arbitrators are now featured in many kinds of commercial contracts. These practices, coupled with plenary judicial enforcement of broadly tailored arbitration provisions, have made arbitration a wide-ranging surrogate for trial in a public courtroom. As a consequence, the arbitration experience has become increasingly similar to civil litigation, and arbitration procedures have become increasingly like the civil procedures they were designed to supplant, including prehearing discovery and motion practice. Not surprisingly, clients and counsel often complain about the costliness and length of arbitration—yet at the same time, ironically, they or their peers bemoan the non-appealability of awards and other features that still distinguish arbitration from litigation. Consider the double-edged lament of one corporate general counsel: "[W]e found arbitration generally is as expensive [as litigation] . . . less predictable, and not appealable. Arbitration is often unsatisfactory because litigators . . . run it exactly like a piece of litigation."

* * *

The growing similarity of arbitration to litigation (as well as the growing use of trial tactics in arbitration) is also reflected in the increased emphasis on the unauthorized practice of law. In recent years, a number of state tribunals or other bodies have considered motions to remove party representatives or vacate an award under this rubric. Several state rulemaking bodies have announced limitations on lawyers from other states representing clients in arbitration. Relatively few issues in arbitration have generated more legal activity than concerns about arbitrator conflict of interest. A host of legal decisions have considered motions to vacate based on an arbitrator's failure to disclose a connection to the case or participants. These concerns have also been among the stimuli for reform of standards governing arbitration, including statutes.

* * *

For some attorneys, arbitration tends to be too much like going to court. In a 2002 survey of experienced commercial arbitrators, three-quarters of respondents expressed the belief that "arbitration is becoming too much like court litigation and thereby losing its promise of providing an expedited and cost-efficient means of resolving commercial disputes." For others, however, even "legalized" forms of arbitration are an unsatisfactory substitute for court trial; critics cite, among other things, the reluctance of arbitrators to grant summary judgments or dispositive relief; the limitations on multiparty practice that result in inefficiencies and potentially incompatible results; the fact that decision makers must be paid by the parties, unlike public judges; the bifurcation of the authority to render and to execute decrees; and the limits on review. The perspectives of counsel reflect the variety of goals and needs that business parties bring to arbitration and suggest that different process options are desired.

* * *

Arbitration hearings are now often preceded by extensive discovery, including depositions. Because discovery has traditionally accounted for the bulk of litigation-related costs, the importation of discovery into arbitration (which traditionally operated with little or no discovery) is particularly noteworthy. Although many arbitrators and some arbitration rules aim to hold the line on excessive discovery, it is not unusual for legal advocates to agree to trial-like procedures for discovery, even to the extent of employing standard civil procedural rules. This should not be surprising as there is a tendency to use the tools with which one is most familiar, and lawyers schooled in trial may predictably rely on their knowledge and experience in the private analog of the process. Trial practice, with its heavy emphasis on prehearing motion practice and intensive discovery, is reinforced by ethical rules enshrining the model of zealous advocacy. For lawyers accustomed to full-fledged discovery, anything less may seem tantamount to inviting claims of malpractice. As one seasoned arbitration practitioner recently observed, "Most lawyers are reluctant to go ahead and try the case. Many times I have tried to shorten the time [frame] and have the hearing sooner, . . . [but] in many instances the lawyers want more time to get prepared."

It is not hard for American lawyers to justify intensive discovery to themselves and their clients. Legitimizing a legal position often requires painstaking reconstruction of past events, a highly labor- and time-intensive activity that requires conscientiously sifting through vast amounts of information, most of which is of little or no relevancy. The expectation—or hope—is that the "mining" effort will ultimately produce a picture that supports the position. Alternatively, it might at least forestall an undesired resolution for months or years.

---

3. DISCOVERY

Professor Stipanowich's just-excerpted passage notes that "discovery has traditionally accounted for the bulk of litigation related costs," and while arbitration "traditionally operated with little or no discovery," it "now often [includes] extensive discovery." This is a sea change, and surely related to the growth of lawyer-ized arbitration.

Nevertheless, parties largely retain ultimate control over the extent to which their arbitration's discovery rises to litigation-like levels. Lawyers work for their clients—the disputing parties—so if parties agree (before or after a dispute arises) to constrain their lawyers' desires for more discovery, lawyers will probably (even if grudgingly) comply. Such parties may need to remain adamant about controlling discovery costs even at the risk of going to the hearing with only an incomplete understanding of the issues, the nature of the opponent's case, and the evidence to be presented.

Discovery in arbitration, like most aspects of arbitration, is primarily determined by the arbitration agreement. Some arbitration agreements provide that discovery may be had in accordance with the Federal Rules of Civil Procedure. Arbitration pursuant to these agreements is unlikely to have much less discovery than litigation.

> "[P]arties increasingly have attempted to build into their contracts procedural safeguards akin to rules of civil procedure. Arbitrators are now charged with judge-like ethical and procedural duties. They must * * * allow more discovery * * * and increasingly conduct hearings under rules of procedure * * *. [T]hese protections have made the arbitration process more like, and sometimes as expensive as, court proceedings."

Scott Atlas & Nancy Atlas, *Potential ADR Backlash*, Disp.Resol.Mag., Summer 2004, 14, 16. In contrast, other parties are writing their arbitration clauses to "place meaningful limits on discovery." John Wilkinson, *Arbitration Contract Clauses: A Potential Key to a Cost-Effective Process*, Disp.Resol.Mag. Fall 2009, at 9.

Many arbitration agreements incorporate the rules of an arbitration organization, such as the American Arbitration Association. These rules typically do not grant the parties rights to broad discovery, but rather grant the arbitrator wide discretion in authorizing discovery. For example, the AAA Commercial Rules, avoiding the word "discovery," provide:

> R-22. Pre-Hearing Exchange and Production of Information
>
> (a) *Authority of arbitrator*. The arbitrator shall manage any necessary exchange of information among the parties with a view to achieving an efficient and economical resolution of the dispute, while at the same time promoting equality of treatment and safeguarding each party's opportunity to fairly present its claims and defenses.
>
> (b) *Documents*. The arbitrator may, on application of a party or on the arbitrator's own initiative:
>
> i. require the parties to exchange documents in their possession or custody on which they intend to rely;
>
> ii. require the parties to update their exchanges of the documents on which they intend to rely as such documents become known to them;
>
> iii. require the parties, in response to reasonable document requests, to make available to the other party documents, in the responding party's possession or custody, not otherwise readily available to the party seeking the documents reasonably believed by the party seeking the documents to exist and to be relevant and material to the outcome of disputed issues; and
>
> iv. require the parties, when documents to be exchanged or produced are maintained in electronic form, to make such documents available in the form most convenient and economical for the party in possession of such documents, unless the arbitrator determines that there is good cause for requiring the documents to be produced in a different form. The parties should attempt to agree in advance upon, and the arbitrator may determine, reasonable search parameters to balance the need for production of electronically stored documents relevant and material to the outcome of disputed issues against the cost of locating and producing them.
>
> R-23. Enforcement Powers of the Arbitrator
>
> The arbitrator shall have the authority to issue any orders necessary to enforce the provisions of rules R-21 and R-22 and to otherwise achieve a fair, efficient and economical resolution of the case, including, without limitation:

(a) conditioning any exchange or production of confidential documents and information, and the admission of confidential evidence at the hearing, on appropriate orders to preserve such confidentiality;

(b) imposing reasonable search parameters for electronic and other documents if the parties are unable to agree;

(c) allocating costs of producing documentation, including electronically stored documentation;

(d) in the case of willful non-compliance with any order issued by the arbitrator, drawing adverse inferences, excluding evidence and other submissions, and/or making special allocations of costs or an interim award of costs arising from such non-compliance; and

(e) issuing any other enforcement orders which the arbitrator is empowered to issue under applicable law.[34]

Some courts, especially in the employment discrimination context, have indicated that they will not enforce arbitration agreements without confidence that there will be sufficient discovery to allow claimants to gather necessary evidence. See, e.g., Cole v. Burns Int'l Security Services, 105 F.3d 1465 (D.C.Cir.1997) (enforcing an employee's agreement to arbitrate statutory employment discrimination claims, but only because):

> the arbitration arrangement (1) provides for neutral arbitrators, (2) provides for more than minimal discovery, (3) requires a written award, (4) provides for all of the types of relief that would otherwise be available in court, and (5) does not require employees to pay either unreasonable costs or any arbitrators' fees or expenses as a condition of access to the arbitration forum.

Id. at 1482. On the other hand, a Supreme Court case (excerpted in Section 3.C.2.b) indicates that the FAA would preempt (hypothetical) state law holding arbitration agreements unconscionable unless they provide for as much discovery as is available in litigation. AT & T Mobility LLC v. Concepcion, 563 U.S. 333, 343 (2011) (FAA would preempt hypothetical state law "finding unconscionable or unenforceable as against public policy consumer arbitration agreements that fail to provide for judicially monitored discovery"). So perhaps the emerging black-letter law is that enforcement of adhesive arbitration agreements is consistent with arbitration having less discovery than litigation, but not too much less.

One discovery tool in litigation is the subpoena. FAA § 7 authorizes the arbitrators to "summon in writing any person to attend before them or any of them as a witness and in a proper case to bring with him or them any book, record, document, or paper which may be deemed material as evidence in the case."[35] This arbitrator power to issue subpoenas, not only to the parties, but also to *unrelated third parties*, is in some tension with the standard view of arbitration as a "creature of contract" because contracts ordinarily cannot impose duties on non-parties. Accordingly, courts are understandably likely to police arbitrators' subpoena power

[34] See, e.g., Am.Arbitration Ass'n, *Commercial Arbitration Rules*, R-22 and R-23 (2013).

[35] 9 U.S.C. § 7.

somewhat more carefully when directed to non-parties than when directed toward the parties themselves.

Courts are split on whether FAA § 7 authorizes subpoenas of non-parties for pre-hearing discovery or only for the hearing itself. Compare In re Security Life Insurance Co. of America, 228 F.3d 865, 870–71 (8th Cir.2000) ("implicit in an arbitration panel's power to subpoena relevant documents for production at a hearing is the power to order the production of relevant documents for review by a party prior to the hearing"), with CVS Health Corp. v. Vividus, LLC, 878 F.3d 703, 708 (9th Cir. 2017) ("We hold that section 7 of the FAA does not grant arbitrators the power to order third parties to produce documents prior to an arbitration hearing. We affirm the district court's denial of HMC's petition to enforce the arbitrators' subpoena."); Life Receivables Trust v. Syndicate 102 at Lloyd's of London 549 F.3d 210, 216–17 (2d Cir.2008) ("we join the Third Circuit in holding that section 7 of the FAA does not authorize arbitrators to compel pre-hearing document discovery from entities not party to the arbitration proceedings.")

Some parties seeking to enforce arbitral subpoenas of non-parties for pre-hearing discovery do so in state courts. The Revised Uniform Arbitration Act (RUAA) authorizes subpoenas of non-parties for pre-hearing discovery for testimony and specifically authorizes depositions, which traditionally are rare in arbitration.[36] However, these provisions of RUAA "can be waived or varied by agreement of the parties"[37] so presumably have no effect on arbitration arising out of an arbitration agreement that, expressly or by incorporating arbitration organization rules, limits discovery.

Depositions can be an effective, but costly and time-consuming, form of discovery. While most arbitration statutes do not mention depositions, the Texas version of the Uniform Arbitration Act says that arbitrators may authorize a deposition "*for discovery or evidentiary purposes* to be taken of an adverse witness," such a deposition to be taken "in the manner provided by law for a deposition in a civil action pending in a district court." Tex.Civ.Prac. & Rem.Code § 171.050.

If depositions of adverse witnesses have not been taken prior to the hearing, lawyers may feel compelled at the hearing itself to engage in protracted cross-examination that can become "a 'fishing expedition'—in effect, a deposition with the arbitrators looking on." Thomas J. Stipanowich, *Rethinking American Arbitration*, 63 Indiana L.J. 425, 451 (1988). See also John Wilkinson, *Streamlining Arbitration of the Complex Case*, Disp. Res. J., Aug.–Oct. 2000 at pp. 8, 11 ("I have witnessed many cross-examinations at arbitration hearings that plod down one dead-end street after another, while the questioner endlessly gropes for any testimony that might be of help"). Alternatively, an arbitration proceeding may be adjourned or continued at the arbitrator's discretion, to allow a party to study and respond to information revealed as a result of testimony or document production; in this respect,

[36] "If an arbitrator permits discovery under subsection (c), the arbitrator may order a party to the arbitration proceeding to comply with the arbitrator's discovery-related orders, issue subpoenas for the attendance of a witness and for the production of records and other evidence at a discovery proceeding, and take action against a noncomplying party to the extent a court could if the controversy were the subject of a civil action in this State." Unif. Arbitration Act § 17(d) (2000).

[37] Id. cmt.1.

arbitration is more like a trial in the civil law systems of continental Europe than a trial in the United States, which once begun, is likely to proceed more or less continuously. (See Section 5.D.1's comparison of civil law and U.S. trials.)

What sanctions can arbitrators impose for the failure to comply with their discovery orders? Compare Kashner Davidson Sec. Corp. v. Mscisz, 531 F.3d 68, 76 (1st Cir. 2008) (appellant failed to timely fulfill arbitrators' discovery orders; arbitrators' sanction was dismissal of appellants claims *with* prejudice; the First Circuit vacated this sanction as a "manifest disregard of the law," since lesser sanctions had not even been imposed, much less been proven ineffective, and relevant arbitration rules state that in "extraordinary cases, [arbitrators] may * * * dismiss a claim * * * with prejudice as a sanction for intentional failure to comply with an order of the arbitrator(s) if lesser sanctions have proven ineffective"), with Polin v. Kellwood, 103 F.Supp.2d 238, 267–68 (S.D.N.Y. 2000) (arbitrators awarded sanctions against the employee's attorney in the amount of half the employer's fees and expenses, totaling over $150,000, for having misled the panel, unduly prolonged the hearings, and for having committed "contempt of the panel" by making "highly defamatory" statements about the chairman to the AAA; held, award confirmed; under the AAA Rules for the Resolution of Employment Disputes, arbitrators were expressly authorized to grant any relief "that would have been available to the parties had the matter been heard in court").

4. PRIVILEGE

Suppose at an arbitration hearing the arbitrator orders the claimant (plaintiff) to produce certain documents; the claimant refuses to comply, asserting that this material consists of the confidential communication of information to the claimant's lawyer and is thus exempt from subpoena on the basis of the attorney-client privilege. The arbitrator then announces that following her usual practice, she will conclude that the evidence if produced would have been unfavorable to the claimant; the arbitrator's award is in favor of the respondent (defendant). On the claimant's motion to vacate the award, what should be the result? The California Evidence Code makes the testimonial privileges applicable in all "proceedings,"[38] a term that Code defines to include arbitration and any other hearing "in which, pursuant to law, testimony can be compelled to be given."[39] It further provides that if a privilege is exercised not to testify or disclose information, "the trier of fact may not draw any inference therefrom as to the credibility of the witness or as to any matter at issue in the proceeding."[40]

[38] Cal.Evidence Code § 910 ("Except as otherwise provided by statute, the provisions of this division apply in all proceedings. The provisions of any statute making rules of evidence inapplicable in particular proceedings, or limiting the applicability of rules of evidence in particular proceedings, do not make this division inapplicable to such proceedings").

[39] Id. § 901 ("'Proceeding' means any action, hearing, investigation, inquest, or inquiry (whether conducted by a court, administrative agency, hearing officer, arbitrator, legislative body, or any other person authorized by law) in which, pursuant to law, testimony can be compelled to be given").

[40] Id. § 913 ("If in the instant proceeding or on a prior occasion a privilege is or was exercised not to testify with respect to any matter, or to refuse to disclose or to prevent another from disclosing any matter, neither the presiding officer nor counsel may comment thereon, no presumption shall arise because of the exercise of the privilege, and the trier of fact may not draw any inference therefrom as to the credibility of the witness or as to any matter at issue in the proceeding").

Arbitration organization rules typically recognize the attorney-client privilege. See, e.g., Am. Arbitration Ass'n, Commercial Arbitration Rules and Mediation Procedures, R-34(c) (2013) ("The arbitrator shall take into account applicable principles of legal privilege, such as those involving the confidentiality of communications between a lawyer and client"). Similarly, "courts have held, in the main, that arbitrators should honor legal privileges as would judges."[41] The D.C. Circuit declined to vacate a labor arbitration award challenged by a party claiming the arbitrator interpreted the attorney-client privilege too broadly. Howard Univ. v. Metro. Campus Police Officer's Union, 512 F.3d 716, 722 (D.C.Cir.2008) ("Although [appellant] is correct that testimony by an attorney describing statements made in open negotiations would not be subject to the attorney-client privilege in a federal court, the arbitrator was not bound by the particulars of federal law governing the attorney-client privilege * * * [a]ccordingly, the question is not whether the arbitrator correctly applied federal law; the question is whether her decision to exclude the evidence out of a concern for a client's asserted interest in confidentiality amounted to 'misconduct'").

Odfjell ASA v. Celanese AG, 380 F.Supp.2d 297 (S.D.N.Y. 2005), provides a nice illustration of the elaborate procedural tangles that claims of privilege in arbitration may create. In an arbitration involving allegations of bid rigging in the parcel tanker shipping industry, the arbitrators issued a subpoena to O'Brien, the former general counsel of Stolt-Nielsen, to testify and produce documents. (Neither Stolt-Nielsen nor O'Brien were parties to the proceedings.) The court granted the claimant's motion to enforce the subpoena saying Stolt's claim of attorney-client privilege "should first be heard and determined by the arbitrator." At an evidentiary hearing, the arbitral panel overruled most of the objections to O'Brien's testimony, but nevertheless—because of the threat of disciplinary action raised by Stolt's counsel—O'Brien refused to answer certain questions and to produce certain documents. The claimants asked the court to compel compliance with the arbitral subpoenas, and at the same time to "defer a substantive review of the arbitration panel's privilege rulings until the confirmation process." But the court decided nevertheless to consider the issue immediately—because the alleged privilege was a "separate issue" from the merits of the arbitration, and because as a non-party Stolt would be effectively unable to appeal the issue after the arbitration was completed. The court ultimately held that the arbitration panel had "abused its discretion" in not allowing Stolt to submit "supporting factual material" in support of its claim of privilege—concerning, for example, whether the subpoenaed testimony implicated only O'Brien's "non-legal responsibilities" at the company. Since such a refusal amounted to a "denial of elementary fairness," the court remanded the question to the arbitrators for further proceedings.

---

[41] James H. Carter, *The Attorney-Client Privilege and Arbitration*, ADR Currents vol. 2, no. 1, Winter 1996–97, at 1, 15. See also Gary B. Born, International Commercial Arbitration in the United States 840 (1994) ("In general, lower U.S. courts have assumed that privileges are unaffected either by the parties' agreement to arbitrate or the fact that it is the arbitral tribunal (rather than a court) that has ordered discovery.").

5. EVIDENCE

Rules of evidence are historically intertwined with the jury, so arbitration's lack of a jury fits with arbitration's typically minimal rules of evidence. Evidentiary rules, like other aspects of arbitration, are primarily determined by arbitration agreements, many of which incorporate the rules of an arbitration organization such as the American Arbitration Association. The AAA's Commercial Arbitration Rules allow parties to offer into evidence whatever is relevant and material:

> The parties may offer such evidence as is relevant and material to the dispute and shall produce such evidence as the arbitrator may deem necessary to an understanding and determination of the dispute. Conformity to legal rules of evidence shall not be necessary. All evidence shall be taken in the presence of all of the arbitrators and all of the parties, except where any of the parties is absent, in default or has waived the right to be present.[42]

This AAA rule's command that the parties *shall* produce evidence the arbitrator deems necessary is typical of most arbitration in allowing arbitrators a more active fact-finding role than is permitted of juries and, in common law countries like the United States, judges. In the U.S., judges and juries are typically passive triers-of-fact, receiving only the evidence presented by the parties. In contrast, some arbitrators are more inquisitorial, sometimes questioning witnesses, or making other investigations into evidence. See, e.g., Am. Arbitration Ass'n, Commercial Arbitration Rules, R-36 (2013) ("An arbitrator finding it necessary to make an inspection or investigation in connection with the arbitration shall direct the AAA to so advise the parties. The arbitrator shall set the date and time and the AAA shall notify the parties. Any party who so desires may be present at such an inspection or investigation. In the event that one or all parties are not present at the inspection or investigation, the arbitrator shall make an oral or written report to the parties and afford them an opportunity to comment.")

Some arbitrations have no rules of evidence so the parties may present whatever evidence they like and the arbitrators can give to it whatever weight they like. Arbitrators' general openness to admitting evidence is due in part to the fact that "refusing to hear evidence pertinent and material to the controversy" is one of the few grounds for vacating the arbitration award, FAA § 10(a)(3), while hearing evidence that would not be admissible in court is not a ground for vacatur.

In *Bowles Financial Group, Inc. v. Stifel, Nicolaus & Co., Inc.*, 22 F.3d 1010 (10th Cir.1994), the claimant's lawyer introduced evidence that would not have been admissible in litigation by "deliberately, intentionally, affirmatively and repeatedly communicat[ing] to the arbitrators an offer of settlement" from the respondent, arguing that the settlement offer "evidenced [the respondent's] admission of liability." "Counsel also indicated he routinely submitted settlement offers to the arbitrators in the cases where he represented clients in arbitration." The arbitrators, "after receiving the settlement offer, commented they would not consider it," but they subsequently made an award to the claimant that exceeded the offer. The court

[42] Am.Arbitration Ass'n, Commercial Arbitration Rules, R-34(a) (2013).

held that the respondent "has not proven it was subjected to a fundamentally unfair hearing":

> Had [the claimant's] counsel done before a court of law what he did before the arbitrators, significant sanctions would have been imposed and a mistrial ordered. But however well-established may be the judicial rules of evidence, they legitimately did not apply to this arbitration.

"This court has no power to judicially impose our rules of evidence on an arbitration proceeding." Id. at 1013. See also WHD, LP. v. Mayflower Capital, LLC, 673 S.E.2d 168, 2009 WL 368335, at *5 (N.C.App.2009) (refusing to vacate arbitration award where arbitrator may have relied on evidence that would not have been admissible in litigation); Mantle v. Upper Deck Co., 956 F.Supp. 719 (N.D.Tex.1997) (arbitrator reviewed allegedly privileged material, including the "mental impressions" of respondent's general counsel concerning "his assessment of the settlement value" of the case; "it is not widely held that arbitrators are so impressionable that exposure to prejudicial documents inexorably leads to partiality"); United States ex rel. National Roofing Services, Inc. v. Lovering-Johnson, Inc., 53 Supp.2d 1142 (D. Kan. 1999) ("if [the parties] wished to arbitrate under rules which prohibit the introduction or consideration of settlement offer evidence, they should contract for such rules").

In contrast, an arbitrator's reliance on rules of evidence to exclude testimony risks vacatur of the arbitration award on the ground that a party has been denied a "fair hearing." For example, in *Tempo Shain Corp. v. Bertek, Inc.*, 120 F.3d 16 (2d Cir. 1997), the dispute in arbitration involved alleged fraudulent inducement to enter into a contract. The witness at issue—a party's former president who was intimately involved in the contract negotiations and allegedly was the only person who could testify about certain aspects of the negotiations—became temporarily unavailable to testify after his wife was diagnosed with a reoccurrence of cancer. The party asked the arbitrators to keep "the record open until [the witness] could testify," but the arbitrators denied this request on the ground that the testimony would be cumulative. The Second Circuit did not defer to the arbitrators' decision because they had given no reasonable basis for their denial. Id. at 20. While the Second Circuit recognized that "undue judicial intervention would inevitably judicialize the arbitration process, thus defeating the objective of providing an alternative to judicial dispute resolution," the court found that "because [the witness] as sole negotiator for [the party] was the only person who could have testified in rebuttal of appellees' fraudulent inducement claim, and the documentary evidence did not adequately address such testimony, there was no reasonable basis for the arbitrators to conclude that [the witnesses] testimony would have been cumulative with respect to those issues." Id. at 21.

On the other hand, courts have often denied motions to vacate arbitration awards because of evidence excluded by the arbitrators. For instance, in *Rosenweig v. Morgan Stanley*, 494 F.3d 1328 (11th Cir. 2007), the Eleventh Circuit confirmed an award against Morgan Stanley finding that the arbitrators' refusal to allow Morgan Stanley additional cross-examination of Rosenweig, its former employee, did not amount to misconduct. The arbitrators did not explain their reasons for denying the additional cross-examination. However, the court determined that the evidence from additional cross-examination, concerning a client list contained in disks produced by Rosenweig, would have been cumulative and immaterial, and for this reason, Morgan Stanley was not deprived of a fair hearing. Id. at 1334.

Perhaps to avoid possible vacatur, arbitrators often tend to admit most proffered evidence and to consider it "for whatever it may be worth." This may be especially pronounced in labor arbitration, where "[i]n general, the need for informality in arbitration has led to the belief that the application of the rules of evidence should not operate as a 'strait-jacket' as arbitrators should be allowed to "receive any evidence 'for what it is worth.'"[43] However, some lawyers criticize "too many arbitrators [who] let everything remotely relevant in, no matter how prejudicial, cumulative, incredible, suspect or otherwise useless, for fear that ruling out anything may lead to vacatur."[44] When lawyers object in arbitration to the introduction of what, in litigation, would be inadmissible evidence, they often do this less in a futile attempt to keep the evidence out, and more to emphasize its unreliability, and thus perhaps to reduce the weight it might have for the arbitrator.

The propensity of arbitrators to admit proffered evidence "for whatever it may be worth" often includes what would be "hearsay" in a court,[45] and this clearly is not a ground for overturning an award. See ARMA, S.R.O. v. BAE Systems Overseas, Inc., 961 F.Supp.2d 245, 263, 271 (D.D.C.2013) (denying motion to vacate based on claim that admission of hearsay, specifically alleged misstatements and unverified opinions, was misconduct denying petitioner a "fundamentally fair hearing"; "In general, it is not enough for the party seeking vacatur to complain that the arbitrator made procedural missteps. An arbitrator has substantial leeway to admit any evidence that it finds useful—even hearsay evidence"); Swenson v. Bishman Inv. Properties, Ltd., 870 F.Supp.2d 1049, 1065 (D. Idaho 2012) (denying motion to vacate award despite arguments the arbitrator improperly relied on hearsay evidence, stating "[a]rbitrators may rely on hearsay evidence and they obviously can reach their own conclusions as to the accuracy of evidence before them").

On the other hand, "[w]hile it is indisputably correct that arbitrators are not bound by the rules of evidence and may consider hearsay, it does not follow that arbitrators are prohibited from excluding hearsay evidence." LJL 33rd St. Assocs., LLC v. Pitcairn Props., 725 F.3d 184, 194–95 (2d Cir. 2013). Accordingly, the Second Circuit said it did "not agree with the district court that the arbitrator's exclusion of Pitcairn's exhibits constituted 'misconduct' in violation of § 10(a)(3) of the FAA."

Should the arbitrator be expected or even required to decide a case based solely on the evidence received at the hearing? After all, one of the advantages of arbitration is that the parties may choose an arbitrator with expertise in the subject matter, so perhaps an arbitrator, unlike a judge, should be expected to draw on such a background. In one dispute, for example, the arbitrators awarded the business

[43] Michael Z. Green, *No Strict Evidence Rules in Labor and Employment Arbitration*, 15 Tex. Wesleyan L. Rev. 533, 536 (2009).

[44] Bruce A. McAllister & Amy Bloom, *Evidence in Arbitration*, 34 J. Mar.L. & Com. 35, 36 (2003).

[45] Michael Z. Green, *No Strict Evidence Rules in Labor and Employment Arbitration*, 15 Tex. Wesleyan L. Rev. 533 (2009) ("Since arbitrators are not bound by the strict rules of evidence applicable in court, there originally developed a practice of admitting hearsay 'for what it is worth'") (citing Barton Center, 121 Lab. Arb. Rep. (BNA) 249, 253 (2005) (Kravit, Arb.) (citations omitted)).

buyer of goods money damages for non-delivery even though no evidence as to the market price of the goods had been introduced. Judge Learned Hand dismissed the seller's argument that this constituted arbitral 'misconduct,' remarking that if the arbitrators "were of the trade, they were justified in resorting to their personal acquaintance with its prices." When the parties have chosen arbitration, Hand added, "they must be content with its informalities; they may not hedge it about with those procedural limitations which it is precisely its purpose to avoid." American Almond Prods. Co. v. Consolidated Pecan Sales Co., 144 F.2d 448, 450–51 (2d Cir.1944). See also In the Matter of the Arbitration between Oinoussian Steamship Corp. of Panama and Sabre Shipping Corp., 224 F.Supp. 807 (S.D.N.Y.1963) (arbitrators allegedly relied on trade custom not mentioned at hearing; "it would be carrying coals to Newcastle to require presentation of evidence to experts in the field"); Rent-A-Center Inc. v. Barker, 633 F.Supp.2d 245, 252 (W.D. La. 2009) ("Arbitrators who are 'familiar with the practices and customs of the calling' may resort to their personal knowledge in making an award without any extraneous evidence") (citing Learned Hand's opinion in *American Almond.*).

However, the arbitrator's relative freedom in supplementing the evidence introduced by the parties is not license to make an independent investigation into the facts of the dispute. Where the quality of goods is in dispute, an arbitrator who gives samples of the goods to his own salesmen for the purpose of obtaining an opinion as to "merchantability" is inviting a court to vacate his award for "misconduct." See Stefano Berizzi Co. v. Krausz, 239 N.Y. 315, 146 N.E. 436 (1925) (Cardozo, J.) ("The plaintiff, knowing nothing of the evidence, had no opportunity to rebut or even to explain it"). So is the arbitrator who, in attempting to fix the rental value of commercial real estate, asks his assistant to stand outside the shops in question to carry out a "pedestrian count." Top Shop Estates v. Danino, [1985] E.G.L.R. 9 (Q.B. 1984) (arbitrator had been "acting under a misapprehension of his function," which is not "to play the part of a Perry Mason where he feels that the submissions or evidence of the parties might usefully be supplemented").

QUESTIONS TO REVIEW AND SYNTHESIZE

1. Arbitration has generally become increasingly similar to litigation in what respects?
2. Compare typical rules of evidence in arbitration with rules of evidence in court.
3. David Schwartz writes that "the simpler procedures and presumably lower process costs of arbitration" may be fine for individuals' simple disputes with businesses, but arbitration is worse than litigation for plaintiffs in "complex individual employment disputes and both employment and consumer class actions." In these more-complex cases, Schwartz says claimants need litigation's more elaborate procedures, particularly its more extensive discovery, because "proof is relatively complex and the pre-litigation distribution of evidence is largely in the possession of the defendant. Therefore, extensive discovery is required for the plaintiff to meet his burden of proof." David S. Schwartz, *Claim-Suppressing Arbitration: The New Rules*, 87 Ind. L.J. 239, 240–42 (2012). What determines how extensive the discovery is in a particular arbitration?

4. Beside generally greater discovery, in what other procedural ways might litigation tend to be better than arbitration for plaintiffs with complex cases?

D. MULTI-PARTY DISPUTES

1. INTRODUCTION

In litigation, rules of civil procedure encourage courts to consolidate related cases and to join multiple parties in a single action if their disputes arise out of the same transaction or occurrence.[46] Consolidation or joinder can avoid multiple litigation over the same facts, thus saving time and money and helping to avoid inconsistent results. These same goals are also reasons for arbitrators to consolidate cases and to join parties in a single proceeding. The obstacle to doing so, however, is the contractual nature of arbitration. Parties who have not agreed to arbitrate have a right to litigate rather than arbitrate. And parties who have agreed to arbitrate have a right to arbitrate rather than litigate.

> Multi-party arbitration is arbitration's equivalent of squaring the circle. The conundrum arises because steps that may be perceived as necessary for the "efficient administration of justice"—consolidating related cases, joining all parties in a single arbitration, avoiding an ungainly number of arbitrators sitting on a tribunal—can run counter to the consensual nature of arbitration, which is generally considered its inviolable foundation.[47]

2. CLAIMS BY OR AGAINST THOSE NOT PARTY TO THE ARBITRATION AGREEMENT

a. PARTY PLAINTIFF VS. NON-PARTY DEFENDANT

Consider, for example, an arbitration clause in a contract between Buyer and Seller for the sale of goods. If Buyer sues Seller on a claim covered by the arbitration clause then Seller will be able to obtain a stay of the litigation and an order compelling Buyer to arbitrate. But what if Buyer also sues the manufacturer of the goods, the lender who financed Buyer's purchase, an insurance company involved in the transaction, or the individual salesperson who made the sale? Can those parties compel Buyer to arbitrate its claims against them, even though they are not parties to the arbitration agreement?

Courts generally treat these as questions about the scope of the arbitration agreement between Buyer and Seller. Contracts often confer rights on those who are not party to the contract, and we call these fortunate parties "intended (third-party) beneficiaries" of the contract.[48] For example, if the arbitration clause in the agreement between Buyer and Seller is written broadly to cover "all disputes, claims, or controversies arising from or relating to this Contract or the relationships which

---

[46] See, e.g., Fed.R.Civ.P. 14 (third-party practice), 19 (joinder of persons needed for just adjudication), 20 (permissive joinder of parties), 22 (interpleader), 23 (class actions), and 24 (intervention).

[47] Stephen R. Bond, *"'Equality' Is Required When Naming Arbitrators, Cour de Cassation Rules,"* 3(3) World Arb. & Med. Rep. at p. 70 (March 1992).

[48] See generally E. Allan Farnsworth, Contracts ch.10 (4th ed.2004).

result from this Contract," then Buyer is required to arbitrate its claims against defendants (such as the manufacturer or salesperson) who are not party to the arbitration agreement if those defendants move to compel arbitration of Buyer's claims against them.[49] In contrast, if the arbitration clause is expressly limited to disputes between Buyer and Seller then Buyer may litigate against defendants other than the seller.[50]

The previous paragraph referred to intended third-party beneficiaries of another party's promise to arbitrate as "fortunate" because those third-party beneficiaries can compel arbitration but, without more, cannot be compelled to arbitrate. Parties to a contract can grant rights to non-parties but generally cannot impose duties on non-parties.

However, legal doctrines outside of contract law can impose duties, including the duty to arbitrate, on parties who are not parties to the arbitration agreement. Such "'traditional principles' of state law [that] allow a contract to be enforced by or against nonparties to the contract [include] 'assumption, piercing the corporate veil, alter ego, incorporation by reference, third-party beneficiary theories, waiver and estoppel,'" according to the following Supreme Court case.

Arthur Anderson LLP v. Carlisle

Supreme Court of the United States, 2009.
556 U.S. 624, 129 S.Ct.1896, 173 L.Ed.2d 832.

■ JUSTICE SCALIA delivered the opinion of the Court.

Section 3 of the Federal Arbitration Act (FAA) entitles litigants in federal court to a stay of any action that is "referable to arbitration under an agreement in writing." Section 16(a)(1)(A), in turn, allows an appeal from "an order . . . refusing a stay of any action under section 3." We address in this case whether appellate courts have jurisdiction under § 16(a) to review denials of stays requested by litigants who were not parties to the relevant arbitration agreement, and whether § 3 can ever mandate a stay in such circumstances.

I

Respondents Wayne Carlisle, James Bushman, and Gary Strassel set out to minimize their taxes from the 1999 sale of their construction-equipment company. Arthur Andersen LLP, a firm that had long served as their company's accountant, auditor, and tax adviser, introduced them to Bricolage Capital, LLC, which in turn referred them for legal advice to Curtis, Mallet-Prevost, Colt & Mosle, LLP. According to respondents, these advisers recommended a "leveraged option strategy" tax shelter designed to create illusory losses through foreign-currency-

[49] Sherer v. Green Tree Servicing, LLC, 548 F.3d 379, 383 (5th Cir.2008) ("the language of the Loan Agreement demonstrates that Sherer has agreed to arbitrate his claims that arise against nonsignatories whose 'relationships . . . result from th[e] [a]greement.' Sherer is bound by the language of the Loan Agreement, and Green Tree, as a nonsignatory whose relationship resulted from the Loan Agreement, may therefore compel Sherer to arbitrate his claims.")

[50] Monsanto Co. v. Benton Farm, 813 So.2d 867 (Ala.2001); Ex parte Martin, 703 So.2d 883, 888 (Ala.1996). The same is true of an arbitration clause expressly limited to disputes between general contractor and subcontractor; it does not cover disputes between subcontractor and a third party. In re Application of Diesel Constr. Co., Inc., 234 N.Y.S.2d 349 (N.Y.Sup.Ct., Special Term 1962).

exchange options. As a part of the scheme, respondents invested in various stock warrants through newly created limited liability companies (LLCs), which are also respondents in this case. The respondent LLCs entered into investment-management agreements with Bricolage, specifying that "[a]ny controversy arising out of or relating to this Agreement or the br[ea]ch thereof, shall be settled by arbitration conducted in New York, New York in accordance with the Commercial Arbitration Rules of the American Arbitration Association."

As with all that seems too good to be true, a controversy did indeed arise. The warrants respondents purchased turned out to be almost entirely worthless, and the Internal Revenue Service (IRS) determined in August 2000 that the "leveraged option strategy" scheme was an illegal tax shelter. The IRS initially offered conditional amnesty to taxpayers who had used such arrangements, but petitioners failed to inform respondents of that option. Respondents ultimately entered into a settlement program in which they paid the IRS all taxes, penalties, and interest owed.

Respondents filed this diversity suit in the Eastern District of Kentucky against Bricolage, Arthur Andersen, and others (all except Bricolage and its employees hereinafter referred to as petitioners), alleging fraud, civil conspiracy, malpractice, breach of fiduciary duty, and negligence. Petitioners moved to stay the action, invoking § 3 of the FAA and arguing that the principles of equitable estoppel demanded that respondents arbitrate their claims under their investment agreements with Bricolage. The District Court denied the motions.

Petitioners filed an interlocutory appeal, which the Court of Appeals for the Sixth Circuit dismissed for want of jurisdiction. We granted certiorari.

II

Ordinarily, courts of appeals have jurisdiction only over "final decisions" of district courts. 28 U.S.C. § 1291. The FAA, however, makes an exception to that finality requirement, providing that "[a]n appeal may be taken from . . . an order . . . refusing a stay of any action under section 3 of this title." 9 U.S.C. § 16(a)(1)(A). By that provision's clear and unambiguous terms, any litigant who asks for a stay under § 3 is entitled to an immediate appeal from denial of that motion—regardless of whether the litigant is in fact eligible for a stay. * * *

The courts that have declined jurisdiction over § 3 appeals of the sort at issue here have done so by conflating the jurisdictional question with the merits of the appeal. They reason that because stay motions premised on equitable estoppel seek to expand (rather than simply vindicate) agreements, they are not cognizable under §§ 3 and 4, and therefore the relevant motions are not actually "under" those provisions. The dissent makes this step explicit, by reading the appellate jurisdictional provision of § 16 as "calling for a look-through" to the substantive provisions of § 3. Jurisdiction over the appeal, however, "must be determined by focusing upon the category of order appealed from, rather than upon the strength of the grounds for reversing the order." The jurisdictional statute here unambiguously makes the underlying merits irrelevant, for even utter frivolousness of the underlying request for a § 3 stay cannot turn a denial into something other than "[a]n order . . . refusing a stay of any action under section 3." 9 U.S.C. § 16(a).

* * *

III

Even if the Court of Appeals were correct that it had no jurisdiction over meritless appeals, its ground for finding this appeal meritless was in error. We take the trouble to address that alternative ground, since if the Court of Appeals is correct on the merits point we will have awarded petitioners a remarkably hollow victory. We consider, therefore, the Sixth Circuit's underlying determination that those who are not parties to a written arbitration agreement are categorically ineligible for relief.

Section 2—the FAA's substantive mandate—makes written arbitration agreements "valid, irrevocable, and enforceable, save upon such grounds as exist at law or in equity for the revocation of a contract." * * * Section 3, in turn, allows litigants already in federal court to invoke agreements made enforceable by § 2. That provision requires the court, "on application of one of the parties," to stay the action if it involves an "issue referable to arbitration under an agreement in writing." 9 U.S.C. § 3.

Neither provision purports to alter background principles of state contract law regarding the scope of agreements (including the question of who is bound by them). Indeed § 2 explicitly retains an external body of law governing revocation (such grounds "as exist at law or in equity").[5] And we think § 3 adds no substantive restriction to § 2's enforceability mandate. "[S]tate law," therefore, is applicable to determine which contracts are binding under § 2 and enforceable under § 3 "*if* that law arose to govern issues concerning the validity, revocability, and enforceability of contracts generally." Because "traditional principles" of state law allow a contract to be enforced by or against nonparties to the contract through "assumption, piercing the corporate veil, alter ego, incorporation by reference, third-party beneficiary theories, waiver and estoppel," 21 R. Lord, Williston on Contracts § 57:19, p. 183 (4th ed.2001), the Sixth Circuit's holding that nonparties to a contract are categorically barred from § 3 relief was error.

Respondents argue that, as a matter of federal law, claims to arbitration by nonparties are not "referable to arbitration *under* an agreement in writing," 9 U.S.C. § 3 (emphasis added), because they "seek to bind a signatory to an arbitral obligation *beyond* that signatory's strictly contractual obligation to arbitrate". Perhaps that would be true if § 3 mandated stays only for disputes between parties to a written arbitration agreement. But that is not what the statute says. It says that stays are required if the claims are "referable to arbitration under an agreement in writing." If a written arbitration provision is made enforceable against (or for the benefit of) a third party under state contract law, the statute's terms are fulfilled.[6]

---

5 We have said many times that federal law requires that "questions of arbitrability . . . be addressed with a healthy regard for the federal policy favoring arbitration." Moses H. Cone Memorial Hospital v. Mercury Constr. Corp., 460 U.S. 1, 24–25, 103 S.Ct. 927, 74 L.Ed.2d 765 (1983). Whatever the meaning of this vague prescription, it cannot possibly require the disregard of state law permitting arbitration by or against nonparties to the written arbitration agreement.

6 We thus reject the dissent's contention that contract law's longstanding endorsement of third-party enforcement is "a weak premise for inferring an intent to allow third parties to obtain a § 3 stay". It seems

* * *

Respondents may be correct in saying that courts' application of equitable estoppel to impose an arbitration agreement upon strangers to the contract has been "somewhat loose." But we need not decide here whether the relevant state contract law recognizes equitable estoppel as a ground for enforcing contracts against third parties, what standard it would apply, and whether petitioners would be entitled to relief under it. These questions have not been briefed before us and can be addressed on remand. It suffices to say that no federal law bars the State from allowing petitioners to enforce the arbitration agreement against respondents and that § 3 would require a stay in this case if it did.

We hold that the Sixth Circuit had jurisdiction to review the denial of petitioners' requests for a § 3 stay and that a litigant who was not a party to the relevant arbitration agreement may invoke § 3 if the relevant state contract law allows him to enforce the agreement. The judgment of the Court of Appeals for the Sixth Circuit is reversed, and the case is remanded for further proceedings consistent with this opinion.

It is so ordered.

■ JUSTICE SOUTER, with whom THE CHIEF JUSTICE and JUSTICE STEVENS join, dissenting.

Section 16 of the Federal Arbitration Act (FAA) authorizes an interlocutory appeal from the denial of a motion under § 3 to stay a district-court action pending arbitration. The question is whether it opens the door to such an appeal at the behest of one who has not signed a written arbitration agreement. Based on the longstanding congressional policy limiting interlocutory appeals, I think the better reading of the statutory provisions disallows such an appeal, and I therefore respectfully dissent.

* * *

Massachusetts' highest court summarized the relevant law as follows:

> Equitable estoppel typically allows a nonsignatory to compel arbitration in either of two circumstances: (1) when a signatory must rely on the terms of the written agreement in asserting its claims against the nonsignatory or (2) when a signatory raises allegations of substantially interdependent and concerted misconduct by both the nonsignatory and one or more of the signatories to the contract.
>
> * * *
>
> Essentially, if a party's claims are so intimately founded in and closely related to an agreement which also mandates arbitration, the party opposing arbitration is equitably estopped from denying the arbitrability of its claims, even against a nonsignatory. * * * Courts frequently rule in favor of nonsignatories in such circumstances because "it would be unfair

---

to us not weak at all, in light of the terms of the statute. There is no doubt that, where state law permits it, a third-party claim is "referable to arbitration under an agreement in writing." It is not our role to conform an unambiguous statute to what we think "Congress probably intended."

> to allow the signatory to rely on the agreement in formulating its claims but to disavow availability of the arbitration clause of that same agreement.

Machado v. System4 LLC, 471 Mass. 204, 211, 28 N.E.3d 401, 409–11 (2015) (compelling arbitration of plaintiffs' claims against non-signatories because "[t]hese claims are inextricably intertwined with and relate directly to the franchise agreements containing the arbitration provision.")

b. NON-PARTY PLAINTIFF VS. PARTY DEFENDANT

Plaintiffs, like defendants, can be intended third-party beneficiaries of another party's promise to arbitrate. For instance, in *Topolski v. Helena Ass'n of Realtors, Inc.*, 15 P.3d 414 (Mont.2000), the real estate broker's client sought arbitration against the broker and the court ordered the broker to arbitrate, even though the client's contract with the broker lacked an arbitration clause, because the broker had agreed to a real estate association's rules requiring brokers to arbitrate clients' claims. Section 2.A.4 showed that securities broker-dealers' duties to arbitrate customer disputes upon customer request similarly arise from an analogous process.

Sometimes, plaintiffs want to be third-party beneficiaries of contracts containing arbitration clauses but to litigate, rather than arbitrate, their claims. For instance, a plaintiff injured while test driving an auto dealer's car "could be considered" a third-party beneficiary of the dealer's insurance policy—the contract between the dealer and its insurer. Ex Parte Dyess, 709 So.2d 447, 449–51 (Ala.1997). If that plaintiff brings a breach-of-contract claim against the dealer's insurer then the insurer may rely on the policy's arbitration clause to require the plaintiff to arbitrate, rather than litigate, his claims against the insurer. In other words, if the plaintiff wants to enforce some of the policy's terms (by suing on them) then he "cannot pick and choose the portions of the contract that he wants to apply." See also Friedman v. Yula, 679 F.Supp.2d 617, 628 (E.D.Pa.2010) ("having embraced the written agreement between Robert and Defendants to prove his claims and his damages, Allan cannot now walk away from the arbitration clauses in the Agreements. * * * Therefore, Plaintiff Allan Friedman must be compelled to arbitration claims [sic] under the Joinder Agreement.")

However, several courts hold that this reasoning—plaintiff "cannot pick and choose the portions of the contract that he wants to apply"—applies only to plaintiffs whose claims rest on the contract containing the arbitration clause, as opposed to non-contract claims, such as tort claims. Fleetwood Enters., Inc. v. Gaskamp, 280 F.3d 1069 (5th Cir.2002); E.I. DuPont de Nemours & Co. v. Rhone Poulenc Fiber & Resin, 269 F.3d 187 (3d Cir.2001). Nevertheless, such a plaintiff might be required to arbitrate due to non-contractual doctrines such as those noted above: estoppel, agency, and corporate veil-piercing. For example, *Peltz v. Sears, Roebuck & Co.*, 367 F.Supp.2d 711 (E.D. Pa. 2005). During an extremely hot summer in Philadelphia, a couple died of heat exposure in their home when their air-conditioner malfunctioned and Sears failed to repair it promptly. The plaintiff filed a survival action for negligence and breach of warranty; as Administrator of the decedent's estate, the plaintiff was naturally thought to "stand in [the decedent's] shoes" and so was obligated to arbitrate pursuant to the arbitration clause in the maintenance agreement between the decedent and Sears. In addition—and more importantly—the plaintiffs had brought a *wrongful death action* on behalf of the decedent's *beneficiaries*; here the court held that even if the wrongful death claim "cannot be said to derive from [the decedent's] claims," the plaintiff was nonetheless "estopped from avoiding arbitration" because the wrongful death claims "rely upon" the maintenance agreement.

3. CONSOLIDATION OF, AND STAYS PENDING, RELATED PROCEEDINGS

a. INTRODUCTION

In a number of common multi-party fact patterns, several related players have an interest in resolving a controversy that has arisen out of a single transaction. For example:

> (i) The Owner of a new building formed separate contracts with the General Contractor (who is responsible for construction) and the Architect (who acts as the Owner's representative in designing and overseeing the project). Owner may make a claim against Contractor for alleged defects in construction; Contractor may answer that any defects are attributable to Architect's failings in specifying materials or in inspecting the work. Should Contractor's defense be upheld, Owner may wish to assert a claim against Architect for negligence. Another common scenario is a claim by Contractor against Owner: Contractor may claim that it was unable to comply with the plans and specifications for the project because they called for the use of materials that were unobtainable; this, Contractor asserts, caused Contractor delay and costs. Should Contractor's claim be upheld, Owner's position will be that Owner is entitled to indemnification from Architect for anything Owner owes to Contractor.[51]
>
> (ii) An owner of a cargo ship leases the ship to a Charterer. The Charterer subcharters (subleases) the vessel to someone interested in carrying cargo for particular voyages. During the course of one such voyage, the ship may suffer structural damage. Shipowner will seek compensation from Charterer; Charterer in turn seeks indemnification from the Sub-charterer who is responsible for the damage.[52]
>
> (iii) The Egyptian Government purchased wheat from four American suppliers; it then chartered a vessel from a Shipper to carry the cargo from Texas to Egypt. During loading, it was discovered that the wheat contained insects; Shipper had to delay loading to fumigate the cargo, and claimed damages for the delay from the Government. The Government took the position that it could not be held liable: "The flour must have been contaminated either before loading, in which case the

---

[51] See, e.g., Consolidated Pacific Engineering, Inc. v. Greater Anchorage Area Borough, 563 P.2d 252 (Alaska 1977); Litton Bionetics, Inc. v. Glen Construction Co., Inc., 292 Md. 34, 437 A.2d 208 (1981).

[52] See Miller, *Consolidated Arbitrations in New York Maritime Disputes*, 14 Int'l Bus.Lawyer 58 (1986).

Suppliers would be liable, or after loading, in which case [the Shipper] would be liable."[53]

In these cases, the party "in the middle"—for example, the Owner in case (i)—likely wants a single proceeding to resolve the interrelated disputes. If the Owner must first assert a claim against Contractor, and only later seek to hold Architect responsible, Owner is faced with more than just the duplication of time and expense inherent in separate proceedings. Owner also faces the real possibility of inconsistent results in the two forums. In arbitration, the Owner may be unable to overcome the Contractor's defense based on deficiencies in the project specifications. In a *later* litigation, however, a court may find that the defect was caused by poor workmanship rather than by the Architect's negligence in preparing the plans—leaving the Owner "holding the bag" alone. While the court granting issue preclusive effect to the arbitration award might prevent this bad result for Owner, Section 3.E.3 noted obstacles to giving arbitration awards such issue preclusive effect. In such a case, the Owner would much prefer to be able to sit back and let the Contractor and Architect fight out between themselves the cause of the construction defects.

b. CONSOLIDATING MULTIPLE ARBITRATIONS

What if *both* contracts (between Owner and Contractor, and between Owner and Architect) contain arbitration clauses? In such a case the Owner may wish to have the various arbitration proceedings "consolidated"—that is, heard jointly before a common arbitrator. The Contractor or the Architect, on the other hand, may object.

Rules of at least one arbitration organization, the Judicial Arbitration and Mediation Service (JAMS) generally authorizes consolidation: "Unless the Parties' Agreement or applicable law provides otherwise, JAMS, if it determines that the Arbitrations so filed have common issues of fact or law, may consolidate Arbitrations."[54] On the other hand, an arbitration organization may be reluctant to consolidate separate arbitration proceedings unless all the parties consent or unless all the agreements explicitly provide for consolidation,[55] because the arbitration organization may fear that consolidation against the will of a party would impair the enforceability of the resulting award. So, parties in the Owner's position sometimes seek a court order consolidating the separate arbitrations. Once a court issues such an order, the arbitration organization is usually willing to administer the consolidated arbitrations.

"If the parties haven't expressly provided for consolidation in their agreements, then for a court to order consolidation would violate the principle that arbitration is

[53] In the Matter of the Arbitration Between the Egyptian Co. for Maritime Transport and Hamlet Shipping Co., Inc., 1982 A.M.C. 874 (S.D.N.Y.1981).

[54] Rule 6(e), JAMS Comprehensive Arbitration Rules & Procedures (2014) https://www.jamsadr.com/files/Uploads/Documents/JAMS-Rules/JAMS_comprehensive_arbitration_rules-2014.pdf.

[55] See, e.g., Consolidation, *Drafting Dispute Resolution Clauses A Practical Guide*, Am. Arbitration Ass'n, at 27 (last visited Sept. 29, 2018)("Since arbitration is a process based on voluntary contractual participation, parties may not be required to arbitrate a dispute without their consent. However, parties can provide for the consolidation of two or more separate arbitrations into a single proceeding or permit the joinder of a third party into an arbitration."), https://www.adr.org/sites/default/files/document_repository/Drafting%20Dispute%20Resolution%20Clauses%20A%20Practical%20Guide.pdf.

consensual." True or false? Compare Dominique Hascher, *Consolidation of Arbitration by American Courts: Fostering or Hampering International Commercial Arbitration*, 1 J. Int'l Arb. 127, 134 (1984) (true; "if it had been the parties' intention to submit their disputes to a multiparty arbitration setting, they would have so provided in their contracts"), with Alan Rau & Edward Sherman, *Tradition and Innovation in International Arbitration Procedure*, 30 Tex. Int'l L.J. 89, 113–115 (1995) (false; "as in most cases of contractual silence we are left with the need for some sort of default rule"; the problem of multiparty disputes is best approached "as one more inquiry into the choice of an appropriate presumption").

Some states' arbitration statutes authorize consolidation of separate arbitrations.[56] For instance, a California statute says:

> A party to an arbitration agreement may petition the court to consolidate separate arbitration proceedings, and the court may order consolidation of separate arbitration proceedings when:
>
> (1) Separate arbitration agreements or proceedings exist between the same parties; or one party is a party to a separate arbitration agreement or proceeding with a third party; and
>
> (2) The disputes arise from the same transactions or series of related transactions; and
>
> (3) There is common issue or issues of law or fact creating the possibility of conflicting rulings by more than one arbitrator or panel of arbitrators.

Cal.Code Civ.Proc. § 1281.3. "In the event that the arbitration agreements in consolidated proceedings contain inconsistent provisions, the court shall resolve such conflicts and determine the rights and duties of the various parties to achieve substantial justice under all the circumstances." Id.

The Revised Uniform Arbitration Act follows California's lead. RUAA § 10(a) states that

> (a) Except as otherwise provided in subsection (c), upon [motion] of a party to an agreement to arbitrate or to an arbitration proceeding, the court may order consolidation of separate arbitration proceedings as to all or some of the claims if:
>
> (1) there are separate agreements to arbitrate or separate arbitration proceedings between the same persons or one of them is a party to a separate agreement to arbitrate or a separate arbitration proceeding with a third person;
>
> (2) the claims subject to the agreements to arbitrate arise in substantial part from the same transaction or series of related transactions;
>
> (3) the existence of a common issue of law or fact creates the possibility of conflicting decisions in the separate arbitration proceedings; and

---

[56] "Except as otherwise provided in subsection (c.) of this section, *upon application of a party to an agreement to arbitrate or to an arbitration proceeding, the Court may order consolidation of separate arbitration proceedings as to all or some of the claims if*: * * *." N.J. Stat. Ann. § 2A:23B–10.

(4) prejudice resulting from a failure to consolidate is not outweighed by the risk of undue delay or prejudice to the rights of or hardship to parties opposing consolidation.

RUAA § 10 (c) adds that a court may nevertheless not order consolidation "of the claims of a party to an agreement to arbitrate which prohibits consolidation." The New Mexico Court of Appeals applied RUAA § 10 to order, over the objection of the defendant homebuilder, consolidation of several homeowners' arbitrations against the homebuilder. Lyndoe v. D.R. Horton, Inc., 287 P.3d 357, 359, 361, 364 (N.M. Ct. App. 2012) (affirming district court's order consolidating arbitrations; "In our view, consolidation of the individual homeowners' arbitrations is consistent with the purpose of arbitration, which is to further judicial economy by providing a quick, informal, and less costly alternative to judicial resolution of disputes").

Some state courts consolidating separate arbitrations find their power to do so "as an incident of the jurisdiction statutorily conferred on a court generally to enforce arbitration agreements."[57] At least one federal court supported consolidation by stressing that "the same considerations of adjudicative economy that argue in favor of consolidating closely related court cases argue for consolidating closely related arbitrations."[58]

However, the general tendency of courts is to refuse to order consolidation of related arbitrations in the absence of express consent of the parties to all the agreements.[59] "A court is not permitted to interfere with private arbitration agreements in order to impose its own view of speed and economy."[60] And even if

---

57 Litton Bionetics, Inc. v. Glen Construction Co., Inc., 437 A.2d 208, 217–18 (Md. 1981)(contractor brought claim against owner who filed negligence counterclaim against both contractor and architect, and sought to compel consolidation; held: court's statutory power to enforce arbitration agreements "embraces the power to order consolidation in appropriate cases, and since the contracts do not confer a right to arbitrate separately, the policy of the AAA cannot prevail over the [state] statute").

58 Connecticut General Life Ins. Co. v. Sun Life Assurance Co. of Canada, 210 F.3d 771 (7th Cir.2000) ("we cannot see any reason why" the court should "place its thumb on the scale, insisting that it be 'clear,' rather than merely more likely than not, that the parties intended consolidation"; "practical considerations [are] relevant to disambiguating a contract, because parties to a contract generally aim at obtaining sensible results in a sensible way"):

59 Lefkovitz v. Wagner, 395 F.3d 773, 780 (7th Cir. 2005)("generally, consolidation of arbitration is permissible only if the applicable arbitration clause or clauses authorize it"); Seretta Constr., Inc. v. Great Am. Ins. Co., 869 So. 2d 676, 678–79 (Fla. Dist. Ct. App. 2004)(no Florida statutory or caselaw support "for the consolidation of the arbitration proceedings"; "we believe the better approach is to follow the federal courts and the states that have held that a court cannot order consolidation of arbitration proceedings arising from separate agreements to arbitrate, absent the parties agreement to allow such consolidation."); Ga. Cas. & Sur. Co. v. Excalibur Reinsurance Corp., 4 F. Supp. 3d 1362, 1368 (N.D. Ga. 2014)(" If the FAA or a state arbitration act lacking a statutory consolidation provision applies, then a court may only consolidate the arbitration if the contracts expressly permit consolidation. Alternatively, if a state arbitration act that allows courts to impose consolidation regardless of the contracts' terms governs the contracts, then a court may order consolidation where the statutory requirements are satisfied").

60 American Centennial Ins. Co. v. National Casualty Co., 951 F.2d 107 (6th Cir. 1991); see also PaineWebber, Inc. v. Fowler, 791 F.Supp. 821 (D. Kans. 1992)("reading consolidation clauses into these contracts" defeats the purpose of protecting "the contractual integrity of arbitration agreements"); Rolls-Royce Industrial Power, Inc. v. Zurn EPC Services, Inc., 2001 WL 1397881 (N.D. Ill.)("there is no textual evidence to suggest that [the respondent] would have wanted to participate in consolidated proceedings with third parties who were non-signatories to the agreement"); Government of the United Kingdom v. Boeing Co., 998 F.2d 68 (2d Cir.1993); Glencore, Ltd. v. Schnitzer Steel Prods. Co., 189 F.3d 264 (2d Cir. 1999)("*Boeing*'s conclusion that there is no source of authority in either the FAA or the Federal Rules of Civil Procedure for the district court to order consolidation absent authority granted by the contracts . . . applies with equal force to a court's order of joint hearing").

a court would generally be willing to order that the Owner-Contractor and the Owner-Architect arbitrations be heard together, if the separate arbitration agreements cannot be harmonized—for example one agreement calls for arbitration in Texas and the other in California, or if the agreements call for administration by different institutions—most courts will be reluctant to consolidate the arbitrations. See, e.g., Parker v. McCaw, 125 Cal.App.4th 1494, 24 Cal.Rptr.3d 55 (2005) (to order consolidation before a single arbitrator would not "achieve substantial justice" where one agreement provides for a single arbitrator but the other calls for a three-person panel; "the contractual right to three arbitrators is substantial and may not be altered by the court"); Biber Partnership, P.C. v. Diamond Hill Joint Venture, LLC, 960 A.2d 774, 775, 778 (N.J.Super.Ct.App.Div.2008) (Biber, architectural firm, sought to consolidate arbitration of disputes between engineering firm (McManus) and building owner under settlement contract between Biber and McManus; consolidation was sought twenty months after settlement agreement; "Biber and McManus entered into a settlement agreement under which the parties agreed to submit their disputes to arbitration"; consolidation is inappropriate not only because of undue delay, but also because it would substantially alter the terms of the settlement agreement; terms with architectural firm would be altered because firm only agreed to arbitration in contract, not settlement, and before a single specific arbitrator as opposed to a different panel of three arbitrators).

c. ESCAPING ARBITRATION IN MULTI-PARTY DISPUTES

Suppose, now, that the agreement between Owner and Contractor contains a clause providing for the arbitration of all disputes, but the agreement between Owner and Architect has no arbitration clause. Owner will not be able to resolve all related disputes at the same time through consolidated arbitration because parties are only obligated to arbitrate when they have agreed to it. In contrast, a practical advantage of litigation is that a court with jurisdiction over all the interested parties can bring them all into the action: In a lawsuit against Contractor, Owner would be able to join a claim "in the alternative" against Architect (see Fed.R.Civ.P. 20(a)); if Owner is a defendant, Owner can "implead" Architect as a "third-party defendant." (See Fed.R.Civ.P. 14(a)). And if there are pending separate "actions involving a common question of law or fact," a court "may order a joint hearing or trial of any or all of the matters in issue in the actions" or may "order all the actions consolidated." (Fed. R.Civ.P. 42(a)).

As Owner will not be able to resolve all related disputes at the same time through consolidated arbitration, Owner may prefer to avoid arbitration completely. Some Owner-Contractor agreements in fact contain an "escape clause," freeing the Owner from any obligation to submit disputes with the Contractor to arbitration if the Owner, "in order to fully protect its interests, desires in good faith to bring in or make a party to any [dispute] * * * the Architect, or any other third party who has not agreed to participate in and be bound by the same arbitration proceeding."[61]

But suppose that the Owner has not been able through negotiation to obtain such an "escape clause," and suppose that the Owner is a party to an arbitration

[61] See Garden Grove Community Church v. Pittsburgh-Des Moines Steel Co., 140 Cal.App.3d 251, 191 Cal.Rptr. 15 (1983).

agreement with the Contractor, but not with the Architect. In such a case, is there any way to ensure that all the claims are heard at the same time in a single proceeding? When the Contractor demands arbitration, the Owner may argue that for the sake of "efficiency," a court should simply refuse to compel arbitration so that the entire dispute can be resolved in one judicial proceeding.

The United States Supreme Court confronted this fact pattern in *Moses H. Cone Memorial Hospital v. Mercury Construction Corp.*, 460 U.S. 1 (1983). Here, Owner had filed a state court action against Contractor—seeking a declaratory judgment that their dispute was not arbitrable—and also against Architect, claiming indemnity for any liability to Contractor. Contractor then brought an action in *federal* court against Owner, under Section 4 of the FAA, to compel arbitration. Since the Owner had taken the care in its own action to join a defendant who was not subject to an arbitration agreement, Owner was then in a position to argue that Contractor's action should be stayed—in order that the entire dispute could be disposed of in the parallel *state* action. Otherwise, Owner asserted, there would have to be "piecemeal litigation." The Supreme Court held that it was an abuse of discretion for the district court to grant a stay of the federal action, which at the time was "running well ahead of the state suit." To the Court, Owner's argument was misconceived: if the dispute between Owner and Contractor were in fact arbitrable, then "piecemeal litigation" was inevitable no matter *which* court, state or federal, decided the question of arbitrability because "the relevant federal law *requires* piecemeal resolution when necessary to give effect to an arbitration agreement." More recent federal courts have continued to require separate resolution of related disputes rather than allow a party (such as Owner) out of its arbitration agreement to consolidate in one litigation all related disputes.[62]

Even if an overall dispute must be settled in "piecemeal" fashion in separate proceedings, it should at least be possible for any lawsuit (say, between the Owner and the Architect) to be stayed until the conclusion of the arbitration between the Owner and the Contractor. See Catlin Syndicate 2003 v. Traditional Air Conditioning, Inc., 2018 WL 3040375, at *2, *7 (E.D.N.Y. June 18, 2018) (plaintiff sued general contractor (GC) with whom plaintiff had an agreement to arbitrate, and air-conditioning subcontract (A/C sub) whose contract with GC did not have an arbitration clause; court granted GC's motion to compel arbitration and stay litigation pending arbitration because "there is sufficient factual and legal overlap [between claims against GC and claims against A/C sub] to warrant a stay").

In contrast to federal courts requiring "piecemeal" resolution of related disputes, some states hold that the "prospect of multiple proceedings carrying a potential for inconsistent findings provides a basis for overriding the freedom to

---

[62] Wiles v. Palm Springs Grill, LLC, No. 15-CV-81597-KAM, 2016 WL 4248315, at *3 (S.D. Fla. Aug. 11, 2016)("Though not raised by Plaintiff, and addressed only briefly by Defendants in a footnote, the Court notes that the arbitration agreement is solely between Plaintiff and Wild West. Defendants Ciceroni and Schneider are not parties to the arbitration agreement. This does not affect the Court's obligation to refer the dispute between Wild West and Plaintiff to arbitration. . .In such a scenario, the Court has discretion to proceed with the litigation between the non-arbitrating parties or to stay the litigation pending the outcome of the arbitration"); Golden Gate Nat'l Senior Care, LLC v. Beavens, 123 F. Supp. 3d 619, 637 (E.D. Pa. 2015) ("Having found that the estate's survival claims are subject to a valid and enforceable arbitration agreement, I must compel arbitration and stay the Berks County proceedings. . .However, I have discretion to deny a stay of count five since Ms. Beavens and her sister are not bound by the arbitration agreement").

contract for arbitration." County of Jefferson v. Barton-Douglas Contractors, Inc., 282 N.W.2d 155 (Iowa 1979). For instance, California's arbitration statute permits a court to *stay arbitration,* or *refuse enforcement* of an arbitration agreement, if one of the parties is also a party to pending *litigation* with a third party "arising out of the same transaction or series of related transactions," and if there is a "possibility of conflicting rulings on a common issue of law or fact." Cal.Code Civ.Proc. § 1281.2. Is such a refusal or stay of arbitration pursuant to the California statute preempted by the FAA?

The Supreme Court was faced with precisely this question in *Volt Information Sciences, Inc. v. Board of Trustees of the Leland Stanford Junior University*, 489 U.S. 468 (1989), discussed in Section 3.C.5. Volt had entered into a construction contract with Stanford under which Volt was to install a system of electrical conduits on the Stanford campus. The contract contained an agreement to arbitrate all disputes between the parties "arising out of or relating to this contract or the breach thereof," and it also contained a choice-of-law clause providing that "[t]he Contract shall be governed by the law of the place where the Project is located." During the course of the project, a dispute developed regarding compensation for extra work: Stanford filed an action against Volt in the state courts of California alleging fraud and breach of contract, and in the same action Stanford also sought indemnity from two other companies involved in the construction project, with whom it did not have arbitration agreements. Volt moved to compel arbitration, and Stanford in turn moved to stay arbitration pursuant to Section 1281.2. Relying on this legislation, the California courts denied Volt's motion to compel arbitration and stayed the arbitration proceedings pending the outcome of the litigation. The reasoning was that "by specifying that their contract would be governed by 'the law of the place where the project is located,' the parties had incorporated the California rules of arbitration, including § 1281.2, into their arbitration agreement."

The Supreme Court agreed with the state courts, and California courts continue to refuse or to stay arbitration in multiparty disputes under Section 1281.2 by continuing to rely on *Volt.*[63]

4. CLASS ACTIONS IN ARBITRATION

Section 3.C.2.b excerpted *AT&T Mobility LLC v. Concepcion*, 563 U.S. 333 (2011), and said *Concepcion* addresses the arbitration-law issue that has, over the last decade or two, likely received the most attention from interest groups—class actions, and in particular adhesive arbitration agreements "waiving" the parties'

[63] See Williams v. Atria Las Posas, 24 Cal. App. 5th 1048, 1053, 1055, 235 Cal. Rptr. 3d 341, 346–47 (2018)("Atria contends that because the arbitration agreement provides for the application of the Federal Arbitration Act (FAA), the procedural rules of the FAA apply here to the exclusion of section 1281.2(c). On this point, Atria is mistaken"; "Accordingly, we will remand to the trial court for it to determine whether the conditions of section 1281.2(c) have been met, and if so, to exercise its discretion on whether to stay or deny arbitration"); Avila v. S. Cal. Specialty Care, Inc., 20 Cal. App. 5th 835, 841, 230 Cal. Rptr. 3d 42, 46–47 (2018)("As noted above, the agreement here does not even mention the FAA, much less expressly adopt its procedural rules. . .Any state law procedural provisions regarding arbitration are valid unless they defeat the rights granted by the FAA to equal enforcement of arbitration clauses. Defendants argue section 1281.2, subdivision (c), places arbitration agreements "on an unequal footing than other contracts," but do not cite any case where California or federal courts reach that conclusion. Indeed, there is ample case law to the contrary, including from the California Supreme Court, which has held that section 1281.2, subdivision (c), does not defeat the rights granted by the FAA, and is therefore not preempted").

rights to participate in class actions. However, if no such waiver has occurred and parties have a dispute that—but for a pre-dispute arbitration clause—would have been litigated as a class action, then it might be resolved in classwide arbitration, which is a class action with rulings by an arbitrator, rather than a judge.

Classwide arbitration was rare until the Supreme Court's 2003 decision in *Green Tree Financial Corp. v. Bazzle*, 539 U.S. 444 (2003), which involved an arbitration agreement that neither permitted nor prohibited class arbitration, but rather was silent on that question. *Bazzle* held that it was for the arbitrator, rather than a court, to interpret this silence, and many post-*Bazzle* arbitrators interpreted such "silent" contracts to permit class arbitration. AAA and JAMS were among the arbitration organizations to develop special rules for handling the growing number of demands for class arbitration.[64] The AAA's "Supplementary Rules" closely track Rule 23 of the Federal Rules of Civil Procedure, and depart in a number of substantial ways from usual arbitration procedures.

Class arbitration's growth was set back by the Supreme Court's 2010 decision in *Stolt-Nielsen S.A. v. AnimalFeeds International Corp.*, 559 U.S. 662 (2010), which interpreted arbitration agreement silence on class arbitration as a prohibition of it. While the arbitrators in *Stolt-Nielsen* "imposed class arbitration even though the parties concurred that they had reached 'no agreement' on that issue," the Court said "the differences between bilateral and class-action arbitration are too great for arbitrators to presume, consistent with their limited powers under the FAA, that the parties' mere silence on the issue of class-action arbitration constitutes consent to resolve their disputes in class proceedings." The *Stolt-Nielsen* Court held that "a party may not be compelled under the FAA to submit to class arbitration unless there is a contractual basis for concluding that the party agreed to do so." Id. at 1775. See also Oxford Health Plans LLC v. Sutter, 569 U.S. 564, 566 (2013) ("The parties agreed that the arbitrator should decide whether their contract authorized class arbitration, and he determined that it did").

AT&T Mobility LLC v. Concepcion, 563 U.S. 333, 336 (2011), excerpted in Section 3.C.2.b, enforced an adhesion contract providing for arbitration of all disputes between the parties, and requiring that claims be brought in the parties' "individual capacity, and not as a plaintiff or class member in any purported class or representative proceeding." While such class-waiver clauses were often unenforceable under California's "*Discover Bank* rule," *Concepcion* found that rule of state law preempted by the FAA. In doing so, *Concepcion* said:

> [T]he "changes brought about by the shift from bilateral arbitration to class-action arbitration" are "fundamental." This is obvious as a structural matter: Classwide arbitration includes absent parties, necessitating additional and different procedures and involving higher stakes. Confidentiality becomes more difficult. And while it is theoretically possible to select an arbitrator with some expertise relevant to the class-certification question, arbitrators are not generally

---

[64] Am.Arbitration Ass'n, *AAA Policy on Class Arbitration* (2005), available at https://www.adr.org/sites/default/files/document_repository/AAA%20Policy%20on%20Class%20Arbitrations.pdf (last visited Oct. 16, 2019); JAMS, JAMS Class Action Procedures (2009), http://www.jamsadr.com/rules-class-action-procedures/ (last visited Dec. 13, 2010).

knowledgeable in the often-dominant procedural aspects of certification, such as the protection of absent parties. The conclusion follows that class arbitration, to the extent it is manufactured by *Discover Bank* rather than consensual, is inconsistent with the FAA.

First, the switch from bilateral to class arbitration sacrifices the principal advantage of arbitration—its informality—and makes the process slower, more costly, and more likely to generate procedural morass than final judgment. "In bilateral arbitration, parties forgo the procedural rigor and appellate review of the courts in order to realize the benefits of private dispute resolution: lower costs, greater efficiency and speed, and the ability to choose expert adjudicators to resolve specialized disputes." But before an arbitrator may decide the merits of a claim in classwide procedures, he must first decide, for example, whether the class itself may be certified, whether the named parties are sufficiently representative and typical, and how discovery for the class should be conducted. A cursory comparison of bilateral and class arbitration illustrates the difference. According to the American Arbitration Association (AAA), the average consumer arbitration between January and August 2007 resulted in a disposition on the merits in six months, four months if the arbitration was conducted by documents only. As of September 2009, the AAA had opened 283 class arbitrations. Of those, 121 remained active, and 162 had been settled, withdrawn, or dismissed. Not a single one, however, had resulted in a final award on the merits. For those cases that were no longer active, the median time from filing to settlement, withdrawal, or dismissal—not judgment on the merits—was 583 days, and the mean was 630 days.

Second, class arbitration *requires* procedural formality. The AAA's rules governing class arbitrations mimic the Federal Rules of Civil Procedure for class litigation. Compare AAA, Supplementary Rules for Class Arbitrations (effective Oct. 8, 2003), online at http://www.adr.org/sp.asp?id=21936, with Fed. Rule Civ. Proc. 23. And while parties can alter those procedures by contract, an alternative is not obvious. If procedures are too informal, absent class members would not be bound by the arbitration. For a class-action money judgment to bind absentees in litigation, class representatives must at all times adequately represent absent class members, and absent members must be afforded notice, an opportunity to be heard, and a right to opt out of the class. At least this amount of process would presumably be required for absent parties to be bound by the results of arbitration.

We find it unlikely that in passing the FAA Congress meant to leave the disposition of these procedural requirements to an arbitrator. Indeed, class arbitration was not even envisioned by Congress when it passed the FAA in 1925; as the California Supreme Court admitted in *Discover Bank*, class arbitration is a "relatively recent development." And it is at the very least odd to think that an arbitrator would be entrusted with ensuring that third parties' due process rights are satisfied.

> Third, class arbitration greatly increases risks to defendants. Informal procedures do of course have a cost: The absence of multilayered review makes it more likely that errors will go uncorrected. Defendants are willing to accept the costs of these errors in arbitration, since their impact is limited to the size of individual disputes, and presumably outweighed by savings from avoiding the courts. But when damages allegedly owed to tens of thousands of potential claimants are aggregated and decided at once, the risk of an error will often become unacceptable. Faced with even a small chance of a devastating loss, defendants will be pressured into settling questionable claims. Other courts have noted the risk of "in terrorem" settlements that class actions entail and class arbitration would be no different.
>
> Arbitration is poorly suited to the higher stakes of class litigation. In litigation, a defendant may appeal a certification decision on an interlocutory basis and, if unsuccessful, may appeal from a final judgment as well. Questions of law are reviewed *de novo* and questions of fact for clear error. In contrast, 9 U.S.C. § 10 allows a court to vacate an arbitral award *only* where the award "was procured by corruption, fraud, or undue means"; "there was evident partiality or corruption in the arbitrators"; "the arbitrators were guilty of misconduct in refusing to postpone the hearing . . . or in refusing to hear evidence pertinent and material to the controversy[,] or of any other misbehavior by which the rights of any party have been prejudiced"; or if the "arbitrators exceeded their powers, or so imperfectly executed them that a mutual, final, and definite award . . . was not made."

Id. at 347–48. Perhaps largely because of *Stolt-Nielsen* and *Concepcion*, class arbitrations since 2011 have been few and far between. While a Consumer Financial Protection Bureau study found 280 class arbitrations between 2003 and 2009[65] after 2010, the Bureau discovered just two AAA class arbitrations, attributing the decline to the Supreme Court's decision in *Stolt-Nielsen*.[66] In 2018, the AAA's class action case docket contained only 74 pending class arbitrations, 12 clause construction awards, and 4 final awards since 2011.[67]

QUESTIONS TO REVIEW AND SYNTHESIZE

1. Suppose X has separate contracts—each containing an arbitration clause—with Y and Z, but Y and Z have no contract with each other, and a dispute arises in which X has suffered a loss for which, under any plausible application of law to facts, either Y or Z is liable, but which of them is liable will require a hearing to admit and assess evidence. Why is X likely to want a single consolidated arbitration

---

[65] Consumer Fin. Prot. Bureau, *Arbitration Study: Report to Congress, Pursuant to Dodd-Frank Wall Street Reform and Consumer Protection Act § 1028(a)*, p. 86–88 (Mar. 2015). https://files.consumerfinance.gov/f/201503_cfpb_arbitration-study-report-to-congress-2015.pdf.

[66] *Id.* at n. 157 ("The small number of class arbitrations filed * * * may be attributable to the Supreme Court's decision in April 2010 in *Stolt-Nielsen S.A. v. Animalfeeds Int'l Corp.*, 130 S. Ct. 1758 (2010)").

[67] Am. Arbitration Ass'n, *Class Action Case Docket* (Accessed Jun. 20, 2018) https://apps.adr.org/CaseDocketApp/faces/CaseSearchPage.jsf;jsessionid=10LWyXwhrok5oDnvocoJWNJ-MEMGQA56ceQBDVy0d-urrg-MxhJ9!1447871939.

including all three parties? What will determine whether X can get a single arbitration, or must have an arbitration with Y and a separate arbitration with Z?

2. Same question as #1 except that the contract between X and Z contains no arbitration clause.

3. Same question as #2 except that X and Z have no contract at all.

4. Why is classwide arbitration now rare?

CHAPTER 5

INTERNATIONAL ARBITRATION

A. COMMERCIAL ARBITRATION AND PUBLIC LAW ARBITRATION

This book began by defining arbitration as private (non-government) adjudication, and this definition fits the vast majority of what is commonly called international commercial arbitration. "When parties [from different nations] agree to arbitrate their disputes, they give up the right to have those disputes decided by a national court. Instead, they agree that their disputes will be resolved privately, outside any court system."[1] That usual absence of national governments as either parties or adjudicators makes such arbitration technically *trans*national, rather than

[1] Margaret L. Moses, The Principles and Practice of International Commercial Arbitration 20 (3d ed. 2017).

*inter*national, but this book and most others nevertheless refer to it as international commercial arbitration.

In contrast, some other international arbitration truly is between nations because one or more parties is a national government (State). Arbitration involving claims against States generally involves claims for which no national court would have jurisdiction to enter judgment against a defending State because the doctrine of sovereign immunity prevents such jurisdiction. So arbitration between States, unlike most other arbitration, is not a private-sector alternative to litigation in government courts, but rather an alternative to the other ways States interact, such as diplomacy and war. For example, the Permanent Court of Arbitration (PCA)[2] resolves "territorial, treaty, and human rights disputes between states, as well as commercial and investment disputes,"[3] and the Iran-United States Claims Tribunal was established in 1981 to resolve claims arising out of the Iran Hostage Crisis.[4]

Sovereign immunity generally deprives courts of jurisdiction to enter judgment, not only on claims between States, but also on claims against States by private parties who are citizens of different States. So foreign investors often fear their investments will be vulnerable to expropriation by the host State with sovereign immunity preventing any recourse in court. To overcome this fear, host states adopt treaties committing to arbitration of foreign investors' claims against a State—commonly known as international investment arbitration—which makes foreign investors more likely to invest believe they will have more effective recourse against the host State if a dispute arises.

Enforcement of an arbitration award against a State may face an obstacle not likely present in international commercial arbitration, let alone domestic arbitration: how does a party enforce an arbitration award against a State whose national courts are part of the State and thus share the State's opposition to enforcement of the award? Moreover, the line between the State and private parties is not as sharp in many nations as it is in the United States, so even an international commercial arbitration award against a nominally private party may face obstacles to enforcement in that party's home courts similar to the obstacles of enforcing an award against a State. This problem of enforcing international commercial arbitration awards is the focus of the most important body of law governing such arbitration: the United Nations Convention on the Recognition and Enforcement of Foreign Arbitral Awards, also known as the "New York Convention."

---

[2] For the text of the Convention of July 29, 1989, see Treaties and Other International Agreements of the United States of America 1776–1949, Vol. I, 230–46 (Charles I. Bevans ed., 1968).

[3] https://pca-cpa.org/en/about/introduction/.

[4] Declaration of the Government of the Democratic and Popular Republic of Algeria, Jan. 19, 1981, 1 Iran-U.S.C.T.R. 3; Declaration of the Government of the Democratic and Popular Republic of Algeria Concerning the Settlement of Claims by the Government of the United States of America and the Government of the Islamic Republic of Iran, Jan. 19, 1981, 1 Iran-U.S.C.T.R. 9.

B. INTERNATIONAL COMMERCIAL ARBITRATION: SOURCES OF LAW

1. TREATIES, PRIMARILY THE NEW YORK CONVENTION

a. BASIC PROVISIONS

The New York Convention (the full text of which appears in Appendix B) was adopted in 1958. The United States ratified (or "acceded to") it in 1970.[5] By April 2018, 159 national governments had become parties to the Convention ("Contracting states").[6] This widespread adoption of the Convention has made it "the single most important pillar on which the edifice of international arbitration rests."[7] The Convention might even "lay claim to be the most effective instance of international legislation in the entire history of commercial law."[8]

The main goal driving adoption of the New York Convention was strengthened enforcement of "foreign" arbitral awards—that is, arbitration awards rendered abroad, "in the territory of a State other than the State where the recognition and enforcement of such awards are sought." Accordingly, it begins "[t]his Convention shall apply to the recognition and enforcement of arbitral awards made in the territory of a State other than the State where the recognition and enforcement of such awards are sought."[9]

Parties often choose as the site of an international arbitration a "neutral" location in which neither party has its principal place of business or substantial assets. Consequently, a claimant who wins an arbitration award can only enforce that award by taking it to some jurisdiction in which the respondent has assets. While many arbitration awards are paid without enforcement action, awards tend to be paid more promptly when enforcement seems a live and imminent alternative. Under the Convention, enforcement in other jurisdictions of a foreign arbitral award is considerably more simple and certain than would be the enforcement of the judgment of a foreign court. (See Section 2.B.1 elaborating this point.)

The key provision of the New York Convention (on the Recognition and Enforcement of Foreign Arbitral Awards) is Article III, which establishes a state's general obligation to recognize and enforce foreign arbitral awards. It requires Contracting States to enforce such awards "in accordance with the rules of procedure" used in the enforcing state with respect to domestic awards. The Convention contains a narrow list of grounds upon which "[r]ecognition and enforcement of the award may be refused." See Art. V. In such a case a court "may" then refuse to enforce the award. (The exceptions are therefore permissive, within

---

[5] In that same year, §§ 201–208 were added to the FAA in order to provide a mechanism for enforcing agreements and awards falling within the Convention.

[6] For the current status, see http://www.uncitral.org/uncitral/en/uncitral_texts/arbitration/NYConvention_status.html. Taiwan, which is not a signatory to the Convention, constitutes perhaps the only exception to this statement.

[7] J. Gillis Wetter, *The Present Status of the International Court of Arbitration of the ICC: An Appraisal*, 1 Am. Rev. Int'l Arb. 91, 93 (1990).

[8] Lord Mustill, *Arbitration: History and Background*, 6(2) J. of Int'l Arb. 43, 49 (1989).

[9] New York Convention, art. I(1).

the discretion of the enforcing court.)[10] The grounds that can be asserted by a party against whom enforcement is sought, in order to contest enforcement of a foreign award, are set out in Art. V(1): Some of these are similar to grounds for vacatur under section 10 of the "domestic" FAA,[11] including:

- due process violations such as the denial of a fair hearing or "the opportunity to present [a party's] claim in a meaningful manner";[12]
- irregular composition of the arbitral tribunal; and
- an award that exceeds the contractual authority of the arbitrator or one that deals with an "inarbitrable" subject matter.

In addition to requiring enforcement of arbitration awards rendered in another State, the New York Convention also requires enforcement of executory arbitration agreements.[13] The New York Convention's remedy for breach of such agreements, like the remedy under FAA §§ 3 and 4, is specific performance, that is, a court order to arbitrate.[14] While the New York Convention requires enforcement of executory arbitration agreements, its provisions on that topic reflect less "drafting attention" than the drafters gave to its provisions on enforcing arbitration awards.[15]

b. U.S. RATIFICATION AND IMPLEMENTATION OF THE NEW YORK AND PANAMA CONVENTIONS

In 1970, the United States ratified the New York Convention and Congress enacted FAA §§ 201–208 to make the Convention enforceable in United States

---

[10] Cf. Jan Paulsson, *May or Must Under the New York Convention: An Exercise in Syntax and Linguistics*, 14 Arb. Int'l 227, 229 (1998) ("four of the five official languages of the Convention clearly leave room for judicial discretion. Only the French text contains a hint of a contrary intention, but it is not explicit").

[11] See, e.g., Polimaster Ltd. v. RAE Sys., Inc., 623 F.3d 832, 836 (9th Cir. 2010) ("The grounds for refusing confirmation of an award under the Federal Arbitration Act (FAA), 9 U.S.C. § 10, generally track those under the New York Convention, although they are not coextensive."); Management & Technical Consultants S.A. v. Parsons-Jurden Int'l Corp., 820 F.2d 1531 (9th Cir.1987) ("In interpreting the grounds specified [for overturning awards], it is generally recognized that the Convention tracks the Federal Arbitration Act").

[12] E.g., Iran Aircraft Industries v. Avco Corp., 980 F.2d 141 (2d Cir.1992). At a pre-hearing conference the claimant had requested guidance as to the appropriate method for proving certain of its claims, which were based on voluminous invoices. The "neutral" arbitrator expressed reluctance about "getting kilos and kilos of invoices" and approved the claimant's proposal that its claims be documented by audited accounts receivable ledgers. However, by the time of the actual hearing, two of the three arbitrators had resigned and been replaced, and the panel ultimately disallowed certain claims that were asserted "solely on the basis of an affidavit and a list of invoices, even if the existence of the invoices was certified by an independent audit." The court held that the panel had "misled" the claimant, "however unwittingly," and enforcement of the award was denied under art. V(1)(b) of the Convention.

[13] New York Convention, art. II(1).

> Each Contracting State shall recognize an agreement in writing under which the parties undertake to submit to arbitration all or any differences which have arisen or which may arise between them in respect of a defined legal relationship, whether contractual or not, concerning a subject matter capable of settlement by arbitration.

[14] *Id.* art. II(3).

> The court of a Contracting State, when seized of an action in a matter in respect of which the parties have made an agreement within the meaning of this article, shall, at the request of one of the parties, refer the parties to arbitration, unless it finds that the said agreement is null and void, inoperative or incapable of being performed.

[15] Gary B. Born, International Commercial Arbitration 710 (2009) ("Article II was added to the Convention in the closing days of negotiations. Little drafting attention was given to the Article.").

courts.[16] The ratification came with the reservation that it would be applied "on the basis of reciprocity, to the recognition and enforcement of only those awards made in the territory of another Contracting State."[17] As a result, an arbitration award rendered in another Contracting State (or an agreement to arbitrate in another Contracting State) is generally enforceable in United States courts. An arbitration award rendered elsewhere in the world may be enforceable in United States courts, but the New York Convention does not make it so.

In addition, the United States and most States in the Western Hemisphere have ratified the Inter-American Convention on International Commercial Arbitration (also known as the Panama Convention), the full text of which appears in Appendix C.[18] The New York Convention does not govern "[i]f a majority of the parties to the arbitration agreement are citizens of a State or States" that have signed the Inter-American Convention,[19] which also enforces arbitration awards. The Inter-American Convention was modeled on the New York Convention and the Second Circuit has stated that "Congress intended the Inter-American Convention to reach the same results as those reached under the New York Convention." Productos Mercantiles E Industriales, S.A. v. Faberge USA, Inc., 23 F.3d 41, 45 (2d Cir.1994).[20]

However, while Article 1 of the Inter-American Convention provides that arbitration agreements are "valid," one of the Convention's "major deficiencies" is that it lacks a provision obligating courts to enforce arbitration agreements by ordering parties to arbitration.[21] Nevertheless, some U.S. courts have ordered parties to arbitration in reliance on FAA § 307, which provides that FAA "Chapter 1 [9 U.S.C. §§ 1–16] applies to actions and proceedings brought under this chapter to the extent chapter 1 is not in conflict with this chapter or the Inter-American Convention

---

[16] 9 U.S.C. § 201.

[17] See http://www.newyorkconvention.org/countries (listing ratifying states and their reservations). See also New York Convention, art. I(3) ("When signing, ratifying or acceding to this Convention, or notifying extension under article X hereof, any State may on the basis of reciprocity declare that it will apply the Convention to the recognition and enforcement of awards made only in the territory of another Contracting State.")

[18] 9 U.S.C. § 305(1). See Inter-American Convention on International Commercial Arbitration, Jan. 30, 1975, 1975 O.A.S.T.S. No.42, 14 I.L.M. 336, available at http://www.oas.org/DIL/CIDIPI_convention_arbitration.htm (last visited Aug.1, 2011). See generally John P. Bowman, The Panama Convention and Its Implementation under the Federal Arbitration Act (2002).

[19] 9 U.S.C. § 305(1). For a list of signatories, see Department of International Law, http://www.oas.org/juridico/english/sigs/b-35.html (last visited Mar.11, 2017).

[20] See also Corporacion Mexicana De Mantenimiento Integral, S. De R.L. De C.V. v. Pemex-Exploracion Y Produccion, 832 F.3d 92, 105 (2d Cir. 2016) ("The domestic enforcement of foreign arbital awards is governed by two international Conventions: the Inter-American Convention on International Commercial Arbitration ('Pana Convention') and the Convention on the Recognition and Enforcement of Foreign Arbitral Awards ('New York Convention'). . .[t]here is no substantive difference between the two."): TermoRio S.A. E.S.P. v. Electranta S.P., 487 F.3d 928, 933 (D.C. Cir. 2007) ("[T]he relevant provisions of the Panama Convention and the New York Convention are substantively identical.")

[21] Claus von Wobeser, *The Influence of the New York Convention in Latin America and on the Inter-American Convention on International Commercial Arbitration*, 2 No. 1 Disp. Resol. Int'l 43, 51 (May, 2008).

as ratified by the United States."[22] In this indirect fashion, some courts have applied FAA § 2 and § 4 to order arbitration in Inter-American Convention cases.[23]

Another unusual aspect of the Panama Convention is Article 3, which says "In the absence of an express agreement between the parties, the arbitration shall be conducted in accordance with the rules of procedure of the Inter-American Commercial Arbitration Commission [ICAC]." See also FAA § 306. Unusual for an international convention to incorporate, as positive law, the rules of a private institution. ICAC rules call for administered arbitration, and in the United States the AAA, as the "national section" of the ICAC, administers these arbitrations.[24]

c. U.S. EXCEPTIONS FROM NEW YORK CONVENTION

i. *Not "Considered as Commercial"*

The New York Convention's applicability to foreign arbitration agreements and awards is subject to two important exceptions in United States courts. One is that the New York Convention permits a ratifying State to "declare that it will apply the Convention only to differences arising out of legal relationships whether contractual or not, which are *considered as commercial* under the national law of the State making such declaration."[25] And FAA § 202 says arbitration agreements and awards "fall[ ] under the Convention" only if "arising out of a legal relationship, whether contractual or not, which is considered as commercial, including a transaction, contract, or agreement described in section 2 of this title."

However, the Supreme Court broadly interprets FAA § 2's "involving commerce" language, incorporated into FAA § 202. Consequently, the definition of "commercial" in United States law may be "the broadest of any signatory to the Convention."[26] For example, employment relationships are generally considered "commercial" by United States courts,[27] but courts of other States might disagree. What sorts of disputes might not be "considered as commercial"? Perhaps examples would include "family law disputes, state boundary disputes, and disputes presenting political issues." Christopher R. Drahozal, Commercial Arbitration: Cases and Problems 346 (3d ed.2013). See also Island Territory of Curacao v. Solitron Devices, Inc., 356 F.Supp. 1, 13 (S.D.N.Y.1973) ("Research has developed nothing to show what the purpose of the 'commercial' limitation was. We may logically speculate

---

[22] 9 U.S.C. § 307.

[23] Paramedics Electromedicia Comercial Ltda. v. Medical Sys. Info. Techs., Inc., 2003 WL 23641529 (S.D.N.Y. June 4, 2003) (FAA§ 4); Siderurgica del Orinoco (SIDOR), CA v. Linea Naviera de Cabotaje, C.A., 1999 WL 632870 (S.D.N.Y. Aug. 19, 1999) (FAA § 2).

[24] *Inter-American Commercial Arbitration Commission Rules*, Am. Arbitration Ass'n, https://www.adr.org/sites/default/files/Inter-American%20Commercial%20Arbitration%20Commission%20Rules-%20English.pdf (last visited Jul. 29, 2018). See generally John P. Bowman, The Panama Convention and Its Implementation Under the Federal Arbitration Act 23–33 (2002).

[25] Article I(3)(emphasis added).

[26] Macneil, Speidel & Stipanowich, Federal Arbitration Law § 44.9.3.3 (1999).

[27] Rogers v. Royal Caribbean Cruise Line, 547 F.3d 1148, 1155 (9th Cir.2008) ("The employment contracts of seafarers 'aris[e] out of legal relationship[s] . . . which [are] considered as commercial,' and therefore those contracts 'fall[ ] under the [C]onvention.'"); Bautista v. Star Cruises, 396 F.3d 1289, 1297–1300 (11th Cir.2005).

that it was to exclude matrimonial and other domestic relations awards, political awards, and the like.")

ii. Arbitration Between U.S. Parties

The New York Convention's applicability to foreign arbitration agreements and awards in United States courts is subject to another exception found in FAA § 202. The New York Convention does not govern an arbitration agreement or award "entirely between citizens of the United States" unless their "relationship involves property located abroad, envisages performance or enforcement abroad, or has some other reasonable relation with one or more foreign states."[28] Courts have held that agreeing to arbitrate in another State is not, without more, enough of a relation with a foreign state to bring the arbitration within the coverage of the Convention.

One of these cases involved a yacht owned by an American couple—and whose home port is Freeport, New York—that was struck by a wave and beached on Long Island while on a short journey from Connecticut; a professional salvor—also from Freeport—towed the vessel approximately six miles to a marina. Before it performed services, however, the salvage company insisted that the owners sign Lloyd's Standard Form of Salvage Agreement. This agreement said that the salvor's compensation shall be fixed by a Lloyd's Arbitration Panel in London. When the salvor initiated arbitration in London, the owners resisted by filing an action in federal court in New York. This case lacks any foreign connection except that the agreed place of arbitration is abroad.

In such cases courts have regularly declined to order arbitration in London, on the ground that the NY Convention did not apply. See Jones v. Sea Tow Services Freeport NY Inc., 30 F.3d 360 (2d Cir.1994)(lower court was held to have "exceeded its jurisdiction" in ordering arbitration in England, since "the relation with a foreign state that is required to invoke the Convention is lacking"). So "the saving grace in this case is that the [owners] will be able to defend in the United States, rather than in a foreign forum, the salvage claim asserted against them." See also Reinholtz v. Retriever Marine Towing & Salvage, 1993 WL 414719 (S.D.Fla.1993). In *Reinholtz* the parties had actually proceeded to arbitration in London; the court held that the resulting award in favor of the salvors could not be enforced, because there was missing the "requisite link to another nation" needed to bring it under the Convention. To the same effect is *Brier v. Northstar Marine, Inc.*, 1993 A.M.C. 1194, 1992 WL 350292 (D.N.J.) (salvor's motion for an order compelling arbitration in London was denied; excluding "purely domestic matters between citizens of the United States * * * would not appear to do any harm to the purposes of the Convention * * * and has the salutary effect of minimizing the expansion of federal jurisdiction into areas traditionally the province of the state judiciary").[29]

---

[28] 9 U.S.C. § 202.

[29] See also Ensco Offshore Co. v. Titan Marine L.L.C., 370 F. Supp. 2d 594, 601 (S.D. Tex. 2005) (granting Texas rig owner's motion for a declaration that the arbitration clause compelling arbitration in London with Florida salvor was invalid because there was "not a reasonable link between the legal relationship and England or any other foreign state"; court did not order arbitration anywhere); Nomanbhoy v. Vahanvaty, No. 11 C 2456, 2011 WL 6736052, at *5 (N.D. Ill. Dec. 21, 2011)(denying Illinois CEO of Illinois company's motion to confirm an arbitration award under the New York Convention from an arbitration in Sri Lanka, between CEO and CEO's siblings and niece who were also shareholders of the company, holding the parties'

These cases seem to rest on two distinct propositions:

- In order for the agreement to arbitrate outside the U.S. to be "cognizable under the Convention," the "reasonable relation" test of FAA § 202 must be satisfied—that is, it is necessary, *even where the arbitration is to be held abroad, to identify some "reasonable relation" that the transaction has with a foreign state;*
- And on this fact pattern, no such "reasonable relation" can be found—"there is no connection with England independent of the" arbitration agreement itself. As the court put it in *Reinholtz*, the argument that the arbitration clause providing for arbitration in London provides the requisite link to another nation is "circular," since "the arbitration agreement itself must possess, not supply, the requisite nexus to a foreign forum to allow a federal court to assert jurisdiction under the Convention."

However, both of these propositions may be in tension with the language and structure of the Convention's Art. I(1), which provides:

> This Convention shall apply to the recognition and enforcement of arbitral awards made in the territory of a State other than the State where the recognition and enforcement of such awards are sought, and arising out of differences between persons, whether physical or legal. It shall also apply to arbitral awards not considered as domestic awards in the State where their recognition and enforcement are sought.

The second sentence of Art. I(1) was added to create category of awards that a state may choose to treat as "non-domestic"—and which *by definition* can apply only in those cases where enforcement is sought in the country *where the award was rendered.* When the Convention was being drafted, one delegation proposed an amendment to exclude from the Convention some awards rendered abroad but nevertheless considered by the enforcing state as "domestic"; this amendment was rejected by over two-thirds of the votes cast. Thus, the applicability of the Convention to awards handed down in another state "does not depend on the existence of any factor connecting the [dispute] with a foreign state. This is not unreasonable as domestic disputes are not seldom referred to foreign arbitration which appears to be particularly well-suited to accommodate the needs of a specific trade." 1 Giorgio Gaja, International Commercial Arbitration: New York Convention at I.A.3 & n.17 (1984). So FAA § 202's exclusion of awards "entirely between citizens of the United States" unless their "relationship involves property located abroad, envisages performance or enforcement abroad, or has some other

agreement did not meet the reasonable relationship requirement of 9 U.S.C. 202 because the legal relationship at issue, the parties' ownership and operation of the company which had no property or operations in a foreign state, was completely domestic; court did not order arbitration anywhere); Armstrong v. NCL (Bahamas) Ltd., 998 F. Supp. 2d 1335 (S.D. Fla. 2013)(denying Bahamian employer's motion to compel arbitration in the U.S. under Bahamian law, as a Seaman who fell from stage on which he was performing while aboard a ship brought action in state court against his employer. The court held a provision in the employee's employment agreement stating arbitration must occur under Bahamian Law in the county of citizenship of the employee (the United States) was unenforceable because the parties' relationship did not have sufficient foreign nexus for removal jurisdiction under the Convention on Recognition and Enforcement of Foreign Arbitral Award because the plaintiff worked only aboard the ship and was never requested to perform work or services on foreign soil; court did not order arbitration anywhere.).

reasonable relation with one or more foreign states" could be read to define the scope of "non-domestic" awards *rendered within the United States*—and not limit the obligation to enforce awards rendered elsewhere, such as London.

As for the proposition that two U.S. parties agreeing to arbitrate in England lack connection with England independent of the agreement itself, Ian R. Macneil, et al., Federal Arbitration Law § 44.9.4 (1999), ask: "If an agreement to arbitrate in a foreign jurisdiction and under its laws does not 'envisage . . . enforcement abroad' [within the language of 202], what does?"

In *Brier*, a magistrate judge—after first rejecting the assertion that the contract was a product of fraud or coercion—found that since the arbitration clause "failed to satisfy the foreign relation requirement" of § 202, it was therefore "unenforceable and invalid." It apparently followed that it was "impossible" for the court even to stay the litigation under § 3 of the FAA; the owner was allowed to proceed to discovery. In *Reinholtz*, the court granted summary judgment to the salvors as to liability and "deferred resolution of the issue of damages * * * until trial." The sweeping implication of both cases, then, is that arbitration agreements and awards that do not fall within the Convention are simply dead letters—and that the court may therefore itself proceed to determine salvage. In contrast, an alternative position is that even if an agreement is not sufficiently "international" to be enforced by the NY Convention, it can be enforced under the domestic FAA.

d. AWARDS MADE IN THE U.S. BUT "NOT CONSIDERED AS DOMESTIC"

In addition to generally making enforceable in United States courts arbitration awards rendered in another Contracting State, the New York Convention also applies to awards made in the United States if those awards are "not considered as domestic."[30] As an oft-cited Second Circuit case, *Bergesen v. Joseph Muller Corp.*,[31] put it,

> awards "not considered as domestic" denotes awards which are subject to the Convention not because made abroad, but because made within the legal framework of another country, e.g., pronounced in accordance with foreign law or involving parties domiciled or having their principal place of business outside the enforcing jurisdiction.[32]

An award rendered in the United States may be "not considered as domestic" (and thus governed by the New York Convention) even if the arbitration was between United States citizens, so long as it involved performance abroad. See Lander Co.,

---

[30] New York Convention, art. I(1) ("This Convention * * * shall also apply to arbitral awards not considered as domestic awards in the State where their recognition and enforcement are sought.").

[31] 710 F.2d 928, 932 (2d Cir.1983).

[32] Id. at 932. See also Ledee v. Ceramiche Ragno, 684 F.2d 184, 187 (1st Cir.1982) (relevant question is "Is a party to the agreement not an American citizen, or does the commercial relationship have some reasonable relation with one or more foreign states?"); Kaliroy Produce Co., Inc. v. Pacific Tomato Growers, Inc., 730 F.Supp.2d 1036, 1039 (D.Ariz.2010) (award rendered in Arizona "is non-domestic and within the scope of the Convention" because the case "involves one foreign party (ALP) and two domestic parties (PTG and Kaliroy), and principally involved conduct and contract performance in the United States and Mexico. Moreover, the Tribunal applied Arizona law in issuing the Award."); Matter of Arbitration Between Trans Chemical Ltd. and China Nat. Machinery Import and China National Machinery Import and Export Corp., 978 F.Supp. 266, 297 (S.D.Tex.1997) ("adopt[ing] the Bergesen definition of 'nondomestic' as encompassing actions to confirm arbitration awards rendered in the United States between two foreign parties.").

Inc. v. MMP Investments, Inc., 107 F.3d 476, 482 (7th Cir.1997) (agreement between two U.S. companies by which one was to become the exclusive distributor of the other's products in Poland; arbitration to take place in New York; court held governed by both the Convention and the FAA). Accord Freudensprung v. Offshore Technical Services, Inc., 379 F.3d 327, 341 (5th Cir.2004); Bergesen v. Joseph Muller Corp., 710 F.2d 928, 934 (2d Cir.1983) ("no reason to assume that Congress did not intend to provide overlapping coverage between the Convention and the Federal Arbitration Act.").

Why would it even matter whether, in some abstract sense, the Convention "applies" to awards rendered within the United States? After all, where an arbitration is to take place within the U.S., doesn't the FAA already provide a ready framework within which courts enforce arbitration agreements and awards? What is the significance, then, for such arbitrations, of the scheme of the Convention? The answer is that there are a number of ways in which the enforcement scheme of the Convention may differ from that of the "domestic" FAA. And while some of these disparities are of marginal or disappearing significance, others may have real impact.

Perhaps the greatest significance of the Convention for U.S. arbitrations is with respect to the jurisdiction of federal courts. Section 3.C.2.c showed that the domestic FAA confers no subject matter jurisdiction, so a plaintiff in federal court seeking to compel arbitration or to confirm an award must point to an independent source of federal jurisdiction, such as diversity of citizenship. By contrast, a case falling within the New York Convention is automatically "deemed to arise under the laws and treaties of the United States"—so federal courts have jurisdiction to entertain such motions even in the absence of diversity and regardless of the amount in controversy. See FAA § 203. In addition, the rights given by FAA § 205 to state court defendants, allowing them to remove to federal court cases falling within the Convention, are considerably broader than rights under the general federal removal statute (28 U.S.C. § 1441).

Application of the New York Convention may also matter with respect to the time to confirm an award. Section 9 of the FAA provides that a party may apply for an order confirming the award "at any time within one year after the award is made." The Second Circuit holds that this is a statute of limitations, so summary confirmation under the statute is barred after a year has passed.[33] In contrast, under the Convention, a motion to confirm may be made within three years after the award.

Finally, when a court grants an order compelling arbitration under § 4 of the FAA, it must direct the parties to arbitrate "in accordance with the terms of

[33] Photopaint Technologies, LLC v. Smartlens Corp., 335 F.3d 152, 155–60 (2d Cir. 2003) ("Our construction of the text is not inevitable, but it is intuitive: for example, tax returns may be filed anytime up to April 15, but one senses at once that the phrase is permissive only up to a point"; moreover, "this result advances important values of finality"). In contrast, three circuits permit confirmation after the one-year period of § 9. An award that has been neither confirmed nor vacated has the same effect as a contract between the parties, so it can still be the subject of an ordinary action on the contract, even after the time for making a statutory motion to confirm has expired. Courts that find the one-year period in § 9 to be merely "permissive" rely on the fact that "an action at law remains a viable alternative to confirmation proceedings"; as a consequence, they hold, "reading § 9 as a strict statute of limitations would be an exercise in futility," Sverdrup Corp. v. WHC Constructors Inc., 989 F.2d 148, 151 (4th Cir. 1993). See also Wachovia Sec., Inc. v. Gangale, 125 Fed.Appx. 671, 676 (6th Cir. 2005); Val-U Const. Co. of S.D. v. Rosebud Sioux Tribe, 146 F.3d 573, 581 (8th Cir. 1998).

agreement." However, § 4 also provides that the arbitration proceedings ordered by the court "shall be within the district in which the petition for an order directing such arbitration is filed." These two provisions must be taken together: So where an arbitration agreement calls for arbitration to take place in New York, a federal district court in Texas may under § 4 lack any power to compel arbitration at all: Arbitration in New York would not be "within the district in which the petition" was filed, and arbitration in Texas would not be "in accordance with the terms of the agreement." By contrast, in cases falling within the Convention, any court with jurisdiction over the parties is empowered to order that arbitration be held "in accordance with the agreement at any place therein provided for, whether that place is within or without the United States." See FAA § 206. See also Oil Basins Ltd. v. Broken Hill Proprietary Co. Ltd., 613 F.Supp. 483, 487 (S.D.N.Y.1985) (§ 4 is superseded by § 206 only "to the extent that the parties specify an arbitration site in the contract"; where "no place was specified explicitly or implicitly," court could order the parties to arbitrate only in its own district).

QUESTIONS TO REVIEW AND SYNTHESIZE

1. The New York Convention's applicability to foreign arbitration agreements and awards is subject to what two important exceptions in United States courts?
2. What is sovereign immunity and how is it related to international arbitration?

2. NATIONAL LAW

a. IMPLEMENTING LEGISLATION

International commercial arbitration is governed not only by the New York Convention and other treaties, but also by national arbitration law. "In virtually all Contracting States, the New York Convention has been implemented through national legislation."[34] While many States have implemented the New York Convention by adopting the United Nations Commission for International Trade Law (UNCITRAL) Model Law on International Arbitration,[35] the United States has not.[36] Instead, the United States legislation implementing the New York Convention is Chapter 2 of the FAA.[37] The United States legislation implementing the Panama Convention is Chapter 3 of the FAA.[38] These chapters of the FAA are the core of the United States' national law on international commercial arbitration. In addition, one might say Chapter 1 of the FAA also implements the New York and Panama Conventions because FAA Chapters 2 and 3 provide that "Chapter 1 applies to actions and proceedings brought under this chapter to the extent that chapter is not in conflict with this chapter or the Convention as ratified by the United States." 9 U.S.C. §§ 208, 307. Finally, U.S. law on international commercial arbitration

---

[34] Gary B. Born, International Commercial Arbitration 99 (2009).

[35] See https://uncitral.un.org/en/texts/arbitration/modellaw/commercial_arbitration/status (table displaying all of the States that have adopted UNCITRAL.)

[36] However, California, Texas and a few other U.S. states have enacted the UNCITRAL Model Law. *Id.*

[37] 9 U.S.C. §§ 201–08.

[38] 9 U.S.C. §§ 301–07.

includes a substantial body of case law. This case law has grown large enough that the American Law Institute has produced a Restatement on The United States Law of International Commercial Arbitration.[39]

If an arbitration agreement or award is covered by (within the scope of) the New York Convention or other treaty then the treaty might be expected to supersede any conflicting national law. But national courts have not always readily subordinated their national laws to the treaties. See Margaret L. Moses, The Principles and Practice of International Commercial Arbitration 25 (3d ed.2017) (the New York Convention "should supercede domestic law regarding the proper form of an arbitration agreement. However, State courts have not always viewed the Convention as superceding their domestic law.") For example, the United States Supreme Court has held "that an Act of Congress * * * is on a full parity with a treaty, and that when a statute which is subsequent in time is inconsistent with a treaty, the statute to the extent of conflict renders the treaty null." Breard v. Greene, 523 U.S. 371, 376 (1998) (quotations omitted). At least one court has refused to enforce an international commercial arbitration award on constitutional grounds. See Base Metal Trading, Ltd. v. OJSC "Novokuznetsky Aluminium Factory," 283 F.3d 208, 214, 211 (4th Cir. 2002) (action to confirm a foreign arbitration award dismissed for lack of personal jurisdiction; "[D]ue process requires Base Metal to establish that NKAZ's contacts with Maryland are 'continuous and systematic.' Yet, sufficient minimum contacts are simply not present in this case").[40] In sum, "the practical effect" of the New York Convention depends on national law—including case law interpreting the Convention and statutes implementing it—and therefore varies from State to State.[41] With national law on arbitration continuing to vary from State to State, cases can turn on the question of which State's arbitration law governs. This question is generally determined by the seat of arbitration.

b. WHICH STATE'S ARBITRATION LAW?: THE "SEAT" OF ARBITRATION

The place (or "seat") of an international commercial arbitration is significant because, under widely recognized choice-of-law principles, the seat State's *arbitration* law governs the dispute even if some other state's *substantive* law governs the underlying contract and merits of the dispute. In other words, an arbitration clause may be governed by a different body of law than the overall contract in which it is embedded. See, e.g., Gulf Petro Trading Co. v. Nigerian Nat. Petroleum Corp., 288 F. Supp. 2d 783, 793 (N.D. Tex. 2003), aff'd, 115 F. App'x 201 (5th Cir. 2004)(parties "contracted that their disputes would be arbitrated in Switzerland, applying Nigerian law"); Deutsche Schachtbau-Und Tiefbohrgesellschaft v. Ras Al Khaimah National Oil Co., [1987] 2 Lloyd's L. Rep. 246 (C.A.), rev'd on other grounds, [1988] 2 Lloyd's Law Rep. 293 (H.L. 1988) (ICC arbitration held in Geneva; even if "the proper law of the substantive contract" was the law of Ras Al Khaimah, United Arab Emirates, where the contract was to

[39] See http://www.ali.org/index.cfm?fuseaction=projects.proj_ip&projectid=20. See George A. Bermann, Jack J. Coe, Jr., Christopher R. Drahozal & Catherine A. Rogers, *Restating the U.S. Law of International Commercial Arbitration*, 113 Penn St. L. Rev. 1333 (2009).

[40] For contrary authority on that personal jurisdiction issue, see Christopher R. Drahozal, Commercial Arbitration: Cases and Problems 620–22 (3d ed.2013).

[41] Gary B. Born, International Commercial Arbitration 99 (2009).

be performed, "the proper law of the arbitration" was Swiss; "an arbitration agreement constitutes a self-contained contract collateral or ancillary to the substantive agreement and * * * not be governed by the same law as that agreement"); XL Ins. Ltd. v. Owens Corning, [2000] 2 Lloyd's L. Rep. 500 (Q.B.) ("parties' freedom of choice includes freedom to choose different systems of law to govern different aspects of their relationship").

The many possible issues likely governed by the seat's arbitration law include arbitrator selection, the arbitration process, and the enforcement (confirmation) or setting aside (vacatur) of the arbitration award.[42] With the seat's arbitration law governing all this, the choice of seat may be a topic of negotiation at the time parties are forming an arbitration agreement. "Parties will tend to choose a country that is not the place of business of either party, so they will be in a 'neutral' forum."[43] The seat can, many authorities suggest, be different from where the arbitration hearing actually occurs. If, for example, the parties want English arbitration law to apply, they can contractually designate England as the seat of arbitration and then hold the arbitration hearings in some other country.[44]

The parties' contract can select the seat of arbitration directly by naming it or indirectly by delegating the choice to the arbitration organization selected to administer the arbitration, such as the International Chamber of Commerce. See, e.g., United States Lines, Inc. v. Liverpool & London Steamship Protection & Indemnity Ass'n, Ltd., 833 F.Supp. 350 (S.D.N.Y.1993) (arbitration clause did not specify venue but provided that if the parties could not agree on an arbitrator, the arbitrator was to be appointed by the President of the Law Society of England; "the Law Society has made it clear that its practice would be to appoint an English arbitrator, and that arbitrator would decide whether England or the United States is the more appropriate venue"; held, parties are "directed to arbitrate at the time and place set by the arbitrator" named by the Law Society).

Another such organization is the American Arbitration Association. When the AAA's International Centre for Dispute Resolution decides the seat (or "locale") of arbitration, it will consider:

1. Location of parties and attorneys.
2. Location of witnesses and documents.
3. Location of records.
4. Where the evidence is located (i.e. location of a construction site).
5. Consideration of the relative difficulty in traveling and cost to parties.
6. Place of performance of the contract.
7. Place of previous court actions.

---

[42] Gary B. Born, International Commercial Arbitration 1307–08 (2009).

[43] Margaret L. Moses, The Principles and Practice of International Commercial Arbitration 52 (3d ed. 2017).

[44] "England is one of the leading jurisdictions in the world for international commercial arbitration (the other two top contenders are France and Switzerland)." S.I. Strong, *Border Skirmishes: The Intersection Between Litigation and International Commercial Arbitration*, 2012 J. Disp. Resol. 1, 5 (2012).

8. Location of most appropriate panel.
9. Any other reasonable arguments that might affect the locale determination.[45]

What if the parties neither select the seat of arbitration directly nor by delegating seat-choice to an arbitration organization? If such parties cannot resolve their dispute about where to seat the arbitration they may litigate the question in national courts. However, most States' arbitration laws deny courts the power to select an arbitral seat. Instead, most States' arbitration laws give arbitrators and arbitration organizations the power to select an arbitral seat, but these laws only apply to arbitrations already seated within that State.[46] Accordingly, some States' arbitration laws hold that arbitration clauses that do not specify an arbitral seat or a means of selecting the arbitral seat are invalid. And when national courts do decide the arbitral seat, there is a risk that different States' courts will select different arbitral seats for the same case. See Tonicstar Ltd v. Am. Home Assur. Co. [2004] EWHC 1234 (Q.B.). This case involved parallel judicial proceedings in New York and England, and later requests for arbitration in both England and New York. The English courts issued an antisuit injunction to prevent the respondents from getting a U.S. court to compel arbitration in New York. The English court reasoned that the dispute was more closely connected to England, and that English courts should therefore decide the arbitral seat. Although there was no conflicting US court decision, such a scenario is conceivable.

Gabrielle Kaufmann-Kohler, *Identifying and Applying the Law Governing the Arbitration Procedure: The Role of the Law of the Place of Arbitration*[*]

International Council for Commercial Arbitration,
Congress series no. 9 (Paris/1999), 336, 342–65.

What Is the Place of Arbitration?

So arbitrations are generally governed by the law of the place where they are held. But is the place a legal connection or a physical, geographical location? How is it selected? Can part or even all procedural steps be carried out elsewhere?

Pursuant to Art. 20(1) of the [UNCITRAL Model Law on International Arbitration (see supra Section 5.B.2.a)], the parties are free to select the place of arbitration. They may do so directly or by delegation to an institution. In the absence of an agreement by the parties, the arbitrators have the power to choose the place, which they must do taking into account "the circumstances of the case, including the convenience of the parties". This latter phrase refers to the *legal*

---

[45] American Arbitration Association, Locale Determinations: ICDR, available at https://www.icdr.org/sites/default/files/document_repository/ICDR_IARC_Standards.pdf.

[46] Gary B. Born, International Commercial Arbitration 1704 (2009) ("[T]he absence of agreement on the arbitral seat arguably prevents application of [national arbitration law] statutory mechanisms that empower the arbitrators to select an arbitral seat."). So a court may refuse to select a seat and refuse to grant anyone else the power to select a seat. In sum, circularity or bootstrapping problem arises.

[*] [A revised version of this article appeared as Gabrielle Kaufmann-Kohler, *Le lieu de l'arbitrage à l'aune de la mondialisation: réflexions à propos de deux formes récentes d'arbitrage*, [1998] Rev. de l'arb. 517.—Eds.]

convenience as well, especially to the suitability of the applicable procedural law. Indeed, in addition to its factual significance (the arbitration is in principle expected to be held there), the choice of the place has legal consequences under the Model Law: it determines the applicability of the Model Law and the place of origin of the award for enforcement purposes.

According to the second paragraph of Art. 20, subject to the parties' contrary agreement, the arbitral tribunal may meet at any place it considers appropriate "for consultation among its members, for hearing witnesses, experts or the parties, or for inspection of goods, other property or documents". * * * [A]ll stages of the arbitration are covered in [this] version. Therefore, an arbitration may take place in its entirety outside the place of arbitration, which is reduced to "nothing but a fiction."

Recognizing that the Model Law attached legal consequences to the "constructive" place of arbitration determined pursuant to Art. 20(1) and that no "genuine link" was required between that place and the actual location of the proceedings, Norway made a proposal during drafting, pursuant to which the "constructive" place of the arbitration would lack at least part of its legal consequences, if "there is no genuine link between that place and the actual arbitral proceedings". The proposal was not followed up and the provision was adopted without a requirement for any kind of link between the "constructive" and the actual place of arbitration. This makes sense: the constructive place is often chosen for its neutrality, i.e., for its absence of connection to either party, while the actual place may be chosen precisely for the opposite reason, because it shows a link to a party due, for instance, to the presence of witnesses.

There was general agreement about the contents of Art. 20 when it was drafted. Hence, the countries adopting the Model Law enacted it without significant changes. Germany, as a newcomer to the Model Law club, deserves a special mention. Its Sect. 1043 ZPO is almost identical to Art. 20. Schlosser views the second paragraph (allowing that procedural steps be taken abroad) as a hidden way out of the rigidity of the territorial connection newly adopted by German arbitration law, since the entire proceedings can be conducted abroad.[53]

Recent non-Model Law legislations provide the same rules. Among these, English law calls for a particular comment. Sect. 3 of the English Arbitration Act 1996 expressly states that the seat in the meaning of the Act is a legal, juridical connection. In *Naviera Amazonica Peruana SA v. Compañia Internacional de Seguros del Peru*, Lord Justice Kerr for the English Court of Appeal had emphasized the "distinction between the legal localisation of an arbitration on the one hand and the appropriate or convenient geographical locality for hearings of arbitration on the other hand".[55] This distinction is confirmed by Sects. 43 and 2(3)(a) of the

[53] This is how I understand the statement that it is not necessary for parties and arbitrators *ever* to meet in Germany for the arbitration to be German. See also F.A. Mann, "Where is an Award Made?", Arbitration International (1985) p. 107 et seq. (the award is made at the arbitral seat, which is "by no means necessarily identical with the place or places where hearings are being held" or, further, which is "independent of the place of meetings of the arbitrators, hearings with the parties").

[55] Decision of 10 November 1987, *Yearbook* XIII (1988) p. 157. The same decision confirms that * * * there is a presumption that the law of the place where the arbitration is held has the strongest connection

Act, which permit a court to secure attendance of witnesses present in the United Kingdom, provided the hearing takes place there, even though the seat of the arbitration is located abroad.

Similarly, the Swiss Supreme Court has recently stressed the same distinction, as well as the legal nature of the place or seat:

> By choosing a Swiss legal domicile [*ein schweizerisches Rechtsdomizil*] for the arbitral tribunal, the parties manifestly intended to submit their dispute to Swiss arbitration law, not to provide for an exclusive location for meetings among arbitrators at the place of arbitration. . . . [T]he determination of a given place of arbitration is of significance to the extent that the award is deemed to be rendered at such place. It is irrelevant that a hearing was effectively held or that the award was effectively issued there.

Indeed, although there is no statutory provision to this effect, it is generally accepted that hearings and meetings in a Swiss arbitration may take place outside of Switzerland.

Most major arbitration rules confirm the parties' freedom to choose the place of arbitration and the possibility to hold meetings and hearings elsewhere. * * * Interestingly, the 1998 ICC (International Chamber of Commerce) Rules contain new provisions on this very subject. Pursuant to Art. 14(2) and (3), the arbitral tribunal may "after consultation with the parties, conduct hearings and meetings at any location it considers appropriate, unless otherwise agreed by the parties" and "deliberate at any location it considers appropriate". This codifies existing practice and confirms the broad consensus found in recent legislations.

Sports Arbitration

Before our traveller brings his sightseeing memories home, he will make two additional stops: one at the Olympic Games and one in cyberspace. Let us start with the Olympics.

The Court of Arbitration for Sport (CAS) is an arbitration institution dealing with the resolution of international disputes related to sports. [See Section 2.B.4] * * *

CAS has its main office in Lausanne and local offices in the USA and in Australia, which provide the logistics for proceedings held locally and managed in consultation with the main office. In addition, CAS sets up a special arbitration body for the duration of the Olympic Games, which resolves all disputes arising during the Games on site, as a rule within 24 hours. * * *

Wherever a CAS arbitration takes place physically, [CAS rules provide that] it always has its legal place or seat in Lausanne. This applies to all CAS arbitrations, wherever the hearings take place, whether they are managed by the Lausanne office exclusively or in conjunction with a decentralized office, and it includes arbitrations handled on the site of the Olympic Games.

---

and should thus govern and vice versa (i.e., a choice of a given procedural law implies a choice of a place). * * *

There are three main reasons for the choice of a sole seat, regardless of the actual place of arbitration. First, that choice provides a uniform procedural regime for all CAS arbitrations, not only in terms of applicable rules under the Code, but also with respect to the arbitration law governing the proceedings. The Games move around, but the legal framework is stable.

Second, conducting the arbitration at the site of the Games is intended to make arbitration as convenient as possible for the parties and to resolve disputes as expeditiously as possible. It is not meant to have any legal significance.

Third, the equal treatment so achieved is consistent with the equal standards that govern the activities giving rise to disputes, i.e., sports competition. A time on a stopwatch is the same wherever the race takes place. It is further consistent—which may be of even greater significance here—with the choice of substantive law governing sports disputes. According to Art. 17 of the CAS ad hoc Rules, the arbitral tribunal must resolve the dispute "pursuant to the Olympic Charter, the applicable regulations, general principles of law and the rules of law, the application of which it deems appropriate".

All these sets of rules (except possibly for the last one, which in practice never comes to bear) are transnational, universal, global. Their application is not dependent on a territorial nexus, nor is it restricted territorially. This global substantive law is matched by a uniform procedural law thanks to the choice of a sole seat for all CAS arbitrations.

* * *

[T]he example of sports arbitration is striking because it demonstrates that the legal place of an arbitration can become pure fiction for perfectly legitimate reasons.

Online Arbitration

Leaving the Olympics, the traveller now takes the leap into cyberspace to observe that online arbitration is just another illustration of a purely fictional (or fictitious?) place of arbitration.

Imagine an arbitration where the request [for arbitration] and later written pleadings are filed, procedural orders issued, and all other communications sent by electronic mail, where procedural hearings take the form of so-called "chats" (even if the term is not really flattering . . .), and witnesses are heard by videoconference.

An unreal, imaginary world? No. Although still very limited in scope, several dispute resolution mechanisms of this kind already exist.* * * * Another example of online dispute resolution are the proposed [World Intellectual Property Organization] WIPO-administered Internet domain name procedures.

Where do online arbitrations physically take place? "In cyberspace" is an easy, but wrong answer: cyberspace is misnamed, "there is no 'there' there", no space, simply a telecommunication network. So where then? Nowhere? Or at the places where the participants access the network? Maybe, but for purposes of connection to a given arbitration law, such a plurilocalization is highly impracticable. The real problem is that on the Internet our traditional concept of place, which implies space, distances, territories, borders, is meaningless. There is no such thing as a physical place of online arbitrations.[98] If the territorial connection is to stand, then we are left to rely on a legal place, which by essence will be nothing but a fiction.

* * *

Virtual arbitration is not limited to full online arbitrations administered by specialized institutions. Tribunals in conventional "real-space" arbitrations, are starting to use electronic communication tools too, for instance to hear a far away witness unable to travel or to save travel expenses.

Because it saves time and costs, which are major concerns to present-day users of arbitration, it is likely that electronic communication will increasingly be used in arbitrations. WIPO intends to make its online mechanism available for intellectual property arbitrations other than domain name disputes. * * * And "traditional" arbitrators, even if they are no computer freaks, will increasingly resort to new telecommunication facilities.

* * *

A Paradox which Fosters Uniformity

Having returned from his trip, the traveler tells of two main evolutions. First, the territorial connection nowadays prevails, primarily because it is easy to handle and provides certainty. In other words, to identify the law applicable to the arbitration procedure, one must define the place of arbitration. Second, that place is increasingly viewed as a fiction which has no necessary connection to the physical location of the proceedings. This trend is evident, even if in the great majority of cases the legal place still coincides with the physical location. With the continuing globalization of the world and the changes brought about by the technological revolution, this evolution cannot but gain in importance. * * * The choice of a place ends up being nothing but a choice of the law governing the arbitration. It delocalizes the arbitration proceedings, removing the authority of the local lex arbitri and the powers of the local courts to supervise the proceedings and set aside the award.

Delocalization, denationalization, deterritorialization gave rise to passionate arguments a number of years ago. Will the once-heated debate be revived by phenomena such as online, Olympic or similar delocalized arbitrations?

If it is accepted that the (legal) place may be a fiction, then the issue of delocalization becomes moot, because delocalization is in fact achieved, though indirectly. One of the main purposes of delocalization as it was once discussed was to eliminate the unintended effects of peculiarities of the law of the place where the arbitration happened to be held. By the choice of an arbitration-friendly fictional place of arbitration, that goal is fully met. It is not threatened by uncertainties or conflicts about competent courts, if courts consistently apply the concept of a legal place or seat and accept jurisdiction in aid and control of arbitration only at that place. * * * [If] by way of the choice of a place, one can avoid inhospitable features of the law where the dispute is physically heard, then denationalization loses much of its practical interest. Not to speak of the fact that

[98] At best, if one really insists on determining a place, there are multiple places, which is of little help to identify the applicable law.

the increasing uniformity of arbitration laws makes the search for hospitable fora less of a necessity.

* * *

Conclusion and Outlook

At the close of his journey, the traveller cannot but conclude that the role of the law of the place of arbitration keeps decreasing. Based on his observations, one can see four reasons for this decline. First, in a "global village", geographical places tend to be immaterial. The activities giving rise to disputes are increasingly globalized; technological communication means abolish distances; the place is becoming a non-issue.

Second, legal places follow suit, with a growing acceptance of the place as a pure fiction and a powerful wave of uniformization of arbitration laws, which tend to become interchangeable.

Third, this uniformization process goes together with a general consensus over two hard-core principles of arbitration law, procedural autonomy and its due process limitation.

Fourth and last is * * * the emergence of a worldwide arbitration culture, which runs parallel to the normalization of arbitral proceedings and—if this writer can be forgiven the term—the "standardization" of the international arbitrator.

The notion that CAS arbitrations necessarily have their "site" in Lausanne was first tested in the New South Wales Court of Appeal, in Australia, in 2000. The Judo Federation of Australia (JFA) had nominated Angela Raguz as a member of the 2000 Australian Olympic Team in the women's under/52 kg category. The nomination was challenged by Rebecca Sullivan, another member of the "JFA Shadow Team," who alleged that she was entitled to the nomination on the grounds of selection criteria contained in an agreement between the JFA and the Australian Olympic Committee (AOC). After an internal JFA Appeal Tribunal rejected the challenge, Sullivan initiated an arbitration proceeding with the CAS office in Sydney. A hearing took place in Sydney 24 days later, and at the end of the hearing, the panel announced its decision in favor of Sullivan: After finding that the selection of Raguz had been in error—that the "points" awarded Sullivan throughout her competitions had been added incorrectly—the panel ordered the JFA to nominate Sullivan to the team instead of Raguz.

Raguz challenged the award in the Australian courts. In order to be eligible for selection to the Olympic Team, each athlete had been required to sign a Team Membership Agreement; the court had no difficulty in finding that by doing so, each had become a party to an "integrated scheme"—including a consent to CAS arbitration—which bound the JFA, the AOC, "and all the relevant athletes." The Team Membership Agreement provided that any decision of the CAS "will be final and binding on the parties and * * * neither party will institute or maintain proceedings in any court or tribunal other than [the CAS]."

The critical problem was the jurisdiction of the courts of Australia: Under Australian legislation, a court could entertain an appeal on a question of law arising out of an arbitral award, unless (1) there was an "exclusion agreement" which "excludes the right of appeal," and (2) if the arbitration agreement was a "domestic arbitration agreement"—that is, one that "does not provide, expressly or by implication, for arbitration *in a country other than Australia*." It was apparent that the CAS arbitration clause did in fact constitute an "exclusion agreement"—but was the agreement a "domestic" one? The court concluded that it was not: The legislation, it held, was concerned "with the legal place of the arbitration"—a "juridical concept"—rather than the "physical place of the arbitration." The statutory scheme of judicial review should not change every time there was a "temporary change of hearing venue"; the legislature obviously wished to permit parties "to select a single legal place of arbitration and to leave the choice of the physical location of hearings to the felt necessities of a specific dispute." Since under the CAS rules the "seat" of every CAS panel was deemed be Lausanne Switzerland, the "exclusion agreement" was valid, and so the appeal was dismissed. Raguz v. Sullivan, [2000] NSWCA 240; 15(10) Mealey's Int'l Arb. Rep. (Oct. 2000), at p. D-1.

QUESTIONS TO REVIEW AND SYNTHESIZE

1. What determines the seat of an international commercial arbitration?
2. What makes the seat important?
3. The CAS example showed what benefits of being able to hold arbitration hearings anywhere while keeping Lausanne, Switzerland the seat for all CAS arbitrations?

C. FORMATION OF ENFORCEABLE INTERNATIONAL COMMERCIAL ARBITRATION AGREEMENTS

1. COURTS REFER THE PARTIES TO ARBITRATION

In addition to the critical obligation to enforce foreign arbitration *awards*, the New York Convention, in Art. II, obligates each contracting state to "recognize an agreement in writing" under which the parties have agreed to arbitrate a dispute "concerning a subject matter capable of settlement by arbitration." Where a court is "seized of an action in respect of which the parties have made" an arbitration agreement, then the court must "refer the parties to arbitration, unless it finds that the said agreement is null and void, inoperative or incapable of being performed."

The phrase "refer to arbitration" "[lacks] a precise legal meaning" so the Convention merely "mandates a result but leaves Contracting States free as to the means by which they are to achieve it."[47] Outside of common-law countries, the usual method for a court to give effect to an arbitration agreement is to *dismiss* an action or to "declare that it has no jurisdiction"; by contrast, in common law countries statutes more commonly provide that a court shall *stay* judicial proceedings pending the completion of the arbitration proceedings.[48] FAA § 3

[47] Aron Broches, *The 1985 UNCITRAL Model Law on International Commercial Arbitration: An Exercise in International Legislation*, 18 Netherlands Yrbk. of Int'l Law 3, 16–17 (1987).

[48] See Restatement (Third) of International Commercial Arbitration § 2.1 (Am. Law Inst. 2017) ("(b) A court enforces an international arbitration agreement by either or both of the following: (1) staying or

provides for a stay, rather than dismissal, and some American courts have found that a stay pending arbitration is an appropriate method in Convention cases of "referring" the parties to arbitration.[49] In other cases—where there is perhaps "no question" as to the arbitrability of the claims and "it appears that the grant of a stay serves no function other than that of postponing the inevitable dismissal of such actions until the completion of arbitration"—dismissal for "lack of subject matter jurisdiction" may be the appropriate means of complying with the Convention.[50] In contrast, other U.S. courts hold "the plain language of § 3 affords a district court no discretion to dismiss a case where one of the parties applies for a stay pending arbitration."[51]

2. ARBITRATION AGREEMENT THAT IS "NULL AND VOID, INOPERATIVE OR INCAPABLE OF BEING PERFORMED"

New York Convention, Art. II, allows a court to refuse to enforce an arbitration agreement that it finds to be "null and void, inoperative or incapable of being performed." What does this mean? If, as is likely, differing national laws have varying requirements concerning the validity of arbitration clauses, what body of law will then determine whether the agreement is enforceable?

For example, suppose that an arbitration agreement provides for arbitration to take place in Italy. One party sues in the United States; the defendant moves to compel arbitration, and the plaintiff argues that the arbitration agreement is not enforceable under Italian law. The agreement fails to comply with Italian law, plaintiff asserts, because under Italian law arbitration clauses are unenforceable (a) where the agreement does not appear above the signatures of both parties, (b) if all of the defendants to a lawsuit are not parties to the agreement, or (c) if they call for an even number of arbitrators. In such circumstances, some courts in the United States have nevertheless stayed the litigation once they were convinced that an "agreement in writing" exists under *U.S.* law. See Marchetto v. DeKalb Genetics

---

dismissing judicial proceedings regarding a dispute that is subject to the agreement; or (2) compelling arbitration of a dispute that is subject to the agreement.").

[49] Todd v. Steamship Mut. Underwriting Ass'n (Bermuda) Ltd., 601 F.3d 329, 332 (5th Cir. 2010) ("[T]he Convention and its implementing legislation do not explicitly authorize staying litigation pending arbitration, and thus parties whose arbitration agreements fall under the Convention have had to seek authority for stays under 9 U.S.C. § 3, a provision of the domestic FAA.") (internal citations omitted), Aggarao v. MOL Ship Mgmt. Co., 675 F.3d 355, 375 (4th Cir. 2012) ("Because neither the Convention nor the Convention Act prohibits the issuance of a stay of proceedings, the authority conferred in § 3 of the FAA is incorporated into the Convention Act.").

[50] See Filanto, S.p.A. v. Chilewich Int'l Corp., 789 F.Supp. 1229, 1241–42 (S.D.N.Y.1992) (court issued final judgment containing a mandatory injunction to arbitrate and held that staying action and retaining jurisdiction "would serve no purpose" since the entire dispute "will be resolved by arbitration"); *see* Lindo v. NCL (Bahmas), Ltd., 652 F.3d 1257, 1287 (11th Cir. 2011) (affirming order to dismiss plaintiff-appellant's complaint, and affirming district court's order to compel arbitration pursuant to the New York Convention).

[51] Lloyd v. Hovensa, LLC., 369 F.3d 263, 269 (3d Cir.2004). See also Adair Bus Sales, Inc. v. Blue Bird Corp., 25 F.3d 953, 955 (10th Cir.1994) ("where a defendant moved for a stay pending arbitration under 9 U.S.C. § 3, the District court erred in instead entering a dismissal and the proper course would have been to enter the stay"). For the contrary view, see, e.g., Soucy v. Capital Mgmt. Servs., L.P., No. 14 C 5935, 2015 WL 404632, at *6 (N.D. Ill. Jan. 29, 2015) ("The Seventh Circuit . . . has repeatedly affirmed district courts' decisions dismissing suits where all of the claims must be arbitrated according to the agreement."); Knall Bev., Inc. v. Teamsters Local Union No. 293 Pension Plan, 744 F.3d 419, 421 (6th Cir. 2014) ("district court correctly ruled that the Act requires that this claim be arbitrated, and properly dismissed the case without prejudice.").

Corp., 711 F.Supp. 936 (N.D.Ill.1989) ("The possibility that Italian law might divest a panel of Italian arbitrators of jurisdiction is not determinative of this court's duty to enforce an otherwise valid arbitration agreement"; "underlying the Supreme Court's willingness to enforce arbitration agreements is the assumption that signatory nations to the Convention will honor arbitration agreements and reject challenges to arbitration based on legal principles unique to the signatory nation").

Other United States cases similarly apply U.S. law to determine whether the parties have formed an international arbitration agreement.[52] This is understandable, as Article II of the New York Convention provides courts with little guidance about how to determine whether the parties have formed an arbitration agreement. Article II provides no legal rules on mutual assent, offer and acceptance, consideration, or any other topics that might play a role in determining whether the parties have formed an arbitration agreement. Nor does Article II tell courts where to look to find such legal rules. In other words, Article II lacks a choice-of-law rule. It does not say, for example, to apply the law of the State in which the agreement was allegedly formed. Or to apply the law of the State in which the alleged agreement would be performed (the "seat" of arbitration). With all this lacking from Article II, it is understandable that United States courts apply their own national law to determine whether the parties have formed an international arbitration agreement.

On the other hand, several commentators have criticized this practice and tried to develop an alternative approach.[53] This alternative approach begins by noting that:

> Article II's terms reflect the fact that the New York Convention was, until late in its drafting process, directly solely at the recognition of arbitral awards, and not arbitration agreements. When Article II of the Convention was expanded, to require recognition of arbitration agreements, relatively little thought was directed towards choice-of-law or other issues relating to the new provisions.[54]

In contrast, New York Convention Art. V(1)(a) does have a choice-of-law rule on the enforcement of arbitration *awards,* and several commentators would apply this choice-of-law rule also to issues about arbitration agreement formation.[55] For example, Albert Jan van den Berg argues that Art. II "can be deemed to incorporate Art. V(1)(a)," and, failing a contrary designation by the parties, "the law applicable to the arbitration agreement" is "the law of the country where the award *will be made"?* Albert Jan van den Berg, The New York Convention of 1958: Towards a Uniform Judicial Interpretation 127 (1981). Alan Scott Rau sees good sense in concluding that a State's obligations under the Convention are "congruent for both agreements and awards". Alan Scott Rau, *The New York Convention in American Courts*, 7 Amer. Rev. of Int'l Arb. 213, 233 & fn. 81 (1996). However, United States

---

[52] Gary B. Born, International Commercial Arbitration at 461, nn. 252–53.

[53] Id. at 460–66.

[54] Id. at 462.

[55] See id. at nn. 263–64. Article V(1)(a) of the Convention provides that enforcement of an award may be refused if the arbitration "agreement is not valid under the law to which the parties have subjected it or, failing any indication thereon, under the law of the country where the award was made." In other words, under Article V(1)(a)'s choice-of-law rule, the relevant State's law is the law the parties have chosen in a choice-of-law clause ("the law to which the parties have subjected it") or, if there is no party choice of law, then the relevant State's law is the law of the country where the award was made, that is, the "seat" of arbitration.

courts have declined to hold that Art. II incorporates Article V's choice of law rule. Rhone Mediterranee Compagnia Francese Di Assicuraziono E Riassicurazoni v. Achille Lauro, 712 F.2d 50, 53 (3d Cir. 1983) (Article V's choice-of-law rule is not incorporated into Article II(1) because Article II(3)'s ambiguity was "deliberate"); Meadows Indem. Co. v. Baccala & Shoop Ins. Sers., Inc., 760 F.Supp. 1036, 1042 (E.D.N.Y. 1991) (Article II(3) does not incorporate Article V's choice-of-law rule). So United States courts are likely to apply United States law to issues of whether an international arbitration agreement has been formed, except when those issues relate to the one formation topic addressed in the New York Convention, the requirement of a writing.

3. "AGREEMENT IN WRITING"

Under domestic United States law, an oral arbitration agreement is likely unenforceable[56] and many other States' national laws also enforce only written arbitration agreements.[57] Similarly, the New York Convention suggests that only written arbitration agreements are enforceable, as it provides that "Each Contracting State shall recognize an *agreement in writing* under which the parties undertake to submit to arbitration."[58] It then defines "agreement in writing" to "include an arbitral clause in a contract or an arbitration agreement, signed by the parties or contained in an exchange of letters or telegrams."[59]

The reference to "letters or telegrams" evokes the technology of the era in which the Convention was written, over half a century ago. In contrast, international commercial arbitration agreements formed through more-modern electronic communication, such as email, may be enforceable but few reported cases have addressed the question.[60] However, the Convention on the Use of Electronic Communications in International Contracts (ECC)[61] provides that "[w]here the law requires that a communication or a contract should be in writing, or provides consequences for the absence of a writing, that requirement is met by an electronic communication if the information contained therein is accessible so as to be usable

[56] FAA § 2 requires courts to enforce only "written" arbitration agreements, as do most state arbitration statutes. See 9 U.S.C. § 2; Unif. Arbitration Act §§ 1, 2, 7 U.L.A. 102, 240 (2005). "The requirement of a writing of the FAA is distinct from any statute of frauds that might otherwise apply to the transaction." Christopher R. Drahozal, Commercial Arbitration: Cases and Problems 93 (2d ed.2006).

[57] See, e.g., UNCITRAL Model Law, art. 7 (Option I, as amended); Swis PILA, art. 178(I); English Arbitration Act, § 5; French Code of Civil Procedure, art. 1443.

[58] New York Convention, art. II(1).

[59] New York Convention, art. II(2). Whether an "agreement in writing" in fact occurred can be a fact-intensive inquiry. See, e.g., Filanto, S.p.A. v. Chilewich Intern. Corp., 789 F.Supp. 1229, 1236–37 (S.D.N.Y.1992).

[60] See also Chloe Z Fishing Co., Inc. v. Odyssey Re (London) Ltd., 109 F.Supp.2d 1236, 1250 (S.D.Cal.2000) ("Under plaintiffs' unduly restrictive definition, only a written message sent in an envelope with a signature or a message transmitted by telegraph would satisfy the letter and telegram requirements respectively. However, the Court finds that Article II section 2 of the Convention could not have intended to exclude all other forms of written communications regularly utilized to conduct commerce in the various signatory nations by failing to provide an exhaustive list of 'letters' or 'telegrams.'") But see Decision of the Hologaland Court of Appeal, 16 August 1999, Yearbook on Commercial Arbitration XXVII, at 519 (2002) (exchange of emails did not satisfy writing requirement).

[61] G.A. Res. 60/21, U.N. Doc. A/Res/60/21, U.N. Sales No E.07.V.2 (Dec. 9, 2005), available at http://www.uncitral.org/pdf/english/texts/electcom/06-57452_Ebook.pdf.

for subsequent reference." Art.9(2). The ECC applies to the New York Convention. Id. art. 20(1).

Even if the communications technology used by the parties fits within the Convention's definition of "agreement in writing," the arbitration agreement may not be enforceable due to the signature requirement. As noted above, New York Convention Article II(2) defines "agreement in writing" to "include an arbitral clause in a contract or an arbitration agreement, *signed by the parties* or contained in an exchange of letters or telegrams." To what does this signature requirement apply? Most United States courts hold that the signature requirement does not apply to "an exchange of letters or telegrams,"[62] but does apply to both "an arbitral clause in a contract or an arbitration agreement."[63] In other words, most courts hold that the signature requirement applies to both the typical pre-dispute arbitration agreement (the "arbitral clause in a contract") and a standalone "arbitration agreement," which is more often formed post-dispute and called a "submission agreement," but does not apply to an arbitration agreement formed by "an exchange of letters or telegrams." These cases and similar issues under the Panama Convention are summarized in the following case.

Freaner v. Valle

United States District Court, Southern District of California, 2013.
966 F.Supp.2d 1068.

■ JANIS L. SAMMARTINO, DISTRICT JUDGE.

Presently before the Court is Plaintiff Ariel Freaner's ("Plaintiff," or "Freaner") Motion to Compel Arbitration of the 2009 Contract, as well as Defendants Enrique Martin Lutteroth Valle ("Valle") and Hotelera Coral, S.A. de C.V.'s ("Hotelera Coral," and collectively, "Defendants") response in opposition.

* * *

Having considered the parties' arguments and the law, the Court (1) DENIES Freaner's motion to compel arbitration.

* * *

This case arises out of a contract dispute between Freaner, a graphic and web designer in San Diego, California, and Hotelera Coral, a resort hotel located in Baja California, Mexico. On June 23, 2008, the parties entered into a Service Agreement, memorialized in a signed, printed contract, pursuant to which Freaner was to provide marketing services and products to Hotelera Coral, including, among other things, design and development of a new web site, development of advertising

[62] See Standard Bent Glass Corp. v. Glassrobots Oy, 333 F.3d 440, 449–50 (3d Cir.2003).

[63] See id.; Kahn Lucas Lancaster, Inc. v. Lark International Ltd., 186 F.3d 210, 217 (2d Cir.1999) ("Grammatically, the comma immediately following 'an arbitration agreement' serves to separate the series ('an arbitral clause in a contract or an arbitration agreement') from the modifying phrase ('signed by the parties or contained in an exchange of letters or telegrams'), and suggests that the modifying phrase is meant to apply to both elements in the series. Indeed, this comma can serve no other grammatical purpose.") But see Sphere Drake Insurance PLC v. Marine Towing, Inc., 16 F.3d 666, 667–69 (5th Cir.1994) (signature not required to enforce "arbitral clause in a contract").

concepts and strategies, and design and production of print advertising materials. Hotelera Coral was to pay $76,592 to Freaner in six installments.

* * *

The June 2008 Service Agreement also includes a provision requiring the parties to settle their disputes through binding arbitration. The arbitral clause reads as follows:

> Arbitration. Any controversy or claim arising out of or related to this Agreement, or breach thereof, shall be submitted to and resolved by binding arbitration. The arbitration will be conducted in San Diego, California by a single neutral arbitrator and in accordance with the then current rules of the American Arbitration Association. The arbitrator shall have the power to enter any award that could be entered by a judge of the trial court of the State of California, and only such power, and shall follow the law. The parties agree to abide by and perform any award rendered by the arbitrator. The arbitrator shall issue the award in writing and therein shall state the essential findings and conclusions on which the award is based. Judgment on the award may be entered in any court having jurisdiction thereof.

In the Spring of 2009, the parties began negotiating another contract. Freaner initiated the negotiations by sending Defendants a document marked as a proposal, which set forth two alternatives. Defendants reviewed the proposal and the parties subsequently agreed on the first alternative, pursuant to which Freaner would provide specified design and creative services in exchange for $4,000 per month from Hotelera Coral for a 12-month term.

Freaner then sent Defendants a printed contract that incorporated the terms that the parties had discussed. This printed contract contained the same arbitral clause as the June 2008 Service Agreement.

The parties disagree as to the events that followed, as discussed more extensively below. It is undisputed, however, that Defendants never signed the printed contract. It is also undisputed that Defendants began paying Freaner $4,000 per month beginning in July 2009 and that Freaner began providing services as specified in the printed contract.

Around May 2010, Defendants became upset because Freaner failed to deliver print advertising materials that Defendants had requested, and paid for, months earlier. The relationship between the parties broke down shortly thereafter and their agreement was not renewed for the following year.

On March 31, 2011, Freaner sent Defendants a letter demanding compensation for numerous services that he allegedly rendered between June 2008 and October 2010. Freaner alleged that he was entitled to $174,080 in unpaid compensation.

2. Procedural Background

On June 17, 2011, Freaner filed suit for breach of contract in the Superior Court of the State of California for the County of San Diego. In his complaint, he alleged breach of the June 2008 Service Agreement and sought damages in excess of $170,000.

On August 15, 2011, Defendants filed a motion to compel arbitration of Freaner's breach of contract claim. On the same day, Defendants also removed the action to this Court, invoking the Inter-American Convention on International Commercial Arbitration, also known as the Panama Convention, and its implementing legislation, 9 U.S.C. §§ 301–307.

On September 2, 2011, Defendants filed a counterclaim for breach of contract, alleging that Freaner breached the parties' 2009 agreement. On the same day, Freaner filed a motion to compel arbitration of the June 2008 Service Agreement. On September 13, 2011, Freaner filed a motion to remand the action back to Superior Court. On September 27, 2011, Freaner filed an answer to Defendants' counterclaim.

On November 17, 2011, the Court denied Freaner's motion to remand because this action is related to an arbitration agreement falling under the Panama Convention, such that removal was proper under 9 U.S.C. § 205, which is incorporated by reference in cases falling under the Panama Convention by 9 U.S.C. § 302.

* * *

[Freaner commenced] arbitration on March 23, 2012. On that day, Freaner filed an arbitral demand with the AAA's International Centre for Dispute Resolution ("ICDR"). Freaner's arbitral demand sought relief under the June 2008 Service Agreement and under the unsigned, printed contract that Freaner sent to Defendants in 2009.

* * *

Freaner filed his motion to compel arbitration on February 15, 2013. Defendants filed a response in opposition on March 4, 2013 * * *.

MOTION TO COMPEL ARBITRATION

1. Standard of Review

A. *Applicability of the Inter-American Convention on International Commercial Arbitration*

The arbitration clause invoked by Freaner in this action is governed by the Inter-American Convention on International Commercial Arbitration, also known as the Panama Convention. The Panama Convention is an international treaty that provides a regional framework for ensuring that national courts recognize and enforce arbitration agreements and arbitral awards relating to international commercial transactions.

The Panama Convention was originally promulgated on January 30, 1975 and signed by the United States on June 9, 1978. The United States subsequently ratified the Convention on October 9, 1986 and legislation implementing the Convention, now codified as Chapter 3 of the FAA, 9 U.S.C. §§ 301–307, was signed into law on August 15, 1990. The U.S. deposited the ratified treaty with the

Organization of American States ("OAS") on September 27, 1990, and the Convention went into force 30 days later, on October 27, 1990.

The Panama Convention is based, in large part, on the more widely known United Nations Convention on the Recognition and Enforcement of Arbitral Awards of June 10, 1958, also known as the New York Convention. The New York Convention was implemented by legislation now codified at Chapter 2 of the FAA, 9 U.S.C. §§ 201–208. The two Conventions share many of the same features and characteristics and Congress has even indicated that the two Conventions are "intended to achieve the same results." See Energy Transp., Ltd. v. M.V. San Sebastian, 348 F.Supp.2d 186, 198 (S.D.N.Y.2004) (quoting H.R.Rep. No. 101–501, at 4 (1990), reprinted in 1990 U.S.C.C.A.N. 675, 678). The legislation implementing the Panama Convention incorporates by reference several crucial provisions of the legislation implementing the New York Convention, further demonstrating the close relationship between the two Conventions. See 9 U.S.C. § 302 (incorporating by reference §§ 202, 203, 204, 205, and 207).

Although the text of the Panama Convention is largely silent as to the Convention's field of application, this omission is addressed by the implementing legislation. Section 202, incorporated by reference by virtue of Section 302, provides, in relevant part:

> An arbitration agreement or arbitral award arising out of a legal relationship, whether contractual or not, which is considered as commercial . . . falls under the Convention. An agreement or award arising out of such a relationship which is entirely between citizens of the United States shall be deemed not to fall under the Convention unless that relationship involves property located abroad, envisages performance or enforcement abroad, or has some other reasonable relation with one or more foreign states.

This broad definition suggests that most arbitration agreements and arbitral awards relating to international commercial transactions will fall under either the New York or Panama Conventions.

* * *

Section 305 provides that the Panama Convention must apply if "a majority of the parties to the arbitration agreement are citizens of a State or States that have ratified or acceded to the Panama Convention and are member States of the Organization of American States. . . ." In all other cases, Section 305 indicates that the New York Convention must govern.

Here, the alleged arbitration agreement consists of an arbitral clause in a printed contract for design and advertising services between Freaner, a citizen of the United States, and Valle, a citizen of Mexico, as well as Hotelera Coral, an entity incorporated under the laws of Baja California, Mexico. Thus, the arbitration agreement falls under the Panama Convention because (1) it evidences a transaction that is both international and commercial in nature, (2) it does not arise out of a relationship that is entirely between citizens of the United States or, alternatively, it has a reasonable relation to a foreign state, namely, Mexico, (3) it designates the seat of the arbitration as San Diego, California, which lies within the

United States, a nation that has acceded to the Convention, and (4) all parties to the agreement are citizens of States that have acceded to the Convention and are member States of the OAS, namely, the United States and Mexico.

B. *Enforcement of Arbitration Agreements Falling Under the Panama Convention*

The Panama Convention provides that arbitration agreements are presumptively valid. Article 1 of the Convention states: "An agreement in which the parties undertake to submit to arbitral decision any differences that may arise or have arisen between them with respect to a commercial transaction is valid."

The Convention is conspicuously silent, however, as to a court's duty or power to compel arbitration or to stay litigation pending an arbitral proceeding. Similarly, the Convention does not enumerate any grounds upon which a court might refuse to enforce an arbitration agreement, nor does it specify any criteria upon which a court should rely in establishing the substantive validity of such an agreement.

These "lacunae" in the Convention's text are largely addressed by the Convention's implementing legislation. * * * Section 303(a) explicitly authorizes courts to refer parties to arbitration in actions falling under the Panama Convention. Moreover, Section 307 requires the residual application of Chapter 1 of the FAA, the law governing domestic arbitration, so long as it does not conflict with Chapter 3 or with the Panama Convention. See, e.g., Productos Mercantiles E Industriales, S.A. v. Faberge USA, Inc., 23 F.3d 41, 45 (2d Cir.1994).

Accordingly, Section 2 of the FAA, which establishes the substantive validity of domestic arbitration agreements, also applies to arbitration agreements falling under the Panama Convention. * * * Section 2 provides that an arbitration agreement "shall be valid, irrevocable, and enforceable, save upon such grounds as exist at law or in equity for the revocation of any contract."

* * *

2. Analysis

Freaner moves to compel arbitration of Defendants' counterclaim on the ground that the parties' agreement is embodied in a printed contract that includes a binding arbitration clause. Defendants resist arbitration and offer three arguments in support of their position: (1) The arbitral clause contained in the printed contract is invalid under the Panama Convention because the contract is not signed by both parties * * *.

A. *Proper Forum for Resolving Defendant's Jurisdictional Challenges*

Freaner's position in this action is that any challenge to the arbitrator's jurisdiction over the dispute is for the arbitrator to resolve. * * *

The proper forum for resolving disputes regarding an arbitrator's jurisdiction is typically a matter left to the agreement of the parties. See Howsam v. Dean Witter Reynolds, 537 U.S. 79, 82–3, 123 S.Ct. 588, 154 L.Ed.2d 491 (2002); First Options of Chi., Inc. v. Kaplan, 514 U.S. 938, 943–45, 115 S.Ct. 1920, 131 L.Ed.2d 985 (1995). It is presumed, however, that parties have not agreed to arbitrate disputes regarding the existence or validity of an arbitration agreement. Howsam, 537 U.S. at 83, 123 S.Ct. 588; First Options, 514 U.S. at 945, 115 S.Ct. 1920. This presumption may only be overcome by "clear and unmistakable" evidence. First Options, 514 U.S. at 945, 115 S.Ct. 1920.

The proper forum for resolving jurisdictional disputes also depends, in large part, on the type of jurisdictional challenge advanced by the party resisting arbitration. * * * Arguments that challenge the validity or legality of a contract as a whole do not impeach a related arbitration clause and are typically considered appropriate for arbitral resolution. See Buckeye Check Cashing, Inc. v. Cardegna, 546 U.S. 440, 449, 126 S.Ct. 1204, 163 L.Ed.2d 1038 (2006). Similarly, arguments that generally challenge *both* the contract as a whole *and* the arbitration clause should be initially determined by the arbitrator. Id. On the other hand, arguments that specifically challenge the validity or legality of the arbitration agreement, as distinguished from the contract as a whole, call into question the legitimacy of the arbitrator's role and so are presumptively for judicial determination. See id.; First Options, 514 U.S. at 943–44, 115 S.Ct. 1920.

Importantly, however, arguments that deny the very *existence* of a contract follow a different line of reasoning. See Buckeye, 546 U.S. at 444 n. 1, 126 S.Ct. 1204 ("The issue of the contract's validity is different from the issue whether any agreement between the alleged obligor and obligee was ever concluded."). Although such challenges are directed at both the contract and the arbitration clause, they are nonetheless unfit for arbitral resolution because it is "virtually impossible" to conceive how a party advancing such an argument could be said to have agreed to arbitrate the question of the arbitrator's jurisdiction. * * * For this reason, a fundamental dispute regarding contract formation is presumptively for judicial resolution, absent other compelling reasons to allow the arbitrator to consider such a challenge. * * *

Here, Defendants' challenges to the arbitrator's jurisdiction are all appropriate for judicial resolution. First, the Panama Convention appears to establish formal validity as a gateway issue that a court must decide prior to referring a matter to arbitration. See Article 1 of the Panama Convention. Moreover, a challenge to the formal validity of an arbitration agreement is best characterized as a challenge directed specifically at the arbitration agreement, rather than at the contract as a whole. Such a challenge is therefore presumptively for resolution by the Court. See Buckeye, 546 U.S. at 449, 126 S.Ct. 1204.

* * *

It would be unfair to compel Defendants to arbitrate a dispute over mutual assent to the contract because the implication of their argument is that they never agreed to arbitrate any issues at all.

* * * Accordingly, the Court proceeds to consider each of Defendants' challenges to the arbitrator's jurisdiction over Defendants' breach-of-contract counterclaim.

B. Merits of Defendants' Jurisdictional Challenges

(1) The Panama Convention's Form Requirements

Article 1 of the Panama Convention provides, in relevant part:

> An agreement in which the parties undertake to submit to arbitral decision any differences that may arise or have arisen between them with respect to a commercial transaction is valid. The agreement shall be set forth in an instrument signed by the parties, or in the form of an exchange of letters, telegrams, or telex communications.

There is little case law discussing this specific provision, * * * yet Article 1's express language suggests that a valid arbitration agreement may take only two forms. First, the arbitration agreement may consist of a writing—either a submission agreement or an arbitral clause in a contract—that is signed by the parties. Second, the arbitration agreement may consist of an exchange of writings, in which case there is no requirement for a signature.

(a) "[A]n instrument signed by the parties"

When an agreement to arbitrate is evidenced only by an arbitral clause in a printed contract, the Panama Convention plainly requires that the contract be signed by the parties. This interpretation is confirmed by analogous authority interpreting Article II(1) of the New York Convention, which sets forth the requirements for the formal validity of an arbitration agreement. Article II(1) of the New York Convention provides, in relevant part:

> Each Contracting State shall recognize an agreement in writing under which the parties undertake to subject to arbitration all or any differences which have arisen or which may arise between them in respect of a defined legal relationship, whether contractual or not, concerning a subject matter capable of settlement by arbitration.

Furthermore, Article II(2) states:

> The term "agreement in writing" shall include an arbitral clause in a contract or an arbitration agreement, signed by the parties or contained in an exchange of letters or telegrams.

The domestic case law reveals at least two conflicting interpretations of these foundational provisions of the New York Convention. * * * Some courts hold that Article II(2) requires only a submission agreement to be signed by the parties in order to be valid. On this reading, an arbitral clause in an unsigned contract is valid so long as the parties manifested their consent to the contract in any form. See, e.g., Sphere Drake Ins. PLC v. Marine Towing, Inc., 16 F.3d 666, 669 (5th Cir.1994). A majority of courts conclude, however, that Article II(2) requires that both types of arbitration agreements be signed by the parties in order to be valid.[5] See, e.g., Standard Bent Glass Corp. v. Glassrobots Oy, 333 F.3d 440, 449 (3d Cir.2003); Kahn Lucas Lancaster, Inc. v. Lark Int'l Ltd., 186 F.3d 210, 214 (2d Cir.1999), partially

[5] Foreign courts also take divergent approaches to the interpretation of Article II(2). Most refuse, however, to give effect to arbitral clauses in unsigned contracts, even when there has been oral or tacit acceptance of the contract by the party resisting arbitration. * * *

abrogated on other grounds by Sarhank Grp. v. Oracle Corp., 404 F.3d 657, 660 n. 2 (2d Cir.2005).

The more demanding interpretation of Article II(2) appears to be logically and grammatically correct, but it has the lamentable effect of rendering invalid many arbitration agreements that arise from informal commercial relationships. Consequently, enforcement of the signed writing requirement in such circumstances has been widely criticized, with several commentators arguing that interpretation of the New York Convention as a "minimum" standard of formal validity is clearly misguided and out of step with commercial practice.

According to these scholars, the New York Convention in fact permits courts to give effect to a broad range of arbitration agreements beyond those enumerated in Article II(2). First, Article VII(l) of the New York Convention explicitly allows parties to rely on provisions of national law if they are more favorable to arbitration than the Convention itself. Article VII(1) can be read to allow parties to invoke the less demanding standard of formal validity articulated in Section 2 of the FAA.[6]

Second, Article II(2) can be interpreted as a non-exhaustive list of the types of arbitration agreements that satisfy the Convention's standard of formal validity. This approach would allow courts to add, over time, new types or categories of agreements that merit recognition and enforcement.

The Panama Convention discloses subtle, yet important, differences when compared with the New York Convention, however. Upon inspection of the two treaties, it appears that the textual, or legal, bases that may justify departure from, or modification of, the New York Convention's form requirements are absent from the Panama Convention.

To begin with, the express language of Article 1 of the Panama Convention clearly indicates that an arbitration agreement consisting exclusively of an arbitral clause in a contract is not valid unless the contract is signed by the parties. Unlike Article II(2) of the New York Convention, which can be plausibly interpreted to relieve the parties of this burden, the Panama Convention is unambiguous as to the need for signatures.

The Panama Convention also does not include a "more-favorable-right" provision, similar to the New York Convention's Article VII(1). Article VII(1) permits for reliance on national laws that are more favorable to arbitration than the Convention itself. The Panama Convention does not appear to provide the parties to an arbitration agreement with this choice of law.

Finally, Article 1 of the Panama Convention cannot reasonably be interpreted as a non-exhaustive list of valid arbitration agreements. Unlike Article II(2) of the New York Convention, Article 1 of the Panama Convention does not set forth a list that begins with the ambiguous term "include," nor does it contain any other textual guides indicating that the form requirement is meant to change or expand over time. The requirement of Article 1 appears to be exclusive.

---

[6] Section 2 of the FAA requires courts to give effect to a "written provision" evidencing an agreement to arbitrate. The signatures of the parties are not required, nor is there a need for both parties to manifest assent in writing.

In short, the Panama Convention provides no apparent grounds for enforcing an arbitral clause in an unsigned contract, absent a separate manifestation of assent in writing. This result may be out of step with contemporary commercial practice, but it appears to be sound in light of slight, yet meaningful, variations between the Panama and New York Conventions. Unlike the New York Convention, the Panama Convention seems not to contemplate reliance on less demanding national law standards of formal validity, such as Section 2 of the FAA.

Here, Freaner's argument that Defendants accepted the printed contract by performance or, alternatively, by spoken words, does not satisfy this Court's reading of Article 1 of the Panama Convention. Freaner's contention that Defendants accepted the printed contract in a separate, unsigned e-mail raises the prospect that a valid arbitration agreement may have been formed through an "exchange of letters." This requirement is discussed below.

(b) "[A]n exchange of letters"

Article 1 of the Panama Convention provides that an arbitration agreement may also take the form of an "exchange of letters, telegraphs, or telex communications." An exchange involving contemporary forms of communication that leave a record, such as fax or e-mail, is also believed to be sufficient.

This provision of the Convention requires that each party consent to the arbitration agreement in writing. The analogous terms of Article II(2) of the New York Convention support this reading, as most courts have refused to give effect under Article II(2) to an arbitral clause in a printed contract that is sent by one party and orally or tacitly accepted by another party. Thus, Article 1's "exchange of letters" provision does not simply codify principles of mutual assent, but rather imposes a standard of formal validity for arbitration agreements that the parties cannot evade.

Nonetheless, Article 1 recognizes as valid any exchange of writings that evidences assent to an arbitration agreement. The exchange need not consist of a written offer and a written acceptance.

Here, Freaner contends that a valid arbitration agreement is set forth in an exchange of e-mails between himself and Jose Humberto Guillin, Hotelera Coral's administrative manager. Guillin sent Freaner an e-mail on December 9, 2009, which read as follows:

> GOOD AFTERNOON
>
> ARIEL
>
> CAN YOU PLEASE SEND ME THE CONTRACT IN FORCE, I
>
> HAVE AN AUDIT.
>
> GREETINGS
>
> HBTO

Freaner responded to Guillin on December 10, 2009 with an e-mail that read as follows:

> Good afternoon. I attach contract in force.

The printed contract containing the arbitral clause was attached to Freaner's e-mail.

On December 11, 2009, Guillin responded with an e-mail that read as follows:

> received and confirmed.

Freaner apparently contends that Guillin's final e-mail constituted a written acceptance of the printed contract. That argument is untenable, however. Freaner's e-mail to Guillin does not constitute an offer creating a power of acceptance. Moreover, Guillin did not have actual or apparent authority to conclude such an agreement with Freaner on behalf of Valle or Hotelera Coral.

More pertinently, the exchange does not evidence Defendants' assent to the printed contract because it does not show that Defendants had at any point accepted the printed contract, tacitly or otherwise. Neither Guillin's generic request for "the contract in force," nor his subsequent e-mail confirming receipt, is specific or substantial enough to show that Defendants had already assented to the contract attached to Freaner's December 10, 2009 e-mail.

Guillin did not participate in the contract negotiations with Freaner. He was aware that Hotelera Coral was paying Freaner for design and advertising services on a monthly basis, but did not know which terms, if any, governed the parties' relationship. Freaner either was, or should have been, aware of Guillin's limited role by the time he received Guillin's e-mail, nearly five months after Defendants' purported acceptance of the printed contract. This e-mail exchange, viewed in isolation or in light of the course of dealing between the parties, does not evidence Defendants' assent to the contract.

Accordingly, the Court declines to give effect to the arbitral clause in the printed contract. The Court DENIES Freaner's motion to compel arbitration because the alleged arbitration agreement is invalid under Article 1 of the Panama Convention.

* * *

Suppose a written proposal to arbitrate is sent by one party and then accepted orally—or even tacitly—by the other party. In such circumstances, under ordinary principles of American contract law—as well as under the domestic law of many other jurisdictions—a court might well find that an enforceable arbitration agreement has been created. See Zambia Steel & Bldg. Supplies Ltd. v. James Clark & Eaton Ltd., [1986] 2 Lloyd's Law Rep. 225 (C.A. 1986) ("assent to the written terms may be proved by other evidence," and so "any evidence which proves that the party has agreed to be bound by an agreement to [arbitrate] contained in a document or documents is sufficient to make the document or documents an agreement in writing"). But do these facts allow us to find an "agreement in writing" within the meaning of the New York Convention? The drafters apparently intended for the answer in such a case to be "no." See Albert Jan van den Berg, The New York Convention of 1958: Towards a Uniform Judicial Interpretation 196 (1981) ("The text of Article II(2) does not leave any doubt on this point"; the legislative history also "confirms that the drafters of the Convention wished to exclude the oral or tacit acceptance of a written proposal to arbitrate"). See Basis Yield Alpha Fund (Master) v. Goldman Sachs Grp., 115 A.D.3d 128, 132 (N.Y. App. Div. 2014) (noting that "[i]n support of its motion to compel arbitration, Goldman relied on a mandatory arbitration clause set forth in a document entitled 'General Terms and Conditions' that was attached to a November 10, 2006 email [to Basis]" and that "the motion court properly held that the purported document containing an arbitration clause did not meet the writing requirements of the New York Convention, which defines an 'agreement in writing' to include 'an arbitral clause in a contract or an arbitration agreement, signed by the parties or contained in an exchange of letters or telegrams'. . .The document, which was attached to an email, was never signed by Basis, nor referred to in any exchange of correspondence between the parties.")

QUESTIONS TO REVIEW AND SYNTHESIZE

1. What sources of law determine whether parties have formed an international commercial arbitration agreement?
2. What is the relationship between the Panama Convention and the New York Convention and when does each apply?
3. What sort of writings may constitute an enforceable international commercial arbitration agreement and when must they be signed to be enforceable?

D. CONDUCT OF INTERNATIONAL COMMERCIAL ARBITRATION

1. OVERVIEW

The New York Convention does not mandate arbitration's procedures, so parties can, in their arbitration agreement, choose their arbitration's rules of procedure and evidence, along with its location, language, governing law, and other matters. "In essence, the parties create their own private system of justice." Margaret L. Moses, The Principles and Practice of International Commercial Arbitration 20 (3d ed. 2017) Rather than creating their own, completely customized, system of justice, parties to many international commercial arbitration agreements incorporate the rules of an arbitration organization, such as the International Chamber of Commerce or the London Court of International Arbitration.

International commercial arbitration procedures often blend procedures familiar in legal systems (like that of the U.S.) based on the English common law and procedures used in the civil law systems prevalent in continental Europe, South America, and East Asia. One major difference between the common law and civil law traditions is "that what common lawyers think of as a trial in civil proceedings does not exist in the civil law world." John Henry Merryman & Rogelio Perez-Perdomo, The Civil Law Tradition 113 (3d ed. 2007). While a trial in the United States brings together the parties, lawyers, judge, and jury in a single, concentrated event, civil law systems use "an entirely different approach" with "no such thing as a trial in our [common law] sense; there is no single, concentrated event. The typical civil proceeding in a civil law country is actually a series of isolated meetings of and written communications between counsel and the judge, in which evidence is introduced, testimony is given, procedural motions and rulings are made, and so on." Why this major difference between common law and civil law systems? "The reason is that the right to a jury in civil actions, traditional in the common law world, has never taken hold in the civil law world." Following the civil law approach of a series of isolated meetings at which some, but not all, evidence is introduced would not be practical with a jury because the "lay jury cannot easily be convened, adjourned, and reconvened several times in the course of a single action without causing a great deal of inconvenience." So in common law systems a trial must be a single, concentrated event. In contrast, civil law systems can spread out the case over several appearances with each involving the examination of only one witness or the introduction of "only one or two pieces of material evidence." Id. at 114.

Consequently, international commercial arbitration procedures generally look somewhat "civilian" to a lawyer trained in the United States, which is not only a common law jurisdiction, but the common law jurisdiction with the most broadly applicable civil jury right.

2. PRE-HEARING

a. SELECTION OF ARBITRATORS

Although an international commercial arbitration might have a single arbitrator, or any number of them, the most common number of arbitrators is three. The prevalence of three as the number of arbitrators explains why discussions of international commercial arbitration often refer, not to "the arbitrator," but to "the tribunal." While a single arbitrator tends to save time and money, "when the parties are from different cultural or legal backgrounds, a party may want at least one arbitrator to have some knowledge and understanding of its own culture and legal system." Margaret L. Moses, The Principles and Practice of International Commercial Arbitration 51 (3d ed. 2017). Also, international commercial disputes tend to be large, and "when there are substantial amounts of money at stake, most parties feel more comfortable with three arbitrators."

Many international commercial arbitration agreements provide for *tripartite* arbitration, in which each party picks one arbitrator and those two agree on the third. This method of arbitrator selection is also the usual method under the rules of important international arbitration organizations, such as the International Chamber of Commerce and London Court of International Arbitration.

b. PLEADINGS

While litigation generally begins with a complaint filed and served by the plaintiff, and domestic arbitration typically begins with a *demand* for arbitration filed and served by the *claimant*, the international arbitration analog is often called (more politely) a *request* for arbitration or *notice* of arbitration. This document typically states the basic substantive claims, the relief sought, and the jurisdiction of the arbitrators conferred by the agreement to arbitrate. The request for arbitration may also include the claimant's views about the appropriate number or manner of selecting arbitrators and, if that is tripartite arbitration, the request for arbitration may also include claimant's nomination of an arbitrator.

The respondent served with a request for arbitration may answer the claimant's allegations and assert counterclaims. The respondent may nominate an arbitrator or object to the arbitrators' jurisdiction to hear the dispute, perhaps arguing that there is no enforceable arbitration agreement or that any such agreement does not cover this dispute. Any pleading should be drafted to be "understandable and persuasive to readers from other legal and linguistic backgrounds." Gary B. Born, International Commercial Arbitration 1798 (2009).

c. DISCOVERY

Like other aspects of international commercial arbitration procedure, discovery is governed primarily by the arbitration agreement, so parties can jointly choose the amount and types of discovery that will be required in their arbitration. Parties typically chose to arbitrate under the rules of an arbitration organization, and those rules generally give arbitrators broad discretion over the amount and types of discovery (or, as it may be called, "disclosure") they will require. "The prevailing view is, and is increasingly firmly-held, * * * that, even absent express authorization, the power to order discovery or disclosure is inherent in an international arbitral tribunal's mandate. This does not obligate a tribunal, in a particular case, to permit or order discovery, but instead (absent contrary agreement) leaves the decision whether or not to order discovery to the tribunal's discretion." Gary B. Born, International Commercial Arbitration 1891 (2009).

Discovery in international commercial arbitration "is usually materially less extensive and intrusive" than in litigation in common law systems like the United States. International commercial arbitration procedures often consist of compromises between the common law and civil law traditions, and in most of the civil law systems prevalent in continental Europe, South America, and East Asia, "[e]vidence-taking is largely controlled by the court and the parties have no (or virtually no) right to demand relevant materials from one another or from witnesses." Id. at 1821, 1893–94. Depositions and interrogatories are not prevalent in international commercial arbitration, so exchanging documents is usually the only discovery.

If a party disobeys an international commercial arbitration tribunal's order to disclose, the arbitrators are likely to draw adverse inferences and may seek court enforcement of their discovery orders. Some national laws authorize courts to help parties in arbitration obtain discovery from recalcitrant opponents and non-parties. For instance, a United States statute gives federal courts the power to order discovery from specified persons "for use in a proceeding in a foreign or international tribunal," 28 U.S.C. § 1782, and some courts have held that this covers an international commercial arbitration tribunal. Roger P. Alford, *Ancillary Discovery to Prove Denial of Justice*, 53 Va. J. Int'l L. 127, 133–42 (2012).

3. HEARING

a. GENERAL COMPARISON WITH TRIAL

International commercial arbitration hearings often differ from trials in the U.S. and domestic arbitration hearings in ways that seem to follow from international commercial arbitration's frequent blending of the common law and civil law traditions. While trials and hearings in the U.S. and other legal systems based on the English common law generally allow parties (through their lawyers) great latitude in presenting their cases—including the direct and cross-examination of witnesses—"arbitrators with civil law backgrounds (principally in Continental Europe, Japan, Korea and China) can often be expected to adopt somewhat more 'inquisitorial' procedures, with the tribunal being primarily responsible for identifying issues, seeking evidence and probing the record." Gary B. Born, International Commercial Arbitration 1787 (2009). Also, civil law systems favor proof through documents, rather than witness testimony, and international commercial arbitration tends to rely more heavily on documentary evidence and written witness statements than on oral testimony.

b. RULES OF EVIDENCE

The New York Convention does not create rules of evidence for arbitration. Many States' national arbitration laws incorporate the UNCITRAL Model Law on International Arbitration, which in Art. 19(2) provides that "[t]he power conferred upon the arbitral tribunal includes the power to determine the admissibility, relevance, materiality and weight of any evidence." This arbitrator discretion over evidentiary matters also typically results from U.S. national law (the FAA) enforcing agreements to arbitrate pursuant to the rules of an arbitration organization that gives arbitrators the power to decide evidentiary issues.

However, parties may not wish to give arbitrators complete discretion over evidentiary issues, so some international commercial arbitration clauses include an agreement that the arbitration be conducted according to the International Bar Association (IBA) Rules on the Taking of Evidence in International Commercial Arbitration.[64] "These rules provide a good harmonization of civil and common law approaches to taking evidence, and provide parties with a fair amount of certainty about the tribunal will deal with documents, witnesses, and experts." Margaret L. Moses, The Principles and Practice of International Commercial Arbitration, 53 (3d ed. 2017).

c. NO HEARING; DISPOSITIVE MOTIONS

While much litigation in the United States ends on a grant of a motion to dismiss or for summary judgment, such motions are generally less likely to succeed in arbitration, including international commercial arbitration. However, that does not mean a live hearing is required for an international commercial arbitration award to be enforceable in court. Just as domestic arbitration may result in a default award against a party who does not participate in arbitration, the same is true internationally. A more difficult situation arises when arbitrators decide to forgo live testimony and decide the case on the documentary evidence submitted, despite a party's request for a live hearing. While there is some domestic United States authority in favor of confirming such awards, a leading scholar of international commercial arbitration writes that "[o]ral hearings are mandatory in virtually all

[64] http://www.ibanet.org/Publications/publications_IBA_guides_and_free_materials.aspx.

international arbitrations (save where the parties agree otherwise). * * * Failure to hear oral evidence, when requested by a party to do so, would invite a challenge to the resulting award for failure to afford the protesting party the opportunity to present its case." Gary B. Born, International Commercial Arbitration 1831–32 (2009).

d. WRITTEN AWARDS; REASONED OPINIONS

Some domestic arbitration awards are brief and conclusory, but international commercial awards tend to be lengthy, thorough discussions of the parties' arguments and the arbitrators' analysis and conclusions. In short, they resemble the opinions issued by many courts.

4. REMEDIES

Money damages are by far the most common remedy awarded in international commercial arbitration, but such arbitrators also fairly often issue injunctions and order the losing party to pay the prevailing party's costs of arbitration, including its legal fees. Courts generally uphold all these remedies but, in contrast, awards of punitive damages "are arguably contrary to public policy in some civil law jurisdictions." Gary B. Born, International Commercial Arbitration 2487 (2009).

QUESTIONS TO REVIEW AND SYNTHESIZE

1. In international commercial arbitration, what does "the tribunal" refer to?
2. Litigation in the U.S. often begins with a "complaint" or a "petition." The analogous document often goes under what names in international commercial arbitration?
3. What is the UNCITRAL Model Law on International Arbitration, and why is it important?

E. ENFORCEMENT AND VACATUR OF INTERNATIONAL COMMERCIAL ARBITRATION AWARDS

1. ENFORCEMENT OF INTERNATIONAL COMMERCIAL ARBITRATION AWARDS

The New York Convention's main purpose is to make arbitration awards rendered in one State enforceable in the courts of other States. Accordingly, the Convention begins "[t]his Convention shall apply to the recognition and enforcement of arbitral awards made in the territory of a State other than the State where the recognition and enforcement of such awards are sought." Art. I(1). The Convention states that "[e]ach Contracting State shall recognize arbitral awards as binding and enforce them," Art. III, and the Convention permits only a narrow list of grounds upon which "[r]ecognition and enforcement of the award may be refused." Art. V.

To recognize and enforce an award, the Convention prescribes a fairly quick and easy process:

> 1. To obtain the recognition and enforcement mentioned in the preceding article, the party applying for recognition and enforcement shall, at the time of the application, supply:
>
> (a) The duly authenticated original award or a duly certified copy thereof;
>
> (b) The original agreement referred to in article II or a duly certified copy thereof.
>
> 2. If the said award or agreement is not made in an official language of the country in which the award is relied upon, the party applying for recognition and enforcement of the award shall produce a translation of these documents into such language. The translation shall be certified by an official or sworn translator or by a diplomatic or consular agent.

Art. IV. The speed and ease of this process is facilitated by national courts' "taking a practical and relatively flexible approach" to it, for example by excusing non-compliance with the translation requirement where the award could nonetheless be comprehended by the court. Gary B. Born, International Commercial Arbitration 2703 (2009).

The Convention's distinction between award recognition and enforcement generally relates to which party—claimant or respondent—prevailed in arbitration. Prevailing claimants typically seek award enforcement to collect the money or other remedy awarded in arbitration, while prevailing respondents typically seek award recognition to increase the award's finality and preclude further arbitration or litigation of the claim respondent defeated in arbitration.

In implementing the New York Convention, Chapter 2 of the FAA provides:

> Within three years after an arbitral award falling under the Convention is made, any party to the arbitration may apply to any court having jurisdiction under this chapter for an order confirming the award as against any other party to the arbitration. The court shall confirm the award unless it finds one of the grounds for refusal or deferral of recognition or enforcement of the award specified in the said Convention.[65]

This provision enables federal[66] courts to confirm awards "falling under" the Convention. For example, if an arbitration tribunal seated outside the United States awards the claimant money damages from the respondent and the respondent has assets in the United States then the claimant does not need to involve a court at the seat of the arbitration. The claimant can get a federal court to confirm the award, which converts the award into a judgment of the court. A confirmed award is enforced in the same manner as other court judgments: through orders to turn over property, judicial liens, etc. Conversely, if an arbitration tribunal seated in the United States awards the claimant money damages from the respondent and the respondent

[65] 9 U.S.C. § 207.

[66] An action to confirm an award falling under the Convention triggers the original, but not exclusive, jurisdiction of the federal courts. 9 U.S.C. § 203. Such an action may be brought in state court but the defendant may then remove it to federal court. 9 U.S.C. § 205.

has assets abroad, say in England, then the claimant does not need to involve a U.S. court before seeking enforcement of the award by an English court.

2. VACATING (SETTING ASIDE) INTERNATIONAL COMMERCIAL ARBITRATION AWARDS

A party displeased with an international arbitration award has two ways to prevent or limit enforcement of the award. First, that party can try to persuade a court at the seat of arbitration to "set aside" (vacate), rather than confirm, the award. The standards for vacatur are found, not in the New York Convention, but in the arbitration law of the State that is the seat of arbitration. Vacatur by a court at the seat nearly always prevents enforcement of the award by the courts of any State. Second, even if the court at the seat of arbitration confirms the award, that confirmation only makes the award enforceable in that State so the party displeased with the award can seek to prevent other States' courts from recognizing and enforcing it.[67] This (non) enforcement is governed by the New York Convention, which provides:

> 1. Recognition and enforcement of the award may be refused, at the request of the party against whom it is invoked, only if that party furnishes to the competent authority where the recognition and enforcement is sought, proof that:
>
> (a) The parties to the agreement referred to in article II were, under the law applicable to them, under some incapacity, or the said agreement is not valid under the law to which the parties have subjected it or, failing any indication thereon, under the law of the country where the award was made; or
>
> (b) The party against whom the award is invoked was not given proper notice of the appointment of the arbitrator or of the arbitration proceedings or was otherwise unable to present his case; or
>
> (c) The award deals with a difference not contemplated by or not falling within the terms of the submission to arbitration, or it contains decisions on matters beyond the scope of the submission to arbitration, provided that, if the decisions on matters submitted to arbitration can be separated from those not so submitted, that part of the award which contains decisions on matters submitted to arbitration may be recognized and enforced; or
>
> (d) The composition of the arbitral authority or the arbitral procedure was not in accordance with the agreement of the parties, or, failing such agreement, was not in accordance with the law of the country where the arbitration took place; or
>
> (e) The award has not yet become binding on the parties, or has been set aside or suspended by a competent authority of the country in which, or under the law of which, that award was made.

---

[67] As noted above, confirmation by the seat is not required before a court outside the seat can enforce an award. See § 71.

2. Recognition and enforcement of an arbitral award may also be refused if the competent authority in the country where recognition and enforcement is sought finds that:

(a) The subject matter of the difference is not capable of settlement by arbitration under the law of that country; or

(b) The recognition or enforcement of the award would be contrary to the public policy of that country.

These grounds for denying recognition and enforcement to awards are permissive. The Convention does not require States to invoke the grounds in Article V, but merely permits States to do so.

a. ONLY THE SEAT CAN VACATE (SET ASIDE) THE AWARD

While the New York Convention's main purpose is to make arbitration awards rendered in one State enforceable in the courts of other States, Article V(i)(e) says that "[r]ecognition and enforcement of the award may be refused [if the award] has been set aside or suspended by a competent authority of the country in which, or under the law of which, that award was made." As a result, a party displeased with an international arbitration award can get a national court (of the State that is the seat of the arbitration) to vacate ("set aside" or annul) the award and then use that vacatur as a defense to enforcement of the award in other States. Crucially, the standards for vacatur are found, not in the New York Convention, but in the national law of the arbitration's seat.

William Laurence Craig, *Uses and Abuses of Appeal from Awards*

4 Arbitration International 174, 174–79, 182–85, 190–92 (1988).

International arbitration has become the ordinary way of resolving international commercial disputes. One of the reasons for this success has been the relative ease with which awards rendered in a foreign jurisdiction can be enforced at the debtor's domicile or in any jurisdiction where the debtor has assets. That ease has been due, in large part, to the New York Convention of 1958, a treaty which provides that the courts of each signatory country will enforce arbitration awards from other countries. The Convention provides relatively few grounds for courts to deny recognition and enforcement of foreign awards. The same spirit which gave rise to the Convention has also led many jurisdictions to look favourably upon enforcing foreign awards even where the Convention does not apply. The internal laws of some countries have provided for even more liberal enforcement of foreign awards than envisioned in the New York Convention.

The rising number of international commercial arbitration awards—and wide dissemination of information about these awards in a number of excellent publications—has produced an increasingly cohesive practice among nations in the recognition and enforcement of awards. In other words, recognition and enforcement of foreign awards is a success story; and the present system can be expected to continue its process toward a uniform international system for recognition and enforcement of awards.

On the other hand, however, no international agreements control how national courts supervise arbitrations taking place on their own territory. Each State is free to apply whatever measures of judicial control it wishes to international arbitration taking place within its own jurisdiction. The most dramatic judicial intervention in the arbitral process is appeal or judicial review at the seat of arbitration. A successful appeal cuts the award off "at its roots" and leaves it unenforceable anywhere because the New York Convention provides that "recognition and enforcement of the award may be refused" on proof that "the award. . . . has been set aside or suspended by a competent authority in which, or under the laws of which, that award was made."

Unlike the unifying trend in recognition and enforcement of foreign awards, judicial review is heteroclite, changing rapidly by reforms of arbitration laws in various jurisdictions. Appeal of arbitration awards is a field of frequently unpredictable results. With more and more awards involving important parties and substantial amounts of money, one may expect ever more testing of judicial review at the seat of arbitration. A party disappointed with an arbitration award will try to have the award set aside at the seat of arbitration because success means that the New York Convention, with its limited grounds for refusing the enforcement of an award, will never come into play.

* * *

There are two basic ways by which a party disgruntled with an arbitration award can test it judicially. First, he can oppose recognition and enforcement of the award in any jurisdiction where the winner seeks judicial enforcement of the award. If he succeeds in opposing enforcement, he defeats the award only in that jurisdiction. The winner may still try to enforce the award in any other jurisdiction where the loser has assets.

The alternative is to take the offensive and seek "judicial review" of the award in the jurisdiction where it was rendered. I will refer to the jurisdiction where the award was rendered as the arbitration's home jurisdiction or as the seat of arbitration. When judicial review in the home jurisdiction nullifies, vacates, overturns or reverses the arbitral award, it cannot be enforced anywhere.

* * *

[It] should be recognised that parties can in a certain measure influence the extent and scope of judicial review. The choice of the seat of arbitration is effectively a choice of law with respect to judicial review of the award. The parties may agree to hold their arbitration in a jurisdiction which guarantees rights of full appeal or what is commonly called ordinary appeal. Ordinary appeal allows a court to conduct a complete review of the arbitrator's decision on the merits, regarding both factual and legal determinations. In some cases ordinary appeal permits the judge to substitute his own decision if he finds that the arbitral tribunal erred. More frequently, parties will seek to hold their arbitration at a place providing only for judicial review or "extraordinary" appeal—appeal only for fundamental irregularities which tainted the arbitral decision.

* * *

It is no surprise that the relationship between arbitrations and judicial review at the seat of the arbitration has not been regulated in a New York Convention fashion. Setting any international standards for how courts should handle arbitrations rendered in their jurisdiction would be a far greater invasion of a State's sovereignty than are international standards for honoring an arbitration award from abroad. Arbitrations in the "home jurisdiction" are much more likely to involve domestic concerns. In large, relatively self-contained economies, the majority of arbitrations will be purely domestic affairs. The relationship between an arbitration and the courts of its home jurisdiction is built on a far different model than the relationship between an arbitration and a foreign court.

Yet a large number of the arbitrations conducted in the world today do not have any meaningful link to their home jurisdiction. Often, the jurisdiction is home to the arbitration without being home to either side in the dispute. In fact, this is a natural result of the nature of international arbitration. Arbitration is often chosen because neither side wants to end up in the courts of the other. Similarly, each side may be suspicious of holding an arbitration in the other side's country. A third country with a proper image of neutrality becomes the chosen site of arbitration. Hence, cities such as Geneva, Stockholm, and Vienna become favored sites for international arbitrations.

Arbitration in a third country is also a natural consequence of the fact that international arbitration is centered on a few arbitration institutions, such as the London Court of International Arbitration (LCIA), the International Chamber of Commerce in Paris, the International Centre for Settlement of Investment Disputes (ICSID) in Washington, or the Stockholm Chamber of Commerce. While all these institutions permit arbitrations under their auspices to be held all over the world, there is an understandable tendency to hold the arbitration in the city where the institution is headquartered. A Brazilian and a Danish company which have agreed to arbitrate their contract by ICC Rules may pick Paris as the seat of arbitration simply because they have no reason to pick any other place and they know the ICC is headquartered there.

The most extreme example of the lack of connection between the dispute and the seat of arbitration arises when the parties have failed to elect a venue in their contract and the seat of arbitration is chosen by the arbitral institution. In the case of the ICC, when the parties have not chosen a seat of arbitration, the ICC will select a neutral site, often based on the domicile of the president of the arbitral tribunal or simply on a location convenient for the parties and arbitrators. It is sometimes said that the result of this exercise is a site equally inconvenient to everyone. More important, the result of this exercise may be selection of a site of arbitration which neither of the parties contemplated in contracting.

The result is a large number of international arbitrations which have nothing to do with the home jurisdiction, except that they use conference rooms in the home jurisdiction's Hilton hotel. The arbitration involves no national of the home jurisdiction, involves no direct financial impact on the home jurisdiction, and applies a substantive law foreign to the home jurisdiction. In the case where the arbitration institution chooses the venue, the seat of arbitration is not even a conscious choice of the parties. Even the procedural rules of the arbitration tend to be those of an arbitration institution, with the procedural law of the home jurisdiction relegated to the second string.

Few of the traditional interests of the courts in overseeing domestic arbitration remain. There is no national to protect; there is no national interest to protect; there may be little domestic law that the arbitral panel can be accused of having misunderstood or misapplied. All that is left is the most abstract of sovereign interests—a pure concern of the government for what happens on its sovereign territory.

The principal interest the national courts have in these kinds of arbitration might arguably be termed interests of national prestige. Arbitral awards from a particular jurisdiction could come to have a certain reputation and that reputation indirectly but inevitably would reflect on the judiciary of that nation. Such subjective feelings hardly seem to be a sufficient foundation upon which to construct a theory of judicial review, however. Nor is it a sufficiently principled response to say that judicial review of international awards should follow the model of domestic review simply because the controlling legislation makes no distinction and judges have been trained to think that way.

This is not to say that a nation hosting international arbitrations has absolutely no legitimate interests in policing those arbitrations. While the principal criterion of determining the applicability of the New York Convention is simply whether the award is "foreign", the "nationality" of the award will have some relevance in determining whether the award was final and, for countries using the reciprocity section, whether the award comes from another signatory State. Courts may have the reaction that an award rendered on their territory should not enter the international stream of enforcement and attain the status of international currency without facing at least the prospects of judicial review. That is, the national judiciary could feel that it is performing its judicial duty or its government's international duty. Judicial review could stem from a sense of national responsibility in the international arena. Finally, courts may demand to exercise some judicial review on the theory that a government has some responsibility to see that justice is done—or, at least, that injustice is not done—within its frontiers.

Consider the distinction between attempts to "set aside" or vacate an award at the seat of arbitration, and resistance to enforcement of that award elsewhere. In *International Standard Elec. Corp. v. Bridas Sociedad Anonima Petrolera, Industrial Y Comercial*, 745 F.Supp. 172 (S.D.N.Y. 1990), a joint venture agreement provided that it would be "governed by and construed under and in accordance with the laws of the State of New York." The International Chamber of Commerce, which was to administer the arbitration, named a Mexican lawyer chair of the three-arbitrator panel—and "since the parties here are an American Company and an Argentine Company, it is not difficult to understand why" the ICC selected Mexico City as the place of arbitration. The arbitrators awarded the claimant damages of almost $7 million, plus $1 million in legal fees, and costs of $400,000. The respondent moved in a U.S. district court to vacate the award, while the claimant "cross petitioned to enforce" it under Art. III of the New York Convention. The federal court in New York held that it lacked jurisdiction to set aside the award because

> the contested language in Article VI(e) of the Convention, ". . . the competent authority of the country under the law of which, [the] award was made" refers exclusively to procedural and not substantive law, and more precisely, to the regimen or scheme of arbitral procedural law under which the arbitration was conducted, and not the substantive law of contract which was applied in the case.
>
> In this case, the parties subjected themselves to the procedural law of Mexico. Hence, since the situs, or forum of the arbitration is Mexico, and the governing procedural law is that of Mexico, only the courts of Mexico have jurisdiction under the Convention to vacate the award. ISEC's petition to vacate the award is therefore dismissed.[68]

The court then turned to the claimant's cross-petition, and proceeded to enforce the award.

Bridas is just one example of U.S. courts' recognition that only the courts at the seat of arbitration have jurisdiction to vacate the arbitration award. Another example involved KBC, a Cayman Islands builder of electric generating stations, contracting with Pertamina, an energy company owned by the Republic of Indonesia, to build and operate a power plant in Indonesia. Among the many opinions in this litigation—which metastasized at an alarming rate—see Karaha Bodas Co., L.L.C v. Perusahaan Pertambangan Minyak Dan Gas Bumi Negara, at 335 F.3d 357 (5th Cir. 2003), and at 364 F.3d 274 (5th Cir. 2004). The contract contained an arbitration clause under which "the site of the arbitration shall be Geneva, Switzerland"; it also recited that "in accordance with Section 641 of the Indonesian Code of Civil Procedure," neither party "shall appeal to any court from the decision of the arbitral panel," and that the parties "waive the applicability" of certain provisions in the Indonesian Code (among them provisions imposing time limits on the arbitral process and requiring that the arbitrators be "bound by strict rules of law").

The government of Indonesia later suspended the project, so KBC instituted arbitration proceedings, and an *ad hoc* arbitral tribunal rendered an award—reciting that it was "made in Geneva"—in the claimant's favor. KBC sought to enforce its award in the United States, as well as in Hong Kong and Canada. While these enforcement proceedings were pending, Pertamina sought to have the award vacated in Switzerland. The Swiss courts dismissed the annulment proceedings on the ground that court costs had not been paid. Having failed in this attempt, Pertamina then sought to have the award set aside in Indonesia—and this time, unsurprisingly, it was successful. What effect should an American court give to the Indonesian decree of annulment? Should it decline to enforce the award?

The Fifth Circuit concluded that the parties' agreement designating Switzerland as the site of arbitration "presumptively designated Swiss procedural law as the *lex arbitri,* in the absence of any express statement making another country's procedural law applicable." And there can be "*only one national court*

[68] Id. at 178.

system that has jurisdiction to consider an application for annulment of an award." "Such 'exclusive' primary jurisdiction in the courts of a single country is consistent with the New York Convention's purpose; facilitates the 'orderliness and predictability' necessary to international commercial agreements; and implements the parties' choice of a neutral forum." It followed, then, that the action of the Indonesian courts in setting aside the award could not be a defense to enforcement under the Convention; the court affirmed a summary judgment of enforcement in favor of KBC.

Such a holding could have been predicted, but the same court—a year earlier—had nevertheless held it to be an "abuse of discretion" to issue an antisuit injunction, with the effect of *prohibiting* Pertamina from pursuing annulment proceedings in Indonesia:

> By allowing concurrent enforcement and annulment actions, as well as simultaneous enforcement actions in third countries, the Convention necessarily envisions multiple proceedings that address the same substantive challenges to an arbitral award. * * * Inasmuch as the Convention provides for multiple proceedings and a more limited role for enforcement jurisdictions, Pertamina's actions in Indonesia, even if spurious, are less vexatious and oppressive than they would be outside of this treaty structure. * * * Not only did KBC contract to arbitrate its dispute in a foreign country (Switzerland), but it also instituted enforcement proceedings in several countries, including the United States. Indeed, but for Pertamina's initiation of a law suit in Indonesia, or perceived bias there, KBC conceivably might have attempted enforcement there as well.

In these circumstances—and "given the absence of a practical, positive effect that any injunction could have"—the court concluded that "more weighty considerations of comity" militated against the injunction; the antisuit injunction could only "have the practical effect of showing a lack of mutual respect for the judicial proceedings of other sovereign nations" and would amount to "an assertion of authority not contemplated by the New York Convention." Although there was indeed "strong evidence" suggesting that Switzerland was "the paramount country of primary jurisdiction under the Convention,"—and indeed that Pertamina "appears to be" "acting in bad faith by pursuing annulment in Indonesia"—that "is an issue that is not directly before us today." "A sovereign country has the competence to determine its own jurisdiction and grant the kinds of relief it deems appropriate."

b. EFFECT OF VACATUR BY SEAT

Vacatur of an award by a court of the State that is the seat of arbitration nearly always prevents the award from being enforced by the courts of other States. See, e.g., TermoRio S.A., E.S.P. v. Electranta S.P., 487 F.3d 928, 936 (D.C. Cir. 2007) ("An arbitration award does not exist to be enforced in other Contracting States if it has been lawfully 'set aside' by a competent authority in the State in which the award was made.") This view has been carried forward into certain national laws: Legislation in both Italy and the Netherlands, for example, makes it *mandatory* for local courts to refuse enforcement of an arbitral award that has been set aside in the state where it was rendered.[69]

In contrast, however, French law "does not permit nonenforcement on the ground that the award has been set aside by the courts of the country where the arbitration took place." See W. Laurence Craig, *Some Trends and Developments in the Laws and Practice of International Commercial Arbitration*, 30 Tex. Int'l L.J. 1, 32 (1995). And the following U.S. case enforced an arbitration award after it had been set aside by the seat State's court, Egypt.

Chromalloy Aeroservices v. Arab Republic of Egypt

United States District Court, District of Columbia, 1996.
939 F.Supp. 907.

■ JUNE L. GREEN, DISTRICT JUDGE.

I. Introduction

This matter is before the Court on the Petition of Chromalloy Aeroservices, Inc., ("CAS") to Confirm an Arbitral Award, and a Motion to Dismiss that Petition filed by the Arab Republic of Egypt ("Egypt"), the defendant in the arbitration. This is a case of first impression. The Court GRANTS Chromalloy Aeroservices' Petition to Recognize and Enforce the Arbitral Award, and DENIES Egypt's Motion to Dismiss, because the arbitral award in question is valid, and because Egypt's arguments against enforcement are insufficient to allow this Court to disturb the award.

II. Background

This case involves a military procurement contract between a U.S. corporation, Chromalloy Aeroservices, Inc., and the Air Force of the Arab Republic of Egypt.

On June 16, 1988, Egypt and CAS entered into a contract under which CAS agreed to provide parts, maintenance, and repair for helicopters belonging to the Egyptian Air Force. On December 2, 1991, Egypt terminated the contract by notifying CAS representatives in Egypt. On December 4, 1991, Egypt notified CAS headquarters in Texas of the termination. On December 15, 1991, CAS notified Egypt that it rejected the cancellation of the contract "and commenced arbitration proceedings on the basis of the arbitration clause contained in Article XII and Appendix E of the Contract." Egypt then drew down CAS' letters of guarantee in an amount totaling some $11,475,968.

---

[69] See Roy Goode, *The Role of the Lex Loci Arbitri in International Commercial Arbitration*, 17 Arb. Int'l 19, 24 (2001). Art. 840(5) C.p.c. (Italy), available at https://www.jus.uio.no/lm/italy.arbitration/840.html ("The Court of Appeal shall refuse recognition or enforcement of the foreign award if in the opposition proceedings the party against whom the award is invoked proves any of the following circumstances. . . the award. . . has been set aside by a competent authority of the State in which, or under the law of which, it was made."); Art. 1076(1)(A)(e) Rv. (Netherlands), available at http://www.dutchcivillaw.com/civilprocedureleg.htm ("* * *an arbitral award made in a foreign State may be recognised in the Netherlands and its enforcement may be sought in the Netherlands * * * unless the party against whom recognition or enforcement is sought, asserts and proves that: * * * the arbitral award has been reversed by a competent authority of the country in which that award is made).

On February 23, 1992, the parties began appointing arbitrators, and shortly thereafter, commenced a lengthy arbitration. On August 24, 1994, the arbitral panel [rendered an award substantially in favor of CAS]. On October 28, 1994, CAS applied to this Court for enforcement of the award. On November 13, 1994, Egypt filed an appeal with the Egyptian Court of Appeal, seeking nullification of the award. * * * On December 5, 1995, Egypt's Court of Appeal at Cairo issued an order nullifying the award. * * *

Egypt argues that this Court should deny CAS' Petition to Recognize and Enforce the Arbitral Award out of deference to its court. CAS argues that this Court should confirm the award because Egypt "does not present any serious argument that its court's nullification decision is consistent with the New York Convention or United States arbitration law."

III. Discussion

* * *

B. Chromalloy's Petition for Enforcement

* * *

1. The Standard under the Convention

This Court must grant CAS's Petition to Recognize and Enforce the arbitral "award unless it finds one of the grounds for refusal . . . of recognition or enforcement of the award specified in the . . . Convention." 9 U.S.C. § 207. Under the Convention, "Recognition and enforcement of the award may be refused" if Egypt furnishes to this Court "proof that . . . [t]he award has . . . been set aside . . . by a competent authority of the country in which, or under the law of which, that award was made." Convention, Article V(1) & V(1)(e) (emphasis added), 9 U.S.C. § 201 note. In the present case, the award was made in Egypt, under the laws of Egypt, and has been nullified by the court designated by Egypt to review arbitral awards. Thus, the Court *may,* at its discretion, decline to enforce the award.

While Article V provides a discretionary standard, Article VII of the Convention *requires* that, "The provisions of the present Convention *shall not* . . . deprive any interested party of any right he may have to avail himself of an arbitral award in the manner and to the extent allowed by the law . . . of the count[r]y where such award is sought to be relied upon." In other words, under the Convention, CAS maintains all rights to the enforcement of this Arbitral Award that it would have in the absence of the Convention. Accordingly, the Court finds that, if the Convention did not exist, the [FAA] would provide CAS with a legitimate claim to enforcement of this arbitral award. Jurisdiction over Egypt in such a suit would be available under 28 U.S.C. §§ 1330 (granting jurisdiction over foreign states "as to any claim for relief in personam with respect to which the foreign state is not entitled to immunity . . . under sections 1605–1607 of this title") and 1605(a)(2) (withholding immunity of foreign states for "an act outside . . . the United States in connection with a commercial activity of the foreign state elsewhere and that act causes a direct effect in the United States").

2. Examination of the Award under 9 U.S.C. § 10

* * *

In the present case, the language of the arbitral award that Egypt complains of reads:

> The Arbitral tribunal considers that it does not need to decide the legal nature of the contract. It appears that the Parties rely principally for their claims and defences, on the interpretation of the contract itself and on the facts presented. Furthermore, the Arbitral tribunal holds that the legal issues in dispute are not affected by the characterization of the contract.

[The] arbitrators in the present case made a procedural decision that allegedly led to a misapplication of substantive law. After considering Egypt's arguments that Egyptian administrative law should govern the contract, the majority of the arbitral panel held that it did not matter which substantive law they applied-civil or administrative. At worst, this decision constitutes a mistake of law, and thus is not subject to review by this Court.

In the United States, "[W]e are well past the time when judicial suspicion of the desirability of arbitration and of the competence of arbitral tribunals inhibited the development of arbitration as an alternative means of dispute resolution." Mitsubishi Motors Corp. v. Soler Chrysler-Plymouth, Inc., 473 U.S. 614, 626–27, 105 S.Ct. 3346, 3354, 87 L.Ed.2d 444 (1985). In Egypt, however, "[I]t is established that arbitration is an exceptional means for resolving disputes, requiring departure from the normal means of litigation before the courts, and the guarantees they afford." (Nullification Decision at 8.) Egypt's complaint that, "[T]he Arbitral Award is null under Arbitration Law, . . . because it is not properly 'grounded' under Egyptian law," reflects this suspicious view of arbitration, and is precisely the type of technical argument that U.S. courts are not to entertain when reviewing an arbitral award.

The Court's analysis thus far has addressed the arbitral award, and, as a matter of U.S. law, the award is proper. See Sanders v. Washington Metro. Area Transit Auth., 819 F.2d 1151, 1157 (D.C.Cir.1987) (holding that, "When the parties have had a full and fair opportunity to present their evidence, the decisions of the arbitrator should be viewed as conclusive as to subsequent proceedings, absent some abuse of discretion by the arbitrator"). The Court now considers the question of whether the decision of the Egyptian court should be recognized as a valid foreign judgment.

As the Court stated earlier, this is a case of first impression. There are no reported cases in which a court of the United States has faced a situation, under the Convention, in which the court of a foreign nation has nullified an otherwise valid arbitral award. This does not mean, however, that the Court is without guidance in this case. To the contrary, more than twenty years ago, in a case involving the enforcement of an arbitration clause under the FAA, the Supreme Court held that:

> An agreement to arbitrate before a specified tribunal is, in effect, a specialized kind of forum-selection clause. . . . The invalidation of such an agreement . . . would not only allow the respondent to repudiate its solemn promise but would, as well, reflect a parochial concept that all disputes must be resolved under our laws and in our courts.

Scherk v. Alberto-Culver Co., 417 U.S. 506, 519, 94 S.Ct. 2449, 2457, 41 L.Ed.2d 270 (1974) In *Scherk,* the Court forced a U.S. corporation to arbitrate a dispute arising under an international contract containing an arbitration clause. In so doing, the Court relied upon the FAA, but took the opportunity to comment upon the purposes of the newly acceded-to Convention:

> The delegates to the Convention voiced frequent concern that courts of signatory countries in which an agreement to arbitrate is sought to be enforced should not be permitted to decline enforcement of such agreements on the basis of parochial views of their desirability or in a manner that would diminish the mutually binding nature of the agreements. . . . [W]e think that this country's adoption and ratification of the Convention and the passage of Chapter 2 of the United States Arbitration Act provide strongly persuasive evidence of congressional policy consistent with the decision we reach today. *Id.* at n. 15.

The Court finds this argument equally persuasive in the present case, where Egypt seeks to repudiate its solemn promise to abide by the results of the arbitration.[4]

C. The Decision of Egypt's Court of Appeal

1. The Contract

"The arbitration agreement is a contract and the court will not rewrite it for the parties." The Court "begin[s] with the 'cardinal principle of contract construction': that a document should be read to give effect to all its provisions and to render them consistent with each other." Article XII of the contract requires that the parties arbitrate all disputes that arise between them under the contract. Appendix E, which defines the terms of any arbitration, forms an integral part of the contract. The contract is unitary. Appendix E to the contract defines the "Applicable Law Court of Arbitration." The clause reads, in relevant part:

> "It is * * * understood that both parties have irrevocably agreed to apply Egypt (sic) Laws and to choose Cairo as seat of the court of arbitration. * * * The decision of the said court shall be final and binding and cannot be made subject to any appeal or other recourse." (Appendix E ("Appendix") to the Contract.)

This Court may not assume that the parties intended these two sentences to contradict one another, and must preserve the meaning of both if possible. Egypt argues that the first quoted sentence supersedes the second, and allows an appeal to an Egyptian court. Such an interpretation, however, would vitiate the second sentence, and would ignore the plain language on the face of the contract. The Court concludes that the first sentence defines choice of law and choice of forum

[4] The fact that this case concerns the enforcement of an arbitral *award,* rather than the enforcement of an agreement to arbitrate, makes no difference, because without the knowledge that judgment will be entered upon an award, the term "binding arbitration" becomes meaningless.

for the hearings of the arbitral panel. The Court further concludes that the second quoted sentence indicates the clear intent of the parties that any arbitration of a dispute arising under the contract is not to be appealed to any court. This interpretation, unlike that offered by Egypt, preserves the meaning of both sentences in a manner that is consistent with the plain language of the contract. The position of the latter sentence as the seventh and final paragraph, just before the signatures, lends credence to the view that this sentence is the final word on the arbitration question. In other words, the parties agreed to apply Egyptian Law to the arbitration, but, more important, they agreed that the arbitration ends with the decision of the arbitral panel.

2. The Decision of the Egyptian Court of Appeal

The Court has already found that the arbitral award is proper as a matter of U.S. law, and that the arbitration agreement between Egypt and CAS precluded an appeal in Egyptian courts. The Egyptian court has acted, however, and Egypt asks this Court to grant *res judicata* effect to that action.

The "requirements for enforcement of a foreign judgment . . . are that there be 'due citation' [*i.e.,* proper service of process] and that the original claim not violate U.S. public policy." Tahan v. Hodgson, 662 F.2d 862, 864 (D.C.Cir.1981) (citing Hilton v. Guyot, 159 U.S. 113, 202, 16 S.Ct. 139, 158, 40 L.Ed. 95 (1895)). The Court uses the term "public policy" advisedly, with a full understanding that, "[J]udges have no license to impose their own brand of justice in determining applicable public policy." Correctly understood, "[P]ublic policy emanates [only] from clear statutory or case law, 'not from general considerations of supposed public interest.'" Id.

The U.S. public policy in favor of final and binding arbitration of commercial disputes is unmistakable, and supported by treaty, by statute, and by case law. The Federal Arbitration Act "and the implementation of the Convention in the same year by amendment of the Federal Arbitration Act," demonstrate that there is an "emphatic federal policy in favor of arbitral dispute resolution," particularly "in the field of international commerce." Mitsubishi v. Soler Chrysler-Plymouth, 473 U.S. 614, 631, 105 S.Ct. 3346, 3356, 87 L.Ed.2d 444 (1985) (internal citation omitted); cf. Revere Copper & Brass Inc., v. Overseas Private Investment Corporation, 628 F.2d 81, 82 (D.C.Cir.1980) (holding that, "There is a strong public policy behind judicial enforcement of binding arbitration clauses"). A decision by this Court to recognize the decision of the Egyptian court would violate this clear U.S. public policy.

* * *

4. Choice of Law

Egypt argues that by choosing Egyptian law, and by choosing Cairo as the sight of the arbitration, CAS has for all time signed away its rights under the Convention and U.S. law. This argument is specious. When CAS agreed to the choice of law and choice of forum provisions, it waived its right to sue Egypt for breach of contract in the courts of the United States in favor of final and binding arbitration of such a dispute under the Convention. Having prevailed in the chosen forum, under the chosen law, CAS comes to this Court seeking recognition and enforcement of the award. The Convention was created for just this purpose. It is untenable to argue that by choosing arbitration under the Convention, CAS has waived rights specifically guaranteed by that same Convention.

5. Conflict between the Convention & the FAA

As a final matter, Egypt argues that, "Chromalloy's use of [A]rticle VII [to invoke the Federal Arbitration Act] contradicts the clear language of the Convention and would create an impermissible conflict under 9 U.S.C. § 208," by eliminating all consideration of Article V of the Convention. See Vimar Seguros y Reaseguros, S.A. v. M/V Sky Reefer, 515 U.S. 528, 533, 115 S.Ct. 2322, 2325, 132 L.Ed.2d 462 (1995) (holding that, "[W]hen two statutes are capable of coexistence . . . it is the duty of the courts, absent a clearly expressed congressional intention to the contrary, to regard each as effective"). As the Court has explained, however, Article V provides a permissive standard, under which this Court *may* refuse to enforce an award. Article VII, on the other hand, mandates that this Court *must* consider CAS' claims under applicable U.S. law. * * *

Article VII does not eliminate all consideration of Article V; it merely requires that this Court protect any rights that CAS has under the domestic laws of the United States. There is no conflict between CAS' use of Article VII to invoke the FAA and the language of the Convention.

IV. Conclusion

The Court concludes that the award of the arbitral panel is valid as a matter of U.S. law. The Court further concludes that it need not grant *res judicata* effect to the decision of the Egyptian Court of Appeal at Cairo. Accordingly, the Court GRANTS Chromalloy Aeroservices' Petition to Recognize and Enforce the Arbitral Award, and DENIES Egypt's Motion to Dismiss that Petition.

Chromalloy relied on Art. VII of the New York Convention, which provides "The provisions of the present Convention shall not * * * deprive any interested party of any right he may have to avail himself of an arbitral award in the manner and to the extent allowed by the law * * * of the count[r]y where such award is sought to be relied upon." But whether Chromalloy "would have been able to enforce an award rendered in Egypt in a United States court in the absence of the New York Convention is doubtful. Thus, it is difficult to see what more favorable rights of domestic law Article VII could have pointed to in this case." Stephen T. Ostrowski & Yuval Shany, Note, *Chromalloy: United States Law and International Arbitration at the Crossroads*, 73 N.Y.U. L. Rev. 1650, 1675–77 (1998)

Perhaps in *Chromallory* the arbitration award was fine and the Egyptian court's nullification of it was a gross injustice, so we see the benefit of *Chromalloy* enforcing the award. But suppose a case in which the arbitration award is grossly unjust and the seat court's nullification of it sensible? Then under *Chromallory* "the winner of a defective award could fail in enforcement in any forum and still continue to go to others in an effort at enforcement, harassing the other party and forcing it either to settle for a nuisance value factored by the number of jurisdictions in which it could be pursued or to expend great amounts of time and effort to block and block again enforcement efforts without ever securing a terminal annulment." W. Michael Reisman, Systems of Control in International Adjudication and Arbitration 117 (1992)

Chromalloy was likely motivated, at least in part, by suspicions about the behavior of the Egyptian courts in overturning an arbitral award rendered against the Egyptian Government. The Cairo court referred at one point to the "irreparable serious harm" that the award would supposedly inflict on Egypt. The attorney for Chromalloy has written that while his client "could present no 'smoking gun' to demonstrate conclusively that the Egyptian court, or the country's entire judiciary, was biased or corrupt, it was able to show that Egyptian courts have had a disturbing propensity to nullify awards in favor of foreign parties against Egyptians or its government for seemingly arbitrary reasons." Gary H. Sampliner, *Enforcement of Foreign Arbitral Awards After Annulment in Their Country of Origin*, 11 (9) Mealey's Int'l Arb. Rep., Sept. 1996 at 22, 28. In these circumstances, was it preferable for the court to rest its decision on Art. VII of the New York Convention rather than relying on the discretionary standard of Art. V(1)(e)?

Chromalloy is not unique but courts generally decline to enforce under their own domestic arbitration law awards that have been vacated by a court of the State that is the seat of arbitration. See, e.g., Baker Marine (Nig.) Ltd. v. Chevron (Nig.) Ltd., 191 F.3d 194 (2d Cir. 1999). Baker Marine and Danos jointly entered a contract with Chevron to provide barge services. The contract specified that the arbitration "procedure * * * shall be governed by the substantive laws of the Federal Republic of Nigeria" and that the contracts "shall be interpreted in accordance with the laws of the Federal Republic of Nigeria." After Baker Marine charged Chevron and Danos with violating the contracts, the parties submitted to arbitration before arbitration panels in Lagos; one panel awarded Baker Marine $2.23 million in damages against Danos and a second panel awarded Baker Marine $750,000 in damages against Chevron. The Nigerian courts later set aside the two awards—concluding, in the Chevron action, that the arbitrators had improperly awarded punitive damages, gone beyond the scope of the submissions, incorrectly admitted parole evidence, and made inconsistent awards; and in the Danos action, that the award was unsupported by the evidence.

Baker Marine moved for confirmation in New York, but the district court relied on Article V(1)(e) in declining to enforce the awards, holding that under the Convention and principles of comity, "it would not be proper to enforce a foreign arbitral award under the Convention when such an award has been set aside by the Nigerian courts." The Second Circuit affirmed:

> It is sufficient answer [to Baker Marine's argument] that the parties contracted in Nigeria that their disputes would be arbitrated under the laws of Nigeria. The governing agreements make no reference whatever to United States law. Nothing suggests that the parties intended United States domestic arbitral law to govern their disputes. Furthermore, Baker Marine has made no contention that the Nigerian courts acted contrary to Nigerian law.

Can *Baker Marine* be squared with the earlier decision in *Chromalloy*? The Second Circuit purported to "distinguish" *Chromalloy* on the ground that unlike the petitioner in that case, "Baker Marine is not a United States citizen, and it did not initially seek confirmation of the award in the United States. Furthermore, Chevron and Danos did not violate any promise in appealing the arbitration award within Nigeria." Furthermore, the court noted, "as a practical matter, mechanical application of domestic arbitral law to foreign awards under the Convention would seriously undermine finality and regularly produce conflicting judgments." If a party whose arbitration award has been vacated at the site of the award can automatically obtain enforcement of the awards under the domestic laws of other nations, a losing party will have every reason to pursue its adversary "with enforcement actions from country to country until a court is found, if any, which grants the enforcement."

QUESTIONS TO REVIEW AND SYNTHESIZE

1. What two litigation paths are generally available to a party seeking to prevent or limit enforcement of an arbitration award rendered against it?
2. Which body of law governs the setting aside (vacatur) of an international commercial arbitration award?
3. Why did *Chromalloy* decline to recognize the decision of the Egyptian court to set aside the award?

3. NON-ENFORCEMENT OF INTERNATIONAL COMMERCIAL ARBITRATION AWARDS

The Convention's grounds for denying recognition and enforcement are discussed in the following subsections.

a. ARBITRATION AGREEMENT INVALID

Article V(1)(a) of the New York Convention says recognition and enforcement of an arbitration award may be refused if "The parties to the agreement referred to in article II were, under the law applicable to them, under some incapacity, or the said agreement is not valid under the law to which the parties have subjected it or, failing any indication thereon, under the law of the country where the award was made." This provision refers to and relates to Article II, which generally requires enforcement of executory arbitration agreements. While Article V(1)(a) has a choice-of-law rule not found in Article II,[70] generally, "the same substantive analysis that applies in the context of the enforcement of [executory] arbitration agreements is equally applicable in resolving an application to recognize [or deny enforcement to] an arbitral award." 2 Gary B. Born, International Commercial Arbitration 2780 (2009). But see China Minmetals Materials Import & Export Co., Ltd. v. Chi Mei Corp., 334 F.3d 274, 286 & fn. 13 (3d Cir. 2003)(court should not enforce an award "where the parties did not reach a valid agreement to arbitrate, at least in the absence of a waiver of the objection to arbitration by the party opposing enforcement";

---

[70] Article V(1)(a) provides that enforcement of an award may be refused if the arbitration "agreement is not valid under the law to which the parties have subjected it or, failing any indication thereon, under the law of the country where the award was made." Under this choice-of-law rule, the relevant State's law is the law the parties have chosen in a choice-of-law clause ("the law to which the parties have subjected it") or, if there is no party choice of law, then the relevant State's law is the law of the country where the award was made, that is, the "seat" of arbitration.

however, there remains "some distinction" between Art. II and Art. V, since the former "explicitly requires 'an agreement in writing' while [the latter, by contrast], requires only that the parties have reached an agreement as to arbitrability under ordinary contract principles"). Compare id. at 292–3 (Alito, J., concurring and writing "separately to elaborate on the importance of Art. IV(1)(b)" of the Convention; to "comport with fundamental principles of arbitration," a party seeking enforcement must produce an "agreement in writing within the meaning of Art. II").

b. INADEQUATE OPPORTUNITY TO PRESENT CASE

Article V(1)(b) of the New York Convention says recognition and enforcement of an arbitration award may be refused if "[t]he party against whom the award is invoked was not given proper notice of the appointment of the arbitrator or of the arbitration proceedings or was otherwise unable to present his case." Cases relying on Article V(1)(b) in denying enforcement to an arbitration award include facts like: lack of an oral hearing, inadequate notice of the hearing, and denial of an opportunity to present evidence. In an example of the latter, the Second Circuit held that arbitrators (the Iran-United States Claims Tribunal) denied a party (Avco) the opportunity to present its claim by first "approving the method of proof proposed by Avco, namely the submission of Avco's audited accounts receivable ledgers," and then ruling against Avco because it did not submit actual invoices. Iran Aircraft Industries v. Avco Corp., 980 F.2d 141 (2d Cir.1992) ("Having thus led Avco to believe it had used a proper method to substantiate its claim, the Tribunal then rejected Avco's claim for lack of proof. * * *We believe that by so misleading Avco, however unwittingly, the Tribunal denied Avco the opportunity to present its claim in a meaningful manner.")

Apart from such relatively rare cases, showing that a party lacked an opportunity to present its case may require an uncertain and fact-intensive inquiry about the extent to which arbitrators can reasonably be expected to accommodate the schedule of a party or its witnesses. Courts generally defer to arbitrators' judgment about the timing and conduct of the arbitration proceedings. See, e.g., Parsons & Whittemore Overseas Co., Inc. v. Societe Generale De L'Industrie du Papier (RAKTA), 508 F.2d 969, 973–74 (2d Cir.1974) (rejecting Article V(1)(b) argument).

c. ARBITRATORS EXCEEDED THEIR JURISDICTION

Article V(1)(c) of the New York Convention says recognition and enforcement of an arbitration award may be refused if "The award deals with a difference not contemplated by or not falling within the terms of the submission to arbitration, or it contains decisions on matters beyond the scope of the submission to arbitration, provided that, if the decisions on matters submitted to arbitration can be separated from those not so submitted, that part of the award which contains decisions on matters submitted to arbitration may be recognized and enforced." This ground for non-enforcement resembles FAA § 10(a)(4), which permits courts to vacate an arbitration award where, among other things, "the arbitrators exceeded their powers."

Courts and commentators generally speak interchangeably of arbitrators exceeding their powers, exceeding their authority, or exceeding their jurisdiction. Importantly, however, whether one calls it the arbitrators' "power," or "authority," or "jurisdiction," it comes from the parties. It is jurisdiction conferred by contract, not by statute or other law, so arbitrators exceed this jurisdiction when they decide matters beyond the scope of the arbitration agreement. This is clear in Article V(1)(c) of the New York Convention which refers to "matters beyond the scope of the submission to arbitration."

Courts will enforce an arbitration award on a claim only if the parties agreed to arbitrate that claim. That the parties agreed to arbitrate *some* claim is not enough. They must have agreed to arbitrate *that* claim. However, courts generally presume that the arbitrators acted within their powers. See Management & Technical Consultants S.A. v. Parsons-Jurden Intern. Corp., 820 F.2d 1531, 1534 (9th Cir.1987) (stating, in a case to enforce a foreign arbitral award, "Federal arbitration law has established a presumption that an arbitral body has acted within its powers"); Parsons & Whittemore Overseas Co., Inc. v. Societe Generale De L'Industrie du Papier (RAKTA), 508 F.2d 969, 976 (2d Cir.1974) (referring to the "powerful presumption that the arbitral body acted within its powers.") Courts rarely decline to enforce awards as beyond the submission to arbitration. Albert Jan van den Berg, New York Convention of 1958: Refusals of Enforcement, 18(2) ICC Int'l Ct. Arb. Bull. 15, 24 (2007) (finding only two reported cases, neither of which was from the United States).

Parties often take this issue away from courts by giving it to arbitrators. That is, parties often agree to arbitrate pursuant to an arbitration organization's rules giving the arbitrators power to decide whether particular claims are within the scope of the arbitration agreement. "As a practical matter, parties in many international commercial arbitrations will be found to have submitted disputes over the scope of their arbitration clause to the arbitrators for resolution. That is in large part because the terms of most institutional arbitration rules expressly provide that jurisdictional questions are for arbitral resolution." Gary B. Born, International Commercial Arbitration 932 (2009).[71] Where parties have done this, the arbitrators' "jurisdictional decision should generally not be subject to subsequent judicial review." Id. at 2802 (Vol 2).

d. IMPROPER ARBITRAL PROCEDURE OR COMPOSITION OF ARBITRAL AUTHORITY

Article V(1)(d) of the New York Convention says recognition and enforcement of an arbitration award may be refused if "[t]he composition of the arbitral authority or the arbitral procedure was not in accordance with the agreement of the parties, or, failing such agreement, was not in accordance with the law of the country where the arbitration took place." The gist of this provision is that arbitration procedure is a matter of contract; it is governed by the parties' agreement and if that agreement has gaps then the law of the seat of arbitration fills those gaps. Cases relying on Article

[71] See, e.g., *International Chamber of Commerce Rules of Arbitration*, Art. 6, https://iccwbo.org/dispute-resolution-services/arbitration/rules-of-arbitration/#article_6.

V(1)(d) in denying enforcement to an arbitration award include facts such as the arbitrators' failure to:

- render an award or conduct the proceedings within prescribed time limits,
- conduct the arbitration in the agreed arbitral seat,
- make a reasoned award,
- apply agreed rules of procedure, or
- apply provisions regarding consolidation of arbitrations.

Id. at 2765–68. That said, courts are generally reluctant (even in cases with facts like those just listed) to overturn awards for arbitrators' minor violations of agreed procedures. A leading commentator states that "the most difficult issues that arise under Article V(1)(d) involve cases where the parties' agreed arbitral procedures violate the mandatory laws of the arbitral seat," and "the weight of authority is that for purposes of Article V(1)(d), the parties' agreed arbitral procedures must be given effect, regardless of the law of the arbitral seat." Id. at 2768.

e. SET ASIDE BY COURT AT SEAT OF ARBITRATION

As noted in Section E.2.b of this chapter, Article V(1)(e) of the New York Convention says recognition and enforcement of an arbitration award may be refused if "The award has not yet become binding on the parties, or has been set aside or suspended by a competent authority of the country in which, or under the law of which, that award was made." Whether a particular award has "become binding on the parties" can be in some cases be debated, but confirmation of an award by a court in the arbitral seat is not necessary to make an award binding. Courts generally hold awards to be binding even when a party displeased with the award might still seek to have it set aside by a court in the arbitral seat. Id. at 2818–19.

A related provision is Article VI of the Convention which provides:

> If an application for the setting aside or suspension of the award has been made to a competent authority referred to in article V(1)(e), the authority before which the award is sought to be relied upon may, if it considers it proper, adjourn the decision on the enforcement of the award and may also, on the application of the party claiming enforcement of the award, order the other party to give suitable security.

At least one United States court has adjourned its enforcement pending a decision by a court at the seat of arbitration, India, on whether to set aside the award. Fertilizer Corp. of India v. IDI Management, Inc., 517 F.Supp. 948, 956–59 (S.D.Ohio 1981) ("The award is presently before the Indian courts for a ruling."); id. at 962 ("this Court has determined to adjourn its decision on enforcement of the Nitrophosphate Award until the Indian courts decide with finality whether the award is correct under Indian law. FCI, of course, may apply to this Court for suitable security, as provided by Article VI.") See also Europcar Italia, S.p.A. v. Maiellano Tours, Inc., 156 F.3d 310, 317–18 (2d Cir. 1998) (listing factors courts should consider when deciding whether to adjourn enforcement proceedings to await the outcome of parallel foreign proceedings).

f. NON-ARBITRABILITY

Article V(2)(a) of the New York Convention says recognition and enforcement of an arbitration award may be refused if "the competent authority in the country where recognition and enforcement is sought finds that: The subject matter of the difference is not capable of settlement by arbitration under the law of that country."[72] This provision relates to Article II(1), discussed above, which requires enforcement of agreements to arbitrate only disputes "concerning a subject matter capable of settlement by arbitration." Generally, "if arbitration of a claim cannot be compelled under Article II(1), because it is non-arbitrable, then an arbitral award dealing with that claim is unenforceable under Article V(2)(a), subject only to possible waiver arguments." 2 Gary B. Born, International Commercial Arbitration 2863 (2009). However, if non-enforcement of an award (Art. V) is sought in a different State than non-enforcement of an executory agreement (Art. II) than different standards may apply. Inarbitrability has not often been relied on by courts in declining enforcement of awards. Albert Jan van den Berg, *New York Convention of 1958: Refusals of Enforcement*, 18(2) ICC Int'l Ct. Arb. Bull. 1 (2007).

g. PUBLIC POLICY

Article V(2)(b) of the New York Convention says recognition and enforcement of an arbitration award may be refused if "the competent authority in the country where recognition and enforcement is sought finds that * * * [t]he recognition or enforcement of the award would be contrary to the public policy of that country." This provision has been interpreted narrowly by United States courts. As the Second Circuit recognized long ago,

> [a]n expansive construction of this defense would vitiate the Convention's basic effort to remove preexisting obstacles to enforcement. Additionally, considerations of reciprocity—considerations given express recognition in the Convention itself—counsel courts to invoke the public policy defense with caution lest foreign courts frequently accept it as a defense to enforcement of arbitral awards rendered in the United States.

Parsons & Whittemore Overseas Co., Inc. v. Societe Generale De L'Industrie du Papier (RAKTA), 508 F.2d 969, 973–74 (2d Cir.1974).[73] Therefore, the court held "enforcement of foreign arbitral awards may be denied on this basis only where enforcement would violate the forum state's most basic notions of morality and justice." Id. at 974. For an example, see Karen Mar. Ltd. v. Omar Int'l, Inc., 322 F. Supp. 2d 224, 229 (E.D.N.Y. 2004) (contract undertaking to boycott Israel violated U.S. anti-boycott law; "if [e]nforcement of the award * * * legitimized or perpetuated the Arab boycott of Israel, [enforcement] would violate basic American notions of morality and justice.") Similarly, one commentator observes that courts, especially in developed countries, exercise "a substantial degree of restraint and

[72] New York Convention, art. V(2)(a).

[73] Accord Fertilizer Corp. of India v. IDI Management, Inc., 517 F.Supp. 948 (S.D.Ohio 1981).

moderation in the application of public policies under Article V(2)(b)," while, in contrast, "some less-developed states have taken relatively expansive views of public policy, relying on the doctrine's 'unruly' character to refuse recognition to foreign arbitral awards on a variety of grounds." Gary B. Born, International Commercial Arbitration 2833, 2859 (2009).

QUESTIONS TO REVIEW AND SYNTHESIZE

1. When does the New York Convention permit a court to refuse to recognize or enforce an arbitration award?
2. What facts would support a party's argument that the court should set aside an award because the party did not have an adequate opportunity to present its case?
3. Is the public policy ground to deny recognition or enforcement of an award used often in the US?

F. DRAFTING AN INTERNATIONAL COMMERCIAL ARBITRATION CLAUSE

Compared to purely domestic transactions, transnational ventures—involving parties of different nationalities, or performance in different nations—tend to be larger and more complex and thus to warrant considerable care at the drafting stage. The potential involvement of more than one legal system should motivate parties and lawyers to think, not only about whether to include an arbitration clause, but also about which courts will be available to intervene in the arbitral process or to enforce or vacate the resulting arbitration award. The following excerpts discuss several key provisions that parties should consider when drafting an international arbitration clause.

Margaret L. Moses, *The Principles and Practice of International Commercial Arbitration*

46–47, 50–52 (3d ed. 2017).

The arbitration agreement serves the critical function of creating a framework for the parties' own private dispute resolution system outside of national courts. To ensure proper functioning of system, the agreement should be drafted with great care. A well-drafted arbitration clause has a significant impact on how well the parties resolve the dispute—how efficiently, how fairly, and how successfully. Unfortunately, in negotiating and drafting a contract, attorneys and parties too often do not focus on drafting the arbitration clause. * * *

There are several reasons for the sad neglect of the arbitration clause. First, the clause is frequently left until the end of the negotiations, after the major issues have been resolved. At that point, parties may think they do not have sufficient energy or resources to engage in more negotiations over the arbitration clause. Second, the lawyers who draft arbitration clauses tend to be transactional lawyers, who may have little understanding or knowledge about the arbitration process or the significance of the arbitration clause. And third, parties simply may not believe they will encounter disputes that would be worth the transaction costs of researching, understanding, and negotiating an arbitration clause that is anything more than boilerplate.

Increasingly, however, lawyers are recognizing that the stakes in arbitration may be high, and that a well-drafted clause can make an enourmous difference in the ability of the parties to resolve a dispute efficiently and effectively. * * * Even among experienced lawyers who have some understanding of arbitration, there can still be disagreement about whether the client is better served by a short and simple clause or by a more extensive and complex clause. Much depends on the kind of transaction at issue, the likelihood that a dispute may develop, and the ultimate value that a potential dispute would likely have.

* * *

1. Choice of Arbitrators

* * * [P]arties will need to make some important decisions. In determining whether to have one or three arbitrators, for example, a party should consider how complicated the transaction is, the likelihood that a dispute will arise, and the estimated value of the potential dispute. * * * With one arbitrator instead of three, it should be easier to schedule hearings. Moreover, the costs would be lower, and the proceedings and award should move forward more quickly, because there would be no need for members of a tribunal [three arbitrators] to confer and debate over various points.

On the other hand, in complex, high-value disputes, parties generally prefer to have three arbitrators. Although having three arbitrators is much more expensive than having one, and scheduling the hearings can be difficult, most parties feel more comfortable with three arbitrators when substantial amounts of money are at stake. With respect to the complexity of the issues, three minds are generally better than one at absorbing all the necessary information and arriving at a reasonable resolution. In addition, when the parties are from different cultural or legal backgrounds, a party may want at least one arbitrator to have some knowledge and understanding of its own culture and legal system. In such a case, the parties may put in their arbitration clause that each party will appoint one arbitrator, and the two party-appointed arbitrators will choose the third arbitrator, who will serve as chair. If the parties do not agree on a method of choosing the arbitrators, selection will occur in accordance with the rules of the administering institution.

Parties also may want to set forth specific qualifications that the arbitrators should have, such as experience or expertise in a particular field, or the ability to speak a particular language. One should be careful, however, not to specify so many characteristics that it becomes impossible to find arbitrators who meet all the qualifications. This could possibly result in invalidating the arbitration clause.

2. Seat of the Arbitration

Choosing the seat of the arbitration is important because generally the arbitration law of the arbitral situs will be the law that governs the arbitration procedure (the *lex arbitri*). Parties want an 'arbitration-friendly' regime—that is, one that will not unduly interfere with the arbitral process. If any court intervention is needed or occurs during or after the arbitration, the local law governing arbitrations will have an impact on the proceedings.

Parties will also tend to choose a country that is not the place of business of either party, so they will be in a 'neutral' forum. In addition, it is important to choose a situs within a country that is a party to the New York Convention (a 'Contracting State'). Many countries have declared they will only enforce arbitration awards that were made in another Contracting State. Thus, if the seat of the arbitration was not within a Contracting State, the award might not be enforceable in the jurisdiction where the losing party's assets are located.

In addition, the arbitration should be held in a place where the infrastructure is sufficiently developed to permit reasonable transportation to and from the location, where basic technology is available (phones, faxes, internet access), and where the political and economic structure is stable. One rule of thumb: Do not hold an arbitration in a place where you would not go on vacation.

3. Language of the Arbitration

Parties should state the language of the arbitration in the arbitration clause. Although some parties assume the language of the contract will be the language of the arbitration, that may not necessarily be the case. The tribunal could decide differently, unless the parties have specifically agreed on a language. A client that had to assume unexpected costs of translating documents and witness testimony because the lawyers had never specified the language in the arbitration clause would not be a happy client.

Eric S. Sherby, *A Checklist for Drafting an International Arbitration Clause*

2010 Bus. L. Today 1, 2 (2010).

* * *

Arbitral institutions (at least the major ones) oversee the work of the arbitrator—to some extent. Also, the conventional wisdom is that it is easier to enforce an award given by an arbitral institution than one given by an ad hoc arbitrator.

But there is a price for that increased accountability and superior chance of enforcement. Arbitral institutions have administrative staff and almost always some professional legal staff.

* * *

The leading international institution is the International Chamber of Commerce (the ICC). Not far behind (at least from an American perspective) is the American Arbitration Association (the AAA), which maintains multiple sets of domestic rules and a set of international rules. In the same tier as the ICC and the AAA is the World Intellectual Property Organization (obviously not for a dispute in, for example, the construction industry).

In connection with sole-arbitrator cases, the rules of each of the ICC, the AAA (international rules), and WIPO include a general preference to appoint an arbitrator from a third-party (neutral) country.

Most international practitioners consider the London Court of International Arbitration to be in a league not far behind the ICC, the AAA, and WIPO. In the United States, in recent years, Judicial Arbitration and Mediation Services (JAMS) has made significant headway in the international field.

* * *

If your clients never have dealings in the Far East, then you likely will not need to be familiar with institutions such as the Chinese European Arbitration Centre or the Hong Kong International Arbitration Centre. However, if your clients do have dealings in the Far East, you should be familiar with those institutions.

* * *

When representing an American company in an international transaction, most American lawyers believe that it is safe to propose the AAA (through its International Rules), with the ICC being a fallback if the non-U.S. company objects to the AAA. It is difficult to argue with that conventional wisdom.

Claudia T. Salomon and J.P. Duffy, *Enforcement Begins when the Arbitration Clause is Drafted*

22 Am. Rev. Int'l Arb. 271, 274–75 (2011).

3. Draft Around Known Enforcement Issues in the Jurisdiction Where Enforcement Is Likely

Practitioners should anticipate where any award is likely to be enforced when drafting international arbitration clauses. If thought is given to where a party may seek to enforce an award, known enforcement issues in that jurisdiction can be anticipated and avoided. For instance, if enforcement is anticipated in India, the drafter may wish to expressly waive application of Part I of the Indian Arbitration and Conciliation Act, 1996, which permits parties that are opposing confirmation of an award to raise broad public policy defenses that can lead to Indian courts reviewing an award on the merits. If enforcement will be sought in Saudi Arabia, the drafter must be aware that Saudi Arabia will not enforce awards that are not Shari'ah-compliant. Accordingly, to the extent possible, the drafter should require the arbitrators to issue a Shari'ah-compliant award.

If enforcement in Qatar is anticipated, drafters may wish to exclude any right to appeal the merits of the award to the Qatari courts. Similarly, drafters may wish to preclude any right to appeal questions of law to the English courts if the arbitration is seated in England or Wales and that right of appeal is not foreclosed by the institutional rules chosen by the parties. Those are merely a few examples of potential issues thoughtful drafters can work around if careful consideration is given to the place where enforcement is likely to be sought. Drafters should therefore seek to determine where enforcement will be most likely and should review any unique enforcement issues or requirements in that jurisdiction.

QUESTIONS TO REVIEW AND SYNTHESIZE

1. What are some important considerations when drafting an international arbitration clause?
2. Why might parties want more than one arbitrator, despite the increased cost?

G. INTERNATIONAL PUBLIC LAW ARBITRATION

1. OVERVIEW OF INTERNATIONAL PUBLIC LAW ARBITRATION

International arbitration basically divides into commercial arbitration and public law arbitration. As we have seen throughout this chapter, international commercial arbitration is similar to domestic arbitration because each is a private-sector alternative to government courts. In the international commercial context, "[w]hen parties agree to arbitrate their disputes, they give up the right to have those disputes decided by a national court. Instead, they agree that their disputes will be resolved privately, outside any court system." Margaret L. Moses, The Principles and Practice of International Commercial Arbitration 20 (3d. ed.2017).

In contrast, the word "arbitration" in the international public law context typically does not refer to a private-sector alternative to government courts. International public law disputes generally involve claims by and against States—claims for which there is no national court with jurisdiction to enter judgment against the defending State because the doctrine of sovereign immunity prevents such jurisdiction. See, e.g., Andreas F. Lowenfeld, International Litigation and Arbitration ch.7 (3d ed.2006). Sovereign immunity is less of a force in commercial arbitration than in public law arbitration because sovereign immunity often does not protect a State insofar as it is engaged in "commercial," rather than governmental, activity. See, e.g., 28 U.S.C. § 1605 ("A foreign state shall not be immune from the jurisdiction of courts of the United States or of the States in any case—* * * in which the action is based upon a commercial activity carried on in the United States by the foreign state.")

When States "arbitrate" their public law disputes with each other, they are not giving up the right to have those disputes decided by a national court because they never had any such right. So international public law arbitration is not an alternative to international litigation, but rather an alternative to the other ways States interact, such as diplomacy and war. The same is also generally true of public international law arbitration involving claims against States by private parties who are citizens of different States; for example, investment arbitration generally involves foreign investors claims against states—claims that would otherwise be barred by sovereign immunity.

Because the claims in public international law arbitration are generally against States, enforcement of an award arising out of such arbitration may face an obstacle not likely present in international commercial arbitration, let alone domestic arbitration: how does a party enforce an arbitration award against a State whose national courts are part of the State and thus share the State's opposition to enforcement of the award?

Public international arbitration agreements can be divided into three types. See, e.g., Thomas Buergenthal & Sean D. Murphy, Public International Law in a Nutshell 71–72 (4th ed.2007). The first consists of an arbitration clause that is included in a treaty with the purpose of resolving disputes regarding the application of that treaty. A prominent example of this first type is investment arbitration. The second type of public international arbitration agreement "consists of treaties whose sole function is to establish a method for the resolution and arbitration of whatever disputes might arise between the parties in the future." Id. And the third type includes post-dispute arbitration agreements, such as the one establishing the Iran-U.S. Claims Tribunal. These three types of public international law arbitration are discussed in the following three sections.

2. INVESTMENT ARBITRATION

When the parties to a major transnational business transactions consist entirely of private-sector businesses from the most economically-developed parts of the world, their contracts often provide for international *commercial* arbitration of any disputes. In contrast, other transnational business transactions involve a country's government (a State) as a party. This is especially likely when the transaction will exploit natural resources (e.g., mining) or require a large investment in a less-developed country. With at least one State as a party, arbitration arising out of such transactions is international *public law* arbitration, and commonly falls under the heading of "investment arbitration." "The paradigmatic commercial arbitration case involves contract claims arising out of business transactions between private parties. Investment disputes, on the other hand, always involve claims against state party respondents concerning their interference with investments made by foreign investors (often, but not always, in state-sponsored projects). The private-public distinction also holds true for the sources that govern the disputes." Irene M. Ten Cate, *International Arbitration and the Ends of Appellate Review*, 44 N.Y.U. J. Int'l L. & Pol. 1109, 1113 (2012).

While international *commercial* arbitration arises out of an ordinary contract between the parties (either a pre-dispute arbitration agreement or a post-dispute submission agreement), the "contract" underlying investment arbitration is typically quite different. Generally, the State in which the investment occurred (the "host" State) previously consented to arbitration by acceding (agreeing) to a treaty providing for the arbitration of investment disputes or by enacting similar legislation. Such a treaty or legislation amounts to a standing offer to arbitrate disputes with any investor fulfilling the requirements of the treaty or legislation.

States typically make such offers to attract foreign investment. Historically, as noted in Section 2.B.3, investors had been vulnerable to host State seizure of assets (expropriation) or regulation tantamount to expropriation. "The investment may be considerable which may need years for the investor to recover. In developing countries foreign investment often relates to core components of the national economy. These factors make foreign investment particularly vulnerable to possible interference by the host state." Julian D. Lew, Loukas A. Mistelis & Stefan M. Kroll, Comparative International Commercial Arbitration 764 (2003). The doctrine of sovereign immunity might prevent investors from bringing a claim against the host State in the investor's home courts or the courts of the host State, so the only remedy available to the investor would be diplomatic or military support from its home State against the host State. With investors' home states generally reluctant to provide such support, investors continue to fear expropriation and similar actions by host states. Reducing these fears is a goal of international investment treaties and their arbitration provisions. Enforcing an international investment arbitration award against a State "may be difficult, but political repercussions of treaty-based arbitration claims have compelled countries to honor awards—obviating the investor's need to pursue collection through the courts." Michael S. Greco & Ian Meredith, *Getting to Yes Abroad: Arbitration as a Tool in Effective Commercial and Political Risk Management*, Bus.L.Today, March/April 2007, at 23, 25.

The terms of international investment treaties vary. In most, host states do not forego a right of expropriation altogether. Rather, host states limit the circumstances permitting expropriation and provide for compensating the foreign investor. See Jeswald W. Salacuse, The Law of Investment Treaties 288 (2010). Host states agree to provide foreign investors with the better of treatment provided to investments of nationals of the host State or of investments of nationals of any other country. Investment treaties usually prohibit the host country from requiring the investment project to export a percentage of its production, use local content, or hire local workers. Id. at 329. Investment treaties ensure that the investor can transfer money freely between the host State and the investor's home State.

The number of parties to international investment treaties varies. Some involve only two countries, that is, they are bilateral investment treaties (BITs). A typical BIT, as elaborated in Section 2.B.3, obligates the host State to provide foreign investors protection against various forms of expropriation and discrimination by the State.[74] For example, in the Supreme Court's 2014 case of *BG Grp., PLC v. Republic of Argentina*, excerpted below, a British investor in Argentina argued "that Argentina's new laws and regulatory practices violated provisions in the [BIT] forbidding the 'expropriation' of investments and requiring that each nation give 'fair and equitable treatment' to investors from the other." 572 U.S. 25, 30 (2014).

BG Group PLC v. Republic of Argentina

Supreme Court of the United States, 2014.
572 U.S. 25, 134 S.Ct. 1198, 188 L.Ed.2d 220.

■ JUSTICE BREYER delivered the opinion of the Court.

Article 8 of an investment treaty between the United Kingdom and Argentina contains a dispute-resolution provision, applicable to disputes between one of

[74] "To facilitate the flow of capital to lesser-developed countries, the United States and other Western nations have entered into more than 2,800 BITs with capital-importing countries. A critical feature of these treaties is that they protect the foreign investor against expropriation or other conduct." Peter B. Rutledge, Arbitration and the Constitution 51–52 (2013).

those nations and an investor from the other. See Agreement for the Promotion and Protection of Investments, Art. 8(2), Dec. 11, 1990, 1765 U. N. T. S. 38 (hereinafter Treaty). The provision authorizes either party to submit a dispute "to the decision of the competent tribunal of the Contracting Party in whose territory the investment was made," *i.e.*, a local court. Art. 8(1). And it provides for arbitration

> "(i) where, after a period of eighteen months has elapsed from the moment when the dispute was submitted to the competent tribunal . . ., the said tribunal has not given its final decision; [or]
>
> "(ii) where the final decision of the aforementioned tribunal has been made but the Parties are still in dispute." Art. 8(2)(a).

The Treaty also entitles the parties to agree to proceed directly to arbitration. Art. 8(2)(b).

This case concerns the Treaty's arbitration clause, and specifically the local court litigation requirement set forth in Article 8(2)(a). The question before us is whether a court of the United States, in reviewing an arbitration award made under the Treaty, should interpret and apply the local litigation requirement *de novo*, or with the deference that courts ordinarily owe arbitration decisions. That is to say, who—court or arbitrator—bears primary responsibility for interpreting and applying the local litigation requirement to an underlying controversy? In our view, the matter is for the arbitrators, and courts must review their determinations with deference.

In the early 1990's, the petitioner, BG Group plc, a British firm, belonged to a consortium that bought a majority interest in an Argentine entity called MetroGAS. MetroGAS was a gas distribution company created by Argentine law in 1992, as a result of the government's privatization of its state-owned gas utility. Argentina distributed the utility's assets to new, private companies, one of which was MetroGAS. It awarded MetroGAS a 35-year exclusive license to distribute natural gas in Buenos Aires, and it submitted a controlling interest in the company to international public tender. BG Group's consortium was the successful bidder.

At about the same time, Argentina enacted statutes providing that its regulators would calculate gas "tariffs" in U. S. dollars, and that those tariffs would be set at levels sufficient to assure gas distribution firms, such as MetroGAS, a reasonable return.

In 2001 and 2002, Argentina, faced with an economic crisis, enacted new laws. Those laws changed the basis for calculating gas tariffs from dollars to pesos, at a rate of one peso per dollar. The exchange rate at the time was roughly three pesos to the dollar. The result was that MetroGAS' profits were quickly transformed into losses. BG Group believed that these changes (and several others) violated the Treaty; Argentina believed the contrary.

In 2003, BG Group, invoking Article 8 of the Treaty, sought arbitration. The parties appointed arbitrators; they agreed to site the arbitration in Washington, D. C.; and between 2004 and 2006, the arbitrators decided motions, received evidence, and conducted hearings. BG Group essentially claimed that Argentina's new laws and regulatory practices violated provisions in the Treaty forbidding the "expropriation" of investments and requiring that each nation give "fair and equitable treatment" to investors from the other. Argentina denied these claims, while also arguing that the arbitration tribunal lacked "jurisdiction" to hear the dispute. According to Argentina, the arbitrators lacked jurisdiction because: (1) BG Group was not a Treaty-protected "investor"; (2) BG Group's interest in MetroGAS was not a Treaty-protected "investment"; and (3) BG Group initiated arbitration without first litigating its claims in Argentina's courts, despite Article 8's requirement. In Argentina's view, "failure by BG to bring its grievance to Argentine courts for 18 months renders its claims in this arbitration inadmissible."

In late December 2007, the arbitration panel reached a final decision. It began by determining that it had "jurisdiction" to consider the merits of the dispute. In support of that determination, the tribunal concluded that BG Group was an "investor," that its interest in MetroGAS amounted to a Treaty-protected "investment," and that Argentina's own conduct had waived, or excused, BG Group's failure to comply with Article 8's local litigation requirement. The panel pointed out that in 2002, the President of Argentina had issued a decree staying for 180 days the execution of its courts' final judgments (and injunctions) in suits claiming harm as a result of the new economic measures. In addition, Argentina had established a "renegotiation process" for public service contracts, such as its contract with MetroGAS, to alleviate the negative impact of the new economic measures. But Argentina had simultaneously barred from participation in that "process" firms that were litigating against Argentina in court or in arbitration. These measures, while not making litigation in Argentina's courts literally impossible, nonetheless "hindered" recourse "to the domestic judiciary" to the point where the Treaty implicitly excused compliance with the local litigation requirement. Requiring a private party in such circumstances to seek relief in Argentina's courts for 18 months, the panel concluded, would lead to "absurd and unreasonable result[s]."

On the merits, the arbitration panel agreed with Argentina that it had not "expropriate[d]" BG Group's investment, but also found that Argentina had denied BG Group "fair and equitable treatment." It awarded BG Group $185 million in damages.

In March 2008, both sides filed petitions for review in the District Court for the District of Columbia. BG Group sought to confirm the award under the New York Convention and the Federal Arbitration Act. Argentina sought to vacate the award in part on the ground that the arbitrators lacked jurisdiction. See § 10(a)(4) (a federal court may vacate an arbitral award "where the arbitrators exceeded their powers").

The District Court denied Argentina's claims and confirmed the award. But the Court of Appeals for the District of Columbia Circuit reversed. In the appeals court's view, the interpretation and application of Article 8's local litigation requirement was a matter for courts to decide *de novo*, *i.e.*, without deference to the views of the arbitrators. The Court of Appeals then went on to hold that the circumstances did not excuse BG Group's failure to comply with the requirement. Rather, BG Group must "commence a lawsuit in Argentina's courts and wait eighteen months before filing for arbitration." Because BG Group had not done so, the arbitrators lacked authority to decide the dispute. And the appeals court ordered the award vacated. * * *

As we have said, the question before us is who—court or arbitrator—bears primary responsibility for interpreting and applying Article 8's local court litigation provision. Put in terms of standards of judicial review, should a United States court review the arbitrators' interpretation and application of the provision *de novo*, or with the deference that courts ordinarily show arbitral decisions on matters the parties have committed to arbitration? Compare, e.g., First Options of Chicago, Inc. v. Kaplan, 514 U. S. 938, 942 (1995) (example where a "court makes up its mind about [an issue] independently" because the parties did not agree it should be arbitrated), with Oxford Health Plans LLC v. Sutter, 133 S. Ct. 2064 (2013) (example where a court defers to arbitrators because the parties "'bargained for'" arbitral resolution of the question (quoting Eastern Associated Coal Corp. v. Mine Workers, 531 U. S. 57, 62, 121 S. Ct. 462, 148 L. Ed. 2d 354 (2000))).

In answering the question, we shall initially treat the document before us as if it were an ordinary contract between private parties. Were that so, we conclude, the matter would be for the arbitrators. We then ask whether the fact that the document in question is a treaty makes a critical difference. We conclude that it does not.

Where ordinary contracts are at issue, it is up to the parties to determine whether a particular matter is primarily for arbitrators or for courts to decide. See, e.g., Steelworkers v. Warrior & Gulf Nav. Co., 363 U. S. 574, 582, 80 S. Ct. 1347, 4 L. Ed. 2d 1409 (1960) ("[A]rbitration is a matter of contract and a party cannot be required to submit to arbitration any dispute which he has not agreed so to submit"). If the contract is silent on the matter of who primarily is to decide "threshold" questions about arbitration, courts determine the parties' intent with the help of presumptions.

On the one hand, courts presume that the parties intend courts, not arbitrators, to decide what we have called disputes about "arbitrability." These include questions such as "whether the parties are bound by a given arbitration clause," or "whether an arbitration clause in a concededly binding contract applies to a particular type of controversy." Howsam v. Dean Witter Reynolds, Inc., 537 U. S. 79, 84, 123 S. Ct. 588, 154 L. Ed. 2d 491 (2002); accord, Granite Rock Co. v. Teamsters, 561 U. S. 287, 299–300, 130 S. Ct. 2847, 177 L. Ed. 2d 567 (2010) (disputes over "formation of the parties' arbitration agreement" and "its enforceability or applicability to the dispute" at issue are "matters . . . the court must resolve" (internal quotation marks omitted)). See First Options, supra, at 941, 943–947, 115 S. Ct. 1920, 131 L. Ed. 2d 985 (court should decide whether an arbitration clause applied to a party who "had not personally signed" the document containing it); AT&T Technologies, Inc. v. Communications Workers, 475 U. S. 643, 651, 106 S. Ct. 1415, 89 L. Ed. 2d 648 (1986) (court should decide whether a particular labor-management layoff dispute fell within the arbitration clause of a collective-bargaining contract); John Wiley & Sons, Inc. v. Livingston, 376 U. S. 543, 546–548, 84 S. Ct. 909, 11 L. Ed. 2d 898 (1964) (court should decide whether an arbitration provision survived a corporate merger). See generally AT&T Technologies, supra, at 649, 106 S. Ct. 1415, 89 L. Ed. 2d 648 ("Unless the parties clearly and unmistakably provide otherwise, the question of whether the parties agreed to arbitrate is to be decided by the court, not the arbitrator").

On the other hand, courts presume that the parties intend arbitrators, not courts, to decide disputes about the meaning and application of particular procedural preconditions for the use of arbitration. See Howsam, supra, at 86, 123 S. Ct. 588, 154 L. Ed. 2d 491 (courts assume parties "normally expect a forum-based decisionmaker to decide forum-specific *procedural* gateway matters" (emphasis added)). These procedural matters include claims of "waiver, delay, or a like defense to arbitrability." Moses H. Cone Memorial Hospital v. Mercury Constr. Corp., 460 U. S. 1, 25, 103 S. Ct. 927, 74 L. Ed. 2d 765 (1983). And they include the satisfaction of "'prerequisites such as time limits, notice, laches, estoppel, and other conditions precedent to an obligation to arbitrate.'" Howsam, supra, at 85, 123 S. Ct. 588, 154 L. Ed. 2d 491 (quoting the Revised Uniform Arbitration Act of 2000 § 6, Comment 2, 7 U. L. A. 13 (Supp. 2002); emphasis deleted). See also § 6(c) ("An arbitrator shall decide whether a condition precedent to arbitrability has been fulfilled"); § 6, Comment 2 (explaining that this rule reflects "the holdings of the vast majority of state courts" and collecting cases).

The provision before us is of the latter, procedural, variety. The text and structure of the provision make clear that it operates as a procedural condition precedent to arbitration. It says that a dispute "shall be submitted to international arbitration" if "one of the Parties so requests," as long as "a period of eighteen months has elapsed" since the dispute was "submitted" to a local tribunal and the tribunal "has not given its final decision." Art. 8(2). It determines *when* the contractual duty to arbitrate arises, not *whether* there is a contractual duty to arbitrate at all. Cf. 13 R. Lord, Williston on Contracts § 38:7, pp. 435, 437; § 38:4, p. 422 (4th ed. 2013) (a "condition precedent" determines what must happen before "a contractual duty arises" but does not "make the *validity* of the contract depend on its happening" (emphasis added)). Neither does this language or other language in Article 8 give substantive weight to the local court's determinations on the matters at issue between the parties. To the contrary, Article 8 provides that *only* the "arbitration decision shall be final and binding on both Parties." Art. 8(4). The litigation provision is consequently a purely procedural requirement—a claims-processing rule that governs when the arbitration may begin, but not whether it may occur or what its substantive outcome will be on the issues in dispute.

Moreover, the local litigation requirement is highly analogous to procedural provisions that both this Court and others have found are for arbitrators, not courts, primarily to interpret and to apply. See Howsam, supra, at 85, 123 S. Ct. 588, 154 L. Ed. 2d 491 (whether a party filed a notice of arbitration within the time limit provided by the rules of the chosen arbitral forum "is a matter presumptively for the arbitrator, not for the judge"); John Wiley, supra, at 555–557, 84 S. Ct. 909, 11 L. Ed. 2d 898 (same, in respect to a mandatory prearbitration grievance procedure that involved holding two conferences). See also Dialysis Access Center, LLC v. RMS Lifeline, Inc., 638 F. 3d 367, 383 (CA1 2011) (same, in respect to a prearbitration "good faith negotiations" requirement); Lumbermens Mut. Cas. Co. v. Broadspire Management Servs., Inc., 623 F. 3d 476, 481 (CA7 2010) (same, in respect to a prearbitration filing of a "Disagreement Notice").

Finally, as we later discuss in more detail, we can find nothing in Article 8 or elsewhere in the Treaty that might overcome the ordinary assumption. It nowhere demonstrates a contrary intent as to the delegation of decisional authority between judges and arbitrators. Thus, were the document an ordinary contract, it would call for arbitrators primarily to interpret and to apply the local litigation provision.

We now relax our ordinary contract assumption and ask whether the fact that the document before us is a treaty makes a critical difference to our analysis. The Solicitor General argues that it should. He says that the local litigation provision may be "a condition on the State's consent to enter into an arbitration agreement." He adds that courts should "review de novo the arbitral tribunal's resolution of objections based on an investor's non-compliance" with such a condition. And he recommends that we remand this case to the Court of Appeals to determine whether the court-exhaustion provision is such a condition.

We do not accept the Solicitor General's view as applied to the treaty before us. As a general matter, a treaty is a contract, though between nations. Its interpretation normally is, like a contract's interpretation, a matter of determining the parties' intent. And where, as here, a federal court is asked to interpret that intent pursuant to a motion to vacate or confirm an award made in the United States under the Federal Arbitration Act, it should normally apply the presumptions supplied by American law. See New York Convention, Art. V(1)(e) (award may be "set aside or suspended by a competent authority of the country in which, or under the law of which, that award was made").

The Solicitor General does not deny that * * * the presumption that parties intend procedural preconditions to arbitration to be resolved primarily by arbitrators * * * applies both to ordinary contracts and to similar provisions in treaties when those provisions are not also "conditions of consent." And, while we respect the Government's views about the proper interpretation of treaties, we have been unable to find any other authority or precedent suggesting that the use of the "consent" label in a treaty should make a critical difference in discerning the parties' intent about whether courts or arbitrators should interpret and apply the relevant provision.

We are willing to assume with the Solicitor General that the appearance of this label in a treaty can show that the parties, or one of them, thought the designated matter quite important. But that is unlikely to be conclusive. For parties often submit important matters to arbitration. And the word "consent" could be attached to a highly procedural precondition to arbitration, such as a waiting period of several months, which the parties are unlikely to have intended that courts apply without saying so. See, *e.g.*, Agreement on Encouragement and Reciprocal Protection of Investments, Art. 9, Netherlands-Slovenia, Sept. 24, 1996, Netherlands T. S. No. 296 ("Each Contracting Party hereby consents to submit any dispute . . . which they can not [*sic*] solve amicably within three months . . . to the International Center for Settlement of Disputes for settlement by conciliation or arbitration"), While we leave the matter open for future argument, we do not now see why the presence of the term "consent" in a treaty warrants abandoning, or increasing the complexity of, our ordinary intent-determining framework.

In any event, the treaty before us does *not* state that the local litigation requirement is a "condition of consent" to arbitration. Thus, we need not, and do not, go beyond holding that, in the absence of explicit language in a treaty demonstrating that the parties intended a different delegation of authority, our ordinary interpretive framework applies. We leave for another day the question of interpreting treaties that refer to "conditions of consent" explicitly. See, e.g., United States-Korea Free Trade Agreement, Art. 11.18, Feb. 10, 2011 (provision entitled "Conditions and Limitations on Consent of Each Party" and providing that "[n]o claim may be submitted to arbitration under this Section" unless the claimant waives in writing "any right" to press his claim before an "administrative tribunal or court"), North American Free Trade Agreement, Arts. 1121–1122, Dec. 17, 1992, 32 I. L. M. 643–644 (providing that each party's "[c]onsent to [a]rbitration" is conditioned on fulfillment of certain "procedures," one of which is a waiver by an investor of his right to litigate the claim being arbitrated). See also 2012 U. S. Model Bilateral Investment Treaty, Art. 26 (entitled "Conditions and limitations on Consent of Each Party"), online at www.ustr.gov/sites/default/files/BIT%20text%20for%20ACIEP%20Meeting.pdf. And we apply our ordinary presumption that the interpretation and application of procedural provisions such as the provision before us are primarily for the arbitrators.

A treaty may contain evidence that shows the parties had an intent contrary to our ordinary presumptions about who should decide threshold issues related to arbitration. But the treaty before us does not show any such contrary intention. We concede that the local litigation requirement appears in (1) of Article 8, while the Article does not mention arbitration until the subsequent paragraph, (2). Moreover, a requirement that a party exhaust its remedies in a country's domestic courts before seeking to arbitrate may seem particularly important to a country offering protections to foreign investors. And the placing of an important matter prior to any mention of arbitration at least arguably suggests an intent by Argentina, the United Kingdom, or both, to have courts rather than arbitrators apply the litigation requirement.

These considerations, however, are outweighed by others. As discussed *supra*, the text and structure of the litigation requirement set forth in Article 8 make clear that it is a procedural condition precedent to arbitration—a sequential step that a party must follow before giving notice of arbitration. The Treaty nowhere says that the provision is to operate as a substantive condition on the formation of the arbitration contract, or that it is a matter of such elevated importance that it is to be decided by courts. International arbitrators are likely more familiar than are judges with the expectations of foreign investors and recipient nations regarding the operation of the provision. See Howsam, supra, at 85, 123 S. Ct. 588, 154 L. Ed. 2d 491 (comparative institutional expertise a factor in determining parties' likely intent). And the Treaty itself authorizes the use of international arbitration associations, the rules of which provide that arbitrators shall have the authority to interpret provisions of this kind. Art. 8(3) (providing that the parties may refer a dispute to the International Centre for the Settlement of Investment Disputes (ICSID) or to arbitrators appointed pursuant to the arbitration rules of the United Nations Commission on International Trade Law (UNCITRAL)).

The upshot is that our ordinary presumption applies and it is not overcome. The interpretation and application of the local litigation provision is primarily for the arbitrators. Reviewing courts cannot review their decision *de novo*. Rather, they must do so with considerable deference.

The dissent interprets Article 8's local litigation provision differently. In its view, the provision sets forth not a condition precedent to arbitration in an already-binding arbitration contract (normally a matter for arbitrators to interpret), but a substantive condition on Argentina's consent to arbitration and thus on the contract's formation in the first place (normally something for courts to interpret). It reads the whole of Article 8 as a "unilateral standing offer" to arbitrate that Argentina and the United Kingdom each extends to investors of the other country. And it says that the local litigation requirement is one of the essential "'terms in which the offer was made.'"

While it is possible to read the provision in this way, doing so is not consistent with our case law interpreting similar provisions appearing in ordinary arbitration contracts. Consequently, interpreting the provision in such a manner would require us to treat treaties as warranting a different kind of analysis. And the dissent does so without supplying any different set of general principles that might guide that analysis. That is a matter of some concern in a world where foreign investment and related arbitration treaties increasingly matter.

Even were we to ignore our ordinary contract principles, however, we would not take the dissent's view. As we have explained, the local litigation provision on its face concerns arbitration's timing, not the Treaty's effective date; or whom its arbitration clause binds; or whether that arbitration clause covers a certain kind of dispute. Cf. Granite Rock, 561 U. S., at 296–303, 130 S. Ct. 2847, 177 L. Ed. 2d 567 (ratification date); First Options, 514 U. S., at 941, 943–947, 115 S. Ct. 1920, 131 L. Ed. 2d 985 (parties); AT&T Technologies, 475 U. S., at 651, 106 S. Ct. 1415, 89 L. Ed. 2d 648 (kind of dispute). The dissent points out that Article 8(2)(a) "does not simply require the parties to wait for 18 months before proceeding to arbitration," but instructs them to *do* something—to "submit their claims for adjudication." That is correct. But the something they must do has no direct impact on the resolution of their dispute, for as we previously pointed out, Article 8 provides that only the decision of the arbitrators (who need not give weight to the local court's decision) will be "final and binding." Art. 8(4). The provision, at base, is a claims-processing rule. And the dissent's efforts to imbue it with greater significance fall short.

The treatises to which the dissent refers also fail to support its position. Those authorities primarily describe how an offer to arbitrate in an investment treaty can be accepted, such as through an investor's filing of a notice of arbitration. They do not endorse the dissent's reading of the local litigation provision or of provisions like it.

To the contrary, the bulk of international authority supports our view that the provision functions as a purely procedural precondition to arbitrate. See 1 G. Born, International Commercial Arbitration 842 (2009) ("A substantial body of arbitral authority from investor-state disputes concludes that compliance with procedural mechanisms in an arbitration agreement (or bilateral investment treaty) is not ordinarily a jurisdictional prerequisite").

In sum, we agree with the dissent that a sovereign's consent to arbitration is important. We also agree that sovereigns can condition their consent to arbitrate by writing various terms into their bilateral investment treaties. But that is not the issue. The question is whether the parties intended to give courts or arbitrators primary authority to interpret and apply a threshold provision in an arbitration contract—when the contract is silent as to the delegation of authority. We have already explained why we believe that where, as here, the provision resembles a claims-processing requirement and is not a requirement that affects the arbitration contract's validity or scope, we presume that the parties (even if they are sovereigns) intended to give that authority to the arbitrators.

Argentina correctly argues that it is nonetheless entitled to court review of the arbitrators' decision to excuse BG Group's noncompliance with the litigation requirement, and to take jurisdiction over the dispute. It asks us to provide that review, and it argues that even if the proper standard is "a [h]ighly [d]eferential" one, it should still prevail. Having the relevant materials before us, we shall provide that review. But we cannot agree with Argentina that the arbitrators "'exceeded their powers'" in concluding they had jurisdiction. (quoting 9 U. S. C. § 10(a)(4)).

The arbitration panel made three relevant determinations:

(1) "As a matter of treaty interpretation," the local litigation provision "cannot be construed as an absolute impediment to arbitration,"

(2) Argentina enacted laws that "hindered" "recourse to the domestic judiciary" by those "whose rights were allegedly affected by the emergency measures," that sought "to prevent any judicial interference with the emergency legislation," and that "excluded from the renegotiation process" for public service contracts "any licensee seeking judicial redress,";

(3) under these circumstances, it would be "absurd and unreasonable" to read Article 8 as requiring an investor to bring its grievance to a domestic court before arbitrating.

The first determination lies well within the arbitrators' interpretive authority. Construing the local litigation provision as an "absolute" requirement would mean Argentina could avoid arbitration by, say, passing a law that closed down its court system indefinitely or that prohibited investors from using its courts. Such an interpretation runs contrary to a basic objective of the investment treaty. Nor does Argentina argue for an absolute interpretation.

As to the second determination, Argentina does not argue that the facts set forth by the arbitrators are incorrect. Thus, we accept them as valid.

The third determination is more controversial. Argentina argues that neither the 180-day suspension of courts' issuances of final judgments nor its refusal to allow litigants (and those in arbitration) to use its contract renegotiation process, taken separately or together, warrants suspending or waiving the local litigation requirement. We would not necessarily characterize these actions as rendering a domestic court-exhaustion requirement "absurd and unreasonable," but at the same time we cannot say that the arbitrators' conclusions are barred by the Treaty. The arbitrators did not "'stra[y] from interpretation and application of the agreement'" or otherwise "'effectively "dispens[e]"'" their "'own brand of . . . justice.'" Stolt-Nielsen S. A. v. AnimalFeeds Int'l Corp., 559 U. S. 662, 671, 130 S. Ct. 1758, 176 L. Ed. 2d 605 (2010) (providing that it is only when an arbitrator engages in such activity that "'his decision may be unenforceable'" (quoting Major League Baseball Players Assn. v. Garvey, 532 U. S. 504, 509, 121 S. Ct. 1724, 149 L. Ed. 2d 740 (2001) (*per curiam*)).

Consequently, we conclude that the arbitrators' jurisdictional determinations are lawful. The judgment of the Court of Appeals to the contrary is reversed.

It is so ordered.

■ JUSTICE SOTOMAYOR, concurring in part.

I agree with the Court that the local litigation requirement at issue in this case is a procedural precondition to arbitration (which the arbitrators are to interpret), not a condition on Argentina's consent to arbitrate (which a court would review *de novo*). Importantly, in reaching this conclusion, the Court acknowledges that "the treaty before us does *not* state that the local litigation requirement is a 'condition of consent' to arbitration." The Court thus wisely "leave[s] for another day the question of interpreting treaties that refer to 'conditions of consent' explicitly." I join the Court's opinion on the understanding that it does not, in fact, decide this issue.

I write separately because, in the absence of this express reservation, the opinion might be construed otherwise. The Court appears to suggest in dictum that a decision by treaty parties to describe a condition as one on their consent to arbitrate "is unlikely to be conclusive" in deciding whether the parties intended for the condition to be resolved by a court. Because this suggestion is unnecessary to decide the case and is in tension with the Court's explicit reservation of the issue, I join the opinion of the Court with the exception of Part IV-A-1.

The Court's dictum on this point is not only unnecessary; it may also be incorrect. It is far from clear that a treaty's express use of the term "consent" to describe a precondition to arbitration should not be conclusive in the analysis. We have held, for instance, that "a gateway dispute about whether the parties are bound by a given arbitration clause raises a 'question of arbitrability' for a court to decide." Howsam v. Dean Witter Reynolds, Inc., 537 U. S. 79, 84, 123 S. Ct. 588, 154 L. Ed. 2d 491 (2002). And a party plainly cannot be bound by an arbitration clause to which it does not consent. See Granite Rock Co. v. Teamsters, 561 U. S. 287, 299, 130 S. Ct. 2847, 177 L. Ed. 2d 567 (2010) ("Arbitration is strictly 'a matter of consent'" (quoting Volt Information Sciences, Inc. v. Board of Trustees of Leland Stanford Junior Univ., 489 U. S. 468, 479, 109 S. Ct. 1248, 103 L. Ed. 2d 488 (1989))).

Consent is especially salient in the context of a bilateral investment treaty, where the treaty is not an already agreed-upon arbitration provision between known parties, but rather a nation state's standing offer to arbitrate with an amorphous class of private investors. In this setting, a nation-state might reasonably wish to condition its consent to arbitrate with a previously unspecified investor counterparty on the investor's compliance with a requirement that might be deemed "purely procedural" in the ordinary commercial context,. Moreover, as THE CHIEF JUSTICE notes, "[i]t is no trifling matter" for a sovereign nation to "subject itself to international arbitration" proceedings, so we should "not presume that any country . . . takes that step lightly."

Consider, for example, the United States-Korea Free Trade Agreement, which as the Court recognizes, includes a provision explicitly entitled "Conditions and Limitations on Consent of Each Party." That provision declares that "[n]o claim may be submitted to arbitration" unless a claimant first waives its "right to initiate or continue before any administrative tribunal or court . . . any proceeding with respect to any measure alleged to constitute a breach" under another provision of the treaty. If this waiver condition were to appear without the "consent" label in a binding arbitration agreement between two commercial parties, one might characterize it as the kind of procedural "'condition precedent to arbitrability'" that we presume parties intend for arbitrators to decide. Howsam, 537 U. S., at 85, 123 S. Ct. 588, 154 L. Ed. 2d 491. But where the waiver requirement is expressly denominated a "condition on consent" in an international investment treaty, the label could well be critical in determining whether the states party to the treaty intended the condition to be reviewed by a court. After all, a dispute as to consent is "the starkest form of the question whether the parties have agreed to arbitrate." And we ordinarily presume that parties intend for courts to decide such questions because otherwise arbitrators might "force unwilling parties to arbitrate a matter they reasonably would have thought a judge . . . would decide." First Options of Chicago, Inc. v. Kaplan, 514 U. S. 938, 945, 115 S. Ct. 1920, 131 L. Ed. 2d 985 (1995).

Accordingly, if the local litigation requirement at issue here were labeled a condition on the treaty parties' "consent" to arbitrate, that would in my view change the analysis as to whether the parties intended the requirement to be interpreted by a court or an arbitrator. As it is, however, all parties agree that the local litigation requirement is not so denominated. Nor is there compelling reason to suppose the parties silently intended to make it a condition on their consent to arbitrate, given that a local court's decision is of no legal significance under the treaty, and given that the entire purpose of bilateral investment agreements is to "reliev[e] investors of any concern that the courts of host countries will be unable or unwilling to provide justice in a dispute between a foreigner and their own government". Moreover, Argentina's conduct confirms that the local litigation requirement is not a condition on consent, for rather than objecting to arbitration on the ground that there was no binding arbitration agreement to begin with, Argentina actively participated in the constitution of the arbitral panel and in the proceedings that followed. See Eastern Airlines, Inc. v. Floyd, 499 U. S. 530, 546, 111 S. Ct. 1489, 113 L. Ed. 2d 569 (1991) (treaty interpretation can be informed by parties' postenactment conduct).[1]

---

[1] The dissent discounts the significance of Argentina's conduct on the ground that Argentina "object[ed] to the [arbitral] tribunal's jurisdiction to hear the dispute." But there is a difference between arguing that a party has failed to comply with a procedural condition in a binding arbitration agreement and arguing that noncompliance with the condition negates the existence of consent to arbitrate in the first place. Argentina points to no evidence that its objection was of the consent variety. This omission is notable because Argentina knew how to phrase its arguments before the arbitrators in terms of consent; it argued separately that it had not consented to arbitration with BG Group on the ground that BG was not a party to the license underlying the dispute. *First Options of Chicago, Inc.* v. *Kaplan*, 514 U. S. 938, 115 S. Ct. 1920, 131 L. Ed. 2d 985 (1995), is not to the contrary, as that case held that "arguing the arbitrability issue to an arbitrator" did not constitute "clea[r] and unmistakabl[e]" evidence sufficient to override an indisputably applicable

In light of these many indicators that Argentina and the United Kingdom did not intend the local litigation requirement to be a condition on their consent to arbitrate, and on the understanding that the Court does not pass on the weight courts should attach to a treaty's use of the term "consent,"

I concur in the Court's opinion.

■ CHIEF JUSTICE ROBERTS, with whom JUSTICE KENNEDY joins, dissenting.

The Court begins by deciding a different case, "initially treat[ing] the document before us as if it were an ordinary contract between private parties." The "document before us," of course, is nothing of the sort. It is instead a treaty between two sovereign nations: the United Kingdom and Argentina. No investor is a party to the agreement. Having elided this rather important fact for much of its analysis, the majority finally "relax[es] [its] ordinary contract assumption and ask[s] whether the fact that the document before us is a treaty makes a critical difference to [its] analysis." It should come as no surprise that, after starting down the wrong road, the majority ends up at the wrong place.

I would start with the document that *is* before us and take it on its own terms. That document is a bilateral investment treaty between the United Kingdom and Argentina, in which Argentina agreed to take steps to encourage U. K. investors to invest within its borders (and the United Kingdom agreed to do the same with respect to Argentine investors). The Treaty does indeed contain a completed agreement for arbitration—between the signatory countries. Art. 9. The Treaty also includes, in Article 8, certain provisions for resolving any disputes that might arise between a signatory country and an investor, who is not a party to the agreement.

One such provision—completely ignored by the Court in its analysis—specifies that disputes may be resolved by arbitration when the host country and an investor "have so agreed." Art. 8(2)(b), 1765 U. N. T. S. 38. No one doubts that, as is the normal rule, whether there was such an agreement is for a court, not an arbitrator, to decide. See First Options of Chicago, Inc. v. Kaplan, 514 U. S. 938, 943–945, 115 S. Ct. 1920, 131 L. Ed. 2d 985 (1995).

When there is no express agreement between the host country and an investor, they must form an agreement in another way, before an obligation to arbitrate arises. The Treaty by itself cannot constitute an agreement to arbitrate with an investor. How could it? No investor is a party to that Treaty. Something else must happen to *create* an agreement where there was none before. Article 8(2)(a) makes clear what that something is: An investor must submit his dispute to the courts of the host country. After 18 months, or an unsatisfactory decision, the investor may then request arbitration.

Submitting the dispute to the courts is thus a condition to the formation of an agreement, not simply a matter of performing an existing agreement. Article 8(2)(a) constitutes in effect a unilateral *offer* to arbitrate, which an investor may

---

presumption that a court was to decide whether the parties had agreed to arbitration. Id., at 944, 946, 115 S. Ct. 1920, 131 L. Ed. 2d 985. The question here, by contrast, is whether that presumption attaches to begin with—that is, whether the local litigation requirement was a condition on Argentina's consent to arbitrate (which would trigger the presumption) or a procedural condition in an already binding arbitration agreement (which would not). That Argentina apparently took the latter position in arbitration is surely relevant evidence that the condition was, in fact, not one on its consent.

accept by complying with its terms. To be sure, the local litigation requirement might not be absolute. In particular, an investor might argue that it was an implicit aspect of the unilateral offer that he be afforded a reasonable opportunity to submit his dispute to the local courts. Even then, however, the question would remain whether the investor has managed to form an arbitration agreement with the host country pursuant to Article 8(2)(a). That question under Article 8(2)(a) is—like the same question under Article 8(2)(b)—for a court, not an arbitrator, to decide. I respectfully dissent from the Court's contrary conclusion.

The majority acknowledges—but fails to heed—"the first principle that underscores all of our arbitration decisions: Arbitration is strictly 'a matter of consent.'" Granite Rock Co. v. Teamsters, 561 U. S. 287, 299, 130 S. Ct. 2847, 177 L. Ed. 2d 567 (2010) (quoting Volt Information Sciences, Inc. v. Board of Trustees of Leland Stanford Junior Univ., 489 U. S. 468, 479, 109 S. Ct. 1248, 103 L. Ed. 2d 488 (1989)). We have accordingly held that arbitration "is a way to resolve those disputes—but only those disputes—that the parties have agreed to submit to arbitration." First Options of Chicago, Inc., supra, at 943, 115 S. Ct. 1920, 131 L. Ed. 2d 985. The same "first principle" underlies arbitration pursuant to bilateral investment treaties. So only if Argentina agreed with BG Group to have an arbitrator resolve their dispute did the arbitrator in this case have any authority over the parties.

The majority opinion nowhere explains when and how Argentina agreed *with BG Group* to submit to arbitration. Instead, the majority seems to assume that, in agreeing with the United Kingdom to adopt Article 8 along with the rest of the Treaty, Argentina thereby formed an agreement with all potential U. K. investors (including BG Group) to submit all investment related disputes to arbitration. That misunderstands Article 8 and trivializes the significance to a sovereign nation of subjecting itself to arbitration anywhere in the world, solely at the option of private parties.

The majority focuses throughout its opinion on what it calls the Treaty's "arbitration clause," but that provision does not stand alone. Rather, it is only part—and a subordinate part at that—of a broader dispute resolution provision. Article 8 is thus entitled "Settlement of Disputes Between an Investor and the Host State," and it opens without so much as mentioning arbitration. Instead it initially directs any disputing investor and signatory country (what the Treaty calls a "Contracting Party") to court. When "an investor of one Contracting Party and the other Contracting Party" have an investment-related dispute that has "not been amicably settled," the Treaty commands that the dispute "*shall be submitted*, at the request of one of the Parties to the dispute, to the decision of the competent tribunal of the Contracting Party in whose territory the investment was made." Art. 8(1), (emphasis added). This provision could not be clearer: Before taking any other steps, an aggrieved investor must submit its dispute with a Contracting Party to that Contracting Party's own courts.

There are two routes to arbitration in Article 8(2)(a), and each passes through a Contracting Party's domestic courts. That is, the Treaty's arbitration provisions in Article 8(2)(a) presuppose that the parties have complied with the local litigation provision in Article 8(1). Specifically, a party may request arbitration only (1) "after a period of eighteen months has elapsed from the moment when the dispute was submitted to the competent tribunal of the Contracting Party in whose territory the investment was made" and "the said tribunal has not given its final decision," Art. 8(2)(a)(i), or (2) "where the final decision of the aforementioned tribunal has been made but the Parties are still in dispute," Art. 8(2)(a)(ii), Either way, the obligation to arbitrate does not arise until the Contracting Party's courts have had a first crack at the dispute.

Article 8 provides a third route to arbitration in paragraph 8(2)(b)—namely, "where the Contracting Party and the investor of the other Contracting Party have so agreed." In contrast to the two routes in Article 8(2)(a), this one does not refer to the local litigation provision. That omission is significant. It makes clear that an investor can bypass local litigation only by obtaining the Contracting Party's explicit agreement to proceed directly to arbitration. Short of that, an investor has no choice but to litigate in the Contracting Party's courts for at least some period.

The structure of Article 8 confirms that the routes to arbitration in paragraph (2)(a) are just as much about eliciting a Contracting Party's consent to arbitrate as the route in paragraph 8(2)(b). Under Article 8(2)(b), the requisite consent is demonstrated by a specific agreement. Under Article 8(2)(a), the requisite consent is demonstrated by compliance with the requirement to resort to a country's local courts.

Whereas Article 8(2)(a) is part of a completed *agreement* between Argentina and the United Kingdom, it constitutes only a unilateral standing *offer* by Argentina with respect to U. K. investors—an offer to submit to arbitration where certain conditions are met. That is how scholars understand arbitration provisions in bilateral investment treaties in general.

An offer must be accepted for a legally binding contract to be formed. And it is an "undeniable principle of the law of contracts, that an offer . . . by one person to another, imposes no obligation upon the former, until it is accepted by the latter, *according to the terms in which the offer was made*. Any qualification of, or departure from, those terms, invalidates the offer." Eliason v. Henshaw, 17 U.S. 225, 4 Wheat. 225, 228, 4 L. Ed. 556 (1819) (emphasis added). This principle applies to international arbitration agreements just as it does to domestic commercial contracts.

By incorporating the local litigation provision in Article 8(1), paragraph 8(2)(a) establishes that provision as a term of Argentina's unilateral offer to arbitrate. To accept Argentina's offer, an investor must therefore first litigate its dispute in Argentina's courts—either to a "final decision" or for 18 months, whichever comes first. Unless the investor does so (or, perhaps, establishes a valid excuse for failing to do so, as discussed below, it has not accepted the terms of Argentina's offer to arbitrate, and thus has not formed an arbitration agreement with Argentina.[1]

Although the majority suggests that the local litigation requirement would not be a "condition of consent" even if the Treaty explicitly called it one, the Court's

[1] To be clear, the only question is whether BG Group formed an *arbitration* agreement with Argentina. To say that BG Group never formed such an agreement is not to call into question the validity of its various commercial agreements with Argentina.

holding is limited to treaties that contain no such clear statement. But there is no reason to think that such a clear statement should be required, for we generally do not require "talismanic words" in treaties. Indeed, another arbitral tribunal concluded that the local litigation requirement was a condition on Argentina's consent to arbitrate despite the absence of the sort of clear statement apparently contemplated by the majority. See ICS Inspection & Control Servs. Ltd. v. Argentine Republic, PCA Case No. 2010-9, Award on Jurisdiction, ¶ 262 (Feb. 10, 2012). Still other tribunals have reached the same conclusion with regard to similar litigation requirements in other Argentine bilateral investment treaties. See Daimler Financial Servs. AG v. Argentine Republic, ICSID Case No. ARB/ 05/1, Award, 193, 194 (Aug. 22, 2012); Wintershall Aktiengesellschaft v. Argentine Republic, ICSID Case No. ARB/04/14, Award, 116 (Dec. 8, 2008).

In the face of this authority, the majority quotes a treatise for the proposition that "'[a] substantial body of arbitral authority from investor-state disputes concludes that compliance with procedural mechanisms in an arbitration agreement (or bilateral investment treaty) is not ordinarily a jurisdictional prerequisite.'" But that simply restates the question. The whole issue is whether the local litigation requirement is a mere "procedural mechanism" or instead a condition on Argentina's consent to arbitrate.

BG Group concedes that other terms of Article 8(1) constitute conditions on Argentina's consent to arbitrate, even though they are not expressly labeled as such. See Tr. of Oral Arg. 57 ("You have to be a U. K. investor, you have to have a treaty claim, you have to be suing another party to the treaty. And if those aren't true, *then there is no arbitration agreement*" (emphasis added)). The Court does not explain why the *only other term*—the litigation requirement—should be viewed differently.

Nor does the majority's reading accord with ordinary contract law, which treats language such as the word "after" in Article 8(2)(a)(i) as creating conditions, even though such language may not constitute a "clear statement." The majority seems to regard the local litigation requirement as a condition precedent to *performance* of the contract, rather than a condition precedent to *formation* of the contract. But that cannot be. Prior to the fulfillment of the local litigation requirement, there was no contract be-tween Argentina *and BG Group* to be performed. The Treaty is not such an agreement, since BG Group is of course not a party to the Treaty. Neither the majority nor BG Group contends that the agreement is under Article 8(2)(b), the provision that applies "where the Contracting Party and the investor of the other Contracting Party have so agreed." An arbitration agreement must be *formed*, and Article 8(2)(a) spells out how an investor may do that: by submitting the dispute to local courts for 18 months or until a decision is rendered.

Moreover, the Treaty's local litigation requirement certainly does not resemble "time limits, notice, laches, estoppel," or the other kinds of provisions that are typically treated as conditions on the performance of an arbitration agreement, rather than prerequisites to formation. Unlike a time limit for submitting a claim to arbitration, see *Howsam v. Dean Witter Reynolds, Inc.*, 537 U. S. 79, 85, 123 S. Ct. 588, 154 L. Ed. 2d 491 (2002), the litigation requirement does not simply regulate the timing of arbitration. As the majority recognizes, the provision does not simply require the parties to wait for 18 months before proceeding to arbitration, but instead requires them to submit their claims for adjudication during that period. And unlike a mandatory pre-arbitration grievance procedure, the litigation requirement sends the parties to court—and not just any court, but a court of the host country.

The law of international arbitration and domestic contract law lead to the same conclusion: Because paragraph (2)(a) of Article 8 constitutes only a unilateral standing offer by the Contracting Parties to each other's investors to submit to arbitration under certain conditions, an investor cannot form an arbitration agreement with a Contracting Party under the Treaty until the investor accepts the actual terms of the Contracting Party's offer. Absent a valid excuse, that means litigating its dispute in the Contracting Party's courts to a "final decision" or, barring that, for at least 18 months.

The nature of the obligations a sovereign incurs in agreeing to arbitrate with a private party confirms that the local litigation requirement is a condition on a signatory country's consent to arbitrate, and not merely a condition on performance of a pre-existing arbitration agreement. There are good reasons for any sovereign to condition its consent to arbitrate disputes on investors' first litigating their claims in the country's own courts for a specified period. It is no trifling matter for a sovereign nation to subject itself to suit by private parties; we do not presume that any country—including our own—takes that step lightly. But even where a sovereign nation has subjected itself to suit in its own courts, it is quite another thing for it to subject itself to international arbitration. Indeed, "[g]ranting a private party the right to bring an action against a sovereign state in an international tribunal regarding an investment dispute is a revolutionary innovation" whose "uniqueness and power should not be over-looked." [J. Salacuse, The Law of Investment Treaties 137 (2010)]. That is so because of both the procedure and substance of investor-state arbitration.

Procedurally, paragraph (3) of Article 8 designates the Arbitration Rules of the United Nations Commission on International Trade Law (UNCITRAL) as the default rules governing the arbitration. Those rules authorize the Secretary-General of the Permanent Court of Arbitration at The Hague to designate an "appointing authority" who—absent agreement by the parties—can select the sole arbitrator (or, in the case of a three-member tribunal, the presiding arbitrator, where the arbitrators nominated by each of the parties cannot agree on a presiding arbitrator). UNCITRAL Arbitration Rules, Arts. 6, 8–9 (rev. 2010 ed.). The arbitrators, in turn, select the site of the arbitration (again, absent an agreement by the parties) and enjoy broad discretion in conducting the proceedings. Arts. 18, 17(1).

Substantively, by acquiescing to arbitration, a state permits private adjudicators to review its public policies and effectively annul the authoritative acts of its legislature, executive, and judiciary. Consider the dispute that gave rise to this case: Before the arbitral tribunal, BG Group challenged multiple sovereign acts of the Argentine Government taken after the Argentine economy collapsed in 2001—in particular, Emergency Law 25,561, which converted dollar-denominated tariffs into peso-denominated tariffs at a rate of one Argentine peso to one U. S. dollar;

Resolution 308/02 and Decree 1090/02, which established a renegotiation process for public service contracts; and Decree 214/02, which stayed for 180 days injunctions and the execution of final judgments in lawsuits challenging the effects of the Emergency Law. Indeed, in awarding damages to BG Group, the tribunal held that the first three of these enactments violated Article 2 of the Treaty.

Perhaps they did, but that is not the issue. Under Article 8, a Contracting Party grants to private adjudicators not necessarily of its own choosing, who can meet literally anywhere in the world, a power it typically reserves to its own courts, if it grants it at all: the power to sit in judgment on its sovereign acts. Given these stakes, one would expect the United Kingdom and Argentina to have taken particular care in specifying the limited circumstances in which foreign investors can trigger the Treaty's arbitration process. And that is precisely what they did in Article 8(2)(a), requiring investors to afford a country's own courts an initial opportunity to review the country's enactments and assess the country's compliance with its international obligations. Contrast this with Article 9, which provides for arbitration between the signatory countries of disputes under the Treaty without any preconditions. Argentina and the United Kingdom considered arbitration with particular foreign investors to be different in kind and to require special limitations on its use.

The majority regards the local litigation requirement as toothless simply because the Treaty does not require an arbitrator to "give substantive weight to the local court's determinations on the matters at issue between the parties," but instead provides that "[t]he arbitration decision shall be final and binding on both Parties," Art. 8(4), 1765 U. N. T. S. 38. While it is true that an arbitrator need not defer to an Argentine court's judgment in an investor dispute, that does not deprive the litigation requirement of practical import. Most significant, the Treaty provides that an "arbitral tribunal shall decide the dispute in accordance with . . . the laws of the Contracting Party involved in the dispute." Art. 8(4), I doubt that a tribunal would give no weight to an Argentine court's authoritative construction of Argentine law, rendered in the same dispute, just because it might not be formally bound to adopt that interpretation.

The local litigation requirement can also help to narrow the range of issues that remain in controversy by the time a dispute reaches arbitration. It might even induce the parties to settle along the way. And of course the investor might prevail, which could likewise obviate the need for arbitration.

None of this should be interpreted as defending Argentina's history when it comes to international investment. That history may prompt doubt that requiring an investor to resort to that country's courts in the first instance will be of any use. But that is not the question. Argentina and the United Kingdom reached agreement on the term at issue. The question can therefore be rephrased as whether it makes sense for either Contracting Party to insist on resort to its courts before being compelled to arbitrate anywhere in the world before arbitrators not of its choosing. The foregoing reasons may seem more compelling when viewed apart from the particular episode before us.

Given that the Treaty's local litigation requirement is a condition on consent to arbitrate, it follows that whether an investor has complied with that requirement is a question a court must decide *de novo*, rather than an issue for the arbitrator to decide subject only to the most deferential judicial review. See, e.g., Adams v. Suozzi, 433 F. 3d 220, 226–228 (CA2 2005) (holding that compliance with a condition on formation of an arbitration agreement is for a court, rather than an arbitrator, to determine). The logic is simple: Because an arbitrator's authority depends on the consent of the parties, the arbitrator should not as a rule be able to decide for himself whether the parties have in fact consented. Where the consent of the parties is in question, "reference of the gateway dispute to the court avoids the risk of forcing parties to arbitrate a matter that they may well not have agreed to arbitrate." Howsam, 537 U. S., at 83–84, 123 S. Ct. 588, 154 L. Ed. 2d 491.

This principle is at the core of our arbitration precedents. See Granite Rock Co., 561 U. S., at 299, 130 S. Ct. 2847, 177 L. Ed. 2d 567 (questions concerning "the formation of the parties' arbitration agreement" are for a court to decide *de novo*). The same principle is also embedded in the law of international commercial arbitration. 2 Born 2792 ("[W]here one party denies ever having made an arbitration agreement or challenges the validity of any such agreement, . . . the possibility of de novo judicial review of any jurisdictional award in an annulment action is logically necessary"). See also Restatement (Third) of U. S. Law of International Commercial Arbitration § 4–12(d)(1) (Tent. Draft No. 2, Apr. 16, 2012) ("a court determines de novo . . . the existence of the arbitration agreement").

Indeed, the question in this case—whether BG Group accepted the terms of Argentina's offer to arbitrate—presents an issue of contract formation, which is the starkest form of the question whether the parties have agreed to arbitrate. In *Howsam v. Dean Witter Reynolds, Inc.*, we gave two examples of questions going to consent, which are for courts to decide: "whether the parties are bound by a given arbitration clause" and "whether an arbitration clause in a concededly binding contract applies to a particular type of controversy." In both examples, there is at least a putative arbitration agreement between *the parties to the dispute*. The only question is whether the agreement is truly binding or whether it covers the specific dispute. Here, by contrast, the question is whether the arbitration clause in the Treaty between the United Kingdom and Argentina gives rise to an arbitration agreement between Argentina *and BG Group* at all.

The majority never even starts down this path. Instead, it preempts the whole inquiry by concluding that the local litigation requirement is the kind of "procedural precondition" that parties typically expect an arbitrator to enforce. But as explained, the local litigation requirement does not resemble the requirements we have previously deemed presumptively procedural. It does not merely regulate the timing of arbitration. Nor does it send the parties to non-judicial forms of dispute resolution.

More importantly, all of the cases cited by the majority as examples of procedural provisions involve commercial contracts between two private parties. None of them—not a single one—involves an agreement between sovereigns or an agreement to which the person seeking to compel arbitration is not even a party. The Treaty, of course, is both of those things.

The majority suggests that I am applying "a different kind of analysis" from that governing private commercial contracts, just because what is at issue is a treaty. That is not so: The key point, which the majority never addresses, is that there is no completed agreement whatsoever between Argentina and BG Group. An agreement must be formed, and whether that has happened is—as it is in the private commercial contract context—an issue for a court to decide.

The distinction between questions concerning consent to arbitrate and mere procedural requirements under an existing arbitration agreement can at times seem elusive. Even the most mundane procedural requirement can be recast as a condition on consent as a matter of technical logic. But it should be clear by now that the Treaty's local litigation requirement is not a mere formality—not in Buenos Aires, not in London. And while it is true that "parties often submit important matters to arbitration," our precedents presume that parties do not submit to arbitration the most important matter of all: whether they are subject to an agreement to arbitrate in the first place.

Nor has the majority pointed to evidence that would rebut this presumption by showing that Argentina "'clearly and unmistakably'" intended to have an arbitrator enforce the litigation requirement. Howsam, supra, at 83, 123 S. Ct. 588, 154 L. Ed. 2d 491 (quoting AT&T Technologies, Inc. v. Communications Workers, 475 U. S. 643, 649, 106 S. Ct. 1415, 89 L. Ed. 2d 648 (1986)). As the majority notes, the Treaty incorporates certain arbitration rules that, in turn, authorize arbitrators to determine their own jurisdiction over a dispute. See Art. 8(3). But those rules do not operate until a dispute is properly before an arbitral tribunal, and of course the whole question in this case is whether the dispute between BG Group and Argentina was before the arbitrators, given BG Group's failure to comply with the 18-month local litigation requirement. As a leading treatise has explained, "[i]f the parties have not validly agreed to any arbitration agreement at all, then they also have necessarily not agreed to institutional arbitration rules." 1 Born 870. "In these circumstances, provisions in institutional rules cannot confer any [such] authority upon an arbitral tribunal."

I also see no reason to think that arbitrators enjoy comparative expertise in construing the local litigation requirement. It would be one thing if that provision involved the application of the arbitrators' own rules, or if it were "intertwined" with the merits of the underlying dispute, Neither is true of the litigation requirement. A court can assess compliance with the requirement at least as well as an arbitrator can. Given the structure of Article 8 and the important interests that the litigation requirement protects, it seems clear that the United Kingdom and Argentina thought the same.[2]

---

[2] JUSTICE Sotomayor contends that "Argentina's conduct confirms that the local litigation requirement is not a condition on consent, for rather than objecting to arbitration on the ground that there was no binding arbitration agreement to begin with, Argentina actively participated in the constitution of the arbitral panel and in the proceedings that followed." But as the arbitral tribunal itself recognized, Argentina *did* object to the tribunal's jurisdiction to hear the dispute. And we have held that "merely arguing the arbitrability issue to an arbitrator"—say, by "filing with the arbitrators a written memorandum objecting to the arbitrators' jurisdiction"—"does not indicate a clear willingness to arbitrate that issue, *i.e.*, a willingness to be effectively bound by the arbitrator's decision on that point." First Options of Chicago, Inc. v. Kaplan, 514 U. S. 938, 946, 115 S. Ct. 1920, 131 L. Ed. 2d 985 (1995). The concurrence contends that Argentina "apparently" argued its jurisdictional objection in terms of procedure rather than consent, but the one piece of evidence cited—a negative inference from the *arbitrator's* characterization of Argentina's argument on a subsidiary issue—hardly suffices to distinguish *First Options*.

Although the Court of Appeals got there by a slightly different route, it correctly concluded that a court must decide questions concerning the interpretation and application of the local litigation requirement *de novo*. At the same time, however, the court seems to have simply taken it for granted that, because BG Group did not submit its dispute to the local courts, the arbitral award in BG Group's favor was invalid. Indeed, the court addressed the issue in a perfunctory paragraph at the end of its opinion and saw "'only one possible outcome'": "that BG Group was required to commence a lawsuit in Argentina's courts and wait eighteen months before filing for arbitration."

That conclusion is not obvious. A leading treatise has indicated that "[i]t is a necessary implication from [a unilateral] offer that the offeror, in addition, makes a subsidiary offer by which he or she promises to accept a tender of performance." On this understanding, an offeree's failure to comply with an essential condition of the unilateral offer "will not bar an action, if failure to comply with the condition is due to the offeror's own fault."

It would be open to BG Group to argue before the Court of Appeals that this principle was incorporated into Article 8(2)(a) as an implicit aspect of Argentina's unilateral offer to arbitrate. Such an argument would find some support in the background principle of customary international law that a foreign individual injured by a host country must ordinarily exhaust local remedies—unless doing so would be "futile." In any event, the issue would be analyzed as one of contract formation, and therefore would be for the court to decide. I would accordingly vacate the decision of the Court of Appeals and remand the case for such an inquiry.

I respectfully dissent.

Investment arbitration arises not only from BITs but also from broader treaties on international trade, such as the North American Free Trade Agreement (NAFTA) involving the United States, Canada, and Mexico. Chapter 11 of NAFTA gives investors of one contracting State the right to initiate binding arbitration against another contracting State under the ICSID Convention, the ICSID Additional Facility Rules, or as an ad hoc arbitration under UNCITRAL Rules.[75] NAFTA arbitration awards are enforceable in domestic courts. See, e.g., International Thunderbird Gaming Corp. v. United Mexican States, 473 F.Supp.2d 80 (D.D.C.2007), aff'd, 255 Fed.Appx. 531 (D.C.Cir.2007). The International Centre for Settlement of Investment Disputes (ICSID) was created by the World Bank to resolve investment disputes, and unlike arbitration awards under the New York Convention, ICSID awards are directly enforceable in signatory states, without any method of review in national courts. Instead, when a party challenges an ICSID award, the Chairman of the Administrative Council of ICSID can appoint an ad hoc committee to review, and possibly annul (vacate), awards. Gary B. Born, International Commercial Arbitration 105 (2009).

---

[75] North American Free Trade Agreement, art. 1120, Jan. 1, 1994, available at http://www.sice.oas.org/Trade/NAFTA/NAFTATCE.ASP.

An illustrative NAFTA arbitration involved a Mexican subsidiary of a U.S. company (Metalclad) that owned a development site for a waste disposal facility in Mexico. Although Mexican federal officials had approved the facility—and had assured Metalclad that no further permissions were necessary—municipal officials later refused to issue a municipal construction permit; after construction began at the site, a state "Ecological Decree" declared the entire area an "ecological preserve [to protect] species of cacti"—which of course had the effect of proscribing the project entirely. Metalclad brought a claim against Mexico under Chapter 11 of NAFTA. Tripartite arbitration hearings took place in Washington, where ICSID is located, but "it was proposed by the Tribunal, and agreed by the parties, that the place of the arbitration would be Vancouver", which is in British Columbia, Canada. The arbitral panel ultimately awarded Metalclad $16,685,000 in damages, having made two critical findings:

- Mexico's various conflicting state and federal decrees were inconsistent with NAFTA's requirement of "transparency": There appeared to be "no clear rule" as to whether a municipal permit was required, and in any event no established practice or procedure governing permit applications. So Mexico had "failed to ensure a transparent and predictable framework for Metalclad's business planning and investment"; "transparency" was understood "to include the idea that all relevant legal requirements for the purpose of initiating, completing and successfully operating investments should be capable of being readily known to all affected investors," and "that there should be no room for doubt or uncertainty."
- In addition, the Mexican state environmental decree was tantamount to an "expropriation" without compensation.

The award was challenged in the British Columbia Supreme Court, which proceeded to review it under the province's International Commercial Arbitration Act. Like most modern legislation, the Act made no provision for judicial review of awards for legal error, but the court vacated the tribunal's first holding on the familiar ground of excess of power—that the arbitrators "had made decisions on matters beyond the scope of the submission to arbitration" Because the tribunal had grounded its decision "on the basis of transparency," and there are "no transparency obligations contained in Chapter 11 of NAFTA." It is true that Art. 1105 of NAFTA requires states to accord investments "fair and equitable treatment" "in accordance with international law"—and the situation might have been very different if the arbitrators had "simply *interpret[ed]*" this language "to include a minimum standard of transparency." But the tribunal had not purported to "interpret the wording of Article 1105," but rather, it "*misstated* the applicable law to include transparency obligations." So although the tribunal's second holding was upheld, the award was "partially set aside"—with the result that interest could only be awarded Metalclad for the period following the date of the Ecological Degree. See United Mexican States v. Metalclad Corp., [2001] BCSC 664, 89 B.C.L.R. (3d) 359 (2001).

Does this use of the rhetoric of "jurisdiction" represent a heightened standard of judicial review, at odds with the usual deference courts give arbitral tribunals? Would such heightened review be justified by the fact that—as the Government of

Mexico argued—NAFTA decisions "have significant public policy ramifications" on issues of general concern, including public health and the environment? See Gus van Harten, *Judicial Supervision of NAFTA Chapter 11 Arbitration: Public or Private Law?*, 21 Arb. Int'l 493 (2005)("the principle of party autonomy—so central to commercial arbitration"—may be less relevant to NAFTA since the treaty standards "could be viewed as analogous to rules of domestic public law that protect individuals by limiting state authority"); Charles H. Brower, *Investor-State Disputes Under NAFTA: The Empire Strikes Back*, 40 Colum. J. Transnat'l L. 43 (2001)("The prospect of lengthy annulment proceedings by itself threatens to diminish investor confidence"; "[i]f municipal courts take the annulment process one step further by permitting the easy reopening of awards, they will cripple a system of neutral adjudication designed to promote the flow of capital across the borders of NAFTA Parties").

3. TREATIES FOCUSED ON ARBITRATION OF FUTURE PUBLIC LAW DISPUTES

The Permanent Court of Arbitration (PCA), established by the 1899 Hague Convention on the Pacific Settlement of International Disputes, is a panel of persons nominated by the (hundred or so) contracting States. "Where contracting states wish to go to arbitration, they are entitled to choose the members of the tribunal from the panel. Thus, [the PCA] is in essence machinery facilitating the establishment of arbitral tribunals." Malcom N. Shaw, International Law 953 (5th ed.2003). The PCA says its caseload includes "territorial, treaty, and human rights disputes between states, as well as commercial and investment disputes."[76] The PCA's website contains a partial list of its cases; that list shows no cases between 1935 and 1998, but dozens of cases more recently.

The International Court of Justice (ICJ), also known as World Court, was created as part of the United Nations in 1945. Judges are elected to it when they receive a majority vote in each of the U.N. Security Council and General Assembly. The ICJ adjudicates two types of cases: contentious and advisory. In contentious cases, only states may be parties. See Statute of the International Court of Justice, Stat 1055, 33 UN Treaty Ser 993, Art 34 (June 26, 1945). In contrast, an advisory opinion may be given in response to any legal question at the request of whatever body may be authorized by or in accordance with the Charter of the United Nations to make such a request. Id. at Art 65. See Michael P. Scharf & Margaux Day, *The International Court of Justice's Treatment of Circumstantial Evidence and Adverse Inferences*, 13 Chi. J. Int'l L. 123 (2012). The ICJ most often receives a case through the parties' agreement to submit their existing dispute—a post-dispute arbitration agreement. However, pre-dispute agreements to resolve disputes before the ICJ are found in various treaties. Examples include the 1948 Genocide Convention, the 1965 Convention on Investment Disputes, the 1965 Convention on the Elimination of All Forms of Racial Discrimination, and the 1970 Hague Convention on Hijacking. See Malcom N. Shaw, International Law 977 (5th ed.2003). While some see "the record of compliance" with ICJ decisions as "only marginally satisfactory," ICJ decisions

[76] https://pca-cpa.org/en/about/introduction/.

have an impact "on a political level," and thus "should not necessarily be exclusively evaluated on the legal plane" of enforcement. Failure to comply violates the U.N. Charter and would ultimately be enforceable by the Security Council but each of its five permanent members (China, France, Russia, the United Kingdom, and the United States) maintains a veto power. Id.

The two institutions discussed in this section—the Permanent Court of Arbitration and the International Court of Justice (or World Court)—both have the word "court" in their names. This may suggest a higher level of "governmental-ness," than is found in international investment arbitration or the Iran-United States Claims Tribunal discussed in the next section. Relatedly, some scholars distinguish international "adjudication" before the PCA or ICJ from international "arbitration" before other bodies—perhaps because "arbitration" tends to connote "non-governmental-ness." See e.g., Stephen E. Gent, *The Politics of International Arbitration and Adjudication*, 2 Penn St. J. L. & Int'l Aff. 66, 67 (2013) ("The two methods primarily differ with respect to the identity of the third party. In arbitration, an individual, state, NGO, or panel of states hands down a decision. On the other hand, adjudication is conducted by an international court, such as the International Court of Justice.")

4. PUBLIC INTERNATIONAL ARBITRATION TRIBUNALS ARISING OUT OF POST-DISPUTE ARBITRATION AGREEMENTS

The leading example of a public international arbitration tribunal established by post-dispute agreement is the Iran-United States Claims Tribunal. It was established in 1981 through the Algiers Declarations as part of the resolution of the Iran Hostage Crisis. The Tribunal hears two categories of claims: private claims, which are claims brought by a national of one State against the other State, and inter-governmental claims, which are claims brought by one State against the other, alleging either a violation of the Algiers Declarations or breach of contract. The Tribunal has decided nearly 4,000 cases and awarded more than $2.5 billion approximately $1 billion to Iran and Iranian nationals and a substantially higher amount to the United States and United States nationals. See Yulia Andreeva, et al., *International Courts*, 43 Int'l Law. 425, 439 (2009). "While successful U.S. nationals were paid out of a security account in the Netherlands, in cases where Iran prevailed but the U.S. national refused to pay, Iran successfully enforced its awards in U.S. Courts through resort to the New York Convention." Thomas Buergenthal & Sean D. Murphy, Public International Law in a Nutshell 76–77 (4th ed.2007) (citing Iran v. Gould, 887 F.2d 1357 (9th Cir.1989)).

QUESTIONS TO REVIEW AND SYNTHESIZE

1. In what fundamental respect is international commercial arbitration similar to domestic (U.S.) arbitration and different from international public law arbitration? To put it another way, what makes international arbitration "commercial" or "public law"?
2. In what important sense is investment arbitration "public law" rather than "commercial"?

3. Why was *BG Group PLC v. Republic of Argentina*, litigated in U.S. courts under U.S. law, rather than in the courts of the United Kingdom or Argentina and under one of those States' laws?

4. In reversing the circuit court's decision that interpretation of the Argentina-U.K. treaty's "local litigation requirement" was for courts to decide de novo, rather than with deference to the views of the arbitrators, Justice Breyer's opinion for the *BG Group* Court relied on the Court's opinion (also authored by Justice Breyer) in *Howsam* v. *Dean Witter Reynolds, Inc.*, for what rule?

CHAPTER 6

PROCESSES SIMILAR TO ARBITRATION

A. PRIVATE JUDGING ("RENT-A-JUDGE") AND THE "SHORT TRIAL"

While litigation is adjudication in a court or other government forum, and arbitration is adjudication in a private (non-government) forum, private judging is somewhere in between. It is adjudication in a quasi-government forum.

Private judging is authorized by statute in only a few states. These statutes generally call the private judge a "referee" and generally permit only post-dispute agreements to send a case to private judging. Like an arbitration agreement, agreements to use a referee can determine the identity of the adjudicator as well as the time and place of a hearing or trial. Compare:

- N.H.Rev.Stat.Ann. § 519:9 (2013) ("The superior court with the consent of the parties shall, and without the consent of the parties may, commit to one or more referees any cause at law or in equity, or the determination of any question of fact pending in court wherein the parties are not, as matter of right, entitled to a trial by jury; and with the consent of the parties shall so commit any other cause or the determination of any other question of fact");
- N.Y. C.P.L.R. 4301 ("A referee to determine an issue or to perform an act shall have all the powers of a court in performing a like function"); id. 4317 ("The parties may stipulate that any issue shall be determined by a referee. Upon the filing of the stipulation with the clerk, the clerk shall forthwith enter an order referring the issue for trial to the referee named therein. Where the stipulation does not name a referee, the court shall designate a referee.");
- Tex.Civ.Prac. & Rem.Code §§ 151.001 (West 2005) ("On agreement of the parties, in civil or family law matters pending in a district court, statutory probate court, or statutory county court, the judge in whose court the case is pending may order referral of the

case as provided by this chapter and shall stay proceedings in the judge's court pending the outcome of the trial. Any or all of the issues in the cases, whether an issue of fact or law, may be referred.");

- Wash.Rev.Code.Ann § 4.48.010 (2015) ("The court shall order all or any of the issues in a civil action, whether of fact or law, or both, referred to a referee upon the written consent of the parties which is filed with the clerk.")

Private judging typically has many traits more like ordinary civil litigation than arbitration. For instance, state law on private judging may require privately-judged trials to be:

(1) governed by the same rules of procedure and evidence used in ordinary litigation;[1]

(2) exposed to public view;[2]

(3) adjudicated only by a former judge;[3] and

(4) subject to appeal in the same manner as other trial verdicts.[4]

With all those similarities to ordinary litigation, private judging basically amounts to an ordinary bench trial—except that the parties select and pay for the judge and hearing room. For instance, the Texas statute cautions: "The state or a unit of local government may not pay any costs related to a trial under this chapter"; "A trial under this chapter may not be held in a public courtroom, and a public employee may not be involved in the trial during regular working hours". Tex.Civ.Prac. & Rem.Code § § 151.009(c), 151.010. See also Cal. Rule of Court 3.907 ("A party who has elected to use the services of a privately compensated referee * * * is deemed to have elected to proceed outside the courthouse; therefore, court facilities and court personnel must not be used, except upon a finding by the presiding judge that the use would further the interests of justice.")

California seems to lead the nation in the use of private judging, perhaps because California's courts have long tended to be especially crowded, or because California enforces *pre*-dispute agreements to use private judging. A California statute provides that a court may "refer" a pending action to any person (the "referee") chosen by the parties in a pre- or post-dispute agreement:

> to hear and determine any or all of the issues in an action or proceeding, whether of fact or of law, and to report a statement of decision; [or] to ascertain a fact necessary to enable the court to determine an action or proceeding.

Cal.Civ.Proc.Code § 638. After hearing the case, California referees are to report their decision in writing to the court within twenty days after the close of testimony;

---

1 Tex.Civ.Prac. & Rem.Code § 151.005 (West 2005).

2 Cal.Ct.R. 2.833.

3 Ala. Code § 12–11A–2 ("Persons who may act as private judges shall: (1) Have been, but are not actively serving as, a judge of a district, circuit, or probate court and have served in the capacity of judge for at least six consecutive years."); Tex.Civ.Prac. & Rem.Code § 151.003 (West 2015).

4 Id. § 151.013.

judgment must then be entered on the referees' decision "in the same manner as if the action had been tried by the court." Id. §§ 643, 644. See also Cal.Const.art. VI, § 21; Cal.Civ.Proc.Code §§ 638–645 (2015).

California's private judging was first "used primarily in technical and complex business litigation involving substantial amounts of money."[5] However, its use has grown in family law matters.

> Private judging was once reserved for high net worth litigants; it had the cache of a rarified legal experience. Due to an overwhelmed judicial system, family law attorneys are routinely considering private judging to resolve smaller cases.
>
> Family law judges openly discuss the privatization of family law as a positive development especially when it comes to trying cases in excess of ten days.
>
> The cost of retaining a private judge was once the prime barrier for most family law litigants. Now, access to a judge trumps costs. A private judge in San Mateo County or San Francisco County charges approximately $400–$650 per hour.
>
> While the hourly fee of a private judge may seem high, family law attorneys are learning that the overall financial cost of litigating in private court may be far less than in public court. The cost savings is due to ease of access to the judge, case management, and faster case resolution.
>
> At retention, the private judge meets with the parties and their attorneys where rules and process are discussed. Communication between the private judge and attorneys is typically by email and telephone conference. Usually discovery is not allowed unless permitted by the judge and the scope of discovery is determined. Tight control of the discovery process is a major cost savings, as litigators well know. The private judge's role is equal parts case management and adjudication. When a ruling is needed, the private judge has only one case on the docket instead of twenty cases.
>
> The post-recession environment highlights the contrast between public and private judging when a case is set for trial. Due to crowded dockets in the family law departments, trials can be set a year out. Worse, where the trial estimate is longer than three days, the case will be transferred from the allpurpose family law judge to the civil trial division where the assigned judge may have little or no experience in family law. Worse still, it is not uncommon to have a fifteen-day trial spread over many months. In contrast, a private judge stays with the case from start to finish and the judge will be selected by the parties for his/her experience in the trial issues. Trials will be concluded faster because the private judge has more available time.

---

[5] Barlow F. Christensen, *Private Justice: California's General Reference Procedure*, 1982 Am.Bar Found.Research J. 79, 82.

> It should be noted that private judging is not truly "private" as Hon. Jill S. Robbins Ret. noted in her article: "The Private Judge: California Anomaly or Wave of the Future." The private judge must file all original pleadings submitted to him or her with the Superior Court. Also, the private judge must make reasonable accommodation for the presence of the public and media at hearings. Ronald S. Granberg echoed this point in his May 9, 2014 presentation to the San Mateo County Bar Association, Family Law Section, on the topic of "Divorce Privacy vs. Govenmental Transparency." Mr. Granberg suggests that if privacy is the attorney's goal, then arbitration should be considered in place of private judging.

H. Yvonne Seeley & Kimberly A. Madigan, *The Impact of the Budget Cutbacks on California Family Law Courts*, Aspatore, 2014 WL 3689592, at *4 (July 2014). See also J. Scott Vowell, *Update on Private Judging in Alabama*, 79 Ala. Law. 400, 402 (2018) (Alabama's Private Judge Act "has been used primarily in domestic relations cases").

Other states have devised different sorts of hybrids between litigation and arbitration, some of which envisage a greater role for the public court system—such as Nevada's "short trial." A Nevada statute says all cases with $50,000 or less at issue "must be submitted to nonbinding arbitration * * * unless the parties have agreed or are otherwise required to submit the action to an alternative method of resolving disputes established by the Supreme Court * * *, including, without limitation, a settlement conference, mediation or a *short trial*." Nev. Stat. § 38.250 (emphasis added). Such an agreement must be "entered into at the time of the dispute and not be a part of any previous agreement between the parties," and must be entered into "knowingly and voluntarily." Id.

Accordingly, the Nevada Supreme Court has promulgated "Short Trial Rules." Short trials are conducted by judges whom parties may select from a state-maintained panel; they may select either sitting district court judges, or "pro tempore judges" from the panel. "Pro tempore judges" are either practicing attorneys with 10 years civil trial experience or retired judges. They are paid $150 per hour—with a maximum of $1500 for the entire case—for which the parties are equally responsible unless stipulated otherwise. While serving, they have "all the powers and authority of a district court judge." If a jury is used, jurors are chosen from the county jury pool. The default size is four persons, three of whom have to concur for a valid verdict. The local court is to provide courtroom space. Nev. Short Trial R. 3, 14, 22, 23, 26, 28.

Under Nevada's short-trial rules, the trial is to be calendared no later than 240 days after the parties' written stipulation agreeing to enter the program. Nev. Short Trial R.12. Each party is allowed only three hours to present its case, unless a different time is stipulated to and approved by the presiding judge. Nev. Short Trial R.21. As is common in many forms of arbitration, the parties are to create a "joint evidentiary booklet" including all evidence to be presented; any evidentiary objections are to be raised at a pre-trial conference or else deemed waived. Nev. Short Trial R.18. A judgment under the short-trial program may not exceed $50,000 per plaintiff exclusive of attorneys' fees and costs unless the parties agree otherwise; either party may appeal an adverse judgment directly to the state supreme court, unless they have agreed "that the results of the short trial are binding." Nev. Short Trial R.26; R.32–33.

QUESTIONS TO REVIEW AND SYNTHESIZE

1. What are some aspects of private judging that are more similar to civil litigation than to arbitration? Conversely, what are some aspects of private judging that are more similar to arbitration?
2. Because private judging allows parties to bypass the queue of cases awaiting trial, private judging has been labeled "Rent-A-Judge" and criticized as, "an unconstitutional, elitist institution that unfairly grants privileges to the wealthy." Anne S. Kim, Note, *Rent-A-Judges and the Cost of Selling Justice*, 44 Duke L.J. 166, 199 (1994). Is that criticism strongest when directed at private judging, arbitration, or Nevada's "Short Trial"?
3. The Judicial Council of California approved rules to govern private judging. Cal. Rule of Court 3.924 requires referees to disclose to the parties "Any significant personal or professional relationship the referee has or has had with a party, attorney, or law firm in the instant case, including the number and nature of any other proceedings in the past 24 months in which the referee has been privately compensated by a party, attorney, law firm, or insurance company in the instant case for any services, including, but not limited to, service as an attorney, expert witness, or consultant or as a judge, referee, arbitrator, mediator, settlement facilitator, or other alternative dispute resolution neutral." How is this rule similar to and different from the California disclosure requirements for arbitrators, discussed in Section 4.B.5.b?
4. The excerpt on private judging in California family law "noted that private judging is not truly 'private' as * * * [t]he private judge must file all original pleadings submitted to him or her with the Superior Court [and] must make reasonable accommodation for the presence of the public and media at hearings. Ronald S. Granberg * * * suggests that if privacy is the attorney's goal, then arbitration should be considered in place of private judging." What did you learn in Sections 2.G, 3.B.4, and 5.B.1.c.i about the law governing of arbitration of divorce and other family cases?

B. BUSINESS COURTS

Several states have business courts with some features commonly associated with arbitration, such as specialized, expert adjudicators, and expedited case management procedures emphasizing resolution of disputes through negotiation, mediation, or other forms of Alternative Dispute Resolution. Much as arbitration's speed, (relative to trial,) has long been thought to attract businesses, delays in ordinary courts seem to have been a major reason behind the creation of business courts.

> The modern business court movement traces its origins to New York in the early 1990s. Litigants in business cases were frustrated by backlog, expense, and inconsistent case management. In response to these complaints, New York initiated a pilot project in Manhattan whereby each business case was assigned to a single judge throughout the litigation. In

> determining which cases should be assigned to these judges, New York drew up a laundry list of cases that would qualify as "commercial." These cases were then automatically assigned to judges in the newly-created Commercial Division as long as they satisfied certain jurisdictional requirements.
>
> As word began to trickle out that the reforms in New York had enabled the courts in that state to resolve business disputes more quickly, other states started creating business courts of their own. * * * By 2011, business courts had been established in nineteen states across the United States.
>
> These new business courts were, in most cases, created by the judiciary rather than the legislature. The supreme court of a state or, in some cases, the chief judge of a particular court would issue an order mandating that "business" cases be assigned to a particular trial judge whose docket would thereafter be comprised primarily or exclusively of such cases. * * *
>
> Although these new business courts resembled New York's in most respects, they took a variety of tacks in how they defined what constituted a "commercial" or "business" case eligible for assignment to the court. * * *
>
> * * *
>
> A number of states have also excluded certain categories of cases from the business court's jurisdiction[, such as] personal injury or individual products liability, * * * wrongful death claims, noncommercial landlord-tenant disputes, and employment law cases. These exclusions were in many cases driven by the need to win support for the court among plaintiffs' lawyers, who had expressed concerns that business court judges might be biased in favor of business interests; these lawyers did not want to litigate personal injury suits, for example, before a business court.
>
> Against this backdrop, business court advocates have identified three principal rationales for creating these courts. First, such courts are said to result in a higher quality of decisions in individual cases and to generate more and better-reasoned decisions in the fields of corporate and commercial law. * * *

John F. Coyle, *Business Courts and Interstate Competition*, 53 Wm. & Mary L. Rev. 1915, 1922–27 (2012). "Outside of New York, however, there is virtually no published statistical evidence—or any definitive statements by state officials with access to internal court data—that the creation of business courts results in the more efficient resolution of business cases." Id. at 1980.

While business courts have some similarities to arbitration, important differences between the two processes remain. Unlike arbitration, parties in business courts generally must take whichever judge the court assigns. Also, business courts tend to:

1. have lower filing fees than arbitration, as government subsidizes the cost of business courts;
2. generally lack the confidentiality of arbitration; and
3. generally have full rights to appeal, as opposed to the narrower grounds for vacating an arbitration award.

Christopher R. Drahozal, *Business Courts and the Future of Arbitration*, 10 Cardozo J. Conflict Resol. 491, 492–98, 498–500 (2009).

In contrast, a Delaware statute tried to create a business court similar to arbitration on all three of these factors, and even described this court's process as "arbitration" in granting its Court of Chancery "the power to arbitrate business disputes." This forum had high filing fees ($12,000), appeal only under the deferential standards of FAA § 10, and confidential proceedings barring public access. This confidentiality—"[a]ttendance at the proceeding is limited to 'parties and their representatives,' and all 'materials and communications' produced during the arbitration are protected from disclosure in judicial or administrative proceedings"—combined with the governmental-ness ("state action") in Delaware's business court violates the First Amendment's right of public access to trials, according to the following Third Circuit case.

Delaware Coalition for Open Government, Inc. v. Strine

United States Court of Appeals for the Third Circuit, 2013.
733 F.3d 510, 41 Media L. Rep. 2685.

■ SLOVITER, CIRCUIT JUDGE.

This appeal requires us to decide whether the public has a right of access under the First Amendment to Delaware's state-sponsored arbitration program. Chancellor Strine and the judges of the Delaware Chancery Court ("Appellants"), who oversee the arbitrations, appeal a judgment on the pleadings entered in favor of the Delaware Coalition for Open Government (the "Coalition"). The District Court found that Delaware's proceedings were essentially civil trials that must be open to the public. Appellants dispute the similarities and argue that the First Amendment does not mandate a right of public access to Delaware's proceedings.

In early 2009, in an effort to "preserve Delaware's preeminence in offering cost-effective options for resolving disputes, particularly those involving commercial, corporate, and technology matters," Delaware amended its code to grant the Court of Chancery "the power to arbitrate business disputes." H.B. 49, 145th Gen. Assemb. (Del. 2009). As a result, the Court of Chancery created an arbitration process as an alternative to trial for certain kinds of disputes. As currently implemented, the proceeding is governed both by statute and by the Rules of the Delaware Court of Chancery.

Delaware's government-sponsored arbitrations are not open to all Delaware citizens. To qualify for arbitration, at least one party must be a "business entity formed or organized" under Delaware law, and neither party can be a "consumer". The statute is limited to monetary disputes that involve an amount-in-controversy of at least one million dollars.

Once qualified parties have consented "by agreement or by stipulation" to avail themselves of the proceeding, they can petition the Register in Chancery to start arbitration. The fee for filing is $12,000, and the arbitration costs $6,000 per day after the first day. After receiving a petition the Chancellor selects a Chancery Court judge to hear the arbitration. The arbitration begins approximately ninety days after the petition is filed, and, as the parties agreed in oral argument, is conducted in a Delaware courthouse during normal business hours. Regular Court of Chancery Rules 26–37, governing depositions and discovery, apply to the proceeding, but the rules can be modified by consensual agreement of the parties.

The Chancery Court judge presiding over the proceeding "[m]ay grant any remedy or relief that [s/he] deems just and equitable and within the scope of any applicable agreement of the parties." Once a decision is reached, a final judgment or decree is automatically entered. Both parties have a right to appeal the resulting "order of the Court of Chancery" to the Delaware Supreme Court, but that court reviews the arbitration using the deferential standard outlined in the Federal Arbitration Act. Arbitrations can therefore only be vacated in relatively rare circumstances, such as when a party can prove that the "award was procured by corruption, fraud, or undue means" or that the "arbitrator [ ] w[as] guilty of misconduct." 9 U.S.C. § 10.

Both the statute and rules governing Delaware's proceedings bar public access. Arbitration petitions are "considered confidential" and are not included "as part of the public docketing system." Attendance at the proceeding is limited to "parties and their representatives," and all "materials and communications" produced during the arbitration are protected from disclosure in judicial or administrative proceedings.

If one of the parties appeals to the Supreme Court of Delaware for enforcement, stay, or vacatur, the record of the proceedings must be filed "with the Supreme Court in accordance with its Rules." "The petition and any supporting documents are considered confidential and not of public record until such time, if any, as the proceedings are the subject of an appeal." The Delaware Supreme Court has yet to adopt rules that would govern the confidentiality of appeals from Delaware's arbitration program, and there is no record of a public appeal from an arbitration award.

In the District Court, the Coalition moved for judgment on the pleadings, arguing that the confidentiality of Delaware's government-sponsored arbitration proceedings violated the First Amendment. The District Court granted the Coalition's motion. The judges of the Delaware Chancery Court appeal.

* * *

"The First Amendment, in conjunction with the Fourteenth, prohibits governments from 'abridging the freedom of speech, or of the press. . . .'" Richmond Newspapers, Inc. v. Virginia, 448 U.S. 555, 575, 100 S.Ct. 2814, 65 L.Ed.2d 973 (1980) (quoting U.S. CONST. amend. I). This protection of speech includes a right of public access to trials, a right first elucidated by the Supreme Court in Richmond Newspapers. In that case the Court found that a Virginia trial court had violated the First Amendment by closing a criminal trial to the public. Chief Justice

Burger's opinion for the plurality emphasized the important role public access plays in the administration of justice and concluded that "[t]he explicit, guaranteed rights to speak and publish concerning what takes place at a trial would lose much meaning if access to observe the trial could . . . be foreclosed arbitrarily."

The Court has since found that the public also has a right of access to voir dire of jurors in criminal trials, and to certain preliminary criminal hearings.

We have found a right of public access to civil trials, as has every other federal court of appeals to consider the issue. In addition to finding a right of public access to civil trials, we have also found a First Amendment right of the public to attend meetings of Pennsylvania city planning commissions and post-trial juror examinations. We have declined, however, to extend the right to the proceedings of judicial disciplinary boards, the records of state environmental agencies, deportation hearings, or the voting process.

The Experience and Logic Test

A proceeding qualifies for the First Amendment right of public access when "there has been a tradition of accessibility" to that kind of proceeding, and when "access plays a significant positive role in the functioning of the particular process in question." Press II, 478 U.S. at 10, 8, 106 S.Ct. 2735. The examination of the history and functioning of a proceeding has come to be known as the "experience and logic" test.

* * *

A. Experience

* * *

The litigants in this case disagree over which history is relevant to Delaware's proceedings. The Appellants suggest that we only examine the history of arbitrations, whereas the Coalition suggests we only examine the history of civil trials. Neither suggestion is appropriate in isolation. If we were to only analyze the history of arbitrations as the Appellants suggest, we would be accepting the state's designation of its proceedings as arbitrations at face value. Uncritical acceptance of state definitions of proceedings would allow governments to prevent the public from accessing a proceeding simply by renaming it. A First Amendment right that mandated access to civil trials, but allowed closure of identical "sivel trials" would be meaningless. Thus, the Supreme Court has held that "the First Amendment question cannot be resolved solely on the label we give the event, i.e., 'trial' or otherwise." The Coalition's suggestion—that we rely solely on the history of civil trials—is also flawed. Defining Delaware's proceeding as a civil trial at the outset would beg the question at issue here, and elide the differences between Delaware's arbitration proceeding and other civil proceedings.

* * * [W]e find that an exploration of both civil trials and arbitrations is appropriate here. Exploring both histories avoids begging the question and allows us to fully consider the "judgment of experience."

1. Civil Trials and the Courthouse

As we explained in *Publicker*, there is a long history of access to civil trials. The English history of access dates back to the Statute of Marlborough passed in 1267, which required that "all Causes . . . to be heard, ordered, and determined before the Judges of the King's Courts [were to be heard] openly in the King's Courts." This tradition of openness continued in English Courts for centuries, ensuring that evidence was delivered "'in the open Court and in the Presence of the Parties, their Attorneys, Council, and all By-standers, and before the Judge and Jury. . . .'" Thus, "'one of the most conspicuous features of English justice, that all judicial trials are held in open court, to which the public have free access, . . . appears to have been the rule in England from time immemorial.'"

This tradition of access to trials and the courthouse was adopted by the American colonies and preserved after the American Revolution. Courthouses served a central place in colonial life, encouraging "the active participation of community members" in shaping the "local practice of justice." As courthouses grew increasingly elaborate in the late-eighteenth century, they continued to encourage public viewing, albeit in more formal surroundings. The courtroom also maintained its important public role: "[w]ith juries, spectators from the community, and press all present," the courtroom "became a public state—a familiar, indeed immediately recognizable enclosure, in which the process of rights definition was made public. . . ."

Today, civil trials and the court filings associated with them are generally open to the public. The courthouse, courtroom, and trial remain essential to the way the public conceives of and interacts with the judicial system.

2. Arbitrations

Arbitrations also have a long history. Written records of proceedings resembling arbitrations have been found in England as early as the twelfth century. Early arbitrations involved community participation, and evidence suggests that they took place in public venues. The use of arbitrations to resolve private disputes, however, was limited by English precedent, which prevented the enforcement of binding agreements to arbitrate.

In the American colonies, arbitrations provided a way for colonists who harbored "suspicion of law and lawyers" to resolve disputes in their communities in a "less public and less adversarial" way. By the eighteenth century, however, arbitrations adopted increasingly formal procedures, and at least some appear to have taken place in public.

As the American economy grew, disputes over business transactions led to the further development of arbitration proceedings. These proceedings were occasionally supervised by a member of the judiciary "not acting in his official capacity." The popularity of commercial arbitration, however, was limited by precedent that made agreements to arbitrate essentially unenforceable. It was not until the passage of New York's Arbitration Act of 1920 and the Federal Arbitration Act of 1925, that arbitration agreements began to be treated by the courts like ordinary contracts. These arbitration acts allowed private arbitration to take on the important role it now serves in resolving commercial disputes.

Modern arbitration law has led to the development of an industry devoted to offering arbitration services. Groups such as the American Arbitration Association and JAMS, Inc. facilitate arbitration by appointing arbitrators, organizing hearings, and setting arbitration standards. These arbitrations, unlike some of their antecedents, are distinctly private. Parties engaged in arbitration must pay both for the arbitrations and for the space in which the arbitrations occur, and they usually choose to close their arbitrations to the public.

Although modern arbitration is dominated by private actors, a number of jurisdictions offer alternative dispute resolution procedures as a supplement to civil litigation. These procedures are sometimes called arbitrations, but unlike private arbitrations, they are usually non-binding, and can sometimes be initiated without the parties' consent.

The history of arbitration thus reveals a mixed record of openness. Although proceedings labeled arbitrations have sometimes been accessible to the public, they have often been closed, especially in the twentieth century. This closure, however, can be explained by the private nature of most arbitrations. Confidentiality is a natural outgrowth of the status of arbitrations as private alternatives to government-sponsored proceedings. Indeed, we would be surprised to find that private arbitrations—taking place before private arbitrators in private venues—had historically been accessible to the public.

Taking the private nature of many arbitrations into account, the history of civil trials and arbitrations demonstrates a strong tradition of openness for proceedings like Delaware's government-sponsored arbitrations. Proceedings in front of judges in courthouses have been presumptively open to the public for centuries. History teaches us not that all arbitrations must be closed, but that arbitrations with non-state action in private venues tend to be closed to the public.[2] Although Delaware's government-sponsored arbitrations share characteristics such as informality, flexibility, and limited review with private arbitrations, they differ fundamentally from other arbitrations because they are conducted before active judges in a courthouse, because they result in a binding order of the Chancery Court, and because they allow only a limited right of appeal.

When we properly account for the type of proceeding that Delaware has instituted—a binding arbitration before a judge that takes place in a courtroom—the history of openness is comparable to the history that this court described in *Publicker* and the Supreme Court found in *Richmond Newspapers*. Thus, unlike the "recent-and rebuttable-regulatory (sic) presumption" of openness in deportation hearings we examined in *North Jersey Media Group*, or the "long-standing trend away from openness" in the electoral process we found in *PG Publishing Co.*, the right of access to government-sponsored arbitrations is deeply rooted in the way the judiciary functions in a democratic society. Our experience inquiry therefore counsels in favor of granting public access to Delaware's proceeding because both

---

[2] Understood in this way, the closure of private arbitrations is only of questionable relevance. Meetings by private organizations, for example, are usually closed to the public, yet we did not consider this history of closure when we found a First Amendment right of public access to city planning commissions. Nor did we consider the history of access to votes undertaken by private organizations, when we examined the history of the voting process.

the "place and process" of Delaware's proceeding "have historically been open to the press and general public."

B. Logic

Under the logic prong of the experience and logic test we examine whether "access plays a significant positive role in the functioning of the particular process in question." We consider both the positive role that access plays, and also "the extent to which openness impairs the public good."

> We have recognized that public access to judicial proceedings provides many benefits, including [1] promotion of informed discussion of governmental affairs by providing the public with the more complete understanding of the [proceeding]; [2] promotion of the public perception of fairness which can be achieved only by permitting full public view of the proceedings; [3] providing a significant community therapeutic value as an outlet for community concern, hostility and emotion; [4] serving as a check on corrupt practices by exposing the [proceeding] to public scrutiny; [5] enhancement of the performance of all involved; and [6] discouragement of [fraud].

All of these benefits would accrue with the opening of Delaware's proceeding. Allowing public access to state-sponsored arbitrations would give stockholders and the public a better understanding of how Delaware resolves major business disputes. Opening the proceedings would also allay the public's concerns about a process only accessible to litigants in business disputes who are able to afford the expense of arbitration. In addition, public access would expose litigants, lawyers, and the Chancery Court judge alike to scrutiny from peers and the press. Finally, public access would discourage perjury and ensure that companies could not misrepresent their activities to competitors and the public.

The benefits of openness weigh strongly in favor of granting access to Delaware's arbitration proceedings. In comparison, the drawbacks of openness that Appellants cite are relatively slight. First, Appellants contend that confidentiality is necessary to protect "patented information, trade secrets, and other closely held information." This information, however, is already protected under Delaware Chancery Court Rule 5.1, which provides for the confidential filing of documents, including "trade secrets; sensitive proprietary information; [and] sensitive financial, business, or personnel information" when "the public interest in access to Court proceedings is outweighed by the harm that public disclosure of sensitive, non-public information would cause." These tailored protections are compatible with the First Amendment right of public access.

Second, Delaware argues that confidentiality is necessary to prevent the "'loss of prestige and goodwill'" that disputants would suffer in open proceedings. Although the loss of prestige and goodwill may be unpleasant for the parties involved, it would not hinder the functioning of the proceeding, nor impair the public good. As we have previously held, the exposure of parties to public scrutiny is one of the central benefits of public access.

The Appellants' third argument is that privacy encourages a "less hostile, more conciliatory approach." This may sometimes be true, but even private binding arbitrations can be contentious. Moreover, informality, not privacy, appears to be the primary cause of the relative collegiality of arbitrations. See Alan Scott Rau et al, Processes of Dispute Resolution, 601 (1989) (citing "relative informality" of arbitration as reason for reduced contentiousness); Christopher Baum, The Benefits of Alternative Dispute Resolution in Common Interest Development Disputes, 84 Saint John's L.Rev. 907, 925 (2010) ("Arbitration is also less contentious than litigation because the formal rules of evidence do not apply, unless the parties agree otherwise."). We therefore do not find that a possible reduction in conciliation caused by public access should weigh heavily in our analysis.

Finally, Appellants argue that opening the proceeding would effectively end Delaware's arbitration program. This argument assumes that confidentiality is the sole advantage of Delaware's proceeding over regular Chancery Court proceedings. But if that were true—if Delaware's arbitration were just a secret civil trial—it would clearly contravene the First Amendment right of access. On the contrary: as the Appellants point out in the rest of their brief, there are other differences between Delaware's government-sponsored arbitration and regular Chancery Court proceedings. Arbitrations are entered into with the parties' consent, the parties have procedural flexibility, and the arbitrator's award is subject to more limited review. Thus, disputants might still opt for arbitration if they would like access to Chancery Court judges in a proceeding that can be faster and more flexible than regular Chancery Court trials.[3]

I agree with Judge Roth on the virtues of arbitration. I cannot help but question why the Delaware scheme limits those virtues to litigants whose disputes involve an amount in controversy of at least a million dollars, and neither of whom is a consumer. One wonders why the numerous advantages set forth in Judge Roth's dissenting opinion (which apparently motivated the Delaware legislature) should not also be available to businesspersons with less than a million dollars in dispute. I see no explanation in Judge Roth's dissent for the limitation to rich businesspersons.

In her dissent, Judge Roth states that she believes that I do not appreciate the difference between adjudication and arbitration, i.e., "that a judge in a judicial proceeding derives her authority from the coercive power of the state, while a judge serving as an arbitrator derives her authority from the consent of the parties." Indeed I do.

Delaware's proceedings are conducted by Chancery Court judges, in Chancery Court during ordinary court hours, and yield judgments that are enforceable in the same way as judgments resulting from ordinary Chancery Court proceedings. Delaware's proceedings derive a great deal of legitimacy and authority from the state. They would be far less attractive without their association with the state. Therefore, the interests of the state and the public in openness must be given weight, not just the interests of rich businesspersons in confidentiality.

[3] Even if granting public access to Delaware's arbitrations were to limit their appeal, parties would still have two effective alternatives: private arbitration or public proceedings before the Chancery Court. Thus, Appellants' contention that allowing public access to Delaware's state-sponsored arbitration proceedings would lead to a mass exodus of corporations is overstated.

Like history, logic weighs in favor of granting access to Delaware's government-sponsored arbitration proceedings. The benefits of access are significant. It would ensure accountability and allow the public to maintain faith in the Delaware judicial system. A possible decrease in the appeal of the proceeding and a reduction in its conciliatory potential are comparatively less weighty, and they fall far short of the "profound" security concerns we found compelling in *North Jersey Media Group*.

Because there has been a tradition of accessibility to proceedings like Delaware's government-sponsored arbitration, and because access plays an important role in such proceedings, we find that there is a First Amendment right of access to Delaware's government-sponsored arbitrations. We will therefore affirm the order of the District Court.

■ FUENTES, CIRCUIT JUDGE, concurring:

Today we affirm the District Court's ruling, which concluded that "the right of access applies to the Delaware proceeding created by section 349 of the Delaware Code." Specifically, the District Court held that "the portions of [section 349] and [of] Chancery Court Rules 96, 97, and 98, which make the proceeding confidential, violate that right." I agree. I write separately because, given that not all provisions of § 349 of the Delaware Code or the Chancery Court Rules relating to Judge-run arbitration proceedings are unconstitutional, I think it is necessary to be more specific than the District Court's order in pointing out those that are problematic and those that are not.

I begin with § 349(b), which provides for the confidentiality in arbitration proceedings for business disputes. This section states that:

> Arbitration proceedings shall be considered confidential and not of public record until such time, if any, as the proceedings are the subject of an appeal. In the case of an appeal, the record shall be filed by the parties with the Supreme Court in accordance with its rules, and to the extent applicable, the rules of the Court of Chancery.

I agree with Judge Sloviter that this provision violates the First Amendment right of public access and cannot stand. However, I see nothing wrong with the other provisions of this statute. I do not believe that § 349(a), granting the Chancery Court the power to arbitrate business disputes, or § 349(c), providing for the filing of "applications to vacate, stay, or enforce an [arbitral] order" with the Delaware Supreme Court, violate the public right of access when § 349(b) is removed from the statutory scheme.

Similarly, not all provision of the Court of Chancery Court Rules implementing § 349 arbitrations raise constitutional concerns. Chancery Court Rule 97(a)(4) provides:

> "The Register in Chancery will not include the petition [for arbitration] as part of the public docketing system. The petition and any supporting documents are considered confidential and not part of public record until such time, if any, as the proceedings are the subject of an appeal. In the case of an appeal, the record shall be filed by the parties with the

> Supreme Court in accordance with its Rules, and to the extent applicable, the Rules of this Court."

Chancery Court Rule 98(b) likewise provides that:

> "Arbitration hearings are private proceedings such that only parties and their representatives may attend, unless all parties agree otherwise. An Arbitrator may not be compelled to testify in any judicial or administrative proceeding concerning any matter relating to service as an Arbitrator. All memoranda and work product contained in the case files of an Arbitrator are confidential. Any communication made in or in connection with the arbitration that relates to the controversy being arbitrated, whether made to the Arbitrator or a party, or to any person if made at an arbitration hearing, is confidential. Such confidential materials and communications are not subject to disclosure in any judicial or administrative proceeding with the following exceptions: (1) where all parties to the arbitration agree in writing to waive the confidentiality, or (2) where the confidential materials and communications consist of statements, memoranda, materials, and other tangible evidence otherwise subject to discovery, which were not prepared specifically for use in the arbitration hearing.

Again, I agree with Judge Sloviter that these provisions violate the First Amendment, but I do not find any problem with the remainder of the Chancery Court Rules implementing the § 349 arbitrations. Chancery Court Rule 96, containing certain definitions, is in my view constitutional in its entirety. Similarly, the remaining portions of Rules 97 and 98, which provide for the scope of arbitration, the proper procedures for an arbitration, and the logistics of hearings and dispute resolution, pass constitutional muster when Rules 97(a)(4) and 98(b) are excised from the law.

"The unconstitutionality of a part of an Act does not necessarily defeat or affect the validity of its remaining provisions." Champlin Ref. Co. v. Corp. Comm'n of Okla., 286 U.S. 210, 234, 52 S.Ct. 559, 76 L.Ed. 1062 (1932). It is well-settled that we must "refrain from invalidating more of a statute than is necessary." Even when construing state laws "[w]e prefer . . . to enjoin only the unconstitutional applications of [a] statute while leaving other applications in force, or to sever its problematic portions."

The crux of today's holding is that the proceedings set up by § 349 violate the First Amendment because they are conducted outside the public view, not because of any problem otherwise inherent in a Judge-run arbitration scheme. Thus, Appellants are enjoined only from conducting arbitrations pursuant to § 349(b) of Title 10 of the Delaware Code or Rules 97(a)(4) and 98(b) of the Delaware Chancery Court. Nothing in today's decision should be construed to prevent sitting Judges of the Court of Chancery from engaging in arbitrations without those confidentiality provisions.

Appellants suggest that Judge-run arbitrations will not occur under § 349 unless they are conducted in private. This may be so, but neither Appellants nor the Delaware Legislature have presented us with an alternative confidential arbitration scheme sufficiently devoid of the air of official State-run proceeding that infects the system now before us, sufficient to pass constitutional muster. Nor have they otherwise suggested that we attempt to sever offending portions of the statute to construct such an alternative. Thus, we have no occasion to consider if different arbitration schemes pass constitutional muster, and we are left with no choice other than to sever the confidentiality provisions.

Appellants only severability argument is a very limited one, that invalidating the self-executing aspect of the arbitral awards, Del. Ch. R. 98(f)(3), is enough to cure any constitutional infirmity. But as Appellants themselves describe it, the procedure contemplated in Rule 98(f)(3) is merely "a matter of convenience." It eliminates the need to file the arbitral award in court, a step that is only significant if a party refuses to abide by an arbitrator's award, a rarely occurring contingency. For essentially the reasons stated in Judge Sloviter's opinion, the mere formality of filing that award in Court, which Rule 98(f)(3) skirts, does not alone alter the First Amendment right of access calculus one way or another.

But I reiterate that we do not express any view regarding the constitutionality of a law that may allow sitting Judges to conduct private arbitrations if the system set up by such a law varies in certain respects from the scheme before us today. Indeed, it is likely that the Delaware Legislature has at its disposal several alternatives should it wish to continue to pursue a scheme of Judge-run arbitrations.

With this understanding of the scope of today's decision, I join in Judge Sloviter's opinion and concur in the judgment.

■ ROTH, CIRCUIT JUDGE, dissenting:

The use of arbitration as a method of resolving business and commercial disputes has been increasing both here and abroad. For example, the caseload of the American Arbitration Association's International Center for Dispute Resolution grew by almost 330 per cent between 1994 and 2004. The number of requests for arbitration in the London Court of International Arbitration grew by 300 per cent in the last decade.

There are a number of factors that have caused this growth in arbitration. One is the importance of resolving disputes expeditiously. Businesses in this country and abroad need to get commercial conflicts resolved as quickly as possible so that commercial relations are not disrupted. Another factor in the growth of arbitration is the increase in commercial disputes between businesses located in different countries. In particular, non-U.S. companies, with no familiarity—or with too much familiarity—with the American judicial system, may prefer arbitration with the rules set by the parties to lengthy and expensive court proceedings. In addition, arbitration permits the proceedings to be kept confidential, protecting trade secrets and sensitive financial information. The Supreme Court has summarized these advantages as follows:

> The point of affording parties discretion in designing arbitration processes is to allow for efficient, streamlined procedures tailored to the type of dispute. It can be specified, for example, that the decisionmaker be a specialist in the relevant field, or that proceedings be kept

> confidential to protect trade secrets. And the informality of arbitral proceedings is itself desirable, reducing the cost and increasing the speed of dispute resolution.

AT&T Mobility LLC v. Concepcion, ___ U.S. ___, 131 S.Ct. 1740, 1749, 179 L.Ed.2d 742 (2011).

The State of Delaware has become interested in sponsoring arbitration as a part of its efforts to preserve its position as the leading state for incorporations in the U.S. One of the reasons that Delaware has maintained this position is the Delaware Court of Chancery, where the judges are experienced in corporate and business law and readily available to resolve this type of dispute. Nevertheless, judicial proceedings in the Court of Chancery are more formal, time consuming and expensive than arbitration proceedings. For that reason, the Court of Chancery, as a formal adjudicator of disputes, may not be able to compete with the new arbitration systems being set up in other states and countries.[3]

In order to prevent the diversion elsewhere of complex business and corporate cases, the Delaware Legislature in 2009 enacted legislation to create an arbitration system. The Legislature established the arbitral system in the Court of Chancery where the judges are the most experienced in corporate and business litigation. The Legislature declared that the new system was "intended to preserve Delaware's preeminence in offering cost-effective options for resolving disputes, particularly those involving commercial, corporate, and technology matters."

This Delaware arbitration system is offered to business entities (at least one of which must have been formed or organized under Delaware law; no party can be a consumer) to resolve expensive and complex disputes (for disputes involving solely monetary damages, the amount in controversy must be at least $1,000,000) with the consent of the parties. The arbitrators are judges of the Court of Chancery or others authorized under the Rules of the Court of Chancery. The proceedings are confidential. In my view, such a set-up creates a perfect model for commercial arbitration.

Judge Sloviter urges, however, that the Delaware system violates the First Amendment of the U.S. Constitution. In arriving at this conclusion, she does not rely solely on either the history of arbitration or the history of civil trials. She looks "'not to the practice of the specific public institution involved, but rather to whether the particular type of government proceeding [has] historically been open in our free society'."[4] She classifies that "particular type of government

---

[3] See N.Y. State Bar Ass'n, Task Force on N.Y. Law in Int'l Matters, Final Report 4 (June 25, 2011) ('[J]urisdictions around the world, many with government support, are taking steps to increase their arbitration case load. New arbitration laws were enacted in 2010 and 2011 in France, Ireland, Hong Kong, Scotland, Ghana and other nations to enhance their attractiveness as seats of arbitration. . . . In 2010, at least three jurisdictions established specialized courts to handle international arbitration matters—Australia, India and Ireland. Several other jurisdictions well-known for international arbitration, including France, the United Kingdom, Switzerland, Sweden and China, have designated certain courts or judges to hear cases to challenge or enforce arbitration awards. Among the cited reasons for this focus on arbitration is the governments' recognition of the importance of arbitration to their economies and to their position in today's world of global commerce.').

[4] I believe that Judge Sloviter does not appreciate the difference between adjudication and arbitration, i.e., that a judge in a judicial proceeding derives her authority from the coercive power of the state while a judge serving as an arbitrator derives her authority from the consent of the parties.

proceeding," which would occur in the Delaware arbitration system, as one that has traditionally been open to the public. In my view, her analysis begs the question.

On the other hand, Judge Fuentes, while concurring with Judge Sloviter, is less broad in his conclusion. His concern is with the confidentiality of the proceedings. He concludes that the confidentiality provisions of 10 Del. C. § 349(b) violate the First Amendment right of public access and cannot stand. He also concludes that the confidentiality provisions for docketing and holding hearings found in Chancery Court Rules 97(a)(4) and 98(b) violate the First Amendment. However, Judge Fuentes finds most of the statute and rules to be acceptable. He has no problem with a sitting judge arbitrating business disputes. He has no problem with the self-executing aspect of the arbitral awards.

I do not agree with Judge Fuentes's contention that the Delaware Court of Chancery's arbitration proceedings cannot be confidential. Confidentiality is one of the primary reasons why litigants choose arbitration to resolve disputes—particularly commercial disputes, involving corporate earnings and business secrets.

In this dissent, I will focus on the issue of confidentiality because that is the only area in which Judge Fuentes and I differ. I will not discuss the other issues raised by Judge Sloviter although I could, if necessary, respond to those also. I will limit my discussion to the difference between Judge Fuentes's views and my own.

An examination of confidentiality in arbitration should begin in colonial times. The tradition of arbitration in England and the American colonies reveals a focus on privacy. See Michael Collins, Privacy and Confidentiality in Arbitration Proceedings, 30 Tex. Int'l L.J. 121, 122 (1995) ("In English law . . . it has for centuries been recognized that arbitrations take place in private."); Amy J. Schmitz, Untangling the Privacy Paradox in Arbitration, 545 U. Kan. L.Rev. 1211, 1223 (2006) ("The New York Chamber of Commerce . . . established an arbitral regime at the Chamber's inception in 1765. . . . [and] relied on arbitration's privacy and independence to foster efficient resolution of disputes among the American and British merchants during and after the American Revolutionary War."). In the twentieth century, the modern arbitration bodies began to develop rules for arbitration proceedings that emphasize privacy and confidentiality. See Richard C. Reuben, Confidentiality in Arbitration: Beyond the Myth, 54 U. Kan. L.Rev. 1255, 1271–72 (2006).

Today, the major national and international arbitral bodies continue to emphasize confidentiality. Their rules provide that arbitration proceedings are not open to the public unless the parties agree they will be. Thus, as a rule, arbitration has not "historically been open to the press and the general public."[6]

With this history of arbitration in mind, looking at experience and logic, see *Press-Enterprise Co. v. Superior Court of Calif. for the Cnty. of Riverside,* 478 U.S. 1, 8, 106 S.Ct. 2735, 92 L.Ed.2d 1 (1986), I conclude that, historically, arbitration has

[6] Judge Sloviter states that the "closure of private arbitrations is only of questionable relevance." I disagree. The development of private arbitration is key to understanding the functions of arbitration as a dispute resolution process and its tradition concerning public access and confidentiality.

been private and confidential. Logically, the resolution of complex business disputes, involving sensitive financial information, trade secrets, and technological developments, needs to be confidential so that the parties do not suffer the ill effects of this information being set out for the public—and especially competitors—to misappropriate. For these reasons, there is here no First Amendment right of public access.

In conclusion, then, it appears to me to be very clear that, when the State of Delaware decided to create its arbitration system, it was looking at traditional arbitration, in a confidential setting, before arbitrators experienced in business and corporate litigation. Delaware did not intend the arbitration system to supplant civil trials. Delaware did not intend to preclude the public from attending proceedings that historically have been open to the public. The new system was created to provide arbitration in Delaware to businesses that consented to arbitration—and that would go elsewhere if Delaware did not offer arbitration before experienced arbitrators in a confidential setting.

For the above reasons, I respectfully dissent. I would reverse the judgment of the District Court and uphold the statute and rules which establish the Delaware arbitration system.

Judge Sloviter's opinion for the Third Circuit pointed out that arbitration's "[c]onfidentiality is a natural outgrowth of the status of arbitrations as private alternatives to government-sponsored proceedings." By contrast, "Delaware's government-sponsored arbitrations * * * differ fundamentally from other arbitrations because they are conducted before active judges in a courthouse." In sum, while arbitration can be highly confidential because it is non-governmental adjudication, a government court—even if it calls itself "arbitration"—is subject to a constitutional right of public access.

West Virginia Investment Management Board v. Variable Annuity Life Insurance Company

Supreme Court of Appeals of West Virginia, 2018.
241 W.Va. 148, 820 S.E.2d 416, 2018 Employee Benefits Cas. 198, 043.

■ WALKER, JUSTICE:

This appeal is the latest chapter in a long-existing contractual dispute between the West Virginia Investment Management Board (IMB), the West Virginia Consolidated Public Retirement Board (CPRB) (together, Petitioners) and the respondent, The Variable Annuity Life Insurance Company (VALIC). The first time the parties were before this Court, we reversed summary judgment in favor of VALIC and remanded for further proceedings.[1] This Court also directed that the matter be referred to the Business Court Division. Eventually, the parties agreed to submit the dispute to binding, non-appealable arbitration before a panel of three business court judges due to the complexity of the case. The panel unanimously

---

[1] *West Virginia Investment Management Bd. v. Variable Annuity Life Ins. Co.*, 234 W. Va. 469, 766 S.E.2d 416 (2014) (*IMB I*).

found in favor of VALIC. Petitioners now contend that the creation and makeup of the arbitration panel was illegal. Petitioners additionally argue that the panel, even if validly created, misapplied the law in reliance on erroneous findings of fact, altogether failed to apply the law of the case created in *IMB I*, and neglected to decide all issues before it.

We disagree and find that the Business Court Division Rules provide sufficient flexibility to allow for arbitration by panel if agreed to by the parties. * * * Accordingly, we affirm the order below dismissing the matter from the Business Division docket in reliance on the conclusions reached in the panel's Final Decision.

I. FACTUAL AND PROCEDURAL BACKGROUND

* * * Petitioners filed this action * * *. [T]he circuit court entered summary judgment in favor of VALIC. Petitioners then appealed that order to this Court in *IMB I*.

In *IMB I*, * * * we reversed the grant of summary judgment and remanded the matter for further proceedings consistent with the opinion. We also referred the matter to the Business Court Division.

Following the remand in *IMB I*, the parties engaged in extensive discovery * * *.

Prior to the pretrial conference, Judge Christopher C. Wilkes—the Business Court Division Chair and Presiding Judge—expressed concern, echoed by the parties, that the complexity of the issues involved might prove difficult for resolution by a lay jury. These concerns prompted Judge Wilkes to offer to hold a bench trial or other alternative dispute resolution. The parties reportedly "liked the idea of arbitration, but worried that the case presented too much information for one arbitrator to absorb." In response, Judge Wilkes offered to secure a panel of arbitrators to hear their dispute according to whatever terms were agreed upon by the parties. Counsel for the parties sought the possibility of securing three business court judges to serve as the arbitration panel to be conducted the next day, but it could not be arranged on such short notice. Judge Wilkes advised the parties that he would not serve on the panel, but the parties requested that Judge Wilkes do so because he was already intimately acquainted with the admittedly complex issues, having presided over the case for the past year. The parties then took leave to consult with their respective clients and reconvened, at which time all counsel agreed to the alternative dispute resolution and at the parties' request, Judge Wilkes cancelled the jury trial scheduled to begin the following day. The parties then agreed that they would attempt to mediate the case once more, and asked that Judge Wilkes serve as the mediator since he not only was aware of all issues, but also was available to conduct the mediation the following day due to cancellation of the jury trial. In the event that the mediation was unsuccessful, the parties agreed that the matter would be submitted to binding, non-appealable arbitration before Judge Wilkes, and Business Court Judges Joanna I. Tabit and Paul T. Farrell, who were specifically chosen by the parties. The parties likewise stipulated to detailed parameters for the arbitration. The parties reduced the pertinent points of their agreement to writing and submitted it to the Business Court on September 20, 2016 as a Joint Stipulation:

WHEREAS, the parties came to an agreement to stay this action and submit to binding arbitration if they are not able [to] resolve it through mediation;

NOW THEREFORE, IT IS HEREBY STIPULATED AND AGREED, by and between the parties, as follows:

1. This action will be stayed.

2. The parties have waived their right to trial by jury or bench.

3. The parties shall mediate this dispute before Judge Wilkes on September 20, 2016.

4. In the event the action is not resolved through mediation, the parties shall submit to binding arbitration before a three-judge panel comprise of Judge Wilkes, Judge Joanna I. Tabit, and Judge Paul T. Farrell ("the arbitration"). Any dispute arising prior to the arbitration shall be resolved by Judge Wilkes.

5. The arbitration shall take place over a three-day period that is mutually convenient to the panel members and parties.

    a. On the first day of arbitration, Plaintiffs shall have up to five hours to present a proffer of evidence.

    b. On the second day of arbitration, Defendant shall have up to five hours to present a proffer of evidence.

    c. On the third day of arbitration, both parties shall have up to three hours to present argument.

6. Seven (7) calendar days before the arbitration is scheduled to begin, the parties may submit pre-arbitration memoranda not to exceed twenty-five (25) pages.

7. At the arbitration, the proffers must be drawn from materials and testimony in the discovery record in the case or publicly available sources.

    a. In the event a party intends to proffer testimony of a witness that is not in the discovery record, that testimony must be provided by affidavit in advance of the arbitration.

    b. Any affidavit prepared pursuant to paragraph 6(a), above, shall be served on opposing party by e-mail at least fourteen (14) calendar days before the arbitration is scheduled to begin.

    c. The opposing party may, at their election, depose any witness whose testimony is presented by affidavit. The deposition shall occur prior to the first date the arbitration is scheduled to begin. The deposition shall be limited to the subject matter of the testimony set forth in the affidavit.

8. Within fourteen (14) calendar days following the conclusion of the arbitration, the parties may submit written arguments in memoranda not to exceed (thirty) 30 pages in length.

9. The arbitration panel shall issue a reasoned decision applying West Virginia law within thirty (30) calendar days after the conclusion of the arbitration.

10. The arbitration shall be confidential, except to the extent disclosure is required by law.

11. The decision of the arbitrators is final and non-appealable.

12. Upon issuance of the panel's reasoned decision, the above-captioned action shall be dismissed with prejudice.

13. The parties shall bear their own costs, including attorneys' fees.

After entering the parties' Joint Stipulation, Judge Wilkes conducted a mediation, but not before informing the parties that any information they did not wish him to know as a member of the arbitration panel should be kept confidential from him during the mediation. The mediation was unsuccessful and the matter was scheduled on the court's public docket for a three-day arbitration on January 18–20, 2017, but was continued by agreement of the parties to March 7–9, 2017.

Beginning March 7, 2017, the arbitration took place in Kanawha County's Ceremonial Courtroom. Because the arbitration was to take place in a county courthouse, and relating to the parties' agreement that arbitration be confidential, except to the extent disclosure is required by law, Judge Wilkes explained to the parties that "you cannot preclude the public or anyone from . . . observing [the arbitration]. So I think we're not going to be able to blanket much, if anything, in confidentiality." The parties thereafter made their five-hour proffers of evidence to the panel, presented three-hour oral arguments, and submitted post-arbitration written arguments. On April 28, 2017, the panel issued a unanimous Final Decision in favor of VALIC * * *.

* * *

Despite agreeing that the panel's order would be binding and non-appealable, Petitioners then applied to this Court * * *.

* * *

On appeal, Petitioners argue that the Business Division did not have the authority to conduct an arbitration and that their consent to the arbitration and its terms was ineffective because the proceedings were illegal. As a facet of that argument, Petitioners argue that to deem the proceedings "confidential" was a violation of the public's constitutional right to access to the courts. * * *

VALIC counters that Petitioners have waived any procedural objection to the arbitration by agreeing to it below, but argue that, even so, the Business Court Rules provide the framework for conducting an arbitration and the parties' agreement was not "illegal." * * *

Turning first to the Business Division's authority to conduct arbitrations, Petitioners do not dispute that they agreed to arbitrate, nor do they claim fraud or any other untoward inducement to enter into the agreement. Instead, Petitioners claim that their consent to the arbitration, while willingly given, was nevertheless ineffective because it was made toward an illegal purpose.

* * *

Petitioners' arguments are three-fold. First, Petitioners argue that the Rules of Judicial Conduct preclude Business Division judges from conducting arbitrations. Second, but relatedly, Petitioners argue that the Business Division Rules do not authorize arbitration, generally, and specifically, they do not authorize the makeup of the one impaneled here. Third, Petitioners argue that the confidential nature of the proceedings renders them unconstitutional, and, therefore, void.

Rule 3.9 of the Code of Judicial Conduct states that "[a] judge shall not act as an arbitrator or mediator or perform other judicial functions apart from the judge's official duties." The commentary to that rule provides "[t]his Rule does not prohibit a judge from participating in arbitration, mediation, or settlement conferences *performed as part of assigned judicial duties. . . .*" Trial Court Rule 29.09(h), a specific Business Court Rule, provides that "[t]he Resolution Judge *is authorized to schedule and conduct mediation of the case or any Alternative Dispute Resolution as agreed to by the parties and the Resolution Judge* in an attempt to resolve the case in an expedient and efficient manner." Likewise, Trial Court Rule 29.04(e) defines the Resolution Judge as "[a] member of the Division assigned by order of the Division Chair, with the advice and consent of the Division, to mediate, *arbitrate, or provide any other form of dispute resolution agreed to by the parties. . . .*" When read together, it requires no stretch of reasoning to conclude that arbitration, if that is the agreed-upon Alternative Dispute Resolution, falls within the scope of a Business Division judge's official duties, and therefore does not run afoul of Rule 3.9 of the Code of Judicial Conduct.

Trial Court Rule 29.09(h) is likewise general enough to imbue the Business Court Division with the authority to conduct an arbitration by panel, if agreed to by the parties and the Resolution Judge. The term "any" within that Rule necessarily includes arbitration by panel as a form of alternative dispute resolution, particularly where the Resolution Judge is given the authority to arbitrate generally under Rule 29.04(e). The Business Division's rules to this end are aimed at flexibility and allow some degree of creativity for resolution of particular types of disputes so long as the creature of that creativity is agreed to by the parties involved.[18] Thus, because we do not find that the Business Division wholly lacked authority to conduct an arbitration by panel or otherwise, there is no cause to conclude that the parties' agreement to do so was "illegal."

---

[18] We find no fault in the agreement to submit this matter to arbitration in general, but merely find that the agreement, by its very nature as an *agreement*, and one to arbitrate at that, limits our appellate review. Consistent with the parties' and Judge Wilkes' concerns, our review of the record suggests that this matter was particularly well-suited for arbitration considering the complexity of the issues involved as well as the sheer volume of evidence to be proffered. Business disputes, as contemplated by the creation of the Business Division, often require a departure from the typical civil case structure. As the parties themselves contemplated, arbitration by panel not only provided the parties with three highly-skilled judges to hear their dispute, but likewise allowed the parties to more capably present their cases through an agreed-upon structure unavailable to litigants in civil cases. The parties here were enabled to present their evidence as they saw fit in five hour blocks in order to serve cohesive factual development, were provided *three hours* of legal argument, and were permitted to submit written legal arguments prior to and at the close of the arbitration for consideration. Where the legal arguments are complex, the often-crippling time limitation of closing arguments to a jury cannot be understated, and these parties had the foresight to contract around that limitation.

More troubling are the manifold roles of Judge Wilkes as the Presiding Judge and Resolution Judge, as well as his ultimate position on the arbitration panel in light of Trial Court Rule 29.07, which provides that "the Division Chair may serve as a Presiding *or* Resolution Judge." Here, Division Chair Judge Wilkes began the case as the Presiding Judge and thereafter mediated the case and served on the arbitration panel as the Resolution Judge. The rules inform us that the policy behind having two separate judges assigned to these tasks is in effort to protect the confidentiality of mediation, and, for that reason, communication between the two is limited: "[t]o protect the confidentiality of the mediation process, communication between the presiding judge and the resolution judge regarding the mediation during or after the process shall be limited to procedural status *or other matters agreed to by all parties*." It is clear from the language of Rule 29.04(e) that the parties may agree to full disclosure of information as between the presiding and resolution judges, and that the parties in this case agreed to just that. For that reason, we see no illegality in the makeup of the arbitration panel so as to void the proceedings.

Moreover, the matter before us is not the archetypal waiver issue arising from the parties' failure to lodge an objection: the parties here *explicitly agreed* that Judge Wilkes would mediate the case and then serve on the arbitration panel. Indeed, the parties *asked* Judge Wilkes to mediate the case, and later *asked* him to serve on the arbitration panel after he offered to impanel three new judges. Judge Wilkes further informed the parties that any information they did not wish him to know as a member of the arbitration panel should not be presented to him during the mediation. Given these circumstances, we find that the policy implications of dual roles as presiding judge and resolution judge have been rendered moot by agreement of the parties and the proceedings are not rendered void or illegal for that reason. Further, we find that Petitioners, again by virtue of their agreement, cannot now be heard to complain of the makeup of the panel.

Turning to Petitioners' argument that the arbitration was unconstitutional because it violated the public's constitutional right to access the courts,[21] we find that argument ill-suited to the actual circumstances of the arbitration conducted below. As discussed by Petitioners, the Court of Appeals for the Third Circuit examined this issue in *Delaware Coalition for Open Government, Inc. v. Strine*. In *Strine*, the Third Circuit struck down a Delaware statutory scheme relating to private, court-sponsored arbitration. The *Strine* court reasoned that because the arbitrations were conducted in state courthouses by officials elected by the public, to preclude the public from the proceedings was a violation of the well-instilled constitutional right to access the courts. Petitioners argue that pursuant to *Strine*, the parties' agreement that the proceedings would be confidential was unconstitutional and the award should be vacated. We find *Strine*'s theoretical arguments with regards to the rights of the public persuasive, and, indeed, this Court has also reiterated that "[o]ne fundamental aspect of our Anglo-American system of justice is its openness," and "[w]ith respect to any judicial or quasi-judicial proceeding, the public must always be afforded the opportunity to realize that there is a careful, reasoned and judicious decision-making process at work[.]"

[21] *See* W. VA. Const. art 3, § 17 ("The courts of this state shall be open[.]").

In application to the underlying proceeding, however, the facts in this case are utterly distinct from those in *Strine*, and the outcome necessarily different.

In *Strine*, the Delaware statutory scheme barred public access by providing that the proceedings could only be attended by the parties and their representatives, and that the petition for arbitration and supporting documents would not be included on the public docketing system. In stark contrast, the date, time and location of the parties' arbitration proceedings below were publicly docketed by the court as they would be in any other civil case, and transcripts of the arbitration were available to the public. While the Final Decision was issued under seal, it was unsealed by this Court, and Petitioners do not allege that members of the public ever sought to review the Final Decision and were denied. Likewise, as Judge Wilkes aptly noted prior to the arbitration, "you cannot preclude the public or anyone from . . . observing [the arbitration]. So I think we're not going to be able to blanket much, if anything, in confidentiality." Petitioners do not allege, nor is there any evidence in the record to suggest that anyone was precluded from observing the arbitration. Rather, Petitioners contend that "[t]he hearing was held in the Kanawha County Courthouse, but it was not publicized and it was not attended by the public or press, though the transcript of the three-day proceeding has been placed on the public docket." Seemingly, Petitioners conflate the concepts of publicity and public access. The constitutional right of the public to access the courts requires that the courts be open as a check on the judiciary; it does not require that the court actively provide publicity for already publicly-docketed proceedings, nor does it require actual attendance of the press or the public. Accordingly, we view the parties' agreement to keep matters confidential to the extent allowable by law as little more than an agreed protective order, ultimately rendered moot when this Court unsealed the record. For those reasons, we do not find that the proceedings violated the constitutional right to access the courts.

* * *

Petitioners further contend that there is no such thing as "binding judicial arbitration" because "judicial arbitration, in jurisdictions offering it all, appears to be uniformly of the non-binding variety."[28]

---

[28] Petitioners argue in their reply brief that there are aspects of public policy that suggest that sitting judges should not act as arbitrators. Initially, we observe that the cases on which Petitioners rely analyze other states' statutory schemes or rules relating whether a judge may, within the confines of those statutes or rules, conduct arbitration. As we have already established, this state's framework for the Business Court Division does not preclude arbitration by business court judges. As to general public policy, first, Petitioners argue that sitting judges may not act as arbitrators because *private* arbitration cannot be conducted in public courthouses without running afoul of constitutional access to the courts. As we have previously discussed, this was not a private arbitration and the public was not precluded access. Second, Petitioners argue that sitting judges may not act as arbitrators because arbitrators need not adhere to the Rules of Evidence or other facets of West Virginia law, which conflicts with the duties of an elected judge. But, pursuant to their agreement, and as discussed below, the panel *did* apply West Virginia law. Third, Petitioners argue that judicial arbitrators should not be permitted to "wear both hats," that is, to hear in their judicial capacity grounds for vacating the awards they rendered in their capacity as an arbitrator. This argument is moot on the facts of this case, however, because Petitioners never made such motion to vacate the award below. Thus, Petitioners raise these public policies in the abstract, but has not alleged that any of those public policies were at stake or violated here. Consequently, we find those arguments unavailing under the current factual circumstances.

Addressing Petitioners' initial argument as to whether judicial arbitration may be binding by agreement of the parties, we readily dismiss it. Petitioners cite to the following states' court-annexed arbitration schemes as authority for the proposition that judicial arbitration is uniformly non-binding because the state statutes or rules that create that form of dispute resolution afford the parties the right to appeal by trial de novo: Ariz. Rev. Stat. § 12–133 (2012) (neutral arbitrators and right of appeal with trial de novo); Fla. Stat. § 44.103 (2007) (same); Haw. Rev. Stat. § 601–20 (2000) (non-binding arbitration with neutral arbitrators); Ill. S. Ct. R. 86–87, 93 (neutral arbitrators with right of appeal); Nev. Rev. Stat. 38.250 (2005), Nev. Arb. R. 7, 18 (same); N.C. Gen. Stat. § 7A–37.1 (2013) (same); R.I. Super. Ct. Arb. R. 2, 5 (neutral arbitrators and right of appeal with trial de novo); Wash. Rev. Code § 7.06040–.050 (2011) (same).

A closer review of those statutes and court rules reveals that there is one glaring and consequential difference between the arbitrations conducted under those schemes and the one conducted here: the arbitration conducted in this case was not mandatory.[29] Arizona, Florida, Hawaii, Illinois, Nevada, North Carolina, Rhode Island, and Washington have, by statute or court rule, court-annexed arbitration. Those states *require* that when certain conditions are met,[30] the parties arbitrate their disputes. Accordingly, appeal by trial de novo is a constitutional prerequisite to such mandatory arbitration so as to preserve the right to a jury trial. When examining its statutory scheme, Arizona's courts have discussed that "[t]he right to trial *de novo* is essential to the constitutionality of *compulsory* arbitration, since both the United States and Arizona Constitutions guarantee the right to trial by jury."[31] * * *

* * *

While preserving the availability of right to appeal by trial de novo, all of these states require affirmative conduct or reservation of the right to appeal by trial de novo in the course of the parties' mandatory arbitration. Here, just the opposite occurred: the parties were not subject to mandatory arbitration, but rather willingly entered into a contractual agreement to resolve their dispute through arbitration and explicitly waived their right to a trial by jury or bench and to subsequent appellate review.

Petitioners' reliance on these foreign authorities is further undercut because Petitioners do not argue that in these jurisdictions the parties may not agree to

---

[29] We note that Petitioners also cite to New Jersey's court-annexed arbitration scheme, N.J. Stat. § 2A;23A–1, *et seq.* (1987) (APDRA), as providing parties to an arbitration with the right of appeal, but not by trial de novo. Consonant with the facts of this case, New Jersey's arbitration scheme may be voluntarily invoked by agreement of parties to an already-existing dispute. It provides for limited appellate review, but as New Jersey courts have discussed, "[a]lthough limited judicial review is a central component of the APDRA, the APDRA's procedures are entirely voluntary, and thus, parties are free to invoke its procedure *in toto* or subject to agreed upon modifications." Weinstock v. Weinstock, 377 N.J.Super. 182, 871 A.2d 776 (2005) (internal quotations and citations omitted). Petitioners likewise cite Tennessee's voluntary, nonbinding ADR scheme (Tenn. S. Ct. R. 31) in support of their argument. However, Appendix B of those rules permits parties to "stipulate[ ] in writing that the award shall be final and binding." See Tuetken v. Tuetken, 320 S.W.3d 262 (Tenn. 2010).

[30] In most of these states, these requirements typically center on a given dollar amount in controversy, or particular types of litigants.

[31] *Valler v. Lee*, 190 Ariz. 391, 949 P.2d 51, 53 (Ariz. Ct. App. 1997) (footnote omitted) (emphasis added).

waive appellate review altogether as the parties did here. To the contrary, many of these jurisdictions offering court-annexed arbitration appear to honor the agreement of the parties to limit or otherwise preclude appellate review, whether waiver is contemplated in the court-annexed arbitration framework itself or is provided for under the applicable arbitration statutes.[34]

It follows, then, that while we find the foreign authority advocated by Petitioners inapposite, we must still consider the validity of the parties' agreement to "binding, non-appealable" arbitration under West Virginia law. In the absence of Business Court Division Rules outlining any specific procedure concerning appellate review, or otherwise, for arbitrations conducted in the Business Court Division, consistent with the parties' arguments invoking the provisions therein, we apply the West Virginia Revised Uniform Arbitration Act (the Act).

West Virginia Code § 55–10–6(a) provides that "[e]xcept as otherwise provided in subsections (b) and (c) of this section, a party to an agreement to arbitrate or to an arbitration proceeding may waive or the parties may vary the effect of the requirements of this article to the extent permitted by law." Applicable to these circumstances is subsection (c), which dictates what provisions of the Act may be waived when the agreement to arbitrate is entered after a controversy has arisen. Subsection (c), in relation to appellate review, indicates that the parties may not vary the effects of West Virginia Code § 55–10–22 (party may move arbitrator to modify or correct an award); West Virginia Code § 55–10–24 (party may move court for confirmation of award if no grounds to modify, correct or vacate award); West Virginia Code § 55–10–25 (party may move court for vacation of award if limited circumstances are met); or West Virginia Code § 55–10–26 (party may move court to modify or correct an award). Subsection (c) does not, however, preclude the parties from waiving appellate review to this Court under West Virginia Code § 55–10–30.

This is consistent with the general view relating to the language of an agreement in which parties agree to final, non-appealable arbitration:

> And generally, a contract provision stating that arbitration is "non-appealable" signifies that the parties to the contract may not appeal the merits of the *arbitration*; not that the parties agree to waive a right to appeal the district court's judgment confirming or vacating the arbitration decision.[39]

[34] See, e.g., 16 A.R.S. Rules of Civil Procedure 77(e) (providing that parties may stipulate that arbitration award entered be binding upon parties thereby precluding appellate attack on award except as provided in arbitration act); N.C.R. ARB 9*ee* (court review of arbitration award limited by provisions of arbitration statute); R.I. Super. Ct. R. Arb. 1(b) ("Arbitration by Agreement. The court may submit any other civil action to arbitration under these Arbitration Rules or any modification thereof, pursuant to agreement by the parties approved by the court provided that the parties agree in writing that the award shall be binding."); Valler, 949 P.2d at 53 ("[A]bsent a stipulation by the parties, the resulting arbitration award is nonbinding if a timely appeal is filed." (emphasis added)); Cozzolino v. Cozzolino, No. A 4770 10T1, 2012 WL 6097090 (N.J. Super. Ct. App. Div. Dec. 10, 2012) (precluding appellate review where parties agreed to waive right to appeal arbitration award).

[39] Southco, Inc. v. Reell Precision Mfg. Corp., 331 Fed.Appx. 925, 927 (3d Cir. 2009).

Stated differently,

> "an arbitration agreement . . . between two sophisticated business parties, each represented by counsel, that clearly precludes judicial review of an arbitration award beyond the trial court level, is enforceable." We explained that just as parties may expand review of an arbitration award by contract, they may also "privately contract to further constrict the scope of limited judicial scrutiny by, for instance, eliminating the added layer of appellate review altogether." * * * We also recognized that in "rare circumstances" private restrictions on judicial review would not be upheld, citing as an example a no-appeal clause prohibiting review by the trial court.[40]

Accordingly, we find that by virtue of the agreement that the arbitration would be "final, and non-appealable" these sophisticated parties, both represented by counsel, have waived the right to appellate review of the merits under West Virginia Code § 55–10–30. Given that Petitioners never moved under West Virginia Code §§ 55–10–22, –24, –25 or –26 to modify, correct or vacate the award below, our review would be particularly inappropriate. * * *

* * *

For the foregoing reasons, we affirm the order of the Business Court Division dismissing the underlying matter from its docket in reliance on the conclusions reached in the arbitration panel's final decision.

* * *

■ DAVIS, J., concurring:

* * * I concur in the majority decision. I have chosen to write separately to address two issues involving mediation and arbitration in the Business Court.

First, as pointed out in the majority opinion, the record in this case revealed that the presiding judge acted as a resolution judge for mediation, and also as one of the three members on the arbitration panel. Rule 29 of the Trial Court Rules recognizes two types of judges: presiding judge and resolution judge. Rule 29 does not authorize a presiding judge to act as a resolution judge in a case. Rule 29.07(a) authorizes the Business Court chair to "enter an order assigning Presiding and Resolution Judges." This rule also states that "[t]he Division Chair may serve as a Presiding or Resolution Judge." The presiding judge has the task of conducting an actual trial of a case. This authority is set out under Rule 29.08(a-g). In the definition of resolution judge provided under Rule 29.04(e), it states that the role of the resolution judge is "to mediate, arbitrate, or provide any other form of dispute resolution agreed to by the parties."

For reasons that are not clear from the record, the parties agreed to have the presiding judge act as a resolution judge. This type of arrangement is not contemplated by the Trial Court Rules. In fact, under the definition of resolution judge provided by Rule 29.04(e), it clearly states that "[t]o protect confidentiality of the mediation process, communication between the presiding judge and

---

[40] Cozzolino, 2012 WL 6097090, at *6 (citing Van Duren v. Rzasa-Ormes, 394 N.J. Super. 254, 926 A.2d 372 (App. Div. 2007), aff'd o.b., 195 N.J. 230, 948 A.2d 1285 (2008)).

resolution judge regarding the mediation during or after the process shall be limited to procedural status or other matters agreed to by the parties." This language unquestionably implies that the positions of presiding judge and resolution judge should not be filled by the same person in the same case. Consequently, I believe it was a serious procedural error for the presiding judge in this matter to also serve as a resolution judge. However, this procedural error was waived by the parties through their acquiescence in the arrangement. The decisions of this Court are quite clear in holding that "[a] litigant may not silently acquiesce to an alleged error, or actively contribute to such error, and then raise that error as a reason for reversal on appeal." * * * Insofar as the Petitioners in this case agreed to have the presiding judge also fill the role of a resolution judge, they cannot complain of the error in this arrangement.

A second issue that the Petitioners waived is whether a resolution judge can act as both a mediator and an arbitrator in the same case. Rule 29 does not expressly address this issue. However, Rule 29.08(h) does appear to implicitly allow this arrangement. This provision states that "[t]he Resolution Judge is authorized to schedule and conduct mediation of the case or any Alternative Dispute Resolution as agreed to by the parties and the Resolution Judge in an attempt to resolve the case in an expedient and efficient manner." This provision allows the parties and the resolution judge to agree upon conducting any type of alternative dispute resolution.

The issue of a judge serving as both a mediator and an arbitrator in the same case was addressed in *In re Cartwright*, 104 S.W.3d 706 (Tex. App. 2003). The decision in that case involved a post-divorce property claim that was filed by the former wife. The trial court appointed another trial judge to act as arbitrator to resolve the claim, as required by the divorce decree. The former husband filed a motion objecting to the person named as arbitrator, because she had served as a mediator over a child custody issue during the divorce proceeding. The trial judge denied the motion. The former husband filed a writ of prohibition seeking to preclude enforcement of the trial court's order. The appellate court granted the writ of prohibition for the following reasons:

> [A] mediator is in the position of receiving the parties' confidential information, which may not be revealed to the court or to any other person. If the mediator is later appointed to be the arbitrator between the same parties, he or she is likely to be in the possession of information that either or both of those parties would not have chosen to reveal to an arbitrator.
>
> . . . The mediation process encourages candid disclosures, including disclosures of confidential information, to a mediator. It is the potential for the use of that confidential information that creates the problem when the mediator, over the objection of one of the parties, becomes the arbitrator of the same or a related dispute. Just as it would be improper for a mediator to disclose any confidential information to another arbitrator of the parties' dispute, *it is also improper for the mediator to act as the arbitrator in the same or a related dispute without the express consent of the parties.*

It should be understood that the decision in *Cartwright* recognized that parties may consent to having the same person act as mediator and arbitrator of a dispute. * * *

As previously noted, the parties agreed to having the mediator serve on the arbitration panel. The record also indicates that the parties were told prior to the mediation that they should not disclose anything during that proceeding which they did not want the mediator to know during the arbitration proceeding. Under these facts, the Petitioners again waived any alleged procedural error.

In view of the foregoing, I concur.

QUESTIONS TO REVIEW AND SYNTHESIZE

1. According to Judge Sloviter's opinion for the Third Circuit in *Strine*, what aspects of Delaware's state-sponsored arbitration program made its confidentiality a First Amendment violation?
2. What can Delaware constitutionally do as a result of Judge Fuentes' concurring words: "Appellants are enjoined only from conducting arbitrations pursuant to § 349(b) of Title 10 of the Delaware Code or Rules 97(a)(4) and 98(b) of the Delaware Chancery Court. Nothing in today's decision should be construed to prevent sitting Judges of the Court of Chancery from engaging in arbitrations without those confidentiality provisions."?
3. Is the West Virginia Supreme Court's opinion (excerpted above) in *Investment Management Board* in tension with, or smoothly consistent with, Judge Sloviter's opinion for the Third Circuit in *Strine*?
4. Given the holdings in *Strine* and *Investment Management Board*, which of the proceedings covered in Sections A and B (private judging, short-trial, and business courts) may constitutionally remain confidential?

C. NON-CONTRACTUAL ARBITRATION

1. GENERAL RULE THAT NON-CONTRACTUAL ARBITRATION MUST BE NON-BINDING TO AVOID VIOLATING CONSTITUTIONAL RIGHT TO JURY TRIAL

"Mandatory" arbitration is less popular than "voluntary" arbitration, but people disagree about which arbitration is mandatory. While opponents of adhesive arbitration agreements often call them, and arbitration arising out of them, "mandatory," or even "forced," arbitration, others reserve the phrase "mandatory arbitration" to describe arbitration required by law even in the absence of an agreement (adhesive or not) to arbitrate. Adhesive arbitration agreements are discussed extensively in Chapters 2 and 3; this concluding chapter now discusses *non-contractual* arbitration, that is, arbitration required by law even in the absence of an agreement to arbitrate.

The contrast between contractual and non-contractual arbitration is particularly stark with respect to the constitutional right to a jury trial.[6] While courts routinely hold that arbitration agreements enforceably waive the constitutional right to a trial by jury,[7] non-contractual arbitration lacks such a waiver and thus generally must be non-binding to avoid violating this jury trial right. As the *West Virginia Investment Management Board* case excerpted above said:

> Petitioners cite to the following states' court-annexed arbitration schemes * * * afford[ing] the parties the right to appeal by trial de novo: Ariz. Rev. Stat. § 12–133 (2012) (neutral arbitrators and right of appeal with trial de novo); Fla. Stat. § 44.103 (2007) (same); Haw. Rev. Stat. § 601–20 (2000) (non-binding arbitration with neutral arbitrators); Ill. S. Ct. R. 86–87, 93 (neutral arbitrators with right of appeal); Nev. Rev. Stat. 38.250 (2005), Nev. Arb. R. 7, 18 (same); N.C. Gen. Stat. § 7A–37.1 (2013) (same); R.I. Super. Ct. Arb. R. 2, 5 (neutral arbitrators and right of appeal with trial de novo); Wash. Rev. Code § 7.06040–.050 (2011) (same).
>
> A closer review of those statutes and court rules reveals that there is one glaring and consequential difference between the arbitrations conducted under those schemes and the one conducted here: the arbitration conducted in this case was not mandatory. Arizona, Florida, Hawaii, Illinois, Nevada, North Carolina, Rhode Island, and Washington have, by statute or court rule, court-annexed arbitration. Those states *require* that when certain conditions are met, the parties arbitrate their disputes. Accordingly, appeal by trial de novo is a constitutional prerequisite to such mandatory arbitration so as to preserve the right to a jury trial. When examining its statutory scheme, Arizona's courts have discussed that "[t]he right to trial *de novo* is essential to the constitutionality of *compulsory* arbitration, since both the United States and Arizona Constitutions guarantee the right to trial by jury."

W. Virginia Inv. Mgmt. Bd. v. Variable Annuity Life Ins. Co., 241 W. Va. 148, 820 S.E.2d 416, 426–27 (2018). Similar issues are elaborated in the following case.

---

[6] While the Seventh Amendment is one of the few amendments in the Bill of Rights that constrains only federal, not state, government, see Curtis v. Loether, 415 U.S. 189, 192 n.6 (1974), nearly all state constitutions contain a provision that similarly protects the right to trial by jury. See Eric J. Hamilton, *Federalism and the State Civil Jury Rights*, 65 Stan. L. Rev. 851, 855 (2013) ("Today, forty-seven state constitutions provide for the right to a jury trial in civil cases.").

[7] See, e.g., Credit Acceptance Corp. v. Front, 231 W. Va. 518, 520, 745 S.E.2d 556, 558 (2013)("Credit Acceptance contends that, in both of these cases, the circuit courts erred by concluding that the arbitration agreements were unconscionable based upon the unavailability of arbitration forums named therein, and because the debtors in the agreements waived their respective rights to a jury trial. Because we find that one of the arbitration forums named in the agreements remains available to arbitrate the parties' disputes, and because an arbitration agreement is not rendered unenforceable solely because a party thereto waives his or her right to a jury trial, we reverse both of these cases and remand for entry of orders compelling arbitration."); Harrington v. Atl. Sounding Co., 602 F.3d 113, 126 (2d Cir.2010) ("courts may not rely on the uniqueness of an agreement to arbitrate, which necessarily waives jury trial, as a basis for a state-law holding that enforcement would be unconscionable. It is well-settled that waivers of jury trial are fully enforceable under the FAA."); Caley v. Gulfstream Aerospace Corp., 428 F.3d 1359, 1371 (11th Cir.2005) (the "agreement to arbitrate and waiver of jury trial rights are governed by contract principles and are not subject to the heightened knowing and voluntary standard argued by plaintiffs"); Sydnor v. Conseco Fin. Servicing Corp., 252 F.3d 302, 307 (4th Cir. 2001) ("the right to a jury trial attaches in the context of judicial proceedings after it is determined that litigation should proceed before a court.").

Jersey Cent. Power & Light Co. v. Melcar Utility Co.

Supreme Court of New Jersey, 2013.
59 A.3d 561, 212 N.J. 576.

■ PER CURIAM.

N.J.S.A. 48:2–80(d), a provision appearing in the Underground Facility Protection Act (UFPA), compels parties seeking monetary relief for damages to underground facilities to submit such causes of action, if valued under a specified amount, to the Office of Dispute Settlement (ODS) within the Office of the Public Defender for unspecified "dispute resolution." On its face, the provision fails to preserve a party's ability to have the property damage dispute remain within or return to a judicial setting. It was applied in this matter to compel the dismissal of a Superior Court action for property damage to underground facilities covered by the UFPA.

The essential issue is whether N.J.S.A. 48:2–80(d), as written, impinges on the constitutional right to a jury trial for property damages. We conclude that it does and therefore reverse the judgment that dismissed the Superior Court action for want of jurisdiction.

I.

This case comes before us with the following factual and procedural background. Plaintiff Jersey Central Power & Light Company (JCP&L), * * * like many utilities, places facilities such as transmission lines and stations below ground where they are not visible. * * *

Recognizing the potential hazards posed by such underground facilities, the Legislature enacted the UFPA to protect both the public from the risk of harm and the utility companies from unnecessary losses. * * *

The UFPA carries significant penalties for those who disregard its mandates * * * [and] imposes damages on the operator of underground facilities, to be paid to excavators, for a failure to comply with the marking and locating duty that the UFPA imposes.

* * * The problem with [UFPA N.J.S.A. 48:2–80] subsection (d)'s inclusion of losses suffered by an underground facility operator due to an excavator's negligence is the method that the Legislature has prescribed for the resolution of such disputes. Subsection (d) concludes with the following directory language:

> Any dispute arising from the provisions of this subsection, where the claim is less than $25,000, shall be subject to an alternative dispute resolution process as established within the Office of Dispute Settlement in the Office of the Public Defender. Nothing in this act shall be construed to discourage parties from pursuing alternative dispute resolution processes for an amount greater than $25,000. The parties may by mutual agreement designate another alternative dispute resolution association for all matters.

The instant matter concerns underground electrical lines owned by JCP&L in the vicinity of Robin Street in Rockaway, New Jersey. In September 2007, defendant Melcar Utility Company (Melcar) performed excavation work in the area of Robin

Street for the purpose of installing underground cables for Verizon of New Jersey (Verizon). During the course of that excavation work, JCP&L's underground electrical lines were damaged. In January 2009, JCP&L filed a complaint against Melcar and Verizon in the Special Civil Part of the Law Division, seeking reimbursement for costs incurred in repairing those electrical lines. Melcar filed a third-party complaint against Utiliquest, an entity contracted by JCP&L to mark the location of JCP&L's underground electrical lines, alleging that Utiliquest failed to properly mark the lines' location and, thus, was responsible for JCP&L's loss.

On the day set for trial before the Special Civil Part, Melcar's attorney made an oral motion to dismiss the matter for lack of jurisdiction, citing N.J.S.A. 48:2–80(d). Melcar argued that under subsection (d) the matter had to be heard by the ODS. * * * [T]he court granted the motion and entered an order dismissing JCP&L's complaint without prejudice.

JCP&L appealed, and in a short, unpublished opinion the Appellate Division affirmed the trial court's order. We granted JCP&L's petition for certification. * * *

II.

* * * As the appeal has progressed, we are informed that the ODS now mandates arbitration as its final means of dispute resolution for the subsection (d) matters sent to it by the Legislature. Regardless of this recent turn of events, JCP&L maintains that arbitration must be consensual, except where the Legislature may direct the form of alternative dispute resolution because the constitutional right to jury trial is not implicated. Here, JCP&L claims that the constitutional right is implicated because of the underlying common-law nature of the property damage claim. * * *

Melcar and Utiliquest respond by asserting * * * that JCP&L's argument—that the statute deprives it of its constitutionally guaranteed right to a jury trial—is meritless because JCP&L failed to seek a jury when it filed its complaint in the Special Civil Part. And, they point out that the ODS has posted the procedures that it employs on the website of the Office of the Public Defender, satisfying any notice obligation to affected parties.

The Attorney General echoes the arguments of respondents Melcar and Utiliquest. He maintains that referral to the ODS is both mandatory and constitutional. * * *

* * *

IV.

Our State Constitution guarantees that the "right of trial by jury shall remain inviolate." N.J. Const. art. I, ¶ 9. It is well-established that this protection applies to civil cases only where the right to a jury trial existed at common law and does not normally apply to cases in equity. See Weinisch v. Sawyer, 123 N.J. 333, 343, 587 A.2d 615 (1991) (guaranteeing jury trial right "only to the extent that it existed at common law when the New Jersey Constitution was adopted"). "Only those actions that triggered the right of a jury trial that predated our State Constitutions, and those that were created anew with enactment of New Jersey's 1776 Constitution, the 1844 Constitution, or the 1947 Constitution serve as the basis for that constitutional right today." Ins. Co. of N. Am. v. Anthony Amadei Sand & Gravel, Inc., 162 N.J. 168, 175–76, 742 A.2d 550 (1999) (citations omitted).

When determining if a jury trial is required under the State Constitution, both the historical basis of the cause of action and the relief sought must be considered. The remedy sought "remains the most persuasive factor."

* * *

[T]he various claims actionable under the Consumer Fraud Act (CFA) * * * evidence the difference between those civil causes of action entitled to the constitutional right to a jury trial and those that are not. In Kugler [v. Banner Pontiac-Buick, Opel, Inc., 120 N.J.Super. 572[, 582, 295 A.2d 385] (Ch.Div.1972)] the Attorney General filed a claim in Chancery Court, seeking to permanently enjoin an automobile seller from altering odometer readings on previously driven cars, as well as relief in the form of restitution and statutorily defined monetary damages. The Appellate Division panel explained that injunctive relief was the primary remedy authorized by N.J.S.A. 56:8–8, and that at common law and under the New Jersey Constitution, the right to trial by jury was not recognized in equitable claims. Thus, in finding no jury trial right was violated, the court concluded that "[t]he matter before the court is an action completely unknown to the common law. It arises out of a [provision of a] statute evidencing the Legislature's recognition of the complexities of commercial bargaining in contemporary society and the need for the protection of the consumer."

By way of contrast, in *Zorba Contractors, Inc. v. Housing Authority of Newark*, 362 N.J.Super. 124, 128–30, 827 A.2d 313 (App.Div.2003), the Appellate Division was called on to review whether a constitutional right to a jury trial existed for litigants who commenced an action under N.J.S.A. 56:8–19, another provision of the CFA, against a company that provided plywood and failed to meet fire retardant treatment standards. Because that CFA provision authorizes "legal relief," the panel inferred that a jury trial right should attach. The panel reasoned that "the forms of relief specifically authorized . . . are monetary—compensatory damages, trebling of those damages and attorneys fees—which is a hallmark of a legal action." The panel also noted additional reasons for recognizing a right to a jury trial. The specific provision limits the class of litigants who may recover to those who suffered an "ascertainable loss of moneys or property." Also, the statute requires knowingly, with the intent of inducing reliance, concealing, suppressing, or omitting a material fact to the detriment of another. These elements mirror the elements required to establish common-law fraud. For those reasons, the Appellate Division concluded that a trial by jury constitutionally was required for this common-law fraud-based cause of action.

* * *

With those legal principles and their past application in mind, we turn to address the nature of Melcar's claim in order to determine whether the constitutional right to a jury trial is implicated.

V.

N.J.S.A. 48:2–80(d), on its face, provides no right to a trial by jury. The Legislature instead has required JCP&L and other private litigants seeking monetary relief for property damages included under N.J.S.A. 48:2–80(d) to submit to an undesignated, alternative dispute resolution process to be developed by the ODS. The ODS has chosen arbitration to carry out its assigned task. In the setting presented to us, our prior case law compels the conclusion that mandatory, binding arbitration is impermissible because it effectively denies JCP&L and other private litigants their constitutionally guaranteed right to a trial by jury for a common-law cause of action in negligence.

* * *

The nature of the cause of action addressed in the UFPA, specifically as its provisions deal with property damage incurred by operators of underground facilities as a result of excavations, renders the relief available under subsection (d) of N.J.S.A. 48:2–80 indistinguishable from a common-law action for property damage. Such suits were part of the actions recognized at common law to which a right to jury trial attached at the time that our State Constitution enshrined the continuing civil jury trial right. The Legislature was not at liberty to ignore the right to a civil jury trial for property damages when enacting the UFPA. * * *

VI.

A.

The judicial process in New Jersey uses mandatory, nonbinding arbitration in certain limited circumstances. The Legislature has expressly required that litigants submit to that compelled, nonbinding alternative dispute resolution process in certain instances. * * * We have reviewed those legislative enactments and collected their procedures in Rule 4:21A-1(a):

> (1) Automobile Negligence Actions. All tort actions arising out of the operation, ownership, maintenance or use of an automobile shall be submitted to arbitration in accordance with these rules.
>
> (2) Other Personal Injury Actions. Except for professional malpractice and products liability actions, all actions for personal injury not arising out of the operation, ownership, maintenance or use of an automobile shall be submitted to arbitration in accordance with these rules.
>
> (3) Other Non-Personal Injury Actions. All actions on a book account or instrument of obligation, all personal injury protection claims against plaintiff's insurer, and all other contract and commercial actions that have been screened and identified as appropriate for arbitration shall be submitted to arbitration in accordance with these rules.

* * * Importantly, however, arbitration does not cut off the right to a jury trial. The process concludes with the option of a trial de novo. R. 4:21A-6(c) (preserving jury trial de novo). Indeed, even when the Legislature has acted to compel the use of arbitration, this Court has highlighted the important caveat of permitting a right to a trial de novo following mandatory arbitration whenever the constitutional right to jury trial was implicated.

In Hartsfield v. Fantini, 149 N.J. 611, 615–16, 695 A.2d 259 (1997), we reviewed the legislatively required mandatory arbitration process for certain automobile accident claims with damages totaling less than $15,000. See N.J.S.A. 39:6A–24 to –35. We approved the process in recognition that the Legislature intended for either party to the arbitration to petition the Superior Court and obtain a de novo jury trial on the legal issue presented to the arbitrator.

We similarly analyzed an analogous statutory framework in N.J.S.A. 2A:23A–20(a), which mandates arbitration for certain personal injury actions when damages amount to $20,000 or less. Again, we recognized that either party to the arbitration could petition the court "'within 30 days of the filing of the arbitration decision for a trial de novo.'" In both scenarios, the Legislature "sought to preserve an individual's right to a jury trial by providing that a person dissatisfied with the arbitration award has the right to request a trial de novo."

B.

N.J.S.A. 48:2–80(d) is a unique statute because it retains no option for a trial de novo. Research fails to reveal any other New Jersey statute that has cut off a private litigant's right to a trial by jury for a cause of action rooted in common law by not expressly including the right to a trial de novo.

The Legislature has mandated binding arbitration as the method of dispute resolution in a limited number of circumstances, generally concerning resolution of public sector collective negotiations. Examples include N.J.S.A. 27:25–14 (concerning employer-employee relations within New Jersey Transit Corporation), N.J.S.A. 34:13A–16 (dealing with labor negotiations with public fire and police departments), N.J.S.A. 52:27BB–61 (addressing municipalities and school districts in unsound financial condition), and N.J.S.A. 58:10–23.11(n) (concerning pollution claims arising from discharges into water). In each of those instances, the Legislature clearly stated that arbitration was to be the form of dispute resolution. However, in each of those instances, the Legislature was not addressing the resolution of causes of action recognized at common law. Thus, the Legislature had the ability to prescribe a nonconsensual form of dispute resolution, unmoored to any requirement that it must carry a de novo right to a trial by jury.

Here, the Legislature did not preserve the right to a trial de novo, as it has done on earlier occasions. * * *

N.J.S.A. 48:2–80(d) is unusual in that it is binding on litigants who are effectively suing in negligence under a statutory standard of care for a claim rooted in common-law negligence causing damage to property. We have no recourse except to declare the statute as written to be constitutionally flawed. Neither we, nor the ODS, may write in a right to a trial de novo to save this statute from its constitutional shortcoming. We leave its correction to the Legislature.

Other courts have similarly held that binding, non-contractual arbitration violates the jury trial right. See, e.g., Lisanti v. Alamo Title Ins. of Tex., 55 P.3d 962 (N.M.2002) (state statute requiring arbitration of all title disputes under one million dollars violated state constitutional right to jury trial); Cooper v. Poston, 483 S.E.2d

750, 751 (S.C.1997) (state statute allowing one party unilaterally to divert an action for monetary damages arising out a motor vehicle accident to binding arbitration would "abrogate another party's constitutional right to a jury trial"); Grace v. Howlett, 283 N.E.2d 474 (Ill.1972) (state statute requiring arbitration of certain automobile injury cases violated right to jury trial under Illinois Constitution).

Also similar to the New Jersey law summarized in *Jersey Cent. Power & Light Co.*, courts generally hold that non-contractual arbitration is constitutional if after arbitration either party is entitled to a trial de novo—even if parties who fail to get a better result at trial than they received in arbitration must pay for consuming the additional resources of a trial. See, e.g., Fisher v. Edgerton, 236 Ariz. 71, 336 P.3d 167 (Ct. App. 2014) (prospect of having to pay an opposing party's attorney fees pursuant to statute and rule governing the right of appeal from compulsory arbitration proceedings did not act as an unreasonable or significant burden impairing an appellant's right to a jury trial, and thus, was not unconstitutional); Richardson v. Sport Shinko (Waikiki Corp.), 76 Haw. 494, 880 P.2d 169 (1994) (rule permitting imposition of sanctions if party does not improve at trial on nonbinding arbitration award did not violate right to jury trial under Hawai'i Constitution); Kimbrough v. Holiday Inn, 478 F.Supp. 566 (E.D.Pa.1979) (jury-trial right not violated by local court rule mandating arbitration as a prerequisite to jury trial in certain civil suits for $50,000 or less; unless a party demands a trial de novo within 20 days after award, the arbitration decision becomes a final judgment; to discourage frivolous appeals of arbitration decisions, the rule "imposes upon the party who demands a trial de novo and fails to obtain a more favorable judgment the amount of the arbitration fees and imposes upon the defendant interest on the award from the time it was filed.")

The previous paragraph discusses one way in which the bindingness of adjudication may be a matter of degree. The most binding adjudication is by the court of last resort (typically a jurisdiction's "supreme court") because no higher authority may review it before it is enforced. In contrast, at the least-binding end of the continuum is adjudication subject to de novo review. Somewhere in between on the continuum of bindingness is adjudication subject to de novo review but with sanctions imposed on parties who do not persuade the reviewing court to give them a better result than the "non-binding" adjudicator's decision.

Another way to make "non-binding" adjudication somewhat binding is to allow the non-binding adjudicator's decision (perhaps including formal findings of fact and conclusions of law) to influence the supposedly de novo reviewer. For instance, several states require ostensibly non-binding arbitration of medical malpractice cases by a "medical review" panel,[8] but in some states the panel's decision is

[8] Under some statutes, this required panel must consist of three physicians. See, e.g., Neb.Rev.St. § 44–2841 (each party selects one physician and the two thus chosen select a third; panel also includes attorney who acts in "advisory capacity" and has no vote). Another common pattern is for the panel to consist of a physician, an attorney, and a member of the "general public." See, e.g., Md.Code, Courts & Jud.Proceed. §§ 3–2A–03, 3–2A–04 (state "Health Claims Arbitration Office" circulates lists of arbitrators in each category to the parties, who may strike unacceptable names); Del.Code. Tit. 18, §§ 6804, 6805 (each panel consists of two "health care providers," one attorney, and two "lay persons" chosen from a "list of 100 objective and judicious persons of appropriate education and experience" maintained by the Commissioner of Insurance). Still other states simply provide for a "tripartite board" (with one member named by each party and a chairman selected by the other two members or by the court) without specifying the profession or background of the arbitrators. Under

admissible in any later trial. For instance, Louisiana's statute provides in part: "Any report of the expert opinion reached by the medical review panel shall be admissible as evidence in any action subsequently brought by the claimant in a court of law, but such expert opinion shall not be conclusive and either party shall have the right to call, at his cost, any member of the medical review panel as a witness." La. R.S. 40:1231.8(H). See also Md.Code Ann.Cts. & Jud.Proc. § 3–2A–06(d) ("arbitration award is admissible as evidence in the judicial proceeding. The award shall be presumed to be correct, and the burden is on the party rejecting it to prove that it is not correct.") Making the panel's decision admissible, let alone "presumed to be correct," presumably increases the likelihood the judge or jury will reach a decision similar to the panel's, which can make "non-binding" arbitration somewhat binding.

Perhaps grappling with intermediate degrees of bindingness is *Chrysler Corp. v. Pitsirelos*, 721 So.2d 710 (Fla.1998), in which a consumer won a case before Florida's "New Motor Vehicle Arbitration Board"—to which the consumer *must* submit before filing suit for breach of a new-vehicle's warranty. Either the consumer or the manufacturer in Florida is entitled to a trial de novo after completion of this "mandatory alternative dispute resolution procedure"; at such a trial the decision of the arbitration board is admissible in evidence. In *Pitsirelos*, the trial judge instructed the jury that the board's decision was "presumed to be correct." The state supreme court held, however, that these instructions were erroneous: Indeed, to interpret the statute in this way would raise serious constitutional issues, since it "would diminish the right to have the ultimate decision in a case made by a court." The board's decision should be treated "only as evidence with its weight to be determined by the factfinder." Nevertheless the Florida Supreme Court held that the manufacturer now had the burden of persuasion in establishing why the board's decision was erroneous: "The party appealing the Arbitration Board's decision carries the burden of proof"; to require the prevailing consumer to bear this burden "as if no previous proceeding had been held" would "relegate the mandatory arbitration to simply being a procedural impediment to the consumer."

Another way in which the bindingness of adjudication can be other than all-or-nothing is to make an adjudicator's decision binding on one party but not the other. For instance, some auto manufacturers have agreed to submit warranty disputes to the "Auto Line" arbitration program administered by the Better Business Bureau. In this program, established by a Federal Trade Commission consent order, *General Motors Corp. v. Abrams*, 897 F.2d 34, 37 (2d Cir.1990), the parties usually "do not find it necessary to involve an attorney." The manufacturer generally agrees in advance to be bound by the award. The consumer, however, is free either to reject any unfavorable award and pursue a warranty claim in court, or indeed, to bypass the arbitration process entirely. See https://www.bbb.org/autoline/bbb-auto-line-process/how-bbb-auto-line-works/ (information can be found under "I. Acceptance/ Rejection of Decision.").

---

the various statutes the fees and expenses of the arbitrators may be shared equally by the parties, may be assessed by the arbitrators as an element of costs, or may in some cases come directly from state funds.

2. EXCEPTIONS TO THE GENERAL RULE THAT NON-CONTRACTUAL ARBITRATION MUST BE NON-BINDING TO AVOID VIOLATING CONSTITUTIONAL RIGHT TO JURY TRIAL

a. ENGAGING IN A LICENSED OCCUPATION AS CONSENT TO NON-CONTRACTUAL, YET BINDING, ARBITRATION

While constitutional jury-trial right challenges have been mounted against various mandates of non-contractual arbitration, the mandated arbitration of particular interest to readers of this book may be one imposed on lawyers. Some states require lawyers to arbitrate fee disputes with their clients—if the client chooses arbitration over litigation. Courts have rejected the contention that this non-contractual, yet binding, arbitration violates the lawyer's constitutional right to a jury trial.

Biotechpharma, LLC, et al. v. Ludwig & Robinson, PLLC

District of Columbia Court of Appeals, 2014.
98 A.3d 986.

■ FISHER, ASSOCIATE JUDGE:

BTP, a biotechnology firm, retained L & R as counsel in March 2011 to help resolve a trade secret dispute. The dispute was settled in May 2012, L & R having billed BTP on a monthly basis during the course of its representation. By June 2012 L & R claimed that BTP owed approximately $1.7 million in outstanding legal fees, disbursements, and expenses. In January 2013 L & R brought suit to collect its fees.

Several weeks later, BTP responded to the complaint by filing a motion to stay the trial court proceedings and compel arbitration. In addition to claiming that L & R had expressly agreed to arbitrate the fee dispute, BTP argued that a binding agreement to arbitrate had been formed by operation of law. BTP cited Rule 8 of the D.C. Bar's Attorney/Client Arbitration Board ("ACAB"), which states that if a client files a petition to arbitrate a fee dispute with a lawyer, "the lawyer is deemed to have agreed to arbitrate." Although it was not mentioned in the trial court, D.C. Bar Rule XIII similarly provides that

> [a]n attorney subject to the disciplinary jurisdiction of [the District of Columbia Court of Appeals] shall be deemed to have agreed to arbitrate disputes over fees for legal services . . . when such arbitration is requested by a present or former client, . . . if a substantial portion of the services were performed by the attorney in the District of Columbia. . . .

* * * Ultimately, the trial court denied BTP's motion without clearly explaining why. BTP now appeals from that order.

* * *

[N]o express agreement to arbitrate was ever formed between the parties.[7]

---

[7] By specifying that an attorney "shall be deemed to have agreed to arbitrate" when the client requests it, Bar Rule XIII empowers clients to unilaterally require arbitration, but the rule does not give lawyers the same prerogative. In fact, ACAB Rule 8(b)(ii) specifically notes that for clients, the arbitration

2. Was There an Implied Agreement to Arbitrate?

BTP maintains, in the alternative, that an agreement was formed by operation of law when it (the client) requested arbitration.

* * *

We conclude that a client need not file a formal petition with ACAB in order to request arbitration pursuant to Bar Rule XIII. A formal filing with ACAB certainly would be sufficient to effectuate such a request, but it is not an absolute prerequisite. Here, BTP's counsel informed the trial court that he actually "tried to" file a petition with ACAB. He also said that ACAB "will not accept the petition until [the] Court stays [the] case." Thus, trying to comply with ACAB's requirements, BTP filed a motion in the trial court to stay litigation and compel arbitration.

Even if BTP's efforts to file a petition with ACAB were not enough to constitute a "request" to arbitrate, BTP formally and unequivocally signaled its desire for arbitration by filing a motion to stay litigation and compel arbitration. We hold that a client that files such a motion in court has "requested" arbitration under Bar Rule XIII. Accordingly, L & R "shall be deemed to have agreed to arbitrate" this fee dispute.

C. Validity of D.C. Bar Rule XIII

L & R challenges the validity of D.C. Bar Rule XIII on two grounds. First, it claims that this court lacked authority to promulgate the rule. Second, L & R challenges the rule's constitutionality. * * *

1. Authority to Promulgate D.C. Bar Rule XIII

L & R contends that this court lacked authority to promulgate Bar Rule XIII. Quite to the contrary, this court possesses broad authority to regulate the practice of law, deriving much of this power from the District of Columbia Court Reorganization Act of 1970. A portion of that Act, passed by Congress, provides that "[t]he District of Columbia Court of Appeals shall make such rules as it deems proper respecting the examination, qualification, and admission of persons to membership in its bar, and their censure, suspension, and expulsion." Beyond this broad statutory grant of authority, the court possesses significant inherent authority as well. In *Sitcov v. District of Columbia Bar*, we relied upon the "almost universally accepted" proposition "that the highest court in the jurisdiction is imbued with the inherent authority to define, regulate, and control the practice of law in that jurisdiction." 885 A.2d 289, 297 (D.C.2005) (quoting Brookens v. Comm. on Unauthorized Practice of Law, 538 A.2d 1120, 1125 (D.C.1988)).

Notably, the preamble to the rules we promulgated to govern the District of Columbia Bar cites both the inherent and statutory authority of this court. Taken together, these two sources of authority allow the court to regulate virtually every aspect of legal practice in the District of Columbia, including the substance of fee agreements. *See* D.C. R. Prof. Cond. 1.5. We readily conclude that this power extends to the subject matter of Bar Rule XIII. See In re LiVolsi, 85 N.J. 576, 428 A.2d 1268, 1273 (1981) (holding that if a court has "authority to control the substance

service offered by ACAB "is voluntary. If the client does not agree to arbitrate, the ACAB cannot compel the client to do so." Thus, L & R's two offers to arbitrate did not trigger mandatory arbitration.

of the [attorney-client] fee relationship, then a power of a lesser magnitude determining the procedure for resolving fee disputes must also be within [the court's] province").

L & R nevertheless asserts that the rule impermissibly alters the jurisdiction of the D.C. courts, since it requires lawyers to arbitrate fee disputes that they would otherwise litigate in civil actions. Additionally, L & R claims that this court violated the Home Rule Act by vesting judicial authority in the non-lawyer members of ACAB panels and by limiting the scope of judicial review. In making these claims, L & R cites several cases from other jurisdictions where courts have considered the type of judicial involvement or the scope of judicial review that must be afforded as part of a mandatory arbitration process.

Importantly, the formation of any arbitration agreement pursuant to Bar Rule XIII requires a manifestation of assent by both attorney and client. Clients invoke the rule by requesting arbitration. Attorneys submit to the rule by practicing law in the District of Columbia. Provided that Rule XIII is valid, it does not affect the jurisdiction of the D.C. courts or violate the Home Rule Act any more than any other agreement to arbitrate would do.

The rule need not provide for judicial review beyond that which is ordinarily available following arbitration. See D.C.Code §§ 16–4423 to –4424 (2012 Repl.); A1 Team USA Holdings, LLC v. Bingham McCutchen LLP, 998 A.2d 320, 322 (D.C.2010) (concluding that under the RUAA, "this court's review of an arbitration award is still extremely limited"); Schwartz v. Chow, 867 A.2d 230 (D.C.2005) (upholding decision of the Superior Court confirming an arbitration award by ACAB). Whatever quasi-judicial authority may be vested in ACAB (if any), it is limited to fee disputes between members of this court's bar and clients who have voluntarily chosen to submit to the board's determination. Nothing in the Home Rule Act inhibits this court's ability to thus manage the affairs of its bar. This court did not exceed its authority in promulgating the rule.

2. Constitutionality of D.C. Bar Rule XIII

Separately, L & R challenges D.C. Bar Rule XIII on constitutional grounds, principally claiming that the rule denies lawyers their Seventh Amendment right to a jury trial. The Seventh Amendment's guarantee extends to "suits in which legal rights [are] to be ascertained and determined, in contradistinction to those where equitable rights alone [are] recognized." Curtis v. Loether, 415 U.S. 189, 193, 94 S.Ct. 1005, 39 L.Ed.2d 260 (1974). In *Simler v. Conner* the Supreme Court concluded that the underlying "case was in its basic character a suit to determine and adjudicate the amount of fees owing to a lawyer by a client under a contingent fee retainer contract, a traditionally 'legal' action." 372 U.S. 221, 223, 83 S.Ct. 609, 9 L.Ed.2d 691 (1963). The Court therefore held that the Seventh Amendment guaranteed a jury trial. Here, L & R's complaint alleges that BTP breached a retainer contract under which it owes attorneys' fees. Thus, L & R has initiated "a traditionally 'legal' action" to which, presumptively, a Seventh Amendment right attaches. Consequently, we must address L & R's contention that Bar Rule XIII violates the Seventh Amendment.[13]

Although other jurisdictions impose rules similar to D.C. Bar Rule XIII, no such rule has ever been struck down for denying an attorney's right to a jury trial. Rather, it has been held that attorneys give up that right by practicing law in a jurisdiction subject to the challenged rule. * * *

Federal courts have taken a similar approach in analogous contexts. For example, in *Geldermann v. Commodity Futures Trading Comm'n,* members of a commodities exchange were required by law to submit "to customer-initiated arbitration." 836 F.2d 310, 311 (7th Cir.1987). A member company challenged the rule—in part on Seventh Amendment grounds—claiming that "membership alone is not sufficient to constitute consent to arbitration and therefore cannot establish a waiver of its constitutional right to an Article III forum." The Seventh Circuit disagreed, explaining that consent to observe all applicable rules and regulations was "a precondition of membership" in the exchange. Accordingly, the court held that the company was "not entitled to an Article III forum" and that "the Seventh Amendment [was] not implicated."

Because an arbitration agreement necessarily embodies a waiver of the right to trial by jury, a determination that there is a valid arbitration agreement here would foreclose any claim L & R might have had to a jury trial. See GTFM, LLC v. TKN Sales, Inc., 257 F.3d 235, 244 (2d Cir.2001) (characterizing the factual premise of a Seventh Amendment claim as "purely hypothetical" where one party to a dispute had exercised its statutory right to compel arbitration); Geldermann, 836 F.2d at 323 (holding that where the parties have consented to arbitration, "the Seventh Amendment simply does not apply"); Cremin v. Merrill Lynch, Pierce, Fenner & Smith, Inc., 957 F.Supp. 1460, 1471 (N.D.Ill.1997) (when "claims are properly before an arbitral forum pursuant to an arbitration agreement, the jury trial right vanishes"). A case-specific waiver of the right to a jury trial is not necessary.

Still, L & R contends that it cannot be deemed to have agreed to arbitrate because at least some of its attorneys joined the District of Columbia Bar before this court promulgated Bar Rule XIII in 1995. Lawyers are required to renew their bar membership every year, however, and those who have done so since 1995 cannot now claim immunity from the rule. In any event, the legal work at issue here took place in 2011 and 2012, long after Rule XIII was promulgated. The attorneys' practice of law in this jurisdiction is enough to make them subject to Rule XIII with respect to any fee dispute arising from that practice.

---

[13] Some state courts have held that their respective state constitutions do not guarantee a jury trial for attorneys litigating fee disputes. See, e.g., Shimko v. Lobe, 103 Ohio St.3d 59, 813 N.E.2d 669, 675, 678–81 (2004); Anderson v. Elliott, 555 A.2d 1042, 1043, 1049–50 (Me.1989). These cases do not address the Seventh Amendment question presented here since the "Amendment applies only to proceedings in courts of the United States, and does not in any manner whatever govern or regulate trials by jury in state courts." Minneapolis & St. Louis R.R. Co. v. Bombolis, 241 U.S. 211, 217, 36 S.Ct. 595, 60 L.Ed. 961 (1916). However, "like other provisions of the Bill of Rights," the Seventh Amendment is "fully applicable to courts established by Congress in the District of Columbia." E.R.B. v. J.H.F., 496 A.2d 607, 610 n. 6 (D.C.1985) (citing Pernell v. Southall Realty, 416 U.S. 363, 370, 94 S.Ct. 1723, 40 L.Ed.2d 198 (1974)).

We now turn to whether this court, through Bar Rule XIII, may require such client-initiated arbitration without violating the Constitution. L & R obliquely suggests that the rule places an unconstitutional condition on the privilege of practicing law in the District of Columbia. Again, however, L & R fails to cite a case—and we are not aware of any—where a litigant has prevailed on that theory when challenging a mandatory arbitration system for attorney-client fee disputes. Courts that have considered the issue have held that "[n]o one has an absolute right to practice law," and "[t]he State may impose reasonable conditions and limitations upon those who wish to exercise th[at] privilege."

"The interest of the States in regulating lawyers is especially great," and they "have broad power to establish standards for . . . regulating the practice of professions." Goldfarb v. Virginia State Bar, 421 U.S. 773, 792, 95 S.Ct. 2004, 44 L.Ed.2d 572 (1975). This includes the right to establish and enforce rules governing the reasonableness of attorney fees. *See* D.C. R. Prof. Cond. 1.5. When promulgating Bar Rule XIII, this court sought to provide an informal and efficient means of resolving attorney-client fee disputes, which are one of the principal sources of public dissatisfaction with the legal system. Because clients are at a significant disadvantage in litigating those disputes, the rule protects their ability to present meritorious claims and defenses, and, we believe, thereby fosters public confidence in the bar. Thus, regulation "in the area of fee disputes" is "critically important."

The scope of Bar Rule XIII is well-fitted to its ends. The rule does not, for instance, require lawyers to give up their right to a jury trial in civil cases not involving fee disputes, and arbitration of fee disputes is required only if the client requests it. Moreover, the arbitration system itself provides an impartial tribunal and the other elements of due process. These considerations support our conclusion that requiring lawyers to submit to client-initiated arbitration "is an entirely reasonable exercise of the judicial power to superintend the bar."

In addition to its Seventh Amendment claim, L & R maintains that compulsory arbitration denies lawyers their right to due process. Similar claims have unvaryingly failed in the courts that have heard them. We see no reason to part ways with this consistent body of persuasive precedent. "[D]ue process is not necessarily judicial process. . . . [N]either is the right of appeal essential to due process of law." Rather, "[t]he crux of due process is an opportunity to be heard and the right to adequately represent one's interests." Arbitration procedures under ACAB rules "readily satisfy these minima."

III. Conclusion

There was a valid agreement to arbitrate pursuant to D.C. Bar Rule XIII and the trial court should have enforced it. Accordingly, we vacate the trial court's order denying BTP's motion to stay, and remand the case with instructions to enforce the arbitration agreement.

Similarly, in Shimko v. Lobe, 103 Ohio St. 3d 59, 813 N.E.2d 669 (2014), the Ohio Supreme Court upheld a rule requiring arbitration through a bar association of disputes over the division of fees between lawyers who are not in the same firm:

[T]he court of appeals found that attorneys admitted to the practice of law in Ohio, including Shimko, agree to have a dispute between lawyers arising under this rule submitted to mediation or arbitration. By doing so, they have waived the right to a jury trial in cases involving such fee disputes.

* * *

Shimko correctly asserts that the court's power to regulate the bar "is not absolute and [that] it must be contained by, and act congruently with, the very constitution that provides for its existence." This court may no more disregard or infringe upon the constitutional rights of our citizens in the exercise of its regulatory functions than may any other branch of government. * * *

In particular, the court does not enjoy any special exemption from compliance with Section 5, Article I of the Ohio Constitution, which ensures that "[t]he right of trial by jury shall be inviolate * * *."

* * *

As far as we can ascertain, no other court has considered the constitutional validity of a disciplinary or other court rule compelling arbitration of fee disputes between attorneys. However, several courts have been confronted with a variety of constitutional objections to court rules that require arbitration of attorney-client fee disputes at the client's option. In each case, the rule was upheld against all challenges, including those based upon the right to a jury trial.

In re LiVolsi (1981), 85 N.J. 576, 428 A.2d 1268, involved a number of challenges to N.J.R. 1:20A, which was adopted by the New Jersey Supreme Court as a mechanism for resolving fee disputes between attorneys and their clients. The rule establishes fee-arbitration committees and provides that a committee must arbitrate a dispute upon the request of a client, whether the attorney consents or not, and that the committee's determination is binding on the parties and unappealable. In finding the promulgation of N.J.R. 1:20A to be within the scope of its constitutional power, the Supreme Court of New Jersey explained:

> The heart of the constitutional provisions concerning the judicial system was the concentration of responsibility for its proper functioning in the Supreme Court and Chief Justice. Such responsibility requires appropriate power over courts, judges, practice and procedure, and lawyers. Responsibility for an adversarial judicial system requires responsibility for the adversaries, and control over both.

* * *

The court went on to reject the claim that N.J.R. 1:20A unconstitutionally denies attorneys the right to trial by jury "on the two grounds that in New Jersey attorneys never had an absolute right to trial by jury in fee dispute cases and that recognizing a jury right in such cases would undermine our constitutional authority to regulate the Bar."

* * *

In *Anderson v. Elliott* (Me.1989), 555 A.2d 1042, the Supreme Judicial Court of Maine held that certain Maine Bar Rules promulgated by the court in 1978 do not infringe upon an attorney's right to trial by jury under the Maine Constitution. * * *

See, also, Nodvin v. State Bar of Georgia (2001), 273 Ga. 559, 561, 544 S.E.2d 142 (recognizing the "unique * * * importance" of public confidence in the judicial system as justification for mandatory arbitration of attorney-client fee disputes).

One of Shimko's principal contentions is that *LiVolsi* and *Anderson* are distinguishable because they involve attorney-client fee disputes rather than disputes between attorneys. According to Shimko, "the nature of the relationship between the attorney and client was critical to each of those courts." In particular, Shimko contends that because "the attorney occupies a fiduciary relationship, with a position of superiority over the client * * *, the Supreme Courts of Maine and New Jersey felt it was reasonable for attorneys to submit to non-jury adjudications for fee disputes." On the other hand, the argument continues, attorneys like Shimko and Lobe need no special protection from one another, as they stand "on equal footing and at arms-length, and neither would be hindered or put to a disadvantage by taking the dispute to court." We disagree.

Shimko's argument is built on the erroneous premise that the constitutional validity of the nonjury dispute-resolution mechanisms at issue in *LiVolsi* and *Anderson* was necessarily dependent upon concerns peculiar to the attorney-client relationship. However, a close reading reveals that the critical support for the constitutionality of the compulsory arbitration schemes in those cases was ultimately found to lie not in the fiduciary character of the attorney-client relationship or the attorney's position of dominance over the client, but in the relations existing between the bench and bar, that is, in the recognition that lawyers are officers of the court and essential to the primary judicial function of administering justice. The essential power to control or regulate the fee arrangement between attorney and client is not derived from the attorney's position in relation to the client, but from the attorney's position in relation to the court and the justice system. Moreover, Shimko forgets that the courts in *LiVolsi* and *Anderson* did not purport to exercise any authority or control over the client. It was the attorney who was held in those cases to have entered a regulated profession and who was subjected to professional standards designed to preserve public confidence in the judicial system. In fact, the very rules at issue in *LiVolsi* and *Anderson* are expressly designed to operate at the client's option, thus disclaiming any ability or desire on the court's part to compel the client to arbitrate a fee dispute. And because those decisions reflect the court's broad power to regulate

> the professional activities of its officers, they are indeed significant to the matter at hand.

Shimko v. Lobe, 103 Ohio St. 3d 59, 64–67, 813 N.E.2d 669, 674–78 (2014) (some internal quotations omitted).

b. EQUITABLE RIGHTS SUBJECT TO NON-CONTRACTUAL, YET BINDING, ARBITRATION

The U.S. Constitution's Seventh Amendment, preserving the right to jury trial, and most state constitutional provisions recognizing this right, were enacted prior to the merger of law and equity. Courts generally interpret these constitutional provisions to confer a jury trial right only in cases arising at law, as opposed to cases in equity—as noted in Section 6.C.1's excerpt from *Jersey Cent. Power & Light Co.*, which said the jury right "applies to civil cases only where the right to a jury trial existed at common law and does not normally apply to cases in equity." See also Feltner v. Columbia Pictures Television, Inc., 523 U.S. 340, 347–48 (1998); Pichler v. UNITE, 542 F.3d 380, 388 (3rd Cir.2008); State v. O'Malley, 95 S.W.3d 82 (Mo.2003). That basically means there is a right to a jury trial of claims for money damages, but not for equitable remedies like injunctions and specific performance.

As in *Jersey Cent. Power & Light Co.*, legislatures and administrative agencies have created new claims that did not exist at the time the constitutional provisions regarding the right to a jury trial were enacted. Whether there is a right to a jury trial of these claims is determined by the language of the statute creating the claim and by whether the claim bears more resemblance to a traditional legal or to equitable claim. For instance, *Jersey Cent. Power & Light Co.*'s analogized the claim created by New Jersey's Underground Facility Protection Act to a traditional negligence claim—an action at law.

In contrast, New York's highest court found claims created by New York's "lemon law" arbitration statute analogous to claims for specific performance and restitution; since such remedies were "equitable in nature" they would not in any event "have been triable by jury under the common law." *Motor Vehicle Manufacturers Ass'n of the U.S. v. New York*, 75 N.Y.2d 175, 551 N.Y.S.2d 470, 550 N.E.2d 919 (1990). Nor did the New York law deprive manufacturers of their right to "have a court or public officer adjudicate their disputes" with consumers by "delegating sovereign judicial power to private arbitrators"; The court reasoned that the legislature had "merely created a new limited class of disputes and provided a procedure for resolving them, much in the same way it removed automobile claims from judicial cognizance by the No-Fault Insurance Law." In addition, since "arbitrators are selected pursuant to detailed standards, the procedures they must follow are specified, the grounds for relief defined and their determinations are subject to judicial review," it followed that "the arbitration proceeding remains within the judicial domain." 550 N.E.2d at 924–25.

c. PUBLIC RIGHTS SUBJECT TO NON-CONTRACTUAL, YET BINDING, ARBITRATION

Several federal laws require arbitration of certain disputes under particular federal programs. These disputes may involve claims by private parties against the federal government or claims between private parties relating to the rights and duties specified by the particular federal program. Examples of such federal laws include the Multiemployer Pension Plan Amendments Act (MPPAA),[9] the Comprehensive Environmental Response, Compensation and Liability Act,[10] and the Federal Insecticide, Fungicide, and Rodenticide Act.[11] Although these instances of binding arbitration are mandated by law, even in the absence of an agreement to arbitrate, these mandates do not violate the constitutional right to a jury trial because that right does not attach to claims under these programs. See, e.g., Connors v. Ryan's Coal Co., 923 F.2d 1461 (11th Cir.1991) (lack of jury trial under MPPAA did not violate the Seventh Amendment). The following paragraphs discuss a Supreme Court case addressing a related constitutional challenge, not based on the jury right but rather on Article III of the U.S. Constitution.

The Article III issue arose in the context of pesticide regulations. Pesticide manufacturers are required to register their products with the Environmental Protection Agency (EPA), and to submit research and test data to the EPA concerning the product's health, safety, and environmental effects. The development of a potential commercial pesticide may require the expenditure of millions of dollars annually over a period of several years. Frequently, after one product has been registered, *another* applicant may wish to register the same or a similar product. Can the EPA consider, in support of this second application, data already in its files that had been submitted by the previous registrant?

The Federal Insecticide, Fungicide, and Rodenticide Act (FIFRA) allows the EPA to consider such data (after a 10-year period of exclusive use), but "only if the applicant has made an offer to compensate the original data submitter." 7 U.S.C. § 136a(c)(1)(F)(ii)–(iii). "In effect, the provision instituted a mandatory data-licensing scheme." See Ruckelshaus v. Monsanto Co., 467 U.S. 986, 992 (1984). If the original data submitter and the second applicant fail to agree on the terms of compensation, then either may compel binding arbitration.

A number of pesticide firms challenged this arbitration mandate, claiming that Article III of the Constitution bars Congress from requiring arbitration of disputes concerning compensation "without also affording substantial review by tenured judges of the arbitrator's decision." A unanimous Supreme Court upheld the FIFRA arbitration scheme in *Thomas v. Union Carbide Agricultural Prods. Co.*, 473 U.S. 568 (1985).

In an earlier case, the Supreme Court had suggested that Congress could not establish Article I "legislative courts" to adjudicate "private rights" disputes. Such disputes, involving "the liability of one individual to another under the law as defined," "lie at the core of the historically recognized judicial power." Northern

[9] 29 U.S.C. §§ 1381–1461.

[10] 42 U.S.C. §§ 9601–75.

[11] 7 U.S.C. §§ 136–136y.

Pipeline Construction Co. v. Marathon Pipe Line Co., 458 U.S. 50 (1982). Justice O'Connor, writing for the Court in *Thomas,* found that the situation presented by FIFRA was different:

> [T]he right created by FIFRA is not a purely "private" right, but bears many of the characteristics of a "public" right. Use of a registrant's data to support a follow-on registration serves a public purpose as an integral part of a program safeguarding the public health. Congress has the power, under Article I, to authorize an agency administering a complex regulatory scheme to allocate costs and benefits among voluntary participants in the program without providing an Article III adjudication. It also has the power to condition issuance of registrations or licenses on compliance with agency procedures. Article III is not so inflexible that it bars Congress from shifting the task of data valuation from the agency to the interested parties.
>
> * * * Congress, without implicating Article III, could have authorized EPA to charge follow-on registrants fees to cover the cost of data and could have directly subsidized FIFRA data submitters for their contributions of needed data. Instead, it selected a framework that collapses these two steps into one, and permits the parties to fix the amount of compensation, with binding arbitration to resolve intractable disputes. Removing the task of valuation from agency personnel to civilian arbitrators, selected by agreement of the parties or appointed on a case-by-case basis by an independent federal agency, surely does not diminish the likelihood of impartial decision-making, free from political influence.
>
> * * *
>
> The danger of Congress or the Executive encroaching on the Article III judicial powers is at a minimum when no unwilling defendant is subjected to judicial enforcement power as a result of the agency "adjudication."
>
> We need not decide in this case whether a private party could initiate an action in court to enforce a FIFRA arbitration. But cf. 29 CFR pt. 1440, App. § 37(c) (1984) (under rules of American Arbitration Association, parties to arbitration are deemed to consent to entry of judgment). FIFRA contains no provision explicitly authorizing a party to invoke judicial process to compel arbitration or enforce an award. In any event, under FIFRA, the only potential object of judicial enforcement power is the follow-on registrant who explicitly consents to have his rights determined by arbitration. Finally, we note that FIFRA limits but does not preclude review of the arbitration proceeding by an Article III court. We conclude that, in the circumstances, the review afforded preserves the "appropriate exercise of the judicial function." FIFRA at a minimum allows private parties to secure Article III review of the arbitrator's "findings and determination" for fraud, misconduct, or misrepresentation. This provision protects against arbitrators who abuse or exceed their powers or willfully misconstrue their mandate under the governing law. * * * For

> purposes of our analysis, it is sufficient to note that FIFRA does provide for limited Article III review, including whatever review is independently required by due process considerations.
>
> * * *
>
> Our holding is limited to the proposition that Congress, acting for a valid legislative purpose pursuant to its constitutional powers under Article I, may create a seemingly "private" right that is so closely integrated into a public regulatory scheme as to be a matter appropriate for agency resolution with limited involvement by the Article III judiciary. To hold otherwise would be to erect a rigid and formalistic restraint on the ability of Congress to adopt innovative measures such as negotiation and arbitration with respect to rights created by a regulatory scheme.

Justice Brennan, joined by Justices Marshall and Blackmun, wrote in concurrence:

> Congress has decided that effectuation of the public policies of FIFRA demands not only a requirement of compensation from follow-on registrants in return for mandatory access to data but also an administrative process—mandatory negotiation followed by binding arbitration—to ensure that unresolved compensation disputes do not delay public distribution of needed products. * * * Although a compensation dispute under FIFRA ultimately involves a determination of the duty owed one private party by another, at its heart the dispute involves the exercise of authority by a federal government arbitrator in the course of administration of FIFRA's comprehensive regulatory scheme. As such it partakes of the character of a standard agency adjudication.

The Supreme Court coyly left open in *Thomas* the question "whether a private party could initiate an action in court to enforce a FIFRA arbitration": but a later court answered "yes." "[I]f the phrase 'binding arbitration' is not given its usual meaning, i.e., that the award is enforceable in court, FIFRA's data-compensation scheme could be rendered meaningless." Cheminova A/S v. Griffin L.L.C., 182 F.Supp.2d 68 (D.D.C. 2002). FIFRA arbitration continues to be used and occasionally appears in court. See, e.g., Drexel Chem. Co. v. Albaugh, Inc., 645 F. App'x 467 (6th Cir. 2016); Non-Dietary Exposure Task Force v. Tagros Chemicals India, Ltd., 309 F.R.D. 66 (D.D.C. 2015) (confirming FIFRA arbitration award).

QUESTIONS TO REVIEW AND SYNTHESIZE

1. Place several types of arbitration, including arbitration governed by FAA § 10, on a continuum from most to least binding.
2. When does non-contractual arbitration violate the constitutional right to a jury trial?
3. The *Biotechpharma* case notes that federal courts have rejected Seventh Amendment jury-right challenges to mandates by the Commodity Futures Trading Commission (CFTC), an independent agency established by Congress, and the National Association of Securities Dealers (predecessor of FINRA), requiring members of commodities and securities exchanges to arbitrate customer disputes if their customers request it. Relatedly, Section 2.A.4 quoted an article stating that "securities broker-dealers are obligated to arbitrate consumer disputes whether they

contract to do so or not. While consumer arbitration in other industries is contractual, consumer arbitration in the securities industry is non-contractual for the business. The broker-dealer's duty to arbitrate is imposed by law—SRO rule—rather than assumed by contract." Ware, *What Makes Securities Arbitration Different from Other Consumer and Employment Arbitration?*, 76 U. Cin. L. Rev. 447, 448–52 (2008). With respect to disputes with their clients/customers, DC lawyers and securities broker-dealers have what in common?

APPENDIX A

FEDERAL ARBITRATION ACT 9 U.S.C. §§ 1–16 (1925)

CHAPTER 1. GENERAL PROVISIONS

§ 1. "Maritime Transactions," and "Commerce" Defined; Exceptions to Operation of Title

"Maritime transactions," as herein defined, means charter parties, bills of lading of water carriers, agreements relating to wharfage, supplies furnished vessels or repairs of vessels, collisions, or any other matters in foreign commerce which, if the subject of controversy, would be embraced within admiralty jurisdiction; "commerce," as herein defined, means commerce among the several States or with foreign nations, or in any Territory of the United States or in the District of Columbia, or between any such Territory and another, or between any such Territory and any State or foreign nation, or between the District of Columbia and any State or Territory or foreign nation, but nothing herein contained shall apply to contracts of employment of seamen, railroad employees, or any other class of workers engaged in foreign or interstate commerce.

§ 2. Validity, Irrevocability, and Enforcement of Agreements to Arbitrate

A written provision in any maritime transaction or a contract evidencing a transaction involving commerce to settle by arbitration a controversy thereafter arising out of such contract or transaction, or the refusal to perform the whole or any part thereof, or an agreement in writing to submit to arbitration an existing controversy arising out of such a contract, transaction, or refusal, shall be valid, irrevocable, and enforceable, save upon such grounds as exist at law or in equity for the revocation of any contract.

§ 3. Stay of Proceedings Where Issue Therein Referable to Arbitration

If any suit or proceeding be brought in any of the courts of the United States upon any issue referable to arbitration under an agreement in writing for such arbitration, the court in which such suit is pending, upon being satisfied that the issue involved in such suit or proceeding is referable to arbitration under such an agreement, shall on application of one of the parties stay the trial of the action until such arbitration has been had in accordance with the terms of the agreement, providing the applicant for the stay is not in default in proceeding with such arbitration.

§ 4. Failure to Arbitrate Under Agreement; Petition to United States Court Having Jurisdiction for Order to Compel Arbitration; Notice and Service Thereof; Hearing and Determination

A party aggrieved by the alleged failure, neglect, or refusal of another to arbitrate under a written agreement for arbitration may petition any United States district court which, save for such agreement, would have jurisdiction under Title

28, in a civil action or in admiralty of the subject matter of a suit arising out of the controversy between the parties, for an order directing that such arbitration proceed in the manner provided for in such agreement. Five days' notice in writing of such application shall be served upon the party in default. Service thereof shall be made in the manner provided by the Federal Rules of Civil Procedure. The court shall hear the parties, and upon being satisfied that the making of the agreement for arbitration or the failure to comply therewith is not in issue, the court shall make an order directing the parties to proceed to arbitration in accordance with the terms of the agreement. The hearing and proceedings, under such agreement, shall be within the district in which the petition for an order directing such arbitration is filed. If the making of the arbitration agreement or the failure, neglect, or refusal to perform the same be in issue, the court shall proceed summarily to the trial thereof. If no jury trial be demanded by the party alleged to be in default, or in the matter in dispute is within admiralty jurisdiction, the court shall hear and determine such issue. Where such an issue is raised, the party alleged to be in default may, except in cases of admiralty, on or before the return day of the notice of application, demand a jury trial of such issue, and upon such demand the court shall make an order referring the issue or issues to a jury in the manner provided by the Federal Rules of Civil Procedure, or may specially call a jury for that purpose. If the jury find that no agreement in writing for arbitration was made or that there is no default in proceeding thereunder, the proceeding shall be dismissed. If the jury find that an agreement for arbitration was made in writing and that there is a default in proceeding thereunder, the court shall make an order summarily directing the parties to proceed with the arbitration in accordance with the terms thereof.

§ 5. Appointment of Arbitrators or Umpire

If in the agreement provision be made for a method of naming or appointing an arbitrator or arbitrators or an umpire, such method shall be followed; but if no method be provided therein, or if a method be provided and any party thereto shall fail to avail himself of such method, or if for any other reason there shall be a lapse in the naming of an arbitrator or arbitrators or umpire, or in filling a vacancy, then upon the application of either party to the controversy the court shall designate and appoint an arbitrator or arbitrators or umpire, as the case may require, who shall act under the said agreement with the same force and effect as if he or they had been specifically named therein; and unless otherwise provided in the agreement the arbitration shall be by a single arbitrator.

§ 6. Application Heard as Motion

Any application to the court hereunder shall be made and heard in the manner provided by law for making and hearing of motions, except as otherwise herein expressly provided.

§ 7. Witnesses Before Arbitrators; Fees; Compelling Attendance

The arbitrators selected either as prescribed in this title or otherwise, or a majority of them, may summon in writing any person to attend before them or any of them as a witness and in a proper case to bring with him or them any book, record, document, or paper which may be deemed material as evidence in the case. The fees for such attendance shall be the same as the fees of witnesses before masters of the

United States Courts. Said summons shall issue in the name of the arbitrator or arbitrators, or a majority of them, and shall be signed by the arbitrators, or a majority of them, and shall be directed to the said person and shall be served in all the same manner as subpoenas to appear and testify before the court; if any person or persons so summoned to testify shall refuse or neglect to obey said summons, upon petition the United States court in and for the district in which such arbitrators or a majority of them, are sitting may compel the attendance of such person or persons before said arbitrator or arbitrators, or punish said person or persons for contempt in the same manner provided on February 12, 1925, for securing the attendance of witnesses or their punishment for neglect or refusal to attend in the courts of the United States.

§ 8. Proceedings Begun by Libel in Admiralty and Seizure of Vessel or Property

If the basis of jurisdiction be a cause of action otherwise justiciable in admiralty, then, notwithstanding anything herein to the contrary, the party claiming to be aggrieved may begin his proceeding hereunder by libel and seizure of the vessel or other property of the other party according to the usual course of admiralty proceedings, and the court shall then have jurisdiction to direct the parties to proceed with the arbitration and shall retain jurisdiction to enter its decree upon the award.

§ 9. Award of Arbitrators; Confirmation; Jurisdiction; Procedure

If the parties in their agreement have agreed that a judgment of the court shall be entered upon the award made pursuant to the arbitration, and shall specify the court, then at any time within one year after the award is made any party to the arbitration may apply to the court so specified for an order confirming the award, and thereupon the court must grant such an order unless the award is vacated, modified, or corrected as prescribed in sections 10 and 11 of this title. If no court is specified in the agreement of the parties, then such application may be made to the United States court in and for the district within which such award was made. Notice of the application shall be served upon the adverse party, and thereupon the court shall have jurisdiction of such party as though he had appeared generally in the proceeding. If the adverse party is a resident of the district within which the award was made, such service shall be made upon the adverse party or his attorney as prescribed by law for service of notice of motion in an action in the same court.

§ 10. Same; Vacation; Grounds; Rehearing

(a) In any of the following cases the United States court in and for the district wherein the award was made may make an order vacating the award upon the application of any party to the arbitration—

(1) where the award was procured by corruption, fraud, or undue means;

(2) Where there was evident partiality or corruption in the arbitrators, or either of them;

(3) Where the arbitrators were guilty of misconduct in refusing to postpone the hearing, upon sufficient cause shown, or in refusing to hear evidence pertinent and material to the controversy; or of any other misbehavior by which the rights of any party have been prejudiced; or

(4) Where the arbitrators exceeded their powers, or so imperfectly executed them that a mutual, final, and definite award upon the subject matter submitted was not made.

(b) If an award is vacated and the time within which the agreement required the award to be made has not expired the court may, in its discretion, direct a rehearing by the arbitrators.

(c) The United States district court for the district wherein an award was made that was issued pursuant to section 580 of title 5 may make an order vacating the award upon the application of a person, other than a party to the arbitration, who is adversely affected or aggrieved by the award, if the use of arbitration or the award is clearly inconsistent with the factors set forth in section 572 of title 5.

§ 11. Same; Modification or Correction; Grounds; Order

In either of the following cases the United States court in and for the district wherein the award was made may make an order modifying or correcting the award upon the application of any party to the arbitration—

(a) Where there was an evident material miscalculation of figures or an evident material mistake in the description of any person, thing, or property referred to in the award.

(b) Where the arbitrators have awarded upon a matter not submitted to them, unless it is a matter not affecting the merits of the decision upon the matter submitted.

(c) Where the award is imperfect in matter of form not affecting the merits of the controversy.

The order may modify and correct the award, so as to effect the intent thereof and promote justice between the parties.

§ 12. Notice of Motions to Vacate or Modify; Service; Stay of Proceedings

Notice of a motion to vacate, modify, or correct an award must be served upon the adverse party or his attorney within three months after the award is filed or delivered. If the adverse party is a resident of the district within which the award was made, such service shall be made upon the adverse party or his attorney as prescribed by law for service of notice of motion in an action in the same court. If the adverse party shall be a nonresident then the notice of the application shall be served by the marshal of any district within which the adverse party may be found in like manner as other process of the court. For the purposes of the motion any judge who might make an order to stay the proceedings in an action brought in the same court may make an order, to be served with the notice of motion, staying the proceedings of the adverse party to enforce the award.

§ 13. Papers Filed with Order on Motions; Judgment; Docketing; Force and Effect; Enforcement

The party moving for an order confirming, modifying, or correcting an award shall, at the time such order is filed with the clerk for the entry of judgment thereon, also file the following papers with the clerk:

(a) The agreement: the selection or appointment, if any, of an additional arbitrator or umpire; and each written extension of the time, if any, within which to make the award.

(b) The award.

(c) Each notice, affidavit, or other paper used upon an application to confirm, modify, or correct the award, and a copy of each order of the court upon such an application.

The judgment shall be docketed as if it was rendered in an action.

The judgment so entered shall have the same force and effect, in all respects, as, and be subject to all the provisions of law relating to, a judgment in an action; and it may be enforced as if it had been rendered in an action in the court in which it is entered.

§ 14. Contracts Not Affected

This title shall not apply to contracts made prior to January 1, 1926.

§ 15. Inapplicability of the Act of State Doctrine

Enforcement of arbitral agreements, confirmation of arbitral awards, and execution upon judgments based on orders confirming such awards shall not be refused on the basis of the Act of State doctrine.

§ 16. Appeals

(a) An appeal may be taken from—

(1) an order—

(A) refusing a stay of any action under section 3 of this title,

(B) denying a petition under section 4 of this title to order arbitration to proceed,

(C) denying an application under section 206 of this title to compel arbitration,

(D) confirming or denying confirmation of an award or partial award, or

(E) modifying, correcting, or vacating an award;

(2) an interlocutory order granting, continuing, or modifying an injunction against an arbitration that is subject to this title; or

(3) a final decision with respect to an arbitration that is subject to this title.

(b) Except as otherwise provided in section 1292(b) of title 28, an appeal may not be taken from an interlocutory order—

(1) granting a stay of any action under section 3 of this title;

(2) directing arbitration to proceed under section 4 of this title;

(3) compelling arbitration under section 206 of this title; or

(4) refusing to enjoin an arbitration that is subject to this title.

CHAPTER 2. CONVENTION ON THE RECOGNITION AND ENFORCEMENT OF FOREIGN ARBITRAL AWARDS

§ 201. Enforcement of Convention

The Convention on the Recognition and Enforcement of Foreign Arbitral Awards of June 10, 1958, shall be enforced in United States courts in accordance with this chapter.

§ 202. Agreement or Award Falling Under the Convention

An arbitration agreement or arbitral award arising out of a legal relationship, whether contractual or not, which is considered as commercial, including a transaction, contract, or agreement described in section 2 of this title, falls under the Convention. An agreement or award arising out of such relationship which is entirely between citizens of the United States shall be deemed not to fall under the Convention unless that relationship involves property located abroad, envisages performance or enforcement abroad, or has some other reasonable relation with one or more foreign states. For the purpose of this section a corporation is a citizen of the United States if it is incorporated or has its principal place of business in the United States.

§ 203. Jurisdiction; Amount in Controversy

An action or proceeding falling under the Convention shall be deemed to arise under the laws and treaties of the United States. The district courts of the United States (including the courts enumerated in section 460 of title 28) shall have original jurisdiction over such an action or proceeding, regardless of the amount in controversy.

§ 204. Venue

An action or proceeding over which the district courts have jurisdiction pursuant to section 203 of this title may be brought in any such court in which save for the arbitration agreement an action or proceeding with respect to the controversy between the parties could be brought, or in such court for the district and division which embraces the place designated in the agreement as the place of arbitration if such place is within the United States.

§ 205. Removal of Cases From State Courts

Where the subject matter of an action or proceeding pending in a State court relates to an arbitration agreement or award falling under the Convention, the defendant or the defendants may, at any time before the trial thereof, remove such action or proceeding to the district court of the United States for the district and division embracing the place where the action or proceeding is pending. The procedure for removal of causes otherwise provided by law shall apply, except that the ground for removal provided in this section need not appear on the face of the complaint but may be shown in the petition for removal. For the purposes of Chapter 1 of this title any action or proceeding removed under this section shall be deemed to have been brought in the district court to which it is removed.

§ 206. Order to Compel Arbitration; Appointment of Arbitrators

A court having jurisdiction under this chapter may direct that arbitration be held in accordance with the agreement at any place therein provided for, whether that place is within or without the United States. Such court may also appoint arbitrators in accordance with the provisions of the agreement.

§ 207. Award of Arbitrators; Confirmation; Jurisdiction; Proceeding

Within three years after an arbitral award falling under the Convention is made, any party to the arbitration may apply to any court having jurisdiction under this chapter for an order confirming the award as against any other party to the arbitration. The court shall confirm the award unless it finds one of the grounds for refusal or deferral of recognition or enforcement of the award specified in the said Convention.

§ 208. Chapter 1; Residual Applications

Chapter 1 applies to actions and proceedings brought under this chapter to the extent that chapter is not in conflict with this chapter or the Convention as ratified by the United States.

CHAPTER 3. INTER-AMERICAN CONVENTION ON INTERNATIONAL COMMERCIAL ARBITRATION

§ 301. Enforcement of Convention

The Inter-American Convention on International Commercial Arbitration of January 30, 1975, shall be enforced in United States courts in accordance with this chapter.

§ 302. Incorporation by Reference

Sections 202, 203, 204, 205, and 207 of this title shall apply to this chapter as if specifically set forth herein, except that for the purposes of this chapter "the Convention" shall mean the Inter-American Convention.

§ 303. Order to Compel Arbitration; Appointment of Arbitrators; Locale

(a) A court having jurisdiction under this chapter may direct that arbitration be held in accordance with the agreement at any place therein provided for, whether that place is within or without the United States. The court may also appoint arbitrators in accordance with the provisions of the agreement.

(b) In the event the agreement does not make provision for the place of arbitration or the appointment of arbitrators, the court shall direct that the arbitration shall be held and the arbitrators be appointed in accordance with Article 3 of the Inter-American Convention.

§ 304. Recognition and Enforcement of Foreign Arbitral Decisions and Awards; Reciprocity

Arbitral decision or awards made in the territory of a foreign State shall, on the basis of reciprocity, be recognized and enforced under this chapter only if that State has ratified or acceded to the Inter-American Convention.

§ 305. Relationship Between the Inter-American Convention and the Convention on the Recognition and Enforcement of Foreign Arbitral Awards of June 10, 1958

When the requirements for application of both the Inter-American Convention and the Convention on the Recognition and Enforcement of Foreign Arbitral Awards of June 10, 1958, are met, determination as to which Convention applies shall, unless otherwise expressly agreed, be made as follows:

(1) If a majority of the parties to the arbitration agreement are citizens of a State or States that have ratified or acceded to the Inter-American Convention and are member States of the Organization of American States, the Inter-American Convention shall apply.

(2) In all other cases the Convention on the Recognition and Enforcement of Foreign Arbitral Awards of June 10, 1958, shall apply.

§ 306. Applicable Rules of Inter-American Commercial Arbitration Commission

(a) For the purposes of this chapter the rules of procedure of the Inter-American Commercial Arbitration Commission referred to in Article 3 of the Inter-American Convention shall, subject to subsection (b) of this section, be those rules as promulgated by the Commission on July 1, 1988.

(b) In the event the rules of procedure of the Inter-American Commercial Arbitration Commission are modified or amended in accordance with the procedures for amendment of the rules of that Commission, the Secretary of State, by regulation in accordance with section 553 of title 5, consistent with the aims and purposes of this Convention, may prescribe that such modifications or amendments shall be effective for purposes of this chapter.

§ 307. Chapter 1; Residual Application

Chapter 1 applies to actions and proceedings brought under this chapter to the extent chapter 1 is not in conflict with this chapter or the Inter-American Convention as ratified by the United States.

APPENDIX B

UNITED NATIONS CONVENTION ON THE RECOGNITION AND ENFORCEMENT OF FOREIGN ARBITRAL AWARDS

[The New York Convention]

June 10, 1958

Article I

1. This Convention shall apply to the recognition and enforcement of arbitral awards made in the territory of a State other than the State where the recognition and enforcement of such awards are sought, and arising out of differences between persons, whether physical or legal. It shall also apply to arbitral awards not considered as domestic awards in the State where their recognition and enforcement are sought.

2. The term "arbitral awards" shall include not only awards made by arbitrators appointed for each case but also those made by permanent arbitral bodies to which the parties have submitted.

3. When signing, ratifying or acceding to this Convention, or notifying extension under article X hereof, any State may on the basis of reciprocity declare that it will apply the Convention to the recognition and enforcement of awards made only in the territory of another Contracting State. It may also declare that it will apply the Convention only to differences arising out of legal relationships whether contractual or not, which are considered as commercial under the national law of the State making such declaration.

Article II

1. Each Contracting State shall recognize an agreement in writing under which the parties undertake to submit to arbitration all or any differences which have arisen or which may arise between them in respect of a defined legal relationship, whether contractual or not, concerning a subject matter capable of settlement by arbitration.

2. The term "agreement in writing" shall include an arbitral clause in a contract or an arbitration agreement, signed by the parties or contained in an exchange of letters or telegrams.

3. The court of a Contracting State, when seized of an action in a matter in respect of which the parties have made an agreement within the meaning of this article, shall, at the request of one of the parties, refer the parties to arbitration, unless it finds that the said agreement is null and void, inoperative or incapable of being performed.

Article III

Each Contracting State shall recognize arbitral awards as binding and enforce them in accordance with the rules of procedure of the territory where the award is relied upon, under the conditions laid down in the following articles. There shall not be imposed substantially more onerous conditions or higher fees or charges on the recognition or enforcement of arbitral awards to which this Convention applies than are imposed on the recognition or enforcement of domestic arbitral awards.

Article IV

1. To obtain the recognition and enforcement mentioned in the preceding article, the party applying for recognition and enforcement shall, at the time of the application, supply:

(a) The duly authenticated original award or a duly certified copy thereof;

(b) The original agreement referred to in article II or a duly certified copy thereof.

2. If the said award or agreement is not made in an official language of the country in which the award is relied upon, the party applying for recognition and enforcement of the award shall produce a translation of these documents into such language. The translation shall be certified by an official or sworn translator or by a diplomatic or consular agent.

Article V

1. Recognition and enforcement of the award may be refused, at the request of the party against whom it is invoked, only if that party furnishes to the competent authority where the recognition and enforcement is sought, proof that:

(a) The parties to the agreement referred to in article II were, under the law applicable to them, under some incapacity, or the said agreement is not valid under the law to which the parties have subjected it or, failing any indication thereon, under the law of the country where the award was made; or

(b) The party against whom the award is invoked was not given proper notice of the appointment of the arbitrator or of the arbitration proceedings or was otherwise unable to present his case; or

(c) The award deals with a difference not contemplated by or not falling within the terms of the submission to arbitration, or it contains decisions on matters beyond the scope of the submission to arbitration, provided that, if the decisions on matters submitted to arbitration can be separated from those not so submitted, that part of the award which contains decisions on matters submitted to arbitration may be recognized and enforced; or

(d) The composition of the arbitral authority or the arbitral procedure was not in accordance with the agreement of the parties, or, failing such agreement, was not in accordance with the law of the country where the arbitration took place; or

(e) The award has not yet become binding on the parties, or has been set aside or suspended by a competent authority of the country in which, or under the law of which, that award was made.

2. Recognition and enforcement of an arbitral award may also be refused if the competent authority in the country where recognition and enforcement is sought finds that:

(a) The subject matter of the difference is not capable of settlement by arbitration under the law of that country; or

(b) The recognition or enforcement of the award would be contrary to the public policy of that country.

Article VI

If an application for the setting aside or suspension of the award has been made to a competent authority referred to in article V (1)(e), the authority before which the award is sought to be relied upon may, if it considers it proper, adjourn the decision on the enforcement of the award and may also, on the application of the party claiming enforcement of the award, order the other party to give suitable security.

Article VII

1. The provisions of the present Convention shall not affect the validity of multilateral or bilateral agreements concerning the recognition and enforcement of arbitral awards entered into by the Contracting States nor deprive any interested party of any right he may have to avail himself of an arbitral award in the manner and to the extent allowed by the law or the treaties of the country where such award is sought to be relied upon.

2. The Geneva Protocol on Arbitration Clauses of 1923 and the Geneva Convention on the Execution of Foreign Arbitral Awards of 1927 shall cease to have effect between Contracting States on their becoming bound and to the extent that they become bound, by this Convention.

Article VIII

1. This Convention shall be open until 31 December 1958 for signature on behalf of any Member of the United Nations and also on behalf of any other State which is or hereafter becomes a member of any specialized agency of the United Nations, or which is or hereafter becomes a party to the Statute of the International Court of Justice, or any other State to which an invitation has been addressed by the General Assembly of the United Nations.

2. This Convention shall be ratified and the instrument of ratification shall be deposited with the Secretary-General of the United Nations.

Article IX

1. This Convention shall be open for accession to all States referred to in article VIII.

2. Accession shall be effected by the deposit of an instrument of accession with the Secretary-General of the United Nations.

Article X

1. Any State may, at the time of signature, ratification or accession, declare that this Convention shall extend to all or any of the territories for the international relations of which it is responsible. Such a declaration shall take effect when the Convention enters into force for the State concerned.

2. At any time thereafter any such extension shall be made by notification addressed to the Secretary-General of the United Nations and shall take effect as from the ninetieth day after the day of receipt by the Secretary-General of the United Nations of this notification, or as from the date of entry into force of the Convention for the State concerned, whichever is the later.

3. With respect to those territories to which this Convention is not extended at the time of signature, ratification or accession, each State concerned shall consider the possibility of taking the necessary steps in order to extend the application of this Convention to such territories, subject, where necessary for constitutional reasons, to the consent of the Governments of such territories.

Article XI

1. In the case of a federal or non-unitary State, the following provisions shall apply:

(a) With respect to those articles of this Convention that come within the legislative jurisdiction of the federal authority, the obligations of the federal Government shall to this extent be the same as those of Contracting States which are not federal States;

(b) With respect to those articles of this Convention that come within the legislative jurisdiction of constituent states or provinces which are not, under the constitutional system of the federation, bound to take legislative action, the federal Government shall bring such articles with a favourable recommendation to the notice of the appropriate authorities of constituent states or provinces at the earliest possible moment;

(c) A federal State Party to this Convention shall, at the request of any other Contracting State transmitted through the Secretary-General of the United Nations, supply a statement of the law and practice of the federation and its constituent units in regard to any particular provision of this Convention, showing the extent to which effect has been given to that provision by legislative or other action.

Article XII

1. This Convention shall come into force on the ninetieth day following the date of deposit of the third instrument of ratification or accession.

2. For each State ratifying or acceding to this Convention after the deposit of the third instrument of ratification or accession, this Convention shall enter into force on the ninetieth day after deposit by such State of its instrument of ratification or accession.

Article XIII

1. Any Contracting State may denounce this Convention by a written notification to the Secretary-General of the United Nations. Denunciation shall take effect one year after the date of receipt of the notification by the Secretary-General.

2. Any State which has made a declaration or notification under article X may, at any time thereafter, by notification to the Secretary-General of the United Nations, declare that this Convention shall cease to extend to the territory concerned one year after the date of the receipt of the notification by the Secretary-General.

3. This Convention shall continue to be applicable to arbitral awards in respect of which recognition or enforcement proceedings have been instituted before the denunciation takes effect.

Article XIV

A Contracting State shall not be entitled to avail itself of the present Convention against other Contracting States except to the extent that it is itself bound to apply the Convention.

Article XV

The Secretary-General of the United Nations shall notify the States contemplated in article VIII of the following:

(a) Signatures and ratifications in accordance with article VIII;

(b) Accessions in accordance with article IX;

(c) Declarations and notifications under articles I, X and XI;

(d) The date upon which this Convention enters into force in accordance with article XII;

(c) Denunciations and notifications in accordance with article XIII.

Article XVI

1. This Convention, of which the Chinese, English, French, Russian and Spanish texts shall be equally authentic, shall be deposited in the archives of the United Nations.

2. The Secretary-General of the United Nations shall transmit a certified copy of this Convention to the States contemplated in article VIII.

APPENDIX C

INTER-AMERICAN CONVENTION ON INTERNATIONAL COMMERCIAL ARBITRATION

[The Panama Convention]

January 30, 1975

PREAMBLE

The Governments of the Member States of the Organization of American States, desirous of concluding a convention on international commercial arbitration, have agreed as follows:

Article 1

An agreement in which the parties undertake to submit to arbitral decision any differences that may arise or have arisen between them with respect to a commercial transaction is valid. The agreement shall be set forth in an instrument signed by the parties, or in the form of an exchange of letters, telegrams, or telex communications.

Article 2

Arbitrators shall be appointed in the manner agreed upon by the parties. Their appointment may be delegated to a third party, whether a natural or juridical person. Arbitrators may be nationals or foreigners.

Article 3

In the absence of an express agreement between the parties, the arbitration shall be conducted in accordance with the rules of procedure of the Inter-American Commercial Arbitration Commission.

Article 4

An arbitral decision or award that is not appealable under the applicable law or procedural rules shall have the force of a final judicial judgment. Its execution or recognition may be ordered in the same manner as that of decisions handed down by national or foreign ordinary courts, in accordance with the procedural laws of the country where it is to be executed and the provisions of international treaties.

Article 5

1. The recognition and execution of the decision may be refused, at the request of the party against which it is made, only if such party is able to prove to the competent authority of the State in which recognition and execution are requested:

a. That the parties to the agreement were subject to some incapacity under the applicable law or that the agreement is not valid under the law to which the parties have submitted it, or, if such law is not specified, under the law of the State in which the decision was made; or

b. That the party against which the arbitral decision has been made was not duly notified of the appointment of the arbitrator or of the arbitration procedure to be followed, or was unable, for any other reason, to present his defense; or

c. That the decision concerns a dispute not envisaged in the agreement between the parties to submit to arbitration; nevertheless, if the provisions of the decision that refer to issues submitted to arbitration can be separated from those not submitted to arbitration, the former may be recognized and executed; or

d. That the constitution of the arbitral tribunal or the arbitration procedure has not been carried out in accordance with the terms of the agreement signed by the parties or, in the absence of such agreement, that the constitution of the arbitral tribunal or the arbitration procedure has not been carried out in accordance with the law of the State where the arbitration took place; or

c. That the decision is not yet binding on the parties or has been annulled or suspended by competent authority of the State in which, or according to the law of which, the decision has been made.

d. The recognition and execution of an arbitral decision may also be refused if the competent authority of the State in which the recognition and execution is requested finds:

e. That the subject of the dispute cannot be settled by arbitration under the law of the State; or

2. That the recognition or execution of the decision would be contrary to the public policy ("ordre public") of that State.

Article 6

If the competent authority mentioned in Article 5.1.e has been requested to annul or suspend the arbitral decision, the authority before which such decision is invoked may, if it deems it appropriate, postpone a decision on the execution of the arbitral decision and, at the request of the party requesting execution, may also instruct the other party to provide appropriate guaranties.

Article 7

This Convention shall be open for signature by the Member States of the Organization of American States.

Article 8

This Convention is subject to ratification. The instruments of ratification shall be deposited with the General Secretariat of the Organization of American States.

Article 9

This Convention shall remain open for accession by any other State. The instruments of accession shall be deposited with the General Secretariat of the Organization of American States.

Article 10

This Convention shall enter into force on the thirtieth day following the date of deposit of the second instrument of ratification.

For each State ratifying or acceding to the Convention after the deposit of the second instrument of ratification, the Convention shall enter into force on the thirtieth day after deposit by such State of its instrument of ratification or accession.

Article 11

If a State Party has two or more territorial units in which different systems of law apply in relation to the matters dealt with in this Convention, it may, at the time of signature, ratification or accession, declare that this Convention shall extend to all its territorial units or only to one or more of them.

Such declaration may be modified by subsequent declarations, which shall expressly indicate the territorial unit or units to which the Convention applies. Such subsequent declarations shall be transmitted to the General Secretariat of the Organization of American States, and shall become effective thirty days after the date of their receipt.

Article 12

This Convention shall remain in force indefinitely, but any of the States Parties may denounce it. The instrument of denunciation shall be deposited with the General Secretariat of the Organization of American States. After one year from the date of deposit of the instrument of denunciation, the Convention shall no longer be in effect for the denouncing State, but shall remain in effect for the other States Parties.

Article 13

The original instrument of this Convention, the English, French, Portuguese and Spanish texts of which are equally authentic, shall be deposited with the General Secretariat of the Organization of American States. The Secretariat shall notify the Member States of the Organization of American States and the States that have acceded to the Convention of the signatures, deposits of instruments or ratification, accession, and denunciation as well as of reservations, if any. It shall also transmit the declarations referred to in Article 11 of this Convention.

INDEX

References are to Pages